HOCKEY GUIDE

1987-88 EDITION

Editor/Hockey Guide
LARRY WIGGE

Compiled by
FRANK POLNASZEK

Contributing Editors/Hockey Guide
JOHN HADLEY
BARRY SIEGEL
DAVE SLOAN
STEVE ZESCH

President-Chief Executive Officer
RICHARD WATERS

Editor
TOM BARNIDGE

Director of Books and Periodicals
RON SMITH

D1601271

Published by

The Sporting News

1212 North Lindbergh Boulevard
P.O. Box 56 — St. Louis, MO 63166

Copyright © 1987
The Sporting News Publishing Company

A Times Mirror Company

ISBN 0-89204-258-3   ISSN 0278-4955

TABLE OF CONTENTS

ON THE COVER: Philadelphia goaltender Ron Hextall, The Sporting News' Rookie of the Year, compiled a 3.00 goals-against average in 1986-87 en route to capturing Vezina Trophy honors and being named the Most Valuable Player in the Stanley Cup playoffs.
—Photo by Brian Tremmel

Oilers' 3rd Cup Title Caps Strange NHL Season

By JIM MATHESON

The 1986-87 National Hockey League season was stranger than fiction.

The winningest coach in history, Scotty Bowman, joined the unemployment line. Pat Quinn, who's studying to be a lawyer, passed Loopholes 101 by signing as the general manager for one club while coaching another. A third coach, Tom Webster, was replaced not because he couldn't change players on the fly, but because he couldn't fly, period. An inner-ear problem forced him to stay off airplanes.

Superstar Bryan Trottier opened his mouth to rap the league's officiating. The league bit back with a $1,000 fine. "I wasn't trying to be a martyr," an unrepentant Trottier said. "I had something on my mind, I said it, and I knew I was going to have to pay a price."

You want more? How about former NHL winger Brian Spencer being charged with murder in Florida. "Brian was an unsophisticated kid who grew up in the backwoods (of northern British Columbia) and, in retrospect, he should have stayed there," said Bob Baun, his former teammate with the Toronto Maple Leafs.

How about Marcel Dionne, trying to gain a contract extension, asking to be traded—and having the club go along with it. The NHL's No. 2 all-time scorer was dealt to the New York Rangers March 10 after more than 11 seasons with the Los Angeles Kings. "When I went home to tell my wife, she threw the phone at me," Dionne said.

Or Wayne Gretzky actually playing three games in succession without scoring a point, proving he's not put together with microchips. "Worst I've ever played. I just stink," said Gretzky, who shrugged off the drought in late March to win his seventh straight scoring title. You wanted drama, you got it.

While Gretzky stayed on top, his team waged a season-long struggle to regain its perch. In the end, the Edmonton Oilers captured their third Stanley Cup in four years.

Before the Oilers closed the book on the season, the NHL's coaches played a vigorous game of musical chairs. Coaching changes were made on 10 teams, but Quinn and Bowman hogged the headlines.

A former NHL Coach of the Year with the Philadelphia Flyers, Quinn seemed

One of the strangest sights of last season was Marcel Dionne playing in a Rangers uniform.

happy in Los Angeles as he began his third season with the Kings. Then, on Christmas Eve, he signed with the Vancouver Canucks to become their president and general manager after the season ended.

"This was as big a scandal as the Ivan Boesky insider-trading scandal on Wall Street," Kings left winger Tiger Williams said.

Quinn claimed he had done nothing wrong. He produced a 1984 contract with Los Angeles—which had not been filed with the NHL—that permitted him to shop his services if he had not been offered a new deal before September 1986.

Scotty Bowman, the NHL's all-time winningest coach with 721 regular-season victories, was fired as general manager of the Buffalo Sabres on December 2 after the club lost 18 of its first 23 games.

Indeed, Canucks executive Arthur Griffiths had asked as far back as June 1984 whether Quinn's contract had been registered with the league. He was told that it had not in June 1985, June 1986 and December 5, 1986. Vancouver then started the wheels in motion to sign Quinn as general manager.

After a series of cloak-and-dagger calls and meetings, Quinn signed December 24. In a startling piece of theater, Griffiths gave the Canucks' trainer a sealed envelope with a $100,000 signing bonus for Quinn. The envelope was passed to the Los Angeles trainer on January 2, 1987, at the morning skate before the Canucks-Kings game.

When the dealings became public a week later, all hell broke loose. After considerable deliberation. NHL President John Ziegler rapped Quinn, Vancouver and Los Angeles for the embarrassing situation. "It's clear that at some point, everyone forgot...the integrity of the competition," Ziegler said.

Quinn was expelled from hockey for the remainder of the season for a conflict of interest. He was prohibited from taking over his duties with the Canucks until June 16, after the league's annual meetings. Ziegler fined the Canucks $310,000 and the Kings, who named assistant Mike Murphy as Quinn's replacement, $130,000.

Vancouver sued the league over the summer, claiming Ziegler had overstepped his authority. The case was expected to be heard in the British Columbia Supreme Court in September 1987. Meanwhile, the NHL's Board of Governors voted at the June meetings to back

Ziegler's actions against the two teams.

Quinn reportedly received a five-year contract worth $200,000 his first season in Vancouver with the potential to earn lucrative bonuses for taking the Canucks up the ladder in the NHL's playoff structure. The Canucks have not had at least a .500 record since they were 33-32-15 in 1975-76.

Bowman's firing December 2 did not have the intrigue of "Quinngate," but it sent tremors throughout the league. Bowman entered the season with 718 regular-season wins at St. Louis, Montreal and Buffalo, but the Sabres suffered their worst start ever with five victories in 23 games. Seymour and Northrup Knox, owners of the club, had endured enough. "The Sabres' record under his leadership simply has not met our patient expectations," Seymour Knox said.

Bowman had been the team's general manager and director of hockey operations for the past seven seasons. Craig Ramsay had taken over behind the bench the month before.

Bowman spent the rest of the year relaxing, doing color commentary during the playoffs and writing for a newspaper during Rendez-Vous '87, the two-game All-Star series between the NHL and Soviet Union. His increased presence around the homefront brought an amusing observation from his daughter. "Congratulations, dad, you've made it to the top," she said as he drove her to school one morning. "You must be the highest-paid chauffeur in the world."

Rendez-Vous, February 11 and February 13 in Quebec City, was a smashing

Phil Esposito of the New York Rangers earned his reputation as the Monty Hall of the league's general managers by trading players, removing coaches and even coaching the team himself in two stints covering 43 games.

success at the box office and on the ice. "The winner was hockey itself," said Soviet Coach Viktor Tikhonov.

Philadelphia's Dave Poulin tipped in Mario Lemieux's shot with 75 seconds left in the first game to lift the NHL All-Stars to a 4-3 victory, while rising Soviet star Valeri Kamensky dazzled everyone in the second game with two goals in the Soviets' 5-3 win. "He'll probably be the Soviet player to reckon with in the future," said Chicago Black Hawks defenseman Doug Wilson.

"It was a great spectacle. . . . I'd love to play an eight-game series against them (four in Moscow and four in North America)," said Gretzky, who was chosen most valuable player of the series. His prize was another car, his 11th since joining the NHL. "I'll give this one to my dad," he said. "I gave one to him a couple of years ago but he wouldn't drive it. Said it wasn't his style."

Walter Gretzky laughed softly. "It was a Cadillac. I couldn't see myself driving to work in a Caddy," he said.

Maybe not, but Rendez-Vous was a rich hockey exchange. "The two games had

some of the greatest hockey you'll ever see," said Tikhonov, who may have saved his job with the Soviet victory in the second game.

NHL coaches, however, were joining Bowman in the unemployment line almost weekly.

The Boston Bruins fired Butch Goring and brought in former captain Terry O'Reilly, who toiled for 13 seasons with the team. O'Reilly, who had been studying to be an architect, took over on November 14.

One week later, New York Rangers General Manager Phil Esposito fired Coach Ted Sator (who would succeed Ramsay in Buffalo the next month), took over himself for a few games, then appointed the hard-luck Webster, who eventually had to quit on doctors' orders because of an inner-ear imbalance.

Esposito finished up the season and then, in a stunning move, hired the Quebec Nordiques' fiery coach, Michel Bergeron, on June 18. Quebec received the Rangers' No. 1 draft choice in 1988 and a reported $100,000 as compensation for Bergeron, who had two years left on his Quebec contract.

"At the draft, I happened to walk over to the Quebec table to try and do some trading," said Esposito, the Monty Hall of the league's general managers. "I jokingly said to their GM, Maurice Filion, 'Why don't you let me have Bergeron?' One thing led to another and a deal was struck."

In seven seasons with the Nordiques, Bergeron twice led the team to the Wales Conference finals. After three straight 40-victory seasons, Quebec slipped to 31-39-10 last year. With the appointment of Andre Savard, 33, as Bergeron's successor, Quebec had the youngest coach in the league. Savard had been coaching the Nordiques' Fredericton farm club.

On March 31, with two games left in the season, the Minnesota North Stars fired Lorne Henning as the team struggled trying to make the playoffs. Glen Sonmor took over for Henning, but the coaching change failed to help the North Stars as they missed postseason play for the first time since failing in 1979. Former Rangers Coach Herb Brooks was hired in April after spending the season at St. Cloud (Minn.) State. Brooks previously coached at the University of Minnesota and led the U.S. Olympic team to the gold medal in the 1980 Winter Games.

In other moves after the season:

• The Pittsburgh Penguins dumped Bob Berry after he failed to reach the playoffs in three years. Pierre Creamer, a successful coach at Sherbrooke in the American Hockey League, was hired to take over.

• Black Hawks General Manager Bob Pulford gave up his coaching chores and was succeeded by Calgary Flames assistant Bob Murdoch.

• The Flames were rocked when Bob Johnson quit after five seasons to become executive director of the Amateur Hockey Association of the United States. He reportedly took a pay cut of $100,000 a year but considered the job security more attractive. "I've been coaching all my life, now it's time to start a new career," he said. Terry Crisp, coach of Calgary's AHL affiliate the past two seasons, was appointed as Johnson's successor.

• The Canucks finished the game of musical chairs, hiring Oilers director of player development Bob McCammon to replace Tom Watt as coach.

When players were moved, the teams didn't create a flurry of trading at the March 10 deadline as they had done the year before. But Dionne's move to the Rangers was startling.

"I lost my big brother, my father, my uncle and my friend," said Rookie of the Year Luc Robitaille, who boarded at Dionne's home in Los Angeles.

Dionne was just as shocked to be leaving. He had asked to be traded, trying to bluff Kings General Manager Rogie Vachon into extending his contract, which had one year remaining. "Even after Rogie told me, I still couldn't believe it happened," said Dionne, a 36-year-old center.

For Dionne and a future third-round pick, the Kings received defenseman Tom Laidlaw and center Bobby Carpenter, the once-upon-a-time Boy Wonder who had scored 53 goals for Washington in 1984-85, then fizzled. It was the second time during the season that Carpenter had been traded. The Capitals had dealt him to the Rangers at midseason for center Mike Ridley, left wing Kelly Miller and right wing Bobby Crawford.

For more than a month prior to his trade to the Big Apple, Carpenter had been suspended from the Capitals for being, they said, a disruptive influence.

"I took a lot of heat," Washington General Manager David Poile said of his decision to suspend one of his team's best players, taking the chance that Carpenter's market value would slip while he was idle. "Some said it was the most bizarre thing they'd heard of in sport.

"In a way, Carpenter was a victim of the sports society. He went into a shell because of all the expectations."

When he proved a bust in New York, too, he was on his way to Los Angeles.

In other major trades:

• Just before the season, the Montreal Canadiens acquired Winnipeg Jets goaltender Brian Hayward, who would lead the league with a 2.81 goals against average, for goaltender Steve Penney and left wing Jan Ingman.

• Esposito ignored the lazy tag that had been hung on Walt Poddubny and obtained him from the Toronto Maple Leafs before the season for center Mike Allison. Poddubny rewarded the Rangers with 40 goals and 47 assists.

• The Rangers did, however, part with left wing Brian MacLellan for a third-round draft pick from Minnesota. MacLellan went on to score 32 goals for the North Stars.

• In a multiplayer deal in October, the Rangers traded the rights to defenseman Reijo Ruotsalainen to Edmonton for veteran defenseman Don Jackson.

• In November, Pittsburgh traded high-scoring center Mike Bullard, in his seventh season with the Penguins, to Calgary for center Dan Quinn. Both players scored 28 goals for their new teams.

The defending Stanley Cup champion Montreal Canadiens acquired Brian Hayward from Winnipeg before the 1986-87 season and the goaltender responded with a league-leading 2.81 goals-against average.

• On December 2, a pair of established defensemen changed clubs when Vancouver sent Rick Lanz to Toronto for Jim Benning and center Dan Hodgson.

• Just more than a week later, original Oiler and personal bodyguard to Gretzky, Dave Semenko, was acquired by Hartford when the Whalers lost enforcer Torrie Robertson with a broken leg.

• Goaltender Bob Froese, benched by the Flyers in favor of rookie Ron Hextall, got his wish to be traded when he was dealt to the Rangers at midseason for defenseman Kjell Samuelsson.

• Left wing John Ogrodnick, a 50-goal scorer in 1984-85, was sent from Detroit to Quebec with left wing Basil McRae and right wing Doug Shedden for left wing Brent Ashton, right wing Mark Kumpel and defenseman Gilbert Delorme. Ashton finished the season with 40 goals, 15 in Detroit. Ogrodnick netted 23 for the year while bothered by a tender ankle.

• Preparing for the playoffs and their push to recapture the Stanley Cup, the Oilers acquired high-scoring center Kent Nilsson from the North Stars for a conditional draft choice. The pick turned out to be a second-rounder when Nilsson helped the Oilers to the title.

• The Red Wings also looked for playoff help by dealing for New Jersey Devils center-captain Mel Bridgman in exchange for right wing Chris Cichocki.

• In a blockbuster deal during the '87 NHL draft, the Nordiques sent feisty center Dale Hunter and goaltender Clint Malarchuk to the Capitals for left wing Gaetan Duchesne, center Alan Haworth and Washington's No. 1 spot in the draft.

The Nilsson and Ruotsalainen deals gave hockey's most potent offense two more weapons. Edmonton scored 372 goals to lead the league for the sixth straight year. Gretzky won the scoring title with 183 points, 75 ahead of linemate Jari Kurri. Lemieux and the Oilers' Mark Messier tied for third with 107 points.

Three other players scored 100 points or more: St. Louis Blues center Doug Gilmour, 105; North Stars right winger Dino Ciccarelli, 103, and Winnipeg center Dale Hawerchuk, 100.

Gretzky led all goal-scorers with 62, followed by Philadelphia's Tim Kerr, 58, Kurri and Lemieux, 54, and Ciccarelli, 52.

Mark Messier (above) fires the puck past Soviet goalie Evgeny Belosheikin to give the NHL All-Stars a 1-0 lead in Game 2 of Rendez-Vous '87 at Quebec City. Valeri Kamensky evened the score with a goal against Grant Fuhr and the Soviets won, 5-3, for a split of the two-game series.

New York Islanders right winger Mike Bossy, who had nine straight 50-goal seasons, was hampered by a bad back and scored only 38.

Leaguewide, goals were down, from an average of 7.9 per game in 1985-86, to 7.3 per game last season. Only six clubs topped the 300-goal plateau: the Oilers, Flames, Kings, Flyers, Rangers and Bruins.

Defensively, the Canadiens allowed the fewest goals with 241, four fewer than Philadelphia. The Canadiens earned that distinction on the final day of the season when they defeated the Rangers, 8-2, while the Flyers suffered a 9-5 loss to the Islanders. There was one scoreless tie, between Buffalo (Tom Barrasso in goal) and Montreal (Patrick Roy). Hartford's Mike Liut led the league's goaltenders with four shutouts.

Among noteworthy incidents of rowdyism, Islanders assistant coach Bob Nystrom was suspended for 10 games for going into the stands after an unruly fan. Hextall was dealt an eight-game suspension, effective at the start of the 1987-88 season, for slashing Nilsson in Game 4 of the Stanley Cup finals.

In Boston, Mayor Raymond Flynn urged the league to crack down on fighting following a bench-clearing brawl involving the Bruins and Canadiens on November 20. Flynn threatened to send police to the Garden to arrest players involved in donnybrooks.

"If I were at that game, I would have instructed my police commissioner to go on the ice with the police department and have the Bruins and Montreal Canadiens taken off the ice in handcuffs and arrested," Flynn said.

Though the benches cleared only five times during the season, a melee before the sixth game of the Cup semifinals provoked the league to address free-for-alls. At the summer meetings, officials voted unanimously to take action at the NHL's board of governors meeting in September. "There was a very strong mandate to eliminate—not cut down, but eliminate—brawling," Ziegler said.

The postseason tournament wasn't chock-full of upsets as it had been the year before, when the Stanley Cup contenders couldn't handle the pretenders. Still, there were some twists.

One Saturday night—and Sunday morning—in New York, the Islanders and Capitals played the equivalent of two games. The combatants dragged their feet like 1930s marathon dancers through 128 minutes, 47 seconds of hockey before Islanders center Pat LaFontaine mercifully ended

the fifth-longest game ever. To find one longer, you had to go back to March 23, 1943, when Toronto defeated Detroit, 3-2, in just over 130 minutes.

"I was too tired to have any emotions after the game," said Isles goaltender Kelly Hrudey, who made 73 saves in the 3-2 win. The victory clinched the Patrick Division semifinals for New York, four games to three.

The Oilers also set an NHL record, scoring 13 times against Los Angeles in the second game of their first-round series. Gretzky tied his own playoff record of seven points on one goal and six assists. He also supplanted former Montreal great Jean Beliveau's career playoff record of 176 points.

"The only longer night I can remember was when my wife (Yvonne) went through 24 hours of labor with our first son," said Kings Coach Mike Murphy.

The Islanders and Red Wings also earned footnotes in history, becoming only the third and fourth teams to recover from a 3-1 deficit and win a seven-game series. Previously, the Red Wings had allowed the Maple Leafs to come back in the Cup finals in 1942, while the Isles rebounded against Pittsburgh in the 1975 quarterfinals. This time, the Isles completed the miracle against Washington in the Patrick Division semifinals, while Detroit gained revenge against Toronto in the Norris Division finals.

On the whole, though, the playoffs unfolded as expected. Only the pregame Wrestlemania between the Flyers and Canadiens in the Wales Conference finals scarred the battle for Lord Stanley's Cup.

"It was stupid and ugly," said Montreal defenseman Larry Robinson, his stomach churning after Flyers defenseman Ed Hospodar pummeled Montreal's Claude Lemieux at the end of the pregame warmup.

It had become a ritual of sorts for Lemieux to shoot a puck into the opponents net before going into the locker room. The Flyers had stopped the Montreal winger once after turning the net around the previous two games, but the hijinx touched off a fistic fury this night as both teams charged from the locker rooms back onto the ice, brawling for 15 minutes.

"If you saw your kids doing it, you'd want to kick their (rear)," said Philadelphia General Manager Bobby Clarke. "We allowed our professionals to do it."

But in the end, the icemen of Edmonton and Philadelphia played a ready-made Stanley Cup final, the first to go seven games since Montreal defeated Chicago in 1971.

"It's too bad there had to be a loser," said

Oilers Coach Glen Sather. "This was a great series, absolutely one of the best you'll ever see."

The series had splashes of heavenly drama as the Flyers rallied to win three games that appeared lost. The series had a horror scene, with Hextall swinging his stick like an ax at Nilsson as if he were auditioning for "Nightmare on Elm Street." It had a battle of gladiators, with Grant Fuhr and Hextall locked in a superb goaltending battle. "The best two in hockey," said Flyers Coach Mike Keenan. There was Gretzky weaving his magic, Flyers left wing Brian Propp strangling his critics and the late Kate Smith big as life on a giant video screen at the Spectrum in Philadelphia.

The Oilers quickly took the series lead, two games to none, but the Flyers weren't about to go quietly into the night.

Early in the opening game, the public address announcer in Edmonton announced a plug for Gretzky's hockey video. "You can buy Wayne Gretzky's 'Hockey: My Way' at the Oiler gift shop." The timing was perfect. Gretzky, who had scored only three goals in the playoffs, ended a five-game goal-scoring drought, scoring once and setting up defenseman Paul Coffey for the game-winner in a 4-2 victory. Kurri and left wing Glenn Anderson tallied the other goals.

"Their best players really came through," Keenan conceded.

Gretzky attributed his reawakening to a new pair of skates and to watching Boston Celtics star Larry Bird take charge of a televised playoff game against the Milwaukee Bucks earlier in the day.

"When I don't score, fingers are pointed, even when we're winning," Gretzky said. "But I think I got some inspiration from watching the Celtics and Milwaukee. Boston was losing and Larry Bird took over. It was like he said, 'Give me the ball,' and away the Celtics went.

"I came to the rink in a real positive frame of mind. I felt very confident before the game started."

The second game was a smorgasbord of thrills, chills and spills as Kurri beat the Flyers, 3-2, almost seven minutes into overtime. In the process, the Oilers handed the Flyers only their second loss of the season in games they led entering the third period. The Flyers were 36-1-4 during the regular season when leading after two periods and 9-0 in the playoffs.

Anderson supplied the biggest thrill, scoring an incredible goal with eight minutes left in regulation to tie the game, 2-2. Looking like a tightrope walker trying to keep his balance, he dashed around Flyers defenseman Doug Crossman and beat Hextall with a quick, low shot to the goalie's stick side.

"How did he stay on his feet? I'd have fallen down for sure," said Kurri.

"I don't know how you explain it," said Anderson.

Hextall and Fuhr chilled the shooters, stopping all but five of 68 shots in 67 frantic minutes. Hextall had no chance on Kurri's game-winner as Coffey passed off to the open right winger.

"The Flyers had two guys go after Wayne, who made the pass to Paul," Kurri said. "Hextall came out to challenge and I had half an open net to shoot at."

The spills involved Gretzky, who raised Keenan's ire by supposedly taking a dive in front of referee Andy van Hellemond. "I feel the best player in the world should earn his room rather than try to take advantage of an official," Keenan said.

"I don't know what he's talking about," Gretzky said. "I still can't remember the incident. It must be (his) frustration."

That was understandable, considering how well the Flyers played.

They were even better in Game 3. At least after they fell behind 3-0. "We were close to being in the grave," admitted Flyers winger Rick Tocchet. "But you don't roll over and die in the Stanley Cup finals."

After Edmonton scored its third goal early in the second period, Philadelphia's Murray Craven and Peter Zezel netted power-play goals from the goal mouth. Scott Mellanby and Brad McCrimmon then scored within 17 seconds early in the third to bring the Flyers back into the series. Brian Propp added an empty-net goal, securing a 5-3 victory.

"We just blew it. We were our own worst enemy," Gretzky said as he tried to digest the biggest cough-up since Joe Valachi sang on the Cosa Nostra. The last time a team in the finals had blown such a lead was in 1944. Chicago, after leading 5-2, had lost to Montreal in overtime, 6-5.

Before the game, the Flyers turned to their good-luck charm at the Spectrum. The late Kate Smith returned larger than life on a giant video screen, singing "God Bless America" in a performance taped from May 19, 1974. The Flyers won their first Stanley Cup that day, beating the Boston Bruins, 1-0.

After some serious soul-searching, the Oilers crushed the Flyers, 4-1, in Game 4 and looked poised for a quick Stanley Cup parade. They had won both of their previous two championships in five games, over the Islanders in 1984 and the Flyers in 1985.

An example of the physical play in the Stanley Cup final is exemplified by this collision between Philadelphia captain Dave Poulin and Edmonton's Glenn Anderson.

Gretzky set up the first three goals, by Kurri, Kevin Lowe (shorthanded) and Randy Gregg (power play). "When he decides to take control, he pulls the whole club along with him," Oilers Owner Peter Pocklington said.

"I know a lot of people were expecting us to hit Wayne, but it's like trying to hit a little gnat," Flyers defenseman Mark Howe said in frustration.

Gretzky may have been elusive, but every Oiler wasn't, especially near Hextall. The Flyers goaltender nearly cut Nilsson off at the knees with a vicious slash late in the game. Hextall lashed out at the nearest Oiler seconds after Anderson whacked him in the midsection while going for a loose puck.

"If that had been Mike Schmidt, it would have been out of the ball park," said Nilsson, who caught the two-handed swipe on the back of the leg.

Hextall showed no remorse. "He (Anderson) gave me one. I'd love to give him

one back, but he wasn't there." Hextall was slapped with an eight-game suspension to start the 1987-88 season.

Hextall's stickwork riled up almost everyone, but tempers had flared during the pregame warmup when Lowe accidentally hit Hextall with a flip shot.

"It was my fault," said Lowe, who was trying to bank the puck off the boards while Hextall was stretching. Within seconds, players were snarling at one another, but tempers eventually cooled.

At the end of the game, Sather had a shoving match with a fan. "One guy spit on me," the Oilers' coach said. "I was upset. What if the guy had AIDS?

"I'm wearing a raincoat if we have to come back to Philadelphia," he said, angry that someone would spit on his suit.

Sather and the Oilers would have to return to the Spectrum. In Game 5 at Edmonton, the Flyers charged from behind again, overcoming a 3-1 deficit to win, 4-3, on Tocchet's goal from the crease early in

Flyers goalie Ron Hextall walked off with the Conn Smythe but the Oilers walked off with the Stanley Cup.

the third period.

Propp set up the winning goal after assisting on the first three. The four assists silenced the critics who had pronounced him missing in action every time the playoffs came around.

"We heard they were planning a parade and used it to our psychological advantage," Tocchet said.

The Flyers also had asked to see the Cup in their dressing room that morning. "First time I've ever touched it," Crossman said.

Kate was singing again before the sixth game, prompting some to call the Flyers tacky.

"Did we stop saluting the flag when Betsy Ross died?" countered John Brogan, the Flyers' assistant to the president.

Kate's luck appeared to have worn off, though, when the Oilers took a 2-0 lead after only six and a half minutes. But once again, the Flyers staged a revival meeting and won, 3-2, to force a seventh game.

Propp tied the score, 2-2, beating Fuhr with a 25-footer at 13:04 of the third period. Just over a minute later, little-used J.J. Daigneault scored on a screened shot from about 50 feet.

The Creatures That Wouldn't Die rolled into Edmonton for one final night. "I hope they've run out of lives," Sather said.

"This is all a little hard to believe," said Hextall, his eyes rolling skyward. "If you'd asked me if we could come back this often. . .once, twice, three times from at least two goals down, I'd have said you were crazy."

But that was the storyline as the Oilers and Flyers met for Game 7. In this chapter, however, the miracle was deleted from the plot. The Oilers fired 43 shots at Hextall, who stopped all but three. Messier, Kurri and Anderson gave Edmonton all the offense it needed in a 3-1 victory.

Hextall won the Conn Smythe Trophy as the Most Valuable Player in the playoffs, becoming only the fourth player to win the award on a losing team. (Roger Crozier, in 1966 with Detroit; Glenn Hall, in 1968 with St. Louis, and Reggie Leach, in 1976 with Philadelphia, were the others.)

"This is a great honor, but it would have meant a lot more to me if we won the Stanley Cup," Hextall said. "I'd gladly trade the Smythe for the Stanley any day."

After the Flyers' Murray Craven scored in the game's first two minutes, the Oilers put on a full-court press. They took the lead on Kurri's tally at 14:59 of the second period and added a goal by Anderson in the waning moments of the game. But the impressive part of this Edmonton victory was the Oilers' defense. They limited the Flyers to just eight shots in the final two periods—only two in the third period—and they regained the Stanley Cup in the process.

"This was the greatest feeling," said Oilers defenseman Charlie Huddy. "It was like losing your house, then scraping together enough money to get it back."

"We went through such a long summer, and to win again was so sweet," Gretzky said. "We knew it would be either the best summer of our life if we won or the worst if we lost."

Keenan offered no excuses. "The way they played in the seventh game, they showed they are the world's best team," he said. "But I can't say enough about my team. They're the most wonderful group of athletes I've ever coached."

Wayne Gretzky (left) and Jari Kurri celebrate after Kurri's goal with 5:01 left in the second period of Game 7 gave the Oilers a 2-1 lead over the Flyers. Glenn Anderson added an insurance goal with 2:24 left as Edmonton won the NHL's first seven-game Stanley Cup final in 16 years, four games to three.

National Hockey League

Organized November 22, 1917

NHL Offices

John A. Ziegler, Jr.

Sun Life Building
1155 Metcalfe Street, Suite 960
Montreal, Que., Canada H3B 2W2
Phone—(514) 871-9220
TWX—(610) 421-3260

Central Scouting & Officiating
Suite 200, 1 Greensboro Drive
Rexdale, Ont. M9W 1C8
Phone—(416) 245-2926
TWX—(610) 492-2703

34th Floor
650 Fifth Avenue
33rd Floor
New York, NY 10019
Phone—(212) 398-1100
TWX—(212) 245-8221

Chairman of the Board .... WILLIAM W. WIRTZ
President .... JOHN A. ZIEGLER, JR.
Vice-Chairman ....FRANK A. GRIFFITHS

Secretary.. ROBERT O. SWADOS
Executive Vice-President.. BRIAN F. O'NEILL
Vice-President and General Counsel.. GILBERT STEIN
Vice-President, Finance..KENNETH G. SAWYER
Vice-President, Project Development ....IAN "SCOTTY" MORRISON
Vice-President, Broadcasting ....JOEL NIXON
Vice-President, Marketing-Public Relations ....STEVE RYAN
    Director of Communications ....John Halligan
    Director of Central Registry.. Garry Lovegrove
    Executive Director of Hockey Operations...Jim Gregory
    Director of Officiating...John McCauley
    Director of Information (Prince of Wales Conference).....................................Gerry Helper (New York)
    Director of Media Relations (Clarence Campbell Conference) .... Gary Meagher (Montreal)
    Supervisors of Officials... Bryan Lewis, John Ashley, Matt Pavelich
    Director of Administration...Phil Scheuer
    Director of Security... Frank Torpey
    Assistant Director of Security .... Al Wiseman

National Hockey League

1987-88

Campbell Conference

Smythe Division

Calgary Flames
Edmonton Oilers
Los Angeles Kings
Vancouver Canucks
Winnipeg Jets

Norris Division

Chicago Black Hawks
Detroit Red Wings
Minnesota North Stars
St. Louis Blues
Toronto Maple Leafs

Prince Of Wales Conference

Patrick Division

New Jersey Devils
New York Islanders
New York Rangers
Philadelphia Flyers
Pittsburgh Penguins
Washington Capitals

Adams Division

Boston Bruins
Buffalo Sabres
Hartford Whalers
Montreal Canadiens
Quebec Nordiques

Board of Governors

William D. Hassett, Jr. .... Boston
Seymour H. Knox, III .... Buffalo
Cliff Fletcher .... Calgary
William W. Wirtz.. Chicago
Michael Ilitch.. Detroit
Peter Pocklington .... Edmonton
Howard Baldwin.. Hartford
Dr. Jerry Buss... Los Angeles
Gordon Gund .... Minnesota
Ronald Corey .... Montreal
John J. McMullen... New Jersey

John O. Pickett, Jr.................................... N. Y. Islanders
Richard H. Evans...................................... N. Y. Rangers
Jay T. Snider.. Philadelphia
J. Paul Martha.. Pittsburgh
Marcel Aubut .... Quebec
Michael Shanahan.. St. Louis
Harold E. Ballard .... Toronto
Frank A. Griffiths.. Vancouver
Abe Pollin .... Washington
Barry Shenkarow.. Winnipeg

Boston Bruins

Adams Division

President and Governor.. William D. Hassett, Jr.
General Manager and Alternate Governor.. Harry Sinden
Assistant General Manager .... Tom Johnson
Coach.. Terry O'Reilly
Assistant Coach .... John Cunniff
Goaltending Coach.. Joe Bertagna
Coordinator of Minor League Player Personnel/Scouting .... Bob Tindall
Director of Player Evaluation.. Bart Bradley
Special Assignment Scout .... Jean Ratelle
Scouting Staff.. Jim Morrison, Andre Lachapelle, Joe Lyons,
Don Saatzer, Lars Waldner
Controller .... John J. Dionne
Trainers .... Jim Narrigan, Larry Ness
Director of Public Relations/Marketing.. Nate Greenberg
Assistant Director of Public Relations .... Heidi Holland
Home Ice... Boston Garden
Address .... 150 Causeway Street, Boston, Mass. 02114
Seating Capacity... 14,451
Club colors .... Gold, Black and White
Phone.. (617) 227-3206

Harry Sinden

Tom Johnson

Terry O'Reilly

Boston Bruins 1987-88 Roster

FORWARDS

Name	Hgt.	Wgt.	Place of Birth	Date	1986-87 Club	G.	A.	Pts.
Beraldo, Paul	5:11	175	Hamilton, Ont.	10- 5-67	Sault Ste. Marie	39	51	90
Burridge, Randy	5:09	180	Fort Erie, Ont.	1- 7-66	Moncton-Boston	27	45	72
Byers, Lyndon	6:01	190	Nipawin, Sask.	2-29-64	Moncton-Boston	7	8	15
Carter, John	5:10	175	Winchester, Mass.	5- 3-63	Moncton-Boston	25	31	56
Courtnall, Geoff	6:00	185	Victoria, B.C.	8-18-62	Boston	13	23	36
Crowder, Keith	6:00	195	Windsor, Ont.	1- 6-59	Boston	22	30	52
Hall, Taylor	5:11	185	Regina, Sask.	2-20-64	Vancouver-Fredericton	21	20	41
Johnston, Greg	6:01	190	Barrie, Ont.	1-14-65	Boston	12	15	27
Kasper, Steve	5:08	170	Montreal, Que.	9-28-61	Boston	20	30	50
Lalonde, Todd	6:00	190	Sudbury, Ont.	8- 4-69	Sudbury	5	11	16
Lehman, Tom	6:01	185	Solna, Sweden	2- 3-64	A.I.K.	25	26	51
Linseman, Ken	5:11	175	Kingston, Ont.	8-11-58	Boston	15	34	49
Malmqvist, Staffan	6:02	190	Borlange, Sweden	3-22-68	Leksand	19	19	38
Markwart, Nevin	5:10	185	Toronto, Ont.	12- 9-64	Moncton-Boston	13	12	25
McCarthy, Tom	6:02	200	Toronto, Ont.	7-31-60	Boston-Moncton	30	30	60
Middleton, Rick	5:11	175	Toronto, Ont.	12- 4-53	Boston	31	37	68
Miller, Jay	6:02	205	Wellesley, Mass.	7-16-60	Boston	1	4	5
Neely, Cam	6:01	205	Comox, B.C.	6- 6-65	Boston	36	36	72
Nienhuis, Kraig	6:02	205	Sarnia, Ont.	5- 9-61	Moncton-Boston	14	19	33
Pasin, Dave	6:01	205	Edmonton, Alta.	7- 8-66	Moncton	27	25	52
Podloski, Ray	6:02	210	Edmonton, Alta.	1- 5-66	Moncton	23	27	50
Reid, Dave	6:00	215	Toronto, Ont.	5-15-64	Moncton-Boston	15	25	40
Simmer, Charlie	6:03	205	Terrace Bay, Ont.	3-20-54	Boston	29	40	69
Sweeney, Bob	6:03	210	Concord, Mass.	1-25-64	Moncton-Boston	31	30	61

DEFENSEMEN

Name	Hgt.	Wgt.	Place of Birth	Date	1986-87 Club	G.	A.	Pts.
Blum, John	6:03	205	Detroit, Mich.	10- 8-59	Washington	2	8	10
Bourque, Ray	5:11	210	Montreal, Que.	12-28-60	Boston	23	72	95
Campbell, Wade	6:04	220	Peace River, Alta.	1- 2-61	Moncton-Boston	12	26	38
Cote, Alain	6:00	200	Montmagny, Que.	4- 4-67	Granby-Boston	7	24	31
Hawgood, Greg	5:08	175	Edmonton, Alta.	8-10-68	Kamloops	30	93	123
Hynes, Gord	6:01	165	Montreal, Que.	7-22-66	Moncton	2	19	21
Kluzak, Gord	6:04	210	Climax, Sask.	3- 4-64	Boston	Did not play		
Larson, Reed	6:00	195	Minneapolis, Minn.	7-30-56	Boston	12	24	36
McPherson, Darwin	6:01	195	Flin Flon, Man.	5-16-68	New Westminster	10	22	32
Pedersen, Allen	6:03	180	Edmonton, Alta.	1-13-65	Boston	1	11	12
Premak, Garth	6:01	185	Ituna, Sask.	3-15-68	Kamloops	8	28	36
Quintal, Stephane	6:03	215	Boucherville, Que.	10-22-68	Granby	13	41	54
Simonetti, Frank	6:01	185	Melrose, Mass.	9-11-62	Moncton-Boston	1	1	2
Thelven, Michael	5-11	180	Stockholm, Sweden	1- 7-61	Boston	5	15	20
Wesley, Glen	6:01	190	Red Deer, Alta.	10- 2-68	Portland	16	46	62

GOALTENDERS

Name	Hgt.	Wgt.	Place of Birth	Date	1986-87 Club	Mins.	GA.	SO.
Foster, Norm	5:09	175	Vancouver, B.C.	2-10-65	Michigan State Univ.	1383	90	..
Keans, Doug	5:07	190	Pembroke, Ont.	1- 7-58	Boston	1942	108	0
Ranford, Bill	5:10	170	Brandon, Man.	12-14-66	Boston-Moncton	2414	130	3
Romano, Roberto	5:06	170	Montreal, Que.	10-10-62	Pittsburgh-Balt.-Moncton-Boston	1837	114	0
Taillefer, Terry	6:00	160	Edmonton, Alta.	7-23-65	Boston University	1260	82	0

Buffalo Sabres

Adams Division

Chairman of the Board... Seymour H. Knox III
President .... Northrup R. Knox
Vice-Chairman of the Board .... Robert E. Rich, Jr.
Vice-President and Counsel .... Robert O. Swados
Treasurer.. Joseph T. J. Stewart
Administrative Vice-President.. Mitchell Owen
Vice-President, Finance .... Robert W. Pickel
General Manager .... Gerry Meehan
Coach .... Ted Sator
Assistant Coaches .... Barry Smith, Don Lever
Director of Professional Evaluation and Development... Craig Ramsay
Director of Amateur Evaluation and Development... Don Luce
Director of Scouting .... Rudy Migay
Coordinator of Minor League Professional Development .... Joe Crozier
Scouting Staff... Don Barrie, Jack Bowman, Frank Deegan, Dennis McIvor,
Paul Merritt, Mike Racicot, Frank Zywiec
Director of Communications.. Paul Wieland
Trainer .... Jim Pizzutelli
Assistant Trainer .... Rip Simonick
Equipment/Trainer .... John Heidinger
Home Ice.. Memorial Auditorium
Address .... Memorial Auditorium, Buffalo, N.Y. 14202
Seating Capacity.. 16,433 (including standees)
Club Colors .... Blue, White and Gold
Phone .... (716) 856-7300

| Seymour Knox III | Northrup Knox | Gerry Meehan | Ted Sator |

Buffalo Sabres 1987-88 Roster

FORWARDS	Hgt.	Wgt.	Place of Birth	Date	1986-87 Club	G.	A.	Pts.
Andersson, Mikael	5:11	180	Malmo, Sweden	5-10-66	Rochester-Buffalo	6	23	29
Andreychuk, Dave	6:03	219	Hamilton, Ont.	9-29-63	Buffalo	25	48	73
Arniel, Scott	6:01	188	Cornwall, Ont.	7-17-62	Buffalo	11	14	25
Brydges, Paul	5:11	180	Guelph, Ont.	6-21-65	Rochester-Buffalo	15	19	34
Capello, Jeff	6:01	195	Ottawa, Ont.	9-25-64	Univ. of Vermont	17	26	43
Creighton, Adam	6:05	216	Burlington, Ont.	6- 2-65	Buffalo	18	22	40
Cullen, John	5:10	185	Puslinch, Ont.	8- 2-64	Boston University	23	29	52
Cyr, Paul	5:10	208	Port Alberni, B.C.	10-31-63	Buffalo	11	16	27
Foligno, Mike	6:02	195	Sudbury, Ont.	1-29-59	Buffalo	30	29	59
Fraser, Jay	6:01	203	Ottawa, Ont.	10-26-61	Rochester	8	12	20
Gage, Jody	6:00	188	Toronto, Ont.	11-29-59	Rochester	26	39	65
Gillies, Clark	6:03	214	Moose Jaw, Sask.	4- 7-54	Buffalo	10	17	27
Gretzky, Keith	5:09	160	Brantford, Ont.	2-16-67	Hamilton	35	66	101
Guay, Francois	6:00	186	Gatineau, Que.	6- 8-68	Laval	52	77	129
Hajdu, Richard	6:00	184	Victoria, B.C.	5-10-65	Rochester	7	15	22
Hartman, Mike	6:00	183	Detroit, Mich.	2- 7-67	North Bay-Buffalo	18	27	45
Hogue, Benoit	5:10	177	Repentigny, Que.	10-28-66	Rochester	14	20	34
Jackson, Jim	5:08	190	Oshawa, Ont.	2- 1-60	Rochester	19	38	57
Kaese, Trent	5:11	219	Nanaimo, B.C.	9- 9-67	Calgary Jrs.	31	24	55
Kerr, Kevin	5:10	182	North Bay, Ont.	9-18-67	Windsor	27	41	68
Logan, Bob	6:00	190	Montreal, Que.	2-22-64	Rochester-Buffalo	37	17	54
Ludvig, Jan	5:10	195	Liberec, Czech.	9-17-61	New Jersey	7	9	16
MacIsaac, Allan	6:00	181	Antigonish, N.S.	10-10-67	Guelph	16	16	32
MacVicar, Andrew	6:01	205	Dartmouth, N.S.	3-12-69	Peterborough	6	13	19
Napier, Mark	5:10	185	Toronto, Ont.	1-28-57	Edmonton-Buffalo	13	18	31
Orlando, Gates	5:08	176	Montreal, Que.	11-16-62	Rochester-Buffalo	24	50	74
Parker, Jeff	6:03	194	St. Paul, Minn.	9- 7-64	Rochester-Buffalo	17	11	28
Priestlay, Ken	5:10	176	Vancouver, B.C.	8-24-67	Victoria-Buffalo	54	45	99
Ristau, Andy	6:05	234	Winnipeg, Man.	1-28-61	Rochester	1	1	2
Ruff, Lindy	6:02	196	Warburg, Alta.	2-17-60	Buffalo	6	14	20
Ruutuu, Christian	5:11	180	Lappeen, Finland	2-20-64	Buffalo	22	43	65
Sheppard, Ray	6:01	206	Pembroke, Ont.	5-27-66	Rochester	18	13	31
Smith, Doug	5:11	186	Ottawa, Ont.	5-17-63	Buffalo	16	24	40
Tkachuk, Grant	5:09	175	L. La Biche, Alta.	9-27-68	Saskatoon	46	36	82
Trapp, Doug	6:00	185	Balcarres, Sask.	11-28-65	Rochester	27	35	62
Tucker, John	6:00	193	Windsor, Ont.	9-29-64	Buffalo	17	34	51
Turgeon, Pierre	6:01	200	Rouyn, Que.	8-29-69	Granby	69	85	154

DEFENSEMEN	Hgt.	Wgt.	Place of Birth	Date	1986-87 Club	G.	A.	Pts.
Anderson, Shawn	6:01	196	Montreal, Que.	2- 7-68	Buffalo-Rochester	4	16	20
Baldris, Miguel	6:00	192	Montreal, Que.	1-30-68	St. Jean	7	34	41
Dunn, Richie	6:00	200	Boston, Mass.	5-12-57	Rochester-Buffalo	7	26	33
Dykstra, Steve	6:02	190	Edmonton, Alta.	2- 3-62	Rochester-Buffalo	0	1	1
Fenyves, Dave	5:11	187	Dunnville, Ont.	4-29-60	Rochester-Buffalo	7	16	23
Ferner, Mark	6:00	193	Regina, Sask.	9- 5-65	Rochester-Buffalo	0	15	15
Fogolin, Lee	6:00	200	Chicago, Ill.	2- 7-55	Edmonton-Buffalo	1	5	6
Gasseau, James	6:02	204	Carleton, Que.	5- 4-66	Rochester	0	2	2
Halkidis, Bob	5:11	194	Toronto, Ont.	3- 5-66	Rochester-Buffalo	2	9	11
Herbers, Ian	6:04	210	Sherwood Pk., Alta.	7-18-67	Swift Current	5	8	13
Hofford, Jim	6:00	195	Sudbury, Ont.	10- 4-64	Rochester-Buffalo	1	8	9
Hoover, Tim	5:10	175	North Bay, Ont.	1- 9-65	Flint	3	23	26
Housley, Phil	5:10	179	St. Paul, Minn.	3- 9-64	Buffalo	21	46	67
Johansson, Calle	5:11	198	Goteborg, Sweden	2-14-67	Bjorklovice	2	13	15
Krupp, Uwe	6:06	230	Cologne, W. Germany	6-24-65	Rochester-Buffalo	4	23	27
McSween, Don	5:11	194	Plymouth, Mich.	6- 9-64	Michigan State	7	23	30
Miller, Brad	6:04	215	Edmonton, Alta.	7-23-69	Regina	10	38	48
Moylan, Dave	6:02	185	Tillsonburg, Ont.	8-13-67	Kitchener	6	13	19
Ramsey, Mike	6:03	187	Minneapolis, Minn.	12- 3-60	Buffalo	8	31	39
Reekie, Joe	6:03	215	Petawawa, Ont.	2-22-65	Rochester-Buffalo	1	14	15

GOALTENDERS	Hgt.	Wgt.	Place of Birth	Date	1986-87 Club	Mins.	GA.	SO.
Barrasso, Tom	6:03	206	Boston, Mass.	3-31-65	Buffalo	2501	152	2
Cloutier, Jacques	5:07	169	Noranda, Que.	1- 3-60	Buffalo	2167	137	0
Puppa, Daren	6:03	191	Kirkland Lake, Ont.	3-23-63	Rochester-Buffalo	3314	159	1
Rein, Kenton	5:11	175	Toronto, Ont.	12- 9-67	Prince Albert	2996	159	0
Wakuluk, Darcy	5:11	180	Pincher Creek, Alta.	3-14-66	Rochester	545	26	0

Calgary Flames

Smythe Division

Owners .... Norman Green, Harley Hotchkiss, Norman Kwong, Mrs. Ralph Scurfield,
B. J. Seaman, D. K. Seaman
President, General Manager and Governor .... Cliff Fletcher
V.P., Business and Finance .... Clare Rhyasen
Assistant to the President .... Al Coates
Assistant General Manager .... Al MacNeil
General Counsel .... Howard Mackie & Assoc.
Coach .... Terry Crisp
Assistant Coaches .... Pierre Page, Doug Risebrough
V.P., Sales and Broadcasting .... Leo Ornest
Director of Public Relations .... Rick Skaggs
Assistant Public Relations Director .... Mike Burke
Chief Scout .... Gerry Blair
Coordinator of Scouting .... Ian McKenzie
U.S. and College Scout .... Al Godfrey
Scouting Staff .... Larry Popein, Ray Clearwater
Controller .... Lynne Tosh
Trainer .... Jim "Bearcat" Murray
Equipment Manager .... Bobby Stewart
Home Ice .... The Olympic Saddledome
Address .... P.O. Box 1540, Station M, Calgary, Alta. T2P 3B9
Seating Capacity 16,798
Club colors .... White, Red and Gold
Phone .... (403) 261-0475

Cliff Fletcher

Al MacNeil

Terry Crisp

Pierre Page

Calgary Flames 1987-88 Roster

FORWARDS	Hgt.	Wgt.	Place of Birth	Date	1986-87 Club	G.	A.	Pts.
Bakovic, Peter	6:01	190	Thunder Bay, Ont.	1-31-65	Moncton	17	34	51
Berezan, Perry	6:02	192	Edmonton, Alta.	12- 5-64	Calgary	5	3	8
Bodak, Bob	6:02	190	Thunder Bay, Ont.	5-28-61	Moncton	11	20	31
Bozek, Steve	5:11	175	Kelowna, B.C.	11-26-60	Calgary	17	18	35
Bradley, Brian	5:10	170	Kitchener, Ont.	1-21-65	Calgary-Moncton	22	34	56
Bucyk, Randy	5:11	175	Edmonton, Alta.	11- 9-62	Sherbrooke	24	39	63
Bullard, Mike	5:10	185	Ottawa, Ont.	3-10-61	Pittsburgh-Calgary	30	36	66
Bureau, Marc	6:02	195	Trois Rivieres, Que.	5-19-66	Longueuil	54	58	112
Chernomaz, Rich	5:10	185	Selkirk, Man.	9- 1-63	Maine-New Jersey	41	31	72
Doucet, Benoit	5:10	180	Montreal, Que.	4-23-63	Team Canada	27	31	58
Fleury, Theoren	5:05	153	Oxbow, Sask.	6-29-68	Moose Jaw	61	68	129
Gregoire, Bill	6:00	175	Victoria, B.C.	4- 9-67	Victoria-Calgary Jrs.	13	17	30
Grimson, Stu	6:05	230	Vancouver, B.C.	5-20-65	Univ. of Manitoba	8	8	16
Hull, Brett	5:11	195	Belleville, Ont.	8- 9-64	Moncton-Calgary	51	42	93
Hunter, Tim	6:02	202	Calgary, Alta.	9-10-60	Calgary	6	15	21
Loob, Hakan	5:09	175	Karlstad, Sweden	7- 3-60	Calgary	18	26	44
Mahoney, Scott	6:00	188	Peterborough, Ont.	4-19-69	Oshawa	13	9	22
Matteau, Stephane	6:04	183	Rouyn, Que.	9- 2-69	Hull	27	48	75
McDonald, Lanny	6:00	190	Hanna, Alta.	2-16-53	Calgary	14	12	26
Mercier, Don	6:04	210	Grimshaw, Alta.	1-21-63	Moncton	5	11	16
Mullen, Joe	5:09	180	New York, N.Y.	2-26-57	Calgary	47	40	87
Mullins, Dwight	6:00	190	Calgary, Alta.	2-28-67	Calgary Jrs.-U. of Calgary	16	11	27
Nicoletti, Martin	6:00	202	Lasalle, Que.	1-15-63	Univ. of Trois Rivieres	7	20	27
Nieuwenduk, Joe	6:03	195	Oshawa, Ont.	9-10-66	Cornell-Calgary	26	22	48
Otto, Joel	6:04	220	Elk River, Minn.	10-29-61	Calgary	19	31	50
Patterson, Colin	6:02	195	Rexdale, Ont.	5-11-60	Calgary	13	14	27
Peplinski, Jim	6:03	209	Renfrew, Ont.	10-24-60	Calgary	18	32	50
Pickell, Doug	6:01	185	London, Ont.	5- 7-68	Kamloops	34	24	58
Roberts, Gary	6:01	190	North York, Ont.	5-23-66	Moncton-Calgary	25	27	52
Rucinski, Mike	5:11	193	Wheeling, Ill.	12-12-63	Moncton-Salt Lake City	21	34	55
Simard, Martin	6:03	215	Montreal, Que.	6-25-66	Granby	30	47	77
Tonelli, John	6:01	200	Milton, Ont.	3-23-57	Calgary	20	31	51
Wenaas, Jeff	6:00	185	Eastend, Sask.	9- 1-67	Medicine Hat	42	29	71
Wilson, Carey	6:02	198	Winnipeg, Man.	5-19-62	Calgary	20	36	56

DEFENSEMEN	Hgt.	Wgt.	Place of Birth	Date	1986-87 Club	G.	A.	Pts.
Aloi, Joe	6:03	205	New Haven, Ct.	10-10-68	Hull	2	5	7
Clarke, Bruce	6:00	190	Toronto, Ont.	2-29-64	Colorado-Calgary	..	..	..
DeGray, Dale	6:00	201	Oshawa, Ont.	9- 3-63	Moncton-Calgary	16	29	45
Glynn, Brian	6:04	224	Iserlohn, W. Germany	11-23-67	Saskatoon	2	26	28
Grant, Kevin	6:04	210	Halifax, N.S.	1- 9-69	Kitchener	5	18	23
Guy, Kevan	6:03	202	Edmonton, Alta.	7-16-65	Calgary-Moncton	2	14	16
Lessard, Rick	6:02	198	Timmins, Ont.	1- 9-68	Ottawa	5	37	42
MacInnis, Al	6:02	193	Inverness, N.S.	7-11-63	Calgary	20	56	76
Macoun, Jamie	6:02	197	Newmarket, Ont.	8-17-61	Calgary	7	33	40
McCutcheon, Darwin	6:05	210	Listowel, Ont.	4-19-62	Moncton	1	10	11
Mersch, Mike	6:02	210	Skokie, Ill.	9-29-64	Salt Lake City	3	12	15
Nattress, Ric	6:02	210	Hamilton, Ont.	5-25-62	St. Louis	6	22	28
Pratt, Tom	6:03	185	Lake Placid, N.Y.	8-28-65	Bowling Green State	1	7	8
Reierson, Dave	6:00	185	Bashaw, Alta.	8-30-64	Team Canada	1	17	18
Reinhart, Paul	5:11	195	Kitchener, Ont.	1- 8-60	Calgary	15	54	69
Sabourin, Ken	6:04	204	Scarborough, Ont.	4-28-66	Moncton	1	10	11
Sheehy, Neil	6:02	215	Inter. Falls, Minn.	2- 9-60	Calgary	4	6	10
St. Arnaud, Alain	6:00	194			Moncton	0	1	1
Suter, Gary	6:00	199	Madison, Wis.	6-24-64	Calgary	9	40	49

GOALTENDERS	Hgt.	Wgt.	Place of Birth	Date	1986-87 Club	Mins.	GA.	SO.
Blair, Grant	6:00	160	Stoney Creek, Ont.	8-15-64	Salt Lake City	1421	111	0
Dadswell, Doug	5:10	175	Scarborough, Ont.	2- 7-64	Moncton-Calgary	2401	148	1
D'Amour, Marc	5:10	165	Sudbury, Ont.	4-29-61	Salt Lake City-Binghamton	981	67	0
Kosti, Rick	5:10	185	Kincaid, Sask.	9-13-63	Team Canada	1736	85	2
Lemelin, Rejean	5:11	170	Quebec City, Que.	11-19-54	Calgary	1735	94	2
Vernon, Mike	5:09	155	Calgary, Alta.	2-24-63	Calgary	2957	178	1

Chicago Black Hawks

Norris Division

President .... William W. Wirtz
Vice-President .... Arthur M. Wirtz, Jr.
Vice-President and Assistant to the President .... Thomas N. Ivan
General Manager .... Bob Pulford
Assistant G.M. and Director of Player Personnel .... Jack Davison
Head Coach .... Bob Murdoch
Assistant Coaches .... Wayne Thomas, Darryl Sutter
Scouts .... Jimmy Walker, Don Smith, Dave Lucas,
Michel Dumas, Jim Pappin, Jan Spieczny
Public Relations .... Jim DeMaria
Trainers .... Lou Varga, Randy Lacey
Home Ice .... Chicago Stadium
Address .... 1800 W. Madison Street, Chicago, Illinois 60612
Seating Capacity 17,317
Club colors .... Red, Black and White
Phone .... (312) 733-5300

| **William W. Wirtz** | **Bob Pulford** | **Jack Davison** | **Bob Murdoch** |

Chicago Black Hawks 1987-88 Roster

FORWARDS	Hgt.	Wgt.	Place of Birth	Date	1986-87 Club	G.	A.	Pts.
Belland, Brad	6:00	180	Windsor, Ont.	1- 4-67	Cornwall	28	25	53
Boudreau, Bruce	5:10	170	Toronto, Ont.	1- 9-55	Nova Scotia	35	47	82
Braccia, Rick	6:00	195	Revere, Mass.	9- 5-67	Boston College	4	5	9
Donnelly, Dave	5:11	185	Edmonton, Alta.	2- 2-62	Chicago	6	12	18
Fraser, Curt	6:00	200	Cincinnati, O.	1-12-58	Chicago	25	25	50
Greenough, Glenn	5:11	198	Sudbury, Ont.	7-20-66	Saginaw	38	43	81
Hudson, Mike	6:01	185	Guelph, Ont.	2- 6-67	Sudbury	40	57	97
Lacouture, Bill	6:02	192	Framingham, Mass.	5-28-68	Natick H.S.	15	39	54
LaPlante, Richard	5:11	175	Boucherville, Que.	3-15-67	Univ. of Vermont-Longueuil	19	34	53
Lappin, Mike	5:10	175	Chicago, Ill.	1- 1-69	Northwood Prep	20	42	62
Larmer, Steve	5:10	189	Peterborough, Ont.	6-16-61	Chicago	28	56	84
LaVarre, Mark	5:11	170	Northbrook, Ill.	2-21-65	Nova Scotia-Chicago	20	23	43
Loach, Lonnie	5:10	181	New Liskeard, Ont.	4-14-68	Guelph	31	24	55
Lowes, Glenn	6:00	184	Burlington, Ont.	1-17-68	Toronto Jrs.	10	14	24
Ludzik, Steve	5:11	186	Toronto, Ont.	4- 3-62	Chicago	5	12	17
MacGregor, Brad	6:00	195	Edmonton, Alta.	7-22-64	Nova Scotia-Saginaw	6	13	19
Mackey, David	6:03	190	N. Westminister, B.C.	7-24-66	Saginaw	26	50	76
Marquette, Dale	5:11	187	Prince George, B.C.	3- 8-68	Brandon	41	29	70
Murray, Troy	6:01	195	Calgary, Alta.	7-31-62	Chicago	28	43	71
Nanne, Marty	6:00	180	Edina, Minn.	7-21-67	Univ. of Minnesota	3	4	7
Noonan, Brian	6:01	180	Boston, Mass.	5-29-65	Nova Scotia	25	26	51
Olczyk, Ed	6:01	195	Chicago, Ill.	8-16-66	Chicago	16	35	51
Paterson, Rick	5:09	187	Kingston, Ont.	2-10-58	Chicago-Nova Scotia	6	9	15
Persson, Joakim	5:08	163	Gavle, Sweden	5-15-66	Brynas	9	8	17
Posa, Victor	6:00	193	Bari, Italy	11- 5-66	Saginaw	13	27	40
Presley, Wayne	5:11	172	Detroit, Mich.	3-23-65	Chicago	32	29	61
Reilly, John	6:03	188	Lawrence, Mass.	1- 5-68	Phillips Andover	27	23	50
Rowbothan, Dave	6:01	185	Ottawa, Ont.	1-31-67	Ottawa	26	43	69
Rychel, Warren	6:00	190	Tecumseh, Ont.	5-12-67	Ottawa-Kitchener	16	12	28
Sanipass, Everett	6:01	192	Big Cove, N.B.	2-13-68	Verdun-Granby-Chicago	35	51	86
Savard, Denis	5:10	167	Pt. Gatineau, Que.	2- 4-61	Chicago	40	50	90
Secord, Alan	6:01	212	Sudbury, Ont.	3- 3-58	Chicago	29	30	59
Stapleton, Mike	5:10	163	Sarnia, Ont.	5- 5-66	Team Canada-Chicago	5	10	15
Tepper, Stephen	6:04	205	Santa Ana, Calif.	3-10-69	Westboro	34	18	52
Thayer, Chris	6:02	190	Exeter, N.H.	11- 9-67	Kent H.S.	15	22	37
Torkki, Jari	6:00	163	Finland	8-11-65	Lukko, Finland	27	8	35
Vincelette, Dan	6:01	202	Verdun, Que.	8- 1-67	Drummondville	34	35	69
Watson, Bill	6:01	190	Pine Falls, Man.	3-30-64	Chicago	13	19	32
Werness, Lance	6:00	175	Burnsville, Minn.	3-28-69	Burnsville H.S.	17	29	46
Williams, Sean	6:01	182	Oshawa, Ont.	1-28-68	Oshawa	21	23	44

DEFENSEMEN	Hgt.	Wgt.	Place of Birth	Date	1986-87 Club	G.	A.	Pts.
Badeau, Rene	6:00	190	Trois-Rivieres, Que.	1-31-64	Saginaw	4	14	18
Beck, Brad	5:11	185	Vancouver, B.C.	2-10-64	Saginaw	10	24	34
Bergevin, Marc	5:11	178	Montreal, Que.	8-11-65	Chicago	4	10	14
Brown, Keith	6:01	191	Cornerbrook, Nfld.	5- 6-60	Chicago	4	23	27
Cassidy, Bruce	5:11	176	Ottawa, Ont.	5-20-65	N.S.-Chi.-T. Canada-Sag.	7	26	33
Dagenais, Mike	6:03	198	Gloucester, Ont.	7-22-69	Peterborough	1	17	18
DiFiore, Ralph	6:01	181	Montreal, Que.	4-20-66	Saginaw	1	5	6
Doyon, Mario	6:00	174	Quebec City, Que.	8-27-68	Drummondville	18	47	65
Hamilton, Brad	6:00	175	Calgary, Alta.	3-30-67	Michigan State Univ.	3	27	30
Heed, Jonas	6:00	174	Sodertalje, Sweden	1- 3-67	Sodertalje	0	2	2
Herbert, Rick	6:01	180	Toronto, Ont.	7-10-67	Brandon-Spokane-Saginaw	3	36	39
Kurzawski, Mark	6:03	199	Chicago, Ill.	2-25-68	Windsor	5	23	28
Manson, Dave	6:02	190	Prince Albert, Sask.	1-27-67	Chicago	1	8	9
McGill, Ryan	6:02	197	Sherwood Pk, Alta.	2-28-69	Swift Current	12	36	48
Murray, Bob	5:10	186	Kingston, Ont.	11-26-54	Chicago	6	38	44
Nylund, Gary	6:03	210	Surrey, B.C.	10-23-63	Chicago	7	20	27
O'Callahan, Jack	6:01	189	Charleston, Mass.	7-24-57	Chicago	1	13	14
Paterson, Marc	6:00	185	Ottawa, Ont.	2-22-64	Moncton	6	21	27
Paynter, Kent	6:00	186	Summerside, P.E.I.	4-27-65	Nova Scotia	2	6	8
Pound, Ian	6:01	183	Brockville, Ont.	1-22-67	Kitchener-London-Toronto Jrs.	2	13	15
Randall, Dave	5:10	185	N. Vancouver, B.C.	4- 5-63	No. Mich.-Team Canada	7	25	32
Russell, Cam	6:04	175	Halifax, N.S.	1-12-69	Hull	3	16	19
Williams, Dan	6:02	180	Oak Park, Ill.	4-15-66	Elmira	5	11	16
Wilson, Behn	6:03	210	Toronto, Ont.	12-19-58	Chicago	Did not play		
Wilson, Doug	6:01	187	Ottawa, Ont.	7- 5-57	Chicago	16	32	48
Wilson, Rik	6:00	185	Long Beach, Ca.	6-17-62	Nova Scotia	8	13	21
Yawney, Trent	6:03	183	Hudson Bay, Sask.	9-29-65	Team Canada	4	15	19

GOALTENDERS	Hgt.	Wgt.	Place of Birth	Date	1986-87 Club	Mins.	GA.	SO.
Bannerman, Murray	5:11	185	Ft. Francis, Ont.	4-27-57	Chicago	2059	142	0
Belfour, Ed	5:11	170	Carman, Man.	4-21-65	Univ. of North Dakota	2049	81	3
Clifford, Chris	5:09	139	Kingston, Ont.	5-26-66	Kingston	2596	191	1
Helmuth, Andy	5:10	172	Detroit, Mich.	3-18-67	Guelph	2637	188	3
Mason, Bob	6:01	180	Intl. Falls, Minn.	4-22-61	Washington	2536	137	0
Pang, Darren	5:05	155	Medford, Ont.	2-17-64	Saginaw-Nova Scotia	2883	171	2
Reid, John	5:11	202	Windsor, Ont.	2-18-67	North Bay	2737	142	1
Waite, Jimmy	6:00	163	Sherbrooke, Que.	4-15-69	Chicoutimi	2569	209	2

Detroit
Red Wings
Norris Division

Owner and President... Michael Ilitch
Executive Vice-President.. James Lites
Secretary/Treasurer .... Marian Ilitch
General Counsel... Denise Ilitch-Lites
Vice-President/Marketing .... Rosanne Kozerski-Brown
Vice-President and General Manager .... Jim Devellano
Asst. General Manager/Director of Player Development.. Nick Polano
Head Coach .... Jacques Demers
Assistant Coaches .... Colin Campbell, Don MacAdam
Assistant Coach/Goaltender .... Dave Dryden
Director of Pro Scouting .... Dan Belisle
Director of Public Relations... Bill Jamieson
Director of Scouting/Player Procurement... Neil Smith
USA College/High School Scout .... Billy Dea
Eastern USA Scout .... Jerry Moschella
Western Canada Scout.. Ken Holland
Scouts.. Chris Coury, Frank Michalek, Dave Polano,
Christer Rockstrom, Mike Daski
Director of Advertising Sales/Promotions .... Terry Murphy
Physical Therapist .... Jim Pengelly
Trainer.. Mark Brennan
Assistant Trainer .... Larry Wasylon
Home Ice .... Joe Louis Sports Arena
Address... 600 Civic Center Drive, Detroit, Mich. 48226
Seating Capacity... 19,275
Club colors... Red and White
Phone .... (313) 567-7333

Mike Ilitch   **Jim Devellano**   **Nick Polano**   **Jacques Demers**

Detroit Red Wings 1987-88 Roster

FORWARDS	Hgt.	Wgt.	Place of Birth	Date	1986-87 Club	G.	A.	Pts.
Ashton, Brent	6:01	210	Saskatoon, Sask.	5-18-60	Quebec-Detroit	40	35	75
Aubrey, Pierre	5:10	175	Cap-de-la-Mad., Que.	4-15-60	Adirondack	3	7	10
Barr, David	6:01	190	Toronto, Ont.	11-30-60	St. Louis-Hartford-Detroit	15	17	32
Bissett, Tom	6:01	180	Seattle, Wash.	3-13-66	Michigan Tech	16	19	35
Bjur, Thomas	6:01	207	Stockholm, Sweden	8-28-66	Portland	28	26	54
Bridgman, Mel	6:00	200	Trenton, Ont.	4-28-55	New Jersey-Detroit	10	33	43
Burr, Shawn	6:01	180	Sarnia, Ont.	7- 1-66	Detroit	22	25	47
Chabot, John	6:02	200	Summerside, P.E.I.	5-18-62	Pittsburgh	14	22	36
Fedyk, Brent	6:00	180	Yorkton, Sask.	3- 8-67	Portland	19	21	40
Gallant, Gerard	5:10	185	Summerside, P.E.I.	9- 2-63	Detroit	38	34	72
Gober, Mike	6:00	192	St. Louis, Mo.	4-10-67	Laval	49	47	96
Graves, Adam	5:11	185	Toronto, Ont.	4-12-68	Windsor	45	55	100
Higgins, Tim	6:01	185	Ottawa, Ont.	2- 7-58	Detroit	12	14	26
Holland, Dennis	5:10	164	Vernon, B.C.	1-30-69	Portland	36	77	113
Karlsson, Lars	5:10	176	Karlstad, Sweden	8-18-66	Bjorkloven	10	24	34
King, Kris	6:00	193	Bracebridge, Ont.	2-18-66	Peterborough	23	33	56
Klima, Petr	6:00	190	Chaomutov, Czech.	12-23-64	Detroit	30	23	53
Kocur, Joe	6:00	195	Calgary, Alta.	12-21-64	Detroit	9	9	18
Krentz, Dale	5:11	187	Steinbach, Man.	12-19-61	Adirondack	32	39	71
Kumpel, Mark	6:00	190	Wakefield, Mass.	3- 7-61	Quebec-Detroit	1	9	10
Lamb, Mark	5:09	180	Ponteix, Sask.	8- 3-64	Adirondack-Detroit	16	37	53
Martinson, Steve	6:01	205	Minnetonka, Minn.	6-21-61	Hershey-Adirondack	1	4	5
McKay, Randy	6:01	185	Montreal, Que.	1-25-67	Michigan Tech	5	11	16
Murphy, Joe	6:01	190	London, Ont.	10-16-67	Adirondack-Detroit	21	39	60
Oates, Adam	5:11	185	Westin, Ont.	8-27-62	Detroit	15	32	47
O'Regan, Thomas	5:10	180	Cambridge, Mass.	12-29-61	Adirondack	20	42	62
Potvin, Marc	6:01	185	Ottawa, Ont.	1-29-67	Bowling Green	5	15	20
Probert, Bob	6:03	215	Windsor, Ont.	6- 5-65	Detroit-Adirondack	14	15	29
Scott, Kevin	5:10	170	Vernon, B.C.	11- 3-67	Vernon	56	70	126
Seiling, Ric	6:01	180	Elmira, Ont.	12-15-57	Detroit	3	8	11
Shibicky, Bill	5:11	189	Burnaby, B.C.	1-25-64	Michigan State	43	36	79
Strong, Ken	5:11	175	Toronto, Ont.	5- 9-63	Adirondack	7	13	20
Yzerman, Steve	5:11	180	Cranbrook, B.C.	5- 9-65	Detroit	31	59	90

DEFENSEMEN	Hgt.	Wgt.	Place of Birth	Date	1986-87 Club	G.	A.	Pts.
Bannister, Darin	6:00	185	Calgary, Alta.	1-16-67	Univ. of Ill.-Chicago	4	16	20
Chiasson, Steve	6:01	205	Barrie, Ont.	4-14-67	Detroit	1	4	5
Clifford, Sean	6:01	200	North Bay, Ont.	5-11-67	Ohio State	3	8	11
DeGaetano, Phil	6:01	203	Roslyn, N.Y.	8- 9-63	Adirondack	7	23	30
Delorme, Gilbert	6:01	205	Boucherville, Que.	11-25-62	Quebec-Detroit	4	3	7
Doyle, Rob	5:11	185	Lindsay, Ont.	2-10-64	Colorado College	17	37	54
Halward, Doug	6:01	197	Toronto, Ont.	11- 1-55	Vancouver-Detroit	0	6	6
Hamalainen, Erik	6:01	187	Rauma, Finland	4-20-65	Lukko	8	8	16
Houda, Doug	6:02	190	Blairmore, Alta.	6- 3-66	Adirondack	6	23	29
Korol, David	6:01	175	Winnipeg, Man.	3- 1-65	Adirondack	1	4	5
Kruppke, Gord	6:01	200	Slave Lake, Alta.	4- 2-69	Prince Albert	2	10	12
LaMoine, Mike	6:00	188	Grand Forks, N. Dak.	12- 1-66	Univ. of No. Dakota	2	17	19
Lewis, Dave	6:02	205	Kindersley, Sask.	7- 3-53	Detroit	2	5	7
Luckraft, Mike	6:01	186	Jackson, Mich.	11-28-66	Univ. of Minnesota	0	2	2
Luongo, Chris	6:00	180	Detroit, Mich.	3-17-67	Michigan State	4	16	20
Mayer, Derek	6:00	185	Rossland, B.C.	5-21-67	Univ. of Denver	5	17	22
Melrose, Barry	6:00	205	Kelvington, Sask.	7-15-56	Adirondack	4	9	13
Morton, Dean	6:01	196	Peterborough, Ont.	2-27-68	Oshawa	1	11	12
Norwood, Lee	6:01	198	Oakland, Calif.	2- 2-60	Detroit-Adirondack	6	24	30
O'Connell, Mike	5:09	180	Chicago, Ill.	11-25-55	Detroit	5	26	31
O'Regan, Thomas	5:10	180	Cambridge, Mass.	12-29-61	Adirondack	20	42	62
Quinlan, Craig	6:02	200	St. Paul, Minn.	4- 9-69	Hill Murray H.S.	7	16	23
Racine, Yves	6:00	183	Matane, Que.	2- 7-69	Longueuil	7	43	50
Rose, Jay	6:00	181	Newton, Mass.	7- 6-66	Clarkston Univ.	2	10	12
Schena, Robert	6:01	190	Saugus, Mass.	5- 5-67	Rensselaer Poly Inst.	1	9	10
Sharples, Jeff	6:00	187	Terrace, B.C.	7-28-67	Portland-Detroit	25	36	61
Smith, Dennis	5:11	192	Detroit, Mich.	7-27-64	Adirondack	4	24	28
Smith, James	6:01	215	Castlegar, B.C.	1-18-64	Adirondack	8	27	35
Snepsts, Harold	6:03	210	Edmonton, Alta.	10-24-54	Detroit	1	13	14
Stark, Jan	6:00	190	Vernon, B.C.	2-29-68	Portland	2	14	16
Veitch, Darren	6:00	190	Saskatoon, Sask.	4-24-60	Detroit	13	45	58
Wilkie, Bob	6:02	200	Calgary, Alta.	2-11-69	Swift Current	12	38	50
Zombo, Rick	6:01	195	Des Plaines, Ill.	5- 8-63	Adirondack-Detroit	1	10	11

GOALTENDERS	Hgt.	Wgt.	Place of Birth	Date		Mins.	GA.	SO.
Cheveldae, Tim	5:10	175	Melville, Sask.	2-15-68	Saskatoon	1909	133	2
Eliot, Darren	6:01	175	Milton, Ont.	11-26-61	Los Angeles-New Haven	1643	118	1
Gowans, Mark	6:00	160	Bay City, Mich.	3-26-67	Hamilton	1106	82	0
Hanlon, Glen	6:00	185	Brandon, Man.	2-20-57	Detroit	1963	104	1
Hansch, Randy	5:10	165	Edmonton, Alta.	2- 8-66	Kalamazoo-Adirondack	1470	93	2
King, Scott	6:01	170	Thunder Bay, Ont.	6-25-67	Univ. of Maine	1111	58	0
Reimer, Mark	5:11	170	Calgary, Alta.	3-23-67	Saskatoon	2442	141	1
St. Laurent, Sam	5:10	190	Arvida, Que.	2-16-59	Detroit-Adirondack	1739	114	1
Stefan, Greg	5:11	180	Brantford, Ont.	2-11-61	Detroit	2351	135	1

Edmonton Oilers

Smythe Division

Owner/Governor .... Peter Pocklington
Alternate Governor .... Glen Sather
General Counsels .... Bob Lloyd, Gary Frohlich
President, General Manager and Co-Coach .... Glen Sather
Co-Coach .... John Muckler
Assistant General Manager .... Bruce MacGregor
Assistant Coach .... Ted Green
Director of Player Personnel/Chief Scout .... Barry Fraser
Scouting Staff .... Lorne Davis, Ace Bailey, Ed Chadwick, Matti Vaisanen
Controller .... Werner Baum
Executive Secretary... Diana Hrynchuk
Director of Public Relations... Bill Tuele
Assistant Public Relations Director .... Steve Knowles
Trainer... Barrie Stafford
Assistant Trainer... Lyle Kulchisky
Athletic Therapist .... Peter Millar
Team Physician .... Dr. Gordon Cameron
Home Ice... Northlands Coliseum
Address .... Edmonton, Alta. T5B 4M9
Seating Capacity... 17,502 (Standing 190)
Club colors... Blue, Orange and White
Phone .... (403) 474-8561

Peter Pocklington   **Glen Sather**   **John Muckler**   **Bruce MacGregor**

Edmonton Oilers 1987-88 Roster

FORWARDS

	Hgt.	Wgt.	Place of Birth	Date	1986-87 Club	G.	A.	Pts.
Anderson, Glenn	5:11	185	Vancouver, B.C.	10- 2-60	Edmonton	35	38	73
Buchberger, Kelly	6:02	190	Lagenburg, Sask.	12- 2-66	Nova Scotia	12	20	32
Crawford, Louis	6:00	185	Belleville, Ont.	11- 5-62	Nova Scotia	3	4	7
Graves, Steve	5:10	190	Kingston, Ont.	4- 7-64	Nova Scotia-Edmonton	20	10	30
Gretzky, Wayne	6:00	170	Brantford, Ont.	1-26-61	Edmonton	62	121	183
Hopkins, Dean	6:01	210	Cobourg, Ont.	6- 6-59	Nova Scotia	20	25	45
Hunter, Dave	5:11	200	Petrolia, Ont.	1- 1-58	Edmonton	6	9	15
Issel, Kim	6:03	184	Regina, Sask.	9-25-67	Prince Albert	31	44	75
Krushelnyski, Mike	6:02	200	Montreal, Que.	4-27-60	Edmonton	16	35	51
Kurri, Jari	6:00	190	Helsinki, Finland	5-18-60	Edmonton	54	54	108
Lacombe, Normand	5:11	205	Pierrefonds, Que.	10-18-64	Roch.-Buff.-N.S.-Edm.	13	17	30
MacTavish, Craig	6:00	190	London, Ont.	8-15-58	Edmonton	20	19	39
Matulik, Ivan	6:00	194	Nitra, Czech.	6-17-68	Slovan Bratislava	1	3	4
McClelland, Kevin	6:00	200	Oshawa, Ont.	7- 4-62	Edmonton	12	13	25
McSorley, Marty	6:01	210	Hamilton, Ont.	5-18-63	Edmonton-Nova Scotia	4	6	10
Messier, Mark	6:01	205	Edmonton, Alta.	1-18-61	Edmonton	37	70	107
Metcalfe, Scott	6:00	195	Vramalea, Ont.	1- 6-67	Windsor-Kingston	25	57	82
Moller, Mike	6:00	190	Calgary, Alta.	6-16-62	Nova Scotia-Edmonton	16	34	50
Tikkanen, Esa	5:11	185	Helsinki, Finland	1-25-65	Edmonton	34	44	78
Van Dorp, Wayne	6:05	230	Vancouver, B.C.	5-19-61	Roch.-N.S.-Edmonton	9	6	15

DEFENSEMEN

	Hgt.	Wgt.	Place of Birth	Date	1986-87 Club	G.	A.	Pts.
Barbe, Mario	6:00	195	Cadillac, Que.	3-17-67	Granby	7	25	32
Beukeboom, Jeff	6:04	210	Ajax, Ont.	3-28-65	Edmonton-Nova Scotia	4	15	19
Campedelli, Dominic	6:01	185	Cohasset, Mass.	4- 3-64	Hershey-Nova Scotia	8	17	25
Coffey, Paul	6:00	200	Weston, Ont.	6- 1-61	Edmonton	17	50	67
Dion, Grant	6:00	190	Nelson, B.C.	1-17-64	Muskegon-Nova Scotia	8	19	27
Evans, Shawn	6:02	195	Kingston, Ont.	9- 7-65	Nova Scotia	7	28	35
Huddy, Charlie	6:00	210	Oshawa, Ont.	6- 2-59	Edmonton	4	15	19
Lowe, Kevin	6:02	195	Lachute, Que.	4-15-59	Edmonton	8	29	37
Miner, John	5:10	190	Moose Jaw, Sask.	7-28-65	Nova Scotia	5	28	33
Muni, Craig	6:02	200	Toronto, Ont.	7-19-62	Edmonton	7	22	29
Odelein, Selmar	6:00	195	Quill Lake, Sask.	4-11-66	Nova Scotia	0	1	1
Playfair, Jim	6:03	205	Vanderhoof, B.C.	5-22-64	Nova Scotia	1	21	22
Smith, Steve	6:02	210	Glasgow, Scotland	4-30-63	Edmonton	7	15	22
Tuer, Al	6:00	175	N. Battleford, Sask.	7-19-63	Nova Scotia	1	14	15
Wiemer, Jim	6:04	200	Sudbury, Ont.	1- 9-61	Nova Scotia	9	32	41

GOALTENDERS

	Hgt.	Wgt.	Place of Birth	Date	1986-87 Club	Mins.	GA.	SO.
Beals, Darren	6:00	187	Dartmouth, N.S.	8-28-68	Kitchener-Ottawa	2582	190	1
Fuhr, Grant	5:10	185	Spruce Grove, Alta.	9-28-62	Edmonton	2388	137	0
Moog, Andy	5:09	170	Penticton, B.C.	2-18-60	Edmonton	2461	144	0
Reaugh, Daryl	6:04	200	Prince George, B.C.	2-13-65	Nova Scotia	2637	163	1
Roach, David	5:10	170	Burnaby, B.C.	1-10-65	Michigan Tech Univ.	1811	151	0

Hartford Whalers

Adams Division

Managing General Partner, Chairman and Governor	Howard L. Baldwin
President, G.M. and Alternate Govenor	Emile Francis
Alternate Governor	Donald G. Conrad
Coach	Jack Evans
Assistant General Manager	Bob Crocker
Special Assistant to Managing General Partner	Gordie Howe
Assistant Coach	Claude Larose
Director of Player Personnel	Steve Brklacich
Scouts	David McNab, Leo Boivin
Trainer	Tommy Woodcock
Equipment Manager	Skip Cunningham
V.P., Marketing and Public Relations	William E. Barnes
V.P., Finance and Development	W. David Andrews III
Assistant to Managing General Partner	Camille Beck
Controller	Michael J. Amendola
Director of Public Relations	Phil Langan
Assistant Director of Public Relations	Mark Willand
Chief Statistician	Frank Polnaszek
Home Ice	Hartford Civic Center
Address	One Civic Center Plaza, Hartford, Conn. 06103
Seating Capacity	15,200
Club colors	Blue, Green and White
Phone	(203) 728-3366

Howard Baldwin   **Emile Francis**   **Bob Crocker**   **Jack Evans**

Hartford Whalers 1987-88 Roster

FORWARDS	Hgt.	Wgt.	Place of Birth	Date	1986-87 Club	G.	A.	Pts.
Anderson, John	5:11	180	Toronto, Ont.	3-28-57	Hartford	31	44	75
Babych, Wayne	5:11	195	Edmonton, Alta.	6- 6-58	Hartford-Binghamton	2	5	7
Brant, Chris	6:01	190	Belleville, Ont.	8-26-65	Binghamton-Salt Lake City	27	38	65
Callaghan, Gary	5:11	175	Oshawa, Ont.	8-12-67	Belleville-Kitchener	30	30	60
Channell, Todd	5:10	185	Naperville, Ill.	8- 8-63	Binghamton-Salt Lake City	23	23	46
Churla, Shane	6:01	200	Fernie, B.C.	6-24-65	Binghamton-Hartford	1	6	7
Chyzowski, Ron	5:10	170	Edmonton, Alta.	8-14-65	Northern Michigan Univ.	15	22	37
Courteau, Yves	5:11	183	Montreal, Que.	4-25-64	Hartford-Binghamton	15	28	43
Dineen, Kevin	5:10	180	Quebec City, Que.	10-28-63	Hartford	40	39	79
Evason, Dean	5:10	180	Flin Flon, Man.	8-22-64	Hartford	22	37	59
Ferraro, Ray	5:11	185	Trail, B.C.	8-23-64	Hartford	27	32	59
Francis, Ron	6:02	200	Sault Ste. Marie, Ont.	3- 1-63	Hartford	30	63	93
Gardner, Bill	5:10	170	Toronto, Ont.	3-19-60	Hartford-Binghamton	17	45	62
Gaume, Dallas	5:10	180	Innisfal, Alta.	8-27-63	Binghamton	18	39	57
Gavin, Stewart	5:11	185	Ottawa, Ont.	3-15-60	Hartford	20	22	42
Hull, Jody	6:02	198	Petrolia, Ont.	2- 2-69	Peterborough	18	34	52
Jarvis, Doug	5:09	175	Brantford, Ont.	3-24-55	Hartford	9	13	22
Johnson, Brian	5:10	180	Two Harbors, Minn.	3- 7-65	Univ. of Minn.-Duluth	20	20	40
Kortko, Roger	5:10	175	Hafford, Sask.	2- 1-63	Springfield	16	30	46
Krampotich, Mickey	5:11	185	Hibbing, Minn.	....	Univ. of North Dakota	27	27	54
Lawless, Paul	5:11	185	Scarborough, Ont.	7- 2-64	Hartford	22	32	54
MacDermid, Paul	6:01	200	Chesley, Ont.	4-14-63	Hartford	7	11	18
MacKenzie, Jean Marc	5:10	185	Sydney, N.S.	10-29-66	Sault Ste. Marie-London	48	55	103
Martin, Tom	6:02	195	Victoria, B.C.	5-11-64	Adirondack-Winnipeg	6	6	12
Millar, Mike	5:10	170	St. Catharines, Ont.	4-28-65	Binghamton-Hartford	47	34	81
Robertson, Torrie	5:11	200	Victoria, B.C.	8- 2-61	Hartford	1	0	1
Semenko, Dave	6:03	220	Winnipeg, Man.	7-12-57	Edmonton-Hartford	4	8	12
Tippett, Dave	5:10	180	Moosomin, Sask.	8-25-61	Hartford	9	22	31
Turgeon, Sylvain	6:00	195	Noranda, Que.	1-17-65	Hartford	23	13	36
Verbeek, Brian	5:09	195	Wyoming, Ont.	10-22-66	Salt Lake City	22	15	37
Yake, Terry	5:11	175	New Westminster, B.C.	10-22-68	Brandon	44	58	102

DEFENSEMEN	Hgt.	Wgt.	Place of Birth	Date	1986-87 Club	G.	A.	Pts.
Babych, Dave	6:02	215	Edmonton, Alta.	5-23-61	Hartford	8	33	41
Burt, Adam	6:02	195	Detroit, Mich.	1-15-69	North Bay	4	27	31
Chapman, Brian	6:00	185	Brockville, Ont.	2-10-68	Belleville	4	32	36
Cote, Sylvain	5:11	185	Quebec City, Que.	1-19-66	Hull-Hartford	4	12	16
Cronin, Shawn	6:01	205	Joliet, Ill.	8-20-63	Binghamton-Salt Lake City	8	17	25
Kleinendorst, Scot	6:03	215	Grand Rapids, Minn.	1-16-60	Hartford	3	9	12
Ladouceur, Randy	6:02	220	Brockville, Ont.	6-30-60	Detroit-Hartford	5	9	14
Laforge, Marc	6:02	201	Sudbury, Ont.	1- 3-68	Kingston	2	10	12
McEwen, Mike	6:01	185	Hornepayne, Ont.	8-10-56	Hartford	8	8	16
Murzyn, Dana	6:02	200	Regina, Sask.	12- 9-66	Hartford	9	19	28
Quenneville, Joel	6:01	200	Windsor, Ont.	9-15-58	Hartford	3	7	10
Samuelsson, Ulf	6:01	195	Fagursta, Sweden	3-26-64	Hartford	2	21	23
Shaw, Brad	5:11	180	Cambridge, Ont.	4-28-64	Binghamton-Hartford	9	30	39
Vellucci, Mike	6:01	180	Farmington, Mich.	8-11-66	Salt Lake City	5	30	35
Vichorek, Mark	6:03	200	Moose Lake, Minn.	5- 1-63	Salt Lake City	1	0	1

GOALTENDERS	Hgt.	Wgt.	Place of Birth	Date	1986-87 Club	Mins.	GA.	SO.
Evoy, Sean	6:00	190	Sudbury, Ont.	2-11-66	Oshawa	1702	89	2
Liut, Mike	6:02	195	Weston, Ont.	1- 7-56	Hartford	3476	187	4
Sidorkiewicz, Peter	5:09	180	Dabr. Bialo., Poland	6-29-63	Binghamton	3304	161	4
Weeks, Steve	5:11	165	Scarborough, Ont.	6-30-58	Hartford	1367	78	1
Whitmore, Kay	5:11	165	Sudbury, Ont.	4-10-67	Peterborough	2159	118	1

Los Angeles Kings

Smythe Division

Owner and Governor .... Dr. Jerry Buss
Co-Owner .... Bruce McNall
Alternate Governors .... Ken Doi, Rogie Vachon, Bruce McNall
General Manager .... Rogie Vachon
Head Coach .... Mike Murphy
Assistant Coaches .... Phil Myre, Bryan Maxwell
Administrative Assistant .... John Wolf
Head Amateur Scout .... Ted O'Connor
Scouting Staff .... Ross Tyrell, Alex Smart, Skip Schamehorn,
Jim Anderson, Bob Owen, Serge Blanchard, Gary Sargent, Nick Beverley, Gordon Evanson
Director of Public Relations .... David Courtney
Public Relations Assistant .... Diane Reesman
Trainers .... Pete Demers, Mark O'Neill
Home Ice .... The Forum
Address .... 3900 West Manchester Blvd., P. O. Box 10
The Forum, Inglewood, Calif. 90306
Seating Capacity 16,005
Club Colors .... Purple and Gold
Phone .... (213) 674-6000

Dr. Jerry Buss   **Bruce McNall**   **Rogie Vachon**   **Mike Murphy**

Los Angeles Kings 1987-88 Roster

FORWARDS	Hgt.	Wgt.	Place of Birth	Date	1986-87 Club	G.	A.	Pts.
Batters, Greg	6:01	196	Victoria, B.C.	1-10-67	Victoria	21	40	61
Bourne, Bob	6:03	197	Netherhill, Sask.	6-21-54	Los Angeles	13	9	22
Carpenter, Bobby	6:00	190	Beverley, Mass.	7-13-63	Wash.-N.Y. Rang.-Los Ang.	9	18	27
Carson, Jimmy	6:00	185	Southfield, Mich.	7-20-68	Los Angeles	37	42	79
Couturier, Sylvain	6:02	205	Greenfield Park, Que.	4-23-68	Laval	39	51	90
Currie, Glen	6:01	180	Montreal, Que.	7-18-58	New Haven	12	16	28
Deegan, Shannon	6:02	190	Montreal, Que.	3-19-66	Univ. of Vermont	19	21	40
Duncanson, Craig	6:00	190	Naughton, Ont.	3-17-67	Cornwall-Los Angeles	22	45	67
Edlund, Par	5:11	198	Nynashamn, Sweden	4- 9-67	Sweden Jr. Nationals	5	6	11
Erickson, Bryan	5:09	170	Roseau, Minn.	3- 7-60	Los Angeles	20	30	50
Flanagan, Tim	6:00	185	Red Deer, Alta.	3- 6-67	Calgary Jrs.	13	14	27
Fox, Jim	5:08	175	Coniston, Ont.	5-18-60	Los Angeles	19	42	61
Gratton, Dan	6:00	185	Brantford, Ont.	12- 7-66	New Haven	6	10	16
Guay, Paul	6:00	193	N. Smithfield, R.I.	9- 2-63	Los Angeles-New Haven	3	8	11
Kelly, Paul	6:00	180	Hamilton, Ont.	4-17-67	Guelph	27	48	75
Krakiwski, Sean	6:00	185	Calgary, Alta.	12-29-67	Calgary Jrs.-Spokane	19	42	61
Kudelski, Bob	6:01	200	Springfield, Mass.	3- 3-64	Yale University	25	22	47
McKenna, Sean	6:00	190	Asbestos, Que.	3- 7-62	Los Angeles	14	19	33
McSorley, Chris	5:11	185	Hamilton, Ont.	3-22-62	New Haven-Muskegon	20	19	39
Nicholls, Bernie	6:00	185	Haliburton, Ont.	6-24-61	Los Angeles	33	48	81
Paterson, Joe	6:02	205	Toronto, Ont.	6-25-60	Los Angeles	2	1	3
Phair, Lyle	6:01	195	Pilot Mound, Man.	8-31-61	New Haven-Los Angeles	21	27	48
Robitaille, Luc	6:01	190	Montreal, Que.	2-17-66	Los Angeles	45	39	84
Sykes, Phil	5:10	175	Dawson Creek, B.C.	3-18-59	Los Angeles	6	15	21
Taylor, Dave	6:00	195	Levack, Ont.	12- 4-55	Los Angeles	18	44	62
Wilks, Brian	5:11	175	N. York, Ont.	2-27-66	New Haven	16	20	36
Wilson, Ross	6:03	197	The Pas, Man.	6-26-69	Peterborough	28	11	39
Williams, Tiger	5:11	190	Weyburn, Sask.	2- 3-54	Los Angeles	16	18	34

DEFENSEMEN	Hgt.	Wgt.	Place of Birth	Date	1986-87 Club	G.	A.	Pts.
Baumgartner, Ken	6:01	196	Flin Flon, Man.	3-11-66	New Haven	0	3	3
Duchesne, Steve	6:00	190	Sept-Iles, Que.	6-30-65	Los Angeles	13	25	38
English, John	6:02	190	Toronto, Ont.	5-13-66	New Haven-Flint	1	2	3
Germain, Eric	6:01	195	Quebec City, Que.	6-26-66	Fredericton-Flint	2	10	12
Hammond, Ken	6:01	190	Pt. Credit, Ont.	8-22-63	New Haven-Los Angeles	1	17	18
Hardy, Mark	5:11	187	Semaden, Switzerland..	2- 1-59	Los Angeles	3	27	30
Hayton, Brian	6:00	198	Peterborough, Ont.	1-22-68	Guelph	6	19	25
Kennedy, Dean	6:02	200	Redvers, Sask.	1-18-63	Los Angeles	6	14	20
Laidlaw, Tom	6:02	205	Brampton, Ont.	4-15-58	N.Y. Rangers-Los Angeles	1	13	14
Larocque, Denis	6:01	205	Hawkesbury, Ont.	5-10-67	Guelph	4	10	14
Ledyard, Grant	6:02	190	Winnipeg, Man.	11-19-61	Los Angeles	14	23	37
McBean, Wayne	6:02	195	Calgary, Alta.	2-21-69	Medicine Hat	12	41	53
Playfair, Larry	6:04	220	Fort St. James, B.C.	6-23-58	Los Angeles	2	7	9
Redmond, Craig	5:10	187	Dawson Creek, B.C.	9-22-65	Los Angeles-New Haven	3	9	12
Wells, Jay	6:01	205	Paris, Ont.	5-18-59	Los Angeles	7	29	36

GOALTENDERS	Hgt.	Wgt.	Place of Birth	Date	1986-87 Club	Mins.	GA.	SO.
Fitzpatrick, Mark	6:02	190	Toronto, Ont.	11-13-68	Medicine Hat	2844	159	4
Healy, Glenn	5:09	183	Pickering, Ont.	8-23-62	New Haven	2827	173	1
Jensen, Al	5:10	180	Hamilton, Ont.	11-27-58	Wash.-Bing.-Los Ang.	1312	96	0
Janecyk, Bob	6:01	180	Chicago, Ill.	5-18-57	Los Angeles	420	34	0
Melanson, Roland	5:10	180	Moncton, N.B.	6-28-60	Los Angeles	2734	168	1
Strome, Greg	5:09	160	Muenster, Sask.	7-18-65	Univ. of North Dakota	40	3	0

Minnesota North Stars

Norris Division

Co-Chairmen of the Board	George Gund III and Gordon Gund
President	John Karr
Vice-President, General Manager	Lou Nanne
Assistant General Manager	Glen Sonmor
Administrative Assistant	Murray Oliver
Coach	Herb Brooks
Assistant Coach	J.P. Parise
Chief Scout	Harry Howell
Special Assignment Scout	Dick Bouchard
Director of Public Relations	Dick Dillman
Publications Manager	Joe Janasz
Public Relations Assistant	Joan Preston
Community Relations Director	Patty Connolly
Scouts	Hexi Riihiranta, Les Jackson, George Agar, Gump Worsley, Smokey Cerrone
Trainer	Dick Rose
Assistant Trainer	Dave Smith
Equipment Manager	Mark Baribeau
Home Ice	Metropolitan Sports Center
Address	7901 Cedar Avenue S., Bloomington, Minn. 55420
Seating Capacity	15,449
Club colors	Green, White, Gold and Blac'
Phone	(612) 853-9333

George Gund III	**Gordon Gund**	**Lou Nanne**	**Herb Brooks**

Minnesota North Stars 1987-88 Roster

FORWARDS	Hgt.	Wgt.	Place of Birth	Date	1986-87 Club	G.	A.	Pts.
Acton, Keith	5:09	172	Stouffville, Ont.	4-15-58	Minnesota	16	29	45
Archibald, Dave	6:01	192	Chiliwack, B.C.	4-14-69	Portland	50	57	107
Archibald, Jim	5:11	180	Craik, Sask.	6- 6-61	Springfield-Minnesota	10	17	27
Babe, Warren	6:02	188	Medicine Hat, Alta.	7- 9-68	Kamloops	36	57	93
Bellows, Brian	5:11	195	St. Catharines, Ont.	9- 1-64	Minnesota	26	27	53
Bennett, Eric	6:03	200	Springfield, Mass.	7-24-67	Providence College	15	12	27
Bergen, Todd	6:03	185	Prince Albert, Sask.	7-11-63	Springfield	12	11	23
Bjugstad, Scott	6:01	175	St. Paul, Minn.	6- 2-61	Minnesota-Springfield	10	13	23
Boh, Rick	5:10	182	Kamloops, B.C.	5-18-64	Colorado College	22	42	64
Brooke, Bob	6:02	205	Acton, Mass.	12-16-60	N.Y. Rangers-Minnesota	13	23	36
Broten, Neal	5:09	169	Roseau, Minn.	11-29-59	Minnesota	18	35	53
Carlson, Jack	6:03	205	Virginia, Minn.	8-23-54	Minnesota	0	0	0
Ciccarelli, Dino	5:10	180	Sarnia, Ont.	2- 8-60	Minnesota	52	51	103
Coulis, Tim	6:00	200	Kenora, Ont.	2-24-58	Springfield	12	19	31
DePalma, Larry	6:00	180	Trenton, Mich.	10-27-65	Springfield-Minnesota	11	8	19
Graham, Dirk	5:11	190	Regina, Sask.	7-29-59	Minnesota	25	29	54
Helmer, Tim	6:00	185	Woodstock, Ont.	11- 6-66	Indianapolis	17	17	34
Helminen, Raimo	6:00	183	Tampere, Finland	11- 6-66	N.Y. Rangers-Minnesota	2	5	7
Hodge, Ken	6:02	190	Windsor, Ont.	4-13-66	Boston College	29	33	62
Houck, Paul	5:11	185	N. Vancouver, B.C.	8-12-63	Springfield-Minnesota	29	20	49
Kaminsky, Kevin	5:09	168	Churchbridge, Sask.	3-13-66	Saskatoon	26	44	70
Lawton, Brian	6:00	173	New Brunswick, N.J.	6-29-65	Minnesota	21	23	44
Lomow, Byron	5:11	180	Sherwood Park, Alta.	4-27-65	Indianapolis	28	43	71
Maruk, Dennis	5:08	174	Toronto, Ont.	11-17-55	Minnesota	16	30	46
MacLellan, Brian	6:03	212	Guelph, Ont.	10-17-59	Minnesota	32	31	63
McColgan, Gary	6:00	192	Scarborough, Ont.	3-27-66	Indianapolis	30	25	55
McRae, Basil	6:02	205	Orilla, Ont.	1- 1-61	Detroit-Quebec	11	7	18
Messier, Mitch	6:02	185	Regina, Sask.	8-21-65	Michigan State	44	48	92
Micheletti, Pat	5:10	175	Hibbing, Minn.	12-11-63	Springfield	17	26	43
Pavelich, Mark	5:08	170	Eveleth, Minn.	2-28-58	Minnesota	4	6	10
Payne, Steve	6:02	215	Toronto, Ont.	8-16-58	Minnesota	4	6	10
Plett, Willi	6:03	220	Paraguay, S. America	6- 7-55	Minnesota	6	5	11
Roy, Stephane	5:11	181	Ste. Foy, Que.	6-29-67	Granby-Team Canada	23	44	67
Ruskowski, Terry	5:09	183	Prince Albert, Sask.	12-31-54	Pittsburgh	14	37	51
Servinis, George	5:11	175	Willowdale, Ont.	4-29-62	Indianapolis	41	54	95
Smith, Randy	6:03	180	Saskatoon, Sask.	7-15-65	Springfield-Minnesota	20	44	64
Tarasuk, Al	6:01	195	Edmonton, Alta.	7-27-64	Indianapolis	8	12	20
Toomey, Sean	6:02	190	St. Paul, Minn.	6-27-65	Indianapolis-Minnesota	3	3	6
Weisbrod, John	6:01	185	Synosset, N.Y.	10- 8-68	Choate Prep	13	14	27

DEFENSEMEN	Hgt.	Wgt.	Place of Birth	Date	1986-87 Club	G.	A.	Pts.
Berger, Mike	5:11	193	Edmonton, Alta.	6- 2-67	Spokane-Indianapolis	26	52	78
Boutilier, Paul	5:11	190	Sydney, N.S.	5- 3-63	Boston-Minnesota	7	13	20
Chambers, Shawn	6:02	218	Sterling Heights, Mich.	10-11-66	U. Alas.-Fairbanks-Fort Wayne	8	29	37
Chisholm, Colin	6:02	190	Edmonton, Alta.	2-25-63	Springfield-Minnesota	1	11	12
Gronstrand, Jari	6:03	197	Tampere, Finland	11-14-62	Tappara	1	6	7
Hartsburg, Craig	6:01	195	Stratford, Ont.	6-29-59	Minnesota	11	50	61
Hirsch, Tom	6:04	211	Minneapolis, Minn.	1-27-63	Minnesota	(Did not play)		
Joy, Garth	5:11	179	Kirkland Lake, Ont.	8- 3-63	Hamilton	6	43	49
Keczmer, Dan	6:01	176	Mt. Clemens, Mich.	5-25-68	Lake Superior State	3	5	8
Kolstad, Dean	6:06	200	Edmonton, Alta.	6-16-68	Prince Albert	17	37	54
Lucyk, Carey	6:01	195	Winnipeg, Man.	3- 8-62	Indianapolis	6	26	32
Maxwell, Brad	6:02	195	Brandon, Man.	6- 8-57	Vanc.-N.Y. Rangers-Minnesota	3	18	21
McCrady, Scott	6:01	195	Calgary, Alta.	10-30-68	Medicine Hat	10	66	76
Mullowney, Michael	6:01	190	Brighton, Mass.	1-17-67	Boston College	0	2	2
Musil, Frantisek	6:03	205	Parbudice, Czech.	12-17-64	Minnesota	2	9	11
Perkins, Don	5:11	190	Whitney, Ont.	8-27-67	Indianapolis	2	12	14
Pitlick, Lance	6:01	185	Minneapolis, Minn.	11- 5-67	Univ. of Minnesota	0	9	9
Pryor, Chris	6:00	200	St. Paul, Minn.	1-23-61	Springfield-Minnesota	1	5	6
Roberts, Gordie	6:00	193	Detroit, Mich.	10- 2-57	Minnesota	3	10	13
Rouse, Bob	6:02	215	Surrey, B.C.	6-18-64	Minnesota	2	10	12
Schlamp, Harold	6:02	210	Winnipeg, Ont.	3- 6-63	Indianapolis	7	19	26
Turner, Brad	6:02	190	Winnipeg, Man.	5-25-68	Univ. of Michigan	3	10	13
Viveiros, Emanuel	5:11	160	St. Albert, Alta.	1- 8-66	Springfield-Minnesota	7	36	43
Wilson, Ron	5:10	170	Windsor, Ont.	5-28-55	Minnesota	12	29	41
Zettler, Rob	6:02	190	Sept Iles, Que.	3- 8-68	Sault Ste. Marie	13	22	35

GOALTENDERS	Hgt.	Wgt.	Place of Birth	Date	1986-87 Club	Mins.	GA.	SO.
Beaupre, Don	5:08	162	Kitchener, Ont.	9-19-61	Minnesota	2622	174	1
Casey, Jon	5:10	155	Grand Rapids, Minn.	3-29-62	Springfield-Indianapolis	2570	153	0
Sands, Mike	5:09	146	Sudbury, Ont.	4- 6-63	Springfield-Minnesota	1211	89	0
Takko, Kari	6:02	182	Kaupunki, Finland	6-23-63	Springfield-Minnesota	2375	135	0

Montreal Canadiens

Adams Division

President .... Ronald Corey
Managing Director .... Serge Savard
Senior Vice-President, Corporate Affairs .... Jean Beliveau
Special Ambassador .... Maurice Richard
Vice-President, Forum Operations .... Aldo Giampaolo
Vice-President, Finance and Administration .... Fred Steer
Director of Hockey Personnel and Assistant to Managing Director .... Jacques Lemaire
Coach .... Jean Perron
Assistant Coach .... Jacques Laperriere
Goaltending Instructor .... Francois Allaire
Director of Player Development and Scout .... Claude Ruel
Director of Recruitment and Assistant to Managing Director .... Andre Boudrias
Chief Scout .... Doug Robinson
Director of Special Events .... Camil Desroches
Director of Advertising Sales .... Floyd Curry
Director of Public Relations .... Claude Mouton
Director of Press Relations .... Michele Lapointe
Club Physician .... Dr. D.G. Kinnear
Head Sports Therapist .... Gene Gaudet
Head Trainer .... Eddy Palchak
Assistant Trainers .... Pierre Gervais, Sylvain Toupin
Home Ice .... Montreal Forum
Address .... 2313 St. Catherine Street West, Montreal, Que. H3H 1N2
Seating Capacity 16,074
Club colors .... Red, White and Blue
Phone .... (514) 932-2582

Ronald Corey **Serge Savard** **Jean Beliveau** **Jean Perron**

Montreal Canadiens 1987-88 Roster

FORWARDS	Hgt.	Wgt.	Place of Birth	Date	1986-87 Club	G.	A.	Pts.
Bonar, Graeme	6:03	208	Toronto, Ont.	1-21-66	Sherbrooke	6	6	12
Bryden, Rob	6:03	205	Toronto, Ont.	4- 5-63	Western Michigan Univ.	46	32	78
Carbonneau, Guy	5:11	180	Sept Ilves, Que.	3-18-60	Montreal	18	27	45
Charbonneau, Jose	6:00	190	Ferne Neuve, Que.	11- 2-66	Sherbrooke	14	27	41
Corson, Shayne	6:00	175	Barrie, Ont.	8-13-66	Montreal	12	11	23
Dahlin, Kjell	6:00	175	Timra, Sweden	2- 2-63	Montreal	12	8	20
Desjardins, Martin	5:11	165	Ste. Rose, Que.	1-28-67	Trois-Rivieres-Longueuil	39	62	101
Dundas, Rocky	6:00	200	Edmonton, Alta.	1-30-67	Medicine Hat	35	41	76
Fletcher, Steven	6:03	205	Montreal, Que.	3-31-62	Sherbrooke	15	11	26
Gainey, Bob	6:02	200	Peterborough, Ont.	12-13-53	Montreal	8	8	16
Ganchar, Perry	5:09	180	Saskatoon, Sask.	10-28-63	Sherbrooke	22	29	51
Gilchrist, Brent	5:11	175	Moose Jaw, Sask.	4- 3-67	Spokane	45	55	100
Harlow, Scott	6:00	190	E. Bridgewater, Mass.	10-11-63	Sherbrooke	22	26	48
Keane, Mike	5:10	175	Winnipeg, Man.	5-28-67	Moose Jaw	25	45	70
Kordic, John	6:01	200	Edmonton, Alta.	3-22-65	Montreal-Sherbrooke	9	7	16
Lemieux, Claude	6:01	206	Buckingham, Que.	7-16-65	Montreal	27	26	53
McPhee, Mike	6:01	200	Rivere Bougeois, N.S.	7-14-60	Montreal	18	21	39
Momesso Sergio	6:03	203	Montreal, Que.	9- 4-65	Montreal-Sherbrooke	15	23	38
Naslund, Mats	5:07	160	Timra, Sweden	10-31-59	Montreal	25	55	80
Nesich, Jim	5:11	170	Dearborn, Mich.	2-22-66	Verdun	20	50	70
Nilan, Chris	6:00	200	Boston, Mass.	2- 9-58	Montreal	4	16	20
Pederson, Mark	6:01	196	Prelate, Sask.	1-14-68	Medicine Hat	56	46	102
Richer, Stephane	6:02	200	Ripon, Que.	6- 7-66	Montreal-Sherbrooke	30	23	53
Rouleau, Guy	5:09	175	Beloeil, Que.	2-16-65	Zurich-Sherbrooke	14	16	30
Skrudland, Brian	6:00	188	Peace River, Alta.	7-31-63	Montreal	11	17	28
Smith, Bobby	6:04	210	North Sydney, N.S.	2-12-58	Montreal	28	47	75
Thibaudeau, Gilles	5:10	165	Montreal, Que.	3- 4-63	Sherbrooke-Montreal	28	43	71
Turcotte, Alfie	5:09	175	Gary, Ind.	6- 5-65	Nova Scotia	27	41	68
Vargas, Ernie	6:02	195	St. Paul, Minn.	3- 1-64	Sherbrooke	22	32	.54
Walter, Ryan	6:00	195	New Westminster, B.C.	4-23-58	Montreal	23	23	46

DEFENSEMEN	Hgt.	Wgt.	Place of Birth	Date	1986-87 Club	G.	A.	Pts.
Chelios, Chris	6:01	186	Chicago, Ill.	1-25-62	Montreal	11	33	44
Dufresne, Donald	6:01	190	Rimouski, Que.	4-10-67	Trois-Rivieres-Longueuil	5	29	34
Gingras, Gaston	6:00	185	Temiscamingue, Que.	2-13-59	Monteal	11	34	45
Green, Rick	6:03	210	Belleville, Ont.	2-20-56	Montreal	1	9	10
Hayward, Rick	6:00	173	Toledo, O.	2-25-66	Sherbrooke	2	3	5
Lalor, Mike	6:03	200	Buffalo, N.Y.	3- 8-63	Montreal	0	10	10
Lefebvre, Sylvain	6:02	190	Richmond, Que.	10-14-67	Laval	10	36	46
Ludwig, Craig	6:03	217	Rhinelander, Wis.	3-15-61	Montreal	4	12	16
Robinson, Larry	6:02	217	Winchester, Ont.	6- 2-51	Montreal	13	37	50
Sandelin, Scott	6:00	191	Hibbing, Minn.	8- 8-64	Sherbrooke	7	22	29
Svoboda, Petr	6:01	170	Most, Czechoslovakia	2-14-66	Montreal	5	17	22
Villeneuve, Andre	6:00	175	Alma, Que.	1-19-63	Hershey-Sherbrooke	3	18	21

GOALTENDERS	Hgt.	Wgt.	Place of Birth	Date	1986-87 Club	Mins.	GA.	SO.
Hayward, Brian	5:10	175	Georgetown, Ont.	6-25-60	Montreal	2178	102	1
Perreault, Jocelyn	6:04	210	Montreal, Que.	1- 8-66	Sherbrooke	721	40	0
Riendeau, Vincent	5:09	173	St. Hyacinthe, Que.	4-20-66	Sherbrooke	2362	114	2
Roy, Patrick	6:00	174	Quebec, Que.	10- 5-65	Montreal	2686	131	1

New Jersey Devils

Patrick Division

Chairman..John J. McMullen
President...Lou Lamoriello
Vice President and General Manager ....Max McNab
Coach...Doug Carpenter
Assistant Coaches..Ron Smith, Bob Hoffmeyer
Director of Player Personnel ....Marshall Johnston
Assistant Director of Player Personnel ....David Conte
Scouts....................................Claude Carrier, Frank Jay, Russ LeClair, Ed Thomlinson, Milt Fisher
Athletic Trainer ....Chris Ipson
Director, Public and Media Relations...David Freed
Administrative Assistant, Public Relations and Tickets ....Tom Shine
Public Relations and Marketing Assistant..Susan Ross
Public Relations Assistant...Mike Levine
Executive Offices...Byrne Meadowlands Arena
Home Ice..Byrne Meadowlands Arena
Address ....Meadowlands Arena, P.O. Box 504, East Rutherford, N.J. 07073
Seating Capacity...19,040
Club Colors...Red, Green and White
Phone ....(201) 935-6050

John McMullen

Max McNab

Doug Carpenter

— 36 —

New Jersey Devils 1987-88 Roster

FORWARDS	Hgt.	Wgt.	Place of Birth	Date	1986-87 Club	G.	A.	Pts.
Adams, Greg	6:02	195	Nelson, B.C.	8- 1-63	New Jersey	20	27	47
Andersen, John	6:00	180	Toronto, Ont.	1-18-68	Oshawa	11	13	24
Anderson, David	6:00	195	Vancouver, B.C.	7-30-62	Maine	9	9	18
Anderson, Perry	6:01	215	Barrie, Ont.	10-14-61	New Jersey-Maine	15	13	28
Barakett, Tim	6:00	180	Montreal, Que.	7-27-65	Harvard University	25	29	54
Brady, Neil	6:03	195	Montreal, Que.	4-12-68	Medicine Hat	19	64	83
Brickley, Andy	5:11	200	Melrose, Mass.	8- 9-61	New Jersey	11	12	23
Broten, Aaron	5:10	175	Roseau, Minn.	11-14-60	New Jersey	26	53	79
Brown, Doug	5:11	190	Southborough, Mass.	6-12-64	Maine-New Jersey	24	35	59
Carlsson, Anders	5:11	190	Galve, Sweden	11-25-60	New Jersey-Maine	2	24	26
Charland, Alain	5:09	155	Verdun, Que.	6-28-67	Drummondville	53	75	128
Cichocki, Chris	5:11	185	Detroit, Mich.	9-17-63	Detroit-Adirondack-Maine	33	36	69
Conacher, Pat	5:08	200	Edmonton, Alta.	5- 1-59	Maine	12	14	26
Crowder, Troy	6:04	215	Sudbury, Ont.	5- 8-68	North Bay	11	16	27
Dorion, Dan	5:09	180	New York, N.Y.	3- 2-63	Maine	16	22	38
Floyd, Larry	5:08	180	Peterborough, Ont.	5- 1-61	Maine	30	44	74
Johnson, Mark	5:09	165	Madison, Wis.	9-22-57	Maine	25	26	51
Korn, Jim	6:04	220	Hopkins, Minn.	7-28-57	Buffalo	4	10	14
Lenardon, Tim	6:02	190	Trail, B.C.	5-11-62	Maine-New Jersey	29	36	65
Loiselle, Claude	5:11	195	Ottawa, Ont.	5-29-63	New Jersey	16	24	40
MacLean, John	6:00	195	Oshawa, Ont.	11-20-64	New Jersey	31	36	67
Maley, David	6:02	210	Beaver Dam, Wis.	4-24-63	Montreal-Sherbrooke	7	17	24
McKinley, Jamie	6:02	180	Moncton, N.B.	5- 1-67	Guelph	23	50	73
Muller, Kirk	6:00	205	Kingston, Ont.	2- 8-66	New Jersey	26	50	76
Polak, Gregg	6:02	180	Providence, R.I.	7-16-67	Oshawa	1	0	1
Shanahan, Brendan	6:03	210	Mimico, Ont.	1-23-69	London	39	53	92
Stewart, Al	6:00	195	Fort St. John, B.C.	1-31-64	Maine-New Jersey	15	24	39
Sulliman, Doug	5:09	190	Glace Bay, N.S.	8-29-59	New Jersey	27	26	53
Todd, Kevin	5:10	180	Winnipeg, Man.	5- 4-68	Prince Albert	39	46	85
Tsujiura, Steve	5:06	165	Coaldale, Alta.	2-28-62	Maine	24	41	65
Verbeek, Pat	5:09	190	Sarnia, Ont.	5-24-64	New Jersey	35	24	59
Ysebaert, Paul	6:01	170	Sarnia, Ont.	5-15-66	Bowling Green State	27	58	85

DEFENSEMEN	Hgt.	Wgt.	Place of Birth	Date	1986-87 Club	G.	A.	Pts.
Blessman, John	6:03	210	Toronto, Ont.	4-27-67	Toronto Jrs.	6	24	30
Brumwell, Murray	6:02	190	Calgary, Alta.	3-31-60	Maine-New Jersey	10	38	48
Cirella, Joe	6:03	210	Hamilton, Ont.	5- 9-63	New Jersey	9	22	31
Daneyko, Ken	6:00	200	Windsor, Ont.	4-16-64	New Jersey	2	12	14
Doyle, Shayne	6:01	200	Lindsay, Ont.	4-26-67	Oshawa	9	13	22
Driver, Bruce	6:00	195	Toronto, Ont.	4-29-62	New Jersey	6	28	34
Hepple, Alan	5:10	190	Blaydon-on-Tyne, Eng.	8-16-63	New Jersey	6	19	25
Kurvers, Tom	6:00	205	Bloomington, Minn.	9-14-62	Montreal-Buffalo	6	17	23
Laniel, Marc	6:01	190	Oshawa, Ont.	1- 6-68	Oshawa	14	31	45
Marcinyshyn, Dave	6:03	190	Edmonton, Alta.	2- 4-67	Kamloops	5	27	32
Mark, Gordie	6:04	210	Edmonton, Alta.	9-10-64	Maine-New Jersey	7	15	22
Octeau, Jay	5:10	180	Providence, R.I.	3-24-65	Boston University	5	23	28
Richmond, Steve	6:00	200	Chicago, Ill.	12-11-59	New Jersey	1	7	8
Velischek, Randy	6:01	205	Montreal, Que.	2-10-62	New Jersey	2	16	18
Walker, John	6:04	195	Iserlohn, W. Germany	1-22-64	N. Alberta Institute	33	29	62
Wolanin, Craig	6:03	205	Grosse Pointe, Mich.	7-27-67	New Jersey	4	6	10

GOALTENDERS	Hgt.	Wgt.	Place of Birth	Date	1986-87 Club	Mins.	GA.	SO.
Billington, Craig	5:10	165	London, Ont.	9-11-66	Maine-New Jersey	2255	179	0
Chabot, Frederic	5:10	160	Habartville, Que.	2-12-68	Drummondville	3508	293	1
Chevrier, Alain	5:08	180	Cornwall, Ont.	4-23-61	New Jersey	3153	227	0
Fry, Peter	5:11	170	Victoria, B.C.	4- 1-67	Victoria	2937	255	0
McLean, Kirk	6:01	190	Willowdale, Ont.	6-26-66	Maine-New Jersey	2765	150	1
Sauve, Bob	5:08	165	Mississauga, Ont.	6-17-55	Chicago	2660	159	1

New York Islanders

Patrick Division

Chairman of the Board/Governor	John O. Pickett, Jr.
President and General Manager	William A. Torrey
Vice-President, Finance	Joseph H. Dreyer
Alternate Governor	William M. Skehan
Vice-President/Player Development	Al Arbour
Coach	Terry Simpson
Assistant General Manager/Director of Scouting	Gerry Ehman
Director of Hockey Administration	Darcy Regier
Scouting Staff	Harry Boyd, Richard Green, Hal Laycoe, Mario Saraceno, Jack Vivian, Earl Ingarfield
Publicity Director	Greg Bouris
Assistant Publicity Director	Cathy Schutte
Communications Consultant	Barney Kremenko
Director of Finance	Arthur McCarthy
Controller	Ralph Sellitti
Trainer	Craig Smith
Assistant Trainer	Jim Pickard
Home Ice	Nassau Veterans Memorial Coliseum
Address	Uniondale, N. Y. 11553
Seating Capacity	16,267
Club colors	Blue, White and Orange
Phone	(516) 794-4100

John Pickett   **Bill Torrey**   **Al Arbour**   **Terry Simpson**

New York Islanders 1987-88 Roster

FORWARDS

Name	Hgt.	Wgt.	Place of Birth	Date	1986-87 Club	G.	A.	Pts.
Bassen, Bob	5:10	180	Calgary, Alta.	5- 6-65	N.Y. Islanders	7	10	17
Bossy, Mike	6:00	185	Montreal, Que.	1-22-57	N.Y. Islanders	38	37	75
Burnie, Stu	5:11	185	Orilla, Ont.	5- 7-62	Springfield	21	30	51
Byram, Shawn	6:02	204	Neepawa, Man.	9-12-68	Prince Albert	19	21	40
Clark, Kerry	6:01	190	Virden, Man.	5-13-68	Saskatoon	12	10	22
Coulter, Neal	6:02	190	Toronto, Ont.	1- 2-63	Springfield-N.Y. Islanders	14	14	28
Dalgarno, Brad	6:03	215	Vancouver, B.C.	8-11-67	Hamilton	27	32	59
DiMaio, Rob	5:08	175	Calgary, Alta.	2-19-68	Medicine Hat	27	43	70
Ewen, Dean	6:01	185	St. Albert, Alta.	2-28-69	Spokane	8	14	22
Flatley, Patrick	6:02	197	Toronto, Ont.	10- 3-63	N.Y. Islanders	16	35	51
Gilbert, Greg	6:01	192	Mississauga, Ont.	1-22-62	N.Y. Islanders	6	7	13
Haanpaa, Ari	6:01	185	Nokia, Finland	11-28-65	N.Y. Islanders	6	4	10
Henry, Dale	6:00	205	Prince Albert, Sask.	9-24-64	N.Y. Islanders	3	3	6
Herom, Kevin	5:11	195	Regina, Sask.	7- 6-67	Moose Jaw	34	33	67
Johannesen, Glen	6:02	220	Lac La Ronge, Sask.	2-15-62	Springfield	10	6	16
Kerr, Alan	5:11	195	Hazelton, B.C.	3-28-67	N.Y. Islanders	7	10	17
King, Derek	6:01	210	Hamilton, Ont.	2-11-67	Oshawa-N.Y. Islanders	53	53	106
Kromm, Rich	5:11	180	Trail, B.C.	3-29-64	N.Y. Islanders	12	17	29
Lackten, Kurt	6:00	177	Kamsack, Sask.	4-20-67	Swift Current	20	20	40
Lauer, Brad	6:00	195	Humbolt, Sask.	10-27-66	N.Y. Islanders	7	14	21
LaFontaine, Pat	5:10	177	St. Louis, Mo.	2-22-65	N.Y. Islanders	38	32	70
Makela, Mikko	6:02	193	Tampere, Finland	2-28-65	N.Y. Islanders	24	33	57
McKechney, Garnet	6:01	170	Swift Current, Sask.	4-28-65	Peoria	16	11	27
McLellan, Todd	5:11	185	Melville, Sask.	10- 3-67	Saskatoon	34	39	73
Sexsmith, Dean	6:01	190	Virden, Man.	5-13-68	Seattle	14	24	38
Sutter, Brent	5:11	180	Viking, Alta.	6-10-62	N.Y. Islanders	27	36	63
Sutter, Duane	6:01	195	Viking, Alta.	3-16-60	N.Y. Islanders	14	17	31
Trottier, Bryan	5:11	195	Val Marie, Sask.	7-17-56	N.Y. Islanders	23	64	87
Vukota, Mick	6:02	195	Saskatoon, Sask.	9-14-66	Spokane	25	28	53
Walsh, Mike	6:02	195	New York, N.Y.	4- 3-62	Springfield	20	26	46
Weiss, Tom	6:04	215	Englewood, Calif.	1-31-62	Springfield	6	10	16
Wieck, Doug	6:00	180	Rochester, Minn.	3-12-65	Virginia	28	39	67
Wiest, Rich	5:11	170	Lethbridge, Alta.	6-22-67	Kamloops	19	27	46
Wood, Randy	6:00	195	Princeton, N.J.	10-12-63	Springfield-N.Y. Islanders	24	24	48

DEFENSEMEN

Name	Hgt.	Wgt.	Place of Birth	Date	1986-87 Club	G.	A.	Pts.
Anderson, Will	6:01	195	Kamloops, B.C.	2-11-68	Victoria	17	43	60
Berg, Bill	6:01	190	St. Catharines, Ont.	10-21-67	Toronto Jrs.	3	15	18
Boyd, Randy	5:11	192	Coniston, Ont.	1-23-62	Springfield-N.Y. Islanders	16	47	63
Chynoweth, Dean	6:01	185	Calgary, Alta.	10-30-68	Medicine Hat	3	18	21
Curran, Brian	6:05	215	Toronto, Ont.	11- 5-63	N.Y. Islanders	0	10	10
Diduck, Gerald	6:02	195	Edmonton, Alta.	4- 6-65	Springfield-N.Y. Islanders	8	11	19
Dineen, Gord	6:00	195	Toronto, Ont.	9-21-62	N.Y. Islanders	4	10	14
Finley, Jeff	6:02	185	Edmonton, Alta.	4-14-67	Portland	13	53	66
Howard, Shawn	6:00	180	Anchorage, Alaska	3-20-68	Penticton	25	34	59
Jonsson, Tomas	5:10	185	Falun, Sweden	4-12-60	N.Y. Islanders	6	25	31
Konroyd, Steve	6:01	195	Scarborough, Ont.	2-10-61	N.Y. Islanders	5	16	21
Leiter, Ken	6:01	195	Detroit, Mich.	4-19-61	N.Y. Islanders	9	20	29
Morrow, Ken	6:04	205	Flint, Mich.	10-17-56	N.Y. Islanders	3	8	11
MacPherson, Duncan	6:01	195	Saskatoon, Sask.	2- 3-66	Springfield	1	0	1
Neill, Mike	6:00	195	Kenora, Ont.	8- 6-65	Springfield	3	4	7
Paddock, Gord	6:00	180	Hamiota, Man.	2-15-64	Springfield	6	11	17
Pilon, Richard	6:00	202	Saskatoon, Sask.	4-30-68	Prince Albert	4	21	25
Potvin, Denis	6:00	205	Ottawa, Ont.	10-29-53	N.Y. Islanders	12	30	42
Smith, Vern	6:01	190	Winnipeg, Man.	5-30-64	Springfield	1	10	11

GOALTENDERS

Name	Hgt.	Wgt.	Place of Birth	Date	1986-87 Club	Mins.	GA.	SO.
Gunn, Roydon	5:09	170	Saskatoon, Sask.	8- 5-66	Springfield	1599	107	0
Hackett, Jeff	6:01	175	London, Ont.	6- 1-68	Oshawa	1672	85	2
Hrudey, Kelly	5:10	180	Edmonton, Alta.	1-13-61	N.Y. Islanders	2624	145	0
Kruzich, Gary	5:05	173	Oak Lawn, Ill.	4-22-65	Bowling Green State	2229	123	1
Maneluk, George	5:11	185	Winnipeg, Man.	7-25-67	Brandon	3258	315	0
Smith, Bill	5:10	185	Perth, Ont.	12-12-50	N.Y. Islanders	2240	132	1
Wakelyn, Marty	6:00	180	Victoria, B.C.	7-18-62	Springfield	1144	75	0

New York Rangers

Patrick Division

President and C.E.O. Madison Square Garden Corp. .... Richard H. Evans
Vice-President, Finance and Administration .... Mel Lowell
Treasurer .... Stephen Schwartz
Vice-President and General Manager .... Phil Esposito
Coach... Michel Bergeron
Goaltending Coach and Special Assignment Scout... Ed Giacomin
Assistant to General Manager .... Joe Bucchino
Vice-President, Communications .... John Halligan
Public Relations Assistants.. Matthew Loughran, Barry Watkins
Statistician .... Arthur Friedman
Scouting Staff... Chuck Grillo, Lou Jankowski, Richard Rose,
Lars-Erik Sjoberg, Wayne Cashman
Trainers .... Jerry Maloney, Joe Murphy, Dave Smith
Home Ice .... Madison Square Garden
Address.. 4 Pennsylvania Plaza, New York, N. Y. 10001
Seating Capacity... 17,500
Club colors .... Blue, Red and White
Phone.. (212) 563-8000

Richard Evans   **Phil Esposito**   **Michel Bergeron**   **Joe Bucchino**

New York Rangers 1987-88 Roster

FORWARDS

Name	Hgt.	Wgt.	Place of Birth	Date	1986-87 Club	G.	A.	Pts.
Brubaker, Jeff	6:02	210	Frederick, Md.	2-24-58	Nova Scotia-Hershey	11	18	29
Caufield, Jay	6:04	220	Philadelphia, Pa.	7-17-60	New Haven-N.Y. Rangers	2	1	3
Dahlen, Ulf	6:02	194	Ostersund, Sweden	1-12-67	Bjorkloven	9	12	21
DeBlois, Lucien	5:11	200	Joliette, Que.	6-21-57	N.Y. Rangers	3	8	11
Dionne, Marcel	5:08	190	Drummondville, Que. ...	8- 3-51	Los Angeles-N.Y. Rangers	28	56	84
Donnelly, Mike	5:11	185	Detroit, Mich.	10-10-63	New Haven-N.Y. Rangers	28	35	63
Duguay, Ron	6:02	210	Sudbury, Ont.	7- 6-57	Pittsburgh-N.Y. Rangers	14	25	39
Erixon, Jan	6:00	190	Skelleftea, Sweden	7- 8-62	N.Y. Rangers	8	18	26
Fenton, Paul	6:00	180	Springfield, Mass.	12-22-59	New Haven-N.Y. Rangers	37	38	75
Gagner, Dave	5:10	180	Chatham, Ont.	12-11-64	New Haven-N.Y. Rangers	23	44	67
Jackson, Jeff	6:00	195	Chatham, Ont.	4-24-65	Newmarket-Tor.-N.Y. Rangers ...	16	14	30
Jensen, Chris	5:11	169	Salmon Arm. B.C.	10-28-63	New Haven-N.Y. Rangers	10	16	26
Kisio, Kelly	5:09	170	Wetaskwin, Alta.	9-18-59	N.Y. Rangers	24	40	64
Kulak, Stu	5:10	180	Edmonton, Alta.	3-10-63	Van.-Edm.-N.Y. Rangers	4	2	6
Larouche, Pierre	5:11	175	Taschereau, Que.	11-16-55	N.Y. Rangers	28	35	63
Latos, James	6:01	200	Wakaw, Sask.	1- 4-66		..	..	..
Maloney, Don	6:01	190	Lindsay, Ont.	9- 5-58	N.Y. Rangers	19	38	57
McPhee, George	5:09	170	Guelph, Ont.	7- 2-58	N.Y. Rangers	4	4	8
Mullen, Brian	5:10	180	New York, N.Y.	3-16-62	Winnipeg	19	32	51
Nemeth, Steve	5:08	162	Calgary, Alta.	2-11-67	Kamloops-Team Canada	10	4	14
O'Dwyer, Bill	6:00	190	S. Boston, Mass.	6-25-60	New Haven	22	42	64
Poddubny, Walt	6:01	205	Thunder Bay, Ont.	2-14-60	N.Y. Rangers	40	47	87
Sandstrom, Tomas	6:02	200	Fagersta, Sweden	9- 4-64	N.Y. Rangers	40	34	74
Siltala, Mike	5:10	185	Toronto, Ont.	8- 5-63	New Haven	13	6	19
Stepan, Brad	5:11	193	Hastings, Minn.	8-27-67	Windsor	18	21	39
Tait, Terry	6:02	190	Thunder Bay, Ont.	9-10-63	Flint	26	39	65
Talakoski, Ron	6:03	220	Thunder Bay, Ont.	6- 1-62	New Haven-N.Y. Rangers	2	2	4
Walker, Gord	6:00	175	Castlegar, B.C.	8-12-65	New Haven-N.Y. Rangers	25	20	45
Wheeldon, Simon	5:11	180	Nelson, B.C.	10- 2-68	New Haven	11	28	39

DEFENSEMEN

Name	Hgt.	Wgt.	Place of Birth	Date	1986-87 Club	G.	A.	Pts.
Bell, Bruce	6:00	190	Toronto, Ont.	2-15-65	St. Louis	3	13	16
Brochu, Stephane	6:01	186	Sherbrooke, Que.	8-15-67		..	..	..
Carkner, Terry	6:03	200	Smith Falls, Ont.	3- 7-66	N.Y. Rangers-New Haven	4	19	23
Crossman, Jeff	6:00	200	Toronto, Ont.	12- 3-67	New Haven	2	3	5
Duggan, Ken	6:03	210	Toronto, Ont.	2-21-63	New Haven	0	1	1
Greschner, Ron	6:02	205	Goodsoil, Sask.	12-22-54	N.Y. Rangers	6	34	40
Giles, Curt	5:08	162	The Pas, Man.	11-30-58	Minnesota-N.Y. Rangers	2	20	22
Horava, Miroslav	6:00	198		8-14-61	Kladno	..	..	..
Huber, Willie	6:05	225	Strasskirchen, W. Ger. .	1-15-58	N.Y. Rangers	8	22	30
Jackson, Don	6:03	210	Minneapolis, Minn.	9- 2-56	N.Y. Rangers	1	0	1
Leavins, Jim	5:11	185	Dinsmore, Sask.	7-28-60	New Haven-N.Y. Rangers	7	22	29
Maciver, Norm	5:11	180	Thunder Bay, Ont.	9- 1-64	New Haven-N.Y. Rangers	6	31	37
Melnyk, Larry	6:00	180	Saskatoon, Sask.	2-21-60	N.Y. Rangers	3	12	15
Patrick, James	6:02	185	Winnipeg, Man.	6-14-63	N.Y. Rangers	10	45	55
Poeschek, Rudy	6:01	208	Kamloops, B.C.	9-29-66	Kamloops	13	18	31
Price, Pat	6:02	195	Nelson, B.C.	3-24-55	Que.-Fred.-N.Y. Rangers	0	8	8
Smith, Scott	6:01	185	St. Paul, Minn.	10-16-62	New Haven	0	8	8
Tinordi, Mark	6:04	206	Red Deer, Alta.	5- 9-66	Calgary Jrs.	29	37	66

GOALTENDERS

Name	Hgt.	Wgt.	Place of Birth	Date	1986-87 Club	Mins.	GA.	SO.
Adam, Drago	5:10	157	N. Battleford, Sask.	9-21-66	New Westminster	2827	259	1
Froese, Bob	5:11	180	St. Catharines, Ont.	6-30-58	Philadelphia-N.Y. Rangers	1654	100	0
Scott, Ron	5:08	155	Guelph, Ont.	7-21-60	New Haven-N.Y. Rangers	1809	115	2
Vanbiesbrouck, John	5:10	180	Detroit, Mich.	9- 4-63	N.Y. Rangers	2656	161	0

Philadelphia Flyers
Patrick Division

Chairman of the Executive Committee .... Edward M. Snider
Chairman of the Board Emeritus.. Joseph C. Scott
President .... Jay T. Snider
Executive Vice-President .... Keith Allen
Vice-President, Finance and Administration.. Donn Patton
Vice-President and General Manager.. Bob Clarke
Coach.. Mike Keenan
Assistant General Manager.. Gary Darling
Assistant Coaches .... E.J. McGuire, Paul Holmgren, Bill Barber
Goaltending Instructor .... Bernie Parent
Physical Conditioning and Rehabilitation Coach .... Pat Croce
Scouts.. Jerry Melnyk, Walt Atanas,
Dennis Patterson, Red Sullivan
Vice-President, Communications .... John Brogan
Public Relations Director.. Rodger Gottlieb
Assistant Public Relations Director.. Mark Piazza
Ticket Manager .... Ceil Baker
Vice-President, Sales .... Jack Betson
Director of Team Services.. Joe Kadlec
Director of Broadcast Sales .... Pete Huver
Trainer.. Dave Settlemyre
Assistant Trainer.. Kurt Mundt
Controller.. Bob Baer
Team Physician .... Edward Viner, M.D.
Home Ice .... The Spectrum
Address.. Pattison Place, Philadelphia, Pa. 19148
Seating Capacity.. 17,211
Club colors .... Orange, White and Black
Phone.. (215) 465-4500

Ed Snider   **Bob Clarke**   **Mike Keenan**   **Jay Snider**

Philadelphia Flyers 1987-88 Roster

FORWARDS

Name	Hgt.	Wgt.	Place of Birth	Date	1986-87 Club	G.	A.	Pts.
Berube, Craig	6:02	200	Calihoo, Alta.	12-17-65	Hershey-Philadelphia	7	17	24
Brown, Dave	6:04	215	Saskatoon, Sask.	10-12-62	Philadelphia	7	3	10
Carson, Lindsay	6:01	200	N. Battleford, Sask.	11-21-60	Philadelphia	11	15	26
Craven, Murray	6:02	185	Medicine Hat, Alta.	7-20-64	Philadelphia	19	30	49
Dobbin, Brian	5:11	195	Petrolia, Ont.	8-18-66	Hershey-Philadelphia	28	36	64
Duvall, Harold	5:11	185	Ogdenburg, N.Y.	4-21-64	Colgate Univ.	8	15	23
Eklund, Pelle	5:09	170	Stockholm, Sweden	3-22-63	Philadelphia	14	41	55
Fitzpatrick, Ross	6:01	195	Penticton, B.C.	10- 7-60	Hershey	45	40	85
Freer, Mark	5:10	180	Peterborough, Ont.	7-14-68	Peterborough-Philadelphia	39	44	83
Hawley, Kent	6:03	215	Kingston, Ont.	2-20-68	Ottawa	29	53	82
Hill, Al	6:01	175	Nanaimo, B.C.	4-22-55	Hershey-Philadelphia	13	37	50
Horacek, Tony	6:03	200	Vancouver, B.C.	2- 3-67	Spokane	23	37	60
Kerr, Tim	6:03	225	Windsor, Ont.	1- 5-60	Philadelphia	58	37	95
Kypreos, Nick	6:00	190	Toronto, Ont.	6- 4-66	North Bay-Hershey	49	42	91
Lamoureux, Mitch	5:07	175	Ottawa, Ont.	8-22-62	Hershey	43	46	89
MacWilliams, Mike	6:01	190	Burnaby, B.C.	2-14-67	Medicine Hat	7	17	24
Maxwell, Kevin	5:09	170	Edmonton, Alta.	3-30-60	Hershey	12	20	32
McLay, Dave	5:11	175	Chilliwack, B.C.	5-13-66	Portland	35	42	77
Mellanby, Scott	6:01	200	Montreal, Que.	6-11-66	Philadelphia	11	21	32
Murray, Mike	6:00	185	Kingston, Ont.	8-29-66	Hershey	8	16	24
Nachbaur, Don	6:02	200	Kitimat, B.C.	1-30-59	Hershey-Philadelphia	18	19	37
Poulin, Dave	5:11	185	Timmins, Ont.	12-17-58	Philadelphia	25	45	70
Propp, Brian	5:10	190	Lanigan, Sask.	2-15-59	Philadelphia	31	36	67
Roupe, Magnus	6:01	190	Stockholm, Sweden	3-23-63	Farjestad	11	6	17
Seabrooke, Glen	6:01	175	Peterborough, Ont.	9-11-67	Peterborough-Philadelphia	31	43	74
Sinisalo, Ilkka	6:01	195	Valeakoski, Finland	7-10-58	Philadelphia	10	21	31
Smith, Derrick	6:02	210	Scarborough, Ont.	1-22-65	Philadelphia	11	21	32
Sutter, Ron	5:11	180	Viking, Alta.	12- 2-63	Philadelphia	10	17	27
Tocchet, Rick	6:00	205	Scarborough, Ont.	4- 9-64	Philadelphia	21	26	47
Tookey, Tim	5:11	185	Edmonton, Alta.	8-29-60	Hershey-Philadelphia	51	73	124
Whyte, David	6:03	200	Hingham, Mass.	5- 1-65	Boston College	2	4	6
Zezel, Peter	5:10	205	Toronto, Ont.	4-22-65	Philadelphia	33	39	72

DEFENSEMEN

Name	Hgt.	Wgt.	Place of Birth	Date	1986-87 Club	G.	A.	Pts.
Armstrong, Ian	6:04	200	Peterborough, Ont.	1-25-65	Hershey	0	7	7
Bar, Mark	6:03	200	Toronto, Ont.	2-15-68	Peterborough	2	12	14
Chychrun, Jeff	6:04	185	LaSalle, Que.	5- 3-66	Hershey-Philadelphia	1	17	18
Crossman, Doug	6:02	195	Peterborough, Ont.	6-30-60	Philadelphia	9	31	40
Daigneault, J.J.	5:11	180	Montreal, Que.	10-12-65	Philadelphia	6	16	22
Hospodar, Ed	6:02	205	Bowling Green, O.	2- 9-59	Philadelphia	2	2	4
Huffman, Kerry	6:02	180	Peterborough, Ont.	1- 3-68	Guelph-Philadelphia	4	31	35
Marsh, Brad	6:02	220	London, Ont.	3-31-58	Philadelphia	2	9	11
McCarthy, Kevin	5:11	195	Winnipeg, Man.	7-14-57	Hershey-Philadelphia	6	44	50
McCrimmon, Brad	5:11	200	Dodsland, Sask.	3-29-59	Philadelphia	10	29	39
Murphy, Gord	6:01	180	Willowdale, Ont.	2-23-67	Oshawa	7	30	37
Rumble, Darren	6:01	190	Barrie, Ont.	1-23-69	Kitchener	11	32	43
Samuelsson, Kjell	6:06	230	Tyringe, Sweden	10-18-58	N.Y. Rangers-Philadelphia	3	12	15
Smith, Steve	5:09	200	Trenton, Ont.	4- 4-63	Hershey-Philadelphia	11	26	37
Smyth, Greg	6:03	195	Oakville, Ont.	4-23-66	Hershey-Philadelphia	0	2	2
Stanley, Daryl	6:02	200	Winnipeg, Man.	12- 2-62	Philadelphia	1	2	3
Stevens, John	6:01	185	Completon, N.B.	5- 4-66	Hershey-Philadelphia	1	17	18
Stothers, Mike	6:04	210	Toronto, Ont.	2-22-62	Hershey-Philadelphia	5	11	16

GOALTENDERS

Name	Hgt.	Wgt.	Place of Birth	Date	1986-87 Club	Mins.	GA.	SO.
Gilmour, Darryl	5:11	160	Winnipeg, Man.	2-13-67	Portland	3236	234	2
Hextall, Ron	6:03	175	Brandon, Man.	5- 3-64	Philadelphia	3799	190	1
Jensen, Darren	5:09	165	Creston, B.C.	5-27-60	Hershey	3430	215	0
Kemp, John	6:00	185	Burlington, Ont.	7-31-63	Hershey	1346	80	1
Laforest, Mark	5:10	180	Welland, Ont.	7-10-62	Adirondack-Detroit	2448	117	3

Pittsburgh Penguins
Patrick Division

Chairman of the Board and President.. Edward J. DeBartolo, Sr.
Vice-President .... Marie Denise DeBartolo York
Vice-President and General Counsel .... J. Paul Martha
Vice-President and Treasurer.. Thomas F. Rosetti
General Manager .... Ed Johnston
Assistant General Manager.. Ken Schinkel
Head Coach .... Pierre Creamer
Assistant Coaches .... Clement Jodoin, Rick Kehoe
Head Scout... Paul Goulet
Eastern Scout... Doug Wood
Western Scout... Bruce Haralson
Quebec Scout.. Albert Mandanici
Minnesota Scout .... John Gill
Boston Scout.. Fred Gore
Director of Marketing.. Paul Steigerwald
Director of Press Relations... Cindy Himes
Director of Team Services .... Terry Schiffhauer
Trainer .... Steve Thomas
Equipment Manager .... Ed Neisner
Strength Coach .... Doug McKenney
Home Ice... Civic Arena
Address... Civic Arena, Gate No. 7, Pittsburgh, Pa. 15219
Seating Capacity... 16,033
Club colors .... Black, Gold and White
Phone.. (412) 642-1800

Edward DeBartolo

Paul Martha

Ed Johnston

Pierre Creamer

Pittsburgh Penguins 1987-88 Roster

FORWARDS

Name	Hgt.	Wgt.	Place of Birth	Date	1986-87 Club	G.	A.	Pts.
Aitken, Brad	6:03	205	Scarborough, Ont.	10-30-67	Sault Ste. Marie	27	38	65
Belanger, Roger	6:00	198	St. Catharines, Ont.	12- 1-65	Baltimore-Muskegon	10	13	23
Bourque, Phil	6:00	208	Chelmsford, Mass.	6- 8-62	Baltimore-Pittsburgh	17	19	36
Brown, Rob	5:11	185	Kingston, Ont.	4-10-68	Kamloops	76	136	212
Cain, Kelly	5:06	180	Toronto, Ont.	4-19-68	..	..	..	..
Callander, Jock	6:01	180	Regina, Sask.	4-23-61	Muskegon	54	82	136
Capuano, Dave	6:02	195	Cranston, R.I.	7-27-68	Univ. of Maine	18	41	59
Cunneyworth, Randy	6:00	183	Etobicoke, Ont.	5-10-61	Pittsburgh	26	27	53
Daniels, Jeff	6:01	191	Oshawa, Ont.	6-24-68	Oshawa	14	9	23
Del Col, John	5:10	192	St. Catharines, Ont.	5-11-65	Baltimore	4	5	9
Drulia, Stan	5:10	188	Elmira, N.Y.	1- 5-68	Hamilton	27	51	78
Errey, Bob	5:10	179	Montreal, Que.	9-21-64	Pittsburgh	16	18	34
Frawley, Dan	6:00	193	Sturgeon Falls, Ont.	6- 2-62	Pittsburgh	14	14	28
Giffin, Lee	5:11	181	Chatham, Ont.	4- 1-67	Oshawa-Pittsburgh	32	70	102
Gotaas, Steve	5:10	175	Camrose, Alta.	5-10-67	Prince Albert	53	55	108
Gruhl, Scott	5:11	185	Port Colborne, Ont.	9-13-59	Muskegon	34	39	73
Hannan, Dave	5:10	180	Sudbury, Ont.	11-26-61	Pittsburgh	10	15	25
Johnson, Scott	5:11	196	New Hope, Minn.	10-12-63	Baltimore	8	7	15
Ketola, Marty	5:11	205	Cloquet, Minn.	2-25-65	Colorado College	4	4	8
Kontos, Chris	6:01	195	Toronto, Ont.	12-10-63	New Haven-Pittsburgh	22	26	48
Kurkinen, Risto	5:09	185	Jyvaskyla, Finland	1-21-63	Jypht	41	19	60
Lamb, Jeff	5:11	170		7-14-64	Denver University	10	24	34
Leach, Jamie	6:01	200	Winnipeg, Man.	8-25-69	Hamilton	12	19	31
Lemieux, Mario	6:04	210	Montreal, Que.	10- 5-65	Pittsburgh	54	53	107
Loney, Troy	6:03	206	Bow Island, Alta.	9-21-63	Baltimore-Pittsburgh	21	21	42
Mann, Jimmy	6:00	205	Montreal, Que.	4-17-59		Did Not Play		
Mathiasen, Dwight	6:01	196	Brandon, Man.	5-12-63	Baltimore-Pittsburgh	23	23	46
Mayer, Pat	6:03	225		7-24-61	Muskegon	4	14	18
McLlwain, Dave	6:00	185	Seaforth, Ont.	1- 9-67	North Bay	46	73	119
Michayluk, Dave	5:10	180	Wakaw, Sask.	5-18-62	Muskegon	47	53	100
Mokosak, Carl	6:01	200	Ft. Sask., Alta.	9-22-62	Baltimore-Pittsburgh	23	27	50
Paiement, Wilf	6:01	210	Earlton, Ont.	10-16-55	Buffalo	20	17	37
Quinn, Dan	5:10	176	Ottawa, Ont.	6- 1-65	Calgary-Pittsburgh	31	49	80
Simpson, Craig	6:02	192	London, Ont.	2-15-67	Pittsburgh	26	25	51
Stevens, Kevin	6:03	224	Brockton, Mass.	4-15-65	Boston College	35	35	70
Teevens, Mark	6:00	183	Ottawa, Ont.	6-17-66	Baltimore	15	16	31
Volhoffer, Troy	5:11	185	Regina, Sask.	2- 9-66	Baltimore	11	25	36
Wilson, Mitch	5:08	186	Kelowna, B.C.	2-15-62	Baltimore-Pittsburgh	10	10	20

DEFENSEMEN

Name	Hgt.	Wgt.	Place of Birth	Date	1986-87 Club	G.	A.	Pts.
Bodger, Doug	6:02	209	Chemainus, B.C.	6-18-66	Pittsburgh	11	38	49
Buskas, Rod	6:01	207	Wetaskiwin, Alta.	1- 7-61	Pittsburgh	3	15	18
Charlesworth, Todd	6:01	190	Calgary, Alta.	3-22-65	Baltimore-Pittsburgh	5	21	26
Dahlquist, Chris	6:01	193	Fridley, Minn.	12-14-62	Baltimore-Pittsburgh	1	17	18
Goertz, Dave	5:11	199	Edmonton, Alta.	3-28-65	Muskegon-Baltimore	3	20	23
Hillier, Randy	6:00	190	Toronto, Ont.	3-30-60	Pittsburgh	4	8	12
Hobson, Doug	5:11	181	Prince Albert, Sask.	4- 9-68	Prince Albert	3	20	23
Joseph, Chris	6:02	210	Burnaby, B.C.	9-10-69	Seattle	13	45	58
Johnson, Jim	6:00	186	New Hope, Minn.	8- 9-62	Pittsburgh	5	25	30
Mantha, Moe	6:02	205	Lakewood, O.	1-21-61	Pittsburgh	9	31	40
Paek, Jim	6:00	188	Seoul, S. Korea	4- 7-67	Oshawa	5	17	22
Rowe, Mike	6:01	200	Kingston, Ont.	3- 8-65	Baltimore-Pittsburgh	1	18	19
Schmidt, Norm	5:11	198	Sault Ste. Marie, Ont.	1-24-63	Pittsburgh-Baltimore	5	12	17
Siren, Ville	6:01	193	Tempere, Finland	2-11-64	Pittsburgh	5	17	22
Taylor, Randy	6:02	207		7-30-65	Harvard	3	35	38
Waver, Jeff	5:10	195	St. Boniface, Man.	9-28-68	Hamilton	12	28	40
Wilson, Rob	6:03	192	Toronto, Ont.	7-18-68	Sudbury	1	27	28
Zalapski, Zarley	6:01	196	Edmonton, Alta.	4-22-68	Team Canada	11	29	40

GOALTENDERS

Name	Hgt.	Wgt.	Place of Birth	Date	1986-87 Club	Mins.	GA.	SO.
Cooper, Jeff	5:10	169	Ottawa, Ont.	6-12-62	Muskegon	2673	147	0
Ford, Brian	5:10	168	Edmonton, Alta.	9-22-61	Baltimore	1541	99	0
Guenette, Steve	5:09	162	Montreal, Que.	11-13-65	Baltimore-Pittsburgh	3148	165	5
Meloche, Gilles	5:09	182	Montreal, Que.	7-12-50	Pittsburgh	2343	134	0
Pietrangelo, Frank	5:11	190	Niagara Falls, Ont.	12-17-64	Muskegon	2090	119	0
Riggin, Pat	5:09	175	Kincardine, Ont.	5-26-59	Boston-Moncton-Pittsburgh	2299	118	1
Tabaracci, Richard	5:10	186	Toronto, Ont.	1- 2-69	Cornwall	3347	290	1

Quebec Nordiques

Adams Division

President and Governor .... Marcel Aubut
General Manager.. Maurice Filion
Director of Personnel Development.. Gilles Leger
Director of Recruiting.. Martin Madden
Coach .... Andre Savard
Associate Coaches.. Guy Lapointe, Alain Chainey
Scout-Professional Hockey and Special Assignments.. Simon Nolet
Scouts .... George Armstrong, Serge Aubry, Red Fleming,
Pierre Gauthier, Darwin Bennett
General Counsel... Jean Pelletier
Assistant to the President/Administration .... Jean Laflamme
Assistant to the President/Marketing and Communications... Jean D. Legault
Supervisor of Press Relations... Jean Martineau
Coordinator of Information.. Nicole Bouchard
Supervisor of Public Relations... Marius Fortier
Physician... Dr. Pierre Beauchemin
Trainers.. Rene Lacasse, Rene Lavigueur, Jacques Lavergne
Home Ice.. Quebec Coliseum
Address .... 2205 Ave. du Colisee, Quebec, Que. G1L 4W7
Seating Capacity.. 15,434
Club colors.. Blue, White and Red
Phone .... (418) 529-8441

Marcel Aubut

Maurice Filion

Gilles Leger

Andre Savard

Quebec Nordiques 1987-88 Roster

FORWARDS	Hgt.	Wgt.	Place of Birth	Date	1986-87 Club	G.	A.	Pts.
Cote, Alain	5:10	203	Matane, Que.	5- 3-57	Quebec	12	24	36
Duchesne, Gaetan	5:11	195	Les Saules, Que.	7-11-62	Washington	17	35	52
Eagles, Mike	5:10	180	Sussex, N.B.	3- 7-63	Quebec	13	19	32
Fortier, Marc	6:00	190	Sherbrooke, Que.	2-26-66	Chicoutimi	66	135	201
Gaulin, Jean-Marc	5:10	182	Balve, Germany	3- 3-62	Fredericton	1	1	2
Gerlitz, Paul	5:11	205	Calgary, Alta.	3-23-63	Muskegon-Fredericton	10	11	21
Gillis, Paul	5:11	190	Toronto, Ont.	12-31-63	Quebec	13	26	39
Goulet, Michel	6:01	185	Peribonka, Que.	4-21-60	Quebec	49	47	96
Groulx, Wayne	5:09	176	Welland, Ont.	2- 2-65	Muskegon-Fredericton	28	27	55
Haworth, Alan	5:10	190	Drummondville, Que.	9- 1-60	Washington	25	16	41
Heroux, Yves	5:11	185	Terrebonne, Que.	4-27-65	Fredericton-Muskegon	14	14	28
Hough, Mike	6:01	190	Montreal, Que.	2- 6-63	Quebec-Fredericton	7	11	18
Lafreniere, Jason	5:11	185	St. Catharines, Que.	12- 6-66	Quebec	13	15	28
Lambert, Lane	5:11	180	Melfort, Sask.	11-18-64	New Haven-N.Y. Rang.-Quebec.	10	11	21
Latta, David	6:00	185	Thunder Bay, Ont.	1- 3-67	Kitchener	32	46	78
McRae, Ken	6:01	196	Winchester, Ont.	4-23-68	Hamilton	19	27	46
Malone, Greg	6:00	190	Fredericton, N.B.	3- 8-56	Fredericton-Quebec	13	23	36
Middendorf, Max	6:04	194	Syracuse, N.Y.	8-18-67	Kitchener-Quebec	39	48	87
Miller, Keith	6:02	212	Toronto, Ont.	3-18-67	Guelph	50	31	81
Millier, Pierre	6:00	165	Baie-Comeau, Que.	1-15-68	Chicoutimi	37	57	94
Natyshak, Mike	6:02	212	Belle River, Ont.	11-29-63	Bowling Green Univ.	5	10	15
Nault, Jean-Francois	6:02	180	Montreal, Que.	12- 5-67	Granby	36	49	85
Ogrodnick, John	6:00	190	Ottawa, Ont.	6-20-59	Detroit-Quebec	23	44	67
Peer, Brit	6:00	189	Toronto, Ont.	6-14-66	Muskegon-Peoria	4	3	7
Perkins, Terry	6:01	190	Campbell River, B.C.	7-21-66	Fredericton	10	11	21
Quinney, Ken	5:10	198	New Westminster, B.C.	5-23-65	Fredericton-Quebec	16	34	50
Routhier, Jean-Marc	6:01	177	Quebec, Que.	2- 2-68	Hull	17	18	35
Shedden, Doug	6:00	190	Wallaceburg, Ont.	4-29-61	Detroit-Quebec-Fredericton	18	20	38
Stastny, Anton	6:00	185	Bratislava, Czech.	8- 5-59	Quebec	27	35	62
Stastny, Peter	6:01	195	Bratislava, Czech.	9-18-56	Quebec	24	52	76
Stienburg, Trevor	6:01	185	Kingston, Ont.	5-13-66	Fredericton-Quebec	15	12	27
Zemlak, Richard	6:02	190	Wynyard, Sask.	3- 3-63	Fredericton-Quebec	9	8	17

DEFENSEMEN	Hgt.	Wgt.	Place of Birth	Date	1986-87 Club	G.	A.	Pts.
Albelin, Tommy	6:01	185	Stockholm, Sweden	5-21-64	Djurgardens	7	5	12
Brown, Jeff	6:01	185	Ottawa, Ont.	4-30-66	Quebec-Fredericton	9	36	45
Bzdel, Gerald	6:00	192	Wynyard, Sask.	3-13-66	Seattle	4	15	19
Donnelly, Gord	6:02	195	Montreal, Que.	4- 5-62	Quebec	0	2	2
Finn, Steven	6:00	192	Laval, Que.	8-20-66	Quebec-Fredericton	9	24	33
Guerard, Stephane	6:02	182	St. Elizabeth, Que.	4-12-68	Shawinigan	5	16	21
Julien, Claude	6:00	195	Blind River, Ont.	4-23-60	France-Fredericton	16	56	72
Karalis, Tom	6:01	205	Montreal, Que.	5-24-64	Fredericton-Muskegon	3	12	15
Moller, Randy	6:02	205	Red Deer, Alta.	8-23-63	Quebec	5	9	14
Picard, Robert	6:02	205	Montreal, Que.	5-25-57	Quebec	8	20	28
Poudrier, Daniel	6:02	185	Thetford Mines, Que.	2-15-64	Fredericton-Quebec	8	18	26
Richard, Jean-Marc	5:11	170	St. Raymond, Que.	10- 8-66	Chicoutimi	21	81	102
Rochefort, Normand	6:01	200	Trois-Rivieres, Que.	1-28-61	Quebec	6	9	15
Shaunessy, Scott	6:04	220	Newport, R.I.	1-22-64	Boston University-Quebec	3	13	16
Shaw, David	6:02	187	St. Thomas, Ont.	5-25-64	Quebec	0	19	19

GOALTENDERS	Hgt.	Wgt.	Place of Birth	Date	1986-87 Club	Mins.	GA.	SO.
Brunetta, Mario	6:03	180	Quebec, Que.	1-25-67	Laval	3469	261	1
Gordon, Scott	5:10	175	South Easton, Mass.	2- 6-63	Fredericton	1616	120	0
Gosselin, Mario	5:08	160	Thetford Mines, Que.	6-15-63	Quebec	1625	86	0
Sevigny, Richard	5:08	178	Montreal, Que.	11- 4-57	Fredericton-Quebec	1028	73	1
Tugnutt, Ron	5:11	148	Scarborough, Ont.	10-22-67	Peterborough	1891	88	2

St. Louis Blues

Norris Division

Board of Directors .... Michael F. Shanahan, Jerome V. LaBarbera, Donald E. Lasater,
James Kerley, Lewis N. Wolff
Chairman of the Board.. Michael F. Shanahan
Vice-Chairman.. Jerome V. LaBarbera
President... Jack Quinn
Vice-President/General Manager .... Ronald Caron
Vice-President/Director of Public Relations and Marketing.. Susie Mathieu
Director of Player Development .... Bob Plager
Director of Scouting..Ted Hampson
Assistant Director of Scouting/Eastern Canada and U.S. ....Jack Evans
Western Canada and U.S. Scout.. Pat Ginnell
Head Coach .... Jacques Martin
Assistant Coaches .... Barclay Plager, Doug MacLean, Joe Micheletti
Assistant Director of Public Relations/Media Relations.. Mark Niebling
Assistant Director of Public Relations/Publications .... Jeff Trammel
Trainer .... Norm Mackie
Home Ice...The Arena
Address.. 5700 Oakland Avenue, St. Louis, Missouri 63110
Seating Capacity.. 17,666
Club colors.. Blue, Gold, Red and White
Phone .... (314) 781-5300

Michael Shanahan

Ron Caron

Jack Quinn

Jacques Martin

St. Louis Blues 1987-88 Roster

FORWARDS

Name	Hgt.	Wgt.	Place of Birth	Date	1986-87 Club	G.	A.	Pts.
Beers, Eddy	6:02	195	Zwaag, Netherlands	10-12-59	St. Louis	Did not play		
Bozon, Philippe	5:11	180	Chamoix, France	11-30-66	St. Jean-Peoria	20	21	41
Cavallini, Gino	6:01	215	Toronto, Ont.	11-24-62	St. Louis	18	26	44
Degagne, Rob	5:09	185	Thunder Bay, Ont.	2- 4-65	Peoria	5	11	16
Delcourt, Grant	5:10	180	Kelowna, B.C.	8-13-66	Spokane	34	44	78
Dumont, Marc	6:01	185	Quebec City, Que.	1-28-67	Laval	29	47	76
Evans, Doug	5:09	178	Peterborough, Ont.	6- 2-63	St. Louis-Peoria	3	13	16
Ewen, Todd	6:02	200	Saskatoon, Sask.	3-26-66	St. Louis-Peoria	2	0	2
Federko, Bernie	6:00	195	Foam Lake, Sask.	5-12-56	St. Louis	20	52	72
Finlay, Andrew	6:04	212	Montreal, Que.	1- 3-65	Erie	30	27	57
Fleming, Gerry	6:05	218	Montreal, Que.	10-16-66	University of PEI	20	15	35
Flockhart, Ron	5:11	185	Smithers, B.C.	10-10-60	St. Louis	16	19	35
Gilmour, Doug	5:11	160	Kingston, Ont.	6-25-63	St. Louis	42	63	105
Holmes, Daril	6:06	205	Nepean, Ont.	2-15-67	Kitchener	17	25	41
Hrkac, Tony	5:11	165	Thunder Bay, Ont.	7- 7-66	Univ. of North Dakota	36	50	86
Huard, Bill	6:01	192	Welland, Ont.	6-24-67	Peterborough	14	11	25
Hunter, Mark	6:00	205	Petrolia, Ont.	11-12-62	St. Louis	36	33	69
Lemieux, Jocelyn	5:11	207	Mont Laurier, Que.	11-18-67	St. Louis	10	8	18
MacEachern, Shane	5:11	179	Charlottetown, PEI	12-14-67	Hull	44	58	102
MacLean, Terry	6:01	178	Montreal, Que.	1-14-68	Trois-Rivieres	41	76	117
McKegney, Tony	6:01	198	Montreal, Que.	2-15-58	Minnesota-N.Y. Rangers	31	20	51
Meagher, Rick	5:08	175	Belleville, Ont.	11- 4-53	St. Louis	18	21	39
Moxam, Daran	5:10	183	Sudbury, Ont.	5-25-66	Kitchener	33	36	69
Osborne, Keith	6:01	181	Toronto, Ont.	4- 2-69	North Bay	34	55	89
Paslawski, Greg	5:11	189	Kindersley, Sask.	8-25-61	St. Louis	29	35	64
Pohl, Trevor	5:11	178	Vernon, B.C.	9-14-67	Portland	10	17	27
Pohl, Troy	5:11	175	Vernon, B.C.	9-14-67	Portland	18	21	39
Porter, Don	6:03	195	Geraldton, Ont.	5-25-66	Michigan Tech Univ.	7	3	10
Raglan, Herb	6:00	204	Peterborough, Ont.	8- 5-67	St. Louis	6	10	16
Reeds, Mark	5:10	190	Toronto, Ont.	1-24-60	St. Louis	9	16	25
Ronning, Cliff	5:08	157	Vancouver, B.C.	10- 1-65	St. Louis	11	14	25
Savard, Ray	5:11	185	Port Albert, B.C.	1- 5-67	Regina	46	22	68
Smith, Darin	6:02	204	Vineland Sta., Ont.	2-20-67	North Bay	22	25	47
Stefan, Joe	6:03	180	Brantford, Ont.	2-27-66	St. Catharines	30	75	105
Sutter, Brian	5:11	180	Viking, Alta.	10- 7-58	St. Louis	3	3	6
Thomlinson, Dave	6:01	185	Edmonton, Alta.	8-22-66	Moose Jaw	44	37	81
Turnbull, Perry	6:02	200	Bentley, Alta.	3- 9-59	Winnipeg	1	5	6
Wickenheiser, Doug	6:01	196	Regina, Sask.	3-30-61	St. Louis	13	15	28
Wolak, Mike	5:10	155	Utica, Mich.	4-29-68	Windsor	30	36	66

DEFENSEMEN

Name	Hgt.	Wgt.	Place of Birth	Date	1986-87 Club	G.	A.	Pts.
Benning, Brian	6:00	175	Edmonton, Alta.	6-10-66	St. Louis	13	36	49
Bothwell, Tim	6:03	190	Vancouver, B.C.	5- 6-55	Hartford-St. Louis	6	16	22
Bourgeois, Charlie	6:04	220	Moncton, N.B.	11-19-59	St. Louis	2	12	14
Carlson, Kent	6:03	200	Concord, N.H.	1-11-62	St. Louis	Did not play		
Copple, John	6:00	195	Hamilton, Ont.	8-27-66	Hamilton	10	36	46
Dark, Michael	6:03	225	Sarnia, Ont.	9-17-63	St. Louis-Peoria	4	11	15
Dirk, Robert	6:04	207	Regina, Sask.	8-20-66	Peoria	5	17	22
Dumas, Robert	5:11	195	Sprint River, Alta.	3-19-69	Seattle	8	29	37
Featherstone, Glen	6:04	209	Toronto, Ont.	7- 8-68	Windsor	6	11	17
Jenewein, Scott	6:03	220	Rochester, Minn.	12-21-64	Peoria	0	2	2
Lavoie, Dominic	6:02	187	Montreal, Que.	11-21-67	St. Jean	12	42	54
Maurice, Paul	6:03	192	S. Ste. Marie, Ont.	1-30-67	Windsor	4	15	19
Nordmark, Robert	6:01	190	Lulea, Sweden	8-20-62	Swedish Nationals	7	8	15
Pavese, Jim	6:02	205	New York, N.Y.	5- 8-62	St. Louis	2	9	11
Posavad, Mike	5:11	196	Brantford, Ont.	1- 3-64	St. Louis-Peoria	2	15	17
Ramage, Rob	6:02	210	Byron, Ont.	1-11-59	St. Louis	11	28	39
Thacker, Rod	6:02	200	Kitchener, Ont.	7-16-68	Sault Ste. Marie	1	9	10
Trader, Larry	6:01	190	Barry's Bay, Ont.	7- 6-63	Canadian Nationals	4	16	20
Watson, Jerry	6:00	200	Smithers, B.C.	9-24-66	St. Albert	..	..	..
Whistle, Rob	6:02	195	Thunder Bay, Ont.	4- 4-61	New Haven	4	12	16
Tournier, Marc	5:11	195	S. Ste. Marie, Ont.	2-13-66	Guelph	12	37	49

GOALTENDERS

Name	Hgt.	Wgt.	Place of Birth	Date	1986-87 Club	Mins.	GA.	SO.
Jablonski, Pat	6:00	170	Toledo, Ohio	6-20-67	Windsor	2328	128	3
May, Darrell	6:00	175	Edmonton, Alberta	3- 6-62	Peoria	3420	214	0
Millen, Greg	5:09	175	Toronto, Ont.	6-25-57	St. Louis	2482	146	0
Perry, Alan	5:08	155	Providence, RI	8-30-66	Belleville	843	64	0
Wamsley, Rick	5:11	185	Simcoe, Ont.	5-25-59	St. Louis	2410	142	0
Seymour, Glen	5:10	175	Prince Rupert, B.C.	6-19-67	Portland-Moose Jaw	2405	172	1

Toronto
Maple Leafs
Norris Division

President, Governor and Managing Director.. Harold E. Ballard
Chairman of the Board... Paul McNamara
General Manager.. Gerry McNamara
Coach .... John Brophy
Assistant Coach .... Garry Lariviere
Assistant General Manager...Gord Stellick
Scouts.. Johnny Bower, Frank Currie, Dick Duff,
Floyd Smith, Jack Gardiner, Jim Easdell, Anders Bengston
Publicity Director .... Bob Stellick
Treasurer.. Donald Crump
Box Office Manager ....I.M. 'Patty' Patoff
Trainers... Guy Kinnear, Dan Lemelin, Dan Marr
Home Ice .... Maple Leaf Gardens
Address ....60 Carlton Street, Toronto, Ont. M5B 1L1
Seating Capacity...16,382 (including standees)
Club Colors .... Blue and White
Phone ....(416) 977-1641

Harold Ballard

Gerry McNamara

John Brophy

Toronto Maple Leafs 1987-88 Roster

FORWARDS	Hgt.	Wgt.	Place of Birth	Date	1986-87 Club	G.	A.	Pts.
Alexander, Ken	6:01	186	Dearborn Hts., Mich.	2-25-67	Hamilton	11	26	37
Allison, Mike	6:00	200	Fort Francis, Ont.	3-28-61	Toronto	7	16	23
Armstrong, Tim	5:11	168	Toronto, Ont.	5-12-67	Newmarket	3	0	3
Bean, Tim	6:00	194	Sault Ste. Marie, Ont.	3- 9-67	North Bay	24	39	63
Bellefeuille, Brian	6:02	185	Natick, Mass.	3-21-67	Canterbury	..	..	..
Bernacci, Ron	5:10	175	Hamilton, Ont.	2-21-67	Hamilton	43	47	90
Brennan, Stephen	6:01	190	Winchester, Mass.	3-22-67	New Prep	..	..	..
Clark, Wendel	5:11	197	Kelvington, Sask.	10-25-66	Toronto	37	23	60
Courtnall, Russ	5:11	179	Duncan, B.C.	6- 2-65	Toronto	29	44	73
Dallman, Marty	5:10	190	Niagara Falls, Ont.	2-15-63	Newmarket	24	24	48
Damphousse, Vincent	6:01	195	Montreal, Que.	12-17-67	Toronto	21	25	46
Daoust, Dan	5:11	160	Montreal, Que.	2-29-60	Toronto	4	3	7
Davidson, Sean	5:11	177	Toronto, Ont.	4-13-68	Toronto Jrs.	30	32	62
Defazio, Dean	5:11	185	Ottawa, Ont.	4-16-63	Newmarket	7	13	20
Donahue, Andy	6:01	180	Boston, Mass.	1-17-67	Dartmouth University	0	7	7
Evans, Daryl	5:09	185	Toronto, Ont.	1-12-61	Newmarket-Toronto	28	46	74
Fergus, Tom	6:01	200	Chicago, Ill.	6-16-62	Toronto-Newmarket	21	29	50
Frycer, Miroslav	6:00	185	Opava, Czech.	9-27-59	Toronto	7	8	15
Giguere, Stephane	6:00	182	Montreal, Que.	2-21-68	St. Jean	45	45	90
Hie, Danny	6:00	178	Mississauga, Ont.	6-21-68	Sudbury	6	25	31
Holick, Mark	6:02	185	Saskatoon, Sask.	8- 6-68	Saskatoon	0	1	1
Hulst, Kent	6:00	180	St. Thomas, Ont.	4- 8-68	Belleville	31	30	61
Ihnacak, Miroslav	5:11	175	Poprad, Czech.	2-19-62	Toronto-Newmarket	17	22	39
Ihnacak, Peter	6:01	195	Poprad, Czech.	5- 3-57	Toronto-Newmarket	14	33	47
Jarvis, Wes	5:11	156	Toronto, Ont.	5-30-58	Newmarket	28	50	78
Jobe, Trevor	6:01	192	Lethbridge, Alta.	5-14-67	Moose Jaw	54	33	87
Laxdal, Derek	6:02	195	St. Boniface, Man.	2-21-66	Newmarket-Toronto	24	20	44
Leeman, Gary	5:11	175	Toronto, Ont.	2-19-64	Toronto	21	31	52
MacInnis, Joseph	6:00	165	Cambridge, Mass.	5-25-66	Northeastern Univ.	7	8	15
Maguire, Kevin	6:02	200	Toronto, Ont.	1- 5-63	Newmarket-Toronto	4	2	6
Marois, Daniel	6:01	180	Montreal, Que.	10- 3-68	Chicoutimi	22	26	48
McIntyre, John	6:01	175	Ravenswood, Ont.	4-29-69	Guelph	8	22	30
McRae, Chris	6:00	178	Beaverton, Ont.	8-25-65	Newmarket	3	7	10
Osborne, Mark	6:01	185	Toronto, Ont.	8-13-61	N.Y. Rangers-Toronto	22	25	47
Reynolds, Bobby	5:11	175	Flint, Mich.	7-14-67	Michigan State Univ.	20	13	33
Ruzicka, Vladimir	6:01	175	Czechoslovakia	6- 6-63	Czechoslovakia	..	..	..
Sacco, Joe	6:01	180	Medford, Mass.	2- 4-69	Medford	35	45	80
Smith, Brad	5:11	180	Quebec City, Que.	7-31-54	Toronto	5	7	12
Terrion, Greg	5:11	175	Marmora, Ont.	5- 2-60	Toronto	7	8	15
Thomas, Steve	5:10	185	Stockport, England	7-15-63	Toronto	35	27	62
Vaive, Rick	6:01	190	Ottawa, Ont.	7-14-59	Toronto	32	34	66
Vani, Carmine	5:11	175	Toronto, Ont.	8- 7-64	Newmarket	1	1	2
Verstraete, Leigh	5:11	183	Pincher Creek, Alta.	1- 6-62	Newmarket	9	7	16
Waslen, Gerrard	6:01	187	Humboldt, Sask.	10- 5-62	Newmarket	22	30	52
Wurst, Mike	6:04	210	Edina, Minn.	10- 5-64	Ohio State	..	..	..
Yaremchuk, Ken	5:11	187	Edmonton, Alta.	1- 1-64	Toronto-Newmarket	5	12	17
DEFENSEMEN								
Abrecht, Cliff	6:00	200	Bramalea, Ont.	5-24-63	Newmarket	2	5	7
Blad, Brian	6:02	195	Brockville, Ont.	7-22-67	Belleville	2	6	8
Boland, Sean	6:03	180	Toronto, Ont.	2-18-68	Toronto Jrs.	0	4	4
Buckley, David	6:04	195	Newton, Mass.	1-27-66	Boston College	3	5	8
Capuano, Jack	6:02	210	Cranston, R.I.	7- 7-66	Maine University	10	34	44
Clements, Scott	6:01	205	Sudbury, Ont.	5- 1-62	Newmarket	1	15	16
Fauss, Ted	6:02	206	Clinton, N.Y.	6-30-61	Newmarket-Toronto	0	6	6
Gill, Todd	6:00	185	Brockville, Ont.	11- 9-65	Toronto-Newmarket	5	35	40
Hotham, Greg	5:11	185	London, Ont.	3- 7-56	Newmarket	4	9	13
Hoard, Brian	6:04	195	Hamilton, Ont.	3-10-68	Sault Ste. Marie	4	9	13
Iafrate, Al	6:02	215	Dearborn, Mich.	3-21-66	Toronto	9	21	30
Jensen, Chris	6:02	190	Wilmette, Ill.	6-29-68	Northwood Prep	8	17	25
Johnson, Terry	6:03	210	Calgary, Alta.	11-28-58	Toronto-Newmarket	0	2	2
Kotsopoulos, Chris	6:03	210	Scarborough, Ont.	11-27-58	Toronto	2	10	12
Lanz, Rick	6:02	200	Karlouyvary, Czech.	9-16-61	Vancouver-Toronto	3	25	28
Latal, Jiri	..	..		2- 2-67	Sparta, Czech.	..	..	..
McGill, Bob	6:01	190	Edmonton, Ala.	4-27-62	Toronto	1	4	5
Richardson, Luke	6:04	208	Ottawa, Ont.	3-26-69	Peterborough	13	32	45
Root, Bill	6:01	204	Toronto, Ont.	9- 6-59	Toronto-Newmarket	7	14	21
Salming, Borje	6:01	195	Kiruna, Sweden	4-17-51	Toronto	4	16	20
Serowik, Jeff	6:00	190	Manchester, N.H.	10- 1-67	Lawrence Academy	..	..	..
Shannon, Darryl	6:02	190	Barrie, Ont.	6-21-68	Windsor	23	27	50
Spangler, Ken	5:11	196	Edmonton, Alta.	5- 2-67	Calgary Jrs.	12	24	36
Taylor, Scott	6:02	182	Toronto, Ont.	3-23-68	Kitchener	6	16	22
Weinrich, Alex	6:00	178	Lewiston, Me.	3-12-69	North Yarmouth Acad.	12	20	32

GOALTENDERS	Hgt.	Wgt.	Place of Birth	Date	1986-87 Club	Mins.	GA.	SO.
Bernhardt, Tim	5:09	164	Sarnia, Ont.	1-17-58	Newmarket-Toronto	1726	120	1
Bester, Allan	5:07	155	Hamilton, Ont.	3-26-64	Toronto-Newmarket	1998	116	2
Dowie, Bruce	5:10	170	Oakville, Ont.	12- 9-62	Newmarket	158	13	0
Reese, Jeff	5:09	150	Brantford, Ont.	3-24-66	Newmarket	2823	193	1
Rhodes, Damian	6:00	165	St. Paul, Minn.	5-28-69	Richfield H.S.	673	51	1
Wregget, Ken	6:01	195	Brandon, Man.	3-25-64	Toronto	3026	200	0

Vancouver Canucks

Smythe Division

Chairman of the Board .... Frank A. Griffiths
Assistant to the Chairman.. Arthur R. Griffiths
President and General Manager... Pat Quinn
Vice President and Director of Hockey Operations...Brian Burke
Vice-President, Communications and Marketing... Glen Ringdal
Senior Advisor.. Jack Gordon
Director of Hockey Information .... Darcy Rota
Head Coach .... Bob McCammon
Assistant Coach .... Jack McIlhargey
Director of Scouting .... Mike Penny
Scouts.. Jack McCartan, Ken Slater, Ron Delorme, Ed McColgan, Paul McIntosh
Community Relations Director.. Lynn Harrison
Goodwill Ambassador .... Babe Pratt
Assistant Director of Hockey Information .... Frank Bohmer
Trainers .... Ken Fleger, Larry Ashley
Home Ice .... Pacific Coliseum
Address...100 North Renfrew St., Vancouver, B.C. V5K 3N7
Seating Capacity..16,553
Club Colors .... Black, Red and Gold
Phone ....(604) 254-5141

Frank A. Griffiths

Pat Quinn

Bob McCammon

Vancouver Canucks 1987-88 Roster

FORWARDS

Name	Hgt.	Wgt.	Place of Birth	Date	1986-87 Club	G.	A.	Pts.
Bertuzzi, Brian	6:00	185	Vancouver, B.C.	1-24-66	Fredericton	7	8	15
Bruce, Dave	5:11	177	Thunder Bay, Ont.	10- 7-64	Fredericton-Vancouver	16	13	29
Coxe, Craig	6:04	195	Chula Vista, Calif.	1-21-64	Vancouver-Fredericton	2	12	14
Crawford, Marc	5:11	185	Belleville, Ont.	2-13-61	Fredericton-Vancouver	8	14	22
Hawkins, Todd	6:01	195	Kingston, Ont.	8- 2-66	Belleville	47	40	87
Hodgson, Dan	5:10	175	Fort Vermillion, Alta.	8-29-65	Newmarket-Vancouver	16	25	41
Kirton, Mark	5:10	170	Regina, Sask.	2- 3-58	Fredericton	27	37	64
Lanthier, Jean-Marc	6:02	195	Montreal, Que.	3-27-63	Fredericton	15	38	53
LeBlanc, John	6:01	190	Campellton, N.B.	2-21-64	Fredericton-Vancouver	41	30	71
Lowry, Dave	6:01	185	Sudbury, Ont.	1-14-65	Vancouver	8	10	18
Murphy, Rob	6:03	195	Hull, Que.	4- 7-69	Laval	35	54	89
Noble, Jeff	5:10	167	Mount Forest, Ont.	5-20-68	Kitchener	29	57	86
Pederson, Barry	5:11	185	Big River, Sask.	3-13-61	Vancouver	24	52	76
Peterson, Brent	6:00	190	Calgary, Alta.	2-15-58	Vancouver	7	15	22
Rohlicek, Jeff	6:00	180	Park Ridge, Ill.	1-27-66	Fredericton	19	37	56
Sandlak, Jim	6:03	209	Kitchener, Ont.	12-12-66	Vancouver	15	21	36
Skriko, Petri	5:10	172	Lapeenranta, Finland	3-12-62	Vancouver	33	41	74
Smyl, Stan	5:08	185	Glendon, Alta.	1-28-58	Vancouver	20	23	43
Stern, Ronnie	6:00	195	St. Agathe, Que.	1-11-67	Longueuil	32	39	71
Stevens, Mike	5:11	193	Kitchener, Ont.	12-30-65	Fredericton	7	18	25
Summanen, Raimo	5:11	185	Jyvaskyla, Finland	3- 2-62	Edmonton-Vancouver	14	11	25
Sundstrom, Patrik	6:02	203	Skelleftea, Sweden	12-14-61	Vancouver	29	42	71
Sutter, Rich	5:11	183	Viking, Alta.	12- 2-63	Vancouver	20	22	42
Tambellini, Steve	6:00	184	Trail, B.C.	5-14-58	Vancouver	16	20	36
Tanti, Tony	5:09	185	Toronto, Ont.	9- 7-63	Vancouver	41	38	79
Taylor, Darren	6:02	173	Calgary, Alta.	5-28-67	Seattle	13	13	26
Vilgrain, Claude	6:01	195	Port-au-Prince, Haiti	3- 1-63	Team Canada	28	42	70
Woodley, Dan	6:00	190	Oklahoma City, Okla.	12-29-67	Portland	30	50	80

DEFENSEMEN

Name	Hgt.	Wgt.	Place of Birth	Date	1986-87 Club	G.	A.	Pts.
Agnew, Jim	6:01	185	Hartney, Man.	3-21-66	Fredericton-Vancouver	0	5	5
Bartel, Robin	6:00	200	Drake, Sask.	5-16-61	Fredericton-Vancouver	0	3	3
Benning, Jim	6:00	185	Edmonton, Alta.	4-29-63	Newmarket-Tor.-Van.	3	16	19
Butcher, Garth	6:00	200	Regina, Sask.	1- 8-63	Vancouver	5	15	20
Cochrane, Glen	6:03	207	Kamloops, B.C.	1-29-58	Vancouver	0	0	0
Herniman, Steve	6:03	199	Windsor, Ont.	6- 9-68	Cornwall	2	8	10
Hunt, Curtis	6:00	180	N. Battleford, Sask.	1-28-67	Prince Albert	6	31	37
Lidster, Doug	6:01	195	Kamloops, B.C.	10-18-60	Vancouver	12	51	63
Lyons, Marc	6:01	201	Toronto, Ont.	1- 8-67	Kingston	5	11	16
MacDonald, Brett	6:01	200	Bothwell, Ont.	1- 5-66	Fredericton	0	9	9
Petit, Michel	6:01	205	St. Malo, Que.	2-12-64	Vancouver	12	13	25
Richter, Dave	6:05	220	St. Boniface, Man.	4- 8-60	Vancouver	2	15	17
Veilleux, Steve	6:00	190	Lachenaie, Que.	3- 9-69	Trois-Rivieres	6	22	28

GOALTENDERS

Name	Hgt.	Wgt.	Place of Birth	Date	1986-87 Club	Mins.	GA.	SO.
Brodeur, Richard	5:07	175	Longueuil, Que.	9-15-52	Vancouver	2972	178	1
Caprice, Frank	5:09	160	Hamilton, Ont.	5- 2-62	Fredericton-Vancouver	2076	136	0
Gamble, Troy	5:11	178	New Glasgow, N.S.	4- 7-67	Medicine Hat	2861	213	0
Kilroy, Shawn	5:11	175	Ottawa, Ont.	8-22-64	Kalamazoo	1476	107	0
Young, Wendell	5:08	185	Halifax, N.S.	8- 1-63	Vancouver-Fredericton	2096	153	0

Washington Capitals
Patrick Division

Chairman of the Board and Governor.. Abe Pollin
President and Alternate Governor .... Richard M. Patrick
Legal Counsel and Alternate Governors .... Peter F. O'Malley, David M. Osnos
Vice-President and General Manager .... David Poile
Comptroller .... Ed Stelzer
Coach .... Bryan Murray
Assistant Coach..Terry Murray
Goaltender Coach.. Warren Strelow
Director of Player Personnel and Recruitment .... Jack Button
Assistant Director of Player Recruitment.. Sam McMaster
Scouts ....Gilles Cote, Ron Ferguson, Clare Rothermel, Bob Schmidt,
Hugh Rogers, Bill Stewart, Michael Abbamont
Director of Marketing...Lew Strudler
Director of Public Relations... Lou Corletto
Assistant Director of Marketing .... Debi Angus
Director of Community Relations... Yvon Labre
Director of Promotions... Charles Copeland
Director of Season Subscriptions .... Joanne Kowalski
Trainer.. Stan Wong
Assistant Trainer .... Doug Shearer
Home Ice .... Capital Centre
Address .... Landover, Md. 20785
Seating Capacity...18,130
Club Colors .... Red, White and Blue
Phone ....(301) 386-7000

Abe Pollin　　　　**David Poile**　　　　**Jack Button**　　　　**Bryan Murray**

Washington Capitals 1987-88 Roster

FORWARDS

Name	Hgt.	Wgt.	Place of Birth	Date	1986-87 Club	G.	A.	Pts.
Adams, Greg	6:01	195	Victoria, B.C.	5-31-60	Washington	14	30	44
Arabski, Rob	5:11	170	Brantford, Ont.	7-17-68	Guelph	29	60	89
Bawa, Robin	6:02	190	Chemainos, B.C.	3-26-66	Kamloops	57	56	113
Bergland, Tim	6:03	180	Crookston, Minn.	1-11-65	Univ. of Minnesota	18	17	35
Christian, Dave	5:11	175	Warroad, Minn.	5-12-59	Washington	23	27	50
DiMuzio, Frank	5:11	185	Toronto, Ont.	8-12-67	Ottawa	59	30	89
Druce, John	6:01	187	Peterborough, Ont.	2-23-66	Binghamton	13	9	22
Dumas, Claude	6:01	175	Thetford-Mines, Que.	1-10-67	Granby	50	82	132
Egerton, Jim	6:00	190	Toronto, Ont.	4-15-61	Flint	52	47	99
Franceschetti, Lou	6:00	190	Toronto, Ont.	3-28-58	Washington	12	9	21
Gartner, Mike	6:00	185	Barrie, Ont.	10-29-59	Washington	41	32	73
Gould, Bob	5:11	195	Petrolia, Ont.	9- 2-57	Washington	23	27	50
Greenlaw, Jeff	6:02	215	Toronto, Ont.	2-28-68	Washington	0	3	3
Gustafsson, Bengt	6:00	185	Karlskoga, Sweden	3-23-58	Bofors	..	..	..
Hollett, Steve	6:01	180	St. John's, Nfld.	6-12-67	Sault Ste. Marie	35	41	76
Hunter, Dale	5:09	190	Petrolia, Ont.	7-31-60	Quebec	10	29	39
Huss, Anders	5:11	185	Brynas, Sweden	4- 6-64	Brynas	12	13	25
Jensen, David	6:01	185	Needham, Mass.	8-19-65	Washington-Binghamton	10	13	23
Kastelic, Ed	6:02	215	Toronto, Ont.	1-29-64	Washington-Binghamton	18	12	30
Larter, Tyler	5:11	185	Charlottetown, P.E.I.	3-12-68	Sault. Ste. Marie	34	59	93
Laughlin, Craig	5:11	198	Toronto, Ont.	9-14-57	Washington	22	30	52
Maltais, Steve	6:01	191	Arvida, Que.	1-25-69	Cornwall	32	12	44
Maurice, Mike	6:00	200	Hamilton, Ont.	4-22-66	Kingston	48	44	92
McCrory, Scott	5:10	175	Campbellford, Ont.	2-27-67	Oshawa	51	99	150
Miller, Kelly	5:11	185	Detroit, Mich.	3- 3-63	N.Y. Rangers-Washington	16	26	42
Murray, Rob	6:01	175	Toronto, Ont.	4- 4-67	Peterborough	17	37	54
O'Rear, Ian	5:10	175	Detroit, Mich.	2-16-66	Winsdor	18	46	64
Pivonka, Michal	6:02	192	Kladno, Czech.	1-28-66	Washington	18	25	43
Ridley, Mike	6:01	200	Winnipeg, Man.	7- 8-63	N.Y. Rangers-Washington	31	39	70
Seftel, Steve	6:01	183	Kitchener, Ont.	5-14-68	Kingston	21	43	64
Stromback, Doug	6:00	180	Farmington, Mich.	3- 2-67	Belleville	32	46	78
Sundstrom, Peter	6:00	180	Skelleftea, Sweden	12-14-61	Bjorkloven	22	16	38
Thomson, Jim	6:01	195	Edmonton, Alta.	12-30-65	Binghamton-Washington	13	10	23

DEFENSEMEN

Name	Hgt.	Wgt.	Place of Birth	Date	1986-87 Club	G.	A.	Pts.
Babcock, Bob	5:11	196	Toronto, Ont.	8- 3-68	Sault Ste. Marie	7	8	15
Ballantyne, Jeff	6:02	195	Elmira, Ont.	1- 7-69	Ottawa	2	13	15
Barrett, John	6:00	208	Ottawa, Ont.	7- 1-58	Washington	2	2	4
Beauchesne, Pat	6:02	204	Albertville, Sask.	2-12-67	Moose Jaw	11	33	44
Beaudoin, Yves	6:00	190	Pt.-aux-Trembles, Que.	1- 7-65	Binghamton-Washington	11	25	36
Cavallini, Paul	6:02	202	Toronto, Ont.	10-13-65	Binghamton-Washington	12	26	38
Cousins, Steve	6:03	205	Edmonton, Alta.	6-27-64	Univ. of Alberta	4	15	19
Eakins, Dallas	6:02	195	Dade City, Fla.	1-20-67	Peterborough	3	11	14
Galley, Garry	5:11	190	Montreal, Que.	4-16-63	Los Angeles-Washington	6	21	27
Hatcher, Kevin	6:04	212	Detroit, Mich.	9- 9-66	Washington	8	16	24
Houlder, Bill	6:02	205	Thunderbay, Ont.	3-11-67	North Bay	17	51	68
Jennings, Grant	6:03	202	Hudson Bay, Sask.	5- 5-65	Binghamton	1	5	6
Kellin, Tony	6:02	205	Grand Rapids, Minn.	3-19-63	Binghamton	8	27	35
Langway, Rod	6:03	215	Taiwan, Formosa	5- 3-57	Washington	2	25	27
MacDonald, Kevin	6:00	190	Brockville, Ont.	2-24-66	Peterborough	4	4	8
Murphy, Larry	6:02	206	Scarborough, Ont.	3- 8-61	Washington	23	58	81
Oleniuk, Devon	6:01	186	Kinstin, Sask.	3-28-68	Kamloops	2	10	12
Shaw, Larry	6:00	200	Guelph, Ont.	2-10-67	Peterborough	4	13	17
Smith, Greg	6:00	195	Ponoka, Alta.	7-18-55	Washington	0	9	9
Stevens, Scott	6:01	210	Kitchener, Ont.	4- 1-64	Washington	10	51	61

GOALTENDERS

Name	Hgt.	Wgt.	Place of Birth	Date	1986-87 Club	Mins.	GA.	SO.
Applewaite, Mark	...			6-29-64	York University	..	..	0
Dufour, Michel	5:06	160	Val d'Or, Que.	8-31-62	Fort Wayne-Muskegon	2418	137	0
Malarchuk, Clint	5:11	180	Grande Prairie, Alta.	5- 1-61	Quebec	3092	175	1
Peeters, Pete	6:01	207	Edmonton, Alta.	8-17-57	Washington	2002	107	0
Raymond, Alain	5:10	177	Rimouski, Que.	6-24-65	Fort Wayne	2433	134	1
Simpson, Shawn	5:11	180	Vancouver, B.C.	8-10-68	Sault Ste. Marie	2673	184	0

Winnipeg Jets

Smythe Division

President and Governor.. Barry Shenkarow
Alternate Governors .... John Ferguson, Bill Davis
Vice-President and General Manager... John Ferguson
Assistant G.M. and Director of Scouting and Recruiting.. Mike Smith
Assistant to the General Manager.. Barry Long
Director, Finance and Administration .... Don Binda
Coach .... Dan Maloney
Assistant Coaches .... Bill Sutherland, Rick St. Croix
Chief Scout.. Les Binkley
Eastern Scout .... Tom Savage
Western Scout .... Charlie Hodge
Special Assignments .... Bill Lesuk
Scouts.. Joe Yanetti, Ken Chisholm,
John O'Flaherty, Bruce Southern
Director of Hockey and Media Information... Murray Harding
Vice President of Marketing.. Madeline Hanson
Athletic Therapist.. Chuck Badcock
Equipment Manager .... Jack Stouffer
Home Ice .... Winnipeg Arena
Address... 15-1430 Maroons Road, Winnipeg, Man. R3G 0L5
Seating Capacity.. 15,401
Club Colors... Red, White and Blue
Phone .... (204) 772-9491

Barry Shenkarow

John Ferguson

Mike Smith

Dan Maloney

Winnipeg Jets 1987-88 Roster

FORWARDS	Hgt.	Wgt.	Place of Birth	Date	1986-87 Club	G.	A.	Pts.
Baillargeon, Joel	6:02	215	Charlesbourg, Que.	10- 6-64	Sherbrooke-Winnipeg	9	19	28
Boschman, Laurie	6:00	185	Major, Sask.	6- 4-60	Winnipeg	17	24	41
Butorac, Ali	5:11	203	Sioux St. Marie, Ont.	7-19-64	Adirondack	8	6	14
Cormier, Eric	6:02	201	Bathurst, N.B.	4-10-64	Moncton Univ.	..	..	..
Douris, Peter	6:01	192	Toronto, Ont.	2-19-66	Sherbrooke-Winnipeg	14	28	42
Duncan, Iain	6:01	180	Weston, Ont.	8- 4-63	Bowling Green-Winnipeg	29	42	71
Elyniuk, Pat	6:00	185	Foam Lake, Sask.	10-30-67	Prince Albert	51	62	113
Endean, Craig	5:11	175	Kamloops, B.C.	4-13-68	Seattle-Regina-Winn.	69	78	147
Fowler, Rob	6:01	195	Tewkesbury, Mass.	7- 7-65	Merrimack	..	..	..
Gilhen, Randy	5:10	190	Zweibrucken, W. Ger.	6-13-63	Sherbrooke	36	29	65
Hamel, Gilles	6:00	185	Asbestos, Que.	3-18-60	Winnipeg	27	21	48
Hawerchuk, Dale	5:11	185	Toronto, Ont.	3- 4-63	Winnipeg	47	53	100
Ingman, Jan	6:02	187	Grumms, Sweden	11-25-61	Farjestads	..	..	..
Jarvenpaa, Hannu	6:00	193	Ilves, Finland	5-19-63	Winnipeg	1	8	9
Jones, Brad	6:00	180	Sterling Heights, Mich ..	6-26-65	U. of Michigan-Winnipeg	33	46	79
Kardum, Nevin	6:01	190	Toronto, Ont.	3-30-67	Providence College	..	..	..
LeVasseur, Chris	6:02	200	Grand Rapids, Minn.	3- 6-64	Alaska-Anchorage	..	..	..
MacLean, Paul	6:00	205	Grostenquin, France	3- 9-58	Winnipeg	32	42	74
McBain, Andrew	6:01	195	Toronto, Ont.	2-18-65	Winnipeg	11	21	32
Morris, Frank	5:11	185	Alexandria, Ont.	3-23-63	Concordia Univ.	..	..	..
Neufeld, Ray	6:03	210	St. Boniface, Man.	4-15-59	Winnipeg	18	18	36
Neilsen, Len	5:09	170	Moosejaw, Sask.	3-28-67	Regina	36	100	136
Nill, Jim	6:00	185	Hanna, Alta.	4-11-58	Winnipeg	3	4	7
Ohman, Roger	6:03	215	Stockholm, Sweden	6- 5-67	Farjestads	..	..	..
Palosaari, Esa	6:04	210	Oulu, Finland	6-10-65	Karpat	..	..	..
Rooney, Steve	6:02	195	Canton, Mass.	6-28-63	Montreal-Winnipeg	2	3	5
Schneider, Scott	6:01	180	Rochester, Minn.	5-18-65	Colorado College	21	22	43
Smail, Doug	5:09	175	Moose Jaw, Sask.	9- 2-57	Winnipeg	25	18	43
Steen, Thomas	5:10	195	Tockmark, Sweden	6- 8-60	Winnipeg	17	33	50
Stewart, Ryan	6:02	185	Prince George, B.C.	6- 1-67	Brandon-Portland	12	11	23
Warus, Mike	6:01	190	Sudbury, Ont.	1-16-64	Lake Superior St.	6	15	21
Whitaker, Gord	6:02	205	Edmonton, Alta.	1-24-66	Colorado College	21	17	38
Wilson, Ron	5:09	175	Toronto, Ont.	5-13-56	Winnipeg	3	13	16
Wright, Kory	5:10	180	Anchorage, Alaska	6-10-65	Northern Michigan Univ.	11	14	25

DEFENSEMEN	Hgt.	Wgt.	Place of Birth	Date	1986-87 Club	G.	A.	Pts.
Armstrong, Harry	6:02	195	Anchorage, Alaska	1-30-65	Univ. of Illinois-Chicago	1	3	4
Berry, Brad	6:02	190	Bashaw, Alta.	4- 1-65	Winnipeg	2	8	10
Carlyle, Randy	5:10	200	Sudbury, Ont.	4-19-56	Winnipeg	16	26	42
Cote, Matt	5:10	195	Manotic, Ont.	1-19-66	Lake Superior St.	1	8	9
Dollas, Bobby	6:02	215	Montreal, Que.	1-31-65	Sherbrooke	6	18	24
Ellett, Dave	6:01	200	Cleveland, O.	3-30-64	Winnipeg	13	31	44
Flichel, Todd	6:03	195	Osgoode, Ont.	9-14-64	Bowling Green	4	15	19
Gosselin, Guy	5:10	185	Rochester, Minn.	1- 6-64	Univ. of Minnesota-Duluth	7	8	15
Husgen, Jamie	6:03	205	St. Louis, Mo.	10-13-64	Univ. of Illinois-Chicago	2	8	10
Kyte, Jim	6:05	210	Ottawa, Ont.	3-21-64	Winnipeg	5	5	10
Marchment, Bryan	6:11	198	Scarborough, Ont.	5- 1-69	Belleville	6	38	44
Marois, Mario	5:11	190	Ancienne Lorette, Que.	12-15-57	Winnipeg	4	40	44
Olausson, Fredrik	6:02	200	Vaxsjo, Sweden	10- 5-66	Winnipeg	7	29	36
Pesetti, Ron	5:11	190	Laval, Que.	5- 3-63	Fort Wayne	12	40	52
Taglianetti, Peter	6:02	200	Framingham, Mass.	8-16-63	Sherbrooke-Winnipeg	5	14	19
Watters, Tim	5:11	180	Kamloops, B.C.	7-25-59	Winnipeg	3	13	16
Sambray, Jim	6:01	185	Thunder Bay, Ont.	3-30-64	Thunder Bay	..	..	..

GOALTENDERS	Hgt.	Wgt.	Place of Birth	Date	1986-87 Club	Mins.	GA.	SO.
Berthiaume, Daniel	5:09	150	Longueil, Que.	1-26-66	Winnipeg-Sherbrooke	2178	116	1
Draper, Tom	5:11	180	Outrement, Que.	11-20-66	Vermont Univ.	1662	96	..
Edmonds, Jim	5:10	170	St. Catharines, Ont.	8- 8-65	Cornell Univ.	953	60	..
Essensa, Bob	6:00	160	Toronto, Ont.	1-14-65	Michigan State Univ.	1383	64	..
Penney, Steve	6:01	190	Ste. Foy, Que.	2- 2-61	Winnipeg-Sherbrooke	526	37	0
Quigley, Dave	5:10	155	Cap-La M'd'I'ne, Que.	1-17-65	Univ. of Moncton	..	..	..
Reddick, Eldon	5:08	170	Halifax, N.S.	10- 6-64	Winnipeg	2762	149	0

★ ★ ★ ★ ★ ★ ★ ★ ★ ★ ★ ★ ★ ★ ★ ★ ★

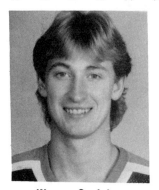

Wayne Gretzky

Tim Kerr

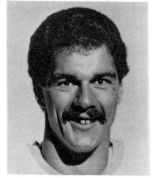

Michel Goulet

The Sporting News
1986-87 NHL All-Star Team

First Team	Position	Second Team
Wayne Gretzky, Edmonton	Center	Mark Messier, Edmonton
Tim Kerr, Philadelphia	Right Wing	Kevin Dineen, Hartford
Michel Goulet, Quebec	Left Wing	Luc Robitaille, Los Angeles
Ray Bourque, Boston	Defense	Larry Murphy, Washington
Mark Howe, Philadelphia	Defense	Paul Coffey, Edmonton
Mike Liut, Hartford	Goalie	Ron Hextall, Philadelphia

THE SPORTING NEWS Player of the Year: Wayne Gretzky, Edmonton
THE SPORTING NEWS Rookie of the Year: Ron Hextall, Philadelphia
THE SPORTING NEWS Coach of the Year: Jacques Demers, Detroit
THE SPORTING NEWS Executive of the Year: John Ferguson, Winnipeg
Note: THE SPORTING NEWS All-Star Team is selected by the NHL Players.

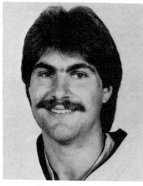

Ray Bourque

Mark Howe

Mike Liut

★ ★ ★ ★ ★ ★ ★ ★ ★ ★ ★ ★ ★ ★ ★ ★ ★

Detroit's Jacques Demers (left), with help from 90-point centerman Steve Yzerman, led the Red Wings to the Campbell Conference finals and was awarded the Jack Adams Trophy as NHL Coach of the Year.

North Stars right winger Dino Ciccarelli finished sixth in scoring with 52 goals and 51 assists for 103 points last season.

1986-87 FINAL NHL STANDINGS

Prince of Wales Conference

Charles F. Adams Division

	G.	W.	L.	T.	Pts.	GF.	GA.
Hartford Whalers	80	43	30	7	93	287	270
Montreal Canadiens	80	41	29	10	92	277	241
Boston Bruins	80	39	34	7	85	301	276
Quebec Nordiques	80	31	39	10	72	267	276
Buffalo Sabres	80	28	44	8	64	280	308

Lester Patrick Division

	G.	W.	L.	T.	Pts.	GF.	GA.
Philadelphia Flyers	80	46	26	8	100	310	245
Washington Capitals	80	38	32	10	86	285	278
New York Islanders	80	35	33	12	82	279	281
New York Rangers	80	34	38	8	76	307	323
Pittsburgh Penguins	80	30	38	12	72	297	290
New Jersey Devils	80	29	45	6	64	293	368

Clarence Campbell Conference

James Norris Division

	G.	W.	L.	T.	Pts.	GF.	GA.
St. Louis Blues	80	32	33	15	79	281	293
Detroit Red Wings	80	34	36	10	78	260	274
Chicago Black Hawks	80	29	37	14	72	290	310
Toronto Maple Leafs	80	32	42	6	70	286	319
Minnesota North Stars	80	30	40	10	70	296	314

Conn Smythe Division

	G.	W.	L.	T.	Pts.	GF.	GA.
Edmonton Oilers	80	50	24	6	106	372	284
Calgary Flames	80	46	31	3	95	318	289
Winnipeg Jets	80	40	32	8	88	279	271
Los Angeles Kings	80	31	41	8	70	318	341
Vancouver Canucks	80	29	43	8	66	282	314

Top 20 Scorers for the Art Ross Memorial Trophy

*Indicates league-leading figure.

	Games	G.	A.	Pts.	Pen.
1. Wayne Gretzky, Edmonton	79	*62	*121	*183	28
2. Jari Kurri, Edmonton	79	54	54	108	41
3. Mario Lemieux, Pittsburgh	63	54	53	107	57
Mark Messier, Edmonton	77	37	70	107	73
5. Doug Gilmour, St. Louis	80	42	63	105	58
6. Dino Ciccarelli, Minnesota	80	52	51	103	92
7. Dale Hawerchuk, Winnipeg	80	47	53	100	54
8. Michel Goulet, Quebec	75	49	47	96	61
9. Tim Kerr, Philadelphia	75	58	37	95	57
Ray Bourque, Boston	78	23	72	95	36
11. Ron Francis, Hartford	75	30	63	93	45
12. Dennis Savard, Chicago	70	40	50	90	108
Steve Yzerman, Detroit	80	31	59	90	43
14. Joe Mullen, Calgary	79	47	40	87	14
Walt Poddubny, New York Rangers	75	40	47	87	49
Bryan Trottier, New York Islanders	80	23	64	87	50
17. Luc Robitaille, Los Angeles	79	45	39	84	28
Steve Larmer, Chicago	80	28	56	84	22
Marcel Dionne, Los Angeles-New York Rangers	81	28	56	84	60
20. Bernie Nicholls, Los Angeles	80	33	48	81	101
Larry Murphy, Washington	80	23	58	81	39

National Hockey League Team-by-Team Individual Scoring

*Indicates league-leading figure.

Boston Bruins

	Games	G.	A.	Pts.	Pen.
Ray Bourque	78	23	72	95	36
Cam Neely	75	36	36	72	143
Charlie Simmer	80	29	40	69	59
Rick Middleton	76	31	37	68	6
Tom McCarthy	68	30	29	59	31
Keith Crowder	58	22	30	52	106
Steve Kasper	79	20	30	50	51
Ken Linseman	64	15	34	49	126
Thomas Gradin	64	12	31	43	18
Geoff Courtnall	65	13	23	36	117
Reed Larson	66	12	24	36	95
Greg Johnston	76	12	15	27	79
Mike Milbury	68	6	16	22	96
Michael Thelven	34	5	15	20	18
Nevin Markwart	64	10	9	19	225
Dwight Foster	47	4	12	16	37
Allen Pedersen	79	1	11	12	71
Kraig Nienhuis	16	4	2	6	2
Dave Reid	12	3	3	6	0
Robert Sweeney	14	2	4	6	21
Lyndon Byers	18	2	3	5	53
Randy Burridge	23	1	4	5	16
Jay Miller	55	1	4	5	208
Mats Thelin	59	1	3	4	69
Wade Campbell	14	0	3	3	24
Doug Keans (Goalie)	36	0	2	2	24
Frank Simonetti	25	1	0	1	17
John Carter	8	0	1	1	0
Bill Ranford (Goalie)	41	0	1	1	8
Cleon Daskalakis (Goalie)	2	0	0	0	0
Alain Cote	3	0	0	0	0
Roberto Romano, Pittsburgh (Goalie)	25	0	0	0	0
Boston (Goalie)	1	0	0	0	0
Totals	26	0	0	0	0

Buffalo Sabres

	Games	G.	A.	Pts.	Pen.
Dave Andreychuk	77	25	48	73	46
Phil Housley	78	21	46	67	57
Christian Ruuttu	76	22	43	65	62
Mike Foligno	75	30	29	59	176
John Tucker	54	17	34	51	21
Adam Creighton	56	18	22	40	26
Doug Smith	62	16	24	40	106
Mike Ramsey	80	8	31	39	109
Wilf Paiement	56	20	17	37	108
Mark Napier, Edmonton	62	8	13	21	2
Buffalo	15	5	5	10	0
Totals	77	13	18	31	2
Paul Cyr	73	11	16	27	122
Clark Gillies	61	10	17	27	81
Scott Arniel	63	11	14	25	59
Tom Kurvers, Montreal	1	0	0	0	0
Buffalo	55	6	17	23	24
Totals	56	6	17	23	24
Lindy Ruff	50	6	14	20	74
Ken Priestlay	34	11	6	17	8
Gilbert Perreault	20	9	7	16	6
Jim Korn	51	4	10	14	158
Shawn Anderson	41	2	11	13	23

Boston Bruins right wing Cam Neely.

	Games	G.	A.	Pts.	Pen.
Bob Logan	22	7	3	10	0
Gates Orlando	27	2	8	10	16
Joe Reekie	56	1	8	9	82
Jeff Parker	15	3	3	6	7
Mike Hartman	17	3	3	6	69
Lee Fogolin, Edmonton	35	1	3	4	17
Buffalo	9	0	2	2	8
Totals	44	1	5	6	25
Don Lever	10	3	2	5	4
Uwe Krupp	26	1	4	5	23
Paul Brydges	15	2	2	4	6
Mark Ferner	13	0	3	3	9
Mikael Andersson	16	0	3	3	0
Bob Halkidis	6	1	1	2	19
Phil Russell	6	0	2	2	12
Bill Hajt	23	0	2	2	4
Jacques Cloutier (Goalie)	40	0	2	2	10
Dave Fenyves	7	1	0	1	0
Richie Dunn	2	0	1	1	2
Steve Dykstra	37	0	1	1	179
Tom Barrasso (Goalie)	46	0	1	1	22
Richard Hajdu	2	0	0	0	0
Doug Trapp	2	0	0	0	0
Daren Puppa (Goalie)	3	0	0	0	2
Jim Hofford	12	0	0	0	40

Calgary Flames

	Games	G.	A.	Pts.	Pen.
Joe Mullen	79	47	40	87	14
Al MacInnis	79	20	56	76	97
Paul Reinhart	76	15	54	69	22
Mike Bullard, Pittsburgh	14	2	10	12	17
Calgary	57	28	26	54	34
Totals	71	30	36	66	51
Carey Wilson	80	20	36	56	42
John Tonelli	78	20	31	51	72
Joel Otto	68	19	31	50	185
Jim Peplinski	80	18	32	50	185
Gary Suter	68	9	40	49	70
Hakan Loob	68	18	26	44	26
Jamie Macoun	79	7	33	40	111
Steve Bozek	71	17	18	35	22
Brian Bradley	40	10	18	28	16
Colin Patterson	68	13	14	27	41
Lanny McDonald	58	14	12	26	54
Tim Hunter	73	6	15	21	357
Gary Roberts	32	5	9	14	85
Dale DeGray	27	6	7	13	29
Neil Sheehy	54	4	6	10	151
Perry Berezan	24	5	3	8	24
Nick Fotiu	42	5	3	8	145
Kari Eloranta	13	1	6	7	9
Joe Nieuwendyk	9	5	1	6	0
Doug Risebrough	22	2	3	5	66
Kevan Guy	24	0	4	4	19
Brian Engblom	32	0	4	4	28
Paul Baxter	18	0	2	2	66
Mike Vernon (Goalie)	54	0	2	2	14
Brett Hull	5	1	0	1	0
Doug Dadswell (Goalie)	2	0	0	0	0
Rejean Lemelin (Goalie)	34	0	0	0	20

Chicago Black Hawks

	Games	G.	A.	Pts.	Pen.
Denis Savard	70	40	50	90	108
Steve Larmer	80	28	56	84	22
Troy Murray	77	28	43	71	59

Calgary Flames defenseman Paul Reinhart.

	Games	G.	A.	Pts.	Pen.
Wayne Presley	80	32	29	61	114
Al Secord	77	29	29	58	196
Ed Olczyk	79	16	35	51	119
Curt Fraser	75	25	25	50	182
Doug Wilson	69	16	32	48	36
Bob Murray	79	6	38	44	80
Bill Watson	51	13	19	32	6
Gary Nylund	80	7	20	27	190
Keith Brown	73	4	23	27	86
Mark LaVarre	58	8	15	23	33
Dave Donnelly	71	6	12	18	81
Rich Preston	73	8	9	17	19
Steve Ludzik	52	5	12	17	34
Darryl Sutter	44	8	6	14	16
Marc Bergevin	66	4	10	14	66
Jack O'Callahan	48	1	13	14	59
Mike Stapleton	39	3	6	9	6
Dave Manson	63	1	8	9	146
Everett Sanipass	7	1	3	4	2
Bob Sauve (Goalie)	46	0	4	4	6
Rick Paterson	22	1	2	3	6
Murray Bannerman (Goalie)	39	0	1	1	4
Darin Sceviour	1	0	0	0	0
Jim Camazzola	2	0	0	0	0
Bruce Cassidy	2	0	0	0	0
Warren Skorodenski (Goalie)	3	0	0	0	0

Detroit Red Wings

	Games	G.	A.	Pts.	Pen.
Steve Yzerman	80	31	59	90	43
Brent Ashton, Quebec	46	25	19	44	17
Detroit	35	15	16	31	22
Totals	81	40	35	75	39
Gerard Gallant	80	38	34	72	216
Darren Veitch	77	13	45	58	52
Petr Klima	77	30	23	53	42
Shawn Burr	80	22	25	47	107
Adam Oates	76	15	32	47	21
Mel Bridgman, New Jersey	51	8	31	39	80
Detroit	13	2	2	4	19
Totals	64	10	33	43	99
Dave Barr, St. Louis	2	0	0	0	0
Hartford	30	2	4	6	19
Detroit	37	13	13	26	49
Totals	69	15	17	32	68
Mike O'Connell	77	5	26	31	70
Lee Norwood	57	6	21	27	163
Tim Higgins	77	12	14	26	124
Bob Probert	63	13	11	24	221
Joey Kocur	77	9	9	18	276
Harold Snepsts	54	1	13	14	129
Ric Seiling	74	3	8	11	49
Mark Kumpel, Quebec	40	1	8	9	16
Detroit	5	0	1	1	0
Totals	45	1	9	10	16
Gilbert Delorme, Quebec	19	2	0	2	14
Detroit	24	2	3	5	33
Totals	43	4	3	7	47
Dave Lewis	58	2	5	7	66
Doug Halward, Vancouver	10	0	3	3	34
Detroit	11	0	3	3	19
Totals	21	0	6	6	53
Rick Zombo	44	1	4	5	59
Steven Chiasson	45	1	4	5	73
Greg Stefan (Goalie)	43	0	4	4	24
Mark Lamb	22	2	1	3	8
Billy Carroll	31	1	2	3	6
Jeff Sharples	3	0	1	1	2

Detroit Red Wings left wing Gerard Gallant.

	Games	G.	A.	Pts.	Pen.
Mark Laforest (Goalie)	5	0	1	1	7
Joe Murphy	5	0	1	1	2
Chris Cichocki	2	0	0	0	2
Ed Johnstone	6	0	0	0	0
Sam St. Laurent (Goalie)	6	0	0	0	0
Dale Krentz	8	0	0	0	0
Glen Hanlon (Goalie)	36	0	0	0	20

Edmonton Oilers

	Games	G.	A.	Pts.	Pen.
Wayne Gretzky	79	*62	*121	*183	28
Jari Kurri	79	54	54	108	41
Mark Messier	77	37	70	107	73
Esa Tikkanen	76	34	44	78	120
Glenn Anderson	80	35	38	73	65
Paul Coffey	59	17	50	67	49
Kent Nilsson, Minnesota	44	13	33	46	12
Edmonton	17	5	12	17	4
Totals	61	18	45	63	16
Mike Krushelnyski	80	16	35	51	67
Craig MacTavish	79	20	19	39	55
Kevin Lowe	77	8	29	37	94
Moe Lemay, Vancouver	52	9	17	26	128
Edmonton	10	1	2	3	36
Totals	62	10	19	29	164
Craig Muni	79	7	22	29	85
Kevin McClelland	72	12	13	25	238
Randy Gregg	52	8	16	24	42
Steve Smith	62	7	15	22	165
Charlie Huddy	58	4	15	19	35
Dave Hunter	77	6	9	15	75
Reijo Ruotsalainen	16	5	8	13	6
Normand Lacombe, Buffalo	39	4	7	11	8
Edmonton	1	0	0	0	2
Totals	40	4	7	11	10
Jeff Beukeboom	44	3	8	11	124
Marty McSorley	41	2	4	6	159
Jaroslav Pouzar	12	2	3	5	6
Danny Gare	18	1	3	4	6
Mike Moller	6	2	1	3	0
Steve Graves	12	2	0	2	0
Grant Fuhr (Goalie)	44	0	2	2	6
Andy Moog (Goalie)	46	0	2	2	8
Dave Lumley	1	0	0	0	0
Wayne Van Dorp	3	0	0	0	25

Hartford Whalers

	Games	G.	A.	Pts.	Pen.
Ron Francis	75	30	63	93	45
Kevin Dineen	78	40	39	79	110
John Anderson	76	31	44	75	19
Ray Ferraro	80	27	32	59	42
Dean Evason	80	22	37	59	67
Paul Lawless	60	22	32	54	14
Stewart Gavin	79	20	21	41	28
Dave Babych	66	8	33	41	44
Sylvain Turgeon	41	23	13	36	45
Ulf Samuelsson	78	2	31	33	162
Dave Tippett	80	9	22	31	42
Dana Murzyn	74	9	19	28	95
Doug Jarvis	80	9	13	22	20
Paul MacDermid	72	7	11	18	202
Mike McEwen	48	8	8	16	32
Randy Ladouceur, Detroit	34	3	6	9	70
Hartford	36	2	3	5	51
Totals	70	5	9	14	121

Edmonton Oilers left wing Esa Tikkanen.

	Games	G.	A.	Pts.	Pen.
Dave Semenko, Edmonton	5	0	0	0	0
Hartford	51	4	8	12	87
Totals	56	4	8	12	87
Scot Kleinendorst	66	3	9	12	130
Joel Quenneville	37	3	7	10	24
Sylvain Cote	67	2	8	10	20
Pat Hughes, St. Louis	43	1	5	6	26
Hartford	2	0	0	0	2
Totals	45	1	5	6	28
Mike Millar	10	2	2	4	0
Mike Liut (Goalie)	59	0	2	2	4
Torrie Robertson	20	1	0	1	98
Bill Gardner	8	0	1	1	0
Shane Churla	20	0	1	1	78
Greg Britz	1	0	0	0	0
Brad Shaw	2	0	0	0	0
Wayne Babych	4	0	0	0	4
Yves Courteau	4	0	0	0	0
Gord Sherven	7	0	0	0	0
Steve Weeks (Goalie)	25	0	0	0	0

Los Angeles Kings

	Games	G.	A.	Pts.	Pen.
Luc Robitaille	79	45	39	84	28
Bernie Nicholls	80	33	48	81	101
Jimmy Carson	80	37	42	79	22
Dave Taylor	67	18	44	62	84
Jim Fox	76	19	42	61	48
Bryan Erickson	68	20	30	50	26
Steve Duchesne	75	13	25	38	74
Grant Ledyard	67	14	23	37	93
Jay Wells	77	7	29	36	155
Morris Lukowich	60	14	21	35	64
Dave Williams	76	16	18	34	*358
Sean McKenna	69	14	19	33	10
Mark Hardy	73	3	27	30	120
Bobby Carpenter, Washington	22	5	7	12	21
N.Y. Rangers	28	2	8	10	20
Los Angeles	10	2	3	5	6
Totals	60	9	18	27	47
Bob Bourne	78	13	9	22	35
Phil Sykes	58	6	15	21	133
Dean Kennedy	66	6	14	20	91
Tom Laidlaw, N.Y. Rangers	63	1	10	11	65
Los Angeles	11	0	3	3	4
Totals	74	1	13	14	69
Larry Playfair	37	2	7	9	181
Craig Redmond	16	1	7	8	8
Paul Guay	35	2	5	7	16
Roland Melanson (Goalie)	46	0	6	6	22
Dave Langevin	11	0	4	4	7
Joe Paterson	45	2	1	3	158
Lyle Phair	5	2	0	2	2
Ken Hammond	10	0	2	2	11
Peter Dineen	11	0	2	2	8
Al Jensen, Washington (Goalie)	6	0	0	0	0
Los Angeles (Goalie)	5	0	1	1	0
Totals	11	0	1	1	0
Darren Eliot (Goalie)	24	0	1	1	18
Brian Wilks	1	0	0	0	0
Craig Duncanson	2	0	0	0	24
Bob Janecyk (Goalie)	7	0	0	0	2

Minnesota North Stars

	Games	G.	A.	Pts.	Pen.
Dino Ciccarelli	80	52	51	103	92
Brian MacLellan	76	32	31	63	69

Los Angeles Kings left wing Luc Robitaille.

	Games	G.	A.	Pts.	Pen.
Craig Hartsburg	73	11	50	61	93
Dirk Graham	76	25	29	54	142
Brian Bellows	65	26	27	53	34
Neal Broten	46	18	35	53	35
Dennis Maruk	67	16	30	46	50
Keith Acton	78	16	29	45	56
Brian Lawton	66	21	23	44	86
Ron Wilson	65	12	29	41	36
Bob Brooke, N.Y. Rangers	15	3	5	8	20
Minnesota	65	10	18	28	78
Totals	80	13	23	36	98
Brad Maxwell, Vancouver	30	1	7	8	28
N.Y. Rangers	9	0	4	4	6
Minnesota	17	2	7	9	31
Totals	56	3	18	21	65
Paul Boutilier, Boston	52	5	9	14	84
Minnesota	10	2	4	6	8
Totals	62	7	13	20	92
Larry DePalma	56	9	6	15	219
Scott Bjugstad	39	4	9	13	43
Gordie Roberts	67	3	10	13	68
Bob Rouse	72	2	10	12	179
Willi Plett	67	6	5	11	263
Frantisek Musil	72	2	9	11	148
Mark Pavelich	12	4	6	10	10
Steve Payne	48	4	6	10	19
Raimo Helminen, N.Y. Rangers	21	2	4	6	2
Minnesota	6	0	1	1	0
Totals	27	2	5	7	2
Jari Gronstrand	47	1	6	7	27
Chris Pryor	50	1	3	4	49
Marc Habscheid	15	2	0	2	2
Paul Houck	12	0	2	2	2
Emanuel Viveiros	1	0	1	1	0
Jim Archibald	1	0	0	0	2
Colin Chisholm	1	0	0	0	0
Sean Toomey	1	0	0	0	0
Randy Smith	2	0	0	0	0
Mike Sands (Goalie)	3	0	0	0	0
Mats Hallin	6	0	0	0	4
Jack Carlson	8	0	0	0	13
Kari Takko (Goalie)	38	0	0	0	14
Don Beaupre (Goalie)	47	0	0	0	16

Montreal Canadiens

	Games	G.	A.	Pts.	Pen.
Mats Naslund	79	25	55	80	16
Bobby Smith	80	28	47	75	72
Claude Lemieux	76	27	26	53	156
Larry Robinson	70	13	37	50	44
Ryan Walter	76	23	23	46	34
Guy Carbonneau	79	18	27	45	68
Gaston Gingras	66	11	34	45	21
Chris Chelios	71	11	33	44	124
Stephane Richer	57	20	19	39	80
Mike McPhee	79	18	21	39	58
Sergio Momesso	59	14	17	31	96
Brian Skrudland	79	11	17	28	107
Shayne Corson	55	12	11	23	144
Petr Svoboda	70	5	17	22	63
Kjell Dahlin	41	12	8	20	0
Chris Nilan	44	4	16	20	266
David Maley	48	6	12	18	55
Bob Gainey	47	8	8	16	19
Craig Ludwig	75	4	12	16	105
Rick Green	72	1	9	10	10
Mike Lalor	57	0	10	10	47
John Kordic	44	5	3	8	151

Montreal Canadiens center Bobby Smith.

	Games	G.	A.	Pts.	Pen.
Gilles Thibaudeau	9	1	3	4	0
Brian Hayward (Goalie)	37	0	2	2	2
Patrick Roy (Goalie)	46	0	1	1	8
Serge Boisvert	1	0	0	0	0
Scott Sandelin	1	0	0	0	0

New Jersey Devils

	Games	G.	A.	Pts.	Pen.
Aaron Broten	80	26	53	79	36
Kirk Muller	79	26	50	76	75
John MacLean	80	31	36	67	120
Pat Verbeek	74	35	24	59	120
Doug Sulliman	78	27	26	53	14
Mark Johnson	68	25	26	51	22
Greg Adams	72	20	27	47	19
Claude Loiselle	75	16	24	40	137
Bruce Driver	74	6	28	34	36
Joe Cirella	65	9	22	31	111
Andy Brickley	51	11	12	23	8
Peter McNab	46	8	12	20	8
Uli Hiemer	40	6	14	20	45
Anders Carlsson	48	2	18	20	14
Perry Anderson	57	10	9	19	105
Randy Velischek	64	2	16	18	54
Jan Ludvig	47	7	9	16	98
Ken Daneyko	79	2	12	14	183
Rich Chernomaz	25	6	4	10	8
Craig Wolanin	68	4	6	10	109
Gordon Mark	36	3	5	8	82
Steve Richmond	44	1	7	8	143
Tim Lenardon	7	1	1	2	0
Timo Blomqvist	20	0	2	2	29
Allan Stewart	7	1	0	1	26
Douglas Brown	4	0	1	1	0
Karl Friesen (Goalie)	4	0	1	1	0
Murray Brumwell	1	0	0	0	2
Kirk McLean (Goalie)	4	0	0	0	0
Chris Terreri (Goalie)	7	0	0	0	0
Craig Billington (Goalie)	22	0	0	0	12
Alain Chevrier (Goalie)	58	0	0	0	17

New York Islanders

	Games	G.	A.	Pts.	Pen.
Bryan Trottier	80	23	64	87	50
Mike Bossy	63	38	37	75	33
Pat LaFontaine	80	38	32	70	70
Brent Sutter	69	27	36	63	73
Mikko Makela	80	24	33	57	24
Patrick Flatley	63	16	35	51	81
Denis Potvin	58	12	30	42	70
Duane Sutter	80	14	17	31	169
Tomas Jonsson	47	6	25	31	36
Rich Kromm	70	12	17	29	20
Ken Leiter	74	9	20	29	30
Randy Boyd	30	7	17	24	37
Brad Lauer	61	7	14	21	65
Steve Konroyd	72	5	16	21	70
Alan Kerr	72	7	10	17	175
Bob Bassen	77	7	10	17	89
Gord Dineen	71	4	10	14	110
Greg Gilbert	51	6	7	13	26
Ken Morrow	64	3	8	11	32
Ari Haanpaa	41	6	4	10	17
Brian Curran	68	0	10	10	356
Dale Henry	19	3	3	6	46
Gerald Diduck	30	2	3	5	67
Neal Coulter	9	2	1	3	7

New Jersey Devils center Aaron Broten.

	Games	G.	A.	Pts.	Pen.
Billy Smith (Goalie)	40	0	2	2	37
Randy Wood	6	1	0	1	4
Mark Hamway	2	0	1	1	0
Kelly Hrudey (Goalie)	46	0	1	1	37
Derek King	2	0	0	0	0

New York Rangers

	Games	G.	A.	Pts.	Pen.
Walt Poddubny	75	40	47	87	49
Marcel Dionne, Los Angeles	67	24	50	74	54
N.Y. Rangers	14	4	6	10	6
Totals	81	28	56	84	60
Tomas Sandstrom	64	40	34	74	60
Kelly Kisio	70	24	40	64	73
Pierre Larouche	73	28	35	63	12
Don Maloney	72	19	38	57	117
James Patrick	78	10	45	55	62
Tony McKegney, Minnesota	11	2	3	5	16
N.Y. Rangers	64	29	17	46	56
Totals	75	31	20	51	72
Ron Greschner	61	6	34	40	62
Ron Duguay, Pittsburgh	40	5	13	18	30
N.Y. Rangers	34	9	12	21	9
Totals	74	14	25	39	39
Willie Huber	66	8	22	30	70
Jan Erixon	68	8	18	26	24
Curt Giles, Minnesota	11	0	3	3	4
N.Y. Rangers	61	2	17	19	50
Totals	72	2	20	22	54
Jeff Jackson, Toronto	55	8	7	15	64
N.Y. Rangers	9	5	1	6	15
Totals	64	13	8	21	79
Larry Melnyk	73	3	12	15	182
Terry Carkner	52	2	13	15	120
Chris Jensen	37	6	7	13	21
Lucien DeBlois	40	3	8	11	27
George McPhee	21	4	4	8	34
Pat Price, Quebec	47	0	6	6	81
N.Y. Rangers	13	0	2	2	49
Totals	60	0	8	8	130
Stu Kulak, Vancouver	28	1	1	2	37
Edmonton	23	3	1	4	41
N.Y. Rangers	3	0	0	0	0
Totals	54	4	2	6	78
Dave Gagner	10	1	4	5	12
Jay Caufield	13	2	1	3	45
Mike Donnelly	5	1	1	2	0
Bob Froese, Philadelphia (Goalie)	3	0	0	0	0
N.Y. Rangers (Goalie)	28	0	2	2	56
Totals	31	0	2	2	56
Gord Walker	1	1	0	1	2
Don Jackson	22	1	0	1	91
Norm Maciver	3	0	1	1	0
Jim Leavins	4	0	1	1	4
John Vanbiesbrouck (Goalie)	50	0	1	1	18
Ron Scott (Goalie)	1	0	0	0	0
Mike Siltala	1	0	0	0	0
Ron Talakoski	3	0	0	0	21
Paul Fenton	8	0	0	0	2
Doug Soetaert (Goalie)	13	0	0	0	14

Philadelphia Flyers

	Games	G.	A.	Pts.	Pen.
Tim Kerr	75	58	37	95	57
Peter Zezel	71	33	39	72	71
Dave Poulin	75	25	45	70	53
Brian Propp	53	31	36	67	45

New York Rangers center Walt Poddubny.

	Games	G.	A.	Pts.	Pen.
Mark Howe	69	15	43	58	37
Pelle Eklund	72	14	41	55	2
Murray Craven	77	19	30	49	38
Rick Tocchet	69	21	26	47	286
Doug Crossman	78	9	31	40	29
Brad McCrimmon	71	10	29	39	52
Scott Mellanby	71	11	21	32	94
Derrick Smith	71	11	21	32	34
Ilkka Sinisalo	42	10	21	31	8
Ron Sutter	39	10	17	27	69
Lindsay Carson	71	11	15	26	141
J.J. Daigneault	77	6	16	22	56
Kjell Samuelsson, N.Y. Rangers	30	2	6	8	50
Philadelphia	46	1	6	7	86
Totals	76	3	12	15	136
Brad Marsh	77	2	9	11	124
Dave Brown	62	7	3	10	274
Ron Hextall (Goalie)	66	0	6	6	104
Glen Seabrooke	10	1	4	5	2
Ed Hospodar	45	2	2	4	136
Brian Dobbin	12	2	1	3	14
Darryl Stanley	33	1	2	3	76
John Stevens	6	0	2	2	14
Al Hill	7	0	2	2	4
Don Nachbaur	23	0	2	2	89
Mark Freer	1	0	1	1	0
Jeff Chychrun	1	0	0	0	4
Jere Gillis	1	0	0	0	0
Greg Smyth	1	0	0	0	0
Ray Allison	2	0	0	0	0
Kevin McCarthy	2	0	0	0	0
Steve Smith	2	0	0	0	6
Mike Stothers	2	0	0	0	4
Tim Tookey	2	0	0	0	0
Craig Berube	7	0	0	0	57
Kerry Huffman	9	0	0	0	2
Glenn Resch (Goalie)	17	0	0	0	0

Pittsburgh Penguins

	Games	G.	A.	Pts.	Pen.
Mario Lemieux	63	54	53	107	57
Dan Quinn, Calgary	16	3	6	9	14
Pittsburgh	64	28	43	71	40
Totals	80	31	49	80	54
Randy Cunneyworth	79	26	27	53	142
Craig Simpson	72	26	25	51	57
Terry Ruskowski	70	14	37	51	147
Doug Bodger	76	11	38	49	52
Moe Mantha	62	9	31	40	44
John Chabot	72	14	22	36	8
Bob Errey	72	16	18	34	46
Jim Johnson	80	5	25	30	116
Dan Frawley	78	14	14	28	218
Kevin LaVallee	33	8	20	28	4
Dave Hannan	58	10	15	25	56
Willy Lindstrom	60	10	13	23	6
Ville Siren	69	5	17	22	50
Warren Young	50	8	13	21	103
Rod Buskas	68	3	15	18	123
Chris Kontos	31	8	9	17	6
Troy Loney	23	8	7	15	22
Randy Hillier	55	4	8	12	97
Dwight Schofield	25	1	6	7	59
Norm Schmidt	20	1	5	6	4
Phil Bourque	22	2	3	5	32
Jim McGeough	11	1	4	5	8
Mitch Wilson	17	2	1	3	83

Pittsburgh Penguins left wing Randy Cunneyworth.

	Games	G.	A.	Pts.	Pen.
Lee Giffin	8	1	1	2	0
Mike Blaisdell	10	1	1	2	2
Neil Belland	3	0	1	1	0
Dwight Mathiasen	6	0	1	1	0
Chris Dahlquist	19	0	1	1	2
Pat Riggin, Boston (Goalie)	10	0	1	1	20
Pittsburgh (Goalie)	17	0	0	0	0
Totals	27	0	1	1	2
Gilles Meloche (Goalie)	43	0	1	1	2
Todd Charlesworth	1	0	1	1	20
Alain Lemieux	1	0	0	0	0
Steve Guenette (Goalie)	2	0	0	0	0
Mike Rowe	2	0	0	0	0
Carl Mokosak	3	0	0	0	4

Quebec Nordiques

	Games	G.	A.	Pts.	Pen.
Michel Goulet	75	49	47	96	61
Peter Stastny	64	24	52	76	43
John Ogrodnick, Detroit	39	12	28	40	6
Quebec	32	11	16	27	4
Totals	71	23	44	67	10
Anton Stastny	77	27	35	62	8
Paul Gillis	76	13	26	39	267
Dale Hunter	46	10	29	39	135
Risto Siltanen	66	10	29	39	32
Alain Cote	80	12	24	36	38
Mike Eagles	73	13	19	32	55
Jeff Brown	44	7	22	29	16
Jason Lafreniere	56	13	15	28	8
Robert Picard	78	8	20	28	71
Doug Shedden, Detroit	33	6	12	18	6
Quebec	16	0	2	2	8
Totals	49	6	14	20	14
David Shaw	75	0	19	19	69
Basil McRae, Detroit	36	2	2	4	193
Quebec	33	9	5	14	149
Totals	69	11	7	18	342
Bill Derlago, Winnipeg	30	3	6	9	12
Quebec	18	3	5	8	6
Totals	48	6	11	17	18
Lane Lambert, N.Y. Rangers	18	2	2	4	33
Quebec	15	5	6	11	18
Totals	33	7	8	15	51
Normand Rochefort	70	6	9	15	46
Mike Hough	56	6	8	14	79
Randy Moller	71	5	9	14	144
Ken Quinney	25	2	7	9	16
Steven Finn	36	2	5	7	40
Jean F. Sauve	14	2	3	5	4
Max Middendorf	6	1	4	5	4
Mario Gosselin (Goalie)	30	0	3	3	20
Richard Zemlak	20	0	2	2	47
Gord Donnelly	38	0	2	2	143
Clint Malarchuk (Goalie)	54	0	2	2	37
Trevor Stienberg	6	1	0	1	12
Greg Malone	6	0	1	1	0
Yves Heroux	1	0	0	0	0
Scott Shaunessy	3	0	0	0	7
Richard Sevigny (Goalie)	4	0	0	0	14
Daniel Poudrier	6	0	0	0	0

St. Louis Blues

	Games	G.	A.	Pts.	Pen.
Doug Gilmour	80	42	63	105	58
Bernie Federko	64	20	52	72	32
Mark Hunter	74	36	33	69	169

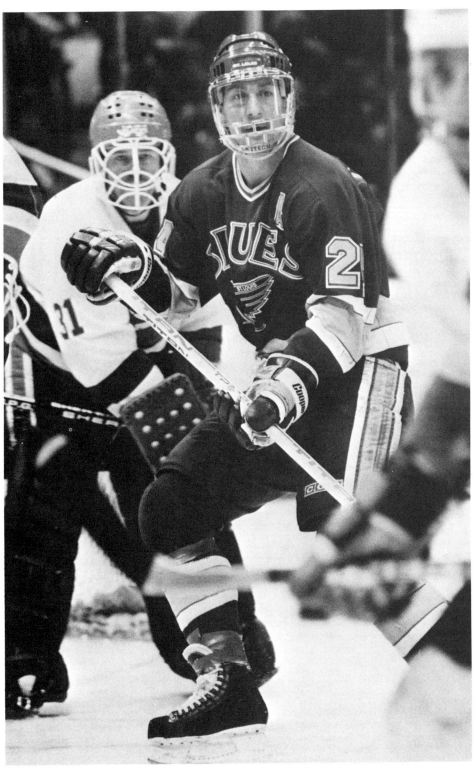

St. Louis Blues center Bernie Federko.

	Games	G.	A.	Pts.	Pen.
Greg Paslawski	76	29	35	64	27
Brian Benning	78	13	36	49	110
Gino Cavallini	80	18	26	44	54
Rick Meager	80	18	21	39	54
Rob Ramage	59	11	28	39	106
Ron Flockhart	60	16	19	35	12
Doug Wickenheiser	80	13	15	28	37
Ric Nattress	73	6	22	28	24
Cliff Ronning	42	11	14	25	6
Mark Reeds	68	9	16	25	16
Tim Bothwell, Hartford	4	1	0	1	0
St. Louis	72	5	16	21	46
Totals	76	6	16	22	46
Jocelyn Lemieux	53	10	8	18	94
Herb Raglan	62	6	10	16	159
Bruce Bell	45	3	13	16	18
Doug Evans	53	3	13	16	91
Charles Bourgeois	66	2	12	14	164
Jim Pavese	69	2	9	11	129
Brian Sutter	14	3	3	6	18
Michael Dark	13	2	0	2	2
Todd Ewen	23	2	0	2	84
Greg Millen (Goalie)	42	0	2	2	12
Mike Posavad	2	0	0	0	0
Larry Trader	5	0	0	0	8
Rick Wamsley (Goalie)	41	0	0	0	10

Toronto Maple Leafs

	Games	G.	A.	Pts.	Pen.
Russ Courtnall	79	29	44	73	90
Rick Vaive	73	32	34	66	61
Steve Thomas	78	35	27	62	114
Wendel Clark	80	37	23	60	271
Gary Leeman	80	21	31	52	66
Tom Fergus	57	21	28	49	57
Mark Osborne, N.Y. Rangers	58	17	15	32	101
Toronto	16	5	10	15	12
Totals	74	22	25	47	113
Vincent Damphousse	80	21	25	46	26
Peter Ihnacak	58	12	27	39	16
Todd Gill	61	4	27	31	92
Al Iafrate	80	9	21	30	55
Rick Lanz, Vancouver	17	1	6	7	10
Toronto	44	2	19	21	32
Totals	61	3	25	28	42
Mike Allison	71	7	16	23	66
Borje Salming	56	4	16	20	42
Miroslav Frycer	29	7	8	15	28
Greg Terrion	67	7	8	15	6
Brad Smith	47	5	7	12	174
Chris Kotsopoulos	43	2	10	12	75
Miroslav Ihnacak	34	6	5	11	12
Ken Yaremchuk	20	3	8	11	16
Dan Daoust	33	4	3	7	35
Bill Root	34	3	3	6	37
Bob McGill	56	1	4	5	103
Ken Wregget (Goalie)	56	0	4	4	20
Daryl Evans	2	1	0	1	0
Ted Fauss	15	0	1	1	11
Terry Johnson	48	0	1	1	104
Tim Bernhardt (Goalie)	1	0	0	0	0
Derek Laxdal	2	0	0	0	7
Val James	4	0	0	0	14
Jerome Dupont	13	0	0	0	23
Kevin Maguire	17	0	0	0	74
Allan Bester (Goalie)	36	0	0	0	8

Toronto Maple Leafs left wing Wendel Clark.

Vancouver Canucks

	Games	G.	A.	Pts.	Pen.
Tony Tanti	77	41	38	79	84
Barry Pederson	79	24	52	76	50
Petri Skriko	76	33	41	74	44
Patrik Sundstrom	72	29	42	71	40
Doug Lidster	80	12	51	63	40
Stan Smyl	66	20	23	43	84
Rich Sutter	74	20	22	42	113
Steve Tambellini	72	16	20	36	14
Jim Sandlak	78	15	21	36	66
Raimo Summanen, Edmonton	48	10	7	17	15
Vancouver	10	4	4	8	0
Totals	58	14	11	25	15
Michel Petit	69	12	13	25	131
Dan Hodgson	43	9	13	22	25
Brent Peterson	69	7	15	22	77
Garth Butcher	70	5	15	20	207
Dave Lowry	70	8	10	18	176
Dave Richter	78	2	15	17	172
David Bruce	50	9	7	16	109
Jim Benning, Toronto	5	0	0	0	4
Vancouver	54	2	11	13	40
Totals	59	2	11	13	44
Marc Crawford	21	0	3	3	67
John LeBlanc	2	1	0	1	0
Craig Coxe	15	1	0	1	31
Wendell Young (Goalie)	8	0	1	1	0
Craig Levie	9	0	1	1	13
Robin Bartel	40	0	1	1	14
Troy Gamble (Goalie)	1	0	0	0	0
Jim Agnew	4	0	0	0	0
Taylor Hall	4	0	0	0	0
Glen Cochrane	14	0	0	0	52
Frank Caprice (Goalie)	25	0	0	0	9
Richard Brodeur (Goalie)	53	0	0	0	2

Washington Capitals

	Games	G.	A.	Pts.	Pen.
Larry Murphy	80	23	58	81	39
Mike Gartner	78	41	32	73	61
Mike Ridley, N.Y. Rangers	38	16	20	36	20
Washington	40	15	19	34	20
Totals	78	31	39	70	40
Scott Stevens	77	10	51	61	285
Craig Laughlin	80	22	30	52	67
Gaetan Duchesne	74	17	35	52	53
Dave Christian	76	23	27	50	8
Bob Gould	78	23	27	50	74
Greg Adams	67	14	30	44	184
Michal Pivonka	73	18	25	43	41
Kelly Miller, N.Y. Rangers	38	6	14	20	22
Washington	39	10	12	22	26
Totals	77	16	26	42	48
Alan Haworth	50	25	16	41	43
Garry Galley, Los Angeles	30	5	11	16	57
Washington	18	1	10	11	10
Totals	48	6	21	27	67
Rod Langway	78	2	25	27	53
Kevin Hatcher	78	8	16	24	144
Lou Franceschetti	75	12	9	21	127
Dave Jensen	46	8	8	16	12
John Blum	66	2	8	10	133
Greg Smith	45	0	9	9	31
John Barrett	55	2	2	4	43
Pete Peeters (Goalie)	37	0	4	4	16
Gary Sampson	25	1	2	3	4

Vancouver Canucks left wing Petri Skriko.

	Games	G.	A.	Pts.	Pen.
Jeff Greenlaw	22	0	3	3	44
Yvon Corriveau	17	1	1	2	24
Ed Kastelic	23	1	1	2	83
Paul Cavallini	6	0	2	2	8
Stephen Leach	15	1	0	1	6
Yves Beaudoin	6	0	0	0	5
Grant Martin	9	0	0	0	4
Jim Thomson	10	0	0	0	35
Bob Crawford, N.Y. Rangers	3	0	0	0	2
Washington	12	0	0	0	0
Totals	15	0	0	0	2
Bob Mason (Goalie)	45	0	0	0	0

Winnipeg Jets

	Games	G.	A.	Pts.	Pen.
Dale Hawerchuk	80	47	53	100	54
Paul MacLean	72	32	42	74	75
Brian Mullen	69	19	32	51	20
Thomas Steen	75	17	33	50	59
Gilles Hamel	79	27	21	48	24
Dave Ellett	78	13	31	44	53
Mario Marois	79	4	40	44	106
Doug Smail	78	25	18	43	36
Randy Carlyle	71	16	26	42	93
Laurie Boschman	80	17	24	41	152
Ray Neufeld	80	18	18	36	105
Fredrick Olausson	72	7	29	36	24
Andrew McBain	71	11	21	32	106
Tim Watters	63	3	13	16	119
Ron Wilson	80	3	13	16	13
Jim Kyte	72	5	5	10	162
Brad Berry	52	2	8	10	60
Hannu Jarvenpaa	20	1	8	9	8
Jim Nill	36	3	4	7	52
Perry Turnbull	26	1	5	6	44
Steve Rooney, Montreal	2	0	0	0	22
Winnipeg	30	2	3	5	57
Totals	32	2	3	5	79
Iain Duncan	6	1	2	3	0
Brad Jones	4	1	0	1	0
Tom Martin	11	1	0	1	49
Craig Endean	2	0	1	1	0
Joel Baillargeon	11	0	1	1	15
Randy Gilhen	2	0	0	0	0
Peter Taglianetti	3	0	0	0	12
Peter Douris	6	0	0	0	0
Steve Penney (Goalie)	7	0	0	0	7
Daniel Berthiaume (Goalie)	31	0	0	0	2
Eldon Reddick (Goalie)	48	0	0	0	8

Complete Goaltending Records

	Games	Mins.	Goals	SO.	Avg.
Brian Hayward	37	2178	102(2)	1	*2.81
Patrick Roy	46	2686	131(6)	1	2.93
MONTREAL TOTALS	80	4864	241	2	2.97
Bob Froese (a)	3	180	8	0	2.67
Glenn Resch	17	867	42(1)	0	2.91
Ron Hextall	*66	*3799	190(4)	1	3.00
PHILADELPHIA TOTALS	80	4846	245	1	3.03
Mike Liut	59	3476	187(3)	*4	3.23
Steve Weeks	25	1367	78(2)	1	3.42
HARTFORD TOTALS	80	4843	270	5	3.35

Mike Liut of the Hartford Whalers led the NHL with four shutouts during the 1986-87 season.

Daniel Berthiaume	31	1758	93(1)	1	3.17
Eldon Reddick	48	2762	149(2)	0	3.24
Steve Penney	7	327	25(1)	0	4.59
WINNIPEG TOTALS	80	4847	271	†2	3.35
Sam St. Laurent	6	342	16	0	2.81
Glen Hanlon	36	1963	104(3)	1	3.18
Mark Laforest	5	219	12	0	3.29
Greg Stefan	43	2351	135(4)	1	3.45
DETROIT TOTALS	80	4875	274	2	3.37
Mario Gosselin	30	1625	86(3)	0	3.18
Clint Malarchuk	54	3092	175(1)	1	3.40
Richard Sevigny	4	144	11	0	4.58
QUEBEC TOTALS	80	4861	276	1	3.41
Bill Ranford	41	2234	124(1)	3	3.33
Doug Keans	36	1942	108(1)	0	3.34
Pat Riggin (b)	10	513	29	0	3.39
Cleon Daskalakis	2	97	7	0	4.33
Roberto Romano (c)	1	60	6	0	6.00
BOSTON TOTALS	80	4846	276	3	3.42
Pete Peeters	37	2002	107(3)	0	3.21
Bob Mason	45	2536	137(3)	0	3.24
Al Jensen (d)	6	328	27(1)	0	4.94
WASHINGTON TOTALS	80	4866	278	0	3.43
Kelly Hrudey	46	2634	145(1)	0	3.30
Billy Smith	40	2252	132(3)	1	3.52
NEW YORK ISLANDERS TOTALS	80	4886	281	1	3.45
Grant Fuhr	44	2388	137(1)	0	3.44
Andy Moog	46	2461	144(2)	0	3.51
EDMONTON TOTALS	80	4849	284	0	3.51
Pat Riggin (b)	17	988	55	0	3.34
Gilles Meloche	43	2343	134(3)	0	3.43
Roberto Romano (c)	25	1438	87(1)	0	3.63
Steve Guenette	2	113	8(2)	0	4.25
PITTSBURGH TOTALS	80	4882	290	††1	3.56
Greg Millen	42	2482	146(3)	0	3.53
Rick Wamsley	41	2410	142(2)	0	3.54
ST. LOUIS TOTALS	80	4892	293	0	3.59
Rejean Lemelin	34	1735	94(4)	2	3.25
Mike Vernon	54	2957	178(2)	1	3.61
Doug Dadswell	2	125	10(1)	0	4.80
CALGARY TOTALS	80	4817	289	3	3.60
Tom Barrasso	46	2501	152(4)	2	3.65
Jacques Cloutier	40	2167	137(1)	0	3.79
Daren Puppa	3	185	13(1)	0	4.22
BUFFALO TOTALS	80	4853	308	2	3.81
Warren Skorodenski	3	155	7	0	2.71
Bob Sauve	46	2660	159	1	3.59
Murray Bannerman	39	2059	142(2)	0	4.14
CHICAGO TOTALS	80	4874	310	1	3.82
Kari Takko	38	2075	119(4)	0	3.44
Don Beaupre	47	2622	174(4)	1	3.98
Mike Sands	3	163	12(1)	0	4.42
MINNESOTA TOTALS	80	4860	314	1	3.88
Richard Brodeur	53	2972	178(3)	1	3.59
Frank Caprice	25	1390	89(2)	0	3.84
Troy Gamble	1	60	4(1)	0	4.00
Wendell Young	8	420	35(2)	0	5.00
VANCOUVER TOTALS	80	4842	314	1	3.89
Allan Bester	36	1808	110(3)	2	3.65
Ken Wregget	56	3026	200(3)	0	3.97
Tim Bernhardt	1	20	3	0	9.00
TORONTO TOTALS	80	4854	319	2	3.94
John Vanbiesbrouck	50	2656	161(6)	0	3.64
Bob Froese (a)	28	1474	92(1)	0	3.74
Ron Scott	1	65	5	0	4.62
Doug Soetaert	13	675	58(1)	0	5.16
NEW YORK RANGERS TOTALS	80	4870	324	0	3.99

Roland Melanson	46	2734	168(3)	1	3.69
Darren Eliot	24	1404	103(5)	1	4.40
Bob Janecyk	7	420	34	0	4.86
Al Jensen (d)	5	300	27(1)	0	5.40
LOS ANGELES TOTALS	80	4858	341	2	4.21
Kirk McLean	4	160	10(1)	0	3.75
Alain Chevrier	58	3153	*227(3)	0	4.32
Chris Terreri	7	286	21(1)	0	4.41
Craig Billington	22	1114	89	0	4.79
Karl Friesen	4	130	16	0	7.38
NEW JERSEY TOTALS	80	4843	368	0	4.56

( )—Empty Net Goals. Do not count against an individual average.
†—Combined shutout by Berthiaume and Reddick against Hartford, January 9, 1987.
††—Combined shutout by Meloche and Romano against Vancouver, January 23, 1987.
(a)—Froese played for Philadelphia and New York Rangers.
(b)—Riggin played for Boston and Pittsburgh.
(c)—Romano played for Pittsburgh and Boston.
(d)—Jensen played for Washington and Los Angeles.

Montreal's Patrick Roy (left) and Buffalo's Tom Barrasso dueled in the NHL's first scoreless game in four years last October 15 in Buffalo. The Sabres and Quebec Nordiques had played the last previous 0-0 tie on February 5, 1983.

NHL Miscellaneous Statistics

(Players are listed alphabetically)

Player — Team	Games	Shots	Goals	Shooting Pct.	PPG	SHG	+/−
Keith Acton, Minnesota	78	126	16	12.7	1	1	− 15
Greg Adams, Washington	67	92	14	15.2	2	0	+ 9
Greg Adams, New Jersey	72	143	20	14.0	6	0	− 16
Jim Agnew, Vancouver	4	1	0	0.0	0	0	Even
Mike Allison, Toronto	71	48	7	14.6	1	3	+ 1
Ray Allison, Philadelphia	2	1	0	0.0	0	0	− 2
Glenn Anderson, Edmonton	80	188	35	18.6	7	1	+ 27
John Anderson, Hartford	76	223	31	13.9	7	0	+ 12
Perry Anderson, New Jersey	57	46	10	21.7	2	0	− 13
Shawn Anderson, Buffalo	41	26	2	7.7	0	0	Even
Mikael Andersson, Buffalo	16	6	0	0.0	0	0	− 2
Dave Andreychuk, Buffalo	77	255	25	9.8	13	0	+ 2
Jim Archibald, Minnesota	1	1	0	0.0	0	0	− 1
Scott Arniel, Buffalo	63	90	11	12.2	0	0	− 1
Brent Ashton, Quebec	46	98	25	25.5	12	2	− 12
Detroit	35	86	15	17.4	3	1	− 3
Totals	81	184	40	21.7	15	3	− 15
Dave Babych, Hartford	66	157	8	5.1	7	0	− 16
Wayne Babych, Hartford	4	2	0	0.0	0	0	− 5
Joel Baillargeon, Winnipeg	11	1	0	0.0	0	0	− 3
Dave Barr, St. Louis	2	3	0	0.0	0	0	+ 1
Hartford	30	25	2	8.0	0	1	− 1
Detroit	37	55	13	23.6	4	0	+ 7
Totals	69	83	15	18.1	4	1	+ 7
John Barrett, Washington	55	37	2	5.4	0	0	− 16
Robin Bartel, Vancouver	40	16	0	0.0	0	0	+ 2
Bob Bassen, N.Y. Islanders	77	59	7	11.9	0	0	− 17
Paul Baxter, Calgary	18	13	0	0.0	0	0	− 5
Yves Beaudoin, Washington	6	4	0	0.0	0	0	− 4
Bruce Bell, St. Louis	45	50	3	6.0	1	0	+ 3
Neil Belland, Pittsburgh	3	4	0	0.0	0	0	Even
Brian Bellows, Minnesota	65	200	26	13.0	8	1	− 13
Brian Benning, St. Louis	78	144	13	9.0	7	0	+ 2
Jim Benning, Toronto	5	3	0	0.0	0	0	Even
Vancouver	54	60	2	3.3	0	0	+ 9
Totals	59	63	2	3.2	0	0	+ 9
Perry Berezan, Calgary	24	31	5	16.1	0	1	+ 4
Marc Bergevin, Chicago	66	56	4	7.1	0	0	+ 4
Brad Berry, Winnipeg	52	39	2	5.1	0	0	+ 6
Craig Berube, Philadelphia	7	4	0	0.0	0	0	+ 2
Jeff Beukeboom, Edmonton	44	24	3	12.5	1	0	+ 7
Scott Bjugstad, Minnesota	39	58	4	6.9	0	0	− 6
Mike Blaisdell, Pittsburgh	10	12	1	8.3	0	0	+ 2
Timo Blomqvist, New Jersey	20	16	0	0.0	0	0	− 3
John Blum, Washington	66	32	2	6.3	0	0	+ 1
Doug Bodger, Pittsburgh	76	176	11	6.3	5	0	+ 6
Serge Boisvert, Montreal	1	0	0	0.0	0	0	Even
Laurie Boschman, Winnipeg	80	161	17	10.6	1	1	− 17
Mike Bossy, N.Y. Islanders	63	226	38	16.8	8	1	− 8
Tim Bothwell, Hartford	4	3	1	33.3	0	0	− 5
St. Louis	72	75	5	6.7	0	0	− 14
Totals	76	78	6	7.7	0	0	− 19
Charles Bourgeois, St. Louis	66	54	2	3.7	0	0	+ 16
Bob Bourne, Los Angeles	78	93	13	14.0	0	3	− 13
Phil Bourque, Pittsburgh	22	23	2	8.7	0	0	− 2
Ray Bourque, Boston	78	334	23	6.9	6	1	+ 44
Paul Boutilier, Boston	52	68	5	7.4	1	0	− 2
Minnesota	10	21	2	9.5	0	0	+ 1
Totals	62	89	7	7.9	1	1	− 1
Randy Boyd, N.Y. Islanders	30	69	7	10.1	3	1	Even
Steve Bozek, Calgary	71	139	17	12.2	2	2	+ 3
Brian Bradley, Calgary	40	64	10	15.6	2	0	+ 6
Andy Brickley, New Jersey	51	55	11	20.0	1	3	− 15
Mel Bridgman, New Jersey	51	73	8	11.0	1	1	− 8
Detroit	13	13	2	15.4	0	1	+ 1
Totals	64	86	10	11.6	1	2	− 7

Player — Team	Games	Shots	Goals	Shooting Pct.	PPG	SHG	+/−
Greg Britz, Hartford	1	0	0	0.0	0	0	Even
Bob Brooke, N.Y. Rangers	15	24	3	12.5	0	0	− 3
Minnesota	65	114	10	8.8	1	1	− 6
Totals	80	138	13	9.4	1	1	− 9
Aaron Broten, New Jersey	80	179	26	14.5	6	0	+ 5
Neal Broten, Minnesota	46	112	18	16.1	5	1	+ 12
Dave Brown, Philadelphia	62	53	7	13.2	0	0	− 7
Douglas Brown, New Jersey	4	10	0	0.0	0	0	− 4
Jeff Brown, Quebec	44	99	7	7.1	3	0	+ 11
Keith Brown, Chicago	73	100	4	4.0	2	0	+ 5
David Bruce, Vancouver	50	76	9	11.8	0	0	+ 2
Murray Brumwell, New Jersey	1	2	0	0.0	0	0	+ 1
Paul Brydges, Buffalo	15	8	2	25.0	0	0	+ 4
Mike Bullard, Pittsburgh	14	42	2	4.8	1	0	− 1
Calgary	57	138	28	20.3	10	0	+ 10
Totals	71	180	30	16.7	11	0	+ 9
Shawn Burr, Detroit	80	153	22	14.4	1	2	+ 2
Randy Burridge, Boston	23	27	1	3.7	0	0	− 6
Rod Buskas, Pittsburgh	68	90	3	3.3	1	0	+ 2
Garth Butcher, Vancouver	70	95	5	5.3	0	0	− 12
Lyndon Byers, Boston	18	14	2	14.3	0	0	− 1
Jim Camazzola, Chicago	2	2	0	0.0	0	0	Even
Wade Campbell, Boston	14	20	0	0.0	0	0	− 1
Guy Carbonneau, Montreal	79	120	18	15.0	0	0	+ 9
Terry Carkner, N.Y. Rangers	52	33	2	6.1	0	0	− 1
Jack Carlson, Minnesota	8	1	0	0.0	0	0	Even
Anders Carlsson, New Jersey	48	35	2	5.7	0	0	− 11
Randy Carlyle, Winnipeg	71	172	16	9.3	5	0	− 6
Bobby Carpenter, Washington	22	47	5	10.6	4	0	− 7
N.Y. Rangers	28	41	2	4.9	1	0	− 12
Los Angeles	10	23	2	8.7	0	0	− 8
Totals	60	111	9	8.1	5	0	− 27
Billy Carroll, Detroit	31	12	1	8.3	0	0	− 9
Jimmy Carson, Los Angeles	80	215	37	17.2	18	0	− 5
Lindsay Carson, Philadelphia	71	100	11	11.0	0	1	− 2
John Carter, Boston	8	12	0	0.0	0	0	+ 3
Bruce Cassidy, Chicago	2	0	0	0.0	0	0	− 1
Jay Caufield, N.Y. Rangers	13	8	2	25.0	0	0	− 2
Gino Cavallini, St. Louis	80	161	18	11.2	4	0	+ 4
Paul Cavallini, Washington	6	6	0	0.0	0	0	− 4
John Chabot, Pittsburgh	72	90	14	15.6	0	0	− 7
Todd Charlesworth, Pittsburgh	1	0	0	0.0	0	0	Even
Chris Chelios, Montreal	71	141	11	7.8	6	0	− 5
Rich Chernomaz, New Jersey	25	44	6	13.6	2	0	− 11
Steve Chiasson, Detroit	45	44	1	2.3	0	0	− 7
Colin Chisholm, Minnesota	1	0	0	0.0	0	0	Even
Dave Christian, Washington	76	152	23	15.1	5	0	− 5
Shane Churla, Hartford	20	2	0	0.0	0	0	− 2
Jeff Chychrun, Philadelphia	1	1	0	0.0	0	0	Even
Dino Ciccarelli, Minnesota	80	255	52	20.4	22	0	+ 10
Chris Cichocki, Detroit	2	0	0	0.0	0	0	− 2
Joe Cirella, New Jersey	65	115	9	7.8	6	0	− 20
Wendel Clark, Toronto	80	246	37	15.0	15	0	− 23
Glen Cochrane, Vancouver	14	2	0	0.0	0	0	Even
Paul Coffey, Edmonton	59	165	17	10.3	10	2	+ 12
Yvon Corriveau, Washington	17	7	1	14.3	0	0	− 4
Shayne Corson, Montreal	55	69	12	17.4	0	1	+ 10
Alain Cote, Boston	3	1	0	0.0	0	0	− 1
Alain Cote, Quebec	80	137	12	8.8	0	2	− 4
Sylvain Cote, Hartford	67	100	2	2.0	0	0	+ 10
Neal Coulter, N.Y. Islanders	9	5	2	40.0	0	0	− 2
Yves Courteau, Hartford	4	4	0	0.0	0	0	− 6
Geoff Courtnall, Boston	65	178	13	7.3	2	0	− 4
Russ Courtnall, Toronto	79	282	29	10.3	3	6	− 20
Craig Coxe, Vancouver	15	7	1	14.3	1	0	− 3
Murray Craven, Philadelphia	77	98	19	19.4	5	3	+ 1
Bobby Crawford, N.Y. Rangers	3	1	0	0.0	0	0	− 1
Washington	12	14	0	0.0	0	0	Even
Totals	15	15	0	0.0	0	0	− 1
Marc Crawford, Vancouver	21	19	0	0.0	0	0	− 8
Adam Creighton, Buffalo	56	109	18	16.5	6	0	+ 4

Player — Team	Games	Shots	Goals	Shooting Pct.	PPG	SHG	+/−
Doug Crossman, Philadelphia	78	122	9	7.4	7	0	+ 18
Keith Crowder, Boston	58	114	22	19.3	4	0	+ 20
Randy Cunneyworth, Pittsburgh	79	169	26	15.4	3	2	+ 14
Brian Curran, N.Y. Islanders	68	34	0	0.0	0	0	+ 3
Paul Cyr, Buffalo	73	131	11	8.4	0	0	− 16
Kjell Dahlin, Montreal	41	53	12	22.6	3	1	− 3
Chris Dahlquist, Pittsburgh	19	15	0	0.0	0	0	− 2
J.J. Daigneault, Philadelphia	77	82	6	7.3	0	0	+ 12
Vincent Damphousse, Toronto	80	142	21	14.8	4	0	− 6
Ken Daneyko, New Jersey	79	113	2	1.8	0	0	− 13
Dan Daoust, Toronto	33	25	4	16.0	0	0	Even
Michael Dark, St. Louis	13	4	2	50.0	0	0	Even
Lucien DeBlois, N.Y. Rangers	40	45	3	6.7	1	0	− 7
Dale DeGray, Calgary	27	57	6	10.5	0	0	− 3
Gilbert Delorme, Quebec	19	22	2	9.1	0	0	− 1
Detroit	24	24	2	8.3	0	0	− 1
Totals	43	46	4	8.7	0	0	− 2
Larry DePalma, Minnesota	56	56	9	16.1	2	0	− 7
Bill Derlago, Winnipeg	30	26	3	11.5	1	0	− 3
Quebec	18	20	3	15.0	0	0	− 4
Totals	48	46	6	13.0	1	0	− 7
Gerald Diduck, N.Y. Islanders	30	54	2	3.7	0	0	− 3
Gord Dineen, N.Y. Islanders	71	59	4	6.8	0	0	− 8
Kevin Dineen, Hartford	78	234	40	17.1	11	0	+ 7
Peter Dineen, Los Angeles	11	5	0	0.0	0	0	− 9
Marcel Dionne, Los Angeles	67	224	24	10.7	9	0	− 8
N.Y. Rangers	14	49	4	8.2	1	0	− 8
Totals	81	273	28	10.3	10	0	− 16
Brian Dobbin, Philadelphia	12	13	2	15.4	0	0	+ 2
Mike Donelly, N.Y. Rangers	5	5	1	20.0	0	0	Even
Dave Donnelly, Chicago	71	64	6	9.4	0	0	− 7
Gord Donnelly, Quebec	38	14	0	0.0	0	0	− 3
Peter Douris, Winnipeg	6	3	0	0.0	0	0	− 1
Bruce Driver, New Jersey	74	132	6	4.5	0	0	− 26
Gaetan Duchesne, Washington	74	108	17	15.7	0	1	+ 18
Steve Duchesne, Los Angeles	75	113	13	11.5	5	0	+ 8
Ron Duguay, Pittsburgh	40	55	5	9.1	0	0	− 8
N.Y. Rangers	34	66	9	13.6	2	1	− 8
Totals	74	121	14	11.6	2	1	− 16
Iain Duncan, Winnipeg	6	7	1	14.3	0	0	+ 1
Craig Duncanson, Los Angeles	2	1	0	0.0	0	0	Even
Richie Dunn, Buffalo	2	1	0	0.0	0	0	+ 2
Jerome Dupont, Toronto	13	5	0	0.0	0	0	− 5
Steve Dykstra, Buffalo	37	21	0	0.0	0	0	− 7
Mike Eagles, Quebec	73	95	13	13.7	0	2	− 15
Pelle Eklund, Philadelphia	72	127	14	11.0	5	0	− 2
Dave Ellett, Winnipeg	78	159	13	8.2	5	0	+ 19
Kari Eloranta, Calgary	13	11	1	9.1	0	0	+ 3
Craig Endean, Winnipeg	2	0	0	0.0	0	0	+ 1
Brian Engblom, Calgary	32	31	0	0.0	0	0	− 7
Bryan Erickson, Los Angeles	68	142	20	14.1	6	2	− 12
Jan Erixon, N.Y. Rangers	68	73	8	11.0	0	1	+ 3
Bob Errey, Pittsburgh	72	138	16	11.6	2	1	− 5
Daryl Evans, Toronto	2	2	1	50.0	1	0	− 2
Doug Evans, St. Louis	53	51	3	5.9	0	0	+ 2
Dean Evason, Hartford	80	124	22	17.7	7	2	+ 4
Todd Ewen, St. Louis	23	11	2	18.2	0	0	− 1
Ted Fauss, Toronto	15	4	0	0.0	0	0	+ 4
Bernie Federko, St. Louis	64	130	20	15.4	9	0	− 25
Paul Fenton, N.Y. Rangers	8	11	0	0.0	0	0	− 5
Dave Fenyves, Buffalo	7	3	1	33.3	0	0	− 3
Tom Fergus, Toronto	57	119	21	17.6	2	1	+ 1
Mark Ferner, Buffalo	13	5	0	0.0	0	0	+ 2
Ray Ferraro, Hartford	80	96	27	28.1	14	0	− 9
Steven Finn, Quebec	36	36	2	5.6	0	0	− 8
Patrick Flatley, N.Y. Islanders	63	113	16	14.2	6	0	+ 17
Ron Flockhart, St. Louis	60	101	16	15.8	2	0	− 9
Lee Fogolin, Edmonton	35	37	1	2.7	0	0	− 2
Buffalo	9	5	0	0.0	0	0	− 2
Totals	44	42	1	2.4	0	0	− 4

Player — Team	Games	Shots	Goals	Shooting Pct.	PPG	SHG	+/−
Mike Foligno	75	185	30	16.2	11	1	+ 13
Dwight Foster, Boston	47	23	4	17.4	0	1	+ 1
Nick Fotiu, Calgary	42	31	5	16.1	0	0	− 3
Jim Fox, Los Angeles	76	162	19	11.7	4	0	− 10
Lou Franceschetti, Washington	75	77	12	15.6	0	0	− 9
Ron Francis, Hartford	75	189	30	15.9	7	0	+ 10
Curt Fraser, Chicago	75	183	25	13.7	3	0	+ 5
Dan Frawley, Pittsburgh	78	109	14	12.8	0	0	− 10
Mark Freer, Philadelphia	1	0	0	0.0	0	0	+ 1
Miroslav Frycer, Toronto	29	52	7	13.5	3	0	− 15
Dave Gagner, N.Y. Rangers	10	16	1	6.3	0	0	− 1
Bob Gainey, Montreal	47	73	8	11.0	0	1	Even
Gerard Gallant, Detroit	80	191	38	19.9	17	0	− 5
Garry Galley, Los Angeles	30	43	5	11.6	2	0	− 9
Washington	18	27	1	3.7	1	0	+ 3
Totals	48	70	6	8.6	3	0	− 6
Bill Gardner, Hartford	8	7	0	0.0	0	0	− 2
Danny Gare, Edmonton	18	22	1	4.5	0	0	+ 2
Mike Gartner, Washington	78	317	41	12.9	5	6	+ 1
Stewart Gavin, Hartford	79	162	20	12.3	3	2	+ 12
Lee Giffin, Pittsburgh	8	8	1	12.5	0	0	+ 2
Greg Gilbert, N.Y. Islanders	51	50	6	12.0	0	0	− 12
Curt Giles, Minnesota	11	5	0	0.0	0	0	+ 2
N.Y. Rangers	61	52	2	3.8	0	0	+ 3
Totals	72	57	2	3.5	0	0	+ 5
Randy Gilhen, Winnipeg	2	3	0	0.0	0	0	− 2
Todd Gill, Toronto	61	51	4	7.8	1	0	− 3
Clark Gillies, Buffalo	61	106	10	9.4	1	0	Even
Jere Gillis, Philadelphia	1	0	0	0.0	0	0	Even
Paul Gillis, Quebec	76	118	13	11.0	0	0	− 5
Doug Gilmour, St. Louis	80	207	42	20.3	17	1	− 2
Gaston Gingras, Montreal	66	173	11	6.4	7	0	− 2
Bobby Gould, Washington	78	156	23	14.7	1	1	+ 18
Michel Goulet, Quebec	75	276	49	17.8	17	0	− 12
Thomas Gradin, Boston	64	87	12	13.8	2	3	+ 4
Dirk Graham, Minnesota	76	197	25	12.7	6	5	− 2
Steve Graves, Edmonton	12	12	2	16.7	0	0	− 2
Rick Green, Montreal	72	38	1	2.6	0	0	− 1
Jeff Greenlaw, Washington	22	9	0	0.0	0	0	+ 2
Randy Gregg, Edmonton	52	59	8	13.6	0	0	+ 36
Ron Greschner, N.Y. Rangers	61	109	6	5.5	1	1	− 6
Wayne Gretzky, Edmonton	79	288	62	21.5	13	7	+ 70
Jari Gronstrand, Minnesota	47	32	1	3.1	0	0	+ 4
Paul Guay, Los Angeles	35	18	2	11.1	0	0	− 14
Kevan Guy, Calgary	24	24	0	0.0	0	0	+ 8
Ari Haanpaa, N.Y. Islanders	41	45	6	13.3	0	0	+ 8
Marc Habscheid, Minnesota	15	14	2	14.3	1	0	− 6
Richard Hajdu, Buffalo	2	1	0	0.0	0	0	+ 1
Bill Hajt, Buffalo	23	11	0	0.0	0	0	Even
Bob Halkidis, Buffalo	6	4	1	25.0	0	0	+ 3
Taylor Hall, Vancouver	4	1	0	0.0	0	0	− 2
Mats Hallin, Minnesota	6	5	0	0.0	0	0	− 3
Doug Halward, Vancouver	10	21	0	0.0	0	0	− 8
Detroit	11	8	0	0.0	0	0	+ 4
Totals	21	29	0	0.0	0	0	− 4
Gilles Hamel, Winnipeg	79	175	27	15.4	1	1	+ 3
Ken Hammond, Los Angeles	10	7	0	0.0	0	0	+ 2
Mark Hamway, N.Y. Islanders	2	1	0	0.0	0	0	− 1
Dave Hannan, Pittsburgh	58	85	10	11.8	0	1	− 2
Mark Hardy, Los Angeles	73	97	3	3.1	0	0	+ 16
Mike Hartman, Buffalo	17	19	3	15.8	0	0	+ 2
Craig Hartsburg, Minnesota	73	189	11	5.8	4	0	− 2
Kevin Hatcher, Washington	78	100	8	8.0	1	0	− 29
Dale Hawerchuk, Winnipeg	80	267	47	17.6	10	0	+ 3
Alan Haworth, Washington	50	143	25	17.5	9	0	+ 3
Raimo Helminen, N.Y. Rangers	21	24	2	8.3	1	0	− 8
Minnesota	6	6	0	0.0	0	0	− 3
Totals	27	30	2	6.7	1	0	− 11
Dale Henry, N.Y. Islanders	19	14	3	21.4	0	0	+ 2
Yves Heroux, Quebec	1	0	0	0.0	0	0	Even

Player — Team	Games	Shots	Goals	Shooting Pct.	PPG	SHG	+/−
Uli Hiemer, New Jersey	40	80	6	7.5	2	0	− 6
Tim Higgins, Detroit	77	110	12	10.9	0	1	− 2
Al Hill, Philadelphia	7	2	0	0.0	0	0	+ 1
Randy Hillier, Pittsburgh	55	51	4	7.8	0	0	+ 12
Dan Hodgson, Vancouver	43	42	9	21.4	4	0	− 9
Jim Hofford, Buffalo	12	8	0	0.0	0	0	− 1
Ed Hospodar, Philadelphia	45	17	2	11.8	0	0	− 8
Paul Houck, Minnesota	12	10	0	0.0	0	0	− 2
Mike Hough, Quebec	56	60	6	10.0	1	1	− 8
Phil Housley, Buffalo	78	202	21	10.4	8	1	− 2
Mark Howe, Philadelphia	69	148	15	10.1	2	4	+ 57
Willie Huber, N.Y. Rangers	66	117	8	6.8	3	1	− 13
Charlie Huddy, Edmonton	58	75	4	5.3	0	0	+ 27
Kerry Huffman, Philadelphia	9	3	0	0.0	0	0	+ 5
Pat Hughes, St. Louis	43	30	1	3.3	0	0	− 6
Hartford	2	3	0	0.0	0	0	− 1
Totals	45	33	1	3.0	0	0	− 7
Brett Hull, Calgary	5	5	1	20.0	0	0	− 1
Dale Hunter, Quebec	46	53	10	18.9	0	0	+ 4
Dave Hunter, Edmonton	77	84	6	7.1	0	0	+ 1
Mark Hunter, St. Louis	74	178	36	20.2	12	0	− 19
Tim Hunter, Calgary	73	66	6	9.1	0	0	− 1
Al Iafrate, Toronto	80	132	9	6.8	0	0	− 18
Miroslav Ihnacak, Toronto	34	65	6	9.2	0	0	+ 3
Peter Ihnacak, Toronto	58	98	12	12.2	4	0	+ 5
Don Jackson, N.Y. Rangers	22	4	1	25.0	0	0	− 1
Jeff Jackson, Toronto	55	42	8	19.0	0	0	− 11
N.Y. Rangers	9	16	5	31.3	2	0	− 3
Totals	64	58	13	22.4	2	0	− 14
Val James, Toronto	4	0	0	0.0	0	0	Even
Hannu Jarvenpaa, Winnipeg	20	36	1	2.8	0	0	− 4
Doug Jarvis, Hartford	80	88	9	10.2	0	2	+ 1
Chris Jensen, N.Y. Rangers	37	70	6	8.6	0	1	− 1
David A. Jensen, Washington	46	49	8	16.3	2	0	− 10
Jim Johnson, Pittsburgh	80	89	5	5.6	0	0	− 6
Mark Johnson, New Jersey	68	193	25	13.0	11	2	− 21
Terry Johnson, Toronto	48	10	0	0.0	0	0	− 5
Greg Johnston, Boston	76	131	12	9.2	0	0	− 7
Ed Johnstone, Detroit	6	0	0	0.0	0	0	+ 1
Brad Jones, Winnipeg	4	8	1	12.5	0	0	+ 2
Tomas Jonsson, N.Y. Islanders	47	99	6	6.1	1	1	− 8
Steve Kasper, Boston	79	110	20	18.2	4	2	− 4
Ed Kastelic, Washington	23	15	1	6.7	1	0	− 3
Dean Kennedy, Los Angeles	66	59	6	10.2	0	0	+ 9
Alan Kerr, N.Y. Islanders	72	97	7	7.2	0	1	− 10
Tim Kerr, Philadelphia	75	261	58	22.2	26	0	+ 38
Derek King, N.Y. Islanders	2	5	0	0.0	0	0	Even
Kelly Kisio, N.Y. Rangers	70	137	24	17.5	4	2	− 5
Scot Kleinendorst, Hartford	66	50	3	6.0	0	0	+ 4
Petr Klima, Detroit	77	209	30	14.4	6	0	− 9
Joey Kocur, Detroit	77	81	9	11.1	2	0	− 10
Steve Konroyd, N.Y. Islanders	72	119	5	4.2	3	0	− 5
Chris Kontos, Pittsburgh	31	38	8	21.1	1	0	− 6
John Kordic, Montreal	44	32	5	15.6	0	0	− 7
Jim Korn, Buffalo	51	35	4	11.4	0	0	− 3
Chris Kotsopoulos, Toronto	43	43	2	4.7	0	0	+ 8
Dale Krentz, Detroit	8	5	0	0.0	0	0	− 2
Rich Kromm, N.Y. Islanders	70	110	12	10.9	0	0	+ 2
Uwe Krupp, Buffalo	26	34	1	2.9	0	0	− 9
Mike Krushelnyski, Edmonton	80	89	16	18.0	4	1	+ 26
Stu Kulak, Vancouver	28	24	1	4.2	1	0	− 11
Edmonton	23	30	3	10.0	0	0	+ 3
N.Y. Rangers	3	2	0	0.0	0	0	− 1
Totals	54	56	4	7.1	1	0	− 9
Mark Kumpel, Quebec	40	47	1	2.1	0	0	− 12
Detroit	5	1	0	0.0	0	0	+ 2
Totals	45	48	1	2.1	0	0	− 10
Jari Kurri, Edmonton	79	211	54	25.6	12	5	+ 35
Tom Kurvers, Montreal	1	2	0	0.0	0	0	+ 1
Buffalo	55	71	6	8.5	1	0	− 10
Totals	56	73	6	8.2	1	1	− 9

Hartford's Doug Jarvis won the Bill Masterton Memorial Trophy in 1986-87 and also set a new NHL record with 962 consecutive regular-season games played.

Player — Team	Games	Shots	Goals	Shooting Pct.	PPG	SHG	+/−
Jim Kyte, Winnipeg	72	62	5	8.1	0	0	+ 4
Normand, Lacombe, Buffalo	39	48	4	8.3	1	0	− 9
Edmonton	1	0	0	0.0	0	0	− 1
Totals	40	48	4	8.3	1	0	− 10
Randy Ladouceur, Detroit	34	25	3	12.0	1	0	− 4
Hartford	36	29	2	6.9	0	0	+ 5
Totals	70	54	5	9.3	1	0	+ 1
Pat LaFontaine, N.Y. Islanders	80	219	38	17.4	19	1	− 10
Jason Lafreniere, Quebec	56	55	13	23.6	7	0	− 3
Tom Laidlaw, N.Y. Rangers	63	36	1	2.8	1	0	− 18
Los Angeles	11	7	0	0.0	0	0	+ 1
Totals	74	43	1	2.3	1	0	− 17
Mike Lalor, Montreal	57	58	0	0.0	0	0	+ 5
Mark Lamb, Detroit	22	8	2	25.0	0	0	Even
Lane Lambert, N.Y. Rangers	18	14	2	14.3	0	0	+ 2
Quebec	15	29	5	17.2	0	0	− 1
Totals	33	43	7	16.3	0	0	+ 1
Dave Langevin, Los Angeles	11	5	0	0.0	0	0	− 3
Rod Langway, Washington	78	76	2	2.6	0	0	+ 11
Rick Lanz, Vancouver	17	39	1	2.6	1	0	− 13
Toronto	44	91	2	2.2	1	0	+ 4
Totals	61	130	3	2.3	2	0	− 9
Steve Larmer, Chicago	80	216	28	13.0	10	0	+ 20
Pierre Larouche, N.Y. Rangers	73	193	28	14.5	8	0	− 7
Reed Larson, Boston	66	209	12	5.7	9	0	+ 9
Brad Lauer, N.Y. Islanders	61	75	7	9.3	1	0	Even
Craig Laughlin, Washington	80	109	22	20.2	11	0	− 3
Kevin LaVallee, Pittsburgh	33	80	8	10.0	5	0	− 2
Mark LaVarre, Chicago	58	46	8	17.4	0	0	+ 11
Paul Lawless, Hartford	60	161	22	13.7	4	0	+ 24
Brian Lawton, Minnesota	66	125	21	16.8	2	0	+ 20
Derek Laxdal, Toronto	2	0	0	0.0	0	0	− 1
Stephen Leach, Washington	15	17	1	5.9	0	0	− 4
Jim Leavins, N.Y. Rangers	4	4	0	0.0	0	0	Even
John LeBlanc, Vancouver	2	4	1	25.0	0	0	+ 1
Grant Ledyard, Los Angeles	67	144	14	9.7	5	0	− 40
Gary Leeman, Toronto	80	196	21	10.7	4	3	− 26
Ken Leiter, N.Y. Islanders	74	159	9	5.7	4	0	+ 1
Moe Lemay, Vancouver	52	86	9	10.5	2	0	− 2
Edmonton	10	7	1	14.3	0	0	+ 2
Totals	62	93	10	10.8	2	0	Even
Alain Lemieux, Pittsburgh	1	0	0	0.0	0	0	− 1
Claude Lemieux, Montreal	76	184	27	14.7	5	0	Even
Jocelyn Lemieux, St. Louis	53	48	10	20.8	1	0	+ 1
Mario Lemieux, Pittsburgh	63	267	54	20.2	19	0	+ 13
Tim Lenardon, New Jersey	7	13	1	7.7	0	0	− 2
Don Lever, Buffalo	10	8	3	37.5	3	0	− 3
Craig Levie, Vancouver	9	8	0	0.0	0	0	+ 3
Dave Lewis, Detroit	58	37	2	5.4	0	0	+ 12
Doug Lidster, Vancouver	80	176	12	6.8	3	0	− 35
Willy Lindstrom, Pittsburgh	60	93	10	10.8	1	0	+ 9
Ken Linseman, Boston	64	94	15	16.0	3	0	+ 15
Bob Logan, Buffalo	22	22	7	31.8	1	0	+ 5
Claude Loiselle, New Jersey	75	145	16	11.0	2	1	− 7
Troy Loney, Pittsburgh	23	48	8	16.7	1	0	Even
Hakan Loob, Calgary	68	129	18	14.0	7	0	− 13
Kevin Lowe, Edmonton	77	99	8	8.1	2	2	+ 41
Dave Lowry, Vancouver	70	74	8	10.8	0	0	− 23
Jan Ludvig, New Jersey	47	56	7	12.5	1	0	− 5
Craig Ludwig, Montreal	75	55	4	7.3	0	0	+ 3
Steve Ludzik, Chicago	52	56	5	8.9	0	0	− 3
Morris Lukowich, Los Angeles	60	105	14	13.3	4	0	Even
Dave Lumley, Edmonton	1	0	0	0.0	0	0	Even
Paul MacDermid, Hartford	72	72	7	9.7	0	0	+ 3
Al MacInnis, Calgary	79	262	20	7.6	7	0	+ 20
Norm Maciver, N.Y. Rangers	3	2	0	0.0	0	0	− 5
John MacLean, New Jersey	80	197	31	15.7	9	0	− 23
Paul MacLean, Winnipeg	72	155	32	20.6	10	0	+ 12
Brian MacLellan, Minnesota	76	146	32	21.9	13	0	− 12
Jamie Macoun, Calgary	79	137	7	5.1	1	0	+ 33

Player — Team	Games	Shots	Goals	Shooting Pct.	PPG	SHG	+/−
Craig MacTavish, Edmonton	79	140	20	14.3	1	4	+ 9
Kevin Maguire, Toronto	17	2	0	0.0	0	0	− 6
Mikko Makela, N.Y. Islanders	80	142	24	16.9	11	0	+ 3
David Maley, Montreal	48	45	6	13.3	0	0	− 1
Greg Malone, Quebec	6	6	0	0.0	0	0	Even
Don Maloney, N.Y. Rangers	72	130	19	14.6	3	3	+ 7
Dave Manson, Chicago	63	42	1	2.4	0	0	− 2
Moe Mantha, Pittsburgh	62	167	9	5.4	8	0	− 6
Gordon Mark, New Jersey	36	31	3	9.7	0	0	− 4
Nevin Markwart, Boston	64	65	10	15.4	0	0	− 6
Mario Marois, Winnipeg	79	193	4	2.1	1	0	− 1
Brad Marsh, Philadelphia	77	81	2	2.5	0	0	+ 9
Grant Martin, Washington	9	5	0	0.0	0	0	− 1
Tom Martin, Winnipeg	11	2	1	50.0	0	0	+ 1
Dennis Maruk, Minnesota	67	144	16	11.1	4	0	+ 5
Dwight Mathiasen, Pittsburgh	6	4	0	0.0	0	0	− 1
Brad Maxwell, Vancouver	30	43	1	2.3	1	0	− 9
N.Y. Rangers	9	10	0	0.0	0	0	− 1
Minnesota	17	33	2	6.1	0	0	+ 3
Totals	56	86	3	3.5	1	0	− 7
Andrew McBain, Winnipeg	71	85	11	12.9	· 1	1	+ 6
Kevin McCarthy, Philadelphia	2	0	0	0.0	0	0	− 1
Tom McCarthy, Boston	68	121	30	24.8	7	0	+ 10
Kevin McClelland, Edmonton	72	76	12	15.8	0	0	− 4
Brad McCrimmon, Philadelphia	71	110	10	9.1	3	2	+ 45
Lanny McDonald, Calgary	58	127	14	11.0	4	0	− 3
Mike McEwen, Hartford	48	86	8	9.3	5	0	− 9
Jim McGeough, Pittsburgh	11	24	1	4.2	0	0	− 5
Bob McGill, Toronto	56	27	1	3.7	0	0	− 2
Tony McKegney, Minnesota	11	15	2	13.3	0	0	+ 2
N.Y. Rangers	64	166	29	17.5	7	2	− 1
Totals	75	181	31	17.1	7	2	+ 1
Sean McKenna, Los Angeles	69	102	14	13.7	0	1	+ 11
Peter McNab, New Jersey	46	49	8	16.3	2	0	− 14
George McPhee, N.Y. Rangers	21	31	4	12.9	0	0	− 2
Mike McPhee, Montreal	79	150	18	12.0	0	2	+ 7
Basil McRae, Detroit	36	21	2	9.5	1	0	− 3
Quebec	33	36	9	25.0	3	0	+ 1
Totals	69	57	11	19.3	4	0	− 2
Marty McSorley, Edmonton	41	32	2	6.3	0	0	− 4
Rick Meagher, St. Louis	80	170	18	10.6	2	2	− 9
Scott Mellanby, Philadelphia	71	118	11	9.3	1	0	+ 8
Larry Melnyk, N.Y. Rangers	73	53	3	5.7	0	0	− 13
Mark Messier, Edmonton	77	208	37	17.8	7	4	+ 21
Max Middendorf, Quebec	6	4	1	25.0	0	0	− 2
Rick Middleton, Boston	76	141	31	22.0	4	4	+ 7
Mike Milbury, Boston	68	59	6	10.2	0	1	+ 22
Mike Millar, Hartford	10	13	2	15.4	1	0	+ 3
Jay Miller, Boston	55	27	1	3.7	0	0	− 11
Kelly Miller, N.Y. Rangers	38	58	6	10.3	2	0	− 5
Washington	39	50	10	20.0	3	1	+ 10
Totals	77	108	16	14.8	5	1	+ 5
Carl Mokosak, Pittsburgh	3	3	0	0.0	0	0	− 4
Mike Moller, Edmonton	6	10	2	20.0	0	0	+ 2
Randy Moller, Quebec	71	106	5	4.7	1	0	− 11
Sergio Momesso, Montreal	59	95	14	14.7	3	0	Even
Ken Morrow, N.Y. Islanders	64	52	3	5.8	0	0	+ 7
Brian Mullen, Winnipeg	69	185	19	10.3	7	0	− 2
Joe Mullen, Calgary	79	206	47	22.8	15	0	+ 18
Kirk Muller, New Jersey	79	193	26	13.5	10	1	− 7
Craig Muni, Edmonton	79	69	7	10.1	0	0	+ 45
Joe Murphy, Detroit	5	3	0	0.0	0	0	Even
Larry Murphy, Washington	80	226	23	10.2	8	0	+ 25
Bob Murray, Chicago	79	177	6	3.4	4	0	− 9
Troy Murray, Chicago	77	127	28	22.0	4	2	+ 14
Dana Murzyn, Hartford	74	135	9	6.7	1	0	+ 18
Frantisek Musil, Minnesota	72	83	2	2.4	0	0	Even
Don Nachbaur, Philadelphia	23	12	0	0.0	0	0	+ 1
Chris Nilan, Montreal	44	68	4	5.9	0	0	+ 2
Mark Napier, Edmonton	62	88	8	9.1	0	1	+ 3

Player — Team	Games	Shots	Goals	Shooting Pct.	PPG	SHG	+/−
Buffalo	15	40	5	12.5	1	0	− 5
Totals	77	128	13	10.2	1	1	− 2
Mats Naslund, Montreal	79	173	25	14.5	10	0	− 3
Ric Nattress, St. Louis	73	133	6	4.5	2	0	− 34
Cam Neely, Boston	75	206	36	17.5	7	0	+ 23
Ray Neufeld, Winnipeg	80	134	18	13.4	5	0	− 13
Bernie Nicholls, Los Angeles	80	227	33	14.5	10	1	− 16
Kraig Nienhuis, Boston	16	25	4	16.0	2	0	− 5
Joe Nieuwendyk, Calgary	9	16	5	31.3	2	0	Even
Jim Nill, Winnipeg	36	12	3	25.0	1	0	+ 1
Kent Nilsson, Minnesota	44	89	13	14.6	8	0	+ 2
Edmonton	17	25	5	20.0	1	0	+ 10
Totals	61	114	18	15.8	9	0	+ 12
Lee Norwood, Detroit	57	101	6	5.9	4	0	− 23
Gary Nylund, Chicago	80	123	7	5.7	2	0	− 9
Jack O'Callahan, Chicago	48	65	1	1.5	1	0	+ 10
Mike O'Connell, Detroit	77	141	5	3.5	3	1	− 25
Adam Oates, Detroit	76	138	15	10.9	4	0	Even
John Ogrodnick, Detroit	39	117	12	10.3	4	1	− 2
Quebec	32	127	11	8.7	2	0	− 6
Totals	71	244	23	9.4	6	1	− 8
Fredrick Olausson, Winnipeg	72	119	7	5.9	1	0	− 3
Ed Olczyk, Chicago	79	181	16	8.8	2	1	− 4
Gates Orlando, Buffalo	27	24	2	8.3	0	0	− 6
Mark Osborne, N.Y. Rangers	58	129	17	13.2	5	0	− 15
Toronto	16	31	5	16.1	1	0	− 1
Totals	74	160	22	13.8	6	0	− 16
Joel Otto, Calgary	68	127	19	15.0	5	0	+ 8
Wilf Paiement, Buffalo	56	117	20	17.1	2	0	+ 2
Jeff Parker, Buffalo	15	10	3	30.0	0	0	+ 1
Greg Paslawski, St. Louis	76	204	29	14.2	5	1	+ 1
Joe Paterson, Los Angeles	45	30	2	6.7	0	0	− 15
Rick Paterson, Chicago	22	4	1	25.0	0	1	+ 1
James Patrick, N.Y. Rangers	78	143	10	7.0	5	0	+ 13
Colin Patterson, Calgary	68	78	13	16.7	0	1	+ 7
Mark Pavelich, MInnesota	12	25	4	16.0	0	0	+ 7
Jim Pavese, St. Louis	69	45	2	4.4	0	0	− 21
Steve Payne, Minnesota	48	67	4	6.0	0	0	− 12
Allen Pedersen, Boston	79	56	1	1.8	0	0	− 15
Barry Pederson, Vancouver	79	184	24	13.0	6	0	− 13
Jim Peplinski, Calgary	80	145	18	12.4	0	2	+ 13
Gilbert Perreault, Buffalo	20	35	9	25.7	1	0	− 2
Brent Peterson, Vancouver	69	71	7	9.9	2	1	− 14
Michel Petit, Vanvouver	69	116	12	10.3	4	0	− 5
Lyle Phair, Los Angeles	5	4	2	50.0	0	0	− 1
Robert Picard, Quebec	78	163	8	4.9	1	1	− 17
Michel Pivonka, Washington	73	117	18	15.4	4	0	− 19
Larry Playfair, Los Angeles	37	20	2	10.0	0	0	− 1
Willi Plett, Minnesota	67	50	6	12.0	0	0	+ 1
Walt Poddubny, N.Y. Rangers	75	253	40	15.8	11	0	+ 16
Mike Posavad, St. Louis	2	0	0	0.0	0	0	+ 1
Denis Potvin, N.Y. Rangers	58	147	12	8.2	8	0	− 6
Daniel Poudrier, Quebec	6	2	0	0.0	0	0	− 2
Dave Poulin, Philadelphia	75	155	25	16.1	1	3	+ 47
Jaroslav Pouzar, Edmonton	12	11	2	18.2	0	0	+ 3
Wayne Presley, Chicago	80	167	32	19.2	7	0	− 18
Rich Preston, Chicago	73	55	8	14.5	0	0	− 8
Pat Price, Quebec	47	22	0	0.0	0	0	− 7
N.Y. Rangers	13	4	0	0.0	0	0	− 8
Totals	60	26	0	0.0	0	0	− 15
Ken Priestlay, Buffalo	34	49	11	22.4	3	0	+ 3
Bob Probert, Detroit	63	56	13	23.2	2	0	− 6
Brian Propp, Philadelphia	53	208	31	14.9	8	5	+ 39
Chris Pryor, Minnesota	50	20	1	5.0	0	0	− 6
Joel Quenneville, Hartford	37	19	3	15.8	0	1	+ 8
Dan Quinn, Calgary	16	27	3	11.1	1	0	− 6
Pittsburgh	64	157	28	17.8	10	3	+ 14
Totals	80	184	31	16.8	11	3	+ 8
Ken Quinney, Quebec	25	22	2	9.1	1	0	+ 2
Herb Raglan, St. Louis	62	58	6	10.3	0	0	+ 6

Player — Team	Games	Shots	Goals	Shooting Pct.	PPG	SHG	+/−
Rob Ramage, St. Louis	59	160	11	6.9	6	0	− 12
Mike Ramsey, Buffalo	80	154	8	5.2	2	1	+ 1
Craig Redmond, Los Angeles	16	18	1	5.6	0	0	− 1
Mark Reeds, St. Louis	68	106	9	8.5	1	0	− 20
Joe Reekie, Buffalo	56	56	1	1.8	0	0	+ 6
Dave Reid, Boston	12	19	3	15.8	0	0	− 1
Paul Reinhart, Calgary	76	120	15	12.5	7	0	+ 7
Stephane Richer, Montreal	57	109	20	18.3	4	0	+ 11
Steve Richmond, New Jersey	44	31	1	3.2	0	0	− 12
Dave Richter, Vancouver	78	31	2	6.5	0	0	− 2
Mike Ridley, N.Y. Rangers	38	81	16	19.8	4	0	− 10
Washington	40	68	15	22.1	6	0	− 1
Totals	78	149	31	20.8	10	0	− 11
Doug Risebrough, Calgary	22	19	2	10.5	0	0	− 2
Gary Roberts, Calgary	32	38	5	13.2	0	0	+ 6
Gordie Roberts, Minnesota	67	43	3	7.0	0	0	− 7
Torrie Robertson, Hartford	20	19	1	5.3	0	0	− 6
Larry Robinson, Montreal	70	122	13	10.7	6	0	+ 24
Luc Robitaille, Los Angeles	79	199	45	22.6	18	0	− 18
Normand Rochefort, Quebec	70	92	6	6.5	0	0	+ 2
Cliff Ronning, St. Louis	42	68	11	16.2	2	0	− 1
Steve Rooney, Montreal	2	2	0	0.0	0	0	Even
Winnipeg	30	23	2	8.7	0	0	− 4
Totals	32	25	2	8.0	0	0	− 4
Bill Root, Toronto	34	31	3	9.7	1	0	− 9
Bob Rouse, Minnesota	72	71	2	2.8	0	0	+ 6
Mike Rowe, Pittsburgh	2	1	0	0.0	0	0	− 2
Lindy Ruff, Buffalo	50	95	6	6.3	0	0	− 12
Reijo Ruotsalainen, Edmonton	16	52	5	9.6	3	0	+ 8
Terry Ruskowski, Pittsburgh	70	71	14	19.7	5	0	+ 8
Phil Russell, Buffalo	6	2	0	0.0	0	0	Even
Christian Ruutu, Buffalo	76	167	22	13.2	3	1	+ 9
Borje Salming, Toronto	56	71	4	5.6	0	1	+ 17
Gary Sampson, Washington	25	14	1	7.1	0	0	− 9
Kjell Samuelsson, N.Y. Rangers	30	20	2	10.0	0	0	− 2
Philadelphia	46	28	1	3.6	0	0	− 9
Totals	76	48	3	6.3	0	0	− 11
Ulf Samuelsson, Hartford	78	104	2	1.9	0	0	+ 29
Scott Sandelin, Montreal	1	0	0	0.0	0	0	+ 1
Jim Sandlak, Vancouver	78	114	15	13.2	2	0	− 4
Tomas Sandstrom, N.Y. Rangers	64	240	40	16.7	13	0	+ 8
Everett Sanipass, Chicago	7	9	1	11.1	0	0	+ 3
Jean Francois Sauve, Quebec	14	14	2	14.3	2	0	− 4
Denis Savard, Chicago	70	237	40	16.9	7	0	+ 15
Darin Sceviour, Chicago	1	1	0	0.0	0	0	Even
Norm Schmidt, Pittsburgh	20	32	1	3.1	1	0	− 8
Dwight Schofield, Pittsburgh	25	9	1	11.1	0	0	+ 4
Glen Seabrooke, Philadelphia	10	10	1	10.0	0	0	+ 2
Al Secord, Chicago	77	179	29	16.2	5	0	− 20
Ric Seiling, Detroit	74	35	3	8.6	0	0	− 4
Dave Semenko, Edmonton	5	1	0	0.0	0	0	Even
Hartford	51	31	4	12.9	0	0	− 6
Totals	56	32	4	12.5	0	0	− 6
Jeff Sharples, Detroit	3	1	0	0.0	0	0	Even
Scott Shaunessy, Quebec	3	0	0	0.0	0	0	− 1
Brad Shaw, Hartford	2	2	0	0.0	0	0	Even
David Shaw, Quebec	75	136	0	0.0	0	0	− 35
Doug Shedden, Detroit	33	51	6	11.8	1	0	+ 3
Quebec	16	29	0	0.0	0	0	− 5
Totals	49	80	6	7.5	1	0	− 2
Neil Sheehy, Calgary	54	45	4	8.9	0	0	+ 11
Gord Sherven, Hartford	7	7	0	0.0	0	0	− 6
Mike Siltala, N.Y. Rangers	1	0	0	0.0	0	0	+ 1
Risto Siltanen, Quebec	66	130	10	7.7	8	0	− 2
Charlie Simmer, Boston	80	137	29	21.2	11	0	+ 20
Frank Simonetti, Boston	25	11	1	9.1	0	0	− 3
Craig Simpson, Pittsburgh	72	133	26	19.5	7	0	+ 11
Ilkka Sinisalo, Philadelphia	42	80	10	12.5	3	1	+ 14
Ville Siren, Pittsburgh	69	84	5	6.0	1	0	+ 8
Petri Skriko, Vancouver	76	224	33	14.7	10	6	− 4
Brian Skrudland, Montreal	79	72	11	15.3	0	1	+ 18

— 99 —

Player — Team	Games	Shots	Goals	Shooting Pct.	PPG	SHG	+/−
Doug Smail, Winnipeg	78	132	25	18.9	0	2	+ 18
Bobby Smith, Montreal	80	197	28	14.2	11	0	+ 6
Brad Smith, Toronto	47	45	5	11.1	0	0	+ 15
Derrick Smith, Philadelphia	71	150	11	7.3	0	0	− 4
Doug Smith, Buffalo	62	158	16	10.1	7	0	− 20
Greg Smith, Washington	45	30	0	0.0	0	0	− 6
Randy Smith, Minnesota	2	0	0	0.0	0	0	− 2
Steve Smith, Philadelphia	2	2	0	0.0	0	0	Even
Steve Smith, Edmonton	62	71	7	9.9	2	0	+ 11
Stan Smyl, Vancouver	66	113	20	17.7	5	2	− 20
Greg Smyth, Philadelphia	1	1	0	0.0	0	0	− 2
Harold Snepsts, Detroit	54	38	1	2.6	0	0	+ 7
Darryl Stanley, Philadelphia	33	22	1	4.5	0	0	+ 6
Mike Stapleton, Chicago	39	54	3	5.6	0	0	− 9
Anton Stastny, Quebec	77	172	27	15.7	6	0	+ 3
Peter Stastny, Quebec	64	157	24	15.3	12	0	− 21
Thomas Steen, Winnipeg	75	143	17	11.9	3	3	+ 7
John Stevens, Philadelphia	6	2	0	0.0	0	0	Even
Scott Stevens, Washington	77	165	10	6.1	2	0	+ 13
Allan Stewart, New Jersey	7	8	1	12.5	0	0	− 4
Trevor Stienberg, Quebec	6	6	1	16.7	0	0	Even
Mike Stothers, Philadelphia	2	2	0	0.0	0	0	Even
Doug Sulliman, New Jersey	78	148	27	18.2	4	1	− 17
Raimo Summanen, Edmonton	48	55	10	18.2	0	0	− 1
Vancouver	10	18	4	22.2	1	0	− 1
Totals	58	73	14	19.2	1	0	− 2
Patrik Sundstrom, Vancouver	72	141	29	20.6	12	1	+ 9
Gary Suter, Calgary	68	152	9	5.9	4	0	− 10
Brent Sutter, N.Y. Islanders	69	177	27	15.3	6	3	+ 23
Brian Sutter, St. Louis	14	22	3	13.6	3	0	− 5
Darryl Sutter, Chicago	44	62	8	12.9	1	0	− 3
Duane Sutter, N.Y. Islanders	80	152	14	9.2	1	0	+ 1
Rich Sutter, Vancover	74	166	20	12.0	3	0	− 17
Ron Sutter, Philadelphia	39	68	10	14.7	0	0	+ 10
Petr Svoboda, Montreal	70	80	5	6.3	1	0	+ 14
Robert Sweeney, Boston	14	13	2	15.4	0	0	− 5
Phil Sykes, Los Angeles	58	62	6	9.7	0	1	+ 10
Peter Taglianetti, Winnipeg	3	2	0	0.0	0	0	− 4
Ron Talakoski, N.Y. Rangers	3	1	0	0.0	0	0	+ 1
Steve Tambellini, Vancouver	72	162	16	9.9	9	0	− 22
Tony Tanti, Vancouver	77	242	41	16.9	15	0	+ 5
Dave Taylor, Los Angeles	67	115	18	15.7	9	1	Even
Greg Terrion, Toronto	67	55	7	12.7	0	2	− 5
Mats Thelin, Boston	59	39	1	2.6	0	0	− 8
Michael Thelven, Boston	34	60	5	8.3	3	0	− 2
Gilles Thibaudeau, Montreal	9	10	1	10.0	0	0	+ 5
Steve Thomas, Toronto	78	245	35	14.3	3	0	− 3
Jim Thomson, Washington	10	5	0	0.0	0	0	− 2
Esa Tikkanen, Edmonton	76	126	34	27.0	6	0	+ 44
Dave Tippett, Hartford	80	120	9	7.5	0	3	+ 1
Rick Tocchet, Philadelphia	69	147	21	14.3	1	1	+ 16
John Tonelli, Calgary	78	150	20	13.3	10	0	− 2
Tim Tookey, Philadelphia	2	1	0	0.0	0	0	Even
Sean Toomey, Minnesota	1	2	0	0.0	0	0	− 1
Larry Trader, St. Louis	5	3	0	0.0	0	0	− 5
Doug Trapp, Buffalo	2	1	0	0.0	0	0	Even
Bryan Trottier, N.Y. Islanders	80	194	23	11.9	13	0	+ 2
John Tucker, Buffalo	54	104	17	16.3	4	0	− 3
Sylvain Turgeon, Hartford	41	137	23	16.8	6	0	− 3
Perry Turnbull, Winnipeg	26	29	1	3.4	0	0	− 2
Rick Vaive, Toronto	73	214	32	15.0	8	1	+ 12
Wayne Van Dorp, Edmonton	3	3	0	0.0	0	0	− 1
Darren Veitch, Detroit	77	164	13	7.9	7	1	+ 14
Randy Velischek, New Jersey	64	39	2	5.1	0	0	− 12
Pat Verbeek, New Jersey	74	143	35	24.5	17	0	− 23
Emanuel Viveiros, Minnesota	1	1	0	0.0	0	0	Even
Gord Walker, N.Y. Rangers	1	1	1	100.0	0	0	+ 2
Ryan Walter, Montreal	76	117	23	19.7	11	0	− 6
Bill Watson, Chicago	51	106	13	12.3	0	0	+ 19
Tim Watters, Winnipeg	63	44	3	6.8	0	0	+ 5
Jay Wells, Los Angeles	77	115	7	6.1	6	0	− 19

Player — Team	Games	Shots	Goals	Shooting Pct.	PPG	SHG	+/−
Doug Wickenheiser, St. Louis	80	131	13	9.9	5	2	− 22
Brian Wilks, Los Angeles	1	0	0	0.0	0	0	− 2
Dave Williams, Los Angeles	76	118	16	13.6	1	0	− 1
Carey Wilson, Calgary	80	140	20	14.3	3	1	− 2
Doug Wilson, Chicago	69	249	16	6.4	7	1	+ 15
Mitch Wilson, Pittsburgh	17	7	2	28.6	0	0	− 3
Ron Wilson, Winnipeg	80	76	3	3.9	0	0	+ 10
Ron Wilson, Minnesota	65	138	12	8.7	6	0	− 9
Craig Wolanin, New Jersey	68	68	4	5.9	0	0	− 31
Randy Wood, N.Y. Islanders	6	4	1	25.0	0	0	− 1
Ken Yaremchuk, Toronto	20	33	3	9.1	0	0	Even
Warren Young, Pittsburgh	50	52	8	15.4	3	0	− 5
Steve Yzerman, Detroit	80	217	31	14.3	9	1	− 1
Richard Zemlak, Quebec	20	2	0	0.0	0	0	Even
Peter Zezel, Philadelphia	71	181	33	18.2	6	2	+ 21
Rick Zombo, Detroit	44	28	1	3.6	0	0	− 6

NHL Departmental Leaders

Goals

1. Wayne Gretzky, Edmonton 62
2. Tim Kerr, Philadelphia 58
3. Mario Lemieux, Pittsburgh 54
   Jari Kurri, Edmonton 54
5. Dino Ciccarelli, Minnesota 52

Assists

1. Wayne Gretzky, Edmonton 121
2. Ray Bourque, Boston 72
3. Mark Messier, Edmonton 70
4. Kevin Dineen, Hartford 69
5. Bryan Trottier, N.Y. Islanders 64

Power-Play Goals

1. Tim Kerr, Philadephia 26
2. Dino Ciccarelli, Minnesota 22
3. Mario Lemieux, Pittsburgh 19
   Pat LaFontaine, N.Y. Islanders 19
5. Luc Robitaille, Los Angeles 18
   Jimmy Carson, Los Angeles 18

Shorthanded Goals

1. Wayne Gretzky, Edmonton 7
2. Petri Skriko, Vancouver 6
   Mike Gartner, Washington 6
   Russ Courtnall, Toronto 6
5. Brian Propp, Philadelphia 5
   Dirk Graham, Minnesota 5
   Jari Kurri, Edmonton 5

Game-Winning Goals

1. Joe Mullen, Calgary 12
2. Mike Gartner, Washington 10
   Tim Kerr, Philadelphia 10
   Jari Kurri, Edmonton 10

Shots on Goal

1. Ray Bourque, Boston 334
2. Mike Gartner, Washington 317
3. Wayne Gretzky, Edmonton 288
4. Russ Courtnall, Toronto 282
5. Michel Goulet, Quebec 276

Shooting Percentage

1. Ray Ferraro, Hartford 28.1
2. Esa Tikkanen, Edmonton 27.0
3. Jari Kurri, Edmonton 25.6
4. Brent Ashton, Quebec 25.5
5. Tom McCarthy, Boston 24.8

Plus/Minus Leaders

1. Wayne Gretzky, Edmonton .... +70
2. Mark Howe, Philadelphia .... +57
3. Dave Poulin, Philadelphia .... +47
4. Craig Muni, Edmonton .... +45
   Brad McCrimmon, Philadelphia .... +45

Penalty Minutes

1. Dave Williams, Los Angeles 358
2. Tim Hunter, Calgary 357
3. Brian Curran, N.Y. Islanders 356
4. Basil McRae, Detroit-Quebec 342
5. Rick Tocchet, Philadelphia 286

Miscellaneous Goaltending Statistics

	Games	W.	L.	T.	Goals	Saves	Sv. Pct.	Goal Interval
Murray Bannerman, Chicago	39	9	18	8	142	978	87.3	14.50
Tom Barrasso, Buffalo	46	17	23	2	152	1046	87.3	16.45
Don Beaupre, Minnesota	47	17	20	6	174	1261	87.9	15.07
Tim Bernhardt, Toronto	1	0	0	0	3	4	57.1	6.67
Daniel Berthiaume, Winnipeg	31	18	7	3	93	716	88.5	18.90
Allan Bester, Toronto	36	10	14	3	110	878	88.9	16.44
Craig Billington, New Jersey	22	4	13	2	89	480	84.4	12.52
Richard Brodeur, Vancouver	53	20	25	5	178	1210	87.2	16.70
Frank Caprice, Vancouver	25	8	11	2	89	552	86.1	15.62
Alain Chevrier, New Jersey	58	24	26	2	227	1563	87.3	13.89
Jacques Cloutier, Buffalo	40	11	19	5	137	897	86.8	15.82
Doug Dadswell, Calgary	2	0	1	1	10	62	86.1	12.50
Cleon Daskalakis, Boston	2	2	0	0	7	44	86.3	13.86
Darren Eliot, Los Angeles	24	8	13	2	103	584	85.0	13.63
Karl Friesen, New Jersey	4	0	2	1	16	64	80.0	8.13
Bob Froese, Philadelphia	3	3	0	0	8	80	90.9	22.50
N.Y. Rangers	28	14	11	0	92	691	88.3	16.02
Totals	31	17	11	0	100	771	88.5	16.54
Grant Fuhr, Edmonton	44	22	13	3	137	1011	88.1	17.43
Troy Gamble, Vancouver	1	0	1	0	4	18	81.8	15.00
Mario Gosselin, Quebec	30	13	11	1	86	669	88.6	18.90
Steve Guenette, Pittsburgh	2	0	2	0	8	44	84.6	14.13
Glen Hanlon, Detroit	36	11	16	5	104	869	89.3	18.88
Brian Hayward, Montreal	37	19	13	4	102	855	89.3	21.35
Ron Hextall, Philadelphia	66	37	21	6	190	1739	90.2	19.99
Kelly Hrudey, N.Y. Islanders	46	21	15	7	145	1073	88.1	18.17
Bob Janecyk, Los Angeles	7	4	3	0	34	188	84.7	12.35
Al Jensen, Washington	6	1	3	1	27	156	85.2	12.15
Los Angeles	5	1	4	0	27	126	82.4	11.11
Totals	11	2	7	1	54	282	83.9	11.63
Doug Keans, Boston	36	18	8	4	108	800	88.1	17.98
Mark Laforest, Detroit	5	2	1	0	12	99	89.2	18.25
Rejean Lemelin, Calgary	34	16	9	1	94	727	88.6	18.46
Mike Liut, Hartford	59	31	22	5	187	1435	88.5	18.59
Clint Malarchuk, Quebec	54	18	26	9	175	1336	88.4	17.67
Bob Mason, Washington	45	20	18	5	137	1107	89.0	18.51
Kirk McLean, New Jersey	4	1	1	0	10	62	86.1	16.00
Roland Melanson, Los Angeles	46	18	21	6	168	1249	88.1	16.27
Gilles Meloche, Pittsburgh	43	13	19	7	134	986	88.0	17.49
Greg Millen, St. Louis	42	15	18	9	146	1003	87.3	17.00
Andy Moog, Edmonton	46	28	11	3	144	1072	88.2	17.09
Pete Peeters, Washington	37	17	11	4	107	821	88.5	18.71
Steve Penney, Winnipeg	7	1	4	1	25	108	81.2	13.08
Daren Puppa, Buffalo	3	0	2	1	13	66	83.5	14.23
Bill Ranford, Boston	41	16	20	2	124	1012	89.1	18.02
Eldon Reddick, Winnipeg	48	21	21	4	149	1105	88.1	18.54
Glenn Resch, Philadelphia	17	6	5	2	42	393	90.3	20.64
Pat Riggin, Boston	10	3	5	1	29	207	87.7	17.69
Pittsburgh	17	8	6	3	55	410	88.2	17.96
Totals	27	11	11	4	84	617	88.0	17.87
Roberto Romano, Pittsburgh	25	9	11	2	87	625	87.8	16.53
Boston	1	0	1	0	6	28	82.4	10.00
Totals	26	9	12	2	93	653	87.5	16.11
Patrick Roy, Montreal	46	22	16	6	131	1073	89.1	20.50
Sam St. Laurent, Detroit	6	1	2	2	16	119	88.1	21.38
Mike Sands, Minnesota	3	0	2	0	12	91	88.3	13.58
Bob Sauve, Chicago	46	19	19	5	159	1338	89.4	16.73
Ron Scott, N.Y. Rangers	1	0	0	1	5	30	85.7	13.00
Richard Sevigny, Quebec	4	0	2	0	11	45	80.4	13.09
Warren Skorodenski, Chicago	3	1	0	1	7	83	92.2	22.14
Billy Smith, N.Y. Islanders	40	14	18	5	132	872	86.9	17.06
Doug Soetaert, N.Y. Rangers	13	2	7	2	58	309	84.2	11.64
Greg Stefan, Detroit	43	20	17	3	135	943	87.5	17.41
Kari Takko, Minnesota	38	13	18	4	119	938	88.7	17.44
Chris Terreri, New Jersey	7	0	3	1	21	151	87.8	13.62
John Vanbiesbrouck, N.Y. Rangers	50	18	20	5	161	1202	88.2	16.50
Mike Vernon, Calgary	54	30	21	1	178	1348	88.3	16.61
Rick Wamsley, St. Louis	41	17	15	6	142	1068	88.3	16.97

	Games	W.	L.	T.	Goals	Saves	Sv. Pct.	Goal Interval
Steve Weeks, Hartford	25	12	8	2	78	535	87.3	17.53
Ken Wregget, Toronto	56	22	28	3	200	1395	87.5	15.13
Wendell Young, Vancouver..................................	8	1	6	1	35	187	84.2	12.00

NOTE: Goals Interval is the average amount of time between goals allowed. Empty Net Goals are not counted.

Goaltending Departmental Leaders

Games Played
1. Ron Hextall, Philadelphia.. 66
2. Mike Liut, Hartford 59
3. Alain Chevrier, New Jersey 58
4. Ken Wregget, Toronto.. 56
5. Clint Malarchuk, Quebec 54
   Mike Vernon, Calgary.. 54

Games Won Leaders
1. Ron Hextall, Philadelphia.. 37
2. Mike Liut, Hartford 31
3. Mike Vernon, Calgary.. 30
4. Andy Moog, Edmonton 28
5. Alain Chevrier, New Jersey 24

Games Lost Leaders
1. Ken Wregget, Toronto.. 28
2. Clint Malarchuk, Quebec 26
   Alain Chevrier, New Jersey 26
4. Richard Brodeur, Vancouver 25
5. Tom Barrasso, Buffalo.. 23

Goals Allowed Leaders
1. Alain Chevrier, New Jersey 227
2. Ken Wregget, Toronto.. 200
3. Ron Hextall, Philadelphia....................................... 190
4. Mike Liut, Hartford 187
5. Richard Brodeur, Vancouver 178
   Mike Vernon, Calgary.. 178

Save Leaders
1. Ron Hextall, Philadelphia....................................... 1739
2. Alain Chevrier, New Jersey 1563
3. Mike Liut, Hartford 1435
4. Ken Wregget, Toronto.. 1395
5. Mike Vernon, Calgary.. 1348

Save Percentage Leaders
1. Warren Skorodenski, Chicago 92.2
2. Bob Froese, Philadelphia....................................... 90.9
3. Glenn Resch, Philadelphia 90.3
4. Ron Hextall, Philadelphia....................................... 90.2
5. Bob Sauve, Chicago 89.4

Goal Interval Leaders
1. Bob Froese, Philadelphia....................................... 22.50
2. Warren Skorodenski, Chicago 22.14
3. Sam St. Laurent, Detroit....................................... 21.38
4. Brian Hayward, Montreal 21.35
5. Glenn Resch, Philadelphia 20.64

Minutes Played
1. Ron Hextall, Philadelphia....................................... 3799
2. Mike Liut, Hartford 3476
3. Alain Chevrier, New Jersey 3153
4. Clint Malarchuk, Quebec 3092
5. Ken Wregget, Toronto.. 3026

Goals-Against Average
1. Bob Froese, Philadelphia....................................... 2.67
2. Warren Skorodenski, Chicago 2.71
3. Sam St. Laurent, Detroit....................................... 2.81
   Brian Hayward, Montreal 2.81
5. Glenn Resch, Philadelphia 2.91

Shutouts
1. Mike Liut, Hartford 4
2. Bill Ranford, Boston 3
3. Rejean Lemelin, Calgary... 2
   Allan Bester, Toronto 2
   Tom Barrasso, Buffalo.. 2

1987 Stanley Cup Playoffs

Top 10 Playoff Scoring Leaders

	Games	G.	A.	Pts.	Pen.
1. Wayne Gretzky, Edmonton	21	5	*29	*34	6
2. Mark Messier, Edmonton	21	12	16	28	16
Brian Propp, Philadelphia	26	12	16	28	10
4. Glenn Anderson, Edmonton	21	14	13	27	59
Pelle Eklund, Philadelphia	26	7	20	27	2
6. Jari Kurri, Edmonton	21	*15	10	25	20
7. Mats Naslund, Montreal	17	7	15	22	11
8. Rick Tocchet, Philadelphia	26	11	10	21	72
9. Larry Robinson, Montreal	17	3	17	20	6
10. Ryan Walter, Montreal	17	7	12	19	10
Kent Nilsson, Edmonton	21	6	13	19	6

*Indicates a league-leading figure.

Preliminary Rounds

(Division Semifinals)

(Best-of-seven Series)

ADAMS DIVISION

	W.	L.	Pts.	GF.	GA.
Quebec Nordiques	4	2	8	27	19
Hartford Whalers	2	4	4	19	27

(Quebec won Adams Division semifinals, 4-2)

Wed. April 8—Quebec 2, at Hartford 3 (a)
Thur. April 9—Quebec 4, at Hartford 5
Sat. April 11—Hartford 1, at Quebec 5
Sun. April 12—Hartford 1, at Quebec 4
Tues. April 14—Quebec 7, at Hartford 5
Thur. April 16—Hartford 4, at Quebec 5 (b)

(a)—Paul MacDermid scored at 2:20 of overtime for Hartford.

(b)—Peter Stastny scored at 6:05 of overtime for Quebec.

	W.	L.	Pts.	GF.	GA.
Montreal Canadiens	4	0	8	19	11
Boston Bruins	0	4	0	11	19

(Montreal won Adams Division semifinal, 4-0)

Wed. April 8—Boston 2, at Montreal 6
Thur. April 9—Boston 3, at Montreal 4 (c)
Sat. April 11—Montreal 5, at Boston 4
Sun. April 12—Montreal 4, at Boston 2

(c)—Mats Naslund scored at 2:38 of overtime for Montreal.

PATRICK DIVISION

	W.	L.	Pts.	GF.	GA.
Philadelphia Flyers	4	2	8	22	13
New York Rangers	2	4	4	13	22

(Philadelphia won Patrick Division semifinal, 4-2)

Wed. April 8—N.Y. Rangers 3, at Philadelphia 3
Thur. April 9—N.Y. Rangers 3, at Philadelphia 8
Sat. April 11—Philadelphia 3, at N.Y. Rangers 0
Sun. April 12—Philadelphia 3, at N.Y. Rangers 6
Tues. April 14—N.Y. Rangers 1, at Philadelphia 3
Thur. April 16—Philadelphia 5, at N.Y. Rangers 0

	W.	L.	Pts.	GF.	GA.
New York Islanders	4	3	8	19	19
Washington Capitals	3	4	6	19	19

(New York Islanders won Patrick Division semifinal, 4-3)

Wed. April 8—N.Y. Islanders 3, at Washington 4
Thur. April 9—N.Y. Islanders 3, at Washington 1
Sat. April 11—Washington 2, at N.Y. Islanders 0
Sun. April 12—Washington 4, at N.Y. Islanders 1
Tues. April 14—N.Y. Islanders 4, at Washington 2
Thur. April 16—Washington 4, at N.Y. Islanders 5
Sat. April 18—N.Y. Islanders 3, at Washington 2 (d)

(d)—Pat LaFontaine scored at 8:47 of fourth overtime for New York.

NORRIS DIVISION

	W.	L.	Pts.	GF.	GA.
Toronto Maple Leafs	4	2	8	15	12
St. Louis Blues	2	4	4	12	15

(Toronto won Norris Division semifinal, 4-2)

Wed. April 8—Toronto 1, at St. Louis 3
Thur. April 9—Toronto 3, at St. Louis 2 (e)
Sat. April 11—St. Louis 5, at Toronto 3
Sun. April 12—St. Louis 1, at Toronto 2
Tues. April 14—Toronto 2, at St. Louis 1
Thur. April 16—St. Louis 0, at Toronto 4

(e)—Rick Lanz scored at 10:17 of overtime for Toronto.

	W.	L.	Pts.	GF.	GA.
Detroit Red Wings	4	0	8	15	6
Chicago Black Hawks	0	4	0	6	15

(Detroit won Norris Division semifinal, 4-0)

Wed. April 8—Chicago 1, at Detroit 3
Thur. April 9—Chicago 1, at Detroit 5
Sat. April 11—Detroit 4, at Chicago 3 (f)
Sun. April 12—Detroit 3, at Chicago 1

(f)—Shawn Burr scored at 4:51 of overtime for Detroit.

	W.	L.	Pts.	GF.	GA.		W.	L.	Pts.	GF.	GA.
Edmonton Oilers	4	1	8	32	20	Winnipeg Jets	4	2	8	22	15
Los Angeles Kings	1	4	2	20	32	Calgary Flames	2	4	4	15	22

(Edmonton won Smythe Division semifinal, 4-1)
Wed. April 8—Los Angeles 5, at Edmonton 2
Thur. April 9—Los Angeles 3, at Edmonton 13
Sat. April 11—Edmonton 6, at Los Angeles 5
Sun. April 12—Edmonton 6, at Los Angeles 3
Tues. April 14—Los Angeles 4, at Edmonton 5

(Winnipeg won Smythe Division semifinal, 4-2)
Wed. April 8—Winnipeg 4, at Calgary 2
Thur. April 9—Winnipeg 3, at Calgary 2
Sat. April 11—Calgary 3, at Winnipeg 2 (g)
Sun. April 12—Calgary 3, at Winnipeg 4
Tues. April 14—Winnipeg 3, at Calgary 4
Thur. April 16—Calgary 1, at Winnipeg 6
(g)—Mike Bullard scored at 3:53 of overtime for Calgary.

Quarterfinal Rounds
(Division Finals)
(Best-of-seven Series)

ADAMS DIVISION

	W.	L.	Pts.	GF.	GA.
Montreal Canadiens	4	3	8	26	21
Quebec Nordiques	3	4	6	21	26

(Montreal won Division final, 4-3)
Mon. April 20—Quebec 7, at Montreal 5
Wed. April 22—Quebec 2, at Montreal 1
Fri. April 24—Montreal 7, at Quebec 2
Sun. April 26—Montreal 3, at Quebec 2 (h)
Tues. April 28—Quebec 2, at Montreal 3
Thur. April 30—Montreal 2, at Quebec 3
Sat. May 2—Quebec 3, at Montreal 5
(h)—Mats Naslund scored at 5:30 of overtime for Montreal.

NORRIS DIVISION

	W.	L.	Pts.	GF.	GA.
Detroit Red Wings	4	3	8	20	18
Toronto Maple Leafs	3	4	6	18	20

(Detroit won Division final, 4-3)
Tues. April 21—Toronto 4, at Detroit 2
Thur. April 23—Toronto 7, at Detroit 2
Sat. April 25—Detroit 4, at Toronto 2
Mon. April 27—Detroit 2, at Toronto 3(i)
Wed. April 29—Toronto 0, at Detroit 3
Fri. May 1—Detroit 4, at Toronto 2
Sun. May 3—Toronto 0, at Detroit 3
(i)—Mike Allison scored at 9:31 of overtime for Toronto.

PATRICK DIVISION

	W.	L.	Pts.	GF.	GA.
Philadelphia Flyers	4	3	8	23	16
New York Islanders	3	4	6	16	23

(Philadelphia won Division final, 4-3)
Mon. April 20—N.Y. Islanders 2, at Philadelphia 4
Wed. April 22—N.Y. Islanders 2, at Philadelphia 1
Fri. April 24—Philadelphia 4, at N.Y. Islanders 1
Sun. April 26—Philadelphia 6, at N.Y. Islanders 4
Tues. April 28—N.Y. Islanders 2, at Philadelphia 1
Thur. April 30—Philadelphia 2, at N.Y. Islanders 4
Sat. May 2—N.Y. Islanders 1, at Philadelphia 5

SMYTHE DIVISION

	W.	L.	Pts.	GF.	GA.
Edmonton Oilers	4	0	8	17	9
Winnipeg Jets	0	4	0	9	17

(Edmonton won Division final, 4-0)
Tues. April 21—Winnipeg 2, at Edmonton 3(j)
Thur. April 23—Winnipeg 3, at Edmonton 5
Sat. April 25—Edmonton 5, at Winnipeg 2
Mon. April 27—Edmonton 4, at Winnipeg 2
(i)—Glenn Anderson scored at 0:36 of overtime for Edmonton.

Semifinal Rounds
(Conference Championships)
(Best-of-seven series)

PRINCE OF WALES CONFERENCE

	W.	L.	Pts.	GF.	GA.
Philadelphia Flyers	4	2	8	22	22
Montreal Canadiens	2	4	4	22	22

(Philadelphia won Conference Title, 4-2)
Mon. May 4—Montreal 3, at Philadelphia 4(k)
Wed. May 6—Montreal 5, at Philadelphia 2
Fri. May 8—Philadelphia 4, Montreal 3
Sun. May 10—Philadelphia 6, at Montreal 3
Tues. May 12—Montreal 5, at Philadelphia 2
Thur. May 14—Philadelphia 4, at Montreal 3
(k)—Ilkka Sinisalo scored at 9:11 of overtime for Philadelphia.

CLARENCE CAMPBELL CONFERENCE

	W.	L.	Pts.	GF.	GA.
Edmonton Oilers	4	1	8	16	10
Detroit Red Wings	1	4	2	10	16

(Edmonton won Conference Title, 4-1)
Tues. May 5—Detroit 3, at Edmonton 1
Thur. May 7—Detroit 1, at Edmonton 4
Sat. May 9—Edmonton 2, at Detroit 1
Mon. May 11—Edmonton 3, at Detroit 2
Wed. May 13—Detroit 3, at Edmonton 6

Finals for the Stanley Cup

(Best-of-seven series)

	W.	L.	Pts.	GF.	GA.
Edmonton Oilers............	4	3	8	22	18
Philadelphia Flyers	3	4	6	18	22

(Edmonton Oilers won Stanley Cup
Championship Series, 4-7)

Sun. May 17—Philadelphia 2, at Edmonton 4
Wed. May 20—Philadelphia 2, at Edmonton 3(I)

Fri.   May 22—Edmonton 3, at Philadelphia 5
Sun. May 24—Edmonton 4, at Philadelphia 1
Tues. May 26—Philadelphia 4, at Edmonton 3
Thur. May 28—Edmonton 2, at Philadelphia 3
Sun. May 31—Philadelphia 1, at Edmonton 3
(I)—Jari Kurri scored at 6:50 of overtime for Edmonton.

Game 1—Sunday, May 17 at Edmonton (Edmonton won, 4-2)

Philadelphia.................0	1	1—2
Edmonton.................. 1	0	3—4

FIRST PERIOD: 1. Edmonton, Gretzky (Kurri, Lowe) 15:06. Penalties: Philadelphia bench (served by Nachbaur) 4:21; Brown, Philadelphia, major 17:42; Buchberger, Edmonton, major 17:42.

SECOND PERIOD: 2. Philadelphia, Propp (Tocchet, Eklund) 16:08. Penalties: Krushelnyski, Edmonton 3:57; McCrimmon, Philadelphia 17:56.

THIRD PERIOD: 3. Edmonton, Anderson (Messier) 0:48; 4. Edmonton, Coffey (Gretzky, Kurri) 7:09; 5. Edmonton, Kurri (Messier, Coffey) 9:11; 6. Philadelphia, Tocchet (Marsh, Eklund) 10:18. Penalties: Tocchet, Philadelphia 13:21; Lowe, Edmonton 13.21.

Shots Against:

Hextall (Philadelphia)..10	8	8 — 26
Fuhr (Edmonton)...10	10	11 — 31

Attendance: 17,502.

Game 2—Wednesday, May 20 at Edmonton (Edmonton won, 3-2)

Philadelphia.................0	2	0	0—2
Edmonton.....................0	1	1	1—3

FIRST PERIOD: No scoring. Penalties: Brown, Philadelphia 2:38; Coffey, Edmonton 8:38; D. Smith, Philadelphia 16:58; Philadelphia bench (served by Carson) 19:52; McCrimmon, Philadelphia 20:00.

SECOND PERIOD: 1. Edmonton, Gretzky (Kurri, Coffey) PPG 0:45; 2. Philadelphia, D. Smith (Mellanby, Sutter) 13:20; 3. Philadelphia, Propp (Tocchet, McCrimmon) 16:23. Penalties: MacTavish, Edmonton 2:59; Samuelsson, Philadelphia 6:21; S. Smith, Edmonton 6:21; Mellanby, Philadelphia 9:08; Coffey, Edmonton 9:08; S. Smith, Edmonton 10:37; Tocchet, Philadelphia 19:25; McSorley, Edmonton 19:25.

THIRD PERIOD: 4. Edmonton, Anderson (Gregg) 11:40. Penalties: Crossman, Philadelphia 12:17; Kurri, Edmonton 16:30.

OVERTIME: 5. Edmonton, Kurri (Coffey, Gretzky) 6:50. Penalties: Craven, Philadelphia 3:16; Anderson, Edmonton 3:16.

Shots Against:

Hextall (Philadelphia)...................................... 9	7	15	3 — 34
Fuhr (Edmonton)..15	12	5	2 — 34

Attendance: 17,502

Game 3—Friday, May 22 at Philadelphia (Philadelphia won, 5-3)

Edmonton.....................2	1	0—3
Philadelphia............... 0	2	3—5

FIRST PERIOD: 1. Edmonton, Messier (MacTavish) SHG 4:14; 2. Edmonton, Coffey (Gretzky, Kurri) 19:51. Penalties: Hunter, Edmonton 2:36; Stanley, Philadelphia 9:47; Krushelnyski, Edmonton 14:04; D. Smith, Philadelphia 17:36.

SECOND PERIOD: 3. Edmonton, Anderson (Messier, Coffey) PPG 1:49; 4. Philadelphia, Craven (Tocchet, Sutter) PPG 9:04; 5. Philadelphia, Zezel (unassisted) PPG 15:20. Penalties: Hextall, Philadelphia (served by Tocchet) 1:12; Edmonton bench (served by Tikkanen) 7:58; Ruotsalainen, Edmonton 11:23; Tikkanen, Edmonton 14:52; Sutter, Philadelphia 17:49.

THIRD PERIOD: 6. Philadelphia, Mellanby (Howe, Sutter) 4:37; 7. Philadelphia, McCrimmon (Mellanby, Sutter) 4:54; 8. Philadelphia, Propp (Samuelsson, Zezel) ENG 19:26. Penalties: McSorley, Edmonton 19:59; Sutter, Philadelphia 17:49.

Shots Against:

Fuhr (Edmonton)...11	14	11 — 36
Hextall (Philadelphia)..8	10	10 — 28

Attendance: 17,222.

Game 4—Sunday, May 24 at Philadelphia (Edmonton won, 4-1)

Edmonton.....................2	1	1—4
Philadelphia............... 0	1	0—1

FIRST PERIOD: 1. Edmonton, Kurri (Gretzky) 5:53; 2. Edmonton, Lowe (Gretzky) SHG 18:44. Penalties: Tikkanen, Edmonton 1:16; D. Smith, Philadelphia 1:16; Lowe, Edmonton 3:32; McCrimmon, Philadelphia 9:35; MacTavish, Edmonton 12:42; Messier, Edmonton 17:28.

SECOND PERIOD: 3. Philadelphia, McCrimmon (Eklund, Propp) PPG 8:17; 4. Edmonton, Gregg (Gretzky) PPG 12:31. Penalties: Gretzky, Edmonton 6:34; Samuelsson, Philadelphia 10:38; Zezel, Philadelphia 13:59; Coffey, Edmonton 19:45; Tocchet, Philadelphia 19:45.

THIRD PERIOD: 5. Edmonton, Krushelnyski (unassisted) 4:17. Penalties: Anderson, Edmonton 1:01; Hextall, Philadelphia (served by Daigneault), misconduct 4:31; Huddy, Edmonton, misconduct 7:39; Tocchet, Philadelphia, misconduct 7:39; Hextall, Philadelphia (served by Mellanby), major 8:50.

Shots Against:

Fuhr (Edmonton)..8	11	9 — 28	
Hextall (Philadelphia)...8	10	11 — 29	

Attendance: 17,222.

Game 5—Tuesday, May 26 at Edmonton (Philadelphia won, 4-3)

Philadelphia............................... 1	2	1—4	
Edmonton.................................. 2	1	0—3	

FIRST PERIOD: 1. Edmonton, Kurri (Gregg, Krushelnyski) PPG 2:58; 2. Edmonton, McSorley (Gretzky) 6:39; 3. Philadelphia, Tocchet (Propp, Eklund) 19:10. Penalties: Tocchet, Philadelphia 2:23; Coffey, Edmonton 2:23; Brown, Philadelphia 2:49; Samuelsson, Philadelphia 10:52; Pouzar, Edmonton 15:10.

SECOND PERIOD: 4. Edmonton, McSorley (Huddy, Pouzar) 1:32; 5. Philadelphia, Crossman (Propp, Eklund) 8:08; 6. Philadelphia, Eklund (Propp, Tocchet) PPG 12:40. Penalties: Messier, Edmonton 12:10; Sutter, Philadelphia 12:48; Krushelnyski, Edmonton 12:48; D. Smith, Philadelphia 18:39; Kurri, Edmonton 18:39.

THIRD PERIOD: 7. Philadelphia, Tocchet, (Propp) 5:26. Penalties: D. Smith, Philadelphia 6:11; Ruotsalainen, Edmonton 6:11.

Shots Against:

Hextall (Philadelphia)...16	10	8 — 34	
Fuhr (Edmonton)..16	6	13 — 35	

Attendance: 17,502.

Game 6—Thursday, May 28 at Philadelphia (Philadelphia won, 3-2)

Edmonton.................................. 2	0	0—2	
Philadelphia............................... 0	1	2—3	

FIRST PERIOD: 1. Edmonton, Lowe (Gretzky, Kurri) SHG 5:08; 2. Edmonton, McClelland (MacTavish, Muni) 15:16. Penalties: McSorley, Edmonton 2:15; Tocchet, Philadelphia 2:15; Hunter, Edmonton 3:22; Coffey, Edmonton 6:04; Poulin, Philadelphia 6:04; McClelland, Edmonton, double minor 8:45; Tocchet, Philadelphia 8:45; Anderson, Edmonton 12:39; Samuelsson, Philadelphia 12:39; Poulin, Philadelphia 15:19; Samuelsson, Philadelphia 20:00; Anderson, Edmonton 20:00.

SECOND PERIOD: 3. Philadelphia, Carson (Brown, Marsh) 7:12. Penalties: Coffey, Edmonton 1:41; Anderson, Edmonton, double minor 9:06; McCrimmon, Philadelphia, double minor 9:06; Crossman, Philadelphia 9:48; McSorley, Edmonton 15:12.

THIRD PERIOD: 4. Philadelphia, Propp (Eklund, Crossman) PPG 13:04; 5. Philadelphia, Daigneault (unassisted) 14:28. Penalties: Messier, Edmonton 0:09; Anderson, Edmonton 12:21.

Shots Against:

Fuhr (Edmonton).. 5	8	10 — 23	
Hextall (Philadelphia)...15	9	8 — 32	

Attendance: 17,222.

Game 7—Sunday, May 31 at Edmonton (Edmonton won, 3-1)

Philadelphia............................... 1	0	0—1	
Edmonton.................................. 1	1	1—3	

FIRST PERIOD: 1. Philadelphia, Craven (Eklund, Crossman) PPG 1:41; 2. Edmonton, Messier (Nilsson, Anderson) 7:45. Penalties: Messier, Edmonton 0:34 Coffey, Edmonton 1:13; Poulin, Philadelphia 4:22.

SECOND PERIOD: 3. Edmonton, Kurri (Gretzky) 14:59. Penalties: Sinisalo, Philadelphia 3:39; Marsh, Philadelphia 12:15; Mellanby, Philadelphia 15:27; S. Smith, Edmonton 15:27; Messier, Edmonton 16:02.

THIRD PERIOD: 4. Edmonton, Anderson (Huddy) 17:36. Penalties: Hextall, Philadelphia (served by Eklund) 4:31; Tocchet, Philadelphia 4:31; McSorley, Edmonton 4:31; MacTavish, Edmonton 4:31; Crossman, Philadelphia 14:16; Tikkanen, Edmonton 14:16.

Shots Against:

Hextall (Philadelphia)...18	13	12 — 43	
Fuhr (Edmonton)..12	6	2 — 20	

Attendance: 17,502.

Team-by-Team Playoff Scoring

Boston Bruins
(Lost Adams Division semifinals to Montreal, 4-0)

	Games	G.	A.	Pts.	Pen.
Cam Neely	4	5	1	6	8
Rick Middleton	4	2	2	4	0
Thomas Gradin	4	0	4	4	0
Ray Bourque	4	1	2	3	0
Ken Linseman	4	1	1	2	22
Tom McCarthy	4	1	1	2	4
Steve Kasper	3	0	2	2	0
Reed Larson	4	0	2	2	2
Randy Burridge	2	1	0	1	2
Keith Crowder	4	0	1	1	4
Lyndon Byers	1	0	0	0	0
Geoff Courtnall	1	0	0	0	0
Charlie Simmer	1	0	0	0	2
Doug Keans (Goalie)	2	0	0	0	4
Bill Ranford (Goalie)	2	0	0	0	0
Dave Reid	2	0	0	0	0
Dwight Foster	3	0	0	0	0
Robert Sweeney	3	0	0	0	0
Wade Campbell	4	0	0	0	11
Greg Johnston	4	0	0	0	0
Nevin Markwart	4	0	0	0	9
Mike Milbury	4	0	0	0	4
Allen Pedersen	4	0	0	0	4
Frank Simonetti	4	0	0	0	6

Calgary Flames
(Lost Smythe Division semifinals to Winnipeg, 4-2)

	Games	G.	A.	Pts.	Pen.
Mike Bullard	6	4	2	6	2
Joe Nieuwendyk	6	2	2	4	0
Brett Hull	4	2	1	3	0
Joe Mullen	6	2	1	3	0
Hakan Loob	5	1	2	3	0
Gary Suter	6	0	3	3	10
Carey Wilson	6	1	1	2	6
Perry Berezan	2	0	2	2	7
Joel Otto	2	0	2	2	6
Kari Eloranta	6	0	2	2	0
Colin Patterson	6	0	2	2	2
Steve Bozek	4	1	0	1	2
Al MacInnis	4	1	0	1	0
Jim Peplinski	6	1	0	1	24
Rejean Lemelin (Goalie)	2	0	1	1	0
Jamie Macoun	3	0	1	1	8
Kevan Guy	4	0	1	1	23
Paul Reinhart	4	0	1	1	6
Doug Risebrough	4	0	1	1	2
Paul Baxter	2	0	0	0	10
Gary Roberts	2	0	0	0	4
John Tonelli	3	0	0	0	4
Lanny McDonald	5	0	0	0	2
Mike Vernon (Goalie)	5	0	0	0	0
Tim Hunter	6	0	0	0	51
Neil Sheehy	6	0	0	0	21

Chicago Black Hawks
(Lost Norris Division semifinals to Detroit, 4-0)

	Games	G.	A.	Pts.	Pen.
Curt Fraser	2	1	1	2	10
Ed Olczyk	4	1	1	2	4
Gary Nylund	4	0	2	2	11

	Games	G.	A.	Pts.	Pen.
Rich Preston	4	0	2	2	4
Marc Bergevin	3	1	0	1	2
Bob Murray	4	1	0	1	4
Wayne Presley	4	1	0	1	9
Denis Savard	4	1	0	1	12
Keith Brown	4	0	1	1	6
Bill Watson	4	0	1	1	0
Dave Donnelly	1	0	0	0	0
Jack O'Callahan	2	0	0	0	2
Darryl Sutter	2	0	0	0	0
Dave Manson	3	0	0	0	10
Dan Vincelette	3	0	0	0	0
Steve Larmer	4	0	0	0	2
Steve Ludzik	4	0	0	0	0
Troy Murray	4	0	0	0	5
Bob Sauve (Goalie)	4	0	0	0	0
Al Secord	4	0	0	0	21
Mike Stapleton	4	0	0	0	2
Doug Wilson	4	0	0	0	0

Detroit Red Wings
(Lost Campbell Conference finals to Edmonton, 4-1)

	Games	G.	A.	Pts.	Pen.
Steve Yzerman	16	5	13	18	8
Gerard Gallant	16	8	6	14	43
Brent Ashton	16	4	9	13	6
Adam Oates	16	4	7	11	6
Shawn Burr	16	7	2	9	20
Mel Bridgman	16	5	2	7	28
Darren Veitch	12	3	4	7	8
Bob Probert	16	3	4	7	63
Lee Norwood	16	1	6	7	31
Joey Kocur	16	2	3	5	71
Mike O'Connell	16	1	4	5	14
Dave Lewis	14	0	4	4	10
Petr Klima	13	1	2	3	4
Greg Stefan (Goalie)	9	0	2	2	0
Harold Snepsts	11	0	2	2	18
Gilbert Delorme	16	0	2	2	14
Dave Barr	13	1	0	1	14
Rick Zombo	7	0	1	1	9
Tim Higgins	12	0	1	1	16
Steve Chiasson	2	0	0	0	19
Jeff Sharples	2	0	0	0	2
Ric Seiling	7	0	0	0	5
Glen Hanlon (Goalie)	8	0	0	0	2
Mark Kumpel	8	0	0	0	4
Mark Lamb	11	0	0	0	11

Edmonton Oilers
(Winners of 1987 Stanley Cup Playoffs)

	Games	G.	A.	Pts.	Pen.
Wayne Gretzky	21	5	*29	*34	6
Mark Messier	21	12	16	28	16
Glenn Anderson	21	14	13	27	59
Jari Kurri	21	*15	10	25	20
Kent Nilsson	21	6	13	19	6
Paul Coffey	17	3	8	11	30
Craig MacTavish	21	1	9	10	16
Esa Tikkanen	21	7	2	9	22
Randy Gregg	18	3	6	9	17
Charlie Huddy	21	1	7	8	21
Marty McSorley	21	4	3	7	65

	Games	G.	A.	Pts.	Pen.
Mike Krushelnyski	21	3	4	7	18
Reijo Ruotsalainen	21	2	5	7	10
Dave Hunter	21	3	3	6	20
Kevin Lowe	21	2	4	6	22
Kevin McClelland	21	2	3	5	43
Steve Smith	15	1	3	4	45
Moe Lemay	9	2	1	3	11
Jaroslav Pouzar	5	1	1	2	2
Craig Muni	14	0	2	2	17
Grant Fuhr (Goalie)	19	0	1	1	0
Andy Moog (Goalie)	2	0	0	0	0
Kelly Buchberger	3	0	0	0	5
Wayne Van Dorp	3	0	0	0	2

Hartford Whalers
(Lost Adams Division semifinals to Quebec, 4-2)

	Games	G.	A.	Pts.	Pen.
Stewart Gavin	6	2	4	6	10
Dean Evason	5	3	2	5	35
Ron Francis	6	2	2	4	6
Scot Kleinendorst	4	1	3	4	20
Kevin Dineen	6	2	1	3	31
Paul MacDermid	6	2	1	3	34
Dana Murzyn	6	2	1	3	29
John Anderson	6	1	2	3	0
Sylvain Turgeon	6	1	2	3	4
Mike McEwen	1	1	1	2	0
Dave Babych	6	1	1	2	14
Ray Ferraro	6	1	1	2	8
Sylvain Cote	2	0	2	2	2
Paul Lawless	2	0	2	2	2
Randy Ladouceur	6	0	2	2	12
Dave Tippett	6	0	2	2	4
Ulf Samuelsson	5	0	1	1	41
Steve Weeks (Goalie)	1	0	0	0	0
Shane Churla	2	0	0	0	42
Pat Hughes	3	0	0	0	0
Dave Semenko	4	0	0	0	15
Doug Jarvis	6	0	0	0	4
Mike Liut (Goalie)	6	0	0	0	2
Joel Quenneville	6	0	0	0	0

Los Angeles Kings
(Lost Smythe Division semifinals to Edmonton, 4-1)

	Games	G.	A.	Pts.	Pen.
Bernie Nicholls	5	2	5	7	6
Jim Fox	5	3	2	5	0
Dave Williams	5	3	2	5	30
Dave Taylor	5	2	3	5	6
Luc Robitaille	5	1	4	5	2
Steve Duchesne	5	2	2	4	4
Bob Bourne	5	2	1	3	0
Bobby Carpenter	5	1	2	3	2
Jimmy Carson	5	1	2	3	6
Mark Hardy	5	1	2	3	10
Jay Wells	5	1	2	3	10
Bryan Erickson	3	1	1	2	0
Dean Kennedy	5	0	2	2	10
Sean McKenna	5	0	1	1	0
Phil Sykes	5	0	1	1	8
Darren Eliot (Goalie)	1	0	0	0	0
Paul Guay	2	0	0	0	0
Joe Paterson	2	0	0	0	0
Morris Lukowich	3	0	0	0	8
Tom Laidlaw	5	0	0	0	2
Grant Ledyard	5	0	0	0	10
Roland Melanson (G)	5	0	0	0	4

Montreal Canadiens
(Lost Prince of Wales Conference finals to Phila., 4-2)

	Games	G.	A.	Pts.	Pen.
Mats Naslund	17	7	15	22	11
Larry Robinson	17	3	17	20	6
Ryan Walter	17	7	12	19	10
Bobby Smith	17	9	9	18	19
Chris Chelios	17	4	9	13	38
Claude Lemieux	17	4	9	13	41
Shayne Corson	17	6	5	11	30
Guy Carbonneau	17	3	8	11	20
Mike McPhee	17	7	2	9	13
Kjell Dahlin	8	2	4	6	0
Brian Skrudland	14	1	5	6	29
Stephane Richer	5	3	2	5	0
Craig Ludwig	17	2	3	5	30
Petr Svoboda	14	0	5	5	10
Sergio Momesso	11	1	3	4	31
Bob Gainey	17	1	3	4	6
Rick Green	17	0	4	4	8
Chris Nilan	17	3	0	3	75
Mike Lalor	13	2	1	3	29
John Kordic	11	2	0	2	19
Gaston Gingras	5	0	2	2	0
Patrick Roy (Goalie)	6	0	0	0	0
Brian Hayward (Goalie)	13	0	0	0	2

New York Islanders
(Lost Patrick Division finals to Philadelphia, 4-3)

	Games	G.	A.	Pts.	Pen.
Bryan Trottier	14	8	5	13	12
Pat LaFontaine	14	5	7	12	10
Mikko Makela	11	2	4	6	8
Patrick Flatley	11	3	2	5	6
Mike Bossy	6	2	3	5	0
Tomas Jonsson	10	1	4	5	6
Alan Kerr	14	1	4	5	25
Steve Konroyd	14	1	4	5	10
Ken Leiter	11	0	5	5	6
Greg Gilbert	10	2	2	4	6
Denis Potvin	10	2	2	4	21
Ken Morrow	13	1	3	4	2
Randy Wood	13	1	3	4	14
Rich Kromm	14	1	3	4	4
Gord Dineen	7	0	4	4	4
Bob Bassen	14	1	2	3	21
Brad Lauer	6	2	0	2	4
Brent Sutter	5	1	0	1	4
Duane Sutter	14	1	0	1	26
Brad Dalgarno	1	0	1	1	0
Randy Boyd	4	0	1	1	6
Gerald Diduck	14	0	1	1	35
Billy Smith (Goalie)	2	0	0	0	0
Ari Haanpaa	6	0	0	0	10
Brian Curran	8	0	0	0	51
Dale Henry	8	0	0	0	2
Kelly Hrudey (Goalie)	14	0	0	0	0

New York Rangers
(Lost Patrick Division semifinals to Philadelphia, 4-2)

	Games	G.	A.	Pts.	Pen.
Pierre Larouche	6	3	2	5	4
Ron Greschner	6	0	5	5	0
Don Maloney	6	2	1	3	6
James Patrick	6	1	2	3	2
Tomas Sandstrom	6	1	2	3	20

	Games	G.	A.	Pts.	Pen.
Ron Duguay	6	2	0	2	4
Marcel Dionne	6	1	1	2	2
Jeff Jackson	6	1	1	2	16
Willie Huber	6	0	2	2	6
Jan Erixon	6	1	0	1	0
George McPhee	6	1	0	1	28
Kelly Kisio	4	0	1	1	2
Pat Price	6	0	1	1	27
Terry Carkner	1	0	0	0	0
Lucien DeBlois	2	0	0	0	2
Jay Caufield	3	0	0	0	12
Stu Kulak	3	0	0	0	2
Bob Froese (Goalie)	4	0	0	0	7
John Vanbiesbrouck (G.)	4	0	0	0	2
Curt Giles	5	0	0	0	6
Tony McKegney	6	0	0	0	12
Larry Melnyk	6	0	0	0	4
Walt Poddubny	6	0	0	0	8

Philadelphia Flyers

(Lost Stanley Cup finals to Edmonton, 4-3)

	Games	G.	A.	Pts.	Pen.
Brian Propp	26	12	16	28	10
Pelle Eklund	26	7	20	27	2
Rick Tocchet	26	11	10	21	72
Doug Crossman	26	4	14	18	31
Tim Kerr	12	8	5	13	2
Peter Zezel	25	3	10	13	10
Mark Howe	26	2	10	12	4
Derrick Smith	26	6	4	10	26
Scott Mellanby	24	5	5	10	46
Lindsay Carson	24	3	5	8	22
Brad McCrimmon	26	3	5	8	30
Ron Sutter	16	1	7	8	12
Brad Marsh	26	3	4	7	16
Ilkka Sinisalo	18	5	1	6	4
Dave Poulin	15	3	3	6	14
Murray Craven	12	3	1	4	9
Tim Tookey	10	1	3	4	2
Kjell Samuelsson	26	0	4	4	25
Al Hill	9	2	1	3	0
Dave Brown	26	1	2	3	59
Don Nachbaur	7	1	1	2	15
J.J. Daigneault	9	1	0	1	0
Ron Hextall (Goalie)	26	0	1	1	43
Glenn Resch (Goalie)	2	0	0	0	0
Greg Smyth	1	0	0	0	2
Mike Stothers	2	0	0	0	7
Craig Berube	5	0	0	0	17
Ed Hospodar	5	0	0	0	2
Darryl Stanley	13	0	0	0	9

Quebec Nordiques

(Lost Adams Division finals to Montreal, 4-3)

	Games	G.	A.	Pts.	Pen.
Peter Stastny	13	6	9	15	12
Michel Goulet	13	9	5	14	35
John Ogrodnick	13	9	4	13	6
Robert Picard	13	2	10	12	10
Anton Stastny	13	3	8	11	6
Risto Siltanen	13	1	9	10	8
Dale Hunter	13	1	7	8	56
Jeff Brown	13	3	3	6	2
Paul Gillis	13	2	4	6	65
Lane Lambert	13	2	4	6	30
Jason Lafreniere	12	1	5	6	2

	Games	G.	A.	Pts.	Pen.
Alain Cote	13	2	3	5	2
Randy Moller	13	1	4	5	23
Basil McRae	13	3	1	4	*99
Normand Rochefort	13	2	1	3	26
Mike Hough	9	0	3	3	26
Steven Finn	13	0	2	2	29
Mike Eagles	4	1	0	1	10
Greg Malone	1	0	0	0	0
Clint Malarchuk (Goalie)	3	0	0	0	0
Mario Gosselin (Goalie)	11	0	0	0	2
Gord Donnelly	13	0	0	0	53

St. Louis Blues

(Lost Norris Division semifinals to Toronto, 4-2)

	Games	G.	A.	Pts.	Pen.
Bernie Federko	6	3	3	6	18
Gino Cavallini	6	3	1	4	2
Doug Gilmour	6	2	2	4	16
Rob Ramage	6	2	2	4	21
Brian Benning	6	0	4	4	9
Mark Hunter	5	0	3	3	10
Bruce Bell	4	1	1	2	7
Greg Paslawski	6	1	1	2	4
Cliff Ronning	4	0	1	1	0
Jocelyn Lemieux	5	0	1	1	6
Mark Reeds	6	0	1	1	2
Jim Pavese	2	0	0	0	2
Rick Wamsley (Goalie)	2	0	0	0	0
Tony Hrkac	3	0	0	0	0
Todd Ewen	4	0	0	0	23
Greg Millen (Goalie)	4	0	0	0	0
Herb Raglan	4	0	0	0	2
Doug Evans	5	0	0	0	10
Tim Bothwell	6	0	0	0	6
Charles Bourgeois	6	0	0	0	27
Rick Meagher	6	0	0	0	11
Ric Nattress	6	0	0	0	2
Doug Wickenheiser	6	0	0	0	2

Toronto Maple Leafs

(Lost Norris Division finals to Detroit, 4-3)

	Games	G.	A.	Pts.	Pen.
Wendel Clark	13	6	5	11	38
Mike Allison	13	3	5	8	15
Dan Daoust	13	5	2	7	42
Russ Courtnall	13	3	4	7	11
Rick Vaive	13	4	2	6	23
Peter Ihnacak	13	2	4	6	9
Vincent Damphousse	12	1	5	6	8
Steve Thomas	13	2	3	5	13
Todd Gill	13	2	2	4	42
Mark Osborne	9	1	3	4	6
Al Iafrate	13	1	3	4	11
Rick Lanz	13	1	3	4	27
Borje Salming	13	0	3	3	14
Brad Smith	11	1	1	2	24
Greg Terrion	13	0	2	2	14
Bill Root	13	1	0	1	12
Tom Fergus	2	0	1	1	2
Gary Leeman	5	0	1	1	14
Ken Wregget (Goalie)	13	0	1	1	4
Allan Bester (Goalie)	1	0	0	0	0
Daryl Evans	1	0	0	0	0
Miroslav Ihnacak	1	0	0	0	0
Kevin Maguire	1	0	0	0	0
Wes Jarvis	2	0	0	0	2

	Games	G.	A.	Pts.	Pen.
Terry Johnson	2	0	0	0	0
Bob McGill	4	0	0	0	0
Ken Yaremchuk	6	0	0	0	0
Chris Kotsopoulos	7	0	0	0	14

	Games	G.	A.	Pts.	Pen.
Dave Jensen	7	0	0	0	2
Greg Smith	7	0	0	0	11

Washington Capitals
(Lost Patrick Division semifinals to N.Y. Islanders, 4-3)

	Games	G.	A.	Pts.	Pen.
Mike Gartner	7	4	3	7	14
Scott Stevens	7	0	5	5	19
Kelly Miller	7	2	2	4	0
Larry Murphy	7	2	2	4	6
Greg Adams	7	1	3	4	38
Dave Christian	7	1	3	4	6
Gaetan Duchesne	7	3	0	3	14
Mike Ridley	7	2	1	3	6
Alan Haworth	6	0	3	3	7
Bob Gould	7	0	3	3	8
Michal Pivonka	7	1	1	2	2
Grant Martin	1	1	0	1	2
Ed Kastelic	5	1	0	1	13
Kevin Hatcher	7	1	0	1	20
John Blum	6	0	1	1	4
Rod Langway	7	0	1	1	2
Craig Laughlin	1	0	0	0	0
Garry Galley	2	0	0	0	0
Pete Peeters (Goalie)	3	0	0	0	2
Bob Mason (Goalie)	4	0	0	0	0
Lou Franceschetti	7	0	0	0	23

Winnipeg Jets
(Lost Smythe Division finals to Edmonton, 4-0)

	Games	G.	A.	Pts.	Pen.
Dale Hawerchuk	10	5	8	13	4
Dave Ellett	10	0	8	8	2
Paul MacLean	10	5	2	7	16
Thomas Steen	10	3	4	7	8
Brian Mullen	9	4	2	6	0
Randy Carlyle	10	1	5	6	18
Laurie Boschman	10	2	3	5	32
Fredrick Olausson	10	2	3	5	4
Doug Smail	10	4	0	4	10
Marois Marios	10	1	3	4	23
Jim Kyte	10	0	4	4	36
Ron Wilson	10	1	2	3	0
Gilles Hamel	8	2	0	2	2
Ray Neufeld	8	1	1	2	30
Iain Duncan	7	0	2	2	6
Andrew McBain	9	0	2	2	10
Brad Berry	7	0	1	1	14
Perry Turnbull	1	0	0	0	10
Jim Nill	3	0	0	0	7
Eldon Reddick (Goalie)	3	0	0	0	0
Daniel Berthiaume (G.)	8	0	0	0	0
Steve Rooney	8	0	0	0	34
Tim Watters	10	0	0	0	21

Complete Stanley Cup Goaltending

	Games	Mins.	Goals	SO.	Avg.
Bob Mason	4	309	9	1	1.75
Pete Peeters	3	180	9(1)	0	3.00
Washington Totals	7	489	19	1	2.33
Allan Bester	1	39	1	0	1.54
Ken Wregget	13	761	29(2)	1	*2.29
Toronto Totals	13	800	32	1	2.40
Greg Millen	4	250	10	0	2.40
Rick Wamsley	2	120	5	0	2.50
St. Louis Totals	6	370	15	0	2.43
Glen Hanlon	8	467	13	*2	1.67
Greg Stefan	9	508	24(3)	0	2.83
Detroit Totals	16	975	40	2	2.46
Grant Fuhr	19	1148	47(2)	0	2.46
Andy Moog	2	120	8	0	4.00
Edmonton Totals	21	1268	57	0	2.70
Billy Smith	2	67	1(1)	0	0.90
Kelly Hrudey	14	842	38(2)	0	2.71
New York Islanders Totals	14	909	42	0	2.77
Glenn Resch	2	36	1	0	1.67
Ron Hextall	*26	*1540	*71(1)	*2	2.77
Philadelphia Totals	26	1576	73	2	2.78
Brian Hayward	13	708	32	0	2.71
Patrick Roy	6	330	22	0	4.00
Montreal Totals	17	1038	54	0	3.12
Daniel Berthiaume	8	439	21	0	2.87
Eldon Reddick	3	166	10(1)	0	3.61
Winnipeg Totals	10	605	32	0	3.17
Mario Gosselin	11	654	37	0	3.39
Clint Malarchuk	3	140	8	0	3.43
Quebec Totals	13	794	45	0	3.40

	Games	Mins.	Goals	SO.	Avg.
Rejean Lemelin	2	101	6	0	3.56
Mike Vernon	5	263	16	0	3.65
Calgary Totals	6	364	22	0	3.63
John Vanbiesbrouck	4	195	11	1	3.38
Bob Froese	4	165	10(1)	0	3.64
New York Rangers Totals	6	360	22	1	3.67
Bob Sauve	4	245	15	0	3.67
Chicago Totals	4	245	15	0	3.67
Steve Weeks	1	36	1	0	1.67
Mike Liut	6	332	25(1)	0	4.52
Hartford Totals	6	368	27	0	4.40
Bill Ranford	2	123	8	0	3.90
Doug Keans	2	120	11	0	5.50
Boston Totals	4	243	19	0	4.69
Roland Melanson	5	260	24(1)	0	5.54
Darren Eliot	1	40	7	0	10.50
Los Angeles Totals	5	300	32	0	6.40

( )—Empty Net Goals. Not counted against an individual goalie's average.

Individual Stanley Cup Leaders

Goals ....Jari Kurri, Edmonton— 15
Assists..Wayne Gretzky, Edmonton— 29
Points...Wayne Gretzky, Edmonton— 34
Penalty Minutes ....Basil McRae, Quebec— 99
Goaltender's average (360 minutes)............................Ken Wregget, Toronto— 2.29
Shutouts .... Glen Hanlon, Detroit— 2
Ron Hextall, Philadelphia— 2

Individual 1986-87 NHL Trophy Winners

ART ROSS TROPHY (Scoring Leader)..Wayne Gretzky, Edmonton
HART MEMORIAL TROPHY (Most Valuable)...Wayne Gretzky, Edmonton
JAMES NORRIS MEMORIAL TROPHY (Top Defenseman) ....Ray Bourque, Boston
VEZINA TROPHY (Top Goaltender)..Ron Hextall, Philadelphia
BILL JENNINGS TROPHY (Goaltending Trophy)....................................Brian Hayward, Montreal
Patrick Roy, Montreal
CALDER MEMORIAL TROPHY (Top Rookie)..Luc Robitaille, Los Angeles
LADY BYNG TROPHY (Most Gentlemanly)...Joe Mullen, Calgary
CONN SMYTHE TROPHY (Playoff MVP)...Ron Hextall, Philadelphia
BILL MASTERTON MEMORIAL TROPHY
(Perseverance, Sportsmanship and Dedication)...Doug Jarvis, Hartford
FRANK J. SELKE TROPHY (Best Defensive Forward)..............................Dave Poulin, Philadelphia
JACK ADAMS AWARD (Coach of the Year)..Jacques Demers, Detroit

Year-By-Year NHL Standings

From 1917-18 through the 1925-26 season, National Hockey League champions played against the Pacific Coast Hockey League for the Stanley Cup. So, only Stanley Cup championships are designated in the following club records for that period.

Key to standings: *—Missed playoffs. †—Eliminated in first round of new playoff format (1974-75). a—Eliminated in quarterfinal round. b—Eliminated in semifinal round. c—Eliminated in final round. xx—Stanley Cup champion.

NOTE: Records for Edmonton Oilers, Hartford Whalers, Quebec Nordiques and Winnipeg Jets include World Hockey Association results prior to their entrance into NHL in 1979-80. Key to WHA standings: *—Missed playoffs. †—Preliminary round (established for 1975-76 season). a—Eliminated in quarterfinal round. b—Eliminated in semifinal round. c—Eliminated in final round. xx—Avco World Cup champion.

Boston Bruins

Season	W.	L.	T.	Pts.	GF.	GA.	Position
1924-25	6	24	0	12	49	119	Sixth
1925-26	17	15	4	38	92	85	Fourth
1926-27	21	20	3	45	97	89	Second—c
1927-28	20	13	11	51	77	70	First—b
1928-29	26	13	5	57	89	52	First—xx
1929-30	38	5	1	77	179	98	First—c
1930-31	28	10	6	62	143	90	First—b
1931-32	15	21	12	42	122	117	Fourth—*
1932-33	25	15	8	58	124	88	First—b
1933-34	18	25	5	41	111	130	Fourth—*
1934-35	26	16	6	58	129	112	First—b
1935-36	22	20	6	50	92	83	Second—a
1936-37	23	18	7	53	120	110	Second—a
1937-38	30	11	7	67	142	89	First—b
1938-39	36	10	2	74	156	76	First—xx
1939-40	31	12	5	67	170	98	First—b
1940-41	27	8	13	67	168	102	First—xx
1941-42	25	17	6	56	160	118	Third—b
1942-43	24	17	9	57	195	176	Second—c
1943-44	19	26	5	43	223	268	Fifth—*
1944-45	16	30	4	36	179	219	Fourth—b
1945-46	24	18	8	56	167	156	Second—c
1946-47	26	23	11	63	190	175	Third—b
1947-48	23	24	13	59	167	168	Third—b
1948-49	29	23	8	66	178	163	Second—b
1949-50	22	32	16	60	198	228	Fifth—*
1950-51	22	30	18	62	178	197	Fourth—b
1951-52	25	29	16	66	162	176	Fourth—b
1952-53	28	29	13	69	152	172	Third—c
1953-54	32	28	10	74	177	181	Fourth—b
1954-55	23	26	21	67	169	188	Fourth—b
1955-56	23	34	13	59	147	185	Fifth—*
1956-57	34	24	12	80	195	174	Third—c
1957-58	27	28	15	69	199	194	Fourth—c
1958-59	32	29	9	73	205	215	Second—b
1959-60	28	34	8	64	220	241	Fifth—*
1960-61	15	42	13	43	176	254	Sixth—*
1961-62	15	47	8	38	177	306	Sixth—*
1962-63	14	39	17	45	198	281	Sixth—*
1963-64	18	40	12	48	170	212	Sixth—*
1964-65	21	43	6	48	166	253	Sixth—*
1965-66	21	43	6	48	174	275	Fifth—*
1966-67	17	43	10	44	182	253	Sixth—*
1967-68	37	27	10	84	259	216	Third—a
1968-69	42	18	16	100	303	221	Second—b
1969-70	40	17	19	99	277	216	Second—xx
1970-71	57	14	7	121	399	207	First—a
1971-72	54	13	11	119	330	204	First—xx
1972-73	51	22	5	107	330	235	Second—a
1973-74	52	17	9	113	349	221	First—c
1974-75	40	26	14	94	345	245	Second—†
1975-76	48	15	17	113	313	237	First—b
1976-77	49	23	8	106	312	240	First—c
1977-78	51	18	11	113	333	218	First—c
1978-79	43	23	14	100	316	270	First—b
1979-80	46	21	13	105	310	234	Second—a
1980-81	37	30	13	87	316	272	Second—†

Season	W.	L.	T.	Pts.	GF.	GA.	Position
1981-82	43	27	10	96	323	285	Second—a
1982-83	50	20	10	110	327	228	First—b
1983-84	49	25	6	104	336	261	First—†
1984-85	36	34	10	82	303	287	Fourth—†
1985-86	37	31	12	86	311	288	Third—†
1986-87	39	34	7	85	301	276	Third—†
	1913	1509	610	4436	12887	11897	

Buffalo Sabres

Season	W.	L.	T.	Pts.	GF.	GA.	Position
1970-71	24	39	15	63	217	291	Fifth—*
1971-72	16	43	19	51	203	289	Sixth—*
1972-73	37	27	14	88	257	219	Fourth—a
1973-74	32	34	12	76	242	250	Fifth—*
1974-75	49	16	15	113	354	240	First—c
1975-76	46	21	13	105	339	240	Second—a
1976-77	48	24	8	104	301	220	Second—a
1977-78	44	19	17	105	288	215	Second—a
1978-79	36	28	16	88	280	263	Second—†
1979-80	47	17	16	110	318	201	First—b
1980-81	39	20	21	99	327	250	First—a
1981-82	39	26	15	93	307	273	Third—†
1982-83	38	29	13	89	318	285	Third—a
1983-84	48	25	7	103	315	257	Second—†
1984-85	38	28	14	90	290	237	Third—†
1985-86	37	37	6	80	296	291	Fifth—*
1986-87	28	44	8	64	280	308	Fifth—*
	646	477	229	1511	4932	4329	

Calgary Flames

Season	W.	L.	T.	Pts.	GF.	GA.	Position
1972-73	25	38	15	65	191	239	Seventh—*
1973-74	30	34	14	74	214	238	Fourth—a
1974-75	34	31	15	83	243	233	Fourth—*
1975-76	35	33	12	82	262	237	Third—†
1976-77	34	34	12	80	264	265	Third—†
1977-78	34	27	19	87	274	252	Third—†
1978-79	41	31	8	90	327	280	Fourth—†
1979-80	35	32	13	83	282	269	Fourth—†
1980-81	39	27	14	92	329	298	Third—b
1981-82	29	34	17	75	334	345	Third—†
1982-83	32	34	14	78	321	317	Second—a
1983-84	34	32	14	82	311	314	Second—a
1984-85	41	27	12	94	363	302	Third—†
1985-86	40	31	9	89	354	315	Second—c
1986-87	46	31	3	95	318	289	Second—†
	529	476	191	1249	4387	4193	

Chicago Black Hawks

Season	W.	L.	T.	Pts.	GF.	GA.	Position
1926-27	19	22	3	41	115	116	Third—a
1927-28	7	34	3	17	68	134	Fifth—*
1928-29	7	29	8	22	33	85	Fifth—*
1929-30	21	18	5	47	117	111	Second—a
1930-31	24	17	3	51	108	78	Second—c
1931-32	18	19	11	47	86	101	Second—a
1932-33	16	20	12	44	88	101	Fourth—*
1933-34	20	17	11	51	88	83	Second—xx
1934-35	26	17	5	57	118	88	Second—a
1935-36	21	19	8	50	93	92	Third—a
1936-37	14	27	7	35	99	131	Fourth—*
1937-38	14	25	9	37	97	139	Third—xx
1938-39	12	28	8	32	91	132	Seventh—*
1939-40	23	19	6	52	112	120	Fourth—a
1940-41	16	25	7	39	112	139	Fifth—b
1941-42	22	23	3	47	145	155	Fourth—a
1942-43	17	18	15	49	179	180	Fifth—*
1943-44	22	23	5	49	178	187	Fourth—c

Season	W.	L.	T.	Pts.	GF.	GA.	Position
1944-45	13	30	7	33	141	194	Fifth—*
1945-46	23	20	7	53	200	178	Third—b
1946-47	19	37	4	42	193	274	Sixth—*
1947-48	20	34	6	46	195	225	Sixth—*
1948-49	21	31	8	50	173	211	Fifth—*
1949-50	22	38	10	54	203	244	Sixth—*
1950-51	13	47	10	36	171	280	Sixth—*
1951-52	17	44	9	43	158	241	Sixth—*
1952-53	27	28	15	69	169	175	Fourth—b
1953-54	12	51	7	31	133	242	Sixth—*
1954-55	13	40	17	43	161	235	Sixth—*
1955-56	19	39	12	50	155	216	Sixth—*
1956-57	16	39	15	47	169	225	Sixth—*
1957-58	24	39	7	55	163	202	Fifth—*
1958-59	28	29	13	69	197	208	Third—b
1959-60	28	29	13	69	191	180	Third—b
1960-61	29	24	17	75	198	180	Third—xx
1961-62	31	26	13	75	217	186	Third—c
1962-63	32	21	17	81	194	178	Second—b
1963-64	36	22	12	84	218	169	Second—b
1964-65	34	28	8	76	224	176	Third—c
1965-66	37	25	8	82	240	187	Second—b
1966-67	41	17	12	94	264	170	First—b
1967-68	32	26	16	80	212	222	Fourth—b
1968-69	34	33	9	77	280	246	Sixth—*
1969-70	45	22	9	99	250	170	First—b
1970-71	49	20	9	107	277	184	First—c
1971-72	46	17	15	107	256	166	First—b
1972-73	42	27	9	93	284	225	First—c
1973-74	41	14	23	105	272	164	Second—b
1974-75	37	35	8	82	268	241	Third—a
1975-76	32	30	18	82	254	261	First—a
1976-77	26	43	11	63	240	298	Third—†
1977-78	32	29	19	83	230	220	First—a
1978-79	29	36	15	73	244	277	First—a
1979-80	34	27	19	87	241	250	First—a
1980-81	31	33	16	78	304	315	Second—†
1981-82	30	38	12	72	332	363	Fourth—b
1982-83	47	23	10	104	338	268	First—b
1983-84	30	42	8	68	277	311	Fourth—†
1984-85	38	35	7	83	309	299	Second—b
1985-86	39	33	8	86	351	349	First—†
1986-87	29	37	14	72	290	310	Third—†
	1597	1738	632	3825	11763	12087	

Detroit Red Wings

Season	W.	L.	T.	Pts.	GF.	GA.	Position
1926-27	12	28	4	28	76	105	Fifth—*
1927-28	19	19	6	44	88	79	Fourth—*
1928-29	19	16	9	47	72	63	Third—a
1929-30	14	24	6	34	117	133	Fourth—*
1930-31	16	21	7	39	102	105	Fourth—*
1931-32	18	20	10	46	95	108	Third—a
1932-33	25	15	8	58	111	93	Second—b
1933-34	24	14	10	58	113	98	First—c
1934-35	19	22	7	45	127	114	Fourth—*
1935-36	24	16	8	56	124	103	First—xx
1936-37	25	14	9	59	128	102	First—xx
1937-38	12	25	11	35	99	133	Fourth—*
1938-39	18	24	6	42	107	128	Fifth—b
1939-40	16	26	6	38	90	126	Fifth—b
1940-41	21	16	11	53	112	102	Third—c
1941-42	19	25	4	42	140	147	Fifth—c
1942-43	25	14	11	61	169	124	First—xx
1943-44	26	18	6	58	214	177	Second—b
1944-45	31	14	5	67	218	161	Second—c
1945-46	20	20	10	50	146	159	Fourth—b
1946-47	22	27	11	55	190	193	Fourth—b
1947-48	30	18	12	72	187	148	Second—c
1948-49	34	19	7	75	195	145	First—c

Season	W.	L.	T.	Pts.	GF.	GA.	Position
1949-50	37	19	14	88	229	164	First—xx
1950-51	44	13	13	101	236	139	First—b
1951-52	44	14	12	100	215	133	First—xx
1952-53	36	16	18	90	222	133	First—b
1953-54	37	19	14	88	191	132	First—xx
1954-55	42	17	11	95	204	134	First—xx
1955-56	30	24	16	76	183	148	Second—c
1956-57	38	20	12	88	198	157	First—b
1957-58	29	29	12	70	176	207	Third—b
1958-59	25	37	8	58	167	218	Sixth—*
1959-60	26	29	15	67	186	197	Fourth—b
1960-61	25	29	16	66	195	215	Fourth—c
1961-62	23	33	14	60	184	219	Fifth—*
1962-63	32	25	13	77	200	194	Fourth—c
1963-64	30	29	11	71	191	204	Fourth—c
1964-65	40	23	7	87	224	175	First—b
1965-66	31	27	12	74	221	194	Fourth—c
1966-67	27	39	4	58	212	241	Fifth—*
1967-68	27	35	12	66	245	257	Sixth—*
1968-69	33	31	12	78	239	221	Fifth—*
1969-70	40	21	15	95	246	199	Third—a
1970-71	22	45	11	55	209	308	Seventh—*
1971-72	33	35	10	76	261	262	Fifth—*
1972-73	37	29	12	86	265	243	Fifth—*
1973-74	29	39	10	68	255	319	Sixth—*
1974-75	23	45	12	58	259	335	Fourth—*
1975-76	26	44	10	62	226	300	Fourth—*
1976-77	16	55	9	41	183	309	Fifth—*
1977-78	32	34	14	78	252	266	Second—a
1978-79	23	41	16	62	252	295	Fifth—*
1979-80	26	43	11	63	268	306	Fifth—*
1980-81	19	43	18	56	252	339	Fifth—*
1981-82	21	47	12	54	270	351	Sixth—*
1982-83	21	44	15	57	263	344	Fifth—*
1983-84	31	42	7	69	298	323	Third—†
1984-85	27	41	12	66	313	357	Third—†
1985-86	17	57	6	40	266	415	Fifth—*
1986-87	34	36	10	78	260	274	Second—b
	1622	1704	640	3884	11736	12073	

Edmonton Oilers

Season	W.	L.	T.	Pts.	GF.	GA.	Position
1972-73	38	37	3	79	269	256	Fifth—*
1973-74	38	37	3	79	268	269	Third—a
1974-75	36	38	4	76	279	279	Fifth—*
1975-76	27	49	5	59	268	345	Fourth—a
1976-77	34	43	4	72	243	304	Fourth—a
1977-78	38	39	3	79	309	307	Fifth—a
1978-79	48	30	2	98	340	266	First—c
1979-80	28	39	13	69	301	322	Fourth—†
1980-81	29	35	16	74	328	327	Fourth—a
1981-82	48	17	15	111	417	295	First—†
1982-83	47	21	12	106	424	315	First—c
1983-84	57	18	5	119	446	314	First—xx
1984-85	49	20	11	109	401	298	First—xx
1985-86	56	17	7	119	426	310	First—a
1986-87	50	24	6	106	372	284	First—xx
	623	464	109	1355	5091	4491	

Hartford Whalers

Season	W.	L.	T.	Pts.	GF.	GA.	Position
1972-73	46	30	2	94	318	263	First—xx
1973-74	43	31	4	90	291	260	First—a
1974-75	43	30	5	91	274	279	First—a
1975-76	33	40	7	73	255	290	Third—b
1976-77	35	40	6	76	275	290	Fourth—a
1977-78	44	31	5	93	335	269	Second—c
1978-79	37	34	9	83	298	287	Fourth—b
1979-80	27	34	19	73	303	312	Fourth—†
1980-81	21	41	18	60	292	372	Fourth—*

Season	W.	L.	T.	Pts.	GF.	GA.	Position
1981-82	21	41	18	60	264	351	Fifth—*
1982-83	19	54	7	45	261	403	Fifth—*
1983-84	28	42	10	66	288	320	Fifth—*
1984-85	30	41	9	69	268	318	Fifth—*
1985-86	40	36	4	84	332	302	Fourth—a
1986-87	43	30	7	93	287	270	First—†
	510	555	130	1150	4346	4586	

Los Angeles Kings

Season	W.	L.	T.	Pts.	GF.	GA.	Position
1967-68	31	33	10	72	200	224	Second—a
1968-69	24	42	10	58	185	260	Fourth—b
1969-70	14	52	10	38	168	290	Sixth—*
1970-71	25	40	13	63	239	303	Fifth—*
1971-72	20	49	9	49	206	305	Seventh—*
1972-73	31	36	11	73	232	245	Sixth—*
1973-74	33	33	12	78	233	231	Third—a
1974-75	42	17	21	105	269	185	Second-†
1975-76	38	33	9	85	263	265	Second—a
1976-77	34	31	15	83	271	241	Second—a
1977-78	31	34	15	77	243	245	Third—†
1978-79	34	34	12	80	292	286	Third—†
1979-80	30	36	14	74	290	313	Second—†
1980-81	43	24	13	99	337	290	Second—†
1981-82	24	41	15	63	314	369	Fourth—a
1982-83	27	41	12	66	308	365	Fifth—*
1983-84	23	44	13	59	309	376	Fifth—*
1984-85	34	32	14	82	339	326	Fourth—†
1985-86	23	49	8	54	284	389	Fifth—†
1986-87	31	41	8	70	318	341	Fourth—†
	592	642	244	1428	5300	5849	

Minnesota North Stars

Season	W.	L.	T.	Pts.	GF.	GA.	Position
1967-68	27	32	15	69	191	226	Fourth—b
1968-69	18	43	15	51	189	270	Sixth—*
1969-70	19	35	22	60	224	257	Third—a
1970-71	28	34	16	72	191	223	Fourth—b
1971-72	37	29	12	86	212	191	Second—a
1972-73	37	30	11	85	254	230	Third—a
1973-74	23	38	17	63	235	275	Seventh—*
1974-75	23	50	7	53	221	341	Fourth—*
1975-76	20	53	7	47	195	303	Fourth—*
1976-77	23	39	18	64	240	310	Second—†
1977-78	18	53	9	45	218	325	Fifth—*
1978-79	28	40	12	68	257	289	Fourth—*
1979-80	36	28	16	88	311	253	Third—b
1980-81	35	28	17	87	291	263	Third—c
1981-82	37	23	20	94	346	288	First—†
1982-83	40	24	16	96	321	290	Second—a
1983-84	39	31	10	88	345	344	First—b
1984-85	25	43	12	62	268	321	Fourth—a
1985-86	38	33	9	85	327	305	Second—†
1986-87	30	40	10	70	296	314	Fifth—*
	581	726	271	1433	5132	5618	

Montreal Canadiens

Season	W.	L.	T.	Pts.	GF.	GA.	Position
1917-18	13	9	0	26	115	84	First and Third
1918-19	10	8	0	20	88	78	Second
1919-20	13	11	0	26	129	113	Second
1920-21	13	11	0	26	112	99	Third
1921-22	12	11	1	25	88	94	Third
1922-23	13	9	2	28	73	61	Second
1923-24	13	11	0	26	59	48	Second—xx
1924-25	17	11	2	36	93	56	Third
1925-26	11	24	1	23	79	108	Seventh
1926-27	28	14	2	58	99	67	Second—c
1927-28	26	11	7	59	116	48	First—b
1928-29	22	7	15	59	71	43	First—b

Season	W.	L.	T.	Pts.	GF.	GA.	Position
1929-30	21	14	9	51	142	114	Second—xx
1930-31	26	10	8	60	129	89	First—xx
1931-32	25	16	7	57	128	111	First—b
1932-33	18	25	5	41	92	115	Third—a
1933-34	22	20	6	50	99	101	Second—a
1934-35	19	23	6	44	110	145	Third—a
1935-36	11	26	11	33	82	123	Fourth—*
1936-37	24	18	6	54	115	111	First—b
1937-38	18	17	13	49	123	128	Third—a
1938-39	15	24	9	39	115	146	Sixth—a
1939-40	10	33	5	25	90	167	Seventh—*
1940-41	16	26	6	38	121	147	Sixth—a
1941-42	18	27	3	39	134	173	Sixth—a
1942-43	19	19	12	50	181	191	Fourth—b
1943-44	38	5	7	83	234	109	First—xx
1944-45	38	8	4	80	228	121	First—b
1945-46	28	17	5	61	172	134	First—xx
1946-47	34	16	10	78	189	138	First—c
1947-48	20	29	11	51	147	169	Fifth—*
1948-49	28	23	9	65	152	126	Third—b
1949-50	29	22	19	77	172	150	Second—b
1950-51	25	30	15	65	173	184	Third—c
1951-52	34	26	10	78	195	164	Second—c
1952-53	28	23	19	75	155	148	Second—xx
1953-54	35	24	11	81	195	141	Second—c
1954-55	41	18	11	93	228	157	Second—c
1955-56	45	15	10	100	222	131	First—xx
1956-57	35	23	12	82	210	155	Second—xx
1957-58	43	17	10	96	250	158	First—xx
1958-59	39	18	13	91	258	158	First—xx
1959-60	40	18	12	92	255	178	First—xx
1960-61	41	19	10	92	254	188	First—b
1961-62	42	14	14	98	259	166	First—b
1962-63	28	19	23	79	225	183	Third—b
1963-64	36	21	13	85	209	167	First—b
1964-65	36	23	11	83	211	185	Second—xx
1965-66	41	21	8	90	239	173	First—xx
1966-67	32	25	13	77	202	188	Second—c
1967-68	42	22	10	94	236	167	First—xx
1968-69	46	19	11	103	271	202	First—xx
1969-70	38	22	16	92	244	201	Fifth—*
1970-71	42	23	13	97	291	216	Third—xx
1971-72	46	16	16	108	307	205	Third—a
1972-73	52	10	16	120	329	184	First—xx
1973-74	45	24	9	99	293	240	Second—a
1974-75	47	14	19	113	374	225	First—b
1975-76	58	11	11	127	337	174	First—xx
1976-77	60	8	12	132	387	171	First—xx
1977-78	59	10	11	129	359	183	First—xx
1978-79	52	17	11	115	337	204	First—xx
1979-80	47	20	13	107	328	240	First—a
1980-81	45	22	13	103	332	232	First—†
1981-82	46	17	17	109	360	223	First—†
1982-83	42	24	14	98	350	286	Second—†
1983-84	35	40	5	75	286	295	Fourth—b
1984-85	41	27	12	94	309	262	First—a
1985-86	40	33	7	87	330	280	Second—xx
1986-87	41	29	10	92	277	241	Second—b
	2213	1317	662	5088	14154	10962	

New Jersey Devils

Season	W.	L.	T.	Pts.	GF.	GA.	Position
1974-75	15	54	11	41	184	328	Fifth—*
1975-76	12	56	12	36	190	351	Fifth—*
1976-77	20	46	14	54	226	307	Fifth—*
1977-78	19	40	21	59	257	305	Second—†
1978-79	15	53	12	42	210	331	Fourth—*
1979-80	20	48	13	51	234	308	Sixth—*
1980-81	22	45	13	57	258	344	Fifth—*
1981-82	18	49	13	49	241	362	Fifth—*
1982-83	17	49	14	48	230	338	Fifth—*

Season	W.	L.	T.	Pts.	GF.	GA.	Position
1983-84	17	56	7	41	231	350	Fifth—*
1984-85	22	48	10	54	263	346	Fifth—*
1985-86	28	49	3	59	300	374	Fifth—*
1986-87	29	45	6	64	293	368	Sixth—*
	254	638	149	655	3117	4415	

New York Islanders

Season	W.	L.	T.	Pts.	GF.	GA.	Position
1972-73	12	60	6	30	170	347	Eighth—*
1973-74	19	41	18	56	182	247	Eighth—*
1974-75	33	25	22	88	264	221	Third—b
1975-76	42	21	17	101	297	190	Second—b
1976-77	47	21	12	106	288	193	Second—b
1977-78	48	17	15	111	334	210	First—a
1978-79	51	15	14	116	358	214	First—b
1979-80	39	28	13	91	281	247	Second—xx
1980-81	48	18	14	110	355	260	First—xx
1981-82	54	16	10	118	385	250	First—xx
1982-83	42	26	12	96	302	226	Second—xx
1983-84	50	26	4	104	357	269	First—c
1984-85	40	34	6	86	345	312	Third—a
1985-86	39	29	12	90	327	284	Third—†
1986-87	35	33	12	82	279	281	Third—a
	599	410	187	1385	4524	3751	

New York Rangers

Season	W.	L.	T.	Pts.	GF.	GA.	Position
1926-27	25	13	6	56	95	72	First—a
1927-28	19	16	9	47	94	79	Second—xx
1928-29	21	13	10	52	72	65	Second—c
1929-30	17	17	10	44	136	143	Third—b
1930-31	19	16	9	47	106	87	Third—b
1931-32	23	17	8	54	134	112	First—c
1932-33	23	17	8	54	135	107	Third—xx
1933-34	21	19	8	50	120	113	Third—a
1934-35	22	20	6	50	137	139	Third—b
1935-36	19	17	12	50	91	96	Fourth—*
1936-37	19	20	9	47	117	106	Third—c
1937-38	27	15	6	60	149	96	Second—a
1938-39	26	16	6	58	149	105	Second—b
1939-40	27	11	10	64	136	77	Second—xx
1940-41	21	19	8	50	143	125	Fourth—a
1941-42	29	17	2	60	177	143	First—b
1942-43	11	31	8	30	161	253	Sixth—*
1943-44	6	39	5	17	162	310	Sixth—*
1944-45	11	29	10	32	154	247	Sixth—*
1945-46	13	28	9	35	144	191	Sixth—*
1946-47	22	32	6	50	167	186	Fifth—*
1947-48	21	26	13	55	176	201	Fourth—b
1948-49	18	31	11	47	133	172	Sixth—*
1949-50	28	31	11	67	170	189	Fourth—c
1950-51	20	29	21	61	169	201	Fifth—*
1951-52	23	34	13	59	192	219	Fifth—*
1952-53	17	37	16	50	152	211	Sixth—*
1953-54	29	31	10	68	161	182	Fifth—*
1954-55	17	35	18	52	150	210	Fifth—*
1955-56	32	28	10	74	204	203	Third—b
1956-57	26	30	14	66	184	227	Fourth—b
1957-58	32	25	13	77	195	188	Second—b
1958-59	26	32	12	64	201	217	Fifth—*
1959-60	17	38	15	49	187	247	Sixth—*
1960-61	22	38	10	54	204	248	Fifth—*
1961-62	26	32	12	64	195	207	Fourth—b
1962-63	22	36	12	56	211	233	Fifth—*
1963-64	22	38	10	54	186	242	Fifth—*
1964-65	20	38	12	52	179	246	Fifth—*
1965-66	18	41	11	47	195	261	Sixth—*
1966-67	30	28	12	72	188	189	Fourth—b
1967-68	39	23	12	90	226	183	Second—a
1968-69	41	26	9	91	231	196	Third—a
1969-70	38	22	16	92	246	189	Fourth—a
1970-71	49	18	11	109	259	177	Second—b

Season	W.	L.	T.	Pts.	GF.	GA.	Position
1971-72	48	17	13	109	317	192	Second—c
1972-73	47	23	8	102	297	208	Third—b
1973-74	40	24	14	94	300	251	Third—b
1974-75	37	29	14	88	319	276	Second—†
1975-76	29	42	9	67	262	333	Fourth—*
1976-77	29	37	14	72	272	310	Fourth—*
1977-78	30	37	13	73	279	280	Fourth—†
1978-79	40	29	11	91	316	292	Third—c
1979-80	38	32	10	86	308	284	Third—a
1980-81	30	36	14	74	312	317	Fourth—b
1981-82	39	27	14	92	316	306	Second—a
1982-83	35	35	10	80	306	287	Fourth—a
1983-84	42	29	9	93	314	304	Fourth—†
1984-85	26	44	10	62	295	345	Fourth—†
1985-86	36	38	6	78	280	276	Fourth—b
1986-87	34	38	8	76	307	323	Fourth—†
	1634	1686	646	3914	12173	12474	

Philadelphia Flyers

Season	W.	L.	T.	Pts.	GF.	GA.	Position
1967-68	31	32	11	73	173	179	First—a
1968-69	20	35	21	61	174	225	Third—a
1969-70	17	35	24	58	197	225	Fifth—*
1970-71	28	33	17	73	207	225	Third—a
1971-72	26	38	14	66	200	236	Fifth—*
1972-73	37	30	11	85	296	256	Second—b
1973-74	50	16	12	112	273	164	First—xx
1974-75	51	18	11	113	293	181	First—xx
1975-76	51	13	16	118	348	209	First—c
1976-77	48	16	16	112	323	213	First—b
1977-78	45	20	15	105	296	200	Second—b
1978-79	40	25	15	95	281	248	Second—a
1979-80	48	12	20	116	327	254	First—c
1980-81	41	24	15	97	313	249	Second—a
1981-82	38	31	11	87	325	313	Third—†
1982-83	49	23	8	106	326	240	First—†
1983-84	44	26	10	98	350	290	Third—†
1984-85	53	20	7	113	348	240	First—c
1985-86	53	23	4	110	335	241	First—†
1986-87	46	26	8	100	310	245	First—c
	816	496	266	1898	5695	4733	

Pittsburgh Penguins

Season	W.	L.	T.	Pts.	GF.	GA.	Position
1967-68	27	34	13	67	195	216	Fifth—*
1968-69	20	45	11	51	189	252	Fifth—*
1969-70	26	38	12	64	182	238	Second—b
1970-71	21	37	20	62	221	240	Sixth—*
1971-72	26	38	14	66	220	258	Fourth—a
1972-73	32	37	9	73	257	265	Fifth—*
1973-74	28	41	9	65	242	273	Fifth—*
1974-75	37	28	15	89	326	289	Third—a
1975-76	35	33	12	82	339	303	Third—†
1976-77	34	33	13	81	240	252	Third—†
1977-78	25	37	18	68	254	321	Fourth—*
1978-79	36	31	13	85	281	279	Second—a
1979-80	30	37	13	73	251	303	Third—†
1980-81	30	37	13	73	302	345	Third—†
1981-82	31	36	13	75	310	337	Fourth—†
1982-83	18	53	9	45	257	394	Sixth—*
1983-84	16	58	6	38	254	390	Sixth—*
1984-85	24	51	5	53	276	385	Fifth—*
1985-86	34	38	8	76	313	305	Fifth—*
1986-87	30	38	12	72	297	290	Fifth—*
	560	780	238	1358	4964	5935	

Quebec Nordiques

Season	W.	L.	T.	Pts.	GF.	GA.	Position
1972-73	33	40	5	71	276	313	Fifth—*
1973-74	38	36	4	80	306	280	Fifth—*

Season	W.	L.	T.	Pts.	GF.	GA.	Position
1974-75	46	32	0	92	331	299	First—c
1975-76	50	27	4	104	371	316	Second—a
1976-77	47	31	3	97	353	295	First—xx
1977-78	40	37	3	83	349	347	Fourth—b
1978-79	41	34	5	87	288	271	Second—b
1979-80	25	44	11	61	248	313	Fifth—*
1980-81	30	32	18	78	314	318	Fourth—†
1981-82	33	31	16	82	356	345	Fourth—b
1982-83	34	34	12	80	343	336	Fourth—†
1983-84	42	28	10	94	360	278	Third—a
1984-85	41	30	9	91	323	275	Second—b
1985-86	43	31	6	92	330	289	First—†
1986-87	31	39	10	72	267	276	Fourth—a
	574	503	116	1264	4815	4551	

St. Louis Blues

Season	W.	L.	T.	Pts.	GF.	GA.	Position
1967-68	27	31	16	70	177	191	Third—c
1968-69	37	25	14	88	204	157	First—c
1969-70	37	27	12	86	224	179	First—c
1970-71	34	25	19	87	223	208	Second—a
1971-72	28	39	11	67	208	247	Third—a
1972-73	32	34	12	76	233	251	Fourth—a
1973-74	26	40	12	64	206	248	Sixth—*
1974-75	35	31	14	84	269	267	Second—†
1975-76	29	37	14	72	249	290	Third—†
1976-77	32	39	9	73	239	276	First—a
1977-78	20	47	13	53	195	304	Fourth—*
1978-79	18	50	12	48	249	348	Third—*
1979-80	34	34	12	80	266	278	Second—†
1980-81	45	18	17	107	352	281	First—a
1981-82	32	40	8	72	315	349	Third—a
1982-83	25	40	15	65	285	316	Fourth—†
1983-84	32	41	7	71	293	316	Second—a
1984-85	37	31	12	86	299	288	First—†
1985-86	37	34	9	83	302	291	Third—b
1986-87	32	33	15	79	281	293	First—†
	629	696	253	1511	5069	5378	

Toronto Maple Leafs

Season	W.	L.	T.	Pts.	GF.	GA.	Position
1917-18	13	9	0	26	108	109	Second, First
1918-19	5	13	0	10	64	92	Third
1919-20	12	12	0	24	119	106	Third
1920-21	15	9	0	30	105	100	First
1921-22	13	10	1	27	98	97	Second—xx
1922-23	13	10	1	27	82	88	Third
1923-24	10	14	0	20	59	85	Third
1924-25	19	11	0	38	90	84	Second
1925-26	12	21	3	27	92	114	Sixth
1926-27	15	24	5	35	79	94	Fifth—*
1927-28	18	18	8	44	89	88	Fourth—*
1928-29	21	18	5	47	85	69	Third—b
1929-30	17	21	6	40	116	124	Fourth—*
1930-31	22	13	9	53	118	99	Second—a
1931-32	23	18	7	53	155	127	Second—xx
1932-33	24	18	6	54	119	111	First—c
1933-34	26	13	9	61	174	119	First—b
1934-35	30	14	4	64	157	111	First—c
1935-36	23	19	6	52	126	106	Second—c
1936-37	22	21	5	49	119	115	Third—a
1937-38	24	15	9	57	151	127	First—c
1938-39	19	20	9	47	114	107	Third—c
1939-40	25	17	6	56	134	110	Third—c
1940-41	28	14	6	62	145	99	Second—b
1941-42	27	18	3	57	158	136	Second—xx
1942-43	22	19	9	53	198	159	Third—b
1943-44	23	23	4	50	214	174	Third—b
1944-45	24	22	4	52	183	161	Third—xx
1945-46	19	24	7	45	174	185	Fifth—*
1946-47	31	19	10	72	209	172	Second—xx

Season	W.	L.	T.	Pts.	GF.	GA.	Position
1947-48	32	15	13	77	182	143	First—xx
1948-49	22	25	13	57	147	161	Fourth—xx
1949-50	31	27	12	74	176	173	Third—b
1950-51	41	16	13	95	212	138	Second—xx
1951-52	29	25	16	74	168	157	Third—b
1952-53	27	30	13	67	156	167	Fifth—*
1953-54	32	24	14	78	152	131	Third—b
1954-55	24	24	22	70	147	135	Third—b
1955-56	24	33	13	61	153	181	Fourth—b
1956-57	21	34	15	57	174	192	Fifth—*
1957-58	21	38	11	53	192	226	Sixth—*
1958-59	27	32	11	65	189	201	Fourth—c
1959-60	35	26	9	79	199	195	Second—c
1960-61	39	19	12	90	234	176	Second—b
1961-62	37	22	11	85	232	180	Second—xx
1962-63	35	23	12	82	221	180	First—xx
1963-64	33	25	12	78	192	172	Third—xx
1964-65	30	26	14	74	204	173	Fourth—b
1965-66	34	25	11	79	208	187	Third—b
1966-67	32	27	11	75	204	211	Third—xx
1967-68	33	31	10	76	209	176	Fifth—*
1968-69	35	26	15	85	234	217	Fourth—a
1969-70	29	34	13	71	222	242	Sixth—*
1970-71	37	33	8	82	248	211	Fourth—a
1971-72	33	31	14	80	209	208	Fourth—a
1972-73	27	41	10	64	247	279	Sixth—*
1973-74	35	27	16	86	274	230	Fourth—a
1974-75	31	33	16	78	280	309	Third—a
1975-76	34	31	15	83	294	276	Third—b
1976-77	33	32	15	81	301	285	Third—a
1977-78	41	29	10	92	271	237	Third—b
1978-79	34	33	13	81	267	252	Third—a
1979-80	35	40	5	75	304	327	Fourth—†
1980-81	28	37	15	71	322	367	Fifth—†
1981-82	20	44	16	56	298	380	Fifth—*
1982-83	28	40	12	68	293	330	Third—†
1983-84	26	45	9	61	303	387	Fifth—*
1984-85	20	52	8	48	253	358	Fifth—*
1985-86	25	48	7	57	311	386	Fourth—a
1986-87	32	42	6	70	286	319	Fourth—a
	1817	1742	633	4267	13002	12723	

Vancouver Canucks

Season	W.	L.	T.	Pts.	GF.	GA.	Position
1970-71	24	46	8	56	229	296	Sixth—*
1971-72	20	50	8	48	203	297	Seventh—*
1972-73	22	47	9	53	233	339	Seventh—*
1973-74	24	43	11	59	224	296	Seventh—*
1974-75	38	32	10	86	271	254	First—a
1975-76	33	32	15	81	271	272	Second—†
1976-77	25	42	13	63	235	294	Fourth—*
1977-78	20	43	17	57	239	320	Third—*
1978-79	25	42	13	63	217	291	Second—†
1979-80	27	37	16	70	256	281	Third—†
1980-81	28	32	20	76	289	301	Third—†
1981-82	30	33	17	77	290	286	Second—c
1982-83	30	35	15	75	303	309	Third—†
1983-84	32	39	9	73	306	328	Third—†
1984-85	25	46	9	59	284	401	Fifth—*
1985-86	23	44	13	59	282	333	Fourth—†
1986-87	29	43	8	66	302	314	Fifth—*
	455	686	211	1121	4434	5212	

Washington Capitals

Season	W.	L.	T.	Pts.	GF.	GA.	Position
1974-75	8	67	5	21	181	446	Fifth—*
1975-76	11	59	10	32	224	394	Fifth—*
1976-77	24	42	14	62	221	307	Fourth—*
1977-78	17	49	14	48	195	321	Fifth—*
1978-79	24	41	15	63	273	338	Fourth—*
1979-80	27	40	13	67	261	293	Fifth—*

Left wing Tony Tanti led Vancouver with 41 goals and 79 points last season.

Season	W.	L.	T.	Pts.	GF.	GA.	Position
1980-81	26	36	18	70	286	317	Fifth—*
1981-82	26	41	13	65	319	338	Fifth—*
1982-83	39	25	16	94	306	283	Third—†
1983-84	48	27	5	101	308	226	Second—a
1984-85	46	25	9	101	322	240	Second—†
1985-86	50	23	7	107	315	272	Second—a
1986-87	38	32	10	86	285	278	Second—†
	384	507	149	917	3496	4053	

Winnipeg Jets

Season	W.	L.	T.	Pts.	GF.	GA.	Position
1972-73	43	31	4	90	285	249	First—c
1973-74	34	39	5	73	264	296	Fourth—a
1974-75	38	35	5	81	322	293	Third—*
1975-76	52	27	2	106	345	254	First—xx
1976-77	46	32	2	94	366	291	Second—c
1977-78	50	28	2	102	381	270	First—xx
1978-79	39	35	6	84	307	306	Third—xx
1979-80	20	49	11	51	214	314	Fifth—*
1980-81	9	57	14	32	246	400	Sixth—*
1981-82	33	33	14	80	319	332	Second—†
1982-83	33	39	8	74	311	333	Fourth—†
1983-84	31	38	11	73	340	374	Third—†
1984-85	43	27	10	96	358	332	Second—a
1985-86	26	47	7	59	295	372	Third—†
1986-87	40	32	8	88	279	271	Third—a
	537	549	109	1183	4632	4687	

NHL Stanley Cup Winners

SEASON	TEAM	COACH
1917-18	Toronto Arenas	Dick Carroll
1919-20	Ottawa Senators	Pete Green
1920-21	Ottawa Senators	Pete Green
1921-22	Toronto St. Pats	Eddie Powers
1922-23	Ottawa Senators	Pete Green
1923-24	Montreal Canadiens	Leo Dandurand
1924-25	Victoria Cougars	Lester Patrick
1925-26	Montreal Maroons	Eddie Gerard
1926-27	Ottawa Senators	Dave Gill
1927-28	New York Rangers	Lester Patrick
1928-29	Boston Bruins	Cy Denneny
1929-30	Montreal Canadiens	Cecil Hart
1930-31	Montreal Canadiens	Cecil Hart
1931-32	Toronto Maple Leafs	Dick Irvin
1932-33	New York Rangers	Lester Patrick
1933-34	Chicago Black Hawks	Tommy Gorman
1934-35	Montreal Maroons	Tommy Gorman
1935-36	Detroit Red Wings	Jack Adams
1936-37	Detroit Red Wings	Jack Adams
1937-38	Chicago Black Hawks	Bill Stewart
1938-39	Boston Bruins	Art Ross
1939-40	New York Rangers	Frank Boucher
1940-41	Boston Bruins	Cooney Weiland
1941-42	Toronto Maple Leafs	Hap Day
1942-43	Detroit Red Wings	Jack Adams
1943-44	Montreal Canadiens	Dick Irvin
1944-45	Toronto Maple Leafs	Hap Day
1945-46	Montreal Canadiens	Dick Irvin
1946-47	Toronto Maple Leafs	Hap Day
1947-48	Toronto Maple Leafs	Hap Day
1948-49	Toronto Maple Leafs	Hap Day
1949-50	Detroit Red Wings	Tommy Ivan
1950-51	Toronto Maple Leafs	Joe Primeau
1951-52	Detroit Red Wings	Tommy Ivan
1952-53	Montreal Canadiens	Dick Irvin
1953-54	Detroit Red Wings	Tommy Ivan
1954-55	Detroit Red Wings	Jimmy Skinner
1955-56	Montreal Canadiens	Toe Blake
1956-57	Montreal Canadiens	Toe Blake
1957-58	Montreal Canadiens	Toe Blake
1958-59	Montreal Canadiens	Toe Blake
1959-60	Montreal Canadiens	Toe Blake
1960-61	Chicago Black Hawks	Rudy Pilous
1961-62	Toronto Maple Leafs	Punch Imlach
1962-63	Toronto Maple Leafs	Punch Imlach
1963-64	Toronto Maple Leafs	Punch Imlach
1964-65	Montreal Canadiens	Toe Blake
1965-66	Montreal Canadiens	Toe Blake
1966-67	Toronto Maple Leafs	Punch Imlach
1967-68	Montreal Canadiens	Toe Blake
1968-69	Montreal Canadiens	Claude Ruel
1969-70	Boston Bruins	Harry Sinden
1970-71	Montreal Canadiens	Al MacNeil
1971-72	Boston Bruins	Tom Johnson
1972-73	Montreal Canadiens	Scotty Bowman
1973-74	Philadelphia Flyers	Fred Shero
1974-75	Philadelphia Flyers	Fred Shero
1975-76	Montreal Canadiens	Scotty Bowman
1976-77	Montreal Canadiens	Scotty Bowman
1977-78	Montreal Canadiens	Scotty Bowman
1978-79	Montreal Canadiens	Scotty Bowman
1979-80	New York Islanders	Al Arbour
1980-81	New York Islanders	Al Arbour
1981-82	New York Islanders	Al Arbour
1982-83	New York Islanders	Al Arbour
1983-84	Edmonton Oilers	Glen Sather
1984-85	Edmonton Oilers	Glen Sather
1985-86	Montreal Canadiens	Jean Perron
1986-87	Edmonton Oilers	Glen Sather

NOTE: 1918-19 series between Montreal and Seattle cancelled after five games because of influenza epidemic.

Stanley Cup Playoff Records

Team

1—Most Stanley Cup Championships: Montreal Canadiens (23).
2—Most Final Series Appearances: Montreal Canadiens (30).
3—Most Years in Playoffs: Montreal Canadiens (57).
4—Most Consecutive Stanley Cup Championships: Montreal Canadiens (5).
5—Most Consecutive Playoff Appearances: Montreal Canadiens (22).
6—Most Goals, One Team, One Game: Edmonton (13) vs. Los Angeles, April 9, 1987.
7—Most Goals, One Team, One Period: Montreal Canadiens (7) vs. Toronto, March 30, 1944—3rd period.
8—Most Consecutive Playoff Game Victories: Edmonton Oilers (12).

Individual

1—Most Years in Playoffs: Gordie Howe (Detroit 19, Hartford 1)—20.
2—Most Consecutive Years in Playoffs: Brad Park (N.Y. Rangers, Boston, Detroit)—17.
3—Most Playoff Games: Henri Richard (Montreal)—180.
4—Most Points in Playoffs: Wayne Gretzky (Edmonton)—209.
5—Most Goals in Playoffs: Mike Bossy (N.Y. Islanders)—85.
6—Most Assists in Playoffs: Wayne Gretzky (Edmonton)—140.
7—Most Shutouts in Playoffs: Jacques Plante (Montreal, St. Louis)—14.
8—Most Games Played by Goaltender: Bill Smith (N.Y. Islanders)—131.
9—Most Points One Year: Wayne Gretzky (Edmonton)—47 in 1984-85.
10—Most Goals One Year:
    Reggie Leach (Philadelphia)—19 in 1975-76.
    Jari Kurri (Edmonton)—19 in 1984-85.
11—Most Assists One Year: Wayne Gretzky (Edmonton)—30 in 1984-85.
12—Most Points By Defenseman One Year: Paul Coffey (Edmonton)—37 in 1984-85.
13—Most Goals By Defenseman One Year: Paul Coffey (Edmonton)—12 in 1984-85.
14—Most Assists By Defenseman One Year: Paul Coffey (Edmonton)—25 in 1984-85.
15—Most Penalty Minutes One Year: Chris Nilan (Montreal)—141 in 1985-86.
16—Most Shutouts One Year:
    Clint Benedict (Montreal Maroons)—4 in 1927-28.
    Dave Kerr (N.Y. Rangers)—4 in 1936-37.
    Frank McCool (Toronto)—4 in 1944-45.
    Terry Sawchuk (Detroit)—4 in 1951-52.
    Bernie Parent (Philadelphia)—4 in 1974-75.
    Ken Dryden (Montreal)—4 in 1976-77.
17—Most Consecutive Shutouts: Frank McCool (Toronto)—3 in 1944-45.
18—Most Points One Game:
    Wayne Gretzky (Edmonton)—7 vs. Calgary, April 17, 1983.
    7 vs. Winnipeg, April 25, 1985.
    7 vs. Los Angeles, April 9, 1987.
19—Most Goals One Game:
    Maurice Richard (Montreal)—5 vs. Toronto, March 23, 1944.
    Darryl Sittler (Toronto)—5 vs. Philadelphia, April 22, 1976.
    Reggie Leach (Philadelphia)—5 vs. Boston, May 6, 1976.
20—Most Assists One Game:
    Mikko Leinonen (N.Y. Rangers)—6 vs. Philadelphia, April 8, 1982.
    Wayne Gretzky (Edmonton)—6 vs. Los Angeles, April 9, 1987.
21—Most Penalty Minutes in Playoffs: Dave (Tiger) Williams (Toronto, Vancouver, Los Angeles)—455.

Individual Awards
Art Ross Trophy
(Leading Scorer—Regular Season)

	Games	G.	A.	Pts.
1917-18—Joe Malone, Montreal	20	44	**	44
1918-19—Newsy Lalonde, Montreal	17	23	9	32
1919-20—Joe Malone, Quebec Bulldogs	24	39	6	45
1920-21—Newsy Lalonde, Montreal	24	33	8	41
1921-22—Punch Broadbelt, Ottawa	24	32	14	46
1922-23—Babe Dye, Toronto	22	26	11	37
1923-24—Cy Denneny, Ottawa	21	22	1	23
1924-25—Babe Dye, Toronto	29	38	6	44
1925-26—Nels Stewart, Montreal Maroons	36	34	8	42
1926-27—Bill Cook, New York Rangers	44	33	4	37
1927-28—Howie Morenz, Montreal	43	33	18	51
1928-29—Ace Bailey, Toronto	44	22	10	32
1929-30—Cooney Weiland, Boston	44	43	30	73
1930-31—Howie Morenz, Montreal	39	28	23	51
1931-32—Harvey Jackson, Toronto	48	28	25	53
1932-33—Bill Cook, New York Rangers	48	28	22	50
1933-34—Charlie Conacher, Toronto	42	32	20	52
1934-35—Charlie Conacher, Toronto	48	36	21	57
1935-36—Dave Schriner, New York Americans	48	19	26	45
1936-37—Dave Schriner, New York Americans	48	21	25	46
1937-38—Gordie Drillon, Toronto	48	26	26	52
1938-39—Toe Blake, Montreal	48	24	23	47
1939-40—Milt Schmidt, Boston	48	22	30	52
1940-41—Bill Cowley, Boston	46	17	45	62
1941-42—Bryan Hextall, New York Rangers	48	24	32	56
1942-43—Doug Bentley, Chicago	50	33	40	73
1943-44—Herbie Cain, Boston	48	36	46	82
1944-45—Elmer Lach, Montreal	50	26	54	80
1945-46—Max Bentley, Chicago	47	31	30	61
1946-47—Max Bentley, Chicago	60	29	43	72
1947-48—Elmer Lach, Montreal	60	30	31	61
1948-49—Roy Conacher, Chicago	60	26	42	68
1949-50—Ted Lindsay, Detroit	69	23	55	78
1950-51—Gordie Howe, Detroit	70	43	43	86
1951-52—Gordie Howe, Detroit	70	47	39	86
1952-53—Gordie Howe, Detroit	70	49	46	95
1953-54—Gordie Howe, Detroit	70	33	48	81
1954-55—Bernie Geoffrion, Montreal	70	38	37	75
1955-56—Jean Beliveau, Montreal	70	47	41	88
1956-57—Gordie Howe, Detroit	70	44	45	89
1957-58—Dickie Moore, Montreal	70	36	48	84
1958-59—Dickie Moore, Montreal	70	41	55	96
1959-60—Bobby Hull, Chicago	70	39	42	81
1960-61—Bernie Geoffrion, Montreal	64	50	45	95
1961-62—Bobby Hull, Chicago	70	50	34	84
1962-63—Gordie Howe, Detroit	70	38	48	86
1963-64—Stan Mikita, Chicago	70	39	50	89
1964-65—Stan Mikita, Chicago	70	28	59	87
1965-66—Bobby Hull, Chicago	65	54	43	97
1966-67—Stan Mikita, Chicago	70	35	62	97
1967-68—Stan Mikita, Chicago	72	40	47	87
1968-69—Phil Esposito, Boston	74	49	77	126
1969-70—Bobby Orr, Boston	76	33	87	120
1970-71—Phil Esposito, Boston	78	76	76	152
1971-72—Phil Esposito, Boston	76	66	67	133
1972-73—Phil Esposito, Boston	78	55	75	130
1973-74—Phil Esposito, Boston	78	68	77	145
1974-75—Bobby Orr, Boston	80	46	89	135
1975-76—Guy Lafleur, Montreal	80	56	69	125
1976-77—Guy Lafleur, Montreal	80	56	80	136
1977-78—Guy Lafleur, Montreal	78	60	72	132
1978-79—Bryan Trottier, New York Islanders	76	47	87	134
1979-80—Marcel Dionne, Los Angeles	80	53	84	137
1980-81—Wayne Gretzky, Edmonton	80	55	109	164
1981-82—Wayne Gretzky, Edmonton	80	92	120	212
1982-83—Wayne Gretzky, Edmonton	80	71	125	196

	Games	G.	A.	Pts.
1983-84—Wayne Gretzky, Edmonton	74	87	118	205
1984-85—Wayne Gretzky, Edmonton	80	73	135	208
1985-86—Wayne Gretzky, Edmonton	80	52	163	215
1986-87—Wayne Gretzky, Edmonton	79	62	121	183

**—Number of assists not recorded.

(Originally Leading Scorer Trophy. Present trophy presented to NHL by Art Ross, former manager-coach of Boston Bruins, in 1947. In event of tie, player with most goals receives the award.)

Hart Memorial Trophy
(Most Valuable Player)

1923-24—Frank Nighbor, Ottawa
1924-25—Billy Burch, Hamilton
1925-26—Nels Stewart, Montreal Maroons
1926-27—Herb Gardiner, Montreal
1927-28—Howie Morenz, Montreal
1928-29—Roy Worters, N.Y. Americans
1929-30—Nels Stewart, Montreal Maroons
1930-31—Howie Morenz, Montreal
1931-32—Howie Morenz, Montreal
1932-33—Eddie Shore, Boston
1933-34—Aurel Joliat, Montreal
1934-35—Eddie Shore, Boston
1935-36—Eddie Shore, Boston
1936-37—Babe Siebert, Montreal
1937-38—Eddie Shore, Boston
1938-39—Toe Blake, Montreal
1939-40—Ebbie Goodfellow, Detroit
1940-41—Bill Cowley, Boston
1941-42—Tom Anderson, N.Y. Americans
1942-43—Bill Cowley, Boston
1943-44—Babe Pratt, Toronto
1944-45—Elmer Lach, Montreal
1945-46—Max Bentley, Chicago
1946-47—Maurice Richard, Montreal
1947-48—Buddy O'Connor, N.Y. Rangers
1948-49—Sid Abel, Detroit
1949-50—Chuck Rayner, N.Y. Rangers
1950-51—Milt Schmidt, Boston
1951-52—Gordie Howe, Detroit
1952-53—Gordie Howe, Detroit
1953-54—Al Rollins, Chicago
1954-55—Ted Kennedy, Toronto

1955-56—Jean Beliveau, Montreal
1956-57—Gordie Howe, Detroit
1957-58—Gordie Howe, Detroit
1958-59—Andy Bathgate, N.Y. Rangers
1959-60—Gordie Howe, Detroit
1960-61—Bernie Geoffrion, Montreal
1961-62—Jacques Plante, Montreal
1962-63—Gordie Howe, Detroit
1963-64—Jean Beliveau, Montreal
1964-65—Bobby Hull, Chicago
1965-66—Bobby Hull, Chicago
1966-67—Stan Mikita, Chicago
1967-68—Stan Mikita, Chicago
1968-69—Phil Esposito, Boston
1969-70—Bobby Orr, Boston
1970-71—Bobby Orr, Boston
1971-72—Bobby Orr, Boston
1972-73—Bobby Clarke, Philadelphia
1973-74—Phil Esposito, Boston
1974-75—Bobby Clarke, Philadelphia
1975-76—Bobby Clarke, Philadelphia
1976-77—Guy Lafleur, Montreal
1977-78—Guy Lafleur, Montreal
1978-79—Bryan Trottier, N.Y. Islanders
1979-80—Wayne Gretzky, Edmonton
1980-81—Wayne Gretzky, Edmonton
1981-82—Wayne Gretzky, Edmonton
1982-83—Wayne Gretzky, Edmonton
1983-84—Wayne Gretzky, Edmonton
1984-85—Wayne Gretzky, Edmonton
1985-86—Wayne Gretzky, Edmonton
1986-87—Wayne Gretzky, Edmonton

Penalty Leaders

	Games	Penalty Minutes
1926-27—Nels Stewart, Montreal Maroons	44	133
1927-28—Eddie Shore, Boston	44	165
1928-29—Merv "Red" Dutton, Montreal Maroons	44	139
1929-30—Joe Lamb, Ottawa Senators	44	119
1930-31—Harvey Rockburn, Detroit	42	118
1931-32—Merv "Red" Dutton, N.Y. Americans	47	107
1932-33—Red Horner, Toronto	47	144
1933-34—Red Horner, Toronto	42	126*
1934-35—Red Horner, Toronto	46	125
1935-36—Red Horner, Toronto	43	167
1936-37—Red Horner, Toronto	48	124
1937-38—Red Horner, Toronto	47	82*
1938-39—Red Horner, Toronto	48	85
1939-40—Red Horner, Toronto	30	87
1940-41—Jimmy Orlando, Detroit	48	99
1941-42—Jimmy Orlando, Detroit	48	81**
1942-43—Jimmy Orlando, Detroit	40	89*
1943-44—Mike McMahon, Montreal Canadiens	42	98
1944-45—Pat Egan, Boston	48	86
1945-46—Jack Stewart, Detroit	47	73
1946-47—Gus Mortson, Toronto	60	133
1947-48—Bill Barilko, Toronto	57	147

	Games	Penalty Minutes
1948-49—Bill Ezinicki, Toronto	52	145
1949-50—Bill Ezinicki, Toronto	67	144
1950-51—Gus Mortson, Toronto	60	142
1951-52—Walter "Gus" Kyle, Boston	69	127
1952-53—Maurice Richard, Montreal Canadiens	70	112
1953-54—Gus Mortson, Chicago	68	132
1954-55—Fernie Flaman, Boston	70	150
1955-56—Lou Fontinato, N.Y. Rangers	70	202
1956-57—Gus Mortson, Chicago	70	147
1957-58—Lou Fontinato, N.Y. Rangers	70	152
1958-59—Ted Lindsay, Chicago	70	184
1959-60—Carl Brewer, Toronto	67	150
1960-61—Pierre Pilote, Chicago	70	165
1961-62—Lou Fontinato, Montreal Canadiens	54	167
1962-63—Howie Young, Detroit	64	273
1963-64—Vic Hadfield, N.Y. Rangers	69	151
1964-65—Carl Brewer, Toronto	70	177
1965-66—Reg Fleming, N.Y. Rangers	69	166
1966-67—John Ferguson, Montreal Canadiens	67	177
1967-68—Barclay Plager, St. Louis Blues	49	153
1968-69—Forbes Kennedy, Philadelphia-Toronto	77	219
1969-70—Keith Magnuson, Chicago	76	213
1970-71—Keith Magnuson, Chicago	76	291
1971-72—Bryan Watson, Pittsburgh Penguins	75	212
1972-73—Dave Schultz, Philadelphia Flyers	76	259
1973-74—Dave Schultz, Philadelphia Flyers	73	348
1974-75—Dave Schultz, Philadelphia Flyers	76	472
1975-76—Steve Durbano, Pittsburgh-Kansas City	69	370
1976-77—Dave Williams, Toronto	77	338
1977-78—Dave Schultz, Los Angeles-Pittsburgh	74	405
1978-79—Dave Williams, Toronto	77	298
1979-80—Jimmy Mann, Winnipeg	72	287
1980-81—Dave Williams, Vancouver	77	333
1981-82—Paul Baxter, Pittsburgh	76	407
1982-83—Randy Holt, Washington	70	275
1983-84—Chris Nilan, Montreal	76	338
1984-85—Chris Nilan, Montreal	77	358
1985-86—Joey Kocur, Detroit	59	377
1986-87—Dave Williams, Los Angeles	76	358

*—Match Misconduct penalty not included in total minutes.
**—Three Match misconduct penalties not included in total minutes. 1946-47 was first season that Match penalties were automatically included in penalty totals.

James Norris Memorial Trophy
(Outstanding Defenseman)

1953-54—Red Kelly, Detroit	1970-71—Bobby Orr, Boston
1954-55—Doug Harvey, Montreal	1971-72—Bobby Orr, Boston
1955-56—Doug Harvey, Montreal	1972-73—Bobby Orr, Boston
1956-57—Doug Harvey, Montreal	1973-74—Bobby Orr, Boston
1957-58—Doug Harvey, Montreal	1974-75—Bobby Orr, Boston
1958-59—Tom Johnson, Montreal	1975-76—Denis Potvin, N.Y. Islanders
1959-60—Doug Harvey, Montreal	1976-77—Larry Robinson, Montreal
1960-61—Doug Harvey, Montreal	1977-78—Denis Potvin, N.Y. Islanders
1961-62—Doug Harvey, N.Y. Rangers	1978-79—Denis Potvin, N.Y. Islanders
1962-63—Pierre Pilote, Chicago	1979-80—Larry Robinson, Montreal
1963-64—Pierre Pilote, Chicago	1980-81—Randy Carlyle, Pittsburgh
1964-65—Pierre Pilote, Chicago	1981-82—Doug Wilson, Chicago
1965-66—Jacques Laperriere, Montreal	1982-83—Rod Langway, Washington
1966-67—Harry Howell, N.Y. Rangers	1983-84—Rod Langway, Washington
1967-68—Bobby Orr, Boston	1984-85—Paul Coffey, Edmonton
1968-69—Bobby Orr, Boston	1985-86—Paul Coffey, Edmonton
1969-70—Bobby Orr, Boston	1986-87—Ray Bourque, Boston

Vezina Trophy

(Awarded to goalkeeper(s) having played a minimum 25 games for the team with fewest goals scored against. Beginning with 1981-82 season, awarded to outstanding goaltender.)

	Games	Goals	SO.	Avg.
1926-27—George Hainsworth, Montreal	44	67	14	1.52
1927-28—George Hainsworth, Montreal	44	48	13	1.09

	Games	Goals	SO.	Avg.
1928-29—George Hainsworth, Montreal	44	43	22	0.98
1929-30—Tiny Thompson, Boston	44	98	3	2.23
1930-31—Roy Worters, New York Americans	44	74	8	1.68
1931-32—Charlie Gardiner, Chicago	48	101	4	2.10
1932-33—Tiny Thompson, Boston	48	88	11	1.83
1933-34—Charlie Gardiner, Chicago	48	83	10	1.73
1934-35—Lorne Chabot, Chicago	48	88	8	1.83
1935-36—Tiny Thompson, Boston	48	82	10	1.71
1936-37—Normie Smith, Detroit	48	102	6	2.13
1937-38—Tiny Thompson, Boston	48	89	7	1.85
1938-39—Frank Brimsek, Boston	43	69	10	1.60
1939-40—Dave Kerr, New York Rangers	48	77	8	1.60
1940-41—Turk Broda, Toronto	48	99	4	2.06
1941-42—Frank Brimsek, Boston	47	112	3	2.38
1942-43—Johnny Mowers, Detroit	50	124	6	2.48
1943-44—Bill Durnan, Montreal	50	109	2	2.18
1944-45—Bill Durnan, Montreal	50	121	1	2.42
1945-46—Bill Durnan, Montreal	40	104	4	2.60
1946-47—Bill Durnan, Montreal	60	138	4	2.30
1947-48—Turk Broda, Toronto	60	143	5	2.38
1948-49—Bill Durnan, Montreal	60	126	10	2.10
1949-50—Bill Durnan, Montreal	64	141	8	2.20
1950-51—Al Rollins, Toronto	40	70	5	1.75
1951-52—Terry Sawchuk, Detroit	70	139	11	1.98
1952-53—Terry Sawchuk, Detroit	70	133	12	1.94
1953-54—Harry Lumley, Toronto	69	128	13	1.85
1954-55—Terry Sawchuk, Detroit	68	132	12	1.94
1955-56—Jacques Plante, Montreal	64	119	7	1.86
1956-57—Jacques Plante, Montreal	61	123	9	2.02
1957-58—Jacques Plante, Montreal	57	119	9	2.09
1958-59—Jacques Plante, Montreal	67	144	9	2.15
1959-60—Jacques Plante, Montreal	69	175	3	2.54
1960-61—John Bower, Toronto	58	145	2	2.50
1961-62—Jacques Plante, Montreal	70	166	4	2.37
1962-63—Glenn Hall, Chicago	66	166	5	2.51
1963-64—Charlie Hodge, Montreal	62	140	8	2.26
1964-65—Terry Sawchuk, Toronto	36	92	1	2.56
John Bower, Toronto	34	81	3	2.38
1965-66—Lorne Worsley, Montreal	48	114	2	2.36
Charlie Hodge, Montreal	21	56	1	2.58
1966-67—Glenn Hall, Chicago	32	66	2	2.38
Denis DeJordy, Chicago	44	104	4	2.46
1967-68—Lorne Worsley, Montreal	40	73	6	1.98
Rogatien Vachon, Montreal	39	92	4	2.48
1968-69—Glenn Hall, St. Louis	41	85	8	2.17
Jacques Plante, St. Louis	37	70	5	1.96
1969-70—Tony Esposito, Chicago	63	136	15	2.17
1970-71—Ed Giacomin, New York Rangers	45	95	8	2.15
Gilles Villemure, N.Y. Rangers	34	78	4	2.29
1971-72—Tony Esposito, Chicago	48	82	9	1.76
Gary Smith, Chicago	28	62	5	2.41
1972-73—Ken Dryden, Montreal	54	119	6	2.26
1973-74—Bernie Parent, Philadelphia	73	136	12	1.89
Tony Esposito, Chicago	70	141	10	2.04
1974-75—Bernie Parent, Philadelphia	68	137	12	2.03
1975-76—Ken Dryden, Montreal	62	121	8	2.03
1976-77—Ken Dryden, Montreal	56	117	10	2.14
Michel Larocque, Montreal	26	53	4	2.09
1977-78—Ken Dryden, Montreal	52	105	5	2.05
Michel Larocque, Montreal	30	77	1	2.67
1978-79—Ken Dryden, Montreal	47	108	5	2.30
Michel Larocque, Montreal	34	94	3	2.84
1979-80—Bob Sauve, Buffalo	32	74	4	2.36
Don Edwards, Buffalo	49	125	4	2.57
1980-81—Richard Sevigny, Montreal	33	71	2	2.40
Michel Larocque, Montreal	28	82	1	3.03
Denis Herron, Montreal	25	67	1	3.50
1981-82—Bill Smith, New York Islanders	46	133	0	2.97
1982-83—Pete Peeters, Boston	62	142	8	2.36
1983-84—Tom Barrasso, Buffalo	42	117	2	2.84
1984-85—Pelle Lindbergh, Philadelphia	65	194	2	3.02
1985-86—John Vanbiesbrouck, N.Y. Rangers	61	184	3	3.32
1986-87—Ron Hextall, Philadelphia	66	190	1	3.00

Bill Jennings Trophy

(Awarded to goalkeeper(s) having played a minimum of 25 games for the team with fewest goals scored against, beginning with 1981-82 season.)

	Games	Goals	SO.	Avg.
1981-82—Denis Herron, Montreal	27	68	3	2.64
Rick Wamsley, Montreal	38	101	2	2.75
1982-83—Roland Melanson, N.Y. Islanders	44	109	1	2.66
Billy Smith, N.Y. Islanders	41	112	1	2.87
1983-84—Pat Riggin, Washington	41	102	4	2.66
Al Jensen, Washington	43	117	4	2.91
1984-85—Tom Barrasso, Buffalo	54	144	5	2.66
Bob Sauve, Buffalo	27	84	0	3.22
1985-86—Bob Froese, Philadelphia	51	116	5	2.55
Darren Jensen, Philadelphia	29	88	2	3.68
1986-87—Brian Hayward, Montreal	37	102	1	2.81
Patrick Roy, Montreal	46	131	1	2.93

Calder Memorial Trophy
(Rookie of the Year)

1932-33—Carl Voss, Detroit
1933-34—Russ Blinco, Montreal Maroons
1934-35—Dave Schriner, N.Y. Americans
1935-36—Mike Karakas, Chicago
1936-37—Syl Apps, Toronto
1937-38—Cully Dahlstrom, Chicago
1938-39—Frank Brimsek, Boston
1939-40—Kilby Macdonald, N.Y. Rangers
1940-41—John Quilty, Montreal
1941-42—Grant Warwick, N.Y. Rangers
1942-43—Gaye Stewart, Toronto
1943-44—Gus Bodnar, Toronto
1944-45—Frank McCool, Toronto
1945-46—Edgar Laprade, N.Y. Rangers
1946-47—Howie Meeker, Toronto
1947-48—Jim McFadden, Detroit
1948-49—Pentti Lund, N.Y. Rangers
1949-50—Jack Gelineau, Boston
1950-51—Terry Sawchuk, Detroit
1951-52—Bernie Geoffrion, Montreal
1952-53—Lorne Worsley, N.Y. Rangers
1953-54—Camille Henry, N.Y. Rangers
1954-55—Ed Litzenberger, Chicago
1955-56—Glenn Hall, Detroit
1956-57—Larry Regan, Boston
1957-58—Frank Mahovlich, Toronto
1958-59—Ralph Backstrom, Montreal
1959-60—Bill Hay, Chicago

1960-61—Dave Keon, Toronto
1961-62—Bobby Rousseau, Montreal
1962-63—Kent Douglas, Toronto
1963-64—Jacques Laperriere, Montreal
1964-65—Roger Crozier, Detroit
1965-66—Brit Selby, Toronto
1966-67—Bobby Orr, Boston
1967-68—Derek Sanderson, Boston
1968-69—Danny Grant, Minnesota
1969-70—Tony Esposito, Chicago
1970-71—Gilbert Perreault, Buffalo
1971-72—Ken Dryden, Montreal
1972-73—Steve Vickers, N.Y. Rangers
1973-74—Denis Potvin, N.Y. Islanders
1974-75—Eric Vail, Atlanta
1975-76—Bryan Trottier, N.Y. Islanders
1976-77—Willi Plett, Atlanta
1977-78—Mike Bossy, N.Y. Islanders
1978-79—Bobby Smith, Minnesota
1979-80—Ray Bourque, Boston
1980-81—Peter Stastny, Quebec
1981-82—Dale Hawerchuk, Winnipeg
1982-83—Steve Larmer, Chicago
1983-84—Tom Barrasso, Buffalo
1984-85—Mario Lemieux, Pittsburgh
1985-86—Gary Suter, Calgary
1986-87—Luc Robitaille, Los Angeles

(Award was originally Leading Rookie Award. Named Calder Trophy in 1936-37 and became Calder Memorial Trophy when NHL President Frank Calder passed away—1942-43 season.)

Lady Byng Memorial Trophy
(Most Gentlemanly Player)

1924-25—Frank Nighbor, Ottawa
1925-26—Frank Nighbor, Ottawa
1926-27—Billy Burch, N.Y. Americans
1927-28—Frank Boucher, N.Y. Rangers
1928-29—Frank Boucher, N.Y. Rangers
1929-30—Frank Boucher, N.Y. Rangers
1930-31—Frank Boucher, N.Y. Rangers
1931-32—Joe Primeau, Toronto
1932-33—Frank Boucher, N.Y. Rangers
1933-34—Frank Boucher, N.Y. Rangers
1934-35—Frank Boucher, N.Y. Rangers
1935-36—Doc Romnes, Chicago
1936-37—Marty Barry, Detroit
1937-38—Gordie Drillon, Toronto
1938-39—Clint Smith, N.Y. Rangers
1939-40—Bobby Bauer, Boston
1940-41—Bobby Bauer, Boston
1941-42—Syl Apps, Toronto

1942-43—Max Bentley, Chicago
1943-44—Clint Smith, Chicago
1944-45—Bill Mosienko, Chicago
1945-46—Toe Blake, Montreal
1946-47—Bobby Bauer, Boston
1947-48—Buddy O'Connor, N.Y. Rangers
1948-49—Bill Quackenbush, Detroit
1949-50—Edgar Laprade, N.Y. Rangers
1950-51—Red Kelly, Detroit
1951-52—Sid Smith, Toronto
1952-53—Red Kelly, Detroit
1953-54—Red Kelly, Detroit
1954-55—Sid Smith, Toronto
1955-56—Earl Reibel, Detroit
1956-57—Andy Hebenton, N.Y. Rangers
1957-58—Camille Henry, N.Y. Rangers
1958-59—Alex Delvecchio, Detroit
1959-60—Don McKenney, Boston

1960-61—Red Kelly, Toronto	1974-75—Marcel Dionne, Detroit
1961-62—Dave Keon, Toronto	1975-76—Jean Ratelle, N.Y. R.-Boston
1962-63—Dave Keon, Toronto	1976-77—Marcel Dionne, Los Angeles
1963-64—Ken Wharram, Chicago	1977-78—Butch Goring, Los Angeles
1964-65—Bobby Hull, Chicago	1978-79—Bob MacMillan, Atlanta
1965-66—Alex Delvecchio, Detroit	1979-80—Wayne Gretzky, Edmonton
1966-67—Stan Mikita, Chicago	1980-81—Butch Goring, N.Y. Islanders
1967-68—Stan Mikita, Chicago	1981-82—Rick Middleton, Boston
1968-69—Alex Delvecchio, Detroit	1982-83—Mike Bossy, N.Y. Islanders
1969-70—Phil Goyette, St. Louis	1983-84—Mike Bossy, N.Y. Islanders
1970-71—John Bucyk, Boston	1984-85—Jari Kurri, Edmonton
1971-72—Jean Ratelle, N.Y. Rangers	1985-86—Mike Bossy, N.Y. Islanders
1972-73—Gil Perreault, Buffalo	1986-87—Joe Mullen, Calgary
1973-74—John Bucyk, Boston	

(Originally Lady Byng Trophy. After winning award seven times, Frank Boucher received permanent possession and a new trophy was donated to NHL in 1936. After Lady Byng's death in 1949, NHL changed name to Lady Byng Memorial Trophy.)

Conn Smythe Trophy
(Most Valuable Player in Playoffs)

1964-65—Jean Beliveau, Montreal	1976-77—Guy Lafleur, Montreal
1965-66—Roger Crozier, Detroit	1977-78—Larry Robinson, Montreal
1966-67—Dave Keon, Toronto	1978-79—Bob Gainey, Montreal
1967-68—Glenn Hall, St. Louis	1979-80—Bryan Trottier, N.Y. Islanders
1968-69—Serge Savard, Montreal	1980-81—Butch Goring, N.Y. Islanders
1969-70—Bobby Orr, Boston	1981-82—Mike Bossy, N. Y. Islanders
1970-71—Ken Dryden, Montreal	1982-83—Billy Smith, N.Y. Islanders
1971-72—Bobby Orr, Boston	1983-84—Mark Messier, Edmonton
1972-73—Yvan Cournoyer, Montreal	1984-85—Wayne Gretzky, Edmonton
1973-74—Bernie Parent, Philadelphia	1985-86—Patrick Roy, Montreal
1974-75—Bernie Parent, Philadelphia	1986-87—Ron Hextall, Philadelphia
1975-76—Reggie Leach, Philadelphia	

Bill Masterton Memorial Trophy
(Presented by Professional Hockey Writers' Association to player who best exemplifies the qualities of perseverance, sportsmanship and dedication to hockey.)

1967-68—Claude Provost, Montreal	1977-78—Butch Goring, Los Angeles
1968-69—Ted Hampson, Oakland	1978-79—Serge Savard, Montreal
1969-70—Pit Martin, Chicago	1979-80—Al MacAdam, Minnesota
1970-71—Jean Ratelle, N.Y. Rangers	1980-81—Blake Dunlop, St. Louis
1971-72—Bobby Clarke, Philadelphia	1981-82—Glenn Resch, Colorado
1972-73—Lowell MacDonald, Pittsburgh	1982-83—Lanny McDonald, Calgary
1973-74—Henri Richard, Montreal	1983-84—Brad Park, Detroit
1974-75—Don Luce, Buffalo	1984-85—Anders Hedberg, N.Y. Rangers
1975-76—Rod Gilbert, N.Y. Rangers	1985-86—Charlie Simmer, Boston
1976-77—Ed Westfall, N.Y. Islanders	1986-87—Doug Jarvis, Hartford

Frank J. Selke Trophy
(Best Defensive Forward)

1977-78—Bob Gainey, Montreal	1982-83—Bobby Clarke, Philadelphia
1978-79—Bob Gainey, Montreal	1983-84—Doug Jarvis, Washington
1979-80—Bob Gainey, Montreal	1984-85—Craig Ramsay, Buffalo
1980-81—Bob Gainey, Montreal	1985-86—Troy Murray, Chicago
1981-82—Steve Kasper, Boston	1986-87—Dave Poulin, Philadelphia

Jack Adams Award
(Coach of the Year)

1973-74—Fred Shero, Philadelphia	1980-81—Red Berenson, St. Louis
1974-75—Bob Pulford, Los Angeles	1981-82—Tom Watt, Winnipeg
1975-76—Don Cherry, Boston	1982-83—Orval Tessier, Chicago
1976-77—Scotty Bowman, Montreal	1983-84—Bryan Murray, Washington
1977-78—Bobby Kromm, Detroit	1984-85—Mike Keenan, Philadelphia
1978-79—Al Arbour, N.Y. Islanders	1985-86—Glen Sather, Edmonton
1979-80—Pat Quinn, Philadelphia	1986-87—Jacques Demers, Detroit

NHL Entry Draft—June 13, 1987

FIRST ROUND

NHL Club	PLAYER	(Pos)	1986-87 CLUB (League)
1—Buffalo	Pierre Turgeon	(C)	Granby (QMJL)
2—New Jersey	Brendan Shanahan	(C)	London (OHL)
3—Boston (from Vancouver)	Glen Wesley	(D)	Portland (WHL)
4—Los Angeles (from Minnesota)	Wayne McBean	(D)	Medicine Hat (WHL)
5—Pittsburgh	Chris Joseph	(D)	Seattle (WHL)
6—Minnesota (from Los Angeles)	David Archibald	(C)	Portland (WHL)
7—Toronto	Luke Richardson	(D)	Peterborough (OHL)
8—Chicago	Jimmy Waite	(G)	Chicoutimi (QMJL)
9—Quebec	Bryan Fogarty	(D)	Kingston (OHL)
10—New York Rangers	Jayson More	(D)	New Westminster (WHL)
11—Detroit	Yves Racine	(D)	Longueuil (QMJL)
12—St. Louis	Keith Osborne	(RW)	North Bay (OHL)
13—New York Islanders	Dean Chynoweth	(D)	Medicine Hat (WHL)
14—Boston	Stephane Quintal	(D)	Granby (QMJL)
15—Quebec (from Washington)	Joe Sakic	(C)	Swift Current (WHL)
16—Winnipeg	Bryan Marchment	(D)	Belleville (OHL)
17—Montreal	Andrew Cassels	(C)	Ottawa (OHL)
18—Hartford	Jody Hull	(RW)	Peterborough (OHL)
19—Calgary	Bryan Deasley	(LW)	University of Michigan
20—Philadelphia	Darren Rumble	(D)	Kitchener (OHL)
21—Edmonton	Peter Soberlak	(LW)	Swift Current (WHL)

SECOND ROUND

NHL Club	PLAYER	(Pos)	1986-87 CLUB (League)
22—Buffalo	Brad Miller	(D)	Regina (WHL)
23—New Jersey	Rickard Persson	(D)	Ostersund, Sweden
24—Vancouver	Rob Murphy	(C)	Laval (QMJL)
25—Calgary (from Minnesota)	Stephane Matteau	(LW)	Hull (QMJL)
26—Pittsburgh	Richard Tabaracci	(G)	Cornwall (OHL)
27—Los Angeles	Mark Fitzpatrick	(G)	Medicine Hat (WHL)
28—Toronto	Daniel Marois	(RW)	Chicoutimi (QMJL)
29—Chicago	Ryan McGill	(D)	Swift Current (WHL)
30—Philadelphia (from Quebec)	Jeff Harding	(RW)	Toronto St. Michael's Jr. B
31—New York Rangers	Daniel Lacroix	(LW)	Granby (QMJL)
32—Detroit	Gordon Kruppke	(D)	Prince Albert (WHL)
33—Montreal (from St. Louis)	John LeClair	(C)	Bellows Free Academy (Vt.)
34—New York Islanders	Jeff Hackett	(G)	Oshawa (OHL)
35—Minnesota (from Boston)	Scott McCrady	(D)	Medicine Hat (WHL)
36—Washington	Jeff Ballantyne	(D)	Ottawa (OHL)
37—Winnipeg	Patrik Eriksson	(C)	Brynas, Sweden
38—Montreal	Eric Desjardins	(D)	Granby (QMJL)
39—Hartford	Adam Burt	(D)	North Bay (OHL)
40—Calgary	Kevin Grant	(D)	Kitchener (OHL)
41—Detroit (from Philadelphia)	Bob Wilkie	(D)	Swift Current (WHL)
42—Edmonton	Brad Werenka	(D)	Northern Michigan University

THIRD ROUND

NHL Club	PLAYER	(Pos)	1986-87 CLUB (League)
43—Los Angeles (from Buffalo)	Ross Wilson	(RW)	Peterborough (OHL)
44—Montreal (from New Jersey)	Mathieu Schneider	(D)	Cornwall (OHL)
45—Vancouver	Steve Veilleux	(D)	Three Rivers (QMJL)
46—N.Y. Rangers (from Minnesota)	Simon Gagne	(RW)	Laval (QMJL)
47—Pittsburgh	Jamie Leach	(RW)	Hamilton (OHL)
48—Minnesota (from Los Angeles)	Kevin Kaminski	(C)	Saskatoon (WHL)
49—Toronto	John McIntyre	(C)	Guelph (OHL)
50—Chicago	Cam Russell	(D)	Hull (QMJL)
51—Quebec	Jim Sprott	(D)	London (OHL)
52—Detroit (from N.Y. Rangers)	Dennis Holland	(C)	Portland (WHL)
53—Buffalo (from Det. & N.J.)	Andrew MacVicar	(LW)	Peterborough (OHL)
54—St. Louis	Kevin Miehm	(C)	Oshawa (OHL)
55—New York Islanders	Dean Ewen	(LW)	Spokane (WHL)
56—Boston	Todd Lalonde	(LW)	Sudbury (OHL)
57—Washington	Steve Maltais	(LW)	Cornwall (OHL)
58—Montreal (from Winnipeg)	Francois Gravel	(G)	Shawinigan (QMJL)
59—St. Louis (from Montreal)	Robert Nordmark	(D)	Lulea, Sweden
60—Chicago (from Hartford)	Mike Dagenais	(D)	Peterborough (OHL)
61—Calgary	Scott Mahoney	(LW)	Oshawa (OHL)
62—Philadelphia	Martin Hostak	(C)	Sparta Praha, Czech.
63—Edmonton	Geoff Smith	(D)	St. Albert (Alta Tier II)

FOURTH ROUND

NHL Club	PLAYER	(Pos)	1986-87 CLUB (League)
64—Edmonton (from Buffalo)	Peter Eriksson	(RW)	Kramfors, Sweden
65—New Jersey	Brian Sullivan	(RW)	Springfield (Mass.) Olympics
66—Vancouver	Doug Torrel	(C)	Hibbing H.S. (Minn.)
67—Boston (from Minnesota)	Darwin McPherson	(D)	New Wesminster (WHL)
68—Pittsburgh	Risto Kurkinen	(LW)	Jypht, Finland
69—N.Y. Rangers (from Los Ang.)	Michael Sullivan	(C)	Boston University
70—Calgary (from Toronto)	Tim Harris	(RW)	Pickering (Ont.) Jr. B
71—Toronto (from Chicago)	Joe Sacco	(LW)	Medford H.S. (Mass.)
72—Quebec	Kip Miller	(C)	Michigan State University
73—Minnesota (from N.Y. Rangers)	John Weisbrod	(C)	Choate Academy (N.Y.)
74—Detroit	Mark Reimer	(G)	Saskatoon (WHL)
75—St. Louis	Darin Smith	(LW)	North Bay (OHL)
76—New York Islanders	George Maneluk	(G)	Brandon (WHL)
77—Boston	Matt Delguidice	(G)	St. Anselm College
78—Washington	Tyler Larter	(C)	Sault Ste. Marie (OHL)
79—Winnipeg	Don McLennan	(D)	University of Denver
80—Montreal	Kris Miller	(D)	Greenway H.S. (Minn.)
81—Hartford	Terry Yake	(C)	Brandon (WHL)
82—St. Louis (from Calgary)	Andy Rymsha	(LW)	Western Michigan University
83—Philadelphia	Tomaz Eriksson	(LW)	Djurgarden, Sweden
84—Buffalo (from Edmonton)	John Bradley	(G)	New Hampton H.S. (R.I.)

FIFTH ROUND

NHL Club	PLAYER	(Pos)	1986-87 CLUB (League)
85—Buffalo	David Pergola	(RW)	Belmont Hill H.S. (Mass.)
86—New Jersey	Kevin Dean	(D)	Culver Military Academy (N.J.)
87—Vancouver	Sean Fabian	(D)	Hill Murray H.S. (Minn.)
88—Minnesota	Teppo Kivela	(C)	Jokerit, Finland
89—Pittsburgh	Jeff Waver	(D)	Hamilton (OHL)
90—Los Angeles	Mike Vukonich	(C)	Duluth Denfeld H.S. (Minn.)
91—Toronto	Mike Eastwood	(C)	Pembroke, Ont.
92—Chicago	Ulf Sandstrom	(RW)	Modo, Sweden
93—Quebec	Rob Mendel	(D)	University of Wisconsin
94—New York Rangers	Eric O'Borsky	(C)	Yale University
95—Detroit	Radomir Brazda	(D)	Pardubice, Czech.
96—Winnipeg (from St. Louis)	Ken Gernander	(C)	Greenway H.S. (Minn.)
97—New York Islanders	Petr Vlk	(LW)	Dukla Jihlava, Czech.
98—Boston	Ted Donato	(C)	Catholic Memorial H.S. (Mass.)
99—Washington	Pat Beauchesne	(D)	Moose Jaw (WHL)
100—Winnipeg	Darrin Amundson	(C)	Duluth East H.S. (Minn.)
101—Montreal	Steve McCool	(D)	Belmont Hill H.S. (Mass.)
102—Hartford	Marc Rousseau	(D)	University of Denver
103—Calgary	Tim Corkery	(D)	Ferris State College
104—Philadelphia	Bill Gall	(RW)	New Hampton H.S. (N.J.)
105—Edmonton	Shaun Van Allen	(C)	Saskatoon (WHL)

SIXTH ROUND

NHL Club	PLAYER	(Pos)	1986-87 CLUB (League)
106—Buffalo	Chris Marshall	(LW)	B.C. High (Mass.)
107—New Jersey	Ben Hankinson	(C)	Edina H.S. (Minn.)
108—Vancouver	Gary Valk	(RW)	Sherwood Park
109—Minnesota	D'Arcy Norton	(LW)	Kamloops (WHL)
110—Pittsburgh	Shawn McEachern	(C)	Matignon H.S. (Mass.)
111—Los Angeles	Greg Batters	(RW)	Victoria (WHL)
112—Toronto	Damian Rhodes	(G)	Richfield H.S. (Minn.)
113—Chicago	Mike McCormick	(D)	Richmond B.C. Tier II
114—Quebec	Garth Snow	(G)	Mount St. Charles H.S. (R.I.)
115—New York Rangers	Ludek Cajka	(D)	Dukla Jihlava, Czech.
116—Detroit	Sean Clifford	(D)	Ohio State University
117—St. Louis	Rob Robinson	(D)	Miami University (O.)
118—New York Islanders	Rob DiMaio	(C)	Medicine Hat (WHL)
119—Boston	Matt Glennon	(LW)	Archbishop Williams H.S. (Mass.)
120—Washington	Rich Defreitas	(D)	St. Mark's H.S. (Conn.)
121—Winnipeg	Joe Harwell	(D)	Hill Murray H.S. (Minn.)
122—Montreal	Les Kuntar	(G)	Nichols H.S. (N.Y.)
123—Hartford	Jeff St. Cyr	(D)	Michigan Tech
124—Calgary	Joe Aloi	(D)	Hull (QMJL)
125—Philadelphia	Tony Link	(D)	Dimond H.S. (Alaska)
126—Edmonton	Radek Toupal	(RW)	Motor Budejovice, Czech.

SEVENTH ROUND

NHL Club	PLAYER	(Pos)	1986-87 CLUB (League)
127—Buffalo	Paul Flanagan	(D)	New Hampton H.S. (Mass.)
128—New Jersey	Tom Neziol	(LW)	Miami University (O.)
129—Vancouver	Todd Fanning	(G)	Ohio State University
130—Minnesota	Timo Kulonen	(D)	Kalpa, Finland
131—Pittsburgh	Jim Bodden	(C)	Chatham (Ont.) Jr. B
132—Los Angeles	Kyosti Karjalainen	(LW)	Brynas, Sweden
133—Toronto	Trevor Jobe	(LW)	Moose Jaw (WHL)
134—Chicago	Stephen Tepper	(RW)	Westboro H.S. (Calif.)
135—Quebec	Tim Hanus	(LW)	Minnetonka H.S. (Minn.)
136—New York Rangers	Clint Thomas	(D)	Bartlett H.S. (Alaska)
137—Detroit	Mike Gober	(LW)	Laval (QMJL)
138—St. Louis	Todd Crabtree	(D)	Governor Dummer H.S. (Mass.)
139—New York Islanders	Knut Walbye	(C)	Furuset, Norway
140—Boston	Rob Cheevers	(C)	Boston College
141—Washington	Devon Oleniuk	(D)	Kamloops (WHL)
142—Winnipeg	Todd Hartje	(C)	Harvard University
143—Montreal	Rob Kelley	(LW)	Matignon H.S. (Mass.)
144—Hartford	Greg Wolf	(D)	Buffalo Regal Midgets
145—Calgary	Peter Ciavaglia	(C)	Nichols H.S. (N.Y.)
146—Philadelphia	Mark Strapon	(D)	Hayward H.S. (Wis.)
147—Edmonton	Tomas Srsen	(LW)	Zetr Brno, Czech.

EIGHTH ROUND

NHL Club	PLAYER	(Pos)	1986-87 CLUB (League)
148—Buffalo	Sean Dooley	(D)	Groton H.S. (Mass.)
149—New Jersey	Jim Dowd	(RW)	Brick H.S. (N.J.)
150—Vancouver	Viktor Tumineu	(C)	Sparta Moscow
151—Minnesota	Don Schmidt	(D)	Kamloops (WHL)
152—Pittsburgh	Jiri Kucera	(RW)	Dukla Jihlava, Czech.
153—Buffalo (from Los Angeles)	Tim Roberts	(C)	Deerfield Academy (Mass.)
154—Toronto	Chris Jensen	(D)	Northwood Prep (N.Y.)
155—Chicago	John Reilly	(LW)	Phillips Andover H.S. (Mass.)
156—Quebec	Jake Enebak	(LW)	Northfield H.S. (Minn.)
157—New York Rangers	Charles Wiegand	(C)	Essex Junction H.S. (Vt.)
158—Detroit	Kevin Scott	(C)	Vernon BCJHL (Tier II)
159—St. Louis	Guy Hebert	(G)	Hamilton College
160—New York Islanders	Jeff Saterdalen	(RW)	Jefferson H.S. (Minn.)
161—Boston	Chris Winnes	(RW)	Northwood Prep (N.Y.)
162—Washington	Thomas Sjogren	(RW)	Vastra Frolunda, Sweden
163—Winnipeg	Markku Kyllonen	(RW)	Joensgo, Finland
164—Montreal	Will Geist	(D)	St. Paul Academy
165—Hartford	John Moore	(C)	Yale University
166—Calgary	Theoren Fleury	(C)	Moose Jaw (WHL)
167—Philadelphia	Darryl Ingham	(RW)	University of Manitoba
168—Edmonton	Age Ellingsen	(D)	Storhamer, Norway

NINTH ROUND

NHL Club	PLAYER	(Pos)	1986-87 CLUB (League)
169—Buffalo	Grant Tkachuk	(LW)	Saskatoon (WHL)
170—New Jersey	John Blessman	(D)	Toronto (OHL)
171—Vancouver	Craig Daly	(D)	New Hampton Prep (Mass.)
172—Minnesota	Jarmo Myllys	(G)	Lukko, Finland
173—Pittsburgh	Jack MacDougall	(RW)	New Prep (Mass.)
174—Los Angeles	Jeff Gawlicki	(LW)	Northern Michigan University
175—Toronto	Brian Blad	(D)	Belleville (OHL)
176—Chicago	Lance Werness	(RW)	Burnsville H.S. (Minn.)
177—Quebec	Jaroslav Sevcik	(LW)	Zetor Brno, Czech.
178—New York Rangers	Eric Burrill	(RW)	Tartan H.S. (Mass.)
179—Detroit	Mikko Haapakoski	(D)	Karpat, Finland
180—St. Louis	Robert Dumas	(D)	Seattle (WHL)
181—New York Islanders	Shawn Howard	(D)	Penticton BCJHL (Tier II)
182—Boston	Paul Ohman	(D)	St. John H.S. (Mass.)
183—Quebec (from Washington)	Ladislav Tresl	(C)	Zetor Brno, Czech.
184—Winnipeg	Jim Fernholz	(RW)	White Bear Lake H.S. (Minn.)
185—Montreal	Eric Tremblay	(D)	Drummondville (QMJL)
186—Hartford	Joe Day	(LW)	St. Lawrence University
187—Calgary	Mark Osiecki	(D)	Madison (USHL)
188—Philadelphia	Bruce McDonald	(RW)	Loomis-Chaffee H.S. (Pa.)
189—Edmonton	Gavin Armstrong	(G)	Rensselaer Poly. Inst.

TENTH ROUND

NHL Club	PLAYER	(Pos)	1986-87 CLUB (League)
190—Buffalo	Ian Herbers	(D)	Swift Current (WHL)
191—New Jersey	Peter Fry	(G)	Victoria (WHL)
192—Vancouver	John Fletcher	(G)	Clarkson College
193—Minnesota	Larry Olimb	(D)	Warroad H.S. (Minn)
194—Pittsburgh	Daryn McBride	(C)	University of Denver
195—Los Angeles	John Preston	(C)	Boston University
196—Toronto	Ron Bernacci	(C)	Hamilton (OHL)
197—Chicago	Dale Marquette	(LW)	Brandon (WHL)
198—Quebec	Darren Nauss	(RW)	North Battleford (Ont.) Tier II
199—New York Rangers	David Porter	(LW)	North Michigan University
200—Detroit	Darin Bannister	(D)	University of Illinois/Chicago
201—St. Louis	David Marvin	(D)	Warroad H.S. (Minn.)
202—New York Islanders	John Herlihy	(RW)	Babson College
203—Boston	Casey Jones	(C)	Cornell University
204—Washington	Chris Clarke	(D)	Pembroke (OHL)
205—N.Y. Rangers (from Winnipeg)	Brett Barnett	(RW)	Wexford (Ont.) Jr. B
206—Montreal	Barry McKinlay	(D)	University of Illinois/Chicago
207—St. Louis (from Hartford)	Andy Cesarski	(D)	Culver Military Academy (N.J.)
208—Calgary	William Sedergren	(D)	Springfield (Mass.) Olympics
209—Philadelphia	Steve Morrow	(D)	Westminster School (N.J.)
210—Edmonton	Mike Tinkham	(RW)	Newburyport H.S. (Mass.)

ELEVENTH ROUND

NHL Club	PLAYER	(Pos)	1986-87 CLUB (League)
211—Buffalo	David Littman	(G)	Boston College
212—New Jersey	Alain Charland	(C)	Drummondville (QMJL)
213—Vancouver	Roger Hansson	(LW)	Rogle, Sweden
214—Minnesota	Mark Felicio	(G)	Northwood Prep (N.Y.)
215—Pittsburgh	Mark Carlson	(LW)	Philadelphia Jrs.
216—Los Angeles	Rostislav Vlach	(RW)	Gottwaldov, Czech.
217—Toronto	Ken Alexander	(LW)	Hamilton (OHL)
218—Chicago	Bill Lacouture	(RW)	Natick H.S. (Mass.)
219—Quebec	Mike Williams	(G)	Ferris State College
220—New York Rangers	Lance Marciano	(D)	Choate Academy (N.Y.)
221—Detroit	Craig Quinlan	(D)	Hill Murray H.S. (Minn.)
222—St. Louis	Dan Rolfe	(D)	Brockville (OHL)
223—New York Islanders	Michael Erickson	(D)	St. John's Hill H.S. (Mass.)
224—Boston	Eric LeMarque	(RW)	Northern Michigan University
225—Washington	Milos Vanik	(C)	Ehc Freiburg, W. Germany
226—Winnipeg	Roger Rougelot	(G)	Madison (USHL)
227—Montreal	Ed Ronan	(RW)	Andover Academy (Mass.)
228—Hartford	Kevin Sullivan	(RW)	Princeton University
229—Calgary	Peter Hasselblad	(D)	Orebro, Sweden
230—Philadelphia	Darius Rusnak	(C)	Bratislava, Czech.
231—Edmonton	Jeff Pauletti	(D)	University of Minnesota

TWELFTH ROUND

NHL Club	PLAYER	(Pos)	1986-87 CLUB (League)
232—Buffalo	Allan MacIsaac	(LW)	Guelph (OHL)
233—Vancouver (from New Jersey)	Neil Eisenhut	(C)	Langley (B.C.) Tier II
234—Vancouver	Matt Evo	(LW)	Country Day H.S. (Mass.)
235—Minnesota	Dave Shields	(C)	University of Denver
236—Pittsburgh	Ake Lilljebjorn	(G)	Brynas, Sweden
237—Los Angeles	Mikael Lindholm	(C)	Brynas, Sweden
238—Toronto	Alex Weinrich	(D)	North Yarmouth Academy (Me.)
239—Chicago	Mike Lappin	(C)	Northwood Prep. (N.Y.)
240—Washington (from Quebec)	Dan Brettschneider	(RW)	Burnsville H.S. (Minn.)
241—Edmonton (from N.Y. Rangers)	Jesper Duus	(D)	Rodoure SK, Denmark
242—Detroit	Tomas Jansson	(D)	Ik Talje, Sweden
243—St. Louis	Ray Savard	(C)	Regina (WHL)
244—New York Islanders	Will Averill	(D)	Belmont Hill H.S. (Mass.)
245—Boston	Sean Gorman	(D)	Matignon H.S. (Mass.)
246—Washington	Ryan Kummu	(D)	Rensselaer Poly. Inst.
247—Winnipeg	Hans Goran Elo	(G)	Djurgarden, Sweden
248—Montreal	Bryan Herring	(C)	Dubuque (USHL)
249—Hartford	Steve Laurin	(G)	Dartmouth College
250—Calgary	Magnus Svensson	(D)	Leksand, Sweden
251—Philadelphia	Dale Roehl	(G)	Minnetonka H.S. (Minn.)
252—Edmonton	Igor Viazmikin	(RW)	USSR

The Buffalo Sabres hope that No. 1 draft choice Pierre Turgeon (above) can be as good or even better than older brother Sylvain, who has scored 139 goals in four seasons with the Hartford Whalers.

INDIVIDUAL RECORDS

SINGLE SEASON RECORDS

1—GOALS
NHL—Wayne Gretzky, Edmonton Oilers—92 (1981-82 season).
WHA—Bobby Hull, Winnipeg Jets—77 (1974-75 season).
CHL—Alain Caron, St. Louis Braves—77 (1963-64 season).
AHL—Paul Gardner, Rochester Americans—61 (1985-86 season).
IHL—Dan Lecours, Milwaukee Admirals—75 (1982-83 season).

2—ASSISTS
NHL—Wayne Gretzky, Edmonton Oilers—163 (1985-86 season).
WHA—Andre Lacroix, San Diego Mariners—106 (1974-75 season).
CHL—Richie Hansen, Salt Lake Golden Eagles—81 (1981-82 season).
AHL—George "Red" Sullivan, Hershey Bears—89 (1953-54 season).
IHL—Dale Yakiwchuk, Milwaukee Admirals—100 (1982-83 season).

3—POINTS
NHL—Wayne Gretzky, Edmonton Oilers—215 (1985-86 season).
WHA—Marc Tardif, Quebec Nordiques—154 (1977-78 season).
CHL—Alain Caron, St. Louis Braves—125 (1963-64 season).
AHL—Paul Gardner, Binghamton—130 (1984-85 season).
IHL—Gary Ford, Muskegon Mohawks—141 (1972-73 season).

4—PENALTY MINUTES
NHL—Dave Schultz, Philadelphia Flyers—472 (1974-75 season).
WHA—Curt Brackenbury, Minnesota Fighting Saints and Quebec Nordiques—365 (1975-76 season).
CHL—Randy Holt, Dallas Black Hawks—411 (1974-75 season).
AHL—Steve Martinson, Hershey Bears—432 (1985-86 season).
IHL—Kevin Evans, Kalamazoo—648 (1986-87 season).

5—SHUTOUTS
NHL—George Hainsworth, Montreal Canadiens—22 (1928-29 season).

Modern Era
NHL—Tony Esposito, Chicago Black Hawks—15 (1969-70 season).
WHA—Gerry Cheevers, Cleveland Crusaders—5 (1972-73 season).
Joe Daley, Winnipeg Jets—5 (1975-76 season).
CHL—Marcel Pelletier, St. Paul Rangers—9 (1963-64 season).
AHL—Gordie Bell, Buffalo Bisons—9 (1942-43 season).
IHL—Charlie Hodge, Cincinnati Mohawks—10 (1953-54 season).

6—GOALS AGAINST AVERAGE
NHL—George Hainsworth, Montreal Canadiens—0.98 (1928-29 season).
WHA—Don McLeod, Houston Aeros—2.57 (1973-74 season).
CHL—Russ Gillow, Oklahoma City Blazers—2.16 (1967-68 season).
AHL—Frank Brimsek, Providence Reds—1.79 (1937-38 season).
IHL—Glenn Ramsay, Cincinnati Mohawks—1.88 (1956-57 season).

CAREER (Regular Season Only)
(No WHA Records Listed for Most Seasons Played.)

1—MOST SEASONS
NHL—Gordie Howe, Detroit Red Wings and Hartford Whalers—26 (1946-47 through 1970-71 and 1979-80).
CHL—Richie Hansen, Fort Worth Texans, Salt Lake Golden Eagles, Wichita Wind—9 (1975-76 through 1983-84 seasons).
AHL—Fred Glover, Indianapolis Caps, St. Louis Flyers, Cleveland Barons—20.
Willie Marshall, Pittsburgh Hornets, Rochester Americans, Hershey Bears, Providence Reds, Baltimore Clippers—20.
IHL—Glenn Ramsay, Cincinnati Mohawks, Fort Wayne Komets, Troy Bruins, Toledo Blades, St. Paul Saints, Omaha Knights, Des Moines Oak Leafs, Toledo Hornets, Port Huron Flags—18 (1956-57 through 1973-74).

2—GAMES PLAYED
NHL—Gordie Howe, Detroit Red Wings and Hartford Whalers—1,767 (26 seasons).
WHA—Andre Lacroix, Philadelphia Blazers, New York Golden Blades, Jersey Knights, San Diego Mariners, Houston Aeros and New England Whalers—551 (7 seasons).
CHL—Richie Hansen, Fort Worth Texans, Salt Lake Golden Eagles, Wichita Wind—575 (9 seasons).
AHL—Willie Marshall, Pittsburgh Hornets, Rochester Americans, Hershey Bears, Providence Reds, Baltimore Clippers—1,205 (20 seasons).
IHL—Glenn Ramsay, Cincinnati Mohawks, Fort Wayne Komets, Troy Bruins, Toledo Blades, St. Paul Saints, Omaha Knights, Des Moines Oak Leafs, Toledo Hornets, Port Huron Flags—1,053 (18 seasons).

3—GOALS SCORED

NHL—Gordie Howe, Detroit Red Wings, Hartford Whalers—801 (26 seasons).
WHA—Marc Tardif, Quebec Nordiques—316 (6 seasons).
CHL—Richie Hansen, Fort Worth Texans, Salt Lake Golden Eagles, Wichita Wind—204 (9 seasons).
AHL—Willie Marshall, Pittsburgh Hornets, Rochester Americans, Hershey Bears, Providence Reds, Baltimore Clippers—523 (20 seasons).
IHL—Joe Kastelic, Fort Wayne Komets, Troy Bruins, Louisville Rebels, Muskegon Zephyrs, Muskegon Mohawks—526 (15 seasons).

4—ASSISTS

NHL—Gordie Howe, Detroit Red Wings, Hartford Whalers—1,049.
WHA—Andre Lacroix, Philadelphia Blazers, Jersey Knights, San Diego Mariners, Houston Aeros, New England Whalers—547 (7 seasons).
CHL—Richie Hansen, Fort Worth Texans, Salt Lake Golden Eagles, Wichita Wind—374 (9 seasons).
AHL—Willie Marshall, Pittsburgh Hornets, Hershey Bears, Rochester Americans, Providence Reds, Baltimore Clippers—852 (20 seasons).
IHL—Len Thornson, Huntington Hornets, Indianapolis Chiefs, Fort Wayne Komets—826 (13 seasons).

5—TOTAL POINTS

NHL—Gordie Howe, Detroit Red Wings, Hartford Whalers—1,850 (26 seasons).
WHA—Andre Lacroix, Philadelphia Blazers, Jersey Knights, San Diego Mariners, Houston Aeros, New England Whalers—798 (7 seasons).
CHL—Richie Hansen, Fort Worth Texans, Salt Lake Golden Eagles, Wichita Wind—578 (9 seasons).
AHL—Willie Marshall, Pittsburgh Hornets, Hershey Bears, Rochester Americans, Providence Reds, Baltimore Clippers—1,375 (20 seasons).
IHL—Len Thornson, Huntington Hornets, Indianapolis Chiefs, Fort Wayne Komets—1,252 (13 seasons).

6—PENALTY MINUTES

NHL—Dave (Tiger) Williams, Toronto Maple Leafs, Vancouver Canucks, Detroit Red Wings, Los Angeles Kings—3,873 (12 seasons).
WHA—Paul Baxter, Cleveland Crusaders, Quebec Nordiques—962 (5 seasons).
CHL—Brad Gassoff, Tulsa Oilers, Dallas Black Hawks—899 (5 seasons).
AHL—Fred Glover, Indianapolis Caps, St. Louis Flyers, Cleveland Barons— 2,402 (20 seasons).
IHL—Gord Malinoski, Dayton Gems, Saginaw Gears—2,175 (9 seasons).

7—SHUTOUTS

NHL—Terry Sawchuk, Detroit Red Wings, Boston Bruins, Los Angeles Kings, New York Rangers, Toronto Maple Leafs—103 (20 seasons).
WHA—Ernie Wakely, Winnipeg Jets, San Diego Mariners, Houston Aeros—16 (6 seasons).
CHL—Michel Dumas, Dallas Black Hawks—12 (4 seasons).
Mike Veisor, Dallas Black Hawks—12 (5 seasons).
AHL—Johnny Bower, Cleveland Barons, Providence Reds—45 (11 seasons).
IHL—Glenn Ramsay, Cincinnati Mohawks, Fort Wayne Komets, Troy Bruins, Toledo Blades, St. Paul Saints, Omaha Knights, Des Moines Oak Leafs, Toledo Hornets, Port Huron Flags—45 (18 seasons).

SINGLE GAME RECORDS

1—GOALS

NHL—Joe Malone, Quebec Bulldogs (January 31, 1920 vs. Toronto St. Pats)—7.

Modern Era

NHL—Syd Howe, Detroit Red Wings (Feb. 3, 1944 vs. N.Y. Rangers)—6.
Gordon Berenson, St. Louis Blues (Nov. 7, 1968 vs. Philadelphia)—6.
Darryl Sittler, Toronto Maple Leafs (Feb. 7, 1976 vs. Boston Bruins)—6.
WHA—Ron Ward, New York Raiders (January 4, 1973 vs. Ottawa)—5.
Ron Climie, Edmonton Oilers (vs. N.Y. Golden Blades, November 6, 1973)—5.
Andre Hinse, Houston Aeros (Jan. 16, 1975 vs. Edmonton)—5.
Vaclav Nedomansky, Toronto Toros (Nov. 13, 1975 vs. Denver Spurs)—5.
Wayne Connelly, Minnesota Fighting Saints (Nov. 27, 1975 vs. Cincinnati Stingers)—5.
Ron Ward, Cleveland Crusaders (Nov. 30, 1975 vs. Toronto Toros)—5.
Real Cloutier, Quebec Nordiques (Oct. 26, 1976 vs. Phoenix Roadrunners)—5.
CHL—Jim Mayer, Dallas Black Hawks (February 23, 1979)—6.
AHL—Bob Heron, Pittsburgh Hornets (1941-42)—6.
Harry Pidhirny, Springfield Indians (1953-54)—6.
Camille Henry, Providence Reds (1955-56)—6.
IHL—Pierre Brillant, Indianapolis Chiefs (Feb. 18, 1959)—6.
Bryan McLay, Muskegon Zephyrs (Mar. 8, 1961)—6.
Elliott Chorley, St. Paul Saints (Jan. 17, 1962)—6.
Joe Kastelic, Muskegon Zephyrs (Mar. 1, 1962)—6.
Tom St. James, Flint Generals (Mar. 15, 1985)—6.

2—ASSISTS

NHL—Billy Taylor, Detroit Red Wings (Mar. 16, 1947 vs. Chicago)—7.
Wayne Gretzky, Edmonton Oilers (Feb. 15, 1980 vs. Washington)—7.

WHA—Jim Harrison, Alberta Oilers (January 30, 1973 vs. New York)—7.
Jim Harrison, Cleveland Crusaders (Nov. 30, 1975 vs. Toronto Toros)—7.
CHL—Art Stratton, St. Louis Braves (1966-67)—6.
Ron Ward, Tulsa Oilers (1967-68)—6.
Bill Hogaboam, Omaha Knights, January 15, 1972—6.
Jim Wiley, Tulsa Oilers, (1974-75)—6.
AHL—Art Stratton, Buffalo Bisons (Mar. 17, 1963 vs. Pittsburgh)—9.
IHL—Jean-Paul Denis, St. Paul Saints (Jan. 17, 1962)—9.

3—POINTS

NHL—Darryl Sittler, Toronto Maple Leafs (Feb. 7, 1976 vs. Boston Bruins)—10.
WHA—Jim Harrison, Alberta Oilers (January 30, 1973 vs. New York)—10.
CHL—Steve Vickers, Omaha Knights (Jan. 15, 1972 vs. Kansas City)—8.
AHL—Art Stratton, Buffalo Bisons (Mar. 17, 1963 vs. Pittsburgh)—9.
IHL—Elliott Chorley, St. Paul Saints (Jan. 17, 1962)—11.
Jean-Paul Denis, St. Paul Saints (Jan. 17, 1962)—11.

4—PENALTY MINUTES

NHL—Randy Holt, Los Angeles Kings (March 11, 1979 vs. Philadelphia)—67.
WHA—Dave Hanson, Birmingham Bulls (Feb. 5, 1978 vs. Indianapolis)—46.
CHL—Gary Rissling, Birmingham Bulls (Dec. 5, 1980 vs. Salt Lake)—49.
AHL—Wally Weir, Rochester Americans (Jan. 16, 1981 vs. New Brunswick)—54.
IHL—Willie Prognitz, Dayton Gems (Oct. 29, 1977)—63.

DEFENSEMEN'S RECORDS
SINGLE SEASON

1—GOALS

NHL—Paul Coffey, Edmonton Oilers (1985-86 season)—48.
WHA—Kevin Morrison, Jersey Knights (1973-74 season)—24.
CHL—Dan Poulin, Nashville South Stars (1981-82 season)—29.
AHL—Greg Tebbutt, Baltimore Skipjacks (1982-83 season)—28.
IHL—Roly McLenahan, Cincinnati Mohawks (1955-56 season)—34.

2—ASSISTS

NHL—Bobby Orr, Boston Bruins (1970-71 season)—102.
WHA—J. C. Tremblay, Quebec Nordiques (1975-76 season)—77.
CHL—Barclay Plager, Omaha Knights (1963-64 season)—61.
AHL—Craig Levie, Nova Scotia Voyageurs (1980-81 season)—62.
IHL—Gerry Glaude, Muskegon Zephyrs (1962-63 season)—86.

3—POINTS

NHL—Bobby Orr, Boston Bruins (1970-71 season)—139.
WHA—J. C. Tremblay, Quebec Nordiques (1972-73 and 1975-76 seasons)—89.
CHL—Dan Poulin, Nashville South Stars (1981-82 season)—85.
AHL—Greg Tebbutt, Baltimore Skipjacks (1982-83 season)—84.
IHL—Gerry Glaude, Muskegon Zephyrs (1962-63 season)—101.

American Hockey League

218 Memorial Avenue, West Springfield, Mass. 01089
Phone— (413) 781-2030

Chairman of the Board—Robert W. Clarke
President and Treasurer—Jack A. Butterfield
Vice-President and General Counsel—Richard F. Canning
Vice-President, Secretary—Gordon C. Anziano

Board Of Governors

Adirondack—Jim Devellano
Baltimore—John M. Haas
Binghamton—Robert Carr
Fredericton—Gilles Leger
Hershey—Frank Mathers
Maine—Ed Anderson
Moncton—Gary O'Neill
New Haven—Macgregor Kilpatrick
Newmarket—Gerry McNamara
Nova Scotia—Bruce McGregor
Rochester—George Bergantz
Sherbrooke—Serge Savard
Springfield—Peter Cooney
Honorary Governor—George Sage

Adirondack Red Wings

President—Michael Ilitch
Governor—Jim Devellano
Executive Vice President—Jim Lites
General Manager—Neil Smith
Dir. of Operations—Jack Kelley
Coach—Bill Dineen
Dir. of Public Relations—John Kelley
Dir. of Marketing and Promotions—Stu Mayer
Trainer—David Casey
Home Ice—Glens Falls Civic Center
Address—1 Civic Center Plaza,
        Glens Falls, N.Y. 12801
Seating Capacity—4,770
NHL Affiliation—Detroit Red Wings
Phone— (518) 798-0366

Baltimore Skipjacks

President—Barton S. Mitchell
Governor—John M. Haas
Alternate Governor—Ken Schinkel
Vice-President—William Sullivan
Secretary—James S. Watson
Treasurer—Gary Fisher
Exec. Vice-Pres.—Walter R. "Bud" Freeman, Jr.
Dir. of Communications—Terry Ficorelli
Director of Marketing and Promotions—Mike Naused
Coach—Gene Ubriaco
Trainer—Tim Ringler
Home Ice—Baltimore Civic Center
Address—Civic Center-Suite 412,
        201 W. Baltimore Street
        Baltimore, Md. 21201
Seating Capacity—11,025
NHL Affiliation—None
Phone— (301) 727-0703

Binghamton Whalers

General Partners—Robert Carr, Jim McCoy,
        Tom Mitchell
Governor—Robert Carr
Coach, Dir. of Hockey Operations—Larry Pleau
Business Manager—Bob Ohrablo
Director of Marketing—Dave Armstrong
Trainer—Jon R. Smith
Executive Assistant—Kim Anderson
Home Ice—Broome County
        Veterans Memorial Arena
Address—1 Stuart Street
        Binghamton, N.Y. 13901
Seating Capacity—4,855

NHL Affiliations—Hartford Whalers and
        Washington Capitals
Phone— (607) 723-8937

Fredericton Express

President/Governor—Gilles Leger
Director of Operations—Michael Doyle
General Manager/Coach—Ron LaPointe
Comptroller—Mary Lifford
Trainer—Marty Flynn
Assistant Comptroller—Cathy Belmore
Equipment Manager—Scott Beckingham
Executive Secretary—Janice Wilson
Home Ice—Aitken Center, University
        of New Brunswick
Seating Capacity—3,548
NHL Affiliations—Quebec Nordiques
        and Vancouver Canucks
Address—Aitken Center, Box 9900
        Fredericton, N.B. E3B 5G4
Phone— (506) 458-9929

Hershey Bears

Board Chairman—Edward R. Book
President—J. Bruce McKinney
Gov., Pres. & Gen. Mgr.—Frank Mathers
Coach—John Paddock
Trainer—Dan Stuck
Publicity and Marketing—Doug Yingst
Home Ice—Hersheypark Arena
Address—P.O. Box 866
        Hershey, Pa. 17033
Seating Capacity—7,286
NHL Affiliation—Philadelphia Flyers
Phone— (717) 534-3380

Maine Mariners

Governor & President—Ed Anderson
Gen. Man./Coach—Mike Milbury
Administrative Assist.—Doug Forester
Office Manager—Susan Small
Dir. Media Relations—Scott Wykoff
Director of Marketing—Dave Ekelund
Group Sales—Joe Ballard
Trainer—Ray Jones
Home Ice—Cumberland County
        Civic Center
Address—P.O. Box 1219
        Portland, Me. 04104
Seating Capacity—6,734
NHL Affiliation—Boston Bruins
Phone— (207) 775-3411

Moncton Hawks

Governor—Gary O'Neill
General Manager/Coach—Rick Bowness
Business Manager—Brian Foster
Director of Marketing, Media Relations
        and Public Relations—Larry Haley
Accountant—Darlene Weir
Home Ice—Moncton Coliseum
Address—P.O. Box 2940, Station A
        Moncton, N.B. E1C 8T8
Seating Capacity—6,904
NHL Affiliation—Winnipeg Jets
Phone— (506) 857-4000

New Haven Nighthawks

Governor—Macgregor Kilpatrick
President—Ken Doi
General Manager—Roy Mlakar
Coach—Robbie Ftorek
Dir. of Press Relations—Jan MacDonald
Trainers—Mark Decola & Scott Smith
Office Manager—Henry Bradbury
Home Ice—Veterans Memorial Coliseum
Address—P.O. Box 1444
        New Haven, Conn. 06506
Seating Capacity—5,636
NHL Affiliations—New York Rangers and
        Los Angeles Kings
Phone—(203) 787-0101

Newmarket Saints

Chairman of the Board—Harold Ballard
Governor—Gerry McNamara
General Manager—Gordon Stellick
Coach—Paul Gardner
Dir. Public Relations—Derek Chalmers
Trainer—Ken Garrett
Home Ice—Newmarket Recreation Complex
Address—Eagle Street
        Newmarket, Que., Ont., L3Y 4W3
Seating Capacity—2,700
NHL Affiliation—Toronto Maple Leafs
Phone—(416) 895-7078

Nova Scotia Oilers

Chairman—R.F. "Tiny" Titus
President—Glen Sather
Governor/Vice President—Bruce McGregor
Director of Operations—John Blackwell
General Manager/Coach—Larry Kish
Controller—Warner Baum
Media Relations and Dir. of Marketing—
        Dean Dachyshyn
Dir. of Player Personnel—Barry Fraser
Director of Admin. and Tickets—Pamela Rudolph
Trainer—Kevin Duguay
Home Ice—Halifax Metro-Centre
Address—5284 Duke Street
        Halifax, N.S. B3J 3L2
Seating Capacity—9,549
NHL Affiliation—Edmonton Oilers
Phone—(902) 429-7600

Rochester Americans

Board Chairman—R. Bruce Davey
Governor and General Manager—George Bergantz
Coach—John Van Boxmeer
P.R. Director—Don Stevens
Asst. Dir. of P.R.—Mike Tedesco

Dir. of Marketing/Sales—Randy Scott
Executive Assistant—Cheryl Barz
Administrative Asst.—Donna Arengi
Trainer—Kent Weisback
Home Ice—War Memorial Auditorium
Address—War Memorial Auditorium,
        100 Exchange Street
        Rochester, N.Y. 14614
Seating Capacity—7,357
NHL Affiliation—Buffalo Sabres
Phone—(716) 454-5335

Sherbrooke Canadiens

President—George Guilbault
Governor—Serge Savard
General Manager—Andre Boudrias
Coach—Pat Burns
Director of Marketing—Alain Trehout
Dir. of Operations—Claude Larose
Asst. Dir. of Operations—Roger Roy
Trainer—Pierre Gervais
Home Ice—Sherbrooke Sports Palace
Address—360 Parc Street
        Sherbrooke, Que. J1E 2J9
Seating Capacity—4,321
NHL Affiliation—Montreal Canadiens
Phone—(819) 566-2114

Springfield Indians

Governor and President—Peter R. Cooney
Alternate Governor—Bill Torrey, James J. Coogan
General Manager—Bruce Landon
Business Manager—Martha Dailey
Broadcaster/Publicity Dir.—John Forslund
Coach—Gord Lane
Trainer—Ed Tyburski
Home Ice—Springfield Civic Center
Address—58 Dwight Street
        Springfield, Mass. 01103
Seating Capacity—7,602
NHL Affiliation—New York Islanders
Phone—(413) 736-4546

Utica Devils

President—Frank DuRoss
Governor—Max McNab
General Manager/Coach—Tom McVie
Dir. of Marketing—Paul D'Aiuto
Media Relations Assist.—Kevin Korzenski
Home Ice—Utica Memorial Coliseum
Address—400 Oriskany St., W.
        Utica, N.Y. 13502
Seating Capacity—4,012
NHL Affiliation—New Jersey Devils
Phone—(315) 724-2126

1986-87 Final AHL Standings

North Division

	G.	W.	L.	T.	Pts.	GF.	GA.
Sherbrooke Canadiens	80	50	28	2	102	328	257
Adirondack Red Wings	80	44	31	5	93	329	296
Moncton Golden Flames	80	43	31	6	92	338	315
Nova Scotia Oilers	80	38	39	3	79	318	315
Maine Mariners	80	35	40	5	75	272	298
Fredericton Express	80	32	43	5	69	292	357

South Division

	G.	W.	L.	T.	Pts.	GF.	GA.
Rochester Americans	80	47	26	7	101	315	263
Binghamton Whalers	80	47	26	7	101	309	259
New Haven Nighthawks	80	44	25	11	99	331	315
Hershey Bears	80	43	36	1	87	329	309
Baltimore Skipjacks	80	35	37	8	78	277	295
Springfield Indians	80	34	40	6	74	296	344
Newmarket Saints	80	28	48	4	60	226	337

NOTE: Ties are a result of shootout losses and are worth one point. These are not included in team losses.

In a shootout, the winning team is credited with a goal. This goal is included in the team "goals for" column and not credited to an individual shooter. The losing team has a goal added to its team "goals against" column and is not charged to an individual goalie.

The following are shootout wins per team: Adirondack (5), Baltimore (4), Binghamton (9), Fredericton (3), Hershey (4), Maine (4), Moncton (2), New Haven (5), Newmarket (10), Nova Scotia (5), Rochester (6), Sherbrooke (4), Springfield (9).

Top 20 Scorers for the John B. Sollenberger Trophy

	Games	G.	A.	Pts.	Pen.
1. Tim Tookey, Hershey	80	51	*73	*124	45
2. Alain Lemieux, Baltimore	72	41	56	97	62
3. Brett Hull, Moncton	67	50	42	92	16
4. Mitch Lamoureux, Hershey	78	43	46	89	122
5. Glenn Merkosky, Adirondack	77	*54	31	85	66
Ross Fitzpatrick, Hershey	66	45	40	85	34
7. Ray Allison, Hershey	78	29	55	84	57
8. Bruce Boudreau, Nova Scotia	78	35	47	82	40
9. Serge Boisvert, Sherbrooke	78	27	54	81	29
10. Wes Jarvis, Newmarket	70	28	50	78	32
11. Mike Millar, Binghamton	61	45	32	77	38
12. Paul Fenton, New Haven	70	37	38	75	45
13. Larry Floyd, Maine	77	30	44	74	50
14. Daryl Evans, Newmarket	74	27	46	73	17
15. Dale Krentz, Adirondack	71	32	39	71	68
16. John LeBlanc, Fredericton	75	40	30	70	27
17. Chris Cichocki, Adirondack	55	31	34	65	27
Maine	7	2	2	4	0
Totals	62	33	36	69	27
18. Geordie Robertson, Adirondack	63	28	41	69	94
19. Alfie Turcotte, Nova Scotia	70	27	41	68	37
Karel Svoboda, Sherbrooke	73	22	46	68	45

Adirondack Red Wings

	Games	G.	A.	Pts.	Pen.
Glenn Merkosky	77	*54	31	85	66
Dale Krentz	71	32	39	71	68
Geordie Robertson	63	28	41	69	94
Tom O'Regan	58	20	42	62	78
Ted Speers	80	24	37	61	39
Joe Murphy	71	21	38	59	61
Eddie Johnstone	61	30	22	52	83
Mark Lamb	49	14	36	50	45
Jim Smith	77	8	27	35	43
Phil DeGaetano	78	7	23	30	75
Doug Houda	77	6	23	29	142
Dennis Smith	64	4	24	28	120
Ken Strong	31	7	13	20	18
Ali Butorac	28	8	6	14	30
Barry Melrose	55	4	9	13	170
Tom Martin	18	5	6	11	57
Neil Magannety	22	7	3	10	7
Pierre Aubry	17	3	7	10	23
Shawn Dineen	29	2	7	9	22
Peter Ekroth	12	1	5	6	12

	Games	G.	A.	Pts.	Pen.
Rick Zombo	25	0	6	6	22
Mark Kumpel	7	2	3	5	0
Bob Probert	7	1	4	5	15
Steve Martinson, Hers.	17	0	3	3	85
Adirondack	14	1	1	2	78
Totals	31	1	4	5	163
Dave Korol	48	1	4	5	67
Lee Norwood	3	0	3	3	0
Wayne Crawford	2	1	1	2	0
Chris Pusey (Goalie)	11	0	1	1	4
Mike O'Neill	24	0	1	1	0
Sam St. Laurent (G.)	25	0	1	1	4
Corrado Micalef (G.)	1	0	0	0	0
John Beukeboom	2	0	0	0	4
Guy Phillips	2	0	0	0	0
Bill Shibicky	2	0	0	0	0
Randy Hansch (Goalie)	10	0	0	0	0
Taras Diakiwski	26	0	0	0	10
Mark Laforest (Goalie)	37	0	0	0	10

Baltimore Skipjacks

	Games	G.	A.	Pts.	Pen.
Alain Lemieux	72	41	56	97	62
Carl Mokosak	67	23	27	50	228
Dwight Mathiason	61	23	22	45	49
Mickey Volcan	72	8	36	44	118
Gary Rissling	66	15	23	38	285
Jim McGeough	45	18	19	37	37
Troy Vollhofer	67	11	25	36	90
Phil Bourque	49	15	16	31	183
Mark Teevens	71	15	16	31	34
Troy Loney	40	13	14	27	134
Todd Charlesworth	75	5	21	26	64
Steve Carlson	67	12	13	25	32
Mike Blaisdell	43	12	12	24	47
Neil Belland	61	6	18	24	12
Michel Therrien	70	7	16	23	48
Roger Belanger	32	9	11	20	14
Mike Rowe	79	1	18	19	64
Mitch Wilson	58	8	9	17	353
Chris Dahlquist	51	1	16	17	50
Warren Young	22	8	7	15	95
Scott Johnson	63	8	7	15	27
Norm Schmidt	36	4	7	11	25
John DelCol	54	4	5	9	100
Mike Richard	9	5	2	7	2
Dwight Schofield	20	1	5	6	58
David Goertz	16	0	3	3	8
Jeff Cornelius	7	0	2	2	25
Steve Guenette (Goalie)	54	0	2	2	13
Brian Ford (Goalie)	32	0	1	1	2
Murray Nystrom	7	0	0	0	19

Binghamton Whalers

	Games	G.	A.	Pts.	Pen.
Mike Millar	61	45	32	77	38
Bill Gardner	50	17	44	61	18
Dallas Gaume	77	18	39	57	31
Grant Martin	63	30	23	53	86
Mark Taylor	67	16	37	53	40
Yves Courteau	57	15	28	43	8
Greg Britz	74	25	16	41	66
Mike Hoffman	74	9	32	41	120
Steve Leach	54	18	21	39	39
Brad Shaw	77	9	30	39	43
Paul Cavallini	66	12	24	36	188
Yves Beaudoin	63	11	25	36	35
Tony Kellin	66	8	27	35	65
Ed Kastelic	48	17	11	28	124
Gary Sampson	37	12	16	28	10
Jim Thomson	57	13	10	23	*360
John Druce	77	13	9	22	131
John Mokosak	72	2	15	17	187
Mark Vichorek	64	1	12	13	63
Wayne Babych	6	2	5	7	6
David Jensen	6	2	5	7	0
Sylvain Cote	12	2	4	6	0
Shane Churla	24	1	5	6	249
Grant Jennings	47	1	5	6	125
Bobby Crawford, N.H.	4	3	0	3	7
Binghamton	5	0	2	2	0
Totals	9	3	2	5	7
Todd Channell	12	1	4	5	4
Jeff Greenlaw	4	0	2	2	0
Sean Cronin	12	0	1	1	60
Peter Sidorkiewicz (G.)	57	0	1	1	10
Jamie Falle (Goalie)	2	0	0	0	0
Bob Mason (Goalie)	2	0	0	0	2
Jean MacKenzie	3	0	0	0	0
Rod Matachuk	3	0	0	0	0
Pete Peeters (Goalie)	4	0	0	0	2
Yvon Corriveau	7	0	0	0	2
Kris King	7	0	0	0	18
Marc D'Amour (Goalie)	8	0	0	0	2
Al Jensen (Goalie)	13	0	0	0	6

Fredericton Express

	Games	G.	A.	Pts.	Pen.
John LeBlanc	75	40	30	70	27
Mark Kirton	80	27	37	64	20
Jeff Rohlicek	70	19	37	56	22
Jean-Marc Lanthier	78	15	38	53	24
Taylor Hall	36	21	20	41	23
Ken Quinney	48	14	27	41	20
Greg Malone	49	13	22	35	50
Trevor Stienburg	48	14	12	26	123
Daniel Poudrier	69	8	18	26	11
Steve Finn	38	7	19	26	73
Mike Stevens	71	7	18	25	258
Doug Shedden, Adir.	5	2	2	4	4
Fredericton	15	12	6	18	0
Totals	20	14	8	22	4
Terry Perkins	44	10	11	21	35
Dunc MacIntyre	37	6	15	21	30
Marc Crawford	25	8	11	19	21
Wayne Groulx	30	11	7	18	8
Jeff Brown	26	2	14	16	16
Richard Zemlak	28	9	6	15	201
Bill Derlago	16	7	8	15	2
Brian Bertuzzi	55	7	8	15	50
Yves Heroux	37	8	6	14	13
Jason Lafreniere	11	3	11	14	0
Dave Bruce	17	7	6	13	73
Craig Coxe	46	1	12	13	168
Allan Measures	29	3	8	11	12
Eric Germain	44	2	8	10	28
Brett MacDonald	49	0	9	9	29
Claude Julien	17	1	6	7	22
Risto Siltanen	6	2	4	6	6
Jim Agnew	67	0	5	5	261
Mike Hough	10	1	3	4	20
Vojtech Kucera	13	1	3	4	10
Wendell Young (Goalie)	30	0	4	4	8

	Games	G.	A.	Pts.	Pen.
Tom Karalis	37	0	3	3	64
Robert Emery	42	2	0	2	63
Jean-Marc Gaulin	17	1	1	2	15
Robin Bartel	10	0	2	2	15
Dwayne Boettger	22	0	2	2	11
Scott Gordon (Goalie)	31	0	2	2	12
Paul Gerlitz	8	0	1	1	0
Richard Sevigny (Goalie)	16	0	1	1	48
Jeff Prendergrast	5	0	0	0	0
Pat Price	7	0	0	0	14
Frank Caprice (Goalie)	12	0	0	0	2

Hershey Bears

	Games	G.	A.	Pts.	Pen.
Tim Tookey	80	51	*73	*124	45
Mitch Lamoureux	78	43	46	89	122
Ross Fitzpatrick	66	45	40	85	34
Ray Allison	78	29	55	84	57
Brian Dobbin	52	26	35	61	66
Kevin McCarthy	74	6	44	50	86
Al Hill	76	13	35	48	124
Steve Smith	66	11	26	37	191
Dave Gans, New Haven	29	10	11	21	20
Hershey	20	7	8	15	28
Totals	49	17	19	36	48
Don Nachbaur	57	18	17	35	274
Jere Gillis	47	13	22	35	32
Kevin Maxwell	56	12	20	32	139
Jeff Brubaker, N. Scotia	47	10	16	26	80
Hershey	12	1	2	3	30
Totals	59	11	18	29	110
John Dzikowski	61	13	13	26	90
Mike Murray	70	8	16	24	10
Craig Berube	63	7	17	24	325
Jeff Chychrun	74	1	17	18	239
Mike Stothers	75	5	11	16	283
John Stevens	63	1	15	16	131
Len Hachborn	17	4	10	14	2
Ian Armstrong	68	0	7	7	148
Brian McKinnon	7	3	2	5	2
Dave McLay	7	1	2	3	15
Greg Smyth	35	0	2	2	158
Kerry Huffman	3	0	1	1	0
Nick Kypreos	10	0	1	1	4
Darren Jensen (Goalie)	59	0	1	1	22
Georges Gagnon (G.)	1	0	0	0	0
Tony Horacek	1	0	0	0	0
John Kemp (Goalie)	30	0	0	0	46

Maine Mariners

	Games	G.	A.	Pts.	Pen.
Larry Floyd	77	30	44	74	50
Chris Cichocki, Adir.	55	31	34	65	27
Maine	7	2	2	4	0
Totals	62	33	36	69	27
Steve Tsujiura	80	24	41	65	73
Tim Lenardon	61	28	35	63	30
Rich Chernomaz	58	35	27	62	65
Doug Brown	73	24	34	58	15
Murray Brumwell	69	10	38	48	30
Dan Dorion	70	16	22	38	47
Alan Stewart	74	14	24	38	143
Pat Conacher	56	12	14	26	47
Alan Hepple	74	6	19	25	137
Rocky Trottier	77	9	14	23	41
Dave Pichette	61	6	16	22	69

	Games	G.	A.	Pts.	Pen.
Bud Stefanski	29	9	12	21	34
Brian Tutt	41	6	15	21	19
David Anderson	59	9	9	18	80
Gordie Mark	29	4	10	14	66
Noel Catterall	80	1	13	14	50
Jan Ludvig	14	6	4	10	46
Archie Henderson	67	4	6	10	246
John McNamara	63	1	9	10	6
Perry Anderson	9	5	4	9	42
Paul Kobylarz	66	2	7	9	43
Uli Hiemer	26	4	3	7	51
Anders Carlsson	6	0	6	6	2
Greg Evtushevski	17	1	1	2	55
Craig Billington (G.)	20	0	1	1	4
Kirk McLean (Goalie)	45	0	1	1	6
Dave Emerson	3	0	0	0	2
Neal Davey	6	0	0	0	2
Shawn MacKenzie (G.)	6	0	0	0	0
Jim Bissett	10	0	0	0	0
Chris Terreri (Goalie)	14	0	0	0	0

Moncton Golden Flames

	Games	G.	A.	Pts.	Pen.
Brett Hull	67	50	42	92	16
Randy Burridge	47	26	41	67	139
Doug Kostynski	74	21	45	66	22
Bob Sweeney	58	29	26	55	81
John Carter	58	25	30	55	60
Dave Pasin	66	27	25	52	47
Peter Bakovic	77	17	34	51	280
Ray Podloski	70	23	27	50	12
Gary Roberts	38	20	18	38	72
Wade Campbell	64	12	23	35	34
Dave Reid	40	12	22	34	23
Dale DeGray	45	10	22	32	57
Bob Bodak	48	11	20	31	75
Brian Bradley	20	12	16	28	8
Kraig Nienhuis	54	10	17	27	44
Marc Paterson	70	6	21	27	112
Gord Hynes	69	2	19	21	21
Don Mercier	74	5	11	16	107
Mike Rucinski	42	5	9	14	14
Darwin McCutcheon	69	1	10	11	187
Ken Sabourin	75	1	10	11	166
Lyndon Byers	27	5	5	10	63
Nevin Markwart	3	3	3	6	11
Landis Chaulk	14	1	0	1	13
Tom McCarthy	2	0	1	1	0
Alain St. Arnaud	3	0	1	1	10
Frank Simonetti	7	0	1	1	6
Pat Riggin (Goalie)	14	0	1	1	6
Maurice Dupuis (Goalie)	2	0	0	0	0
Rob Kivell	3	0	0	0	2
Bill Ranford (Goalie)	3	0	0	0	0
R. Romano, Balt. (G.)	5	0	0	0	0
Moncton (Goalie)	1	0	0	0	0
Totals	6	0	0	0	0
Bill Gregoire	7	0	0	0	29
Dale Rivington	15	0	0	0	4
Cleon Daskalakis (G.)	27	0	0	0	14
Doug Dadswell (Goalie)	42	0	0	0	14

New Haven Nighthawks

	Games	G.	A.	Pts.	Pen.
Paul Fenton	70	37	38	75	45

	Games	G.	A.	Pts.	Pen.
Bill O'Dwyer	65	22	42	64	74
Dave Gagner	56	22	41	63	50
Mike Donnelly	58	27	34	61	52
Lyle Phair	65	19	27	46	77
Mark Lofthouse	47	18	27	45	34
Gordie Walker	59	24	20	44	58
Simon Wheeldon	38	11	28	39	39
Brian Wilks	43	16	20	36	23
Norm MacIver	71	6	30	36	73
Chris Kontos	36	14	17	31	29
Guy Benoit	41	14	15	29	10
Glen Currie	54	12	16	28	16
Jim Leavins	54	7	21	28	16
Mark Raedeke	50	10	15	25	56
Mike Siltala	17	13	6	19	20
Peter Dineen	59	2	17	19	140
Dan Gratton	49	6	10	16	45
Rob Whistle	55	4	12	16	30
Ken Hammond	66	1	15	16	76
Steve Moria	31	5	8	13	8
Chris Jensen	14	4	9	13	41
Terry Carkner	12	2	6	8	56
Scott Smith	39	0	8	8	63
Jim Wiemer	6	0	7	7	6
Lane Lambert	11	3	3	6	19
Jeff Crossman	61	2	3	5	133
Craig Redmond	5	2	2	4	6
Chris McSorley	22	2	2	4	116
Ron Talakoski	26	2	2	4	58
Paul Guay	6	1	3	4	11
Bruce Eakin	4	1	2	3	4
Ken Baumgartner	13	0	3	3	99
Dave Nicholls	6	2	0	2	12
David Langevin	10	1	1	2	7
Peter Sawkins	23	1	1	2	8
Raimo Helminen	6	0	2	2	0
Ron Scott (Goalie)	29	0	2	2	4
Glenn Healy (Goalie)	47	0	2	2	24
Brent Sapergia	2	0	1	1	0
Darren Eliot (Goalie)	4	0	1	1	2
Ken Duggan	13	0	1	1	4
Terry Kleisinger (G.)	1	0	0	0	0
Mark Tinordi	2	0	0	0	2
John English	3	0	0	0	6
Duanne Moeser	3	0	0	0	0
Jay Caufield	13	0	0	0	43

Newmarket Saints

	Games	G.	A.	Pts.	Pen.
Wes Jarvis	70	28	50	78	32
Daryl Evans	74	27	46	73	17
Gerard Waslen	79	22	30	52	64
Marty Dallman, Balt.	6	0	1	1	0
Newmarket	42	24	24	48	44
Totals	48	24	25	49	44
Darek Laxdal	78	24	20	44	69
Miroslav Ihnacak	32	11	17	28	6
Dean Defazio	76	7	13	20	116
Dan Hodgson	20	7	12	19	16
Rich Costello	48	6	11	17	53
Leigh Verstraete	57	9	7	16	179
Terry Martin	72	8	7	15	8
Bill Root	32	4	11	15	23
Scott Clements	70	1	14	15	77
Greg Hotham	51	4	9	13	60
Blake Wesley	79	1	12	13	170
Todd Petkovich	61	3	7	10	71

	Games	G.	A.	Pts.	Pen.
Jeff Jackson	7	3	6	9	13
Chris McRae	51	3	6	9	193
Todd Gill	11	1	8	9	33
Jerome Dupont	29	1	8	9	47
Peter Ihnacak	8	2	6	8	0
Val James	74	4	3	7	71
Cam Plante	19	3	4	7	14
Cliff Abrecht	63	2	5	7	20
Kevin Maguire	51	4	2	6	131
Ken Yaremchuk	14	2	4	6	21
Jim Benning	10	1	5	6	0
Ted Fauss	59	0	5	5	81
Tim Armstrong	5	3	0	3	2
Carmine Vani	27	1	1	2	31
Tim Bernhardt (Goalie)	31	0	2	2	0
Jeff Reese (Goalie)	50	0	2	2	24
Tom Fergus	1	0	1	1	0
Terry Johnson	24	0	1	1	37
Dan Daoust	1	0	0	0	4
Allan Bester (Goalie)	3	0	0	0	0
Bruce Dowie (Goalie)	4	0	0	0	2

Nova Scotia Oilers

	Games	G.	A.	Pts.	Pen.
Bruce Boudreau	78	35	47	82	40
Alfie Turcotte	70	27	41	68	37
Murray Eaves	76	26	38	64	46
Tom McMurchy	67	21	35	56	99
Brian Noonan	70	25	26	51	30
Don Biggs	80	22	25	47	165
Mike Moller	70	14	33	47	28
Dean Hopkins	59	20	25	45	84
Shawn Evans	55	7	28	35	29
Jim Wiemer	59	9	25	34	72
John Miner	45	5	28	33	38
Kelly Buchberger	70	12	20	32	257
Jim Camazzola	48	13	18	31	31
Dominic Campedelli, Sh.	7	3	2	5	2
Hershey	45	7	15	22	70
Nova Scotia	12	0	4	4	7
Totals	64	10	21	31	79
Steve Graves	59	18	10	28	22
Jim Playfair	60	1	21	22	82
Rik Wilson	45	8	13	21	109
Mark LaVarre	17	12	8	20	8
Normand Lacombe, Ro..	13	6	5	11	4
Nova Scotia	10	3	5	8	4
Totals	23	9	10	19	8
Wayne Van Dorp, Roch.	47	7	3	10	192
Nova Scotia	11	2	3	5	37
Totals	58	9	6	15	229
Al Tuer	69	1	14	15	273
Rick Paterson	31	5	7	12	2
Bruce Cassidy	19	2	8	10	4
Butch Goring	10	3	5	8	2
Brad MacGregor	47	2	6	8	6
Kent Paynter	66	2	6	8	57
Jeff Beukeboom	14	1	7	8	35
Lou Crawford	35	3	4	7	48
Grant Dion	14	1	4	5	2
Marty McSorley	7	2	2	4	48
W. Skorodenski (G.)	32	0	2	2	13
Daryl Reaugh (Goalie)	46	0	2	2	8
Victor Posa	2	1	0	1	2
Jim Mollard	2	0	1	1	0
Selmar Odelein	2	0	1	1	2
Tim Cranston	1	0	0	0	2

	Games	G.	A.	Pts.	Pen.
Rene Badeau	2	0	0	0	0
Darren Pang (Goalie)	7	0	0	0	0

Rochester Americans

	Games	G.	A.	Pts.	Pen.
Jody Gage	70	26	39	65	60
Gates Orlando	44	22	42	64	42
Doug Trapp	68	27	35	62	80
Jim Jackson	71	19	38	57	48
Don Lever	57	29	25	54	69
Bob Logan	56	30	14	44	27
Warren Harper	61	13	27	40	50
Benoit Hogue	52	14	20	34	52
Richie Dunn	64	6	26	32	47
Ray Sheppard	55	18	13	31	11
Paul Brydges	54	13	17	30	54
Jack Brownschidle	74	8	22	30	13
Mikael Andersson	42	6	20	26	14
Claude Verret	36	13	12	25	2
Jeff Parker	54	14	8	22	75
Richard Hajdu	58	7	15	22	90
Dave Fenyves	71	6	16	22	57
Uwe Krupp	42	3	19	22	50
Jay Fraser	36	8	12	20	159
Mark Ferner	54	0	12	12	157
Doug Smith	15	5	6	11	35
Jim Hofford	54	1	8	9	204
Bob Halkidis	59	1	8	9	144
Al Conroy	13	4	4	8	40
Shawn Anderson	15	2	5	7	11
Joe Reekie	22	0	6	6	52
Andy Ristau	23	1	1	2	113
Jayson Meyer	3	0	2	2	12
James Gasseau	7	0	2	2	6
Jim Burton	10	0	2	2	4
Marc Tornier	2	0	1	1	2
Darcy Wakaluk (Goalie)	11	0	1	1	12
Mike Craig (Goalie)	23	0	1	1	8
Daren Puppa (Goalie)	57	0	1	1	12
Steve Dykstra	18	0	0	0	77

Sherbrooke Canadiens

	Games	G.	A.	Pts.	Pen.
Serge Boisvert	78	27	54	81	29
Karel Svoboda	73	22	46	68	45
Gilles Thibaudeau	62	27	40	67	26
Randy Gilhen	75	36	29	65	44
Randy Bucyk	70	24	39	63	28
Ernie Vargas	69	22	32	54	52
Perry Ganchar	68	22	29	51	64
Scott Harlow	66	22	26	48	6
Rejean Cloutier	76	7	37	44	182
Peter Douris	62	14	28	42	24
Jose Charbonneau	72	14	27	41	94
Scott Sandelin	74	7	22	29	35
Joel Baillargeon	44	9	18	27	137
Steven Fletcher	70	15	11	26	261
Bobby Dollas	75	6	18	24	87
Luc Gauthier	78	5	17	22	81
Andre Villeneuve, Hers.	5	0	2	2	2
Sherbrooke	51	3	16	19	69
Totals	56	3	18	21	71

	Games	G.	A.	Pts.	Pen.
Peter Taglianetti	54	5	14	19	104
Steve Rooney	22	4	11	15	66
Stephane Richer	12	10	4	14	11
Billy Campbell	60	1	13	14	21
Graeme Bonar	21	6	6	12	7
John Kordic	10	4	4	8	49
Guy Rouleau	10	4	3	7	2
Sergio Momesso	6	1	6	7	10
David Maley	11	1	5	6	25
Rick Hayward	46	2	3	5	153
Kevin Houle	4	0	3	3	0
Len Nielsen	3	1	0	1	0
Steve Penney (Goalie)	4	0	1	1	2
Jamie Husgen	2	0	0	0	0
Daniel Berthiaume (G.)	7	0	0	0	2
Brian Williams	9	0	0	0	6
Jocelyn Perreault (G.)	13	0	0	0	0
Marc Behrend (Goalie)	18	0	0	0	4
Vincent Riendeau (G.)	41	0	0	0	23

Springfield Indians

	Games	G.	A.	Pts.	Pen.
Randy Smith	75	20	44	64	24
Mark Hamway	59	25	31	56	8
Stu Burnie	76	21	30	51	62
Paul Houck	64	29	18	47	58
Randy Wood	75	23	24	47	57
Mike Walsh	67	20	26	46	32
Roger Kortko	75	16	30	46	54
Pat Micheletti	67	17	26	43	39
Emanuel Viveiros	76	7	35	42	38
Randy Boyd	48	9	30	39	96
Tim Coulis	38	12	19	31	212
Jim Archibald	66	10	17	27	303
Neal Coulter	47	12	13	25	63
Todd Bergen	27	12	11	23	14
Dale Henry	23	9	14	23	49
Gord Paddock	78	6	11	17	127
Glenn Johannesen	54	10	6	16	156
Tom Weiss	46	6	10	16	47
Gerald Diduck	45	6	8	14	120
Colin Chisolm	75	1	11	12	141
Vern Smith	41	1	10	11	58
Scott Bjugstad	11	6	4	10	7
Gordon Lane	62	2	6	8	117
Mike Neill	32	3	4	7	67
Bruce Eakin	11	0	5	5	6
Larry DePalma	9	2	2	4	82
Bill Berg	4	1	1	2	4
Alan May	4	0	2	2	11
Chris Pryor	5	0	2	2	17
Duncan MacPherson	26	1	0	1	86
Jon Casey (Goalie)	13	0	1	1	8
Marty Wakelyn (Goalie)	21	0	1	1	6
Royden Gunn (Goalie)	29	0	1	1	17
Gary Johnson (Goalie)	1	0	0	0	0
Carey Lucyk	1	0	0	0	0
Scott Rettew	1	0	0	0	0
Marcel Frere	2	0	0	0	0
Garnet McKechney	2	0	0	0	4
Kari Takko (Goalie)	5	0	0	0	0
Mike Sands (Goalie)	19	0	0	0	0

Complete AHL Goaltending

	Games	Mins.	Goals	SO.	Avg.
Mark Laforest................................	37	2229	105(2)	3	2.83
Corrado Micalef.............................	1	59	5	0	5.08
Chris Pusey....................................	11	617	40(1)	0	3.89
Sam St. Laurent.............................	25	1397	98(4)	1	4.21
Randy Hansch................................	10	544	36	0	3.97
Shootout Losses			5		
Adirondack Totals....................	84	4846	296	4	3.66
Brian Ford	32	1541	99(5)	0	3.85
Steve Guenette	54	3035	157(8)	*5	3.10
Roberto Romano (a).......................	5	274	18	0	3.94
Shootout Losses			8		
Baltimore Totals.....................	91	4850	295	5	3.65
Bob Mason....................................	2	119	4	0	2.02
Peter Sidorkiewicz	57	3304	161(3)	4	2.92
Jamie Falle	2	64	6	0	5.62
Al Jensen......................................	13	684	42(2)	0	3.68
Pete Peeters	4	245	4	1	0.98
Marc D'Amour	8	461	30	0	3.90
Shootout Losses			7		
Binghamton Totals....................	86	4877	259	5	3.19
Frank Caprice................................	12	686	47	0	4.11
Scott Gordon.................................	31	1599	119(1)	0	4.47
Wendell Young...............................	30	1676	118(4)	0	4.22
Richard Sevigny.............................	16	884	62(1)	0	4.21
Shootout Losses			5		
Fredericton Totals....................	89	4845	357	0	4.42
Darren Jensen................................	*60	*3429	*215(6)	0	3.76
John Kemp	30	1349	80	1	3.56
Georges Gagnon.............................	1	40	7	0	10.50
Shootout Losses			1		
Hershey Totals.....................	91	4818	309	1	3.85
Craig Billington.............................	20	1151	70(2)	0	3.65
Kirk McLean...................................	45	2606	140(3)	1	3.22
Chris Terreri	14	765	57(1)	0	4.47
Shawn MacKenzie	6	321	19(1)	1	3.55
Shootout Losses			5		
Maine Totals.....................	85	4843	298	2	3.69
Doug Dadswell...............................	42	2275	138(2)	1	3.64
Cleon Daskalakis	27	1452	118(1)	0	4.88
Bill Ranford	3	180	6	0	2.00
Pat Riggin.....................................	14	798	34(1)	1	2.56
Roberto Romano (a).......................	1	65	3	0	2.77
Maurice Dupuis	2	76	6	0	4.74
Shootout Losses			6		
Moncton Totals.....................	89	4846	315	2	3.90
Glenn Healy	47	2828	173(4)	1	3.67
Ron Scott......................................	29	1744	107(1)	2	3.68
Terry Kleisinger.............................	1	40	4	0	6.00
Darren Eliot..................................	4	239	15	0	3.77
Shootout Losses			11		
New Haven Totals	81	4851	315	3	3.90
Allan Bester	3	190	6	0	1.89
Jeff Reese.....................................	50	2822	193(2)	1	4.10
Tim Bernhardt................................	31	1705	117(2)	1	4.12
Bruce Dowie	4	155	13	0	5.03
Shootout Losses			4		
Newmarket Totals	88	4872	337	2	4.15
Daryl Reaugh	46	2637	163(5)	1	3.71
Warren Skorodenski	32	1813	121(2)	2	4.00
Darren Pang...................................	7	389	21	0	3.24
Shootout Losses			3		
Nova Scotia Totals	85	4839	315	3	3.91
Mike Craig	23	1192	82(2)	0	4.13
Darcy Wakaluk	11	545	26	0	2.86
Daren Puppa..................................	57	3129	146	1	*2.80
Shootout Losses			7		
Rochester Totals.....................	91	4866	263	1	3.24

	Games	Mins.	Goals	SO.	Avg.
Daniel Berthiaume	7	420	23	0	3.29
Vincent Riendeau	41	2363	114(4)	2	2.89
Marc Behrend....................................	19	1124	62	0	3.31
Jocelyn Perreault	13	722	40	0	3.32
Steve Penney	4	199	12	0	3.62
Shootout Losses			2		
Sherbrooke Totals	84	4828	257	2	3.19
Royden Gunn	29	1599	107	0	4.02
Mike Sands......................................	19	1048	77(3)	0	4.41
Gary Johnson	1	19	0	0	0.00
Marty Wakelyn..................................	21	1144	75(1)	0	3.93
Kari Takko	5	300	16	1	3.20
Jon Casey	13	770	56(3)	0	4.36
Shootout Losses			6		
Springfield Totals	88	4880	344	1	4.23

( )—Empty Net Goals. Do not count against a Goaltender's average.
(a)—Romano played for Baltimore and Moncton.

Individual 1986-87 Leaders

Goals	Glenn Merkosky, Adirondack—	54
Assists...	Tim Tookey, Hershey—	73
Points..	Tim Tookey, Hershey—	124
Penalty Minutes	Jim Thomson, Binghamton—	360
Goaltending Average (25 Games)...........................	Daren Puppa, Rochester—	2.80
Shutouts	Steve Guenette, Baltimore—	5

1987 Calder Cup Playoffs
(All series best of seven)

Quarterfinals

Series "A"

	W.	L.	Pts.	GF.	GA.
Sherbrooke..................	4	1	8	25	16
Nova Scotia	1	4	2	16	25

(Sherbrooke wins series, 4 games to 1)

Series "C"

	W.	L.	Pts.	GF.	GA.
Rochester......................	4	1	8	24	17
Hershey	1	4	2	17	24

(Rochester wins series, 4 games to 1)

Series "B"

	W.	L.	Pts.	GF.	GA.
Adirondack	4	2	8	25	17
Moncton	2	4	4	17	25

(Adirondack wins series, 4 games to 2)

Series "D"

	W.	L.	Pts.	GF.	GA.
Binghamton	4	3	8	22	19
New Haven....................	3	4	6	19	22

(Binghamton wins series, 4 games to 3)

Semifinals

Series "E"

	W.	L.	Pts.	GF.	GA.
Sherbrooke..................	4	1	8	27	14
Adirondack	1	4	2	14	27

(Sherbrooke wins series, 4 games to 1)

Series "F"

	W.	L.	Pts.	GF.	GA.
Rochester......................	4	2	8	20	12
Binghamton	2	4	4	12	20

(Rochester wins series, 4 games to 2)

Finals—For the Calder Cup

Series "G"

	W.	L.	Pts.	GF.	GA.
Rochester......................	4	3	8	30	33
Sherbrooke..................	3	4	6	33	30

(Rochester wins series, and Calder Cup, 4 games to 3)

Top 10 Playoff Scorers

	Games	G.	A.	Pts.	Pen.
1. Gates Orlando, Rochester	18	9	13	*22	14
Peter Douris, Sherbrooke	17	7	*15	*22	16
3. Randy Gilhen, Sherbrooke	17	7	13	20	10
4. Jody Gage, Rochester	17	*14	5	19	24
5. Serge Boisvert, Sherbrooke	15	8	10	18	15
6. Perry Ganchar, Sherbrooke	17	9	8	17	37
Jose Charbonneau, Sherbrooke	16	5	12	17	17
8. Ray Sheppard, Rochester	15	12	3	15	2
Bob Logan, Rochester	18	5	10	15	4
Dave Fenyves, Rochester	18	3	12	15	10

Team-by-Team Playoff Scoring

Adirondack Red Wings
(Lost semifinals to Sherbrooke, 4-1)

	Games	G.	A.	Pts.	Pen.
Glenn Merkosky	11	6	8	14	7
Ken Strong	11	6	7	13	12
Tom O'Regan	11	3	9	12	10
Peter Ekroth	11	2	9	11	31
Doug Houda	11	1	8	9	50
Ray Cote	9	2	6	8	2
Dale Krentz	11	3	4	7	10
Neil Magannety	11	3	4	7	5
Dave Korol	11	2	2	4	21
Pierre Aubry	9	1	3	4	32
Joe Murphy	10	2	1	3	33
Barry Melrose	11	1	2	3	107
Steve Martinson	11	2	0	2	*108
Ted Speers	11	2	0	2	4
Shawn Dineen	11	1	1	2	30
Mark Kumpel	1	1	0	1	0
Eddie Johnstone	5	1	0	1	2
Adam Graves	5	0	1	1	0
Ali Butorac	7	0	1	1	11
Phil DeGaetano	10	0	1	1	51
Sam St. Laurent (Goalie)	3	0	0	0	0
Bill Shibicky	3	0	0	0	0
Dennis Smith	6	0	0	0	8
Randy Hansch (Goalie)	10	0	0	0	0

Binghamton Whalers
(Lost semifinals to Rochester, 4-2)

	Games	G.	A.	Pts.	Pen.
Bill Gardner	13	4	8	12	14
Mike Millar	13	7	4	11	27
Paul Cavallini	13	2	7	9	35
Brad Shaw	12	1	8	9	2
Mark Taylor	13	2	6	8	9
Gary Sampson	11	4	2	6	0
Greg Britz	13	3	3	6	6
Yves Courteau	7	1	4	5	12
Grant Martin	12	3	1	4	16
Steve Leach	13	3	1	4	6
Mike Hoffman	13	2	2	4	23
John Druce	12	0	3	3	28
Tony Kellin	5	1	1	2	2
Dallas Gaume	12	1	1	2	7
John Mokosak	9	0	2	2	42
Grant Jennings	13	0	2	2	17
Yvon Corriveau	8	0	1	1	0
Jim Thomson	10	0	1	1	40
Yves Beaudoin	11	0	1	1	6

	Games	G.	A.	Pts.	Pen.
Brian Chapman	1	0	0	0	0
Jean MacKenzie	1	0	0	0	0
Mark Vichorek	2	0	0	0	0
Larry Shaw	3	0	0	0	0
Marc LaForge	4	0	0	0	7
Sean Cronin	10	0	0	0	41
Peter Sidorkiewicz (G.)	13	0	0	0	6

Hershey Bears
(Lost quarterfinals to Rochester, 4-1)

	Games	G.	A.	Pts.	Pen.
Tim Tookey	5	5	4	9	0
Brian Dobbin	5	4	2	6	15
Ross Fitzpatrick	5	1	4	5	10
Ray Allison	5	3	1	4	12
Kevin McCarthy	5	0	4	4	4
Mitch Lamoureux	5	1	2	3	8
Don Nachbaur	5	0	3	3	47
Jeff Brubaker	3	2	0	2	10
Len Hachborn	5	0	2	2	2
Steve Smith	5	0	2	2	8
Kevin Maxwell	3	1	0	1	30
Al Hill	5	0	1	1	2
Tony Horacek	1	0	0	0	0
John Kemp (Goalie)	2	0	0	0	0
Mike Murray	2	0	0	0	0
Greg Smyth	2	0	0	0	19
Ian Armstrong	3	0	0	0	2
John Stevens	3	0	0	0	7
Jeff Chychrun	4	0	0	0	10
Kerry Huffman	4	0	0	0	0
Darren Jensen (Goalie)	4	0	0	0	2
Dave Gans	5	0	0	0	21
Jere Gillis	5	0	0	0	9
Mike Stothers	5	0	0	0	10

Moncton Golden Flames
(Lost quarterfinals to Adirondack, 4-2)

	Games	G.	A.	Pts.	Pen.
Peter Bakovic	6	3	3	6	54
Brian Bradley	6	3	3	6	16
John Carter	6	2	3	5	5
Brett Hull	3	2	2	4	2
Dale DeGray	5	2	1	3	19
Doug Kostynski	6	2	1	3	0
Randy Burridge	3	1	2	3	30
Benoit Douchet	5	0	3	3	18
Bob Bodak	6	1	1	2	18
Dave Pasin	6	1	1	2	14

	Games	G.	A.	Pts.	Pen.
Bob Sweeney	4	0	2	2	13
Bill Gregoire	6	0	2	2	48
Alain St. Arnaud	6	0	2	2	30
Darwin McCutcheon	4	0	1	1	51
Dave Reid	5	0	1	1	0
Dave Reierson	6	0	1	1	12
Ken Sabourin	6	0	1	1	27
Cleon Daskalakis (G.)	1	0	0	0	0
Marc Paterson	3	0	0	0	0
Ray Podloski	3	0	0	0	15
Gord Hynes	4	0	0	0	2
Don Mercier	4	0	0	0	15
Doug Dadswell (Goalie)	6	0	0	0	2

New Haven Nighthawks

(Lost quarterfinals to Binghamton, 4-3)

	Games	G.	A.	Pts.	Pen.
Paul Fenton	7	6	4	10	6
Dave Gagner	7	1	5	6	18
Gordie Walker	7	3	2	5	0
Guy Benoit	6	2	2	4	16
Brian Wilks	7	1	3	4	7
Jim Leavins	7	0	4	4	2
Glen Currie	6	2	1	3	0
Lyle Phair	7	0	3	3	13
Mike Donnelly	7	2	0	2	9
Rob Whistle	7	1	1	2	7
Terry Carkner	3	1	0	1	0
Mark Lofthouse	4	0	1	1	2
Ken Hammond	6	0	1	1	21
Peter Dineen	7	0	1	1	27
Mark Raedeke	7	0	1	1	33
Ron Talakoski	1	0	0	0	0
Jeff Crossman	2	0	0	0	20
Dan Gratton	2	0	0	0	0
Mark Tinordi	2	0	0	0	0
Bill O'Dwyer	3	0	0	0	14
Scott Smith	3	0	0	0	12
Simon Wheeldon	5	0	0	0	6
Ken Baumgartner	6	0	0	0	60
Glenn Healy (Goalie)	7	0	0	0	0
Norm MacIver	7	0	0	0	9

Nova Scotia Oilers

(Lost quarterfinals to Sherbrooke, 4-1)

	Games	G.	A.	Pts.	Pen.
Bruce Boudreau	5	3	3	6	4
Alfie Turcotte	5	2	4	6	2
Tom McMurchy	4	3	2	5	4
Brian Noonan	5	3	1	4	4
Rik Wilson	5	1	3	4	20
Shawn Evans	5	0	4	4	6
Jim Wiemer	5	0	4	4	2
Don Biggs	5	1	2	3	4
John Miner	5	0	3	3	4
Murray Eaves	4	1	1	2	2
Steve Graves	5	1	1	2	2
Normand Lacombe	5	1	1	2	6
Kelly Buchberger	5	0	1	1	23
Rick Paterson	5	0	1	1	10
Al Tuer	5	0	1	1	48
Dean Hopkins	1	0	0	0	5
Mike Moller	1	0	0	0	0
Kent Paynter	2	0	0	0	0
Daryl Reaugh (Goalie)	2	0	0	0	0
Jim Camazzola	3	0	0	0	0

	Games	G.	A.	Pts.	Pen.
Darren Pang (Goalie)	3	0	0	0	2
Dominic Campedelli	5	0	0	0	17
Wayne Van Dorp	5	0	0	0	56

Rochester Americans

(Winners of 1987 Calder Cup Playoffs)

	Games	G.	A.	Pts.	Pen.
Gates Orlando	18	9	13	*22	14
Jody Gage	17	*14	5	19	24
Ray Sheppard	15	12	3	15	2
Bob Logan	18	5	10	15	4
Dave Fenyves	18	3	12	15	10
Uwe Krupp	17	1	11	12	16
Jayson Meyer	18	2	8	10	14
Benoit Hogue	12	5	4	9	8
Jim Jackson	16	5	4	9	6
Doug Trapp	16	0	9	9	5
Don Lever	18	4	3	7	14
Richie Dunn	18	1	6	7	6
Claude Verret	8	3	3	6	0
Ken Priestlay	8	3	2	5	4
Warren Harper	11	1	4	5	18
Jack Brownschidle	12	1	3	4	0
Al Conroy	13	1	3	4	50
Jeff Parker	14	1	3	4	19
Mikael Andersson	9	1	2	3	2
Richard Hajdu	11	1	1	2	9
Jim Hofford	13	1	0	1	57
Jay Fraser	6	0	1	1	17
Paul Brydges	1	0	0	0	0
Andy Ristau	5	0	0	0	31
Darcy Wakaluk (Goalie)	5	0	0	0	0
Bob Halkidis	8	0	0	0	43
Daren Puppa (Goalie)	16	0	0	0	2

Sherbrooke Canadiens

(Lost finals to Rochester, 4-3)

	Games	G.	A.	Pts.	Pen.
Peter Douris	17	7	*15	*22	16
Randy Gilhen	17	7	13	20	10
Serge Boisvert	15	8	10	18	15
Perry Ganchar	17	9	8	17	37
Jose Charbonneau	16	5	12	17	17
David Maley	12	7	7	14	10
Randy Bucyk	17	3	11	14	2
Rejean Cloutier	17	3	9	12	59
Steven Fletcher	17	6	5	11	82
Scott Harlow	15	5	6	11	6
Ernie Vargas	16	6	3	9	13
Brent Gilchrist	10	2	7	9	2
Karel Svoboda	11	2	7	9	4
Peter Taglianett	10	2	5	7	25
Bobby Dollas	16	2	4	6	13
Scott Sandelin	16	2	4	6	2
Luc Gauthier	17	2	4	6	31
Joel Baillargeon	6	2	2	4	27
Mike Keane	9	2	2	4	16
Billy Campbell	9	1	3	4	4
Andre Villeneuve	15	1	2	3	38
Len Nielsen	5	1	1	2	0
Rick Hayward	3	0	1	1	15
Marc Behrend (Goalie)	1	0	0	0	0
Sylvain Lefebvre	1	0	0	0	0
Guy Rouleau	2	0	0	0	0
Jocelyn Perreault (G.)	6	0	0	0	4
Vincent Riendeau (G.)	13	0	0	0	6

Complete Calder Cup Goaltending

	Games	Mins.	Goals	SO.	Avg.
Jocelyn Perreault, Sherbrooke	6	258	9(1)	0	*2.09
Glenn Healy, New Haven	7	427	19(3)	0	2.67
Peter Sidorkiewicz, Binghamton	13	794	36(3)	0	2.72
Daren Puppa, Rochester	*16	*944	*48(2)	*1	3.05
Marc Behrend, Sherbrooke	1	59	3	0	3.05
Darren Pang, Nova Scotia	3	200	11	0	3.30
Cleon Daskalakis, Moncton	1	36	2	0	3.33
Randy Hansch, Adirondack	10	579	34	0	3.52
Vincent Riendeau, Sherbrooke	13	742	47	0	3.80
Doug Dadswell, Moncton	6	326	23	0	4.23
Darren Jensen, Hershey	4	203	15	0	4.43
Darcy Wakaluk, Rochester	5	141	11(1)	0	4.68
John Kemp, Hershey	2	96	9	0	5.63
Sam St. Laurent, Adirondack	3	105	10	0	5.71
Daryl Reaugh, Nova Scotia	2	120	13(1)	0	6.50

( )—Empty Net Goals. Do not count against a Goaltender's average.

Individual AHL Playoff Leaders

Goals	Jody Gage, Rochester—	14
Assists	Peter Douris, Sherbrooke—	15
Points	Gates Orlando, Rochester—	22
	Peter Douris, Sherbrooke—	22
Penalty Minutes	Steve Martinson, Adirondack—	108
Goaltender's Average	Jocelyn Perreault, Sherbrooke—	2.09
Shutouts	Daren Puppa, Rochester—	1

★★★

AHL 1986-87 ALL-STARS

First Team	Position	Second Team
Daren Puppa, Rochester	Goal	Peter Sidorkiewicz, Bing.
Brad Shaw, Binghamton	Defense	Dave Fenyves, Rochester
Richie Dunn, Rochester	Defense	Jack Brownschidle, Rochester
Tim Tookey, Hershey	Center	Alain Lemieux, Baltimore
Brett Hull, Moncton	Right Wing	Serve Boisvert, Sherbrooke
Glenn Merkosky, Adirondack	Left Wing	Paul Fenton, New Haven

★★★

AHL 1986-87 TROPHY WINNERS

John B. Sollenberger Trophy (Leading Scorer) .... Tim Tookey, Hershey
Les Cunningham Plaque (Most Valuable Player) .... Tim Tookey, Hershey
Harry (Hap) Holmes Memorial Trophy (Top Team Goaltending) .... Vincent Riendeau, Sherbrooke
Dudley (Red) Garrett Memorial Trophy (Top Rookie).. Brett Hull, Moncton
Eddie Shore Plaque (Outstanding Defenseman) .... Brad Shaw, Binghamton
Fred Hunt Memorial Award (Sportsmanship, Determination, Dedication)....................... Glenn Merkosky, Adirondack
Louis A.R. Pieri Memorial Award (Top AHL Coach)... Larry Pleau, Binghamton
Baz Bastien Trophy (Coaches pick as top AHL Goalie)... Mark Laforest, Adirondack
Jack Butterfield Trophy (Calder Cup Playoffs MVP) .... Dave Fenyves, Rochester

AHL All-Time Trophy Winners

John B. Sollenberger Trophy
Leading Scorer

(Originally called Wally Kilrea Trophy, later changed to Carl Liscombe Trophy
and during summer of 1955 given current name)

	Games	G.	A.	Pts.	Pen.
1936-37—Jack Markle, Syracuse	48	21	39	60	2
1937-38—Jack Markle, Syracuse	48	22	32	54	8
1938-39—Don Deacon, Pittsburgh	46	24	41	65	41
1939-40—Norm Locking, Syracuse	55	31	32	63	12
1940-41—Les Cunningham, Cleveland	56	22	42	64	10
1941-42—Pete Kelly, Springfield	46	34	44	78	11
1942-43—Wally Kilrea, Hershey	56	31	68	99	8
1943-44—Tommy Burlington, Cleveland	52	33	49	82	17
1944-45—Bob Gracie, Pittsburgh	58	40	55	95	4
Bob Walton, Pittsburgh	58	37	58	95	17
1945-46—Les Douglas, Indianapolis	62	44	46	90	35
1946-47—Phil Hergesheimer, Philadelphia	64	48	44	92	20
1947-48—Carl Liscombe, Providence	68	50	68	118	10
1948-49—Sid Smith, Pittsburgh	68	55	57	112	4
1949-50—Les Douglas, Cleveland	67	32	68	100	27
1950-51—Ab DeMarco, Buffalo	64	37	76	113	35
1951-52—Ray Powell, Providence	67	35	62	97	6
1952-53—Eddie Olson, Cleveland	61	32	54	86	33
1953-54—George Sullivan, Hershey	69	30	89	119	54
1954-55—Eddie Olson, Cleveland	60	41	47	88	48
1955-56—Zellio Toppazzini, Providence	64	42	71	113	44
1956-57—Fred Glover, Cleveland	64	42	57	99	111
1957-58—Willie Marshall, Hershey	68	40	64	104	56
1958-59—Bill Hicke, Rochester	69	41	56	97	41
1959-60—Fred Glover, Cleveland	72	38	69	107	143
1960-61—Bill Sweeney, Springfield	70	40	68	108	26
1961-62—Bill Sweeney, Springfield	70	40	61	101	14
1962-63—Bill Sweeney, Springfield	69	38	65	103	16
1963-64—Gerry Ehman, Rochester	66	36	49	85	26
1964-65—Art Stratton, Buffalo	71	25	84	109	32
1965-66—Dick Gamble, Rochester	71	47	51	98	22
1966-67—Gordon Labossiere, Quebec	72	40	55	95	71
1967-68—Simon Nolet, Quebec	70	44	52	96	45
1968-69—Jeannot Gilbert, Hershey	71	35	65	100	13
1969-70—Jude Drouin, Montreal	65	37	69	106	88
1970-71—Fred Speck, Baltimore	72	31	61	92	40
1971-72—Don Blackburn, Providence	76	34	65	99	12
1972-73—Yvon Lambert, Nova Scotia	76	52	52	104	84
1973-74—Steve West, New Haven	76	50	60	110	41
1974-75—Doug Gibson, Rochester	75	44	72	116	81
1975-76—Jean-Guy Gratton, Hershey	73	35	58	93	38
1976-77—Andre Peloffy, Springfield	79	42	57	99	106
1977-78—Gord Brooks, Philadelphia	81	42	56	98	40
Rick Adduono, Rochester	76	38	60	98	34
1978-79—Bernie Johnston, Maine	70	29	66	95	40
1979-80—Norm Dube, Nova Scotia	77	40	61	101	51
1980-81—Mark Lofthouse, Hershey	74	48	55	103	131
1981-82—Mike Kasczyki, New Brunswick	80	36	82	118	67
1982-83—Ross Yates, Binghamton	77	41	84	125	28
1983-84—Claude Larose, Sherbrooke	80	53	67	120	6
1984-85—Paul Gardner, Binghamton	64	51	79	130	10
1985-86—Paul Gardner, Rochester	71	61	51	112	16
1986-87—Tim Tookey, Hershey	80	51	73	124	45

Les Cunningham Plaque

Most Valuable Player

1947-48—Carl Liscombe, Providence
1948-49—Carl Liscombe, Providence
1949-50—Les Douglas, Cleveland
1950-51—Ab DeMarco, Buffalo
1951-52—Ray Powell, Providence

1952-53—Eddie Olson, Cleveland
1953-54—George "Red" Sullivan, Hershey
1954-55—Ross Lowe, Springfield
1955-56—Johnny Bower, Providence
1956-57—Johnny Bower, Providence

1957-58—Johnny Bower, Cleveland
1958-59—Bill Hicke, Rochester
          Rudy Migay, Rochester (tie)
1959-60—Fred Glover, Cleveland
1960-61—Phil Maloney, Buffalo
1961-62—Fred Glover, Cleveland
1962-63—Denis DeJordy, Buffalo
1963-64—Fred Glover, Cleveland
1964-65—Art Stratton, Buffalo
1965-66—Dick Gamble, Rochester
1966-67—Mike Nykoluk, Hershey
1967-68—Dave Creighton, Providence
1968-69—Gilles Villemure, Buffalo
1969-70—Gilles Villemure, Buffalo
1970-71—Fred Speck, Baltimore
1971-72—Garry Peters, Boston

1972-73—Billy Inglis, Cincinnati
1973-74—Art Stratton, Rochester
1974-75—Doug Gibson, Rochester
1975-76—Ron Andruff, Nova Scotia
1976-77—Doug Gibson, Rochester
1977-78—Blake Dunlop, Maine
1978-79—Rocky Saganiuk, New Brunswick
1979-80—Norm Dube, Nova Scotia
1980-81—Pelle Lindbergh, Maine
1981-82—Mike Kasczyki, New Brunswick
1982-83—Ross Yates, Binghamton
1983-84—Mal Davis, Rochester
          Garry Lariviere, St. Catharines (tie)
1984-85—Paul Gardner, Binghamton
1985-86—Paul Gardner, Rochester
1986-87—Tim Tookey, Hershey

Harry (Hap) Holmes Memorial Trophy
Outstanding Goaltender

	Games	Goals	SO.	Avg.
1936-37—Bert Gardiner, Philadelphia	47	108	4	2.29
1937-38—Frank Brimsek, Providence	48	86	5	1.79
1938-39—Alfie Moore, Hershey	53	105	7	1.98
1939-40—Moe Roberts, Cleveland	56	130	5	2.32
1940-41—Chuck Rayner, Springfield	36	87	6	2.42
1941-42—Bill Beveridge, Cleveland	31	73	8	2.35
1942-43—Gordie Bell, Buffalo	52	125	9	2.40
1943-44—Nick Damore, Hershey	54	133	4	2.46
1944-45—Yves Nadon, Buffalo	30	87	3	2.90
1945-46—Connie Dion, St. Louis-Buffalo	42	124	1	2.95
1946-47—Baz Bastien, Pittsburgh	40	140	7	2.60
1947-48—Baz Bastien, Pittsburgh	68	170	5	2.50
1948-49—Baz Bastien, Pittsburgh	68	175	6	2.57
1949-50—Gil Mayer, Pittsburgh	50	142	4	2.84
1950-51—Gil Mayer, Pittsburgh	71	174	6	2.45
1951-52—Johnny Bower, Cleveland	68	165	3	2.43
1952-53—Gil Mayer, Pittsburgh	62	146	6	2.35
1953-54—Jacques Plante, Buffalo	55	148	3	2.69
1954-55—Gil Mayer, Pittsburgh	64	179	3	2.80
1955-56—Gil Mayer, Pittsburgh	56	151	5	2.70
1956-57—Johnny Bower, Providence	57	138	4	2.42
1957-58—Johnny Bower, Cleveland	64	140	8	2.19
1958-59—Bob Perreault, Hershey	50	134	6	2.68
1959-60—Ed Chadwick, Rochester	67	184	4	2.75
1960-61—Marcel Paille, Springfield	67	188	8	2.81
1961-62—Marcel Paille, Springfield	45	115	2	2.56
1962-63—Denis DeJordy, Buffalo	67	187	6	2.79
1963-64—Roger Crozier, Pittsburgh	44	103	4	2.34
1964-65—Gerry Cheevers, Rochester	72	195	5	2.68
1965-66—Les Binkley, Cleveland	66	192	2	2.93
1966-67—Andre Gill, Hershey	56	161	4	2.90
1967-68—Bob Perreault, Hershey	57	149	6	2.88
1968-69—Gilles Villemure, Buffalo	62	148	6	2.41
1969-70—Gilles Villemure, Buffalo	65	156	8	2.52
1970-71—Gary Kurt, Cleveland	42	101	3	2.67
1971-72—Dan Bouchard, Boston	50	122	4	2.51
Ross Brooks, Boston	30	65	1	2.38
1972-73—Michel Larocque, Nova Scotia	47	114	1	2.50
1973-74—Jim Shaw, Nova Scotia	41	104	3	2.68
Dave Elenbaas, Nova Scotia	39	109	3	2.96
1974-75—Ed Walsh, Nova Scotia	46	128	2	2.77
Dave Elenbaas, Nova Scotia	30	93	1	3.15
1975-76—Dave Elenbaas, Nova Scotia	48	114	5	2.42
Ed Walsh, Nova Scotia	31	91	2	3.06
1976-77—Ed Walsh, Nova Scotia	40	115	3	2.86
Dave Elenbaas, Nova Scotia	31	81	5	2.61
1977-78—Bob Holland, Nova Scotia	38	120	1	3.17
Maurice Barrette, Nova Scotia	39	107	2	2.74
1978-79—Pete Peeters, Maine	35	100	2	2.90
Robbie Moore, Maine	26	84	1	3.38

	Games	Goals	SO.	Avg.
1979-80—Rick St. Croix, Maine	46	132	1	2.90
Robbie Moore, Maine	32	106	1	3.48
1980-81—Pelle Lindbergh, Maine	51	165	1	3.26
Robbie Moore, Maine	25	92	1	3.86
1981-82—Bob Janecyk, New Brunswick	53	153	2	2.85
Warren Skorodenski, New Brunswick	28	70	3	2.55
1982-83—Brian Ford, Fredericton	27	84	0	3.49
Clint Malarchuk, Fredericton	25	78	1	3.11
1983-84—Brian Ford, Fredericton	36	105	2	2.94
1984-85—Jon Casey, Baltimore	46	116	4	2.63
1985-86—Sam St. Laurent, Maine	50	161	1	3.38
Karl Friesen, Maine	35	115	2	3.48
1986-87—Vincent Riendeau, Sherbrooke	41	114	2	2.89

Dudley (Red) Garrett Memorial Trophy
Outstanding Rookie Player

1947-48—Bob Solinger, Cleveland Barons
1948-49—Terry Sawchuk, Indianapolis Caps
1949-50—Paul Meger, Buffalo Bisons
1950-51—Wally Hergesheimer, Cleveland Barons
1951-52—Earl "Dutch" Reibel, Indianapolis Caps
1952-53—Guyle Fielder, St. Louis Flyers
1953-54—Don Marshall, Buffalo Bisons
1954-55—Jimmy Anderson, Springfield Indians
1955-56—Bruce Cline, Providence Reds
1956-57—Boris "Bo" Elik, Cleveland Barons
1957-58—Bill Sweeney, Providence Reds
1958-59—Bill Hicke, Rochester Americans
1959-60—Stan Baluik, Providence Reds
1960-61—Ronald "Chico" Maki, Buffalo Bisons
1961-62—Les Binkley, Cleveland Barons
1962-63—Doug Robinson, Buffalo Bisons
1963-64—Roger Crozier, Pittsburgh Hornets
1964-65—Ray Cullen, Buffalo Bisons
1965-66—Mike Walton, Rochester Americans
1966-67—Bob Rivard, Quebec Aces
1967-68—Gerry Desjardins, Cleveland Barons

1968-69—Ron Ward, Rochester Americans
1969-70—Jude Drouin, Montreal Voyageurs
1970-71—Fred Speck, Baltimore Clippers
1971-72—Terry Caffery, Cleveland Barons
1972-73—Ron Anderson, Boston Braves
1973-74—Rick Middleton, Providence Reds
1974-75—Jerry Holland, Providence Reds
1975-76—Greg Holst, Providence (tie)
    Pierre Mondou, Nova Scotia
1976-77—Rod Schutt, Nova Scotia
1977-78—Norm Dupont, Nova Scotia
1978-79—Mike Meeker, Binghamton
1979-80—Daryl Sutter, New Brunswick
1980-81—Pelle Lindbergh, Maine
1981-82—Bob Sullivan, Binghamton
1982-83—Mitch Lamoureux, Baltimore
1983-84—Claude Verret, Rochester
1984-85—Steve Thomas, St. Catharines
1985-86—Ron Hextall, Hershey
1986-87—Brett Hull, Moncton

Eddie Shore Plaque
Outstanding Defenseman

1958-59—Steve Kraftcheck, Rochester
1959-60—Larry Hillman, Providence
1960-61—Bob McCord, Springfield
1961-62—Kent Douglas, Springfield
1962-63—Marc Reaume, Hershey
1963-64—Ted Harris, Cleveland
1964-65—Al Arbour, Rochester
1965-66—Jim Morrison, Quebec
1966-67—Bob McCord, Pittsburgh
1967-68—Bill Needham, Cleveland
1968-69—Bob Blackburn, Buffalo
1969-70—Noel Price, Springfield
1970-71—Marshall Johnston, Cleveland
1971-72—Noel Price, Nova Scotia
1972-73—Ray McKay, Cincinnati

1973-74—Gordon Smith, Springfield
1974-75—Joe Zanussi, Providence
1975-76—Noel Price, Nova Scotia
1976-77—Brian Engblom, Nova Scotia
1977-78—Terry Murray, Maine
1978-79—Terry Murray, Maine
1979-80—Rick Vasko, Adirondack
1980-81—Craig Levie, Nova Scotia
1981-82—Dave Farrish, New Brunswick
1982-83—Greg Tebbutt, Baltimore
1983-84—Garry Lariviere, St. Catharines
1984-85—Richie Dunn, Binghamton
1985-86—Jim Wiemer, New Haven
1986-87—Brad Shaw, Binghamton

Fred Hunt Memorial Award
AHL Coaches' MVP

1977-78—Blake Dunlop, Maine
1978-79—Bernie Johnston, Maine
1979-80—Norm Dube, Nova Scotia
1980-81—Tony Cassolato, Hershey
1981-82—Mike Kasczyki, New Brunswick

1982-83—Ross Yates, Binghamton
1983-84—Claude Larose, Sherbrooke
1984-85—Paul Gardner, Binghamton
1985-86—Steve Tsujiura, Maine
1986-87—Glenn Merkosky, Adirondack

Louis A. R. Pieri Memorial Award
Outstanding Coach

1967-68—Vic Stasiuk, Quebec
1968-69—Frank Mathers, Hershey
1969-70—Fred Shero, Buffalo
1970-71—Terry Reardon, Baltimore
1971-72—Al MacNeil, Nova Scotia
1972-73—Floyd Smith, Cincinnati
1973-74—Don Cherry, Rochester
1974-75—John Muckler, Providence
1975-76—Chuck Hamilton, Hershey
1976-77—Al MacNeil, Nova Scotia
1977-78—Bob McCammon, Maine
1978-79—Parker MacDonald, New Haven
1979-80—Doug Gibson, Hershey
1980-81—Bob McCammon, Maine
1981-82—Orval Tessier, New Brunswick
1982-83—Jacques Demers, Fredericton
1983-84—Gene Ubriaco, Baltimore
1984-85—Bill Dineen, Adirondack
1985-86—Bill Dineen, Adirondack
1986-87—Larry Pleau, Binghamton

Baz Bastien Trophy
Coaches pick as top AHL Goalie

1983-84—Brian Ford, Fredericton
1984-85—Jon Casey, Baltimore
1985-86—Sam St. Laurent, Maine
1986-87—Mark Laforest, Adirondack

Jack Butterfield Trophy
Calder Cup Playoffs MVP

1983-84—Bud Stefanski, Maine
1984-85—Brian Skrudland, Sherbrooke
1985-86—Tim Tookey
1986-87—Dave Fenyves, Rochester

AHL All-Time Championship Teams

REGULAR SEASON		PLAYOFFS (Calder Cup)	
Div. Championship Team (Coach)		Year	Championship Team (Coach)
E—Philadelphia (Herb Gardiner) W—Syracuse (Eddie Powers)		1936-37	Syracuse Stars (E. Powers)
E—Providence (Bun Cook) W—Cleveland (Bill Cook)		1937-38	Providence Reds (Bun Cook)
E—Philadelphia (Herb Gardiner) W—Hershey (Herb Mitchell)		1938-39	Cleveland Barons (Bill Cook)
E—Providence (Bun Cook) W—Indianapolis (Herb Lewis)		1939-40	Providence Reds (Bun Cook)
E—Providence (Bun Cook) W—Cleveland (Bill Cook)		1940-41	Cleveland Barons (Bill Cook)
E—Springfield (Johnny Mitchell) W—Indianapolis (Herb Lewis)		1941-42	Indianapolis Caps (Herb Lewis)
Hershey (Cooney Weiland)		1942-43	Buffalo Bisons (Art Chapman)
E—Hershey (Cooney Weiland) W—Cleveland (Bun Cook)		1943-44	Buffalo Bisons (Art Chapman)
E—Buffalo (Art Chapman) W—Cleveland (Bun Cook)		1944-45	Cleveland Barons (Bun Cook)
E—Buffalo (Frank Beisler) W—Indianapolis (Earl Seibert)		1945-46	Buffalo Bisons (Frank Beisler)
E—Hershey (Don Penniston) W—Cleveland (Bun Cook)		1946-47	Hershey Bears (Don Penniston)
E—Providence (Terry Reardon) W—Cleveland (Bun Cook)		1947-48	Cleveland Barons (Bun Cook)
E—Providence (Terry Reardon) W—St. Louis (Ebbie Goodfellow)		1948-49	Providence Reds (Terry Reardon)
E—Buffalo (Roy Goldsworthy) W—Cleveland (Bun Cook)		1949-50	Indianapolis Caps (Ott Heller)
E—Buffalo (Roy Goldsworthy) W—Cleveland (Bun Cook)		1950-51	Cleveland Barons (Bun Cook)
E—Hershey (John Crawford) W—Pittsburgh (King Clancy)		1951-52	Pittsburgh Hornets (King Clancy)

Div. Championship Team (Coach)	Year	Championship Team (Coach)
Cleveland (Bun Cook)	1952-53	Cleveland Barons (Bun Cook)
Buffalo (Frank Eddolls)	1953-54	Cleveland Barons (Bun Cook)
Pittsburgh (Howie Meeker)	1954-55	Pittsburgh Hornets (Howie Meeker)
Providence (John Crawford)	1955-56	Providence Reds (John Crawford)
Providence (John Crawford)	1956-57	Cleveland Barons (Jack Gordon)
Hershey (Frank Mathers)	1957-58	Hershey Bears (Frank Mathers)
Buffalo (Bobby Kirk)	1958-59	Hershey Bears (Frank Mathers)
Springfield (Pat Egan)	1959-60	Springfield Indians (Pat Egan)
Springfield (Pat Egan)	1960-61	Springfield Indians (Pat Egan)
E—Springfield (Pat Egan) W—Cleveland (Jack Gordon)	1961-62	Springfield Indians (Pat Egan)
E—Providence (Fern Flaman) W—Buffalo (Billy Reay)	1962-63	Buffalo Bisons (Billy Reay)
E—Quebec (Floyd Curry) W—Pittsburgh (Vic Stasiuk)	1963-64	Cleveland Barons (Fred Glover)
E—Quebec (Bernie Geoffrion) W—Rochester (Joe Crozier)	1964-65	Rochester Americans (Joe Crozier)
E—Quebec (Bernie Geoffrion) W—Rochester (Joe Crozier)	1965-66	Rochester Americans (Joe Crozier)
E—Hershey (Frank Mathers) W—Pittsburgh (Baz Bastien)	1966-67	Pittsburgh Hornets (Baz Bastien)
E—Hershey (Frank Mathers) W—Rochester (Joe Crozier)	1967-68	Rochester Americans (Joe Crozier)
E—Hershey (Frank Mathers) W—Buffalo (Fred Shero)	1968-69	Hershey Bears (Frank Mathers)
E—Montreal (Al MacNeil) W—Buffalo (Fred Shero)	1969-70	Buffalo Bisons (Fred Shero)
E—Providence (Larry Wilson) W—Baltimore (Terry Reardon)	1970-71	Springfield Kings (John Wilson)
E—Boston (Armond Guidolin) W—Baltimore (Terry Reardon)	1971-72	Nova Scotia Voyageurs (Al MacNeil)
E—Nova Scotia (Al MacNeil) W—Cincinnati (Floyd Smith)	1972-73	Cincinnati Swords (Floyd Smith)
N—Rochester (Don Cherry) S—Baltimore (Terry Reardon)	1973-74	Hershey Bears (Chuck Hamilton)
N—Providence (John Muckler) S—Virginia (Doug Barkley)	1974-75	Springfield Indians (Ron Stewart)
N—Nova Scotia (Al MacNeil) S—Hershey (Chuck Hamilton)	1975-76	Nova Scotia Voyageurs (Al MacNeil)
Nova Scotia (Al MacNeil)	1976-77	Nova Scotia Voyageurs (Al MacNeil)
N—Maine (Bob McCammon) S—Rochester (Duane Rupp)	1977-78	Maine Mariners (Bob McCammon)
N—Maine (Bob McCammon) S—New Haven (Parker MacDonald)	1978-79	Maine Mariners (Bob McCammon)
N—New Brunswick (Crozier-Angotti) S—New Haven (Parker MacDonald)	1979-80	Hershey Bears (Doug Gibson)
N—Maine (Bob McCammon) S—Hershey (Bryan Murray)	1980-81	Adirondack Red Wings (Tom Webster, J. P. LeBlanc)
N—New Brunswick (Orval Tessier) S—Binghamton (Larry Kish)	1981-82	New Brunswick (Orval Tessier)
N—Fredericton (Jacques Demers) S—Rochester (Mike Keenan)	1982-83	Rochester (Mike Keenan)
N—Fredericton (Earl Jessiman) S—Baltimore (Gene Ubriaco)	1983-84	Maine (John Paddock)
N—Maine (McVie-Paddock) S—Binghamton (Larry Pleau)	1984-85	Sherbrooke (Pierre Creamer)
N—Adirondack (Bill Dineen) S—Hershey (John Paddock)	1985-86	Adirondack (Bill Dineen)
N—Sherbrooke (Pierre Creamer) S—Rochester (John Van Boxmeer)*	1986-87	Rochester (John Van Boxmeer)

*Rochester awarded division championship based on season series record.

International Hockey League

(Organized, December 21, 1945)

Commissioner—Bud Poile

8650 Commerce Park Place
Suite D
Indianapolis, Ind. 46268
(317) 872-1524
TWX 510-600-2072

Mike Meyers—Director of Information

Colorado Rangers

Governor—Dennis Champine
Director of Hockey Operations—Greg Ahbe
Public Relations—To be announced
Coach—Peter Mahovlich
Director of Marketing—Julia Westland
Home Ice—Denver Coliseum (8,100)
Address—4400 Brighton
  Suite 200
  Denver, Colo. 80216
Affiliation—New York Rangers
Phone—(303) 298-7779

Flint Spirits

Governor—C. J. Shelley
Manager/Coach—Rick Dudley
Director of Public Relations—Steve Violetta
Home Ice—I.M.A. Sports Arena (4,021)
Address—3501 Lapeer Road
  Flint, Mich. 48503
Affiliations—Buffalo Sabres, Detroit Red Wings, Vancouver Canucks and Philadelphia Flyers
Phone—(313) 743-1870

Fort Wayne Komets

Governor—David Welker
General Manager—Bob Chase
Manager and Coach—Rob Laird
Director of Public Relations—To be announced
Director of Marketing—To be announced
Home Ice—Allen County Memorial (8,022)
Address—4000 Parnell Ave.,
  Fort Wayne, Ind. 46805
Affiliation—Washington Capitals
Phone—(219) 484-2581

Kalamazoo Wings

Governor—Ted Parfet
Alt. Gov./Gen. Man.—Bill Inglis
Coach—John Marks
Director of Public Relations—Steve Doherty
Director of Broadcasting—Mike Miller
Home Ice—Wings Stadium (5,121)
Address—3620 Van Rick Dr.,
  Kalamazoo, Mich. 49002
Affiliation—Minnesota North Stars
Phone—(616) 349-9772

Milwaukee Admirals

Governor—Joseph E. Tierney Jr.
Alt. Gov./Gen. Man.—Phil Wittliff
Coach—To be announced
Dir. of Sales and Marketing—Mike Wojciechowski
Dir. of P. R./Communications—Doug Petitt
Home Ice—Wilson Park Ice Arena (3,100 est.)
Address—320 E. Michigan St.
  Milwaukee, Wis. 53202
Affiliations—Edmonton Oilers, Boston Bruins, Hartford Whalers and Toronto Maple Leafs
Phone—(414) 225-2400

Muskegon Lumberjacks

Governor and General Manager—Larry Gordon
Alternate Governor—John Snider
Coach—Rick Ley
Director of Public Relations—Bob Heethuis
Director of Sales—Leo Hunstiger
Home Ice—L.C. Walker Sports Arena (5,061)
Address—470 W. Western Ave.
  Muskegon, Mich. 49440
Affiliation—Pittsburgh Penguins
Phone—(616) 726-5058

Peoria Rivermen

Governor—Harold Hansen
Coach—Pat Kelly
Director of Public Relations—Matt McConnell
Business Manager—Scott Wilson
Home Ice—Peoria Civic Center (9,228)
Address—201 S. W. Jefferson
  Peoria, Ill. 61602
Affiliations—St. Louis Blues and New York Islanders
Phone—(309) 673-8900

Saginaw Hawks

Governor—Eugene Chardoul, M.D.
Alt. Gov./Gen. Man./Coach—Dennis Desrosiers
Director of Public Relations—Jim Nightingale
Home Ice—Saginaw Civic Center (5,463)
Address—118 North Washington
  Saginaw, Mich. 48607
Affiliation—Chicago Black Hawks
Phone—(517) 754-3940

Salt Lake Golden Eagles

Governor—Art Teece
Alt. Gov./Gen. Man.—Marc Amicone
Coach—Paul Baxter
Director of Public Relations—Alisa Acuna
Home Ice—Salt Palace (10,594)
Address—100 S.W. Temple
  Salt Lake City, Utah 84101
Affiliation—Calgary Flames
Phone—(801) 521-6120

1986-87 Final IHL Standings

East Division

	G.	W.	L.	O.	Pts.	GF.	GA.
Muskegon Lumberjacks	82	47	40	5	99	366	286
Saginaw Generals	82	44	32	6	94	383	344
Flint Spirits	82	42	33	7	91	343	361
Kalamazoo Wings	82	36	38	8	80	331	353

West Division

	G.	W.	L.	O.	Pts.	GF.	GA.
Fort Wayne Komets	82	48	26	8	104	343	284
Salt Lake Golden Eagles	82	39	31	12	90	360	357
Milwaukee Admirals	82	41	37	4	86	342	358
Indianapolis Checkers	82	37	38	7	81	360	387
Peoria Rivermen	82	31	42	9	71	264	362

NOTE: O. (Overtime) column includes overtime losses and overtime ties (teams receive a point for either).

Top 20 Scorers for the Leo P. Lamoureux Memorial Trophy

	Games	G.	A.	Pts.	Pen.
1. Jock Callander, Muskegon	82	54	82	*136	110
Jeff Pyle, Saginaw	82	49	*87	*136	34
3. Ron Handy, Indianapolis	82	*55	80	135	57
4. Dave Michayluk, Muskegon	82	47	53	100	69
5. Jim Egerton, Flint	71	52	47	99	227
6. Bobby Francis, Salt Lake	82	29	69	98	86
7. Todd Hooey, Salt Lake	82	47	48	95	60
Michel Mongeau, Saginaw	76	42	53	95	34
George Servinis, Indianapolis	70	41	54	95	54
10. Bob Lakso, Indianapolis	79	39	55	94	6
11. Doug Morrison, Salt Lake	73	48	39	87	24
12. Steve Salvucci, Fort Wayne	74	39	47	86	142
Drew Callander, Muskegon	80	34	52	86	92
Greg Tebbutt, Saginaw	81	27	59	86	215
15. Ron Leef, Fort Wayne	74	23	59	82	40
16. Glenn Greenough, Saginaw	70	38	43	81	63
17. Todd Bjorkstrand, Indianapolis	82	33	47	80	61
18. Hubie McDonough, Flint	82	27	52	79	59
19. Tim Hrynewich, Milwaukee	82	39	37	76	78
20. Colin Chin, Fort Wayne	75	33	42	75	35

Flint Spirits

	Games	G.	A.	Pts.	Pen.
Jim Egerton	71	52	47	99	227
Hubie McDonough	82	27	52	79	59
Simon Wheeldon	41	17	53	70	67
Kurt Kalweit	75	35	34	69	78
Jayson Meyer	73	17	51	68	77
Terry Tait	73	26	39	65	48
Dave Nicholls	60	27	31	58	237
Brian McKinnon	50	16	23	39	40
Mark Kachowski	75	18	13	31	273
Mark Raedeke	21	11	15	26	89
Richard Adolfi, Milw.	50	7	8	15	37
Flint	18	4	7	11	26
Totals	68	11	15	26	63
Tim Hoover	75	3	23	26	26
Ken Duggan	67	2	23	25	51
Frank Perkins	53	8	13	21	223
Jim Andonoff	34	7	11	18	24
Bobby Williams, Milw.	3	0	1	1	0
Flint	22	12	4	16	28
Totals	25	12	5	17	28
Mario Chitaroni	11	2	12	14	14
Andy Ristau	31	5	7	12	267
Warren Harper	15	4	7	11	14

	Games	G.	A.	Pts.	Pen.
Jay Fraser	8	7	3	10	24
Jay Caufield	14	4	3	7	59
Brian Carroll	39	3	3	6	24
Ali Butorac	13	1	5	6	43
Peter Sawkins	29	1	5	6	15
Dwayne Boettger	41	0	6	6	44
Mike O'Neill	12	2	3	5	6
Don Waddell	10	1	4	5	2
Brent Daugherty	11	0	4	4	9
Ron Talakowski	3	2	1	3	12
John English	18	1	2	3	83
Ray LeBlanc (Goalie)	63	0	3	3	20
Scott Robins	3	2	0	2	0
Marc Marchand	8	0	2	2	11
Eric Germain	21	0	2	2	23
Dwayne Moeser	2	0	1	1	0
John Gibson	4	0	1	1	0
Rick Osborn	4	0	1	1	4
Kevin Robinson	4	0	1	1	4
Trent Kaese	1	0	0	0	0
Tim Brantner	2	0	0	0	4
Todd Clarke, Peoria	2	0	0	0	0
Flint	0	0	0	0	0
Totals	2	0	0	0	0

	Games	G.	A.	Pts.	Pen.
Mike Craig (Goalie).......	2	0	0	0	0
Paul Castron................	4	0	0	0	0
John Franzosa (Goalie)..	5	0	0	0	0
Joe Paniccia	5	0	0	0	0
Mark Salvucci..............	5	0	0	0	34
Bob Langley................	7	0	0	0	16
Peter Richards (Goalie)..	8	0	0	0	0
Darcy Wakaluk (Goalie)	9	0	0	0	8

Fort Wayne Komets

	Games	G.	A.	Pts.	Pen.
Steve Salvucci................	74	39	47	86	142
Ron Leef	74	23	59	82	40
Colin Chin	75	33	42	75	35
Paul Pooley	77	28	44	72	47
Jim Burton	58	19	52	71	50
Perry Pooley	82	30	31	61	31
Mike Lekun	68	32	26	58	236
Paul Couture	64	24	31	55	6
Craig Channell	81	12	42	54	90
Ron Pesetti...................	79	12	40	52	62
Rod Matechuk	72	23	23	46	64
Dale Baldwin	59	12	28	40	121
Derek Ray	75	16	23	39	156
Tony Camazzola............	74	21	16	37	137
Dan Ryder	56	4	10	14	18
Bruce Shoebottom	75	2	10	12	309
Shawn Chambers	12	2	6	8	0
Jay Johnston	31	0	8	8	92
Rene Boudreault, Musk..	17	3	1	4	11
Fort Wayne	7	1	0	1	6
Totals	24	4	1	5	17
Dan McFall...................	11	0	5	5	0
Claude Dumas..............	3	1	3	4	2
Darryl Moise.................	33	1	3	4	25
John Baldassari	20	0	4	4	44
John Hilworth	8	1	2	3	9
M. Dufour, Musk. (G.) ...	3	0	0	0	0
Fort Wayne (G.)	41	0	3	3	27
Totals	44	0	3	3	27
Joel Baillargeon............	4	1	1	2	37
Scot Birnie	6	1	0	1	38
Vic Morin	2	0	1	1	2
Doug Rigler	4	0	1	1	2
Tom Strelow	2	0	0	0	0
Grant Jennings	3	0	0	0	0
Bruce Gilles (Goalie)......	5	0	0	0	4
Alain Raymond (Goalie)	45	0	0	0	27

Indianapolis Checkers

	Games	G.	A.	Pts.	Pen.
Ron Handy	82	*55	80	135	57
George Servinis............	70	41	54	95	54
Bob Lakso....................	79	39	55	94	6
Todd Bjorkstrand..........	82	33	47	80	61
Byron Lomow................	81	28	43	71	225
Gary McColgan	75	30	25	55	15
Todd Carlile	50	11	29	40	102
Tim Salmon..................	46	12	24	36	31
Tim Helmer	74	17	17	34	21
Marc Magnan	77	11	21	32	353
Carey Lucyk	73	6	26	32	94
Peter Laviolette.............	72	10	20	30	146
Harold Schlamp	59	7	19	26	175
Mike Nepi	69	5	21	26	197
Allen Tarasuk	46	8	12	20	173

	Games	G.	A.	Pts.	Pen.
Joe West	24	13	6	19	40
Kevin Conway...............	29	11	8	19	29
Don Perkins	36	2	12	14	110
Neil Davey	44	2	11	13	34
Shawn Dineen..............	27	3	8	11	63
Jamie Wansbrough.........	10	3	3	6	0
Sean Toomey................	13	3	3	6	0
Paul Skjodt...................	11	1	4	5	4
Bryan Wells	10	2	2	4	60
Mike Barron	24	1	3	4	13
Ron Sanko	9	2	1	3	13
Mike Berger	4	0	3	3	4
Vessa Surenkin	14	0	3	3	23
Brian McKee.................	4	0	2	2	4
Don Emerson	5	0	2	2	32
Jon Casey (Goalie)	31	0	2	2	28
Mike Zanier (Goalie)......	14	0	1	1	6
Terry Kleisinger, Flint (G)	2	0	0	0	2
Indianapolis (G.)....	4	0	0	0	0
Totals	6	0	0	0	2
Chris Pusey (Goalie)	6	0	0	0	2
Dave Parro (Goalie)	32	0	0	0	12

Kalamazoo Wings

	Games	G.	A.	Pts.	Pen.
Dale Yakiwchuk, Milw. ..	67	27	36	63	111
Kalamazoo...........	16	4	12	16	69
Totals	83	31	48	79	180
Brent Jarrett	63	17	55	72	65
Claude Noel	80	33	37	70	28
Bob Curtis	80	44	24.	68	36
Tom Searle, Milwaukee .	16	3	3	6	9
Kalamazoo...........	64	15	38	53	49
Totals	80	18	41	59	58
Rob Nichols	71	29	27	56	357
Greg Evtushevski, Ind. ...	8	1	6	7	13
Kalamazoo...........	47	23	26	49	114
Totals	55	24	32	56	127
Bill Schafhauser............	82	6	49	55	52
Darcy Roy....................	72	24	27	51	85
Kevin Evans	73	19	31	50	*648
Bill Terry	27	11	22	33	36
Neil Hawryliw	56	9	23	32	84
John Beukeboom	80	8	24	32	270
Allan Measures	37	11	15	26	26
Wade Dawson, Milw.	17	0	3	3	18
Kalamazoo...........	59	7	15	22	146
Totals	76	7	18	25	164
Joe Lunney...................	46	8	12	20	90
Paul Moore	71	8	9	17	163
Mike Greeder	76	3	12	15	232
Morrie Gare	38	5	9	14	73
Brian Rorabeck.............	14	8	4	12	2
Brian Tutt....................	19	2	7	9	10
John Dzikowski.............	21	2	4	6	72
Brad Hammett...............	35	1	5	6	40
Randy Hansch (Goalie)..	16	0	3	3	0
Shawn Kilroy (Goalie)....	25	0	2	2	10
Georges Gagnon (G.)...	43	0	2	2	16
Jim Buwalda.................	1	0	0	0	0
Earl Switzer	1	0	0	0	0

Milwaukee Admirals

	Games	G.	A.	Pts.	Pen.
Tim Hrynewich	82	39	37	76	78
Neil Meadmore, Kal.	14	5	4	9	37

	Games	G.	A.	Pts.	Pen.
Milwaukee	64	30	31	61	122
Totals	78	35	35	70	159
Kevin Schamehorn	82	35	35	70	102
Bill McCreary	74	30	35	65	64
Gord Stafford	71	28	34	62	42
Wayne Crawford, Kal.	52	27	21	48	38
Milwaukee	15	5	8	13	23
Totals	67	32	29	61	61
Doug Kyle	71	21	33	54	23
Cam Plante	56	7	47	54	44
Fred Berry	57	18	31	49	50
Andy Cozzi	63	24	20	44	16
Dwaine Hutton, Flint	48	13	24	37	71
Milwaukee	5	2	3	5	0
Totals	53	15	27	42	71
George White	60	15	27	42	50
Darren McKay	58	9	29	38	64
Blaine Peerless	74	5	31	36	71
Brian Byrnes	82	2	26	28	70
Kelly Hubbard	75	5	18	23	175
Mario Belanger	35	10	9	19	6
Steve Tuite, Muskegon	39	0	4	4	4
Milwaukee	33	4	10	14	22
Totals	72	4	14	18	26
Tim Molle	54	4	13	17	137
Daniel Lecours	12	5	7	12	6
Florent Robidoux	15	2	7	9	16
Brian Martin, Flint	11	1	0	1	15
Milwaukee	5	0	1	1	0
Totals	16	1	1	2	15
Bob McNamara (Goalie)	16	0	2	2	2
Rob Holland (Goalie)	66	0	2	2	9
John Hutchings	3	1	0	1	0
Alan Graves	1	0	0	0	30
Eric LeGros	1	0	0	0	0
Bruce Cullen	2	0	0	0	0
Marc Damphousse	2	0	0	0	0
Jim Ralph (Goalie)	2	0	0	0	2
Chris Tanguay	3	0	0	0	0
Stephen Latour	6	0	0	0	0
Tim Loven	7	0	0	0	0

Muskegon Lumberjacks

	Games	G.	A.	Pts.	Pen.
Jock Callander	82	54	82	*136	110
Dave Michayluk	82	47	53	100	69
Drew Callander	80	34	52	86	92
Scott Gruhl	67	34	39	73	157
Todd Strueby	82	28	41	69	208
Jim Mollard	67	25	38	63	78
Dave Allison	67	11	35	46	337
Wayne Groulx	38	18	22	40	49
Gerry Minor	68	17	22	39	93
Chris McSorley	47	18	17	35	293
Todd Carnelley	71	4	29	33	75
Jim McGeough	18	13	15	28	6
Roy Sommer	65	14	13	27	219
Mike Forbes	67	3	22	25	113
Grant Dion	40	7	15	22	46
Paul Gerlitz	54	10	10	20	26
Dave Goertz	44	3	17	20	44
Pat Mayer	71	4	14	18	387
Yves Heroux	25	6	8	14	31
Terry Perkins	12	4	8	12	31
Tom Karalis	28	3	9	12	94
Dennis Polonich	22	2	9	11	24
Jean-Marc Gaulin	5	1	3	4	6

	Games	G.	A.	Pts.	Pen.
Jiri Kormanik	10	0	4	4	4
Frank Pietrangelo (G.)	35	0	4	4	2
Roger Belanger	5	1	2	3	4
Jeff Cooper (Goalie)	45	0	3	3	4
Doug Speck	8	0	2	2	6
Kurt Rugenius, Flint	6	0	2	2	10
Muskegon	7	0	0	0	6
Totals	13	0	2	2	16
Dave Moore	1	0	0	0	0
Don Keller	4	0	0	0	10

Peoria Rivermen

	Games	G.	A.	Pts.	Pen.
Denis Cyr	81	29	41	70	10
Grant Rezansoff	82	25	44	69	33
Paul Adey	79	35	28	63	40
John Vecchiarelli, Flint	12	4	3	7	23
Peoria	65	18	34	52	91
Totals	77	22	37	59	114
Bobby Simpson, S. L.	9	2	3	5	12
Peoria	58	14	29	43	32
Totals	67	16	32	48	44
John Goodwin	35	13	26	39	30
Bob Fleming	80	11	21	32	185
Tony Curtale	72	8	21	29	126
Garnet McKechney	70	16	11	27	32
Doug Evans	18	10	15	25	39
Charlie Meitner	39	12	10	22	12
Robert Dirk	76	5	17	22	155
Brian Shaw	38	9	12	21	77
Earl Ingarfield	33	8	11	19	18
Mike Posavad	77	2	15	17	77
Wray Brimmer	49	8	8	16	42
Rob DeGagne	26	5	11	16	12
Philippe Bozon	28	4	11	15	17
Michael Dark	42	4	11	15	93
Ken Filbey, Salt Lake	24	5	5	10	11
Peoria	13	0	4	4	0
Totals	37	5	9	14	11
Mike Neill	43	2	10	12	83
Mark Cupolo	37	4	7	11	22
Dale Dunbar	46	2	8	10	32
Brit Peer, Muskegon	11	1	0	1	9
Peoria	20	3	3	6	5
Totals	31	4	3	7	14
Tom Weiss	9	3	3	6	6
Todd Ewen	16	3	3	6	110
Jim Koudys	9	3	2	5	4
Dave Waldie	11	2	3	5	4
Mike Brodzinski	8	2	2	4	4
Scott Jenewein	5	0	2	2	4
Darrell May (Goalie)	58	0	2	2	22
Don Einwechter (Goalie)	23	0	1	1	12
Alan Perry (Goalie)	6	0	0	0	4
Andrew Finley	7	0	0	0	2

Saginaw Generals

	Games	G.	A.	Pts.	Pen.
Jeff Pyle	82	49	*87	*136	34
Michel Mongeau	76	42	53	95	34
Greg Tebbutt	81	27	59	86	215
Glenn Greenough	70	38	43	81	63
Dave Mackey	81	26	49	75	173
Peter Horachek	77	30	34	64	26
Bernie Gallant	66	24	38	62	77

	Games	G.	A.	Pts.	Pen.
Guy Jacob, Peoria.........	2	0	0	0	4
Saginaw..................	76	33	25	58	184
Totals	78	33	25	58	188
Tom St. James	53	30	25	55	33
Michel Caron.................	82	12	36	48	123
Victor Posa	61	13	27	40	203
Brad Beck.......................	82	10	24	34	114
Darin Sceviour..............	37	13.	18	31	4
Carmine Vani, Flint........	14	4	6	10	53
Fort Worth	6	1	1	2	2
Milwaukee.............	2	0	1	1	0
Saginaw......»..........	19	5	10	15	52
Totals	41	10	18	28	107
Kevin Houle	39	6	12	18	27
Rene Badeau	69	4	13	17	121
Bruce Howes..................	81	4	13	17	39
Bruce Cassidy	10	2	13	15	6
Brad MacGregor...........	13	4	8	12	4
Jeff Prendergast, Peoria	18	1	2	3	15
Saginaw.................	26	2	5	7	12
Totals	44	3	7	10	27
Brian Williams	6	1	5	6	8
Ralph DiFiore	36	1	5	6	49
Claude Gagnon............	6	2	2	4	0
Gilles Charbonneau.......	25	1	3	4	35
Chris Delabbio	5	1	1	2	2
Darren Pang (Goalie)	41	0	2	2	12
Graham Herring............	4	0	1	1	0
Doug Voss (Goalie)........	1	0	0	0	0
Mike Klasson	2	0	0	0	14
Rick Herbert	3	0	0	0	0
Roger Dube	5	0	0	0	2
Kerry Laviolette............	5	0	0	0	4
Warren Skorodenski (G.)	6	0	0	0	0
Jocelyn Perreault (G.)....	7	0	0	0	0
Ed Considine	11	0	0	0	9

	Games	G.	A.	Pts.	Pen.
D. Meszaros, Flint (G.)...	9	0	0	0	0
Saginaw (Goalie) ..	7	0	0	0	6
Totals	16	0	0	0	6
Alex Daviault...............	18	0	0	0	38
Rick Knickle (Goalie)......	26	0	0	0	23

Salt Lake Golden Eagles

	Games	G.	A.	Pts.	Pen.
Bobby Francis................	82	29	69	98	86
Todd Hooey	82	47	48	95	60
Doug Morrison	73	48	39	87	24
Steve Harrison	81	13	61	74	40
Tim Ferguson	80	28	39	67	44
Chris Brant	67	27	38	65	107
Gary Stewart	82	8	46	54	188
Todd Channell..............	59	22	19	41	28
Mike Rucinski................	28	16	25	41	19
Brian Verbeek...............	52	22	15	37	119
Mark Odnokon.............	75	15	21	36	67
Mike Vellucci	60	5	30	35	94
Mel Hewitt	76	20	11	31	307
Gary DeGrio	54	12	19	31	10
Pat Ribble....................	80	9	19	28	55
Glen Sharpley	32	10	15	25	14
Shawn Cronin................	53	8	16	24	118
Mike Mersch	43	3	12	15	101
Ted Pearson.................	17	6	8	14	10
Dale Rivington	37	0	9	9	18
Randy Turnbull	60	2	6	8	212
Rick Heinz (Goalie)........	51	0	4	4	31
Grant Blair (Goalie).......	26	0	2	2	21
Mark Vichorek.............	16	1	0	1	32
Chris MacDonald..........	1	0	1	1	2
Bobby Crawford	2	0	1	1	0
Marc D'Amour (Goalie).	10	0	0	0	0

Complete IHL Goaltending

	Games	Mins.	Goals	SO.	Avg.
Mike Craig	2	120	5	0	2.50
Ray LeBlanc	64	3417	222(4)	1	3.90
Dave Meszaros (a)	9	442	34	0	4.62
Peter Richards	8	398	33(1)	1	4.97
John Franzosa	5	192	18	0	5.62
Terry Kleisinger (b)	2	53	5	0	5.66
Darcy Wakaluk	9	350	38	0	6.51
Shootout losses			1		
Flint Totals	99	4972	361	2	4.36
Alain Raymond	45	2433	134(1)	1	3.304
Michel Dufour (c)	40	2247	126(2)	1	3.36
Bruce Gilles	5	289	17	0	3.53
Shootout losses			4		
Fort Wayne Totals	90	4969	284	2	3.43
Dave Parro	32	1780	124(3)	*3	4.18
Jon Casey	31	1794	133(1)	0	4.45
Mike Zanier	14	807	60(2)	0	4.46
Chris Pusey	6	330	36	0	6.55
Terry Kleisinger (b)	4	240	25	0	6.25
Shootout losses			3		
Indianapolis Totals	87	4951	387	3	4.69
Randy Hansch	16	926	60	2	3.89
Georges Gagnon	43	2543	180(1)	0	4.25
Shawn Kilroy	25	1476	107(3)	0	4.35
Shootout losses			2		
Kalamazoo Totals	84	4945	353	2	4.28
Rob Holland	*66	*3915	*268(2)	1	4.11
Jim Ralph	2	120	9	0	4.50
Bob McNamara	16	926	77	0	4.99
Shootout losses			2		
Milwaukee Totals	84	4961	358	1	4.33
Jeff Cooper	45	2673	147(4)	2	*3.300
Frank Pietrangelo	35	2090	119(3)	2	3.42
Michel Dufour (c)	3	179	11	0	3.69
Shootout losses			2		
Muskegon Totals	83	4942	286	4	3.47
Darrell May	58	3420	214(5)	2	3.75
Don Einwechter	23	1233	102	0	4.96
Alan Perry	6	312	36(2)	0	6.92
Shootout losses			3		
Peoria Totals	87	4965	362	2	4.37
Darren Pang	44	2500	151(3)	2	3.62
Dave Meszaros (a)	7	427	28(1)	0	3.93
Warren Skorodenski	6	319	21	0	3.95
Jocelyn Perreault	6	286	21	0	4.41
Rick Knickle	26	1413	113(1)	0	4.80
Doug Voss	1	37	4	0	6.49
Shootout losses			1		
Saginaw Totals	90	4982	344	2	4.14
Rick Heinz	51	3026	201(2)	1	3.99
Marc D'Amour	10	523	37(1)	0	4.24
Grant Blair	25	1431	108(4)	0	4.53
Shootout losses			4		
Salt Lake Totals	86	4980	357	1	4.30

( )—Empty Net Goals. Do not count against a Goaltender's average.
(a)—Meszaros played for Flint and Saginaw.
(b)—Kleisinger played for Flint and Indianapolis.
(c)—Dufour played for Fort Wayne and Muskegon.

Individual 1986-87 Leaders

Goals	Ron Handy, Indianapolis—	55
Assists	Jeff Pyle, Saginaw—	87
Points	Jock Callander, Muskegon—	136
	Jeff Pyle, Saginaw—	136
Penalty Minutes	Kevin Evans, Kalamazoo—	648
Goaltending Average (2,000 Minutes)	Jeff Cooper, Muskegon—	3.30
Shutouts	Dave Parro, Indianapolis—	3

1986-87 Turner Cup Playoffs

(All series best of seven)

Quarterfinals

West Division

Series "A"

	W.	L.	Pts.	GF.	GA.
Fort Wayne	4	2	8	23	18
Indianapolis	2	4	4	18	23

(Fort Wayne wins series, 4 games to 2)

Series "D"

	W.	L.	Pts.	GF.	GA.
Salt Lake	4	2	8	29	22
Milwaukee	2	4	4	22	29

(Salt Lake wins series, 4 games to 2)

East Division

Series "B"

	W.	L.	Pts.	GF.	GA.
Muskegon	4	1	8	16	12
Kalamazoo	1	4	2	12	16

(Muskegon wins series, 4 games to 1)

Series "C"

	W.	L.	Pts.	GF.	GA.
Saginaw	4	2	8	30	24
Flint	2	4	4	24	30

(Saginaw wins series, 4 games to 2)

Semifinals

West Division

Series "E"

	W.	L.	Pts.	GF.	GA.
Salt Lake	4	1	8	24	15
Fort Wayne	1	4	2	15	24

(Salt Lake wins series, 4 games to 1)

East Division

Series "F"

	W.	L.	Pts.	GF.	GA.
Muskegon	4	0	8	21	8
Saginaw	0	4	0	8	21

(Muskegon wins series, 4 games to 0)

Finals for the Turner Cup

Series "G"

	W.	L.	Pts.	GF.	GA.
Salt Lake	4	2	8	28	26
Muskegon	2	4	4	26	28

(Salt Lake wins series, and Turner Cup, 4 games to 2)

Top 10 Playoff Scorers

	Games	G.	A.	Pts.	Pen.
1. Mike Rucinski, Salt Lake	17	9	*18	*27	28
2. Jim McGeough, Muskegon	15	*14	8	22	10
Todd Hooey, Salt Lake	17	*14	8	22	21
4. Chris Brant, Salt Lake	17	11	10	21	23
5. Jock Callander, Muskegon	15	13	7	20	23
6. Todd Channell, Salt Lake	17	8	10	18	8
7. Bobby Francis, Salt Lake	17	9	8	17	13
Doug Morrison, Salt Lake	17	9	8	17	26
9. Dave Michayluk, Muskegon	15	2	14	16	8
10. Ted Pearson, Salt Lake	17	3	12	15	10

Team-by-Team Playoff Scoring

Flint Spirits

(Lost quarterfinals to Saginaw, 4 games to 2)

	Games	G.	A.	Pts.	Pen.
Terry Tait	6	5	2	7	7
Mario Chitaroni	6	5	1	6	6
Bobby Williams	6	2	4	6	4
Trent Kaese	6	4	1	5	9
Hubie McDonough	6	3	2	5	0
Richard Adolfi	6	1	3	4	5
Don Waddell	6	1	3	4	4
Tim Hoover	5	0	4	4	0
John English	6	1	2	3	12
Dave Nichols	5	0	3	3	5
Jim Egerton	6	0	3	3	4
Brian McKinnon	3	1	1	2	0
Mark Kachowski	6	1	1	2	21
Brent Daugherty	6	0	2	2	0
Ken Duggan	6	0	2	2	2
Jim Andonoff	1	0	1	1	2
Ray LeBlanc (Goalie)	4	0	1	1	0
Peter Richards (Goalie)	3	0	0	0	0
Kurt Kalweit	4	0	0	0	0
Todd Clarke	6	0	0	0	0

Fort Wayne Komets

(Lost semifinals to Salt Lake, 4 games to 1)

	Games	G.	A.	Pts.	Pen.
Jim Burton	11	2	11	13	25
Dale Baldwin	11	2	8	10	29

	Games	G.	A.	Pts.	Pen.
Steve Salvucci	11	2	8	10	17
Rod Matechuk	11	4	5	9	12
Perry Pooley	11	5	3	8	4
Ron Leef	11	2	5	7	7
Tony Camazzola	11	4	1	5	44
Shawn Chambers	10	1	4	5	5
Claude Dumas	7	4	0	4	0
Colin Chin	9	3	1	4	12
Paul Couture	8	2	1	3	0
Craig Channell	11	2	1	3	29
Derek Ray	11	2	1	3	10
Paul Pooley	2	1	2	3	2
Mike Lekun	8	1	1	2	46
Ron Pesetti	5	0	2	2	5
Darryl Moise	7	0	2	2	2
Dan Ryder	11	1	0	1	6
Michel Dufour (Goalie)	6	0	0	0	2
Alain Raymond (Goalie)	6	0	0	0	0
Bruce Shoebottom	10	0	0	0	31

Indianapolis Checkers

(Lost quarterfinals to Fort Wayne, 4 games to 2)

	Games	G.	A.	Pts.	Pen.
Byron Lomow	6	3	5	8	21
Ron Handy	6	4	3	7	2
Brian McKee	6	2	3	5	6
Todd Bjorkstrand	6	3	1	4	9
Sean Toomey	5	2	2	4	2
Bob Lakso	6	2	2	4	0
Allen Tarasuk	6	1	2	3	10
Joe West	6	1	2	3	4
Gary McColgan	6	0	2	2	0
Neil Davey	3	0	1	1	2
Carey Lucyk	4	0	1	1	13
Peter Laviolette	5	0	1	1	12
Mike Berger	6	0	1	1	13
Tim Helmer	3	0	0	0	0
Mike Nepi	3	0	0	0	9
Don Perkins	3	0	0	0	4
Vessa Surenkin	3	0	0	0	4
Marc Magnan	6	0	0	0	22
Harold Schlamp	6	0	0	0	24
Mike Zanier (Goalie)	6	0	0	0	0

Kalamazoo Wings

(Lost quarterfinals to Muskegon, 4 games to 1)

	Games	G.	A.	Pts.	Pen.
Dale Yakiwchuk	5	1	4	5	31
Bob Curtis	5	2	2	4	2
Claude Noel	5	1	2	3	0
Joe Lunney	5	2	0	2	6
John Beukeboom	5	1	1	2	16
Allan Measures	5	1	1	2	0
Tom Searle	4	0	2	2	2
Brent Jarrett	5	0	2	2	4
Kevin Evans	3	1	0	1	24
John Dzikowski	5	1	0	1	2
Mike Greeder	5	1	0	1	4
Bill Schafhauser	5	1	0	1	2
Wade Dawson	5	0	1	1	8
Georges Gagnon (G.)	5	0	1	1	12
Neil Hawryliw	5	0	1	1	4
Darcy Roy	5	0	1	1	4
Brad Hammett	1	0	0	0	4
Paul Moore	5	0	0	0	11

Milwaukee Admirals

(Lost quarterfinals to Salt Lake, 4 games to 2)

	Games	G.	A.	Pts.	Pen.
Florent Robidoux	6	3	3	6	13
Kevin Schamehorn	6	3	3	6	6
George White	6	3	3	6	7
Gord Stafford	6	3	2	5	2
Tim Hrynewich	6	2	3	5	2
Cam Plante	5	2	2	4	4
Bill McCreary	6	2	2	4	10
Tim Molle	5	1	3	4	8
Darren McKay	6	0	4	4	13
Neal Meadmore	6	0	4	4	9
Dwaine Hutton	4	3	0	3	0
Wayne Crawford	6	0	3	3	0
Andy Cozzi	5	0	1	1	2
Rob Holland (Goalie)	6	0	1	1	2
Kelly Hubbard	6	0	1	1	5
Blaine Peerless	6	0	1	1	4
Steve Tuite	1	0	0	0	2
Doug Kyle	3	0	0	0	0
Eric Legros	3	0	0	0	0
Brian Byrnes	4	0	0	0	6

Muskegon Lumberjacks

(Lost finals to Salt Lake, 4 games to 2)

	Games	G.	A.	Pts.	Pen.
Jim McGeough	15	*14	8	22	10
Jock Callander	15	13	7	20	23
Dave Michayluk	15	2	14	16	8
Tom Karalis	15	2	12	14	28
Scott Gruhl	15	5	7	12	54
Gerry Minor	15	3	9	12	32
Mike Forbes	15	1	10	11	4
Drew Callander	15	5	5	10	0
Todd Strueby	13	4	6	10	53
Jim Mollard	14	4	5	9	20
Dave Allison	15	4	3	7	20
Grant Dion	13	1	6	7	6
Roy Sommer	15	3	3	6	44
Chris McSorley	15	1	3	4	*87
Dave Goertz	15	0	4	4	14
Pat Mayer	13	1	0	1	53
Jeff Cooper (Goalie)	1	0	0	0	0
Paul Gerlitz	1	0	0	0	2
Todd Carnelley	2	0	0	0	0
Yves Heroux	2	0	0	0	0
Frank Pietrangelo (G.)	15	0	0	0	2

Saginaw Generals

(Lost semifinals to Muskegon, 4 games to 0)

	Games	G.	A.	Pts.	Pen.
Darin Sceviour	10	10	2	12	0
Greg Tebbutt	8	6	5	11	34
Dave Mackey	10	5	6	11	22
Brad MacGregor	10	3	6	9	2
Michel Mongeau	10	3	6	9	10
Jeff Pyle	10	3	6	9	8
Guy Jacob	10	2	7	9	23
Peter Horachek	10	2	3	5	0
Glenn Greenough	10	1	2	3	8
Bruce Cassidy	2	1	1	2	0
Kevin Houle	5	1	1	2	0
Rick Herbert	8	0	2	2	9
Brad Beck	10	0	2	2	24
Victor Posa	7	1	0	1	34

	Games	G.	A.	Pts.	Pen.
Michel Caron	8	0	1	1	9
Bruce Howes	10	0	1	1	2
Gilles Charboneau	2	0	0	0	4
Rick Knickle (Goalie)	2	0	0	0	2
Warren Skordenski (G.)	6	0	0	0	12
Tom St. James	8	0	0	0	4
Rene Badeau	10	0	0	0	4

Salt Lake Golden Eagles
(Winners to 1987 Turner Cup Playoffs)

	Games	G.	A.	Pts.	Pen.
Mike Rucinski	17	9	*18	*27	28
Todd Hooey	17	*14	8	22	21
Chris Brant	17	11	10	21	23
Todd Channell	17	8	10	18	8

	Games	G.	A.	Pts.	Pen.
Bobby Francis	17	9	8	17	13
Doug Morrison	17	9	8	17	26
Ted Pearson	17	3	12	15	10
Steve Harrison	17	4	10	14	12
Gary Stewart	17	3	10	13	29
Gary DeGrio	17	5	5	10	2
Mike Mersch	17	0	10	10	14
Mark Vichorek	17	0	8	8	23
Mel Hewitt	17	3	3	6	*87
Pat Ribble	17	1	5	6	2
Tim Ferguson	17	3	0	3	6
Rick Heinz (Goalie)	16	0	1	1	12
Grant Blair (Goalie)	1	0	0	0	2
Dale Rivington	4	0	0	0	9
Randy Turnbull	10	0	0	0	56

Complete Turner Cup Goaltending

	Games	Mins.	Goals	SO.	Avg.
Michel Dufour, Fort Wayne	6	346	17(1)	0	2.95
Frank Pietrangelo, Muskegon	15	923	46(1)	0	*2.99
Georges Gagnon, Kalamazoo	5	307	16	*1	3.13
Rick Heinz, Salt Lake	*16	*981	*57	0	3.49
Mike Zanier, Indianapolis	6	359	21(2)	0	3.51
Rick Knickle, Saginaw	5	329	21	0	3.83
Alain Raymond, Fort Wayne	6	320	23(1)	0	4.31
Ray LeBlanc, Flint	4	233	17	0	4.38
Warren Skorodenski, Saginaw	6	304	24	0	4.47
Peter Richards, Flint	3	146	12(1)	0	4.93
Rob Holland, Milwaukee	6	360	30	0	5.00
Grant Blair, Salt Lake	1	60	6	0	6.00
Jeff Cooper, Muskegon	1	8	1	0	7.50

( )—Empty Net Goals. Do not count against a Goaltender's average.

Individual IHL Playoff Leaders

Goals	Todd Hooey, Salt Lake—	14
	Jim McGeough, Muskegon—	14
Assists	Mike Rucinski, Salt Lake—	18
Points	Mike Rucinski, Salt Lake—	27
Penalty Minutes	Chris McSorley, Muskegon—	87
	Mel Hewitt, Salt Lake—	87
Goaltending Average	Frank Pietrangelo, Muskegon—	2.99
Shutouts	Georges Gagnon, Kalamazoo—	1

★★

IHL 1986-87 All-Stars

First Team	Position	Second Team
Darrell May, Peoria	Goal	Darren Pang, Saginaw
Jeff Cooper, Muskegon		Ray LeBlanc, Flint
Jim Burton, Fort Wayne	Defense	Jayson Meyer, Flint
Greg Tebbutt, Saginaw	Defense	Bill Schafhauser, Kalamazoo
Jock Callander, Muskegon	Center	Ron Handy, Indianapolis
Jim Egerton, Flint	Right Wing	Todd Hooey, Salt Lake
Steve Salvucci, Fort Wayne	Left Wing	Jeff Pyle, Saginaw
Dave Michayluk, Muskegon		

★★

IHL 1986-87 Trophy Winners

James Gatschene Memorial Trophy (Most Valuable Player).......................Jeff Pyle, Saginaw
Jock Callander, Muskegon
Leo P. Lamoureux Memorial Trophy (Leading Scorer) ....Jock Callander, Muskegon
Jeff Pyle, Saginaw
James Norris Memorial Trophy (Outstanding Goaltender) .... Alain Raymond, Fort Wayne
Michel Dufour, Fort Wayne
Governors Trophy (Outstanding Defenseman)....................................Jim Burton, Fort Wayne
Garry F. Longman Memorial Trophy (Outstanding Rookie)...........Michel Mongeau, Saginaw
Ken McKenzie Trophy (Outstanding American-Born Rookie) ....Ray LeBlanc, Flint
Commissioner's Trophy (Coach of the Year)....................................Wayne Thomas, Salt Lake
Turner Cup Playoff MVP ....Rick Heinz, Salt Lake
Fred A. Huber Trophy (Regular Season Champion) ....Fort Wayne Komets
Joseph Turner Memorial Cup Winner (Playoff Champion)............... Salt Lake Golden Eagles

IHL All-Time Trophy Winners

James Gatschene Memorial Trophy
Most Valuable Player

1946-47—Herb Jones, Det. Auto Club
1947-48—Lyle Dowell, Det. Bright's Goodyears
1948-49—Bob McFadden, Det. Jerry Lynch
1949-50—Dick Kowcinak, Sarnia
1950-51—John McGrath, Toledo
1951-52—Ernie Dick, Chatham
1952-53—Donnie Marshall, Cincinnati
1953-54—No award given
1954-55—Phil Goyette, Cincinnati
1955-56—George Hayes, Grand Rapids
1956-57—Pierre Brillant, Indianapolis
1957-58—Pierre Brillant, Indianapolis
1958-59—Len Thornson, Fort Wayne
1959-60—Billy Reichart, Minneapolis
1960-61—Len Thornson, Fort Wayne
1961-62—Len Thornson, Fort Wayne
1962-63—Len Thornson, Fort Wayne
Eddie Lang, Fort Wayne (tie)
1963-64—Len Thornson, Fort Wayne
1964-65—Chick Chalmers, Toledo
1965-66—Gary Schall, Muskegon

1966-67—Len Thornson, Fort Wayne
1967-68—Len Thornson, Fort Wayne
Don Westbrooke, Dayton (tie)
1968-69—Don Westbrooke, Dayton
1969-70—Cliff Pennington, Des Moines
1970-71—Lyle Carter, Muskegon
1971-72—Len Fontaine, Port Huron
1972-73—Gary Ford, Muskegon
1973-74—Pete Mara, Des Moines
1974-75—Gary Ford, Muskegon
1975-76—Len Fontaine, Port Huron
1976-77—Tom Mellor, Toledo
1977-78—Dan Bonar, Fort Wayne
1978-79—Terry McDougall, Fort Wayne
1979-80—Al Dumba, Fort Wayne
1980-81—Marcel Comeau, Saginaw
1981-82—Brent Jarrett, Kalamazoo
1982-83—Claude Noel, Toledo
1983-84—Darren Jensen, Fort Wayne
1984-85—Scott Gruhl, Muskegon
1985-86—Darrell May, Peoria
1986-87—Jeff Pyle, Saginaw
Jock Callander, Muskegon (tie)

Leo P. Lamoureux Memorial Trophy

Leading Scorer

(Originally called George H. Wilkinson Trophy
from 1946-47 through 1959-60.)

1946-47—Harry Marchand, Windsor
1947-48—Dick Kowcinak, Det. Auto Club
1948-49—Leo Richard, Toledo
1949-50—Dick Kowcinak, Sarnia
1950-51—Herve Parent, Grand Rapids
1951-52—George Parker, Grand Rapids
1952-53—Alex Irving, Milwaukee
1953-54—Don Hall, Johnstown
1954-55—Phil Goyette, Cincinnati
1955-56—Max Mekilok, Cincinnati
1956-57—Pierre Brillant, Indianapolis
1957-58—Warren Hynes, Cincinnati
1958-59—George Ranieri, Louisville
1959-60—Chick Chalmers, Louisville
1960-61—Ken Yackel, Minneapolis
1961-62—Len Thornson, Fort Wayne
1962-63—Moe Bartoli, Minneapolis
1963-64—Len Thornson, Fort Wayne
1964-65—Lloyd Maxfield, Port Huron
1965-66—Bob Rivard, Fort Wayne
1966-67—Len Thornson, Fort Wayne

1967-68—Gary Ford, Muskegon
1968-69—Don Westbrooke, Dayton
1969-70—Don Westbrooke, Dayton
1970-71—Darrel Knibbs, Muskegon
1971-72—Gary Ford, Muskegon
1972-73—Gary Ford, Muskegon
1973-74—Pete Mara, Des Moines
1974-75—Rick Bragnalo, Dayton
1975-76—Len Fontaine, Port Huron
1976-77—Jim Koleff, Flint
1977-78—Jim Johnston, Flint
1978-79—Terry McDougall, Fort Wayne
1979-80—Al Dumba, Fort Wayne
1980-81—Marcel Comeau, Saginaw
1981-82—Brent Jarrett, Kalamazoo
1982-83—Dale Yakiwchuk, Milwaukee
1983-84—Wally Schreiber, Fort Wayne
1984-85—Scott MacLeod, Salt Lake
1985-86—Scott MacLeod, Salt Lake
1986-87—Jock Callander, Muskegon
Jeff Pyle, Saginaw (tie)

James Norris Memorial Trophy

Outstanding Goaltender

1955-56—Bill Tibbs, Troy
1956-57—Glenn Ramsey, Cincinnati
1957-58—Glenn Ramsey, Cincinnati
1958-59—Don Rigazio, Louisville
1959-60—Rene Zanier, Fort Wayne
1960-61—Ray Mikulan, Minneapolis
1961-62—Glenn Ramsey, Omaha
1962-63—Glenn Ramsey, Omaha
1963-64—Glenn Ramsey, Toledo
1964-65—Chuck Adamson, Fort Wayne
1965-66—Bob Sneddon, Port Huron
1966-67—Glenn Ramsey, Toledo
1967-68—Tim Tabor, Muskegon
    Bob Perani, Muskegon
1968-69—Pat Rupp, Dayton
    John Adams, Dayton
1969-70—Gaye Cooley, Des Moines
    Bob Perreault, Des Moines
1970-71—Lyle Carter, Muskegon
1971-72—Glenn Resch, Muskegon
1972-73—Robbie Irons, Fort Wayne

    Don Atchison, Fort Wayne
1973-74—Bill Hughes, Muskegon
1974-75—Bob Volpe, Flint
    Merlin Jenner, Flint
1975-76—Don Cutts, Muskegon
1976-77—Terry Richardson, Kalamazoo
1977-78—Lorne Molleken, Saginaw
    Pierre Chagnon, Saginaw
1978-79—Gord Laxton, Grand Rapids
1979-80—Larry Lozinski, Kalamazoo
1980-81—Claude Legris, Kalamazoo
    Georges Gagnon, Kalamazoo
1981-82—Lorne Molleken, Toledo
    Dave Tardich, Toledo
1982-83—Lorne Molleken, Toledo
1983-84—Darren Jensen, Fort Wayne
1984-85—Rick Heinz, Peoria
1985-86—Rick St. Croix, Fort Wayne
    Pokey Reddick, Fort Wayne
1986-87—Alain Raymond, Fort Wayne
    Michel Dufour, Fort Wayne

Governors Trophy

Outstanding Defenseman

1964-65—Lionel Repka, Fort Wayne
1965-66—Bob Lemieux, Muskegon
1966-67—Larry Mavety, Port Huron
1967-68—Carl Brewer, Muskegon
1968-69—Al Breaule, Dayton
    Moe Benoit, Dayton (tie)
1969-70—John Gravel, Toledo
1970-71—Bob LaPage, Des Moines
1971-72—Rick Pagnutti, Fort Wayne
1972-73—Bob McCammon, Port Huron
1973-74—Dave Simpson, Dayton
1974-75—Murry Flegel, Muskegon
1975-76—Murry Flegel, Muskegon

1976-77—Tom Mellor, Toledo
1977-78—Michel LaChance, Milwaukee
1978-79—Guido Tenesi, Grand Rapids
1979-80—John Gibson, Saginaw
1980-81—Larry Goodenough, Saginaw
1981-82—Don Waddell, Saginaw
1982-83—Jim Burton, Fort Wayne
    Kevin Willison, Milwaukee (tie)
1983-84—Kevin Willison, Milwaukee
1984-85—Lee Norwood, Peoria
1985-86—Jim Burton, Fort Wayne
1986-87—Jim Burton, Fort Wayne

Garry F. Longman Memorial Trophy

Outstanding Rookie

1961-62—Dave Richardson, Fort Wayne
1962-63—John Gravel, Omaha
1963-64—Don Westbrooke, Toledo
1964-65—Bob Thomas, Toledo
1965-66—Frank Golembrowsky, Port Huron
1966-67—Kerry Bond, Columbus
1967-68—Gary Ford, Muskegon
1968-69—Doug Volmar, Columbus
1969-70—Wayne Zuk, Toledo
1970-71—Corky Agar, Flint
    Herb Howdle, Dayton (tie)
1971-72—Glenn Resch, Muskegon
1972-73—Danny Gloor, Des Moines
1973-74—Frank DeMarco, Des Moines

1974-75—Rick Bragnalo, Dayton
1975-76—Sid Veysey, Fort Wayne
1976-77—Ron Zanussi, Fort Wayne
    Garth MacGuigan, Muskegon (tie)
1977-78—Dan Bonar, Fort Wayne
1978-79—Wes Jarvis, Port Huron
1979-80—Doug Robb, Milwaukee
1980-81—Scott Vanderburgh, Kalamazoo
1981-82—Scott Howson, Toledo
1982-83—Tony Fiore, Flint
1983-84—Darren Jensen, Fort Wayne
1984-85—Gilles Thibaudeau, Flint
1985-86—Guy Benoit, Muskegon
1986-87—Michel Mongeau, Saginaw

Ken McKenzie Trophy

Outstanding American-born Rookie

1977-78—Mike Eruzione, Toledo
1978-79—Jon Fontas, Saginaw
1979-80—Bob Janecyk, Fort Wayne
1980-81—Mike Labianca, Toledo
    Steve Janaszak, Fort Wayne (tie)
1981-82—Steve Salvucci, Saginaw

1982-83—Paul Fenton, Peoria
1983-84—Mike Krensing, Muskegon
1984-85—Bill Schafhauser, Kalamazoo
1985-86—Brian Noonan, Saginaw
1986-87—Ray LeBlanc, Flint

Commissioner's Trophy
Coach of the Year

1984-85—Rick Ley, Muskegon
Pat Kelly, Peoria (tie)
1985-86—Rob Laird, Fort Wayne
1986-87—Wayne Thomas, Salt Lake

Turner Cup Playoff MVP

1984-85—Denis Cyr, Peoria
1985-86—Jock Callander, Muskegon
1986-87—Rick Heinz, Salt Lake

IHL All-Time Championship Teams
(Regular season championship award originally called
J.P. McGuire Trophy from 1946-47 through 1953-54.)

Fred A. Huber Trophy Regular Season Champion			Joseph Turner Memorial Cup Winners Playoff Champion	
Championship Team	(Coach)	Year	Championship Team	(Coach)
No Trophy Awarded		1945-46	Detroit Auto Club	(Jack Ward)
Windsor Staffords	(Jack Ward)	1946-47	Windsor Spitfires	(Ebbie Goodfellow)
Windsor Spitfires	(Dent-Goodfellow)	1947-48	Toledo Mercurys	(Andy Mulligan)
Toledo Mercurys	(Andy Mulligan)	1948-49	Windsor Hettche Spitfires	(Jimmy Skinner)
Sarnia Sailors	(Dick Kowcinak)	1949-50	Chatham Maroons	(Bob Stoddart)
Grand Rapid Rockets	(Lou Trudell)	1950-51	Toledo Mercurys	(Alex Wood)
Grand Rapid Rockets	(Lou Trudell)	1951-52	Toledo Mercurys	(Alex Wood)
Cincinnati Mohawks	(Buddy O'Conner)	1952-53	Cincinnati Mohawks	(Buddy O'Conner)
Cincinnati Mohawks	(Roly McLenahan)	1953-54	Cincinnati Mohawks	(Roly McLenahan)
Cincinnati Mohawks	(Roly McLenahan)	1954-55	Cincinnati Mohawks	(Roly McLenahan)
Cincinnati Mohawks	(Roly McLenahan)	1955-56	Cincinnati Mohawks	(Roly McLenahan)
Cincinnati Mohawks	(Roly McLenahan)	1956-57	Cincinnati Mohawks	(Roly McLenahan)
Cincinnati Mohawks	(Bill Gould)	1957-58	Indianapolis Chiefs	(Leo Lamoureux)
Louisville Rebels	(Leo Gasparini)	1958-59	Louisville Rebels	(Leo Gasparini)
Fort Wayne Komets	(Ken Ullyot)	1959-60	St. Paul Saints	(Fred Shero)
Minneapolis Millers	(Ken Yackel)	1960-61	St. Paul Saints	(Fred Shero)
Muskegon Zephyrs	(Moose Lallo)	1961-62	Muskegon Zephyrs	(Moose Lallo)
Fort Wayne Komets	(Ken Ullyot)	1962-63	Fort Wayne Komets	(Ken Ullyot)
Toledo Blades	(Moe Benoit)	1963-64	Toledo Blades	(Moe Benoit)
Port Huron Flags	(Lloyd Maxfield)	1964-65	Fort Wayne Komets	(Eddie Long)
Muskegon Mohawks	(Moose Lallo)	1965-66	Port Huron Flags	(Lloyd Maxfield)
Dayton Gems	(Warren Back)	1966-67	Toledo Blades	(Terry Slater)
Muskegon Mohawks	(Moose Lallo)	1967-68	Muskegon Mohawks	(Moose Lallo)
Dayton Gems	(Larry Wilson)	1968-69	Dayton Gems	(Larry Wilson)
Muskegon Mohawks	(Moose Lallo)	1969-70	Dayton Gems	(Larry Wilson)
Muskegon Mohawks	(Moose Lallo)	1970-71	Port Huron Flags	(Ted Garvin)
Muskegon Mohawks	(Moose Lallo)	1971-72	Port Huron Flags	(Ted Garvin)
Fort Wayne Komets	(Marc Boileau)	1972-73	Fort Wayne Komets	(Marc Boileau)
Des Moines Capitals	(Dan Belisle)	1973-74	Des Moines Capitals	(Dan Belisle)
Muskegon Mohawks	(Moose Lallo)	1974-75	Toledo Goaldiggers	(Ted Garvin)
Dayton Gems	(Ivan Prediger)	1975-76	Dayton Gems	(Ivan Prediger)
Saginaw Gears	(Don Perry)	1976-77	Saginaw Gears	(Don Perry)
Fort Wayne Komets	(Gregg Pilling)	1977-78	Toledo Goaldiggers	(Ted Garvin)
Grand Rapids Owls	(Moe Bartoli)	1978-79	Kalamazoo Wings	(Bill Purcell)
Kalamazoo Wings	(Doug McKay)	1979-80	Kalamazoo Wings	(Doug McKay)
Kalamazoo Wings	(Doug McKay)	1980-81	Saginaw Gears	(Don Perry)
Toledo Goaldiggers	(Bill Inglis)	1981-82	Toledo Goaldiggers	(Bill Inglis)
Toledo Goaldiggers	(Bill Inglis)	1982-83	Toledo Goaldiggers	(Bill Inglis)
Fort Wayne Komets	(Ron Ullyot)	1983-84	Flint Generals	(Dennis Desrosiers)
Peoria Rivermen	(Pat Kelly)	1984-85	Peoria Rivermen	(Pat Kelly)
Fort Wayne Komets	(Rob Laird)	1985-86	Muskegon Lumberjacks	(Rick Ley)
Fort Wayne Komets	(Rob Laird)	1986-87	Salt Lake Golden Eagles	(Wayne Thomas)

All American Hockey League

Commissioner—Tom Prichard; President—Bob Nagy; Public Relations Director—George Willard
401 N. East Ave., Jackson, Mich. 49201; Phone—(517) 787-0968

Carolina Thunderbirds
Owners—John Baker, David Redmond
Coach and General Manager—Pierre Hamel
Director of Public Relations—Jim Riggs
Home Ice—Winston-Salem Memorial Coliseum
Seating Capacity—5,937
Phone— (919) 748-0919

Danville Saints
Owner—Bob Nagy
Home Ice—Palmer Civic Center
Seating Capacity—3,200
Phone—(217) 431-2424

Michigan Stars
Owner—Bob Nagy
Home Ice—Ice Box
Seating Capacity—1,500
Phone—(313) 676-6429

Jackson Americans
Owner—Jerry Desloover
Home Ice—Jackson Sports Arena
Seating Capacity—2,500
Phone— (517) 783-2664

Port Huron
Owner—Grant Judd
Home Ice—McMorran Arena
Seating Capacity—3,500
Phone—(313) 982-0242

Troy Sabres
Owner—Dave Rose
Home Ice—Hobart Arena
Seating Capacity—4,500
Phone—(513) 339-5145

Virginia Lancers
President—Henry Brabham IV
Home Ice—Vinton Sports Complex
Seating Capacity—3,400
Phone— (703) 345-3557

Atlantic Coast Hockey League
(Will not be operating during 1987-88 season.)
1986-87 Final ACHL Standings

	G.	W.	L.	T.	Pts.	GF.	GA.
Virginia Lancers	55	36	19	3	75	288	218
Erie Golden Blades	55	28	27	2	58	250	246
Mohawk Valley Comets	54	23	31	3	49	260	292
Carolina Thunderbirds	54	23	31	2	48	252	278
*Troy Slapshots	6	2	4	0	4	20	36

*Franchise was revoked on November 17, 1986.
NOTE: In ACHL games in 1986-87, if a game remained tied after an overtime, the two teams would take alternating penalty shots to determine a winner. Teams receive a point for overtime shootout losses. There were no shootouts that resulted in ties.

Top 10 ACHL Scorers

	Games	G.	A.	Pts.	Pen.
1. Doug McCarthy, Carolina	54	37	*73	*110	55
2. Peter DeArmas, Virginia	*55	*44	65	109	16
3. Scott Knutson, Carolina	54	33	58	91	16
4. John Torchetti, Virginia	24	18	18	36	63
Carolina	27	21	30	51	27
Totals	51	39	48	87	90
5. Scott Curwin, Virginia	54	26	60	86	95
6. Jeff Eatough, Mohawk Valley	53	43	42	85	93
7. Mario Roberge, Virginia	52	25	43	68	178
Steve Plaskon, Troy	6	4	2	6	10
Mohawk Valley	41	19	43	62	104
Totals	47	23	45	68	114
9. Doug Wieck, Virginia	53	28	39	67	40
10. Joe Demitchell, Troy	6	3	4	7	12
Mohawk Valley	41	28	28	56	88
Totals	47	31	32	63	100

Carolina Thunderbirds

	Games	G.	A.	Pts.	Pen.
Doug McCarthy	54	37	*73	*110	55
Scott Knutson	54	33	58	91	16
John Torchetti, Virginia	24	18	18	36	63
Carolina	27	21	30	51	27
Totals	51	39	48	87	90
Bob Hagan	54	15	43	58	82
Paul Reifenberger	54	21	29	50	36
Joe Curran, Mo. Val.	11	6	7	13	45
Carolina	29	9	24	33	42
Totals	40	15	31	46	87

	Games	G.	A.	Pts.	Pen.
Jeff Grade	52	15	23	38	180
Alan May	42	23	14	37	310
Sean Mangan, Erie	28	7	12	19	50
Carolina	26	0	12	12	29
Totals	54	7	24	31	79
Randy Irving	36	4	26	30	133
Scott Allen	18	15	7	22	2
Jim Lawson	38	8	11	19	16
Bob Dore	25	2	16	18	53
Michel Lanouette	24	5	12	17	104
Bob Bennett	17	6	10	16	13
Mike Albano	16	5	7	12	6
Dan Vlaisavljevich	23	7	4	11	42
Bill McClellan	14	4	7	11	2
Bryan Wells	7	5	5	10	66
Mike Alexander	11	3	6	9	4
Marc Marchand	12	3	4	7	75
Barry Smith, Mo. Val.	8	0	2	2	48
Erie	8	0	2	2	34
Carolina	5	2	0	2	14
Totals	21	2	4	6	96
Alex Daviault	13	2	2	4	70
Cam Colborne	9	1	2	3	7
Dean Byfuglien, M.V.	10	1	2	3	80
Carolina	3	0	0	0	0
Totals	13	1	2	3	80
Tom Allen (Goalie)	26	0	2	2	24
Sonny Sodke	5	1	0	1	29
Chris Pusey (Goalie)	4	0	1	1	2
John Pasquale (Goalie)..	9	0	1	1	2
Stuart Gould, Troy (G.).	4	0	0	0	0
Carolina (Goalie)..	5	0	0	0	0
Totals	9	0	0	0	0
Bruce Gillies (Goalie).....	20	0	0	0	6

Erie Golden Blades

	Games	G.	A.	Pts.	Pen.
Jamie Nadjiwan	50	33	26	59	112
Andrew Finlay	41	30	27	57	44
Charlie Meitner	28	22	31	53	24
Tim Lescarbeau	55	26	24	50	61
Rene Boudreault	36	22	28	50	56
Bob Vanbiesbrouck	50	4	38	42	162
Duanne Moeser	27	20	21	41	41
Darryl Moise	36	4	35	39	66
Jim Cowell, Troy	1	0	0	0	0
Erie	27	7	31	38	32
Totals	28	7	31	38	32
Don Edwardson	29	16	16	32	21
Steve Mologousis	47	12	20	32	85
Scott Robins	28	10	16	26	20
Brian Keates, Mo. Val.	21	5	16	21	18
Erie	9	3	2	5	11
Totals	30	8	18	26	29
Rob Pfoh	32	12	13	25	105
Barry Tabobondung	15	5	13	18	26
Darryl Harpe	9	2	12	14	2
Paul Mancini	13	5	8	13	25
Warren Crowchild	27	3	10	13	10
Bill Nash, Carolina	16	4	4	8	52
Erie	2	0	0	0	26
Totals	18	4	4	8	78
John Michelletto	29	0	8	8	56
Steve Doll, Mo. Val.	4	0	1	1	23
Erie	15	2	4	6	76
Totals	19	2	5	7	99

	Games	G.	A.	Pts.	Pen.
Steve Trethewey, M.V.	2	0	0	0	4
Erie	4	1	3	4	20
Totals	6	1	3	4	24
Lyle Jonathan	15	0	4	4	64
Pete Ventry	10	1	2	3	23
John Holland	13	1	2	3	10
Bob Moise	7	2	0	2	23
Daniel Courcy	2	1	1	2	0
Dave Barry	2	0	2	2	7
Randy Jaycock (Goalie).	40	0	2	2	6
Marty Wakelyn (Goalie)	8	0	1	1	0
Bob Hill (Goalie)	1	0	0	0	0
Ray Fontaine	3	0	0	0	2
Marvin Smith (Goalie) ..	3	0	0	0	0
Dave Tagliarini (Goalie)	8	0	0	0	2

Mohawk Valley Comets

	Games	G.	A.	Pts.	Pen.
Jeff Eatough	53	43	42	85	93
Steve Plaskon, Troy	6	4	2	6	10
Mohawk Valley	41	19	43	62	104
Totals	47	23	45	68	114
Joe Demitchell, Troy	6	3	4	7	12
Mohawk Valley	41	28	28	56	88
Totals	47	31	32	63	100
Dan Lane	37	34	24	58	182
Todd Flanigan, Troy	6	4	1	5	20
Mohawk Valley	43	21	32	53	164
Totals	49	25	33	58	184
Scott Rettew, Troy	1	0	1	1	0
Mohawk Valley	44	21	25	46	79
Totals	45	21	26	47	79
Gilles Charbonneau	30	14	32	46	31
Mark Blizzard	47	19	25	44	248
Andy Martone, Troy	6	1	2	3	0
Mohawk Valley	43	12	25	37	35
Totals	49	13	27	40	35
Tim Loven	40	4	20	24	33
Ed Considine, Troy	1	0	0	0	2
Mohawk Valley	32	4	19	23	172
Totals	33	4	19	23	174
Tadd Tuomie	28	2	15	17	58
Don Herczeg, Troy	4	0	3	3	50
Mohawk Valley	12	2	10	12	91
Totals	16	2	13	15	141
Kurt Rugenius	27	6	8	14	51
Kerry Laviolette	13	5	6	11	18
Bob Palinski	11	5	2	7	16
Dick Popiel	9	2	5	7	62
Paul Castron	8	1	6	7	2
Gasper Paul, Troy	6	1	3	4	4
Mohawk Valley	4	0	2	2	11
Totals	10	1	5	6	15
Erick Grafstrom	5	1	3	4	0
Steve Rachwal	9	3	0	3	28
Curt Cole, Troy	5	1	1	2	9
Mohawk Valley	2	0	1	1	0
Totals	7	1	2	3	9
Tom Goar, Troy	6	0	2	2	8
Mohawk Valley	1	0	1	1	0
Totals	7	0	3	3	8
Tim Flanigan (Goalie)	20	0	3	3	10
Jay Swist	3	1	1	2	4
George Finn	5	1	1	2	18
Kermit Salfi, Troy	1	1	0	1	0
Mohawk Valley	6	0	1	1	0
Totals	7	1	1	2	0

	Games	G.	A.	Pts.	Pen.
Steve McCharles	3	0	2	2	12
Mike Bauers	2	0	1	1	0
Gary Abate	1	0	0	0	0
Brad Courteau	1	0	0	0	0
Gerry Hourihan (Goalie)	1	0	0	0	0
Doug Knowler	1	0	0	0	0
Guy Wherity	1	0	0	0	0
John DePalma	2	0	0	0	15
Greg Barber	3	0	0	0	2
Stuart Frye, Troy (G.)	2	0	0	0	2
Mo. Valley (G.)	4	0	0	0	0
Totals	6	0	0	0	2
Dan Delianedis (Goalie)	35	0	0	0	8

Troy Slapshots

	Games	G.	A.	Pts.	Pen.
Rob Henry	6	3	2	5	9
Jak Bestle	5	1	2	3	4
Mike Chighisola	5	1	1	2	9
Dwight Boss	4	0	2	2	4
Bill Bieren	1	0	1	1	2
Keith Bemis (Goalie)	2	0	0	0	0
Martin Raymond	3	0	0	0	4

Virginia Lancers

	Games	G.	A.	Pts.	Pen.
Peter DeArmas	55	*44	65	109	16
Scott Curwin	54	26	60	86	95
Mario Roberge	52	25	43	68	178
Doug Wieck	53	28	39	67	40
Bob Thebeau	47	23	38	61	64
Tom Diedrich	44	28	24	52	75
Nick Pappas	55	20	24	44	89
Don McCoy	32	22	19	41	21
Matt Muniz	28	18	23	41	10
Tim Brantner	45	6	32	38	232
Bob Manning	50	5	23	28	22
Serge Roberge	49	9	16	25	*353
John Tringale, Carolina	1	1	0	1	0
Virginia	24	6	11	17	8
Totals	25	7	11	18	8
Craig Johnson	24	3	11	14	57
Greg McPhee	12	2	8	10	2
Joe Lunney	4	3	3	6	6
Steve Olson	15	2	4	6	15
Dana Demole (Goalie)	31	0	3	3	2
Cory Goddard (Goalie)	26	0	0	0	6

Individual ACHL Goaltending

	Games	Mins.	Goals	SO.	Avg.
Tom Allen	26	132	99(1)	0	4.49
Chris Pusey	4	238	20(1)	0	5.04
Bruce Gillies	20	1113	96(2)	0	5.17
John Pasquale	9	362	36	0	5.98
Stuart Gould (a)	5	205	23	0	6.73
Carolina Totals	64	3243	278	0	5.14
Bob Hill	1	33	2	0	3.64
Marty Wakelyn	8	480	33	0	4.13
Randy Jaycock	*40	*2229	*163(1)	1	4.39
Marvin Smith	3	180	14	1	4.67
Dave Tagliarini	8	367	30	0	4.99
Steve Doll	1	24	3	0	7.50
Erie Totals	61	3313	246	2	4.46
Dan Delianedis	35	1943	161(4)	0	4.97
Tim Flanigan	20	1150	109	1	5.69
Stuart Frye (b)	4	106	11	0	6.21
Gerry Hourihan	1	60	7	0	7.00
Mohawk Valley Totals	60	3259	292	1	5.38
Stuart Frye (b)	2	125	7	0	3.36
Stuart Gould (a)	4	163	19	0	6.99
Keith Bemis	2	77	10	0	7.79
Troy Totals	8	365	36	0	5.92
Dana Demole	31	1823	108(1)	*3	*3.55
Cory Goddard	26	1503	107(2)	0	4.27
Virginia Totals	57	3326	218	3	3.93

( )—Empty Net Goals. Do not count against a Goaltender's average.
(a)—Gould played for Carolina and Troy.
(b)—Frye played for Mohawk Valley and Troy.

Individual 1986-87 Leaders

Goals	Peter DeArmas, Virginia—	44
Assists	Doug McCarthy, Carolina—	73
Points	Doug McCarthy, Carolina—	110
Penalty Minutes	Serge Roberge, Virginia—	353
Goaltending Average	Dana Demole, Virginia—	3.55
Shutouts	Dana Demole, Virginia—	3*

*Tied single season record.

1986-87 ACHL Playoffs

(All series best of seven)

Semifinals

Series "A"

	W.	L.	Pts.	GF.	GA.
Virginia	4	1	8	30	16
Carolina	1	4	2	16	30

(Virginia wins series, 4 games to 1)

Series "B"

	W.	L.	Pts.	GF.	GA.
Mohawk Valley	4	2	8	36	24
Erie	2	4	5	24	36

(Mohawk Valley wins series, 4 games to 2)

Finals

Series "C"

	W.	L.	Pts.	GF.	GA.
Virginia	4	3	8	26	27
Mohawk Valley	3	4	6	27	26

(Virginia wins series and Bob Payne Trophy,
4 games to 3)

Top 10 Playoff Scorers

	Games	G.	A.	Pts.	Pen.
1. Steve Plaskon, Mohawk Valley	12	9	*17	*26	49
2. Scott Rettew, Mohawk Valley	13	10	10	20	36
Peter DeArmas, Virginia	12	8	12	20	6
4. Joe Demitchell, Mohawk Valley	13	11	8	19	8
5. Dan Lane, Mohawk Valley	13	9	8	17	71
Paul Castron, Mohawk Valley	13	6	11	17	8
7. Matt Muniz, Virginia	12	*13	3	16	2
Don McCoy, Virginia	12	8	8	16	17
9. Scott Curwin, Virginia	12	6	9	15	23
10. Mario Roberge, Virginia	12	5	9	14	62

Team-by-Team Playoff Scoring

Carolina Thunderbirds

(Lost semifinals to Virginia, 4-1)

	Games	G.	A.	Pts.	Pen.
Doug McCarthy	5	2	5	7	0
Bryan Wells	5	4	2	6	40
Bob Dore	5	2	3	5	12
Alan May	5	2	2	4	57
Scott Knutson	5	1	3	4	4
John Torchetti	5	1	3	4	12
Paul Reifenberger	5	1	2	3	0
Jeff Grade	5	0	3	3	17
Marc Marchand	5	2	0	2	26
Cam Colborne	5	1	1	2	0
Jim Lawson	5	0	1	1	2
Sean Mangan	5	0	1	1	0
John Pasquale (Goalie)	1	0	0	0	0
Scott Allen	5	0	0	0	8
Bruce Gillies (Goalie)	5	0	0	0	0

Erie Golden Blades

(Lost semifinals to Mohawk Valley, 4-2)

	Games	G.	A.	Pts.	Pen.
Rene Boudreault	6	5	6	11	15
Andrew Finlay	6	4	4	8	4
Duanne Moeser	6	4	4	8	4
Don Edwardson	6	2	6	8	14
Tim Lescarbeau	6	4	3	7	15
Bob Vanbiesbrouck	6	1	5	6	18
Jim Cowell	6	2	2	4	15
Darryl Harpe	6	0	3	3	4

	Games	G.	A.	Pts.	Pen.
Rob Pfoh	6	1	1	2	26
Steve Mologousis	4	1	0	1	2
Randy Jaycock (Goalie)	4	0	1	1	0
Steve Doll	1	0	0	0	0
Stuart Frye (Goalie)	1	0	0	0	0
Roydon Gunn (Goalie)	1	0	0	0	0
Lyle Jonathan	5	0	0	0	7
Warren Crowchild	6	0	0	0	0
John Micheletto	6	0	0	0	21

Mohawk Valley Comets

(Lost finals to Virginia, 4-3)

	Games	G.	A.	Pts.	Pen.
Steve Plaskon	12	9	*17	*26	49
Scott Rettew	13	10	10	20	36
Joe Demitchell	13	11	8	19	8
Dan Lane	13	9	8	17	71
Paul Castron	13	6	11	17	8
Jeff Eatough	13	5	7	12	46
Brian Keates	12	2	8	10	43
Andy Martone	13	0	9	9	4
Todd Flanigan	13	4	4	8	34
Ed Considine	10	0	6	6	25
Mark Blizzard	11	4	1	5	72
Kurt Rugenius	9	0	5	5	23
Tim Loven	8	0	4	4	20
Tadd Tuomie	7	2	1	3	13
Don Herczeg	2	1	0	1	40
Tim Flanigan (Goalie)	2	0	0	0	2
Dan Delianedis (Goalie)	12	0	0	0	6

Virginia Lancers
(Winners of 1987 ACHL Playoffs)

	Games	G.	A.	Pts.	Pen.
Peter DeArmas	12	8	12	20	6
Matt Muniz	12	*13	3	16	2
Don McCoy	12	8	8	16	17
Scott Curwin	12	6	9	15	23
Mario Roberge	12	5	9	14	62
Bob Thebeau	12	2	12	14	31
Tom Diedrich	12	5	6	11	8
Doug Wieck	12	2	9	11	6
Serge Roberge	12	4	2	6	*104
Bob Manning	12	1	5	6	4
Nick Pappas	12	2	3	5	16
Greg McPhee	9	0	5	5	0
Tim Brantner	12	0	5	5	62
Dana Demole (Goalie)	12	0	0	0	2

Complete ACHL Playoff Goaltending

	Games	Mins.	Goals	SO.	Avg.
Dana Demole, Virginia	*12	*732	39(4)	0	*3.20
Dan Delianedis, Mohawk Valley	*12	714	*43	0	3.61
Tim Flanigan, Mohawk Valley	2	92	7	0	4.57
Randy Jaycock, Erie	4	254	19	0	4.67
Bruce Gillies, Carolina	5	279	27	0	5.80
Stuart Frye, Erie	1	60	7	0	7.00
John Pasquale, Carolina	1	20	3	0	9.00
Roydon Gunn, Erie	1	60	10	0	10.00

Individual ACHL Playoff Leaders

Goals ....Matt Muniz, Virginia— 13*
Assists.. Steve Plaskon, Mohawk Valley— 17
Points.. Steve Plaskon, Mohawk Valley— 26**
Penalty Minutes .... Serge Roberge, Virginia— 104*
Goaltending Average................................. Dana Demole, Virginia— 3.20
Shutouts .... — None

*Established new playoff record.
**Tied playoff record.

★★

ACHL 1986-87 All-Stars

First Team	Position	Second Team
Randy Jaycock, Erie	Goal	Dana Demole, Virginia
		Dan Delianedis, Mo. Valley
Bob Hagan, Carolina	Defense	Andy Martone, Mo. Valley
Bob Thebeau, Virginia	Defense	Bob Manning, Virginia
Tim Brantner, Virginia		Kurt Rugenius, Mo. Valley
Peter DeArmas, Virginia	Center	Andrew Finlay, Erie
Jeff Eatough, Mohawk Valley	Right Wing	Alan May, Carolina
Doug McCarthy, Carolina	Left Wing	Tom Diedrich, Virginia

★★

ACHL 1986-87 Trophy Winners

Most Valuable Player ....Peter DeArmas, Virginia
Top Scorer...Doug McCarthy, Carolina
Rookie of the Year...Scott Knutson, Carolina
Scott Curwin, Virginia (tie)
Top Goaltender...Dana Demole, Virginia
Playoff MVP..Peter DeArmas, Virginia
Dana Demole, Virginia (tie)
Coach of the Year..John Tortorella, Virginia

ACHL Championship Teams

Regular Season Champion Championship Team (Coach)		Bob Payne Trophy Playoff Champion Championship Team (Coach)
Salem Raiders (Pat Kelly)	1981-82	Mohawk Valley Stars (Bill Horton)
Carolina Thunderbirds (Rick Dudley)	1982-83	Carolina Thunderbirds (Rick Dudley)
Carolina Thunderbirds (Rick Dudley)	1983-84	Erie Golden Blades (Bill Horton)
Carolina Thunderbirds (Rick Dudley)	1984-85	Carolina Thunderbirds (Rick Dudley)
Carolina Thunderbirds (Rick Dudley)	1985-86	Carolina Thunderbirds (Rick Dudley)
Virginia Lancers (John Tortorella)	1986-87	Virginia Lancers (John Tortorella)

Most Valuable Player
1981-82—Dave MacQueen, Salem
1982-83—Rory Cava, Carolina
1983-84—Paul O'Neill, Virginia
1984-85—Barry Tabobondung, Erie
1985-86—Joe Curran, Carolina
1986-87—Peter DeArmas, Virginia

Top Scorer
1981-82—Dave MacQueen, Salem
1982-83—Dave Watson, Carolina
1983-84—Rob Clavette, Pinebridge-Erie
1984-85—Paul Mancini, Erie
1985-86—Dave Herbst, Erie
1986-87—Doug McCarthy, Carolina

Rookie of the Year
1984-85—Kurt Rugenius, Mohawk Valley
    Todd Bjorkstrand, Pinebridge (tie)
1985-86—Bobby Williams, New York
1986-87—Scott Knutson, Carolina
    Scott Curwin, Virginia (tie)

Top Goaltender
1981-82—Gilles Moffet, Salem
1982-83—Yves Dechene, Carolina
1983-84—Darrell May, Erie
1984-85—Dan Olson, Carolina
1985-86—Ray LeBlanc, Carolina
1986-87—Dana Demole, Virginia

Playoff MVP
1984-85—Brian Carroll, Carolina
1985-86—Bob Dore, Carolina
1986-87—Peter DeArmas, Virginia
    Dana Demole, Virginia (tie)

Coach of the Year
1981-82—Bill Horton, Mohawk Valley
1982-83—Jim Mikol, Erie
1983-84—Paul O'Neill, Virginia
1984-85—Frank Perkins, Pinebridge
1985-86—Rick Dudley, Carolina
1986-87—John Tortorella, Virginia

MEMORIAL CUP WINNERS

Season	Team
1918-19—	University of Toronto Schools
1919-20—	Toronto Canoe Club
1920-21—	Winnipeg Falcons
1921-22—	Fort William War Veterans
1922-23—	Univ. of Manitoba-Winnipeg
1923-24—	Owen Sound Greys
1924-25—	Regina Pats
1925-26—	Calgary Canadians
1926-27—	Owen Sound Greys
1927-28—	Regina Monarchs
1928-29—	Toronto Marlboros
1929-30—	Regina Pats
1930-31—	Winnipeg Elmwoods
1931-32—	Sudbury Wolves
1932-33—	Newmarket
1933-34—	Toronto St. Michael's
1934-35—	Winnipeg Monarchs
1935-36—	West Toronto Redmen
1936-37—	Winnipeg Monarchs
1937-38—	St. Boniface Seals
1938-39—	Oshawa Generals
1939-40—	Oshawa Generals
1940-41—	Winnipeg Rangers
1941-42—	Portage la Prairie
1942-43—	Winnipeg Rangers
1943-44—	Oshawa Generals
1944-45—	Toronto St. Michael's
1945-46—	Winnipeg Monarchs
1946-47—	Toronto St. Michael's
1947-48—	Port Arthur West End Bruins
1948-49—	Montreal Royals
1949-50—	Montreal Jr. Canadiens
1950-51—	Barrie Flyers
1951-52—	Guelph Biltmores
1952-53—	Barrie Flyers

Season	Team
1953-54—	St. Catharines Tee Pees
1954-55—	Toronto Marlboros
1955-56—	Toronto Marlboros
1956-57—	Flin Flon Bombers
1957-58—	Ottawa-Hull Jr. Canadiens
1958-59—	Winnipeg Braves
1959-60—	St. Catharines Tee Pees
1960-61—	Toronto St. Michael's Majors
1961-62—	Hamilton Red Wings
1962-63—	Edmonton Oil Kings
1963-64—	Toronto Marlboros
1964-65—	Niagara Falls Flyers
1965-66—	Edmonton Oil Kings
1966-67—	Toronto Marlboros
1967-68—	Niagara Falls Flyers
1968-69—	Montreal Jr. Canadiens
1969-70—	Montreal Jr. Canadiens
1970-71—	Quebec Remparts
1971-72—	Cornwall Royals
1972-73—	Toronto Marlboros
1973-74—	Regina Pats
1974-75—	Toronto Marlboros
1975-76—	Hamilton Fincups
1976-77—	New Westminster Bruins
1977-78—	New Westminster Bruins
1978-79—	Peterborough Petes
1979-80—	Cornwall Royals
1980-81—	Cornwall Royals
1981-82—	Kitchener Rangers
1982-83—	Portland Winter Hawks
1983-84—	Ottawa 67's
1984-85—	Prince Albert Raiders
1985-86—	Guelph Platers
1986-87—	Medicine Hat Tigers

Ontario Hockey League

Commissioner—David E. Branch
Chairman of the Board—Dr. Robert Vaughan
655 Dixon Rd., Rexdale, Ontario M9W 1J4
Phone—(416) 243-3100
Director of Information and Statistics—Herb Morell
Director of Officiating—Ken Bodendistel
Director of Central Scouting—Jack Ferguson
Director of Public Relations and Marketing—John Sop

1986-87 Final OHL Standings

Matt Leyden Division

	G.	W.	L.	T.	Pts.	GF.	GA.
Oshawa Generals	66	49	14	3	101	322	201
Peterborough Petes	66	35	34	7	77	267	212
Ottawa 67's	66	33	28	5	71	310	280
Kingston Canadians	66	26	39	1	53	287	316
Belleville Bulls	66	26	39	1	53	292	347
Cornwall Royals	66	23	40	3	49	261	369
Toronto Marlboros	66	22	41	3	47	298	376

Hap Emms Division

	G.	W.	L.	T.	Pts.	GF.	GA.
North Bay Centennials	66	46	18	2	94	357	216
Hamilton Steelhawks	66	39	24	3	81	321	258
Windsor Compuware Spitfires	66	36	25	5	77	287	249
Kitchener Rangers	66	32	31	3	67	293	305
Sault Ste. Marie Greyhounds	66	31	31	4	66	301	299
Guelph Platers	66	29	35	2	60	275	281
London Knights	66	25	39	2	52	259	329
Sudbury Wolves	66	20	44	2	42	285	377

NOTE: Kingston awarded fourth place based on 5-4, won-lost record over Belleville during regular season.

Top 10 Scorers for the Eddie Powers Memorial Trophy

	Games	G.	A.	Pts.	Pen.
1. Scott McCrory, Oshawa	66	51	*99	*150	35
2. Dave McLlwain, North Bay	60	46	73	119	35
3. Mike Richard, Toronto	66	57	50	107	38
4. Derek King, Oshawa	57	53	53	106	74
5. Ron Goodall, Kitchener	66	52	53	105	17
Jean-Marc MacKenzie, London	63	49	56	105	20
7. Mario Chitaroni, Sudbury	63	54	48	102	164
8. Keith Gretzky, Belleville	29	17	36	53	10
Hamilton	35	18	30	48	8
Totals	64	35	66	101	18
9. Adam Graves, Windsor	66	45	55	100	70
Lee Giffin, Oshawa	48	31	69	100	46

Belleville Bulls

	Games	G.	A.	Pts.	Pen.
Todd Hawkins	60	47	40	87	187
Doug Stromback, N. B.	24	10	13	23	13
Belleville	41	22	33	55	10
Totals	65	32	46	78	23
Frank Melone	64	28	39	67	59
Dean Haig, North Bay	23	6	8	14	24
Belleville	44	16	32	48	36
Totals	67	22	40	62	60
Kent Hulst, Windsor	37	18	20	38	49
Belleville	27	13	10	23	17
Totals	64	31	30	61	66
Paul Wilkinson, Ham.	29	10	15	25	38
Belleville	26	16	20	36	22
Totals	55	26	35	61	60
Wilf Payne	65	21	38	59	37
Bryan Marchment	52	6	38	44	238
Brian Chapman	54	4	32	36	142
Peter Choma	64	18	17	35	34
Mike Arthur	66	9	19	28	50
Tony Crisp	61	11	16	27	5
David Haas, London	5	1	0	1	5
Kitchener	4	0	1	1	4
Belleville	55	10	13	23	86
Totals	64	11	14	25	95

	Games	G.	A.	Pts.	Pen.
Scott Shepherd	65	4	20	24	40
Darryl Williams, Ham.	24	2	4	6	36
Belleville	34	7	6	13	72
Totals	58	9	10	19	108
Jim Dean	44	5	14	19	12
Greg Bignell	64	2	10	12	177
John Van Kessel	61	1	10	11	58
Brian Blad, Windsor	15	1	1	2	30
Belleville	20	1	5	6	43
Totals	35	2	6	8	73
Alan Perry (Goalie)	15	0	3	3	10
Derek Langille	42	0	2	2	27
Brian Tessier, King. (G.)	8	0	1	1	4
Toronto (Goalie)	3	0	0	0	0
Belleville (Goalie)	17	0	0	0	4
Totals	28	0	1	1	8
John Robinson	9	0	0	0	2
Doug Barr	32	0	0	0	35
Paul Henriques (Goalie)	35	0	0	0	8

Cornwall Royals

	Games	G.	A.	Pts.	Pen.
Larry Mitchell	66	39	42	81	46
Bill Bennett	60	23	53	76	14
Craig Duncanson	52	22	45	67	88
Brad Belland	50	28	25	53	31
Darren Colbourne, Osh.	17	3	2	5	18
Cornwall	41	17	25	42	33
Totals	58	20	27	47	51
Steve Maltais	65	32	12	44	29
Paul Cain	60	13	27	40	8
Steve Simoni, Ottawa	40	11	15	26	23
Cornwall	19	7	6	13	10
Totals	59	18	21	39	33
Robert Ray	46	17	20	37	158
Mathieu Schneider	63	7	29	36	75
Jason Hannigan	61	16	13	29	76
Luc Sabourin	53	5	24	29	38
Mark Evans	65	5	23	28	75
Mike Ware	50	5	19	24	173
Scott MacDonald, Osh.	20	3	4	7	4
Cornwall	35	6	9	15	10
Totals	55	9	13	22	14
Glen Johnston	48	3	8	11	29
Derek Middleton	53	2	8	10	48
Steve Herniman	64	2	8	10	121
Bob Carroll	47	1	8	9	0
Tom Roman, S.S. Marie	3	0	1	1	11
Cornwall	16	2	3	5	20
Totals	19	2	4	6	31
Allen Murphy	60	2	2	4	13
Ken Resetar	45	1	2	3	39
Pat Holley	18	1	1	2	30
Pat Gooley	20	0	2	2	4
Richard Tabaracci (G.)	59	0	1	1	30
Jack Reimer	1	0	0	0	0
Pat Malone	3	0	0	0	6
Mark Seguin (Goalie)	14	0	0	0	2

Guelph Platers

	Games	G.	A.	Pts.	Pen.
Rob Arabski	64	29	60	89	36
Keith Miller	66	50	31	81	44
Paul Kelly	61	27	48	75	67
Jamie McKinley	57	23	50	73	109
Lonnie Loach	56	31	24	55	42

	Games	G.	A.	Pts.	Pen.
Luciano Fagioli	64	26	29	55	33
Darren Treloar, Pete.	19	5	19	24	14
Guelph	26	9	17	26	8
Totals	45	14	36	50	22
Marc Tournier	63	12	37	49	77
Kerry Huffman	44	4	31	35	20
Allan Maclsaac	63	16	16	32	130
John McIntyre	47	8	22	30	95
Robb Graham	45	13	14	27	37
Brian Hayton	63	6	19	25	113
Rob Zamuner	62	6	15	21	8
Kelly Bradley	64	5	14	19	42
Denis Larocque	45	4	10	14	82
Bill Loshaw	62	1	8	9	149
David Noseworthy	51	0	6	6	31
Sean Whyte	41	1	3	4	13
Steve Perkovic	63	1	3	4	47
Gary Wenzel	4	1	2	3	2
Brian Barron	29	1	1	2	13
Andy Helmuth (Goalie)	48	0	2	2	21
Paul Reynolds	3	1	0	1	5
Greg Snyder	3	0	1	1	0
Nelson Duarte (Goalie)	1	0	0	0	0
Dave McVicker	4	0	0	0	2
Ken Murchison	6	0	0	0	0
Stephane Hebert (G.)	8	0	0	0	0
Dave Thomas	9	0	0	0	7
Scott Luce (Goalie)	18	0	0	0	8

Hamilton Steelhawks

	Games	G.	A.	Pts.	Pen.
Keith Gretzky, Belleville	29	17	36	53	10
Hamilton	35	18	30	48	8
Totals	64	35	66	101	18
Ron Bernacci	66	43	47	90	79
Stan Drulia	55	27	51	78	26
Kirk Tomlinson	65	33	37	70	169
Brad Dalgarno	60	27	32	59	100
Brent Thompson	61	20	35	55	56
Garth Joy	66	6	43	49	56
Ken McRae, Sudbury	21	12	15	27	40
Hamilton	20	7	12	19	25
Totals	41	19	27	46	65
John Copple	66	10	36	46	58
Guy Girouard	65	13	32	45	83
Jeff Waver	63	12	28	40	132
Brad Gratton	59	18	19	37	8
Ken Alexander, Kit.	20	3	14	17	43
Sudbury	9	3	5	8	18
Hamilton	34	5	7	12	46
Totals	63	11	26	37	107
Jamie Leach	64	12	19	31	67
Shawn McCosh	50	11	17	28	49
Brian Martin	20	14	11	25	37
John Purves	28	12	11	23	37
Fred Pennell	57	9	11	20	103
Don Pancoe	44	4	8	12	120
Dennis Vial	53	1	8	9	194
Mark Couture	7	1	2	3	0
Mark Gowans, Osh. (G.)	10	0	1	1	0
Hamilton (G.)	20	0	2	2	2
Totals	30	0	3	3	2
Andy Paquette, Sudbury	2	0	0	0	0
Hamilton	1	0	2	2	0
Totals	3	0	2	2	0
Rob Scriven	4	2	0	2	2
Mike Rosati (Goalie)	26	0	2	2	12

	Games	G.	A.	Pts.	Pen.
Tim Upper	4	0	1	1	7
Matt Leonard	2	0	0	0	2
Mark Bernard (Goalie)	3	0	0	0	0
Joey Simon	4	0	0	0	0
Mark Jovanovic	11	0	0	0	2

Kingston Canadiens

	Games	G.	A.	Pts.	Pen.
Mike Maurice	60	48	44	92	69
Mike Fiset	66	34	47	81	53
Bryan Fogarty	56	20	50	70	46
Steve Seftel	54	21	43	64	55
Andy Rivers	62	21	39	60	19
Scott Pearson	62	30	24	54	101
Kelly Cain, London	5	4	3	7	18
Kitchener	28	18	19	37	48
Kingston	12	3	5	8	15
Totals	45	25	27	52	81
Jamie Henckel, Toronto	19	3	3	6	2
Kingston	39	15	18	33	20
Totals	58	18	21	39	22
Wayne Erskine	61	14	20	34	14
Ted Linseman	61	8	24	32	75
Chad Badawey	66	16	13	29	25
Troy MacNevin	66	4	21	25	46
Marc Lyons	47	5	11	16	32
John Battice	53	5	11	16	25
Peter Liptrott	64	3	11	14	103
Marc Laforge	53	2	10	12	224
Sloan Torti	58	4	1	5	15
Jeff Sirkka	64	0	5	5	156
Alain Laforge	22	1	3	4	6
Chris Lukey	22	1	2	3	19
Andre Belzile	8	0	2	2	4
Chris Clifford (Goalie)	44	0	2	2	24
Franco Giammarco (G.)	17	0	1	1	0
Terry Collett	1	0	0	0	0
Jamie Edwards	1	0	0	0	0
Stephen Gordon	1	0	0	0	0
Curtis Thompson	2	0	0	0	0
Stephen Richard	4	0	0	0	2
John Agazzi	10	0	0	0	7

Kitchener Rangers

	Games	G.	A.	Pts.	Pen.
Ron Goodall	66	52	53	105	17
Jeff Noble	66	29	57	86	55
Max Middendorf, Sud.	31	31	29	60	7
Kitchener	17	7	15	22	6
Totals	48	38	44	82	13
David Latta	50	32	46	78	46
Daran Moxam	56	33	36	69	128
Gary Callaghan, Belle.	4	1	2	3	5
Kitchener	52	29	28	57	18
Totals	56	30	30	60	23
Darren Rumble	64	11	32	43	44
Daril Holmes, Kingston	34	13	15	28	54
Kitchener	30	4	9	13	30
Totals	64	17	24	41	84
Craig Booker	63	15	20	35	108
Warren Rychel, Ottawa	28	11	7	18	57
Kitchener	21	5	5	10	39
Totals	49	16	12	28	96
Kevin Grant	52	5	18	23	125

	Games	G.	A.	Pts.	Pen.
Peter Viskovich, Kingston	31	4	12	16	0
Kitchener	24	3	3	6	2
Totals	55	7	15	22	2
Scott Taylor	53	6	16	22	123
Ed Kister, London	3	2	3	5	6
Kitchener	53	4	13	17	34
Totals	56	6	16	22	40
Paul Epoch	64	3	17	20	68
Dave Moylan, Sudbury	13	5	6	11	41
Kitchener	38	1	7	8	57
Totals	51	6	13	19	98
Mark Montanari	63	9	7	16	112
Richard Borgo	62	5	10	15	29
Doug Jones	44	4	5	9	19
Bruno Lapensee, Corn.	8	3	4	7	16
Kitchener	8	0	0	0	0
Totals	16	3	4	7	16
Allan Lake	46	3	3	6	184
Jim Hulton	50	1	3	4	39
Darren Beals, Ott.(G.)	4	0	0	0	0
Kitchener (Goalie)	45	0	3	3	2
Totals	49	0	3	3	2
David Weiss (Goalie)	35	0	2	2	2
Darrin Baker (Goalie)	1	0	0	0	0
Dave Cassin	1	0	0	0	0
Daryl Noren	4	0	0	0	0
Len Fawcett	9	0	0	0	2
Rick Allain	18	0	0	0	32

London Knights

	Games	G.	A.	Pts.	Pen.
Jean-Marc MacKenzie	63	49	56	105	20
Brendan Shanahan	56	39	53	92	128
Murray Nystrom	60	31	49	80	73
Peter Lisy, Kitchener	5	0	2	2	7
London	57	21	49	70	19
Totals	62	21	51	72	26
Don Martin	63	19	38	57	127
Steve Ewing, Belleville	7	3	2	5	6
Kitchener	21	7	7	14	54
London	28	11	11	22	27
Totals	56	21	20	41	87
Dennis McEwen	63	22	18	40	72
Jim Sprott	66	8	30	38	153
Shane Whelan, Windsor	9	4	5	9	22
London	43	9	14	23	46
Totals	52	13	19	32	68
Brent Daugherty, Sud.	32	6	13	19	81
London	27	4	7	11	40
Totals	59	10	20	30	121
Brad Schlegel	65	4	23	27	24
Trevor Dam	64	6	17	23	88
Shayne Stevenson	61	7	15	22	56
Tim Taylor	34	7	9	16	11
Greg Hankkio, Kitchener	5	0	0	0	2
London	61	5	10	15	42
Totals	66	5	10	15	44
Steven Marcolini, Kit.	5	0	2	2	17
London	29	0	5	5	41
Totals	34	0	7	7	58
Ray Gallagher	9	1	4	5	7
Pat Vachon	26	3	1	4	30
Wayne Smith	41	1	3	4	26
Craig Majaury	39	1	2	3	23
Dave Akey	64	1	2	3	125
Brian Kukulka	1	0	0	0	0
Joe Novak (Goalie)	1	0	0	0	0

	Games	G.	A.	Pts.	Pen.
Andy Doxtator	2	0	0	0	0
Tim Horvat	2	0	0	0	0
Rob Coutts	5	0	0	0	4
A. Hogberg, Sud. (G.)	12	0	0	0	0
London (Goalie)	1	0	0	0	0
Totals	13	0	0	0	0
Paul Holden	16	0	0	0	2
Barry Earhart	22	0	0	0	5
Chris Somers (Goalie)	32	0	0	0	2
Steve Titus (Goalie)	47	0	0	0	6

North Bay Centennials

	Games	G.	A.	Pts.	Pen.
Dave McIlwain	60	46	73	119	35
Nick Kypreos	46	49	41	90	54
Keith Osborne	61	34	55	89	31
Len Soccio	66	31	54	85	56
Darren Turcotte	55	30	48	78	20
Bill Houlder	62	17	51	68	68
Tim Bean	65	24	39	63	134
Mike Gillies	66	33	24	57	17
Darin Smith	59	22	25	47	142
Wayne MacPhee	64	10	36	46	141
Mike Hartman	32	15	24	39	144
Adam Burt	57	4	27	31	138
Troy Crowder, Belleville	21	5	5	10	52
North Bay	35	6	11	17	90
Totals	56	11	16	27	142
Darcy Cahill	52	7	19	26	7
Jason Corrigan	53	5	14	19	25
Jeff Bloemberg	60	5	13	18	91
Brent Bywater	62	1	14	15	80
Shawn Roy	36	0	9	9	6
Rich Stromback	40	1	3	4	79
Chad Gleason	57	1	3	4	88
Greg Capson	22	0	2	2	14
John Reid (Goalie)	47	0	1	1	39
Shawn Foisy	1	0	0	0	0
Shawn Dubois	4	0	0	0	2
Mark Dunning	18	0	0	0	0
Rob Fournier (Goalie)	25	0	0	0	12

Oshawa Generals

	Games	G.	A.	Pts.	Pen.
Scott McCrory	66	51	*99	*150	35
Derek King	57	53	53	106	74
Lee Giffin	48	31	69	100	46
Barry Burkholder, Sud.	2	2	2	4	5
Oshawa	51	31	30	61	68
Totals	53	33	32	65	73
Marc Laniel	63	14	31	45	42
Sean Williams	62	21	23	44	32
Petri Matikainen	50	8	34	42	53
Kevin Miehm	61	12	27	39	19
Gordon Murphy	56	7	30	37	95
Brian Hunt	61	13	22	35	25
Brent Grieve	60	9	19	28	102
John Andersen	45	11	13	24	24
Jeff Daniels	54	14	9	23	22
Scott Mahoney	54	13	9	22	161
Shane Doyle	46	9	13	22	168
Jim Paek	57	5	17	22	75
Greg Watson	57	8	11	19	208
Dean Morton	62	1	11	12	165
Tony Joseph	44	2	5	7	93

	Games	G.	A.	Pts.	Pen.
Sean Evoy (Goalie)	31	0	6	6	4
Ian Fraser	5	2	1	3	0
Jeff Hackett (Goalie)	31	0	2	2	0
Greg Polak	11	1	0	1	23
Mike Short	50	0	1	1	78
Dave Humphreys (G.)	1	0	0	0	0
Jeff McColl	1	0	0	0	0

Ottawa 67's

	Games	G.	A.	Pts.	Pen.
Andrew Cassels	66	26	66	92	28
Frank DiMuzio	61	*59	30	89	57
Kent Hawley	64	29	53	82	86
Guy Larose	66	28	49	77	77
Dave Rowbotham	66	26	43	69	7
Brent Battistelli	61	26	37	63	88
Mike Griffith	65	21	29	50	54
Rick Lessard	66	5	36	41	188
Ransome Drcar	66	4	24	28	112
Mike Rutherford	35	13	12	25	22
John Hanna	22	14	8	22	15
Todd Clarke	42	6	15	21	65
Graydon Almstedt	64	1	17	18	26
Jeff Ballantyne	65	2	13	15	75
Dave Gibbons	48	5	9	14	62
John East	46	3	7	10	21
Matt Giesebrecht	59	4	5	9	18
Denis Chouinard, S.S.M.	28	0	1	1	14
Ottawa	26	3	5	8	22
Totals	54	3	6	9	36
Vern Ray	57	2	3	5	114
Matt Hendricks	9	4	0	4	0
Brian Therrien	4	2	0	2	0
Willie Popp, Ham. (G.)	1	0	0	0	0
Ottawa (G)	40	0	2	2	10
Totals	41	0	2	2	10
Tom Nickolau	3	1	0	1	2
Pat Howie	1	0	1	1	0
Steve Catney	2	0	0	0	0
Scott Cumming (Goalie)	30	0	0	0	6

Peterborough Petes

	Games	G.	A.	Pts.	Pen.
Mark Freer	65	39	43	82	44
Glen Seabrooke	48	30	39	69	29
Kris King	46	23	33	56	160
Rob Murray	62	17	37	54	204
Jody Hull	49	18	34	52	22
Luke Richardson	59	13	32	45	70
Ross Wilson	66	28	11	39	91
Todd Gregory	60	14	22	36	45
Jamey Hicks	55	11	19	30	45
Greg Vey	57	8	22	30	105
Billie McMillan	38	14	14	28	32
Bill Huard	61	14	11	25	61
Andy MacVicar	64	6	13	19	33
Mike Dagenais	56	1	17	18	66
Larry Shaw	61	4	13	17	78
Steve DeGurse	50	5	11	16	62
Dan Jensen	58	4	12	16	46
Dallas Eakins	54	3	11	14	145
Mark Baron	36	2	12	14	38
Kevin MacDonald	48	4	4	8	183
Corey Foster	30	3	4	7	4
Kay Whitmore (Goalie)	36	0	4	4	13
Tie Domi	18	1	1	2	79

	Games	G.	A.	Pts.	Pen.
Rick Franze	2	0	1	1	0
Dave Davidson	5	0	1	1	4
Ron Tugnutt (Goalie)	31	0	1	1	4
Terry Naugler	1	0	0	0	0
Jeff DeNoble	2	0	0	0	0
Mike Hall	4	0	0	0	0

Sault Ste. Marie Greyhounds

	Games	G.	A.	Pts.	Pen.
Mike Oliverio	66	35	58	93	34
Tyler Larter	59	34	59	93	122
Paul Beraldo	63	39	51	90	117
Dan Currie	66	31	52	83	53
Steve Hollett	65	35	41	76	63
Brad Aitken	52	27	38	65	86
Mike Glover	57	26	22	48	107
Troy Mallette	65	20	25	45	157
Mark Haarmann	60	6	30	36	25
Rob Zettler	64	13	22	35	89
Steve Cote	46	9	12	21	25
Steve Bisson	52	5	15	20	38
Bob Babcock	62	7	8	15	243
Brian Hoard, Hamilton	1	0	1	1	0
Belleville	9	0	0	0	31
Sault Ste. Marie	44	4	8	12	137
Totals	54	4	9	13	168
Peter Fiorentino	64	1	12	13	187
Mike Kolodziejczyk	48	4	6	10	35
Rod Thacker, Hamilton	6	0	0	0	0
Ottawa	31	1	3	4	36
Sault Ste. Marie	26	0	6	6	28
Totals	63	1	9	10	64
Rob Reid	54	1	5	6	15
Bob Jones	51	1	4	5	46
Jeff Columbus	47	2	1	3	59
Kent Trolley	9	1	1	2	7
Shawn Simpson (Goalie)	46	0	2	2	15
Mark Harding	4	0	1	1	0
Hal Turner	4	0	1	1	0
Peter Turko	8	0	1	1	0
Glen Chiasson (Goalie)	1	0	0	0	0
Robin Rubic	4	0	0	0	4
Rob Watson (Goalie)	20	0	0	0	8

Sudbury Wolves

	Games	G.	A.	Pts.	Pen.
Mario Chitaroni	63	54	48	102	164
Mike Hudson	63	40	57	97	18
Dean Guitard, Cornwall	8	2	6	8	19
Sudbury	44	17	38	55	120
Totals	52	19	44	63	139
Mark Turner	63	20	33	53	28
Wayne Doucet	64	20	28	48	85
Steve Hedington, Belle.	9	2	2	4	2
Sudbury	42	14	21	35	24
Totals	51	16	23	39	26
Jordan Fois, Hamilton	29	2	8	10	33
Sudbury	35	5	23	28	68
Totals	64	7	31	38	101
Dan Hie, Ottawa	4	3	6	9	16
Hamilton	15	2	14	16	25
Sudbury	19	1	5	6	47
Totals	38	6	25	31	88

	Games	G.	A.	Pts.	Pen.
Rob Wilson	58	1	27	28	135
Jim Way, Belleville	2	0	0	0	0
Sudbury	57	12	13	25	75
Totals	59	12	13	25	75
Mike Siefker, Windsor	33	3	6	9	34
Sudbury	21	5	10	15	13
Totals	54	8	16	24	47
Dean Jalbert	45	8	12	20	48
Todd Lalonde	29	5	11	16	71
Paul DiPietro	49	5	11	16	13
Peter Hughes, Belleville	2	0	0	0	0
Sudbury	58	4	9	13	91
Totals	60	4	9	13	91
Phil Paquette	56	3	9	12	64
Pierre Gagnon	59	2	9	11	68
Justin Corbeil	55	1	9	10	42
Jason Simon, London	33	1	2	3	33
Sudbury	26	2	3	5	50
Totals	59	3	5	8	83
Jeff Smith	7	4	0	4	0
Costa Papista	15	0	4	4	37
Steve Locke, Hamilton	13	0	3	3	2
Sudbury	5	0	0	0	0
Totals	18	0	3	3	2
Greg White	4	1	1	2	0
P. Richards, Ham. (G.)	24	0	0	0	12
Sudbury (G.)	29	0	2	2	45
Totals	53	0	2	2	57
Greg Levert	4	1	0	1	0
Shannon Bolton	7	1	0	1	6
Kevin O'Driscoll	1	0	1	1	0
Steve Boyd	5	0	1	1	0
Jim Smith	5	0	1	1	2
Dave Barrett (Goalie)	1	0	0	0	0
Dino Cirello (Goalie)	1	0	0	0	0
Tony Falvo	1	0	0	0	0
Marcel Tellier	1	0	0	0	2
Aldo Teofilo	1	0	0	0	0
Rick Johnson	2	0	0	0	0
Jim Kennedy	2	0	0	0	0
Derek Thompson	2	0	0	0	0
Vince Edwards	3	0	0	0	19
John Eliopoulos	3	0	0	0	0
Ace Roque	3	0	0	0	0
Sean Ebdon	4	0	0	0	15
Neil McFarlane	4	0	0	0	0
Chuck Petahtegoose	4	0	0	0	0
Andy Stephenson	4	0	0	0	0
Norm Krumpschmid	5	0	0	0	0
Dwayne Newton	5	0	0	0	18
Rick Mitchell	9	0	0	0	2
Ted Mielczarek (Goalie)	17	0	0	0	4
D. Gatenby, S.S.M. (G.)	5	0	0	0	4
Belle. (G.)	3	0	0	0	0
Sud. (G.)	14	0	0	0	8
Totals	22	0	0	0	12

Toronto Marlboros

	Games	G.	A.	Pts.	Pen.
Mike Richard	66	57	50	107	38
Tim Armstrong	66	29	55	84	61
Vito Cramarossa	59	24	50	74	130
Chris Govedaris	64	36	28	64	148
Sean Davidson	66	30	32	62	24
Rob Cimetta	66	21	35	56	65
Mike Jackson	63	17	37	54	78
Dan Resko	65	20	23	43	31

	Games	G.	A.	Pts.	Pen.
Yvon Corriveau	23	14	19	33	23
John Blessman	61	6	24	30	130
John Nelson	63	8	18	26	51
Brian Collinson	65	7	18	25	53
Glenn Lowes	49	10	14	24	118
Jeff Turcotte	22	4	14	18	8
Bill Berg	57	3	15	18	138
Chris Cygan	61	4	13	17	20
Ian Pound, Kitchener	5	0	1	1	15
London	32	2	4	6	62
Toronto	28	0	8	8	49
Totals	65	2	13	15	126
Mike Flanagan	49	1	10	11	49
Paul Stafford	38	1	4	5	15
Ian Rand	33	0	5	5	0
Anthony Cross	7	2	2	4	2
Sean Boland	17	0	4	4	23
Nick Vitucci (Goalie)	47	0	2	2	4
Brian Merko	21	1	0	1	2
Collin Power	3	0	1	1	0
Jack Tootikian	1	0	0	0	0
David Kunda	2	0	0	0	0
George Wood (Goalie)	2	0	0	0	2
Nick Zarafonitis	9	0	0	0	2
Mike Volpe (Goalie)	10	0	0	0	0
Piero Greco, Belle. (G.)	11	0	0	0	0
Tor. (G.)	15	0	0	0	2
Totals	26	0	0	0	2

Windsor Compuware Spitfires

	Games	G.	A.	Pts.	Pen.
Adam Graves	66	45	55	100	70
Scott Metcalfe, Kingston	39	15	45	60	104

	Games	G.	A.	Pts.	Pen.
Windsor	18	10	12	22	52
Totals	57	25	57	82	156
Kevin Kerr	63	27	41	68	*264
Mike Wolak, Kitchener	9	3	6	9	6
Belleville	25	20	16	36	18
Windsor	26	7	14	21	26
Totals	60	30	36	66	50
Ian O'Rear	62	18	46	64	43
Darrin Shannon	60	17	41	58	31
Darryl Shannon	64	23	27	50	83
John Urbanic	53	19	27	46	86
Jean-Paul Gorley	59	18	25	43	19
Brad Stepan	54	18	21	39	58
Brad Hyatt, Hamilton	1	0	0	0	0
Belleville	16	3	8	11	26
Windsor	39	5	16	21	48
Totals	56	8	24	32	74
Peter DeBoer	52	13	17	30	37
Paul Hampton	55	5	25	30	56
Mark Kurzawski	65	5	23	28	96
Ron Jones	49	7	20	27	76
Paul Maurice	63	4	15	19	87
Glen Featherstone	47	6	11	17	154
Geoff Benic	63	9	7	16	169
Kevin White	51	4	2	6	0
Rob LeBlanc	22	1	3	4	7
Scott Laurin	23	0	2	2	2
Rob Flynn	38	0	2	2	46
Peter Ing (Goalie)	28	0	1	1	9
Pat Jablonski (Goalie)	41	0	1	1	16
Joe Ranger	1	0	0	0	7
Bill White, Sudbury (G.)	5	0	0	0	0
Wind. (G.)	3	0	0	0	0
Totals	8	0	0	0	0

Complete OHL Goaltending

	Games	Mins.	Goals	SO.	Avg.
Mark Gowans (a)	10	571	21(1)	0	2.21
Dave Humphreys	1	64	3	0	2.81
Jeff Hackett	31	1672	85(2)	2	3.05
Sean Evoy	31	1702	89	2	3.14
Oshawa Totals	66	4009	201	4	3.01
Ron Tugnutt	31	1891	88(3)	2	*2.79
Kay Whitmore	36	2159	118(3)	1	3.28
Peterborough Totals	66	4050	212	3	3.14
John Reid	47	2737	142(1)	1	3.11
Rob Fournier	25	1281	72(1)	2	3.37
North Bay Totals	66	4018	216	3	3.23
Pat Jablonski	41	2328	128(3)	*3	3.30
Peter Ing	28	1615	105(2)	0	3.90
Bill White (b)	3	111	10(1)	0	5.41
Windsor Totals	66	4054	249	3	3.69
Willie Popp (c)	1	60	1	0	1.00
Peter Richards (d)	24	1399	76(1)	0	3.26
Mike Rosati	26	1334	85	1	3.82
Mark Gowans (a)	20	1106	82(1)	0	4.45
Mark Bernard	3	129	12	0	5.58
Hamilton Totals	66	4028	258	1	3.84
Darren Beals (e)	4	240	11	1	2.75
Willie Popp (c)	40	2232	139(2)	0	3.74
Scott Cumming	30	1567	127(1)	0	4.86
Ottawa Totals	66	4039	280	1	4.16

	Games	Mins.	Goals	SO.	Avg.
Scott Luce	18	1001	55	*3	3.30
Andy Helmuth	48	2637	188(5)	*3	4.28
Stephane Hebert	8	327	28(2)	0	5.14
Nelson Duarte	1	20	3	0	9.00
Guelph Totals	66	3986	281	6	4.23
Shawn Simpson	46	2673	184(2)	0	4.13
Dan Gatenby (f)	5	227	16	0	4.23
Rob Watson	20	1080	90(1)	0	5.00
Glen Chiasson	1	40	6	0	9.00
Sault Ste. Marie Totals	66	4019	299	0	4.46
David Weiss	35	1665	120(1)	0	4.32
Darren Beals (e)	45	2342	179(3)	0	4.59
Darrin Baker	1	20	2	0	6.00
Kitchener Totals	66	4027	305	0	4.54
Chris Clifford	44	2576	188(3)	1	4.38
Brian Tessier (g)	8	506	39	0	4.62
Franco Giammarco	17	924	86	0	5.58
Kingston Totals	66	4006	316	1	4.73
Steve Titus	47	2476	195(3)	1	4.73
Chris Somers	32	1508	120(3)	0	4.77
Anders Hogberg (h)	1	12	3	0	15.00
Joe Novak	1	20	5	0	15.00
London Totals	66	4016	329	1	4.92
Alan Perry	15	843	64(1)	0	4.56
Brian Tessier (g)	17	854	68(2)	0	4.78
Paul Henriques	35	1699	141(1)	0	4.98
Piero Greco (i)	11	466	45(1)	0	5.79
Dan Gatenby (f)	3	135	24	0	10.67
Belleville Totals	66	3997	347	0	5.21
Richard Tabaracci	*59	*3347	*290	1	5.20
Mark Seguin	14	674	79	0	7.03
Cornwall Totals	66	4021	369	1	5.51
Nick Vitucci	47	2456	213(3)	0	5.20
Mike Volpe	10	473	42	0	5.33
Piero Greco (i)	15	831	77	0	5.56
George Wood	2	111	14(1)	0	7.57
Brian Tessier (g)	3	147	26	0	10.61
Toronto Totals	66	4017	376	0	5.62
Dan Gatenby (f)	14	722	54	0	4.49
Peter Richards (d)	29	1714	149(2)	0	5.22
Ted Mielczarek	17	856	84	0	5.89
Anders Hogberg (h)	12	554	63	0	6.82
Bill White (b)	5	139	19	0	8.20
Dino Cirello	1	7	2	0	17.14
Dave Barrett	1	12	4	0	20.00
Sudbury Totals	66	4003	377	0	5.65

( )—Empty Net Goals. Do not count against a Goaltender's average.
(a)—Gowans played for Oshawa and Hamilton
(b)—White played for Windsor and Sudbury.
(c)—Popp played for Hamilton and Ottawa.
(d)—Richards played for Hamilton and Sudbury.
(e)—Beals played for Ottawa and Kitchener.
(f)—Gatenby played for Sault Ste. Marie, Belleville and Sudbury.
(g)—Tessier played for Kingston, Belleville and Toronto.
(h)—Hogberg played for London and Sudbury.
(i)—Greco played for Belleville and Toronto.

Individual 1986-87 Leaders

Goals	Frank DiMuzio, Ottawa—	59
Assists	Scott McCrory, Oshawa—	99
Points	Scott McCrory, Oshawa—	150
Penalty Minutes	Kevin Kerr, Windsor—	264
Goaltender's Average	Ron Tugnutt, Peterborough—	2.79
Shutouts	Andy Helmuth, Guelph—	3
	Scott Luce, Guelph—	3
	Pat Jablonski, Windsor—	3

1987 J. Ross Robertson Cup Playoffs

(All series best of seven)

Super Series

(To determine who hosts Memorial Cup)

Series "A"

	W.	L.	Pts.	GF.	GA.
Oshawa	4	3	8	29	20
North Bay	3	4	6	20	29

(Oshawa wins series, 4 games to 3)

Division Quarterfinals

Leyden Division

Series "B"

	W.	L.	Pts.	GF.	GA.
Ottawa	4	1	8	17	13
Cornwall	1	4	2	13	17

(Ottawa wins series, 4 games to 1)

Series "C"

	W.	L.	Pts.	GF.	GA.
Kingston	4	2	8	18	18
Belleville	2	4	4	18	18

(Kingston wins series, 4 games to 2)

Emms Division

Series "B"

	W.	L.	Pts.	GF.	GA.
Hamilton	4	1	8	22	18
Guelph	1	4	2	18	22

(Hamilton wins series, 4 games to 1)

Series "C"

	W.	L.	Pts.	GF.	GA.
Windsor	4	0	8	17	10
Sault Ste. Marie	0	4	0	10	17

(Windsor wins series, 4 games to 0)

Division Semifinals

Series "D"

	W.	L.	Pts.	GF.	GA.
Oshawa	4	2	8	28	13
Kingston	2	4	4	13	28

(Oshawa wins series, 4 games to 2)

Series "D"

	W.	L.	Pts.	GF.	GA.
North Bay	4	0	8	19	13
Kitchener	0	4	0	13	19

(North Bay wins series, 4 games to 0)

Series "E"

	W.	L.	Pts.	GF.	GA.
Peterborough	4	2	8	24	21
Ottawa	2	4	4	21	24

(Peterborough wins series, 4 games to 2)

Series "E"

	W.	L.	Pts.	GF.	GA.
Windsor	4	0	8	18	10
Hamilton	0	4	0	10	18

(Windsor wins series, 4 games to 0)

Division Finals

Series "F"

	W.	L.	Pts.	GF.	GA.
Oshawa	4	2	8	17	13
Peterborough	2	4	4	13	17

(Oshawa wins series, 4 games to 2)

Series "F"

	W.	L.	Pts.	GF.	GA.
North Bay	4	2	8	27	25
Windsor	2	4	4	25	27

(North Bay wins series, 4 games to 2)

OHL Final Series for the J. Ross Robertson Cup

Series "G"

	W.	L.	Pts.	GF.	GA.
Oshawa	4	3	8	29	25
North Bay	3	4	6	25	29

(Oshawa wins series, and Robertson Cup, 4 games to 3)

Top 10 Playoff Scorers

	Games	G.	A.	Pts.	Pen.
1. Scott McCrory, Oshawa	24	15	*22	*37	20
2. Lee Giffin, Oshawa	23	*17	19	36	14
3. Len Soccio, North Bay	24	9	18	27	36
4. David McIlwain, North Bay	24	7	18	25	40
5. Derek King, Oshawa	17	14	10	24	40
6. Bill Houlder, North Bay	22	4	19	23	20
7. Keith Osborne, North Bay	24	11	11	22	25
Gordon Murphy, Oshawa	24	6	16	22	22
9. Mike Gillies, North Bay	24	12	9	21	4
10. Darren Turcotte, North Bay	18	12	8	20	6

Team-by-Team Playoff Scoring

Belleville Bulls

(Lost division quarterfinals to Kingston, 4 games to 2)

	Games	G.	A.	Pts.	Pen.
Todd Hawkins	6	3	5	8	16
Paul Wilkinson	6	3	4	7	17
Doug Stromback	6	2	2	4	10
Peter Choma	6	1	3	4	7
Bryan Marchment	6	0	4	4	17
David Haas	6	3	0	3	13
Wilf Payne	6	2	0	2	4
Brian Chapman	6	1	1	2	10
Kent Hulst	6	1	1	2	0
Frank Melone	6	1	1	2	8
Greg Bignell	6	0	2	2	15
Jim Dean	6	0	2	2	9
Darryl Williams	6	0	2	2	21
Scott Shepherd	6	1	0	1	2
Mike Arthur	6	0	1	1	9
Tony Crisp	6	0	1	1	0
Dean Haig	6	0	1	1	2
Derek Langille	6	0	0	0	0
Alan Perry (Goalie)	6	0	0	0	4

Cornwall Royals

(Lost division quarterfinals to Ottawa, 4 games to 1)

	Games	G.	A.	Pts.	Pen.
Craig Duncanson	5	4	3	7	20
Larry Mitchell	5	4	2	6	19
Brad Belland	5	1	3	4	8
Darren Colbourne	5	1	2	3	2
Scott MacDonald	5	2	0	2	2
Robert Ray	5	1	1	2	16
Mark Evans	5	0	2	2	27
Steve Simoni	5	0	2	2	10
Jason Hannigan	5	0	1	1	7
Luc Sabourin	5	0	1	1	12
Mike Ware	5	0	1	1	10
Gary St. Pierre	2	0	0	0	0
Steve Herniman	3	0	0	0	0
Paul Cain	5	0	0	0	0
Glen Johnston	5	0	0	0	2
Steve Maltais	5	0	0	0	2
Derek Middleton	5	0	0	0	9
Allen Murphy	5	0	0	0	0
Mathieu Schneider	5	0	0	0	22
Rick Tabaracci (Goalie)	5	0	0	0	2

Guelph Platers

(Lost division quarterfinals to Hamilton, 4 games to 1)

	Games	G.	A.	Pts.	Pen.
Keith Miller	5	6	2	8	0
Darren Treloar	5	2	5	7	0
Paul Kelly	5	2	4	6	0
Jamie McKinley	5	2	3	5	0
Rob Zamuner	5	0	5	5	2
Brian Hayton	5	2	1	3	0
Lonnie Loach	5	2	1	3	2
Allan MacIsaac	5	1	2	3	22
Marc Tournier	5	1	2	3	15
Luciano Fagioli	5	0	2	2	0
Kerry Huffman	5	0	2	2	8
Denis Larocque	5	0	2	2	9
Gary Wenzel	5	0	1	1	0
Kelly Bradley	5	0	0	0	0

	Games	G.	A.	Pts.	Pen.
Andy Helmuth (Goalie)	5	0	0	0	4
Bill Loshaw	5	0	0	0	7
David Noseworthy	5	0	0	0	2
Stephen Perkovic	5	0	0	0	2
Sean Whyte	5	0	0	0	0

Hamilton Steelhawks

(Lost division semifinals to Windsor, 4 games to 0)

	Games	G.	A.	Pts.	Pen.
Keith Gretzky	9	5	9	14	4
Brian Martin	9	5	6	11	16
Brad Dalgarno	9	4	6	10	11
Kirk Tomlinson	9	4	6	10	28
Stan Drulia	9	4	4	8	2
Ron Bernacci	9	2	6	8	6
John Copple	9	1	7	8	12
Jeff Waver	9	0	5	5	23
John Purves	9	2	0	2	12
Ken McRae	7	1	1	2	12
Brent Thompson	7	1	1	2	6
Jamie Leach	9	1	1	2	4
Garth Joy	9	0	2	2	4
Shawn McCosh	6	1	0	1	2
Guy Girouard	9	1	0	1	6
Ken Alexander	9	0	1	1	12
Don Pancoe	9	0	1	1	24
Brad Gratton	1	0	0	0	0
Mark Gowans (Goalie)	3	0	0	0	0
Fred Pennell	7	0	0	0	2
Mike Rosati (Goalie)	7	0	0	0	0
Dennis Vial	8	0	0	0	8

Kingston Canadians

(Lost division semifinals to Oshawa, 4 games to 2)

	Games	G.	A.	Pts.	Pen.
Mike Maurice	12	11	2	13	21
Ted Linseman	12	2	6	8	20
Mike Fiset	10	2	5	7	4
Scott Pearson	9	3	3	6	42
James Henckel	12	1	5	6	2
Bryan Fogarty	12	2	3	5	5
Troy MacNevin	12	2	3	5	15
Steve Seftel	12	1	4	5	9
Wayne Erskine	12	2	2	4	9
John Agazzi	12	1	2	3	15
Andy Rivers	4	0	3	3	0
Chad Badawey	12	1	1	2	4
Sloan Torti	7	1	0	1	4
Andre Belzile	12	1	0	1	6
Marc Laforge	12	1	0	1	79
Peter Liptrott	11	0	1	1	5
Chris Lukey	12	0	1	1	17
Marc Lyons	12	0	1	1	44
Jeff Sirkka	12	0	1	1	34
Franco Giammarco (G.)	1	0	0	0	0
Alain Laforge	2	0	0	0	2
John Battice	5	0	0	0	0
Chris Clifford (Goalie)	12	0	0	0	4

Kitchener Rangers

(Lost division semifinals to North Bay, 4 games to 0)

	Games	G.	A.	Pts.	Pen.
Max Middendorf	4	2	5	7	5
Ed Kister	4	3	2	5	2

	Games	G.	A.	Pts.	Pen.
Gary Callaghan	4	2	3	5	0
Daran Moxam	4	1	2	3	39
Ron Goodall	4	0	3	3	0
David Latta	4	0	3	3	2
Dave Moylan	3	2	0	2	11
Jeff Noble	4	2	0	2	20
Mark Montanari	4	1	1	2	16
Richard Borgo	4	0	1	1	0
Kevin Grant	4	0	1	1	16
Darren Rumble	4	0	1	1	9
Jim Hulton	1	0	0	0	0
Allan Lake	1	0	0	0	7
Darren Beals (Goalie)	2	0	0	0	2
David Weiss (Goalie)	2	0	0	0	0
Daril Holmes	3	0	0	0	7
Craig Booker	4	0	0	0	2
Paul Epoch	4	0	0	0	4
Doug Jones	4	0	0	0	0
Warren Rychel	4	0	0	0	9
Scott Taylor	4	0	0	0	9

North Bay Centennials

(Lost league finals to Oshawa, 4 games to 3)

	Games	G.	A.	Pts.	Pen.
Len Soccio	24	9	18	27	36
David McLlwain	24	7	18	25	40
Bill Houlder	22	4	19	23	20
Keith Osborne	24	11	11	22	25
Mike Gillies	24	12	9	21	4
Darren Turcotte	18	12	8	20	6
Nick Kypreos	24	11	5	16	78
Tim Bean	21	4	12	16	65
Mike Hartman	19	7	8	15	88
Troy Crowder	23	3	9	12	99
Darin Smith	23	3	8	11	84
Wayne MacPhee	24	2	9	11	43
Jeff Bloemberg	21	1	6	7	13
Adam Burt	24	1	6	7	68
Brent Bywater	24	0	6	6	18
Shawn Roy	16	2	3	5	0
Jason Corrigan	6	1	2	3	0
Greg Capson	19	1	1	2	12
Darcy Cahill	11	0	1	1	4
Rick Stromback	19	0	1	1	36
Shawn Dubois	1	0	0	0	0
Mark Dunning	1	0	0	0	0
Chad Gleason	17	0	0	0	11
John Reid (Goalie)	24	0	0	0	18

Oshawa Generals

(Winners of 1987 J. Ross Robertson Cup Playoffs)

	Games	G.	A.	Pts.	Pen.
Scott McCrory	24	15	*22	*37	20
Lee Giffin	23	*17	19	36	14
Derek King	17	14	10	24	40
Gordon Murphy	24	6	16	22	22
Barry Burkholder	26	7	9	16	33
Marc Laniel	26	3	13	16	20
Brian Hunt	26	5	10	15	13
Jim Paek	26	1	14	15	43
Petri Matikainen	21	2	12	14	36
Sean Williams	25	7	5	12	19
Brent Grieve	24	3	8	11	22
John Andersen	25	6	4	10	18
Dean Morton	23	3	6	9	112

	Games	G.	A.	Pts.	Pen.
Kevin Miehm	26	1	8	9	12
Shane Doyle	23	4	4	8	115
Scott Mahoney	26	4	1	5	*117
Jeff Daniels	15	3	2	5	5
Mike Short	17	0	3	3	32
Greg Watson	21	1	1	2	59
Ian Fraser	7	1	0	1	7
Greg Polak	4	0	0	0	5
Sean Evoy (Goalie)	14	0	0	0	9
Jeff Hackett (Goalie)	16	0	0	0	2
Tony Joseph	19	0	0	0	58

Ottawa 67's

(Lost division semifinals to Peterborough, 4 games to 2)

	Games	G.	A.	Pts.	Pen.
Andrew Cassels	11	5	9	14	7
John Hanna	11	6	4	10	13
Guy Larose	11	2	8	10	27
Mike Griffith	11	5	4	9	0
Dave Rowbotham	11	4	5	9	2
Rick Lessard	11	1	7	8	30
Frank DiMuzio	7	5	1	6	21
Mike Rutherford	11	4	2	6	0
Ransome Drcar	11	3	3	6	18
Todd Clarke	11	1	4	5	32
Kent Hawley	11	0	5	5	43
Graydon Almstedt	11	1	1	2	11
Brent Battistelli	9	0	2	2	18
Willie Popp (Goalie)	9	0	2	2	8
John East	11	1	0	1	11
Dave Gibbons	11	0	1	1	11
Scott Cumming (Goalie)	4	0	0	0	4
Jeff Ballantyne	5	0	0	0	9
Vern Ray	9	0	0	0	11
Denis Chouinard	11	0	0	0	5
Matt Giesebrecht	11	0	0	0	2

Peterborough Petes

(Lost division finals to Oshawa, 4 games to 2)

	Games	G.	A.	Pts.	Pen.
Kris King	12	5	8	13	41
Jody Hull	12	4	9	13	14
Bill McMillan	8	4	4	8	5
Ross Wilson	12	3	5	8	16
Mark Freer	12	2	6	8	5
Bill Huard	12	5	2	7	19
Glen Seabrooke	4	3	3	6	6
Greg Vey	12	1	5	6	7
Mike Dagenais	12	4	1	5	20
Rob Murray	3	1	4	5	8
Dallas Eakins	12	1	4	5	37
Luke Richardson	12	0	5	5	24
Andy MacVicar	11	2	1	3	7
Larry Shaw	12	1	2	3	35
Jamey Hicks	12	0	3	3	2
Mark Bar	12	1	1	2	25
Todd Gregory	8	0	2	2	0
Dan Jensen	9	0	1	1	0
Kevin MacDonald	10	0	1	1	16
Corey Foster	1	0	0	0	0
Ron Tugnutt (Goalie)	6	0	0	0	2
Kay Whitmore (Goalie)	7	0	0	0	0
Steve DeGurse	8	0	0	0	12
Tie Domi	10	0	0	0	20

Sault Ste. Marie Greyhounds

(Lost division quarterfinals to Windsor, 4 games to 0)

	Games	G.	A.	Pts.	Pen.
Paul Beraldo	4	3	2	5	6
Dan Currie	4	2	1	3	2
Peter Fiorentino	4	2	1	3	5
Brad Aitken	4	1	2	3	5
Mike Oliverio	4	0	3	3	0
Steve Bisson	4	1	1	2	4
Steve Cote	4	0	2	2	7
Tyler Larter	4	0	2	2	8
Troy Mallette	4	0	2	2	2
Mike Glover	4	1	0	1	15
Steve Hollett	4	0	1	1	7
Shawn Simpson (Goalie)	4	0	1	1	0
Rod Thacker	4	0	1	1	8
Mike Kolodziejczyk	2	0	0	0	0
Rob Reid	2	0	0	0	0
Kent Trolley	2	0	0	0	2
Jeff Columbus	3	0	0	0	0
Bob Jones	3	0	0	0	0
Bob Babcock	4	0	0	0	11
Brian Hoard	4	0	0	0	2
Rob Zettler	4	0	0	0	0

Windsor Compuware Spitfires

(Lost division finals to North Bay, 4 games to 2)

	Games	G.	A.	Pts.	Pen.
Adam Graves	14	9	8	17	32
Brad Hyatt	14	7	7	14	11
Peter DeBoer	14	4	9	13	16
Ian O'Rear	14	2	11	13	25
Darryl Shannon	14	4	8	12	18
Kevin Kerr	14	3	8	11	45
Scott Metcalfe	13	5	5	10	27
Darrin Shannon	14	4	6	10	8
John Urbanic	14	3	6	9	10
Mike Wolak	14	2	7	9	2
Glen Featherstone	14	2	6	8	19
Paul Hampton	14	0	8	8	18
Jean-Paul Gorley	14	4	3	7	4
Mark Kurzawski	14	3	4	7	38
Brad Stepan	13	2	5	7	14
Ron Jones	13	2	4	6	19
Geoff Benic	14	2	1	3	22
Paul Maurice	14	2	1	3	18
Rob LeBlanc	1	0	0	0	0
Kevin White	2	0	0	0	0
Peter Ing (Goalie)	3	0	0	0	0
Pat Jablonski (Goalie)	12	0	0	0	0

Complete Robertson Cup Goaltending

	Games	Mins.	Goals	SO.	Avg.
Sean Evoy	14	720	31	*2	*2.58
Jeff Hackett	15	895	40	0	2.68
Oshawa Totals	26	1615	71	2	2.64
Alan Perry	6	367	18	1	2.94
Belleville Totals	6	367	18	1	2.94
Kay Whitmore	7	366	17	1	2.79
Ron Tugnutt	6	374	21	1	3.37
Peterborough Totals	12	740	38	2	3.08
Pat Jablonski	12	710	38	0	3.21
Peter Ing	3	161	9	0	3.35
Windsor Totals	14	870	47	0	3.24
Willie Popp	9	503	26(1)	0	3.10
Scott Cumming	4	160	10	0	3.75
Ottawa Totals	11	663	37	0	3.35
Rick Tabaracci	5	303	16(1)	0	3.17
Cornwall Totals	5	303	17	0	3.37
Chris Clifford	12	730	42(2)	0	3.45
Franco Giammarco	1	20	2	0	6.00
Kingston Totals	12	750	46	0	3.68
John Reid	*24	*1496	*92(4)	0	3.69
North Bay Totals	24	1496	96	0	3.85
Mike Rosati	7	384	22	0	3.44
Mark Gowans	3	157	14	0	5.35
Hamilton Totals	9	541	36	0	3.99
Shawn Simpson	4	243	17	0	4.20
Sault Ste. Marie Totals	4	243	17	0	4.20
Andy Helmuth	5	300	21(1)	0	4.20
Guelph Totals	5	300	22	0	4.40
David Weiss	2	138	10	0	4.35
Darren Beals	2	120	9	0	4.50
Kitchener Totals	4	258	19	0	4.42

( )—Empty Net Goals. Do not count against a Goaltender's average.

Individual OHL Playoff Leaders

Goals ....Lee Giffin, Oshawa— 17
Assists..Scott McCrory, Oshawa— 22
Points..Scott McCrory, Oshawa— 37
Penalty Minutes ....Scott Mahoney, Oshawa— 117
Goaltender's average...Sean Evoy, Oshawa— 2.58
Shutouts ....Sean Evoy, Oshawa— 2

★★

OHL 1986-87 All-Stars

First Team	Position	Second Team
Ron Tugnutt, Peterborough	Goal	Shawn Simpson, S.S. Marie
Kerry Huffman, Guelph	Defense	Darryl Shannon, Windsor
Bryan Fogarty, Kingston	Defense	Petri Matikainen, Oshawa
Scott McCrory, Oshawa	Center	Dave McIlwain, North Bay
Lee Giffin, Oshawa	Right Wing	Todd Hawkins, Belleville
Derek King, Oshawa	Left Wing	Nick Kypreos, North Bay

★★

OHL 1986-87 Trophy Winners

Red Tilson Trophy (Outstanding Player)..Scott McCrory, Oshawa
Eddie Powers Memorial Trophy (Scoring Champion)...Scott McCrory, Oshawa
Dave Pinkney Trophy (Top Team Goaltending)..Sean Evoy, Oshawa
                                                                                                                                        Jeff Hackett, Oshawa
Max Kaminsky Trophy (Outstanding Defenseman)...Kerry Huffman, Guelph
William Hanley Trophy (Most Gentlemanly) ....Scott McCrory, Oshawa
                                                                                                                                        Keith Gretzky, Hamilton
Emms Family Award (Rookie of the Year) ....Andrew Cassels, Ottawa
Matt Leyden Trophy (Coach of the Year)..Paul Theriault, Oshawa
Jim Mahon Memorial Trophy (Top scoring Right Wing)..Ron Goodall, Kitchener
F.W. Dinty Moore Trophy (Lowest average by a rookie goalie) ....Jeff Hackett, Oshawa
Leo Lalonde Memorial Trophy (Overage Player of Year) ....Mike Richard, Toronto

Historical OHL Trophy Winners

Red Tilson Trophy
(Outstanding Player)

Season	Player	Club
1944-45	Doug McMurdy, St. Catharines	
1945-46	Tod Sloan, St. Michael's	
1946-47	Ed Sanford, St. Michael's	
1947-48	George Armstrong, Stratford	
1948-49	Gil Mayer, Barrie	
1949-50	George Armstrong, Marlboros	
1950-51	Glenn Hall, Windsor	
1951-52	Bill Harrington, Kitchener	
1952-53	Bob Attersley, Oshawa	
1953-54	Brian Cullen, St. Catharines	
1954-55	Hank Ciesla, St. Catharines	
1955-56	Ron Howell, Guelph	
1956-57	Frank Mahovlich, St. Michael's	
1957-58	Murray Oliver, Hamilton	
1958-59	Stan Mikita, St. Catharines	
1959-60	Wayne Connelly, Peterborough	
1960-61	Rod Gilbert, Guelph	
1961-62	Pit Martin, Hamilton	
1962-63	Wayne Maxner, Niagara Falls	
1963-64	Yvan Cournoyer, Montreal	
1964-65	Andre Lacroix, Peterborough	
1965-66	Andre Lacroix, Peterborough	
1966-67	Mickey Redmond, Peterborough	

Season	Player	Club
1967-68	Walt Tkaczuk, Kitchener	
1968-69	Rejean Houle, Montreal	
1969-70	Gilbert Perreault, Montreal	
1970-71	Dave Gardner, Marlboros	
1971-72	Don Lever, Niagara Falls	
1972-73	Rick Middleton, Oshawa	
1973-74	Jack Valiquette, Sault Ste. Marie	
1974-75	Dennis Maruk, London	
1975-76	Peter Lee, Ottawa	
1976-77	Dale McCourt, St. Catharines	
1977-78	Bobby Smith, Ottawa	
1978-79	Mike Foligno, Sudbury	
1979-80	Jim Fox, Ottawa	
1980-81	Ernie Godden, Windsor	
1981-82	Dave Simpson, London	
1982-83	Doug Gilmour, Cornwall	
1983-84	John Tucker, Kitchener	
1984-85	Wayne Groulx, Sault Ste. Marie	
1985-86	Ray Sheppard, Cornwall	
1986-87	Scott McCrory, Oshawa	

Eddie Powers Memorial Trophy
(Scoring Champion)

Season	Player	Club
1933-34	J. Groboski, Oshawa	

Season	Player	Club
1934-35	J. Good, Toronto Lions	
1935-36	John O'Flaherty, West Toronto	
1936-37	Billy Taylor, Oshawa	
1937-38	Hank Goldup, Tor. Marlboros	
1938-39	Billy Taylor, Oshawa	
1939-40	Jud McAtee, Oshawa	
1940-41	Gaye Stewart, Tor. Marlboros	
1941-42	Bob Wiest, Brantford	
1942-43	Norman "Red" Tilson, Oshawa	
1943-44	Ken Smith, Oshawa	
1944-45	Leo Gravelle, St. Michael's	
1945-46	Tod Sloan, St. Michael's	
1946-47	Fleming Mackell, St. Michael's	
1947-48	George Armstrong, Stratford	
1948-49	Bert Giesebrecht, Windsor	
1949-50	Earl Reibel, Windsor	
1950-51	Lou Jankowski, Oshawa	
1951-52	Ken Laufman, Guelph	
1952-53	Jim McBurney, Galt	
1953-54	Brian Cullen, St. Catharines	
1954-55	Hank Ciesla, St. Catharines	
1955-56	Stan Baliuk, Kitchener	
1956-57	Bill Sweeney, Guelph	
1957-58	John McKenzie, St. Catharines	
1958-59	Stan Mikita, St. Catharines	
1959-60	Chico Maki, St. Catharines	
1960-61	Rod Gilbert, Guelph	
1961-62	Andre Boudrias, Montreal	
1962-63	Wayne Maxner, Niagara Falls	
1963-64	Andre Boudrias, Montreal	
1964-65	Ken Hodge, St. Catharines	
1965-66	Andre Lacroix, Peterborough	
1966-67	Derek Sanderson, Niagara Falls	
1967-68	Tom Webster, Niagara Falls	
1968-69	Rejean Houle, Montreal	
1969-70	Marcel Dionne, St. Catharines	
1970-71	Marcel Dionne, St. Catharines	
1971-72	Bill Harris, Toronto	
1972-73	Blake Dunlop, Ottawa	
1973-74	Jack Valiquette, Sault Ste. Marie	
	Rick Adduono, St. Catharines	
1974-75	Bruce Boudreau, Toronto	
1975-76	Mike Kaszycki, Sault Ste. Marie	
1976-77	Dwight Foster, Kitchener	
1977-78	Bobby Smith, Ottawa	
1978-79	Mike Foligno, Sudbury	
1979-80	Jim Fox, Ottawa	
1980-81	John Goodwin, Sault Ste. Marie	
1981-82	Dave Simpson, London	
1982-83	Doug Gilmour, Cornwall	
1983-84	Tim Salmon, Kingston	
1984-85	Dave MacLean, Belleville	
1985-86	Ray Sheppard, Cornwall	
1986-87	Scott McCrory, Oshawa	

Dave Pinkney Trophy
(Top Team Goaltending)

Season	Player	Club
1948-49	Gil Mayer, Barrie	
1949-50	Don Lockhart, Marlboros	
1950-51	Don Lockhart, Marlboros	
	Lorne Howes, Barrie	
1951-52	Don Head, Marlboros	
1952-53	John Henderson, Marlboros	
1953-54	Dennis Riggin, Hamilton	
1954-55	John Albani, Marlboros	
1955-56	Jim Crockett, Marlboros	
1956-57	Len Broderick, Marlboros	
1957-58	Len Broderick, Marlboros	
1958-59	Jacques Caron, Peterborough	
1959-60	Gerry Cheevers, St. Michael's	

Season	Player	Club
1960-61	Bud Blom, Hamilton	
1961-62	George Holmes, Montreal	
1962-63	Chuck Goddard, Peterborough	
1963-64	Bernie Parent, Niagara Falls	
1964-65	Bernie Parent, Niagara Falls	
1965-66	Ted Quimet, Montreal	
1966-67	Peter MacDuffe, St. Catharines	
1967-68	Bruce Mullet, Montreal	
1968-69	Wayne Wood, Montreal	
1969-70	John Garrett, Peterborough	
1970-71	John Garrett, Peterborough	
1971-72	Michel Larocque, Ottawa	
1972-73	Mike Palmateer, Toronto	
1973-74	Don Edwards, Kitchener	
1974-75	Greg Millen, Peterborough	
1975-76	Jim Bedard, Sudbury	
1976-77	Pat Riggin, London	
1977-78	Al Jensen, Hamilton	
1978-79	Nick Ricci, Niagara Falls	
1979-80	Rick LaFerriere, Peterborough	
1980-81	Jim Ralph, Ottawa	
1981-82	Marc D'Amour, Sault Ste. Marie	
1982-83	Peter Sidorkiewicz, Oshawa	
	Jeff Hogg, Oshawa	
1983-84	Darren Pang, Ottawa	
	Greg Coram, Ottawa	
1984-85	Scott Mosey, Sault Ste. Marie	
	Marty Abrams, Sault Ste. Marie	
1985-86	Kay Whitmore, Peterborough	
	Ron Tugnutt, Peterborough	
1986-87	Sean Evoy, Oshawa	
	Jeff Hackett, Oshawa	

Max Kaminsky Trophy
(Outstanding Defenseman)

Season	Player	Club
1969-70	Ron Plumb, Peterborough	
1970-71	Jocelyn Guevremont, Montreal	
1971-72	Denis Potvin, Ottawa	
1972-73	Denis Potvin, Ottawa	
1973-74	Jim Turkiewicz, Peterborough	
1974-75	Mike O'Connell, Kingston	
1975-76	Rick Green, London	
1976-77	Craig Hartsburg, S. Ste. Marie	
1977-78	Brad Marsh, London	
	Rob Ramage, London	
1978-79	Greg Theberge, Peterborough	
1979-80	Larry Murphy, Peterborough	
1980-81	Steve Smith, Sault Ste. Marie	
1981-82	Ron Meighan, Niagara Falls	
1982-83	Allan MacInnis, Kitchener	
1983-84	Brad Shaw, Ottawa	
1984-85	Bob Halkidis, London	
1985-86	Terry Carkner, Peterborough	
	Jeff Brown, Sudbury	
1986-87	Kerry Huffman, Guelph	

William Hanley Trophy
(Most Gentlemanly)

Season	Player	Club
1960-61	Bruce Draper, St. Michael's	
1961-62	Lowell MacDonald, Hamilton	
1962-63	Paul Henderson, Hamilton	
1963-64	Fred Stanfield, St. Catharines	
1964-65	Jimmy Peters, Hamilton	
1965-66	Andre Lacroix, Peterborough	
1966-67	Mickey Redmond, Peterborough	
1967-68	Tom Webster, Niagara Falls	
1968-69	Rejean Houle, Montreal	
1969-74	No award presented	

Season	Player	Club
1974-75	Doug Jarvis, Peterborough	
1975-76	Dale McCourt, Hamilton	
1976-77	Dale McCourt, St. Catharines	
1977-78	Wayne Gretzky, S.S. Marie	
1978-79	Sean Simpson, Ottawa	
1979-80	Sean Simpson, Ottawa	
1980-81	John Goodwin, Sault Ste. Marie	
1981-82	Dave Simpson, London	
1982-83	Kirk Muller, Guelph	
1983-84	Kevin Conway, Kingston	
1984-85	Scott Tottle, Peterborough	
1985-86	Jason Lafreniere, Belleville	
1986-87	Scott McCrory, Oshawa	
	Keith Gretzky, Hamilton	

Emms Family Award
(Rookie of the Year)

Season	Player	Club
1972-73	Dennis Maruk, London	
1973-74	Jack Valiquette, Sault Ste. Marie	
1974-75	Danny Shearer, Hamilton	
1975-76	John Travella, Sault Ste. Marie	
1976-77	Yvan Joly, Ottawa	
1977-78	Wayne Gretzky, S. S. Marie	
1978-79	John Goodwin, Sault Ste. Marie	
1979-80	Bruce Dowie, Toronto	
1980-81	Tony Tanti, Oshawa	
1981-82	Pat Verbeek, Sudbury	
1982-83	Bruce Cassidy, Ottawa	
1983-84	Shawn Burr, Kitchener	
1984-85	Derek King, Sault Ste. Marie	
1985-86	Lonnie Loach, Guelph	
1986-87	Andrew Cassels, Ottawa	

Matt Leyden Trophy
(Coach of the Year)

Season	Coach	Club
1971-72	Gus Bodnar, Oshawa	
1972-73	George Armstrong, Toronto	
1973-74	Jack Bownass, Kingston	
1974-75	Bert Templeton, Hamilton	
1975-76	Jerry Toppazzini, Sudbury	
1976-77	Bill Long, London	
1977-78	Bill White, Oshawa	
1978-79	Gary Green, Peterborough	
1979-80	Dave Chambers, Toronto	
1980-81	Brian Kilrea, Ottawa	
1981-82	Brian Kilrea, Ottawa	
1982-83	Terry Crisp, Sault Ste. Marie	

Season	Coach	Club
1983-84	Tom Barrett, Kitchener	
1984-85	Terry Crisp, Sault Ste. Marie	
1985-86	Jacques Martin, Guelph	
1986-87	Paul Theriault, Oshawa	

Jim Mahon Memorial Trophy
(Top Scoring Right Wing)

Season	Player	Club
1971-72	Bill Harris, Toronto	
1972-73	Dennis Ververgaert, London	
1973-74	Dave Gorman, St. Catharines	
1974-75	Mark Napier, Toronto	
1975-76	Peter Lee, Ottawa	
1976-77	John Anderson, Toronto	
1977-78	Dino Ciccarelli, London	
1978-79	Mike Foligno, Sudbury	
1979-80	Jim Fox, Ottawa	
1980-81	Tony Tanti, Oshawa	
1981-82	Tony Tanti, Oshawa	
1982-83	Ian MacInnis, Cornwall	
1983-84	Wayne Presley, Kitchener	
1984-85	Dave MacLean, Belleville	
1985-86	Ray Sheppard, Cornwall	
1986-87	Ron Goodall, Kitchener	

F.W. Dinty Moore Trophy
(Lowest Average by a Rookie Goalie)

Season	Player	Club
1975-76	Mark Locken, Hamilton	
1976-77	Barry Heard, London	
1977-78	Ken Ellacott, Peterborough	
1978-79	Nick Ricci, Niagara Falls	
1979-80	Mike Vezina, Ottawa	
1980-81	John Vanbiesbrouck, Sault Ste. Marie	
1981-82	Shawn Kilroy, Peterborough	
1982-83	Dan Burrows, Belleville	
1983-84	Jerry Iuliano, Sault Ste. Marie	
1984-85	Ron Tugnutt, Peterborough	
1985-86	Paul Henriques, Belleville	
1986-87	Jeff Hackett, Oshawa	

Leo Lalonde Memorial Trophy
(Overage Player of the Year)

1983-84	Don McLaren, Ottawa	
1984-85	Dunc MacIntyre, Belleville	
1985-86	Steve Guenette, Guelph	
1986-87	Mike Richard, Toronto	

Western Hockey League

(Known as Western Canada Hockey League prior to 1978-79)

President—Ed Chynoweth
Vice-President—Richard Doerksen
Executive Assistant—Norman Dueck
616-5920 Macleod Trail S., Calgary, Alberta T2H 0K2
Phone—(403) 253-8113

Final 1986-87 WHL Standings

East Division

	G.	W.	L.	T.	Pts.	GF.	GA.
Medicine Hat Tigers	72	48	19	5	101	383	264
Saskatoon Blades	72	44	26	2	90	369	282
Prince Albert Raiders	72	43	26	3	89	346	264
Moose Jaw Warriors	72	38	31	3	79	366	321
Regina Pats	72	31	37	4	66	332	356
Swift Current Broncos	72	28	40	4	60	331	393
Calgary Wranglers	72	23	46	3	49	304	390
Brandon Wheat Kings	72	19	49	4	42	282	443

West Division

	G.	W.	L.	T.	Pts.	GF.	GA.
Kamloops Blazers	72	55	14	3	113	496	292
Portland Winter Hawks	72	47	23	2	96	439	355
Spokane Chiefs	72	37	33	2	76	374	350
Victoria Cougars	72	30	41	1	61	334	412
Seattle Thunderbirds	72	21	47	4	46	328	430
New Westminster Bruins	72	18	50	4	40	300	432

Top 20 Scorers for the Bob Brownridge Memorial Trophy

	Games	G.	A.	Pts.	Pen.
1. Rob Brown, Kamloops	63	*76	*136	*212	101
2. Craig Endean, Seattle	17	20	20	40	18
Regina	59	49	57	106	16
Totals	76	69	77	146	34
3. Len Nielsen, Regina	72	36	100	136	32
4. Joe Sakic, Swift Current	72	60	73	133	31
5. Theoren Fleury, Moose Jaw	66	61	68	129	110
6. Adam Morrison, Victoria	65	55	70	125	57
7. Greg Hawgood, Kamloops	61	30	93	123	139
8. Ron Shudra, Kamloops	71	49	70	119	68
9. Robin Bawa, Kamloops	62	57	56	113	91
Pat Elynuik, Prince Albert	64	51	62	113	40
Dennis Holland, Portland	72	36	77	113	96
12. Glen Goodall, Seattle	68	63	49	112	64
13. Steve Gotaas, Prince Albert	68	53	55	108	94
14. Brent Hughes, New Westminster	8	5	4	9	22
Victoria	61	38	61	99	146
Totals	69	43	65	108	168
15. Dave Archibald, Portland	65	50	57	107	40
16. Terry Houlder, Calgary	72	28	77	105	49
17. Mark Pederson, Medicine Hat	69	56	46	102	58
Darcy Norton, Kamloops	71	45	57	102	66
Terry Yake, Brandon	71	44	58	102	64
20. Brent Gilchrist, Spokane	46	45	55	100	71

Brandon Wheat Kings

	Games	G.	A.	Pts.	Pen.
Terry Yake	71	44	58	102	64
Dale Marquette	68	41	29	70	59
Troy Kennedy, N. West..	26	13	17	30	11
Brandon	41	10	26	36	40
Totals	67	23	43	66	51
Mike Morin	67	36	25	61	91
Chad Silver	71	19	30	49	13
Judson Innes, Swift Cur.	1	0	0	0	0
Brandon	42	12	28	40	38
Totals	43	12	28	40	38
Curtis Bateman	58	15	23	38	78
Rick Herbert, Spokane...	2	0	1	1	8
Brandon	65	3	34	37	129
Totals	67	3	35	38	137
Kevin Clemens, M.H.	26	5	4	9	21
Brandon	43	11	16	27	29
Totals	69	16	20	36	50
Korey Sundstrom, Vic. ...	16	7	3	10	8
New Westminister..	13	3	2	5	9
Brandon	40	8	10	18	18
Totals	69	18	15	33	35
Dwayne Wills, N. West..	17	3	13	16	8
Brandon	18	8	9	17	2
Totals	35	11	22	33	10
Murray Rice	54	12	15	27	121
Kevin Green, M.J.	11	1	1	2	0
Brandon	46	13	6	19	7
Totals	57	14	7	21	7
Jeff Odgers	70	7	14	21	150
Kevin Chevaldayoff	70	0	16	16	259
Kevin Yellowaga	52	3	10	13	26
Darren Stolk	71	3	9	12	60
Graham Garden	56	2	10	12	58
Dave Whistle, Kamloops	4	2	1	3	4
Brandon	13	3	3	6	20
Totals	17	5	4	9	24
Troy Arndt	38	1	8	9	154
Blair Lee	15	2	6	8	4
Tye Cameron, Portland..	13	0	2	2	16
Brandon	21	2	2	4	30
Totals	34	2	4	6	46
Ed Brost, Swift Cur.	8	3	2	5	12
Brandon	3	0	0	0	0
Totals	11	3	2	5	12
Perry Fafard	11	2	3	5	8
Kirk Phare	5	1	3	4	9
George Maneluk (G.)	58	0	4	4	19
Corey Cheney, M.H.	25	0	2	2	2
Brandon	1	0	0	0	0
Totals	26	0	2	2	2
Bruce Coverenton	1	0	0	0	2
Brad Newmier	1	0	0	0	0
Steve Cox	2	0	0	0	0
Steve Bray (Goalie)	3	0	0	0	0
Derek Babe (Goalie)	9	0	0	0	0
Chad Gaborieau	9	0	0	0	11

Calgary Wranglers

	Games	G.	A.	Pts.	Pen.
Terry Houlder	72	28	77	105	49
Terry Zaporzan	72	46	46	92	48
Mark Tinordi	61	29	37	66	148

	Games	G.	A.	Pts.	Pen.
Trent Kaese, Swift Cur. ...	2	1	0	1	4
Calgary	68	30	24	54	117
Totals	70	31	24	55	121
Bryan Bosch	68	12	43	55	0
Kevin Heise	68	20	16	36	125
Ken Spangler	49	12	24	36	185
Bill Gregoire, Victoria....	15	6	3	9	41
Calgary	34	7	14	21	132
Totals	49	13	17	30	173
Curt Lehner, Spokane....	26	8	3	11	17
Calgary	28	10	6	16	25
Totals	54	18	9	27	42
Tim Flanagan	45	13	14	27	83
Terry Black	54	12	12	24	49
Kelly Ens	58	11	12	23	76
James Wheatcroft	62	8	14	22	93
Greg Leahy	64	6	16	22	170
Dwight Mullins	31	12	8	20	71
John Heasty	66	5	15	20	122
Rob Krauss	70	3	17	20	130
Peter Schmid, Victoria ...	22	0	6	6	7
Calgary	45	3	9	12	11
Totals	67	3	15	18	18
Brian Puhalsky	11	2	5	7	24
Peter Berthelson	68	1	6	7	45
Sampsa Jakonen	50	4	1	5	51
Grant Chorney, Seattle..	8	0	0	0	20
Regina	25	2	1	3	58
Calgary	12	0	0	0	21
Totals	45	2	1	3	99
Chris Churchill (Goalie) .	40	0	3	3	15
Mark Bassen	4	1	1	2	4
Grant McPhail (Goalie) .	43	0	2	2	8
Steven Young	4	1	0	1	0
Don Blishen (Goalie)	1	0	0	0	0
Roby Goodwin	1	0	0	0	0
Jeff Ferguson (Goalie)...	3	0	0	0	2
Pat Pylypuik	3	0	0	0	14
Paul Thomsen, Victoria ..	2	0	0	0	6
Calgary	1	0	0	0	0
Totals	3	0	0	0	6
Mark Greig	5	0	0	0	0

Kamloops Blazers

	Games	G.	A.	Pts.	Pen.
Rob Brown	63	*76	*136	*212	101
Greg Hawgood	61	30	93	123	139
Ron Shudra	71	49	70	119	68
Robin Bawa	62	57	56	113	91
Darcy Norton	71	45	57	102	66
Warren Babe, Swift Cur.	16	8	12	20	19
Kamloops	52	28	45	73	110
Totals	68	36	57	93	129
Glenn Mulvenna, N.W...	53	24	44	68	43
Kamloops	18	13	8	21	18
Totals	71	37	52	89	61
Kelly Para	72	30	50	80	87
Mark Recchi	40	26	50	76	63
Doug Pickell	70	34	24	58	182
Len Mark	71	23	30	53	47
Rich Wiest, Swift Cur.....	24	6	5	11	60
Kamloops	44	13	22	35	69
Totals	68	19	27	46	129

	Games	G.	A.	Pts.	Pen.
Garth Premak, N.W.	53	7	26	33	16
Kamloops	17	1	2	3	2
Totals	70	8	28	36	18
David Marcinyshyn	68	5	27	32	106
Rudy Poeschek	54	13	18	31	153
Don Schmidt	49	5	21	26	248
Casey MacMillan	58	5	13	18	61
Bill Harrington	46	7	8	15	22
Steve Nemeth	10	10	4	14	0
Devon Oleniuk, Sask.	18	1	3	4	19
Kamloops	37	1	7	8	35
Totals	55	2	10	12	54
Steve Weinke	48	2	9	11	74
Dean Cook (Goalie)	40	0	5	5	9
Stacy Nickel, Reg. (G.)	36	0	4	4	15
Kamloops (Goalie)	10	0	1	1	2
Totals	46	0	5	5	17
Mike Needham	3	1	2	3	0
Wayne MacDonald	14	1	2	3	2
Serge Lajoie	7	0	2	2	0
Calvin MacDonald (G.)	5	0	1	1	0
Kirt Brennan	1	0	0	0	0

Medicine Hat Tigers

	Games	G.	A.	Pts.	Pen.
Mark Pederson	69	56	46	102	58
Neil Brady	57	19	64	83	126
Wayne Hynes	72	38	43	81	78
Rocky Dundas, Spokane	19	13	17	30	69
Medicine Hat	29	22	24	46	63
Totals	48	35	41	76	132
Keith Van Rooyen, Spo.	22	5	26	31	85
Medicine Hat	45	7	38	45	82
Totals	67	12	64	76	167
Scott McCrady	70	10	66	76	157
Jeff Wenaas	70	42	30	72	68
Rob Dimaio	70	27	43	70	130
Dale Kushner	63	34	34	68	250
Ron Bonora	72	31	33	64	91
Guy Phillips	44	27	32	59	36
Wayne McBean	71	12	41	62	163
Trevor Linden	72	14	22	36	59
Kirby Lindal, Spokane	17	6	11	17	25
Medicine Hat	44	7	7	14	26
Totals	61	13	18	31	51
Rod Williams, Brandon	33	6	10	16	98
Regina	18	2	4	6	59
Medicine Hat	16	3	3	6	59
Totals	67	11	17	28	216
Jamie Huscroft, Seattle	21	1	18	19	99
Medicine Hat	14	3	3	6	71
Totals	35	4	21	25	170
Mike MacWilliam, N.W.	40	6	14	20	134
Medicine Hat	4	1	3	4	0
Totals	44	7	17	24	134
Dean Chynoweth	67	3	19	22	285
Mark Kuntz	66	4	14	18	149
Kevin Knopp	65	4	12	16	39
Mark Fitzpatrick (G.)	50	0	8	8	16
Trevor Ellerman	37	1	2	3	6
Mark Woolf	5	1	0	1	0
Kalvin Knibbs	7	1	0	1	0
Kelly Hitchins, Bran. (G.)	12	0	1	1	13
Medicine Hat (G.)	17	0	0	0	4
Totals	29	0	1	1	17
Jason Prosofsky	1	0	0	0	0
Randy Siska	1	0	0	0	2

Moose Jaw Warriors

	Games	G.	A.	Pts.	Pen.
Theoren Fleury	66	61	68	129	110
Trevor Jobe	58	54	33	87	53
Dave Thomlinson, Bran. .	2	0	1	1	9
Moose Jaw	69	44	36	80	117
Totals	71	44	37	81	126
Troy Edwards	69	37	41	78	102
Mike Keane	53	25	45	70	107
Kevin Herom	72	34	33	67	111
Bob Foglietta, Portland..	33	17	17	34	35
Moose Jaw	31	14	15	29	32
Totals	64	31	32	63	67
Lyle Odelein	59	9	50	59	70
Neil Pogany	70	21	25	46	63
Pat Beauchesne	69	11	33	44	151
Lee Trim, Brandon	40	5	16	21	88
Moose Jaw	27	1	9	10	57
Totals	67	6	25	31	145
Jerome Bechard	69	9	18	27	163
Neil Pilon	72	2	23	25	119
Darren Kwiatkowski, Se.	11	1	1	2	16
Moose Jaw	58	8	12	20	97
Totals	69	9	13	22	113
Brian Ilkuf	59	6	8	14	28
Blair Atcheynum, Sask...	21	0	4	4	4
Swift Current	5	2	1	3	0
Moose Jaw	12	3	0	3	2
Totals	38	5	5	10	6
Corey Bealieu	63	2	7	9	188
Jim MacKenzie	65	5	3	8	125
Rob Harvey	28	3	4	7	2
Warren Morrisseau	36	0	5	5	7
Dan Matheson	39	1	3	4	49
Glen Seymour, Port. (G.)	24	0	0	0	9
Moose Jaw (G.)	23	0	2	2	6
Totals	47	0	2	2	15
Glen Gulutzan	1	1	0	1	0
Jim Sykora	5	0	1	1	2
Dean Kuntz (Goalie)	25	0	1	1	9
Mike Fischer	1	0	0	0	0
Kevin Hehr	1	0	0	0	2
Cory Patterson	1	0	0	0	0
Jamie Barnett	3	0	0	0	0
Corey Belitski	3	0	0	0	0
Marti Loftsgard	3	0	0	0	0
Kent Paterson	3	0	0	0	0
Stephen Corfmat	4	0	0	0	2
Dennis Carignan	5	0	0	0	0
Calvin Fendelet	6	0	0	0	2
Rod Kavanagh, P.A.	2	0	0	0	0
Moose Jaw	4	0	0	0	7
Totals	6	0	0	0	7
Lloyd Cox	11	0	0	0	6

New Westminster Bruins

	Games	G.	A.	Pts.	Pen.
Scott Rawson	72	29	48	77	61
Stuart Sage	72	47	29	76	88
Cal Zankowski	71	35	35	70	82
Sean Lebrun, Spokane...	6	2	5	7	9
New Westminster...	55	21	32	53	47
Totals	61	23	37	60	56
Pat Bingham	70	23	14	37	148
Jayson More, Brandon ..	21	4	6	10	62
New Westminster..	43	4	23	27	155
Totals	64	8	29	37	217

	Games	G.	A.	Pts.	Pen.
Mario Desjardins, Kam..	28	7	8	15	8
New Westminster...	19	12	7	19	32
Totals	47	19	15	34	40
Darwin McPherson	65	10	22	32	242
Jeff Cornelius	43	6	20	26	154
Scott Daniels, Kamloops	43	6	4	10	66
New Westminster...	19	4	7	11	30
Totals	62	10	11	21	96
Darren Schwartz	39	6	12	18	135
Gerry Johannson	47	2	15	17	237
Steve Rennie	34	5	8	13	6
Brian McFarlane	22	5	7	12	12
Doneau Menard	65	3	9	12	59
Scott Farrell	67	4	8	12	47
Rene Vinopal	11	3	6	9	8
Link Gaetz	44	2	7	9	52
Jeff Kitsch	34	4	3	7	11
Mark Harding	15	3	2	5	0
Blaine Fomradas	45	2	3	5	42
Tom Nickolau, Brandon.	1	0	0	0	9
New Westminster...	3	1	3	4	9
Totals	4	1	3	4	18
Drago Adam (Goalie) ...	53	0	4	4	16
Kelly Ross	12	2	1	3	5
Brian Kozak	3	1	2	3	0
Mark Ragot	9	1	2	3	0
Randy Olson, Victoria..	3	2	0	2	2
New Westminster...	2	0	0	0	0
Totals	5	2	0	2	2
Mike Bafaro	3	1	1	2	4
Tony Bobbit	1	0	0	0	2
Mike McIntyre	1	0	0	0	0
Aaron Nosky	2	0	0	0	0
Bob Stickney	3	0	0	0	8
Drew Sawtell	5	0	0	0	5
Jason Mager	15	0	0	0	9
Ray Woodley (Goalie)...	32	0	0	0	8

Portland Winter Hawks

	Games	G.	A.	Pts.	Pen.
Dennis Holland	72	36	77	113	96
Dave Archibald	65	50	57	107	40
Dan Woodley	47	30	50	80	81
Dave McLay	57	35	42	77	151
Jeff Finley	72	13	53	66	113
Jamie Nicolls	59	28	37	65	42
Troy Mick	57	30	33	63	60
Glen Wesley	63	16	46	62	72
Jeff Sharples	44	25	35	60	92
Thomas Bjuhr	39	28	26	54	23
Brian Gerrits	68	25	27	52	64
James Latos	69	27	18	45	210
Scott Melnyk	65	21	22	43	63
Brent Fedyk, Regina	12	9	6	15	9
Seattle	13	5	11	16	9
Portland	11	5	4	9	6
Totals	36	19	21	40	24
Troy Pohl	54	18	21	39	142
Roy Mitchell	68	7	32	39	103
Shaun Clouston	70	6	25	31	93
Trevor Pohl	58	10	17	27	219
Ryan Stewart, Brandon..	15	7	9	16	15
Portland	7	5	2	7	12
Totals	22	12	11	23	27
Jay Stark	70	2	14	16	321
Steve Kloepzig	64	3	10	13	177

	Games	G.	A.	Pts.	Pen.
Darryl Gilmour, MJ (G).	31	0	1	1	4
Portland (Goalie)...	24	0	2	2	0
Totals	55	0	3	3	4
Bruce Basken	16	1	0	1	13
Todd Finner	1	0	1	1	0
Jim Swan (Goalie)	18	0	1	1	10
Byron Dafoe (Goalie)	2	0	0	0	0
Chris Eisenhart (Goalie).	14	0	0	0	2

Prince Albert Raiders

	Games	G.	A.	Pts.	Pen.
Pat Elynuik	64	51	62	113	40
Steve Gotaas	68	53	55	108	94
Kevin Todd	71	39	46	85	92
Kim Issel	70	31	44	75	55
Michael Modano	70	32	30	62	26
Dean Kolstad	72	17	37	54	112
Wayde Bucsis	64	18	28	46	21
Shawn Byram, Regina	12	3	3	6	25
Prince Albert	55	16	18	34	122
Totals	67	19	21	40	147
Curtis Hunt	47	6	31	37	101
Rod Dallman	47	13	21	34	240
Ian McAmmond	68	9	23	32	22
Jason Smart	57	9	22	31	62
Darin Kimble	68	17	13	30	190
Dean Braham	72	15	13	28	141
Richard Pilon	68	4	21	25	192
Doug Hobson	69	3	20	23	83
Gord Kruppke	49	2	10	12	129
Reid Simpson	47	3	8	11	105
Todd Nelson	35	1	6	7	10
Brad Bergen	10	1	3	4	8
Paul Thompson, Brand...	2	0	0	0	4
Swift Current	12	1	2	3	34
Prince Albert	14	0	0	0	10
Totals	28	1	2	3	48
Kenton Rein (Goalie)	51	0	3	3	29
Allan Wonitowy	22	0	2	2	7
Andy Kenning	6	0	2	2	13
Scott Frizzell	19	0	2	2	33
Paul Sutcliffe	3	0	1	1	0
Stacey Narowski	14	0	1	1	42
Garvin Weber (Goalie)..	23	0	1	1	0
Trevor Huber	1	0	0	0	0
Shane Kohl	2	0	0	0	2
Jim Hiller	3	0	0	0	12
Stan Reddick (Goalie)....	3	0	0	0	2
Dean Ross (Goalie)	4	0	0	0	2

Regina Pats

	Games	G.	A.	Pts.	Pen.
Craig Endean, Seattle....	17	20	20	40	18
Regina	59	49	57	106	16
Totals	76	69	77	146	34
Len Nielsen	72	36	100	136	32
Ray Savard, Seattle	16	8	6	14	43
Regina	56	38	16	54	134
Totals	72	46	22	68	177
Brad Hornung	61	32	34	66	55
Darren McKechnie	72	29	33	62	34
Mark Janssens	68	24	38	62	209
Gary Dickie	70	27	31	58	85
Brad Miller	67	10	38	48	154

	Games	G.	A.	Pts.	Pen.
Mike Van Slooten, Cal...	44	10	19	29	29
Regina	23	8	8	16	6
Totals	67	18	27	45	35
Chris Tarnowski, Kam. ...	51	3	23	26	67
Regina	20	0	15	15	27
Totals	71	3	38	41	94
Bryan Wells	20	7	15	22	105
Dan Logan, Saskatoon ..	29	4	4	8	9
Regina	25	3	9	12	15
Totals	54	7	13	20	24
Milan Dragicevic	42	5	12	17	76
Cregg Nicol	46	5	11	16	186
Darren Parsons	65	3	13	16	89
Mike Dyck, Brandon	13	1	2	3	10
Regina	29	4	6	10	82
Totals	42	5	8	13	92
Trent Kachur, Sask.	4	0	0	0	2
Regina	41	3	10	13	94
Totals	45	3	10	13	96
Brian Wilkie	33	5	4	9	52
Craig Kalawsky	66	1	8	9	90
Jim Mathieson	40	0	9	9	40
Troy Bakogeorge	25	6	2	8	13
Bob Heeney	25	3	3	6	104
Bob Rioux	14	1	4	5	4
Brent Kilpatrick, Seattle .	6	0	2	2	14
New Westminister..	7	1	1	2	7
Regina	8	0	1	1	26
Totals	21	1	4	5	47
Taras Diakiwski	14	2	1	3	46
Mike Shand	7	1	1	2	10
Rob McKinley, Kam. (G.)	29	0	2	2	6
Regina (Goalie)	15	0	0	0	4
Totals	44	0	2	2	10
Kevin Kowalchuk	2	0	1	1	0
Brent Janke	11	0	1	1	6
Mike Gibson (Goalie)	17	0	1	1	10
Brian Leibel (Goalie)	1	0	0	0	0
Murray Larose	2	0	0	0	0
Layne Meko	2	0	0	0	0
Jeff Stayko (Goalie)	2	0	0	0	0
Scott Reid	7	0	0	0	0
Kevin Kuntz	15	0	0	0	20
Darin McInnis (Goalie)...	18	0	0	0	2
Phil Lepage	29	0	0	0	16

Saskatoon Blades

	Games	G.	A.	Pts.	Pen.
Shaun Van Allen	72	38	59	97	116
Tracey Katelnikoff	72	42	45	87	73
Grant Tkachuk	71	46	36	82	108
Blaine Chrest, Portland..	5	1	4	5	0
Saskatoon	62	27	44	71	17
Totals	67	28	48	76	17
Todd McLellan	60	34	39	73	66
Kevin Kaminski	67	26	44	70	325
Jack Bowkus	53	27	31	58	84
Jason Christie	67	20	30	50	73
Kelly Chase	68	17	29	46	285
Mike Bukta	65	8	36	44	96
Curtis Leschyshyn	70	14	26	40	107
Walter Shutter	60	22	16	38	84
Kory Kocur	62	13	17	30	98
Brian Glynn	44	2	26	28	163
Collin Bauer	61	1	25	26	37
Kerry Clark	54	12	10	22	229
Darryl Daignault	32	10	10	20	27

	Games	G.	A.	Pts.	Pen.
Bryan Larkin	40	3	16	19	56
Marty Prazma	53	1	16	17	79
Tony Twist	64	0	8	8	181
Trent McLellan, P. Albert	4	0	1	1	2
Regina	16	2	2	4	2
Saskatoon	6	0	2	2	0
Totals	26	2	5	7	4
Mark Reimer (Goalie)....	42	0	6	6	4
Tim Cheveldae (Goalie).	33	0	4	4	2
Dean Holoein	7	1	1	2	13
Curtis Chamberlin	1	0	1	1	0
Mark Holick	12	0	1	1	53
Kelly Chotowetz	1	0	0	0	0

Seattle Thunderbirds

	Games	G.	A.	Pts.	Pen.
Glen Goodall	68	63	49	112	64
Larry Bernard	70	40	46	86	159
Brad Melin	65	28	55	83	12
Chris Joseph	67	13	45	58	155
Kent Dochuk	65	22	25	47	141
Victor Gervais	66	13	30	43	58
Scott Neely	41	19	22	41	6
Dean Sexsmith, Brandon	2	0	2	2	2
Prince Albert	35	4	16	20	26
Seattle	28	10	6	16	18
Totals	65	14	24	38	46
Rob Dumas	72	8	29	37	259
Shawn Chambers	28	8	25	33	58
Mike Schwengler, M.H...	55	11	9	20	15
Seattle	17	2	6	8	2
Totals	72	13	15	28	17
Rick Fry	67	14	13	27	31
Darren Taylor	60	13	13	26	112
Ken McIntyre, Regina	10	1	3	4	24
Seattle	46	5	8	13	95
Totals	56	6	11	17	119
Gerald Bzdel, Regina	13	0	3	3	38
Seattle	35	4	9	13	99
Totals	48	4	12	16	137
Rob Flintoft	58	1	9	10	147
Matt Hervey	9	4	5	9	59
Joey Mittelsteadt	61	3	6	9	143
Shannon Travis	64	2	7	9	70
Jason Phillips, Brandon..	7	1	1	2	2
Seattle	8	3	2	5	2
Totals	15	4	3	7	4
Darryl Havrelock	59	1	5	6	156
Todd Sawtell, Spokane..	1	0	0	0	0
Seattle	21	2	3	5	24
Totals	22	2	3	5	24
Gary Grant	27	2	3	5	77
Garnet Kazuik, M. J.	6	1	0	1	0
Regina	6	1	2	3	4
Seattle	2	0	0	0	0
Totals	14	2	2	4	4
Greg Hubert (Goalie)	42	0	3	3	0
Trevor Sim	4	2	0	2	0
Danny Lorenz (Goalie)...	38	0	2	2	6
Trevor Goertzen	3	1	0	1	0
Bruce Dirom	1	0	0	0	0
Boyd Lomow	3	0	0	0	4
Darryl Mitchell	3	0	0	0	2
Barcley Pernata	3	0	0	0	0
Rob Hale	4	0	0	0	5

	Games	G.	A.	Pts.	Pen.
Trent Ciprick, Brandon...	4	0	0	0	5
Seattle..................	1	0	0	0	2
Totals	5	0	0	0	7
Mike McLean, M.J. (G.).	3	0	0	0	7
Seattle (Goalie)	2	0	0	0	0
Totals	5	0	0	0	7
Mark Howell................	9	0	0	0	0

Spokane Chiefs

	Games	G.	A.	Pts.	Pen.
Brent Gilchrist................	46	45	55	100	71
Mark Wingerter.............	72	44	48	92	87
Grant Delcourt	57	34	44	78	75
Mike Berger	65	26	49	75	80
Rob Friesen....................	49	19	46	65	32
Sean Krakiwsky, Cal......	19	3	16	19	20
Spokane...............	38	16	26	42	37
Totals	57	19	42	61	57
Tony Horacek	64	23	37	60	177
Mick Vukota	61	25	28	53	*337
Gregg Delcourt	64	16	31	47	44
Mike Hawes...................	72	24	22	46	117
Mitch Cornett	68	13	33	46	99
Darcy Loewen...............	68	15	25	40	129
Mike Rickert..................	71	8	23	31	126
Travis Green	64	8	17	25	27
Dean Ewen, N. West......	9	2	3	5	28
Spokane...............	57	6	11	17	208
Totals	66	8	14	22	236
Kevin Ekdahl, M.H.	25	0	0	0	22
Spokane...............	32	6	10	16	37
Totals	57	6	10	16	59
Todd Voshell...............	57	1	10	11	170
David Bessason.............	68	1	8	9	47
Murray Duval	27	2	6	8	21
Alex Bell	41	1	5	6	32
Brian Barron	21	1	4	5	21
Todd Oliphant, S. C.	3	0	0	0	0
Spokane...............	15	4	0	4	18
Totals	18	4	0	4	18
Troy Gamble, M.H. (G.)	11	0	1	1	0
Spokane (Goalie) ..	38	0	2	2	23
Totals	49	0	3	3	23
Scott Humeniuk.............	10	2	0	2	2
Kevin Jorgenson............	2	0	0	0	0
Don Henderson, Seattle .	1	0	0	0	0
New Westminster...	1	0	0	0	0
Spokane...............	2	0	0	0	0
Totals	4	0	0	0	0
Artie Feher (Goalie).......	6	0	0	0	0
Trevor Leslie	6	0	0	0	14
Bill Francione (Goalie) ...	10	0	0	0	2
John Colvin (Goalie)......	29	0	0	0	24

Swift Current Broncos

	Games	G.	A.	Pts.	Pen.
Joe Sakic......................	72	60	73	133	31
Peter Soberlak, Kam......	16	2	7	9	26
Swift Current.........	52	31	35	66	19
Totals	68	33	42	75	45
Dan Lambert.................	68	13	53	66	95
Sheldon Kennedy..........	49	23	41	64	43
Todd Sceviour	72	28	31	59	52
Trent Kresse	30	28	28	56	27
Scott Kruger.................	36	19	37	56	32

	Games	G.	A.	Pts.	Pen.
Erin Ginnell, Seattle	17	10	3	13	6
Regina................	27	10	12	22	23
Swift Current.........	29	13	6	19	6
Totals	73	33	21	54	35
Bob Wilkie, Calgary	1	0	1	1	0
Swift Current.........	64	12	37	49	50
Totals	65	12	38	50	50
Tim Tisdale	66	20	29	49	25
Ryan McGill..................	72	12	36	48	226
Kurt Lackten.................	65	20	20	40	97
Garth Lamb, Moose Jaw	15	6	14	20	28
Victoria................	8	2	5	7	14
Swift Current.........	29	1	4	5	13
Totals	52	9	23	32	55
Tim Logan, Moose Jaw..	45	7	10	17	86
Swift Current.........	29	4	6	10	45
Totals	74	11	16	27	131
Lonnie Spink, Kam.	23	1	8	9	20
Swift Current.........	45	2	9	11	11
Totals	68	3	17	20	31
Clarke Polglase	69	2	13	15	33
Terry Baustad, Calgary .	14	2	7	9	0
Moose Jaw	19	0	3	3	7
Swift Current.........	8	0	2	2	2
Totals	41	2	12	14	9
Ian Herbers..................	72	5	8	13	230
Gord Green	57	4	3	7	189
Dave Aldred	33	3	3	6	17
Brent Ruff....................	33	3	3	6	2
Chris Mantyka..............	31	3	2	5	101
Tracy Egeland	48	3	2	5	20
Trevor Kruger (Goalie)...	31	0	2	2	0
Jason Proulx, Kamloops.	13	0	1	1	10
Swift Current.........	41	0	1	1	17
Totals	54	0	2	2	27
Mark Stockham	2	1	0	1	2
Kevin Clayton	1	0	0	0	0
Andres Froid (Goalie)....	1	0	0	0	0
Terry Head	2	0	0	0	0
Gene Patterson (Goalie)	6	0	0	0	0
Mike Wegleitner	7	0	0	0	12
Mike Sutherland (G.)	9	0	0	0	2
Pat Nogier (Goalie).......	42	0	0	0	4

Victoria Cougars

	Games	G.	A.	Pts.	Pen.
Adam Morrison	65	55	70	125	57
Brent Hughes, N. West. .	8	5	4	9	22
Victoria................	61	38	61	99	146
Totals	69	43	65	108	168
Ken Priestlay	33	43	39	82	37
Greg Batters	64	21	40	61	257
Jim Kambeitz................	67	33	27	60	177
Will Andersen...............	69	17	43	60	96
Micah Aivazoff.............	72	18	39	57	112
Len Barrie, Calgary	34	13	13	26	81
Victoria................	34	7	6	13	92
Totals	68	20	19	39	173
Wayne Stripp	66	14	23	37	91
Kent Lewis...................	57	14	21	35	77
Gary Moscaluk, N. W. ..	13	0	8	8	38
Victoria................	38	2	23	25	75
Totals	51	2	31	33	113
Andrew Wolf	65	5	25	30	167
Joel Savage.................	68	14	13	27	48
Clayton Young..............	67	8	16	24	49

	Games	G.	A.	Pts.	Pen.		Games	G.	A.	Pts.	Pen.
Dan Sexton	39	11	11	22	47	Jody Gonek	62	0	4	4	236
Guy Burr	46	8	8	16	31	Dan Pahl	2	0	1	1	0
Tony Hand	3	4	4	8	0	Wade Flaherty (Goalie)	3	0	1	1	0
Chris Calverley	10	1	7	8	6	Barry Harbin	11	0	1	1	4
Steve Chelios	8	2	4	6	8	Mike Doyle (Goalie)	28	0	1	1	13
Randy Hoffart	43	1	5	6	211	Pat Hodgins	1	0	0	0	0
Dwayne Keller	39	0	5	5	40	Stan Marple	3	0	0	0	7
Peter Fry (Goalie)	54	0	5	5	22	Jeff Resler	5	0	0	0	2
Bruce Courtnall	22	1	3	4	36	Ray Clarke	8	0	0	0	6

Complete WHL Individual Goaltending

	Games	Mins.	Goals	SO.	Avg.
George Maneluk	*58	*3258	*315(1)	0	5.80
Kelly Hitchins (a)	12	704	68	0	5.80
Derek Babe	9	374	49(1)	0	7.86
Steve Bray	3	33	9	0	16.36
Brandon Totals	82	4369	443	0	6.08
Grant MacPhail	43	2254	187(1)	0	4.98
Chris Churchill	40	2015	184(1)	0	5.48
Don Blishen	1	20	2	0	6.00
Jeff Ferguson	3	104	15	0	8.65
Calgary Totals	87	4393	390	0	5.33
Dean Cook	40	2181	140	1	3.85
Rob McKinley (b)	29	1426	99(2)	0	4.17
Stacy Nickel (c)	10	528	32	0	3.64
Calvin MacDonald	5	258	19	0	4.42
Kamloops Totals	84	4393	292	1	3.99
Mark Fitzpatrick	50	2844	159(1)	*4	3.35
Troy Gamble (d)	11	646	46	0	4.27
Kelly Hitchins (a)	17	906	58	0	3.84
Medicine Hat Totals	78	4396	264	4	3.60
Darryl Gilmour (e)	31	1776	123(4)	2	4.16
Glen Seymour (f)	23	1185	74	1	3.75
Dean Kuntz	25	1280	102(1)	0	4.78
Mike McLean (g)	3	146	17	0	6.99
Moose Jaw Totals	82	4387	321	3	4.39
Drago Adam	53	2827	259(1)	1	5.50
Ray Woodley	32	1550	171(1)	0	6.62
New Westminster Totals	85	4377	432	1	5.92
Darryl Gilmour (e)	24	1460	111	0	4.56
Chris Eisenhart	14	638	49	0	4.61
Glen Seymour (f)	24	1220	98	0	4.82
Jim Swan	18	952	80	0	5.04
Byron Dafoe	2	128	17	0	7.97
Portland Totals	82	4398	355	0	4.84
Kenton Rein	51	2996	159(2)	0	*3.18
Stan Reddick	3	122	8(1)	0	3.93
Dean Ross	4	152	11(1)	0	4.34
Garvin Weber	23	1095	82	0	4.49
Prince Albert Totals	81	4365	264	0	3.63
Brian Leibel	1	18	1	0	3.33
Rob McKinley (b)	15	722	54	1	4.49
Stacy Nickel (c)	36	1912	146(2)	1	4.58
Mike Gibson	17	696	57(1)	1	4.91
Jeff Stayko	2	100	9	0	5.40
Darin McInnis	18	927	85(1)	1	5.50
Regina Totals	89	4375	356	4	4.88
Mark Reimer	42	2442	141(7)	1	3.46
Tim Cheveldae	33	1909	133(1)	2	4.18
Saskatoon Totals	75	4351	282	3	3.89
Danny Lorenz	38	2103	199	0	5.68
Greg Hubert	42	2220	223(1)	1	6.03
Mike McLean (g)	2	64	7	0	6.56
Seattle Totals	82	4387	430	1	5.88

	Games	Mins.	Goals	SO.	Avg.
Troy Gamble (d)	38	2157	163(2)	0	4.53
Bill Francione	10	449	34	0	4.54
John Colvin	29	1425	112	0	4.72
Artie Feher	6	323	39	0	7.24
Spokane Totals	83	4354	350	0	4.82
Mike Sutherland	9	433	33	0	4.57
Trevor Kruger	31	1595	129(2)	0	4.85
Gene Patterson	6	250	21	0	5.04
Pat Nogier	42	2086	201(1)	0	5.78
Andres Froid	1	23	6	0	15.65
Swift Current Totals	89	4387	393	0	5.37
Peter Fry	54	2937	255(1)	0	5.21
Mike Doyle	28	1282	139	0	6.51
Wade Flaherty	3	127	16(1)	0	7.56
Victoria Totals	85	4346	412	0	5.69

( )—Empty Net Goals. Do not count against a goaltender's average.
(a)—Hitchins played for Brandon and Medicine Hat.
(b)—McKinley played for Kamloops and Regina.
(c)—Nickel played for Kamloops and Regina.
(d)—Gamble played for Medicine Hat and Spokane.
(e)—Gilmour played for Moose Jaw and Portland.
(f)—Seymour played for Moose Jaw and Portland.
(g)—McLean played for Moose Jaw and Seattle.

Individual 1986-87 Leaders

Goals	Rob Brown, Kamloops—	76
Assists	Rob Brown, Kamloops—	136
Points	Rob Brown, Kamloops—	212
Penalty Minutes	Mick Vukota, Spokane—	337
Goaltender's Average	Kenton Rein, Prince Albert—	3.18
Shutouts	Mark Fitzpatrick, Medicine Hat—	4

1987 WHL Playoffs

East Division Quarterfinals
(Best-of-five series)

	W.	L.	Pts.	GF.	GA.		W.	L.	Pts.	GF.	GA.
Moose Jaw	3	0	6	15	5	Prince Albert	3	1	6	20	13
Regina	0	3	0	5	15	Swift Current	1	3	2	13	20
(Moose Jaw wins series, 3 games to 0)						(Prince Albert wins series, 3 games to 1)					

East Division Semifinals
(Best-of-seven series)

	W.	L.	Pts.	GF.	GA.		W.	L.	Pts.	GF.	GA.
Medicine Hat	4	2	8	28	22	Saskatoon	4	0	8	21	12
Moose Jaw	2	4	4	22	28	Prince Albert	0	4	0	12	21
(Medicine Hat wins series, 4 games to 2)						(Saskatoon wins series, 4 games to 0)					

West Division Semifinals
(Best-of-nine series)

	W.	L.	Pts.	GF.	GA.		W.	L.	Pts.	GF.	GA.
Kamloops	5	0	10	31	13	Portland	5	0	10	37	17
Victoria	0	5	0	13	31	Spokane	0	5	0	17	37
(Kamloops wins series, 5 games to 0)						(Portland wins series, 5 games to 0)					

East Division Finals
(Best-of-seven series)

	W.	L.	Pts.	GF.	GA.		W.	L.	Pts.	GF.	GA.
Medicine Hat	4	3	8	28	27	Portland	5	3	10	50	38
Saskatoon	3	4	6	27	28	Kamloops	3	5	6	38	50
(Medicine Hat wins series, 4 games to 3)						(Portland wins series, 5 games to 3)					

West Division Finals
(Best-of-nine series)

Western Hockey League Playoff Finals

(Best-of-seven series)

	W.	L.	Pts.	GF.	GA.
Medicine Hat	4	3	8	30	25
Portland	3	4	6	25	30

(Medicine Hat wins WHL Playoffs, 4 games to 3)

Top 10 WHL Playoff Scorers

	Games	G.	A.	Pts.	Pen.
1. Dan Woodley, Portland	19	*19	17	*36	52
2. Dave Archibald, Portland	20	10	18	28	11
3. Mark Pederson, Medicine Hat	20	*19	7	26	14
Glen Wesley, Portland	20	8	18	26	27
5. Dave McLay, Portland	18	9	15	24	51
6. Greg Hawgood, Kamloops	13	7	16	23	18
Scott McCrady, Medicine Hat	20	2	*21	23	30
8. Guy Phillips, Medicine Hat	20	10	12	22	16
Jeff Sharples, Portland	20	7	15	22	23
Jeff Finley, Portland	20	1	*21	22	27

Team-by-Team Playoff Scoring

Kamloops Blazers

(Lost West Division finals to Portland, 5 games to 3)

	Games	G.	A.	Pts.	Pen.
Greg Hawgood	13	7	16	23	18
Steve Nemeth	13	11	9	20	12
Mark Recchi	13	3	16	19	17
Darcy Norton	13	7	9	16	15
Robin Bawa	13	6	7	13	22
Rob Brown	5	6	5	11	6
Ron Shudra	11	7	3	10	10
Warren Babe	11	4	6	10	8
Glenn Mulvenna	13	4	6	10	10
Kelly Para	13	5	4	9	20
Len Mark	13	2	4	6	8
Richie Wiest	10	1	4	5	16
Rudy Poeschek	13	1	4	5	39
Don Schmidt	13	2	2	4	34
Garth Premak	13	1	3	4	14
Doug Pickell	13	0	4	4	15
Mike Needham	11	2	1	3	5
David Marcinyshyn	13	0	3	3	35
Devon Oleniuk	13	0	2	2	19
Bill Harrington	1	0	0	0	0
Steve Weinke	1	0	0	0	0
Casey MacMillan	2	0	0	0	0
Stacy Nickel (Goalie)	8	0	0	0	4
Dean Cook (Goalie)	9	0	0	0	0

Medicine Hat Tigers

(Winners of 1987 WHL Playoffs)

	Games	G.	A.	Pts.	Pen.
Mark Pederson	20	*19	7	26	14
Scott McCrady	20	2	*21	23	30
Guy Phillips	20	10	12	22	16
Dale Kushner	20	8	13	21	57
Jeff Wenaas	17	9	9	18	28
Rob Dimaio	20	7	11	18	46
Wayne Hynes	20	7	8	15	26
Keith Van Rooyen	18	0	14	14	22
Rocky Dundas	20	4	8	12	44
Ron Bonora	20	6	5	11	20
Wayne McBean	20	2	8	10	40
Trevor Linden	20	5	4	9	17
Dean Chynoweth	13	4	2	6	28
Kirby Lindal	20	3	2	5	12
Neil Brady	18	1	4	5	25
Jamie Huscroft	20	0	3	3	*125
Mark Fitzpatrick (G.)	20	0	2	2	14
Mike MacWilliam	19	1	0	1	35
Mark Kuntz	19	0	1	1	27
Kevin Knopp	3	0	0	0	0
Rod Williams	13	0	0	0	12

Moose Jaw Warriors

(Lost East Division semifinals to Medicine Hat, 4 games to 2)

	Games	G.	A.	Pts.	Pen.
Theoren Fleury	9	7	9	16	34
Mike Keane	9	3	9	12	11
Dave Thomlinson	9	7	3	10	19
Pat Beauchesne	9	2	7	9	16
Bob Foglietta	9	5	3	8	8
Lyle Odelein	9	2	5	7	26
Troy Edwards	9	1	6	7	8
Trevor Jobe	9	4	2	6	4
Kevin Herom	9	3	2	5	24
Jerome Bechard	9	1	4	5	17
Neil Pilon	9	0	5	5	22
Lee Trim	9	1	3	4	15
Rob Harvey	6	1	1	2	2
Brian Ilkuf	9	1	1	2	7
Neil Pogany	9	0	2	2	4
Darren Kwiatkowski	9	0	1	1	12
Dean Kuntz (Goalie)	1	0	0	0	0
Lloyd Cox	3	0	0	0	0
Corey Bealieu	9	0	0	0	17
Jim MacKenzie	9	0	0	0	7
Glen Seymour (Goalie)	9	0	0	0	0

Portland Winter Hawks

(Lost WHL finals to Medicine Hat, 4 games to 3)

	Games	G.	A.	Pts.	Pen.
Dan Woodley	19	*19	17	*36	52

	Games	G.	A.	Pts.	Pen.
Dave Archibald	20	10	18	28	11
Glen Wesley	20	8	18	26	27
Dave McLay	18	9	15	24	51
Jeff Sharples	20	7	15	22	23
Jeff Finley	20	1	*21	22	27
Dennis Holland	20	7	14	21	20
Ryan Stewart	17	7	11	18	34
Brian Gerrits	19	11	6	17	14
Brent Fedyk	14	5	6	11	0
Troy Mick	20	8	2	10	40
Jamie Nicolls	20	6	4	10	17
Troy Pohl	15	3	7	10	30
James Latos	20	5	3	8	56
Scott Melynk	19	4	4	8	37
Jay Stark	20	0	6	6	58
Sean Clouston	19	0	5	5	45
Trevor Pohl	15	2	1	3	37
Roy Mitchell	20	0	3	3	23
Jim Swan (Goalie)	1	0	0	0	0
Steve Kloepzig	4	0	0	0	0
Darryl Gilmour (Goalie)	19	0	0	0	4

Prince Albert Raiders

(Lost East Division semifinals to Saskatoon, 4 games to 0)

	Games	G.	A.	Pts.	Pen.
Steve Gotaas	8	5	6	11	16
Pat Elynuik	8	5	5	10	12
Kevin Todd	8	2	5	7	17
Richard Pilon	7	1	6	7	17
Jason Smart	8	3	3	6	6
Darin Kimble	8	1	5	6	22
Dean Kolstad	8	1	5	6	8
Wayde Bucsis	8	2	3	5	2
Doug Hobson	8	2	3	5	12
Reid Simpson	8	2	3	5	13
Michael Modano	8	1	4	5	4
Curtis Hunt	8	1	3	4	4
Ian McAmmond	8	2	1	3	5
Kim Issel	6	1	2	3	17
Dean Braham	8	2	0	2	10
Shawn Byram	7	1	1	2	10
Rod Dallman	5	0	1	1	32
Garvin Weber (Goalie)	1	0	0	0	0
Alan Wonitowy	1	0	0	0	0
Shane Kohl	2	0	0	0	2
Todd Nelson	4	0	0	0	0
Gord Kruppke	8	0	0	0	9
Kenton Rein (Goalie)	8	0	0	0	2

Regina Pats

(Lost East Division quarterfinals to Moose Jaw,
3 games to 0)

	Games	G.	A.	Pts.	Pen.
Craig Endean	3	5	0	5	4
Len Nielsen	3	0	4	4	0
Milan Dragicevic	3	0	1	1	4
Mark Janssens	3	0	1	1	14
Jim Mathieson	3	0	1	1	2
Dan Logan	1	0	0	0	0
Darrin McInnis (Goalie)	1	0	0	0	0
Brent Janke	2	0	0	0	0
Brian Wilkie	2	0	0	0	2
Troy Bakogeorge	3	0	0	0	2
Gary Dickie	3	0	0	0	6

	Games	G.	A.	Pts.	Pen.
Trent Kachur	3	0	0	0	11
Craig Kalawsky	3	0	0	0	6
Brad Miller	3	0	0	0	6
Darren McKechnie	3	0	0	0	0
Rob McKinley (Goalie)	3	0	0	0	0
Cregg Nicol	3	0	0	0	21
Darren Parsons	3	0	0	0	2
Ray Savard	3	0	0	0	17
Chris Tarnowski	3	0	0	0	6
Mike Van Slooten	3	0	0	0	0

Saskatoon Blades

(Lost East Division finals to Medicine Hat, 4 games to 3)

	Games	G.	A.	Pts.	Pen.
Tracey Katelnikoff	11	8	6	14	12
Jack Bowkus	11	9	4	13	10
Kevin Kaminski	11	5	6	11	45
Shaun Van Allen	11	4	6	10	24
Blaine Chrest	11	3	7	10	0
Kelly Chase	11	2	8	10	37
Jason Christie	11	3	5	8	17
Mike Bukta	11	0	8	8	18
Walter Shutter	11	5	2	7	20
Grant Tkachuk	11	4	3	7	12
Curtis Leschyshyn	11	1	5	6	14
Colin Bauer	11	0	6	6	10
Darryl Daignault	10	2	2	4	10
Brian Glynn	11	1	3	4	19
Todd McLellan	6	1	1	2	2
Mark Reimer (Goalie)	6	0	1	1	2
Dean Holoien	7	0	1	1	8
Kerry Clark	8	0	1	1	23
Tony Twist	11	0	1	1	42
Mark Holick	2	0	0	0	0
Kory Kocur	4	0	0	0	7
Tim Cheveldae (Goalie)	5	0	0	0	0
Bryan Larkin	7	0	0	0	8

Spokane Chiefs

(Lost West Division semifinals to Portland, 5 games to 0)

	Games	G.	A.	Pts.	Pen.
Brent Gilchrist	5	2	7	9	6
Grant Delcourt	5	2	6	8	11
Sean Krakiwsky	5	2	4	6	4
Mark Wingerter	5	3	2	5	9
Kevin Ekdahl	5	4	0	4	9
Tony Horacek	5	1	3	4	18
Todd Voshell	5	0	3	3	14
Greg Delcourt	5	1	1	2	4
Mitch Cornett	5	1	0	1	6
Dean Ewen	5	1	0	1	39
David Bessason	5	0	1	1	0
Rob Friesen	5	0	1	1	4
Mike Hawes	5	0	1	1	16
Scott Humeniuk	1	0	0	0	0
Brian Barron	2	0	0	0	7
Mike Berger	2	0	0	0	2
Todd Oliphant	2	0	0	0	0
Travis Green	3	0	0	0	0
Mick Vukota	4	0	0	0	40
Troy Gamble (Goalie)	5	0	0	0	2
Darcy Loewen	5	0	0	0	16
Mike Rickert	5	0	0	0	10

Swift Current Broncos

(Lost East Division quarterfinals to Prince Albert, 3 games to 1)

	Games	G.	A.	Pts.	Pen.
Tim Tisdale	4	1	4	5	2
Bob Wilkie	4	1	3	4	2
Todd Sceviour	4	3	0	3	0
Sheldon Kennedy	4	0	3	3	4
Tracy Egeland	4	1	1	2	0
Gord Green	4	1	1	2	18
Ian Herbers	4	1	1	2	12
Dan Lambert	4	1	1	2	9
Lonnie Spink	4	1	1	2	0
Erin Ginnell	4	1	0	1	0
Garth Lamb	4	1	0	1	4
Ryan McGill	4	1	0	1	9
Kurt Lackten	3	0	1	1	4
Trevor Kruger (Goalie)	4	0	1	1	0
Clark Polglase	4	0	1	1	2
Joe Sakic	4	0	1	1	0
Dave Aldred	4	0	0	0	0
Tim Logan	4	0	0	0	7
Jason Proulx	4	0	0	0	0

Victoria Cougars

(Lost West Division semifinals to Kamloops, 5 games to 0)

	Games	G.	A.	Pts.	Pen.
Adam Morrison	5	1	5	6	4
Brent Hughes	5	4	1	5	8
Steve Chelios	5	2	2	4	4
Will Andersen	5	1	3	4	6
Clayton Young	5	0	3	3	6
Joel Savage	5	2	0	2	0
Wayne Stripp	5	1	1	2	4
Greg Batters	5	0	2	2	17
Randy Hoffart	5	0	2	2	13
Mike Aivazoff	5	1	0	1	2
Kent Lewis	5	1	0	1	4
Len Barrie	5	0	1	1	15
Jim Kambeitz	5	0	1	1	16
Gary Moscaluk	3	0	0	0	0
Guy Burr	5	0	0	0	0
Peter Fry (Goalie)	5	0	0	0	6
Jody Gonek	5	0	0	0	14
Dwayne Keller	5	0	0	0	6
Andrew Wolf	5	0	0	0	2

Complete WHL Playoff Goaltending

	Games	Mins.	Goals	SO.	Avg.
Stacey Nickel	8	356	24	*1	4.04
Dean Cook	9	440	39	0	5.32
Kamloops Totals	17	796	63	1	4.75
Mark Fitzpatrick	*20	*1224	71(4)	*1	3.48
Medicine Hat Totals	20	1224	75	1	3.68
Dean Kuntz	1	9	0	0	0.00
Glen Seymour	9	535	33	*1	3.70
Moose Jaw Totals	10	544	33	1	3.64
Jim Swan	1	60	3	0	3.00
Darryl Gilmour	19	1167	*83	*1	4.27
Portland Totals	20	1227	86	1	4.21
Garvin Weber	1	35	1	0	1.71
Kenton Rein	8	443	31(2)	0	4.20
Prince Albert Totals	9	478	34	0	4.27
Darrin McInnis	1	45	2	0	2.67
Rob McKinley	3	135	13	0	5.78
Regina Totals	4	180	15	0	5.00
Mark Reimer	6	360	20	0	*3.33
Tim Cheveldae	5	308	20(1)	0	3.90
Saskatoon Totals	11	668	41	0	3.68
Troy Gamble	5	298	35(2)	0	7.05
Spokane Totals	5	298	37	0	7.45
Trevor Kruger	4	240	19(1)	0	4.75
Swift Current Totals	4	240	20	0	5.00
Peter Fry	5	304	31	0	6.12
Victoria Totals	5	304	31	0	6.12

( )—Empty Net Goals. Do not count against a goaltender's average.

Individual WHL Playoff Leaders

Goals	Dan Woodley, Portland—	19
	Mark Pederson, Medicine Hat—	19
Assists	Scott McCrady, Medicine Hat—	21
	Jeff Finley, Portland—	21
Points	Dan Woodley, Portland—	36
Penalty Minutes	Jamie Huscroft, Medicine Hat—	125
Goaltender's Average (60 minutes)	Mark Reimer, Saskatoon—	3.33
Shutouts	Mark Fitzpatrick, Medicine Hat—	1
	Darryl Gilmour, Portland—	1
	Stacey Nickel, Kamloops—	1
	Glen Seymour, Moose Jaw—	1

★★★

1986-87 WHL All-Star Teams

East Division   West Division

East Division	Position	West Division
Kenton Rein, Prince Albert	Goal	Drago Adam, New West.
Wayne McBean, Medicine Hat	Defense	Glen Wesley, Portland
Mark Tinordi, Calgary	Defense	Greg Hawgood, Kamloops
Theoren Fleury, Moose Jaw	Center	Rob Brown, Kamloops
Mark Pederson, Medicine Hat	Left Wing	Brent Hughes, Victoria
Pat Elynuik, Prince Albert	Right Wing	Robin Bawa, Kamloops

★★★

1987 WHL Trophy Winners

Most Valuable Player Trophy	Joe Sakic, Swift Current (East Division)
	Rob Brown, Kamloops (West Division)
Bob Brownridge Memorial Trophy (Top Scorer)	Rob Brown, Kamloops
Stewart "Butch" Paul Memorial Trophy (Rookie of the Year)	Joe Sakic, Swift Current (East Division)
	Dennis Holland, Portland (West Division)
Frank Boucher Memorial Trophy (Most Gentlemanly Player)	Len Nielsen, Regina (East Division)
	Dave Archibald, Portland (West Division)
Top Defenseman Trophy	Wayne McBean, Medicine Hat (East Division)
	Glen Wesley, Portland (West Division)
Top Goaltender	Kenton Rein, Prince Albert (East Division)
	Dean Cook, Kamloops (West Division)
Player of the Year	Rob Brown, Kamloops
Dunc McCallum Memorial Trophy (Coach of the Year)	Graham James, Swift Current (East Division)
	Ken Hitchcock, Kamloops (West Division)
Scott Munro Memorial Trophy (Regular Season Champion)	Kamloops Blazers
Msgr. Athol Murray Memorial Trophy (Playoff Champion)	Medicine Hat Tigers

Historical WHL Trophy Winners

(Canadian Major Junior Hockey League in 1966-67, renamed the Western Canadian Hockey League from 1967-68 to 1976-77. Has been named the Western Hockey League since 1977-78 season).

Most Valuable Player Trophy (Selected by coaches) / Bob Brownridge Memorial Trophy (Top Scorer)

Most Valuable Player Trophy (Selected by coaches)	Year	Bob Brownridge Memorial Trophy (Top Scorer)
Gerry Pinder, Saskatoon	1966-67	Gerry Pinder, Saskatoon (140 pts)
Jim Harrison Estevan	1967-68	Bobby Clarke, Flin Flon (168 pts)
Bobby Clarke, Flin Flon	1968-69	Bobby Clarke, Flin Flon (137 pts)
Reggie Leach, Flin Flon	1969-70	Reggie Leach, Flin Flon (111 pts)
Ed Dyck, Calgary	1970-71	Chuck Arnason, Flin Flon (163 pts)
John Davidson, Calgary	1971-72	Tom Lysiak, Medicine Hat (143 pts)
Dennis Sobchuk, Regina	1972-73	Tom Lysiak, Medicine Hat (154 pts)
Ron Chipperfield, Brandon	1973-74	Ron Chipperfield, Brandon (162 pts)
Bryan Trottier, Lethbridge	1974-75	Mel Bridgman, Victoria (157 pts)
Bernie Federko, Saskatoon	1975-76	Bernie Federko, Saskatoon (187 pts)
Barry Beck, New Westminster	1976-77	Bill Derlago, Brandon (178 pts)
Ryan Walter, Seattle	1977-78	Brian Propp, Brandon (182 pts)
Perry Turnbull, Portland	1978-79	Brian Propp, Brandon (194 pts)
Doug Wickenheiser, Regina	1979-80	Doug Wickenheiser, Regina (170 pts)
Steve Tsujiura, Medicine Hat	1980-81	Brian Varga, Regina (187 pts)
Mike Vernon, Calgary	1981-82	Jock Callander, Regina (190 pts)
Mike Vernon, Calgary	1982-83	Dale Derkatch, Regina (179 pts)
Ray Ferraro, Brandon	1983-84	Ray Ferraro, Brandon (192 pts)
Cliff Ronning, New Westminster	1984-85	Cliff Ronning, New Westminster (197 pts)
Emanuel Viveiros, Prince Albert (East Division) Rob Brown, Kamloops (West Division)	1985-86	Rob Brown, Kamloops (173 pts)
Joe Sakic, Swift Current (East Division) Rob Brown, Kamloops (West Division)	1986-87	Rob Brown, Kamloops (212 pts.)

Stewart "Butch" Paul Memorial Trophy (Rookie of the Year) / Frank Boucher Memorial Trophy (Most Gentlemanly Player)

Stewart "Butch" Paul Memorial Trophy (Rookie of the Year)	Year	Frank Boucher Memorial Trophy (Most Gentlemanly Player)
Ron Garwasiuk, Regina	1966-67	Morris Stefaniw, Estevan
Ron Fairbrother, Saskatoon	1967-68	Bernie Blanchette, Saskatoon
Ron Williams, Edmonton	1968-69	Bob Liddington, Calgary
Gene Carr, Flin Flon	1969-70	Randy Rota, Calgary
Stan Weir, Medicine Hat	1970-71	Lorne Henning, Estevan
Dennis Sobchuk, Regina	1971-72	Ron Chipperfield, Brandon
Rick Blight, Brandon	1972-73	Ron Chipperfield, Brandon
Cam Connor, Flin Flon	1973-74	Mike Rogers, Calgary
Don Murdoch, Medicine Hat	1974-75	Danny Arndt, Saskatoon
Steve Tambellini, Lethbridge	1975-76	Blair Chapman, Saskatoon
Brian Propp, Brandon	1976-77	Steve Tambellini, Lethbridge
John Ogrodnick, N.W.-Keith Brown, Port.	1977-78	Steve Tambellini, Lethbridge
Kelly Kisio, Calgary	1978-79	Errol Rausse, Seattle
Grant Fuhr, Victoria	1979-80	Steve Tsujiura, Medicine Hat
Dave Michayluk, Regina	1980-81	Steve Tsujiura, Medicine Hat
Dale Derkatch, Regina	1981-82	Mike Moller, Lethbridge
Dan Hodgson, Prince Albert	1982-83	Darren Boyko, Winnipeg
Cliff Ronning, New Westminster	1983-84	Mark Lamb, Medicine Hat
Mark Mackay, Moose Jaw	1984-85	Cliff Ronning, New Westminster
Neil Brady, Medicine Hat (East Division) Ron Shudra, Kamloops (West Division) Dave Waldie, Portland (West Division)	1985-86	Randy Smith, Saskatoon (East Division) Ken Morrison, Kamloops (West Division)
Joe Sakic, Swift Current (East Division) Dennis Holland, Portland (West Division)	1986-87	Len Nielsen, Regina (East Division) Dave Archibald, Portland (West Division)

Top Defenseman Trophy / Top Goaltender Trophy

Top Defenseman Trophy	Year	Top Goaltender Trophy
Barry Gibbs, Estevan	1966-67	Ken Brown, Moose Jaw
Gerry Hart, Flin Flon	1967-68	Chris Worthy, Flin Flon
Dale Hoganson, Estevan	1968-69	Ray Martyniuk, Flin Flon
Jim Hargreaves, Winnipeg	1969-70	Ray Martyniuk, Flin Flon
Ron Jones, Edmonton	1970-71	Ed Dyck, Calgary
Jim Watson, Calgary	1971-72	John Davidson, Calgary
George Pesut, Saskatoon	1972-73	Ed Humphreys, Saskatoon
Pat Price, Saskatoon	1973-74	Garth Malarchuk, Saskatoon
Rick LaPointe, Victoria	1974-75	Bill Oleschuk, Saskatoon
Kevin McCarthy, Winnipeg	1975-76	Carey Walker, New Westminster
Barry Beck, New Westminster	1976-77	Glen Hanlon, Brandon

Top Defenseman Trophy

Brad McCrimmon, Brandon	1977-78	Bart Hunter, Portland
Keith Brown, Portland	1978-79	Rick Knickle, Brandon
David Babych, Portland	1979-80	Kevin Eastman, Victoria
Jim Benning, Portland	1980-81	Grant Fuhr, Victoria
Gary Nylund, Portland	1981-82	Mike Vernon, Calgary
Gary Leeman, Regina	1982-83	Mike Vernon, Calgary
Bob Rouse, Lethbridge	1983-84	Ken Wregget, Lethbridge
Wendel Clark, Saskatoon	1984-85	Troy Gamble, Medicine Hat
Emanuel Viveiros, Prince Albert (East Division)	1985-86	Mark Fitzpatrick, Medicine Hat
Glen Wesley, Portland (West Division)		
Wayne McBean, Medicine Hat (East Division)	1986-87	Kenton Rein, Prince Albert (East Division)
Glen Wesley, Portland (West Division)		Dean Cook, Kamloops (West Division)

Top Goaltender Trophy

Player Of The Year
(Selected by fans and media)

Rob Brown, Kamloops	1986-87	Graham James, Swift Current (East Division)
		Ken Hitchcock, Kamloops (West Division)
Emanuel Viveiros, Prince Albert	1985-86	Terry Simpson, Prince Albert
Dan Hodgson, Prince Albert	1984-85	Doug Sauter, Medicine Hat
Ray Ferraro, Brandon	1983-84	Terry Simpson, Prince Albert
Dean Evason, Kamloops	1982-83	Darryl Lubiniecki, Saskatoon
Mike Vernon, Calgary	1981-82	Jack Sangster, Seattle
Barry Pederson, Victoria	1980-81	Ken Hodge, Portland
Doug Wickenheiser, Regina	1979-80	Doug Sauter, Calgary
Brian Propp, Brandon	1978-79	Dunc McCallum, Brandon
Ryan Walter, Seattle	1977-78	Dave King, Billings
		Jack Shupe, Victoria
Kevin McCarthy, Winnipeg	1976-77	Dunc McCallum, Brandon
Bernie Federko, Saskatoon	1975-76	Ernie McLean, New Westminster
Ed Staniowski, Regina	1974-75	Pat Ginnell, Victoria
No Award Given	1973-74	Stan Dunn, Swift Current
No Award Given	1972-73	Pat Ginnell, Flin Flon
No Award Given	1971-72	Earl Ingarfield, Regina
No Award Given	1970-71	Pat Ginnell, Flin Flon
No Award Given	1969-70	Pat Ginnell, Flin Flon
No Award Given	1968-69	Scotty Munro, Calgary

Coach Of The Year
Dunc McCallum Memorial Trophy

Regular Season Champions
Scott Munro Memorial Trophy

Kamloops Blazers	1986-87	Medicine Hat Tigers
Medicine Hat Tigers	1985-86	Kamloops Blazers
Prince Albert Raiders	1984-85	Prince Albert Raiders
Kamloops Junior Oilers	1983-84	Kamloops Junior Oilers
Saskatoon Blades	1982-83	Lethbridge Broncos
Lethbridge Broncos	1981-82	Portland Winter Hawks
Victoria Cougars	1980-81	Victoria Cougars
Portland Winter Hawks	1979-80	Regina Pats
Brandon Wheat Kings	1978-79	Brandon Wheat Kings
Brandon Wheat Kings	1977-78	New Westminster Bruins
New Westminster Bruins	1976-77	New Westminster Bruins
New Westminster Bruins	1975-76	New Westminster Bruins
Victoria Cougars	1974-75	New Westminster Bruins
Regina Pats	1973-74	Regina Pats
Saskatoon Blades	1972-73	Medicine Hat Tigers
Calgary Centennials	1971-72	Edmonton Oil Kings
Edmonton Oil Kings	1970-71	Edmonton Oil Kings
Flin Flon Bombers	1969-70	Flin Flon Bombers
Flin Flon Bombers	1968-69	Flin Flon Bombers
Flin Flon Bombers	1967-68	Estevan Bruins
Edmonton Oil Kings	1966-67	Moose Jaw Canucks

Playoff Champions
Msgr. Athol Murray Memorial Trophy

Quebec Major Junior Hockey League

President and Executive Director—Gilles Courteau
Vice-President—John Horman
Statistician—Douglas Horman
4635 1st Avenue, Room 240
Charlesbourg, Quebec G1G 5W5
Phone—(418) 623-1508

Final 1986-87 QHL Standings

Frank Dilio Division

	G.	W.	L.	T.	Pts.	GF.	GA.
Granby Bisons	70	48	18	4	100	416	318
Shawinigan Cataracts	70	38	26	6	82	408	335
Chicoutimi Segueneens	70	37	28	5	79	411	353
Drummondville Voltigeurs	70	35	35	0	70	353	382
Trois-Rivieres Draveurs	70	28	40	2	58	357	389

Robert Lebel Division

	G.	W.	L.	T.	Pts.	GF.	GA.
Longueuil Chevaliers	70	46	20	4	96	369	259
Laval Titans	70	34	32	4	72	377	340
St. Jean Castors	70	28	41	1	57	332	389
Hull Olympiques	70	26	39	5	57	286	323
Verdun Junior Canadiens	70	14	55	1	29	299	520

Top 10 Scorers for the Jean Beliveau Trophy

	Games	G.	A.	Pts.	Pen.
1. Marc Fortier, Chicoutimi	65	66	*135	*201	39
2. Patrice Lefebvre, Shawinigan	69	57	122	179	144
3. Stephan Lebeau, Shawinigan	65	*77	90	167	60
4. Patrice Tremblay, Chicoutimi	70	76	80	156	34
5. Pierre Turgeon, Granby	58	69	85	154	8
6. Luc Beausoleil, Laval	67	65	87	152	53
7. Claude Dumas, Granby	67	50	82	132	59
8. Francois Guay, Laval	63	52	77	129	67
9. Alain Charland, Drummondville	70	53	75	128	64
10. Stefan Figliuzzi, St. Jean	70	43	78	121	25

Team-by-Team Regular Season QHL Scoring

Chicoutimi Sagueneens

	Games	G.	A.	Pts.	Pen.
Marc Fortier	65	66	*135	*201	39
Patrice Tremblay	70	76	80	156	34
Eric Pinard	63	53	49	102	27
Jean Marc Richard	67	21	81	102	105
Pierre Miller	68	37	57	94	92
Daniel Maurice	68	31	61	92	151
Daniel Bock	66	20	50	70	143
Martin Leroux	67	23	27	50	80
Daniel Marois	40	22	26	48	143
Yves Gaucher	55	22	25	47	304
Carl Larouche	61	11	24	35	84
Eric Nadeau	61	11	18	29	93
Serge Lanthier	67	5	18	23	100
Alain Jobin	69	1	21	22	105
Marco Raposo	21	8	11	19	2
Serge Lauzon	64	5	9	14	145
Serge Vigneault	58	3	11	14	131
Remi Brassard	51	3	8	11	128
Laval Brassard	62	1	10	11	43
Dave Lasalle	50	2	8	10	315
Richard Gravel	28	4	5	9	42
Danny Hunter	23	1	2	3	80
Steve Boivin	17	0	2	2	0
Jimmy Waite (Goalie)	50	0	2	2	12
Sylvain Sevigny	4	1	0	1	4
Sylvain Reid	25	0	1	1	112
Denis Desbiens (Goalie)	37	0	1	1	6
Pierre Martel	1	0	0	0	0
Eric Goulet (Goalie)	2	0	0	0	0

Drummondville Voltigeurs

	Games	G.	A.	Pts.	Pen.
Alain Charland	70	53	75	128	64
Martin Fecteau	64	41	65	106	209
Steve Chartrand	70	45	55	100	28
Martin Bergeron	66	36	58	94	83
Daniel Vincelette	50	34	35	69	288
Mario Doyon	65	18	47	65	150
Daniel Dore	68	23	41	64	229
Eric Tremblay	66	14	47	61	264
Nicolas Beaulieu	69	19	34	53	198

	Games	G.	A.	Pts.	Pen.
Pierre Yves Clement	69	22	19	41	105
Giovanni Iasenza	58	16	17	33	152
Regis Chouinard	53	7	21	28	*459
Gaetan Legault	64	1	18	19	146
Christian Ratthe	67	4	13	17	99
Stephane Therrien	69	5	10	15	42
Christian Lalumiere	61	3	12	15	166
Eric Demers	29	3	11	14	93
Tom Gibbons	55	2	12	14	291
Donald Gagnon	20	2	4	6	41
Jean Eric Landry	58	2	3	5	54
Richard Matte	44	1	4	5	44
Sarto Legault	18	1	2	3	32
Michel Dandeneault	6	1	1	2	7
Bryan Paradis (Goalie)	13	0	2	2	0
Frederic Chabot (G.)	62	0	2	2	14
Francois Girouard	3	0	1	1	0
Alain Bruno	13	0	1	1	17
Dominic Joly	1	0	0	0	0
Stephane Lepine (G.)	2	0	0	0	0
Jean Francois Exantus	6	0	0	0	25

Granby Bisons

	Games	G.	A.	Pts.	Pen.
Pierre Turgeon	58	69	85	154	8
Claude Dumas	67	50	82	132	59
Sylvain Hurteau	68	39	47	86	122
Jean Francois Nault	53	36	49	85	68
Everett Sanipass	35	34	48	82	220
Martin Simard	41	30	47	77	105
Stephane Roy	45	23	44	67	54
Benoit Grouix	59	19	48	67	24
Francis Breault	60	24	33	57	134
Stephane Quintal	67	13	41	54	178
Eric Gravel	62	7	35	42	178
Eric Desjardins	66	14	24	38	75
Stephane Dubois	66	7	28	35	70
Mario Barbe	65	7	25	32	356
Alain Cote	43	7	24	31	185
Daniel Lacroix	54	9	16	25	311
Martin Olivier	51	5	17	22	132
Daniel Charbonneau	58	3	8	11	35
Pierre Paul Landry	57	1	9	10	28
Benoit Adam	50	4	4	8	160
Frederic Simard	10	5	2	7	5
Eric Ricard	42	2	5	7	69
Stefan Camire	47	2	1	3	32
Eric Bohemier (Goalie)	35	0	1	1	15
Stephane Gaucher (G.)	36	0	1	1	0
Sylvain Bonneau (G.)	8	0	0	0	0
James Blanchard (G.)	17	0	0	0	2

Hull Olympiques

	Games	G.	A.	Pts.	Pen.
Benoit Brunet	60	43	67	110	105
Shane MacEachern	69	44	58	102	126
Stephane Matteau	69	27	48	75	113
Daniel Shank	46	26	43	69	325
Kelly Nester	69	25	23	48	82
Raynald Gagne	60	13	32	45	64
Herbert Hohenberger	68	20	23	43	105
Jean Marc Routhier	59	17	18	35	98
Michael McCullough	35	14	19	33	25
Sean Wallington	64	7	22	29	179
Stephane Richer	33	6	22	28	74
Kennie MacDermid	65	9	18	27	40
Joe Foglietta	14	13	13	26	4

	Games	G.	A.	Pts.	Pen.
Hal Turner	46	8	17	25	229
Dominic Emond	51	9	12	21	16
Cam Russell	66	3	16	19	119
Joe Suk	70	7	10	17	37
Guy Dupuis	69	5	10	15	35
Brian Bearskin	16	5	6	11	23
Joseph A. Aloi	58	2	5	7	166
Paul Manson	66	3	2	5	181
Marc Labelle	58	1	4	5	91
Grant Ferrigan (Goalie)	2	0	0	0	0
Graeme Harvey (Goalie)	27	0	0	0	2
Jason Glickman (Goalie)	49	0	0	0	20

Laval Titans

	Games	G.	A.	Pts.	Pen.
Luc Beausoleil	67	65	87	152	53
Francois Guay	63	52	77	129	67
Mike Gober	63	49	47	96	292
Sylvain Couturier	67	39	51	90	77
Rob Murphy	70	35	54	89	86
Eric Aubertin	59	33	51	84	70
Marc Dumont	67	29	47	76	53
Simon Gagne	66	19	35	54	90
Raymond Saumier	57	13	37	50	301
Sylvain Lefebvre	70	10	36	46	44
Patrick Black	65	5	36	41	130
Donald Audette	66	17	22	39	36
Eddy Courtenay	48	15	20	35	12
Stephane Plante	57	9	25	34	226
Daniel Larin	59	8	24	32	211
Eric Bedard	58	8	23	31	18
Vincent Garneau	46	8	11	19	25
Eric Dubois	61	1	17	18	29
Jacques Pinet	61	4	13	17	325
Martin Latreille	59	1	16	17	118
Stuart Lee Marston	16	0	8	8	24
Eric Gobeil	44	0	7	7	12
Fabrice Texier	4	0	4	4	2
Eric Del-Vecchio	24	1	1	2	2
Jean Christian Filippin	9	1	0	1	5
Jean B. Cardinal (G.)	3	0	0	0	0
Eric Vachon (Goalie)	13	0	0	0	0
Mario Brunetta (Goalie)	59	0	0	0	23

Longueuil Chevaliers

	Games	G.	A.	Pts.	Pen.
Marc Bureau	66	54	58	112	68
Martin Desjardins	68	39	61	100	89
Marc Saumier	50	39	49	88	250
Eric Couvrette	55	24	49	73	29
Ronnie Stern	56	32	39	71	266
Simon Massie	56	32	38	70	68
Real Godin	61	18	32	50	0
Yves Racine	70	7	43	50	50
Richard Laplante	50	17	30	47	33
Daniel Gauthier	64	23	22	45	23
Steven Paiement	68	17	21	38	14
Donald Dufresne	67	5	29	34	97
Guy Darveau	64	9	24	33	175
Jean Claude Latour	56	9	22	31	215
Mario Debenedictis	28	13	16	29	27
Andre Brassard	66	3	26	29	164
Michel Thibodeau	65	5	20	25	79
Alain Leveille	59	9	8	17	21
Don McGrath	58	1	14	15	347
Alexandre Fortin	50	4	10	14	50
Martin Vezina	13	0	4	4	6

	Games	G.	A.	Pts.	Pen.
Marc Tremblay	18	1	1	2	66
Robert Desjardins (G.)	57	0	2	2	6
Csaba Kazamer	6	0	1	1	5
Eric Maguire (Goalie)	8	0	1	1	0
Mario Meilleur	2	0	0	0	0
David Baird	6	0	0	0	2
Andre Racicot Jr. (G.)	3	0	0	0	0
Stephane Robinson (G.)	4	0	0	0	0

St. Jean Castors

	Games	G.	A.	Pts.	Pen.
Stefan Figliuzzi	70	43	78	121	25
Stephane Giguere	69	45	45	90	129
Brook Kelly	70	34	44	78	183
Eric Galarneau	69	36	41	77	104
Robert Ouellet	70	29	45	74	26
Dominic Lavoie	64	12	42	54	97
Jan Alston	68	20	32	52	30
Serge Richard	70	20	32	52	62
Steve Cadieux	65	28	22	50	26
Philippe Bozon	25	20	21	41	75
Miguel Baldris	67	7	34	41	72
Regis Tremblay	70	9	25	34	35
Martin Lauzon	69	6	28	34	156
Stephane Provost	66	3	19	22	96
Marco Grondin	57	5	15	20	95
Richard Audette	38	0	12	12	22
Pascal Germain	20	3	8	11	15
Alain Guay	56	4	6	10	83
David Bastille	56	1	9	10	156
Jean Francois Tremblay	31	4	3	7	2
Hugo Berard	38	2	2	4	14
Joel Drolet (Goalie)	52	0	1	1	12
S. Beauregard (G.)	13	0	0	0	0

Shawinigan Cataracts

	Games	G.	A.	Pts.	Pen.
Patrice Lefebvre	69	57	122	179	144
Stephan Lebeau	65	*77	90	167	60
Denis Paul	53	53	63	116	56
Robert Page	70	30	74	104	141
Luc Duval	70	40	58	98	18
Jean Bois	69	35	59	94	112
Patrick Lebeau	66	26	52	78	90
Mario Lanthier	67	9	35	44	12
Rene Corriveau	67	6	37	43	184
Patrick Sauriol	63	24	11	35	17
Stephane Lavigne	69	6	21	27	313
Stephane Carrier	69	2	24	26	154
Dean Bergeron	67	13	10	23	51
Stephane Morin	65	9	14	23	28
Stephane Guerard	31	5	16	21	57
Eric Courchesne	49	7	13	20	64
Serge Pepin	60	4	15	19	16
Christian Bertrand	52	6	12	18	148
Jean Francois Quintin	42	1	9	10	17
Stephane Marcoux	24	2	2	4	28

	Games	G.	A.	Pts.	Pen.
Mario Mercier	28	1	3	4	75
Eric Metivier (Goalie)	27	0	2	2	2
Francois Gravel (Goalie)	40	0	0	0	0

Trois-Rivieres Draveurs

	Games	G.	A.	Pts.	Pen.
Terry MacLean	69	41	76	117	20
Claude Lapointe	70	47	57	104	123
Richard Charette	62	32	55	87	51
Michel Picard	66	33	35	68	53
Michel Beaucaire	63	26	35	61	53
Paul Willett	68	21	34	55	47
Guy Lefebvre	70	20	33	53	51
Jacques Dumais	69	11	39	50	164
Denis Gaudreau	34	10	33	43	94
Benoit Gosselin	64	12	25	37	51
Gaetan Sarault	68	13	21	34	33
Steve Veilleux	62	6	22	28	227
Eric Martin	60	7	10	17	120
Daniel Maillet	66	4	10	14	150
Stephane Guenette	29	3	10	13	40
Serge Theriault	27	2	3	5	15
Martin Jolette	63	1	4	5	51
Alain Dubeau (Goalie)	32	0	3	3	4
Richard Provost	14	1	1	2	9
Benoit Pare (Goalie)	22	0	1	1	2
Ghislain Lefebvre (G.)	29	0	0	0	4
Donald Theriault	31	0	0	0	19

Verdun Junior Canadiens

	Games	G.	A.	Pts.	Pen.
Eric Legros	69	46	55	101	61
Andrew McKim	70	28	59	87	12
Neil Carnes	62	30	55	85	83
Jim Nesich	62	20	50	70	133
Marc Picard	65	15	47	62	23
Dany Ducios	64	27	25	52	261
Norman Desjardins Jr.	66	22	27	49	106
Mario Milani	60	15	27	42	83
Michel Bedard	67	11	24	35	69
Stephane Briand	66	15	18	33	9
Jocelyn Joly	57	14	19	33	189
Marc Poirier	71	11	16	27	37
Martin Cote	67	6	19	25	168
Demetrios Stefanopoulos	64	6	13	19	74
Michel Voyer	62	8	9	17	39
Craig Kitteringham	59	5	11	16	148
Michel Therrien	22	2	8	10	85
Sylvain Mayer	53	2	7	9	309
Robert Rioux	11	3	5	8	2
Scott MacTavish	11	1	2	3	30
Gary Talis	22	1	2	3	38
Pierre Langlois	9	1	1	2	11
Gary Brown	7	0	2	2	9
Peter Lalancette	15	0	2	2	45
Paul Douglas	61	1	0	1	32
J. C. Bergeron (G.)	52	0	1	1	0
Alain Harvey (Goalie)	28	0	0	0	0

Complete QHL Goaltending

	Games	Mins.	Goals	SO.	Avg.
Robert Desjardins, Longueuil	57	3359	182	*2	*3.25
Grant Ferrigan, Hull	2	120	7	1	3.50
Jason Glickman, Hull	49	2696	170	1	3.78
Stephane Gaucher, Granby	36	1821	129	0	4.25
Eric Bohemier, Granby	35	1846	133	1	4.32

	Games	Mins.	Goals	SO.	Avg.
Ghislain Lefebvre, Trois-Rivieres	29	1533	112	1	4.38
Eric Metivier, Shawinigan	27	1551	114	0	4.41
Stephane Beauregard, St. Jean	13	785	58	0	4.43
Mario Brunette, Laval	59	3469	261	1	4.51
Eric Maguire, Langueuil	8	374	30	0	4.81
Francois Gravel, Shawinigan	40	2415	194	0	4.82
Jimmy Waite, Chicoutimi	50	2569	209	*2	4.88
Denis Desbiens, Chicoutimi	37	1666	138	0	4.97
Frederic Chabot, Drummondville	*62	*3508	293	1	5.01
Eric Vachon, Laval	13	658	60	0	5.47
Sylvain Bonneau, Granby	8	263	24	1	5.48
Alain Dubeau, Trois-Rivieres	32	1686	156	0	5.55
Joel Drolet, St. Jean	52	3152	295	0	5.62
Stephane Robinson, Longueuil	4	238	23	0	5.80
Graeme Harvey, Hull	27	1428	139	0	5.84
Jean Claude Bergeron, Verdun	52	2991	*306	0	6.14
Andre Racicot Jr., Longueuil	3	180	19	0	6.33
Benoit Pare, Trois-Rivieres	22	1121	120	0	6.42
James Blanchard, Granby	17	885	98	0	6.64
Bryan Paradis, Drummondville	13	640	71	0	6.66
Jean Bernard Cardinal, Laval	3	129	15	0	6.98
Eric Goulet, Chicoutimi	2	21	3	0	8.57
Alain Harvey, Verdun	28	1341	197	0	8.81
Stephane Lepine, Drummondville	2	64	13	0	12.19

Individual 1986-87 Leaders

Goals	Stephan Lebeau, Shawinigan—	77
Assists	Marc Fortier, Chicoutimi—	135
Points	Marc Fortier, Chicoutimi—	201
Penalty Minutes	Regis Chouinard, Drummondville—	459
Goaltending Average	Robert Desjardins, Longueuil—	3.25
Shutouts	Robert Desjardins, Longueuil—	2
	Jimmy Waite, Chicoutimi—	2

1987 QHL President Cup Playoffs

Quarterfinals

Round-Robin Series
(Top two teams in each division advance to semifinals)

Frank Dilio Division

	W.	L.	T.	Pts.	GF.	GA.
Shawinigan	7	1	0	14	40	37
Chicoutimi	4	4	0	8	47	39
Granby	3	5	0	6	39	44
Drummondville	2	6	0	4	34	40

Robert Lebel Division

	W.	L.	T.	Pts.	GF.	GA.
Laval	5	3	0	10	50	39
Longueuil	5	3	0	10	35	34
Hull	4	4	0	8	38	34
St. Jean	2	6	0	4	35	51

Semifinals

(Best-of-seven series)

Frank Dilio Division

	W.	L.	Pts.	GF.	GA.
Chicoutimi	4	2	8	37	32
Shawinigan	2	4	4	32	37

(Chicoutimi wins series, 4 games to 2)

Robert Lebel Division

	W.	L.	Pts.	GF.	GA.
Longueuil	4	3	8	33	23
Laval	3	4	6	23	33

(Longueuil wins series, 4 games to 3)

Finals

(Best-of-seven series)

	W.	L.	Pts.	GF.	GA.
Longueuil	4	1	8	33	17
Chicoutimi	1	4	2	17	33

(Longueuil wins series, and President Cup, 4 games to 1)

Top 10 Playoff Scorers

	Games	G.	A.	Pts.	Pen.
1. Marc Fortier, Chicoutimi	19	11	*40	*51	20
2. Marc Saumier, Longueuil	20	15	26	41	48
3. Patrice Tremblay, Chicoutimi	19	*22	16	38	22
Daniel Maurice, Chicoutimi	19	10	28	38	54
5. Marc Bureau, Longueuil	20	17	20	37	12
6. Mario Debenedictis, Longueuil	20	16	19	35	10
7. Denis Paul, Shawinigan	14	17	15	32	30
8. Jean Marc Richard, Chicoutimi	18	6	25	31	28
9. Stephan Lebeau, Shawinigan	14	9	20	29	20
Eric Couvrette, Longueuil	20	8	21	29	26

Team-by-Team Playoff Scoring

Chicoutimi Sagueneens
(Lost finals to Longueuil, 4-1)

	Games	G.	A.	Pts.	Pen.
Marc Fortier	19	11	*40	*51	20
Patrice Tremblay	19	*22	16	38	22
Daniel Maurice	19	10	28	38	54
Jean Marc Richard	16	6	25	31	28
Eric Pinard	18	16	10	26	11
Daniel Marois	16	7	14	21	25
Yves Gaucher	17	7	10	17	77
Daniel Bock	19	4	9	13	43
Martin Leroux	19	6	6	12	2
Pierre Millier	15	5	2	7	42
Carl Larouche	18	4	2	6	21
Alain Jobin	18	0	6	6	71
Eric Nadeau	15	1	3	4	52
Laval Brassard	19	0	4	4	15
Serge Lauzon	19	0	4	4	17
Dave Lasalle	13	1	1	2	46
Serge Vigneault	18	1	0	1	49
Richard Gravel	8	0	1	1	2
Remi Brassard	9	0	1	1	8
Serge Lanthier	17	0	1	1	30
Sylvain Reid	3	0	0	0	0
Sylvain Sevigny	3	0	0	0	2
Jimmy Waite (Goalie)	11	0	0	0	0
Denis Desbiens (Goalie)	14	0	0	0	2

Granby Bisons
(Was eliminated in round-robin play)

	Games	G.	A.	Pts.	Pen.
Pierre Turgeon	7	9	6	15	15
Claude Dumas	8	6	6	12	2
Everett Sanipass	8	6	4	10	48
Martin Simard	8	3	7	10	21
Stephane Quintal	8	0	9	9	10
Jean Francois Nault	8	1	6	7	4
Mario Barbe	7	1	5	6	38
Sylvain Hurteau	7	3	2	5	27
Francis Breault	8	3	2	5	14
Eric Desjardins	8	3	2	5	10
Stephane Roy	7	2	3	5	50
Benoit Groulx	8	1	2	3	2
Daniel Lacroix	8	1	2	3	22
Alain Cote	4	0	3	3	2
Daniel Charbonneau	7	0	3	3	6
Eric Gravel	8	0	2	2	6
Stephane Dubois	8	0	1	1	4
Martin Olivier	8	0	1	1	2
Pierre Paul Landry	1	0	0	0	0
Eric Ricard	1	0	0	0	0
Eric Bohemier (Goalie)	3	0	0	0	0
James Blanchard (G.)	6	0	0	0	0
Benoit Adam	7	0	0	0	2

Drummondville Voltiguers
(Was eliminated in round-robin play)

	Games	G.	A.	Pts.	Pen.
Steve Chartrand	8	6	7	13	2
Martin Bergeron	8	5	8	13	0
Daniel Vincelette	8	6	5	11	17
Alain Charland	8	4	6	10	8
Martin Fecteau	7	2	6	8	31
Pierre-Yves Clement	8	4	3	7	27
Eric Tremblay	8	2	5	7	46
Richard Matte	8	2	2	4	9
Mario Dovon	8	1	3	4	30
Christian Ratthe	8	0	3	3	14
Christian Lalumiere	8	2	0	2	5
Giovanni Iasenza	6	0	2	2	23
Tom Gibbons	8	0	2	2	17
Nicolas Beaulieu	6	0	1	1	8
Daniel Dore	8	0	1	1	18
Jean Francois Exantus	1	0	0	0	0
Alain Bruno	3	0	0	0	0
Gaeten Legault	5	0	0	0	4
Frederic Chabot (G.)	8	0	0	0	2
Jean Eric Landry	8	0	0	0	4
Stephane Therrien	8	0	0	0	0

Hull Olympiques
(Was eliminated in round-robin play)

	Games	G.	A.	Pts.	Pen.
Joe Foglietta	8	8	8	16	6
Shane MacEachern	8	6	7	13	8
Benoit Brunet	6	7	5	12	8
Stephane Matteau	8	3	7	10	8
Stephane Richer	8	3	4	7	17
Kelly Nester	8	2	5	7	4
Herbert Hohenberger	8	3	3	6	12
Raynald Gagne	7	1	5	6	2
Hal Turner	8	2	3	5	16
Joe Suk	8	2	1	3	4
Guy Dupuis	8	1	2	3	2
Marc Labelle	7	0	2	2	12
Paul Manson	8	0	2	2	5
Dominic Emond	7	0	1	1	0
Cam Russell	8	0	1	1	16
Grant Ferrigan (Goalie)	1	0	0	0	0
Graeme Harvey (Goalie)	2	0	0	0	0
Sean Wallington	3	0	0	0	2
Jason Glickman (Goalie)	7	0	0	0	4
Joseph A. Aioi	8	0	0	0	13
Kennie MacDermid	8	0	0	0	15

Laval Titans
(Lost semifinals to Longueuil, 4-3)

	Games	G.	A.	Pts.	Pen.
Mike Gober	15	13	14	27	52
Sylvain Couturier	13	12	14	26	19
Luc Beausoleil	15	6	15	21	4
Simon Gagne	15	9	11	20	12
Marc Dumont	15	10	8	18	6
Francois Guay	14	5	13	18	18
Daniel Larin	15	5	7	12	45
Donald Audette	14	2	6	8	10
Rob Murphy	14	3	4	7	15
Eric Aubertin	15	2	5	7	20
Sylvain Lefebvre	15	1	6	7	12
Patrick Black	12	0	6	6	12
Eric Bedard	15	2	2	4	2
Jacques Pinet	14	1	3	4	25
Eric Dubois	14	0	4	4	6
Raymond Saumier	13	1	2	3	76
Stephane Plante	15	1	1	2	17
Martin Latreille	15	0	2	2	6
Mario Brunetta (Goalie)	14	0	1	1	14
Eddy Courtenay	1	0	0	0	0
Eric Vachon (Goalie)	2	0	0	0	0
Eric DelVecchio	3	0	0	0	0
Vincent Garneau	6	0	0	0	0

Longueuil Chevaliers
(Winners of 1987 President Cup Playoffs)

	Games	G.	A.	Pts.	Pen.
Marc Saumier	20	15	26	41	48
Marc Bureau	20	17	20	37	12
Mario Debenedictis	20	16	19	35	10
Eric Couvrette	20	8	21	29	26
Richard Laplante	20	8	14	22	10
Ronnie Stern	19	11	9	20	55
Martin Desjardins	19	8	10	18	18
Yves Racine	20	3	11	14	14
Steven Paiement	20	4	6	10	22
Andre Brassard	15	0	10	10	51
Daniel Gauthier	18	4	5	9	15
Donald Durresne	20	1	8	9	38
Guy Darveau	15	1	7	8	23
Simon Massie	16	3	4	7	10
Don McGrath	19	1	5	6	*96
Real Godin	20	1	5	6	0
Michel Thibodeau	19	1	4	5	10
Alain Leveille	14	0	1	1	0
Alexandre Fortin	15	0	1	1	20
Marc Tremblay	1	0	0	0	0
Eric Maguire (Goalie)	2	0	0	0	0
Jean Claude Latour	9	0	0	0	27
Robert Desjardins (G.)	19	0	0	0	0

St. Jean Castors
(Was eliminated in round-robin play)

	Games	G.	A.	Pts.	Pen.
Stefan Figliuzzi	8	5	6	11	0
Philippe Bozon	8	5	5	10	30
Serge Richard	8	3	7	10	0
Brook Kelly	8	3	6	9	10
Dominic Lavoie	8	2	7	9	2
Stephane Giguere	8	3	5	8	11
Steve Cadieux	8	1	7	8	4
Jan Alston	8	4	3	7	9
Robert Ouellet	8	3	4	7	0
Regis Tremblay	8	2	3	5	15
Richard Audette	8	1	3	4	0
Eric Galarneau	7	0	4	4	8
Marco Grondin	5	1	2	3	0
Martin Lauzon	7	1	2	3	0
Stephane Brochu	8	0	2	2	11
Jean Franco Tremblay	8	1	0	1	0
Joel Drolet (Goalie)	4	0	0	0	0
S. Beauregard (G.)	5	0	0	0	0
Alain Guay	5	0	0	0	2
Miguel Baldris	8	0	0	0	9
Stephane Provost	8	0	0	0	6

Shawinigan Cataracts
(Lost semifinals to Chicoutimi, 4-2)

	Games	G.	A.	Pts.	Pen.
Denis Paul	14	17	15	32	30
Stephan Lebeau	14	9	20	29	20
Patrice Lefebvre	12	9	16	25	19
Luc Duval	14	9	9	18	15
Robert Page	14	8	9	17	45
Stephane Guerard	12	2	9	11	36
Eric Courchesne	14	2	9	11	14
Jean Bois	13	4	6	10	46
Stephane Carrier	14	0	9	9	54
Patrick Lebeau	13	2	6	8	17
Serge Pepin	14	2	6	8	11
Stephane Lavigne	8	1	4	5	58
Mario Lanthier	12	2	2	4	0
Patrick Sauriol	14	2	2	4	2
Stephane Morin	14	1	3	4	27
Dean Bergeron	14	2	1	3	9
Jean Francois Quintin	10	0	2	2	2
Rene Corriveau	14	0	2	2	56
Mario Mercier	3	0	1	1	17
Eric Metivier (Goalie)	3	0	0	0	4
Stephane Dugal	6	0	0	0	30
Christian Bertrand	7	0	0	0	33
Francois Gravel (Goalie)	11	0	0	0	0

Complete 1986 President Cup Goaltending

	Games	Mins.	Goals	SO.	Avg.
Robert Desjardins, Longueuil	*19	*1125	*66	0	*3.52
Francois Gravel, Shawinigan	11	678	47	0	4.16
Jason Glickman, Hull	7	386	27	0	4.20
Grant Ferrigan, Hull	1	28	2	0	4.29
Graeme Harvey, Hull	2	67	5	0	4.48
Mario Brunetta, Laval	14	820	63	0	4.61
Denis Desbiens, Chicoutimi	14	599	46	0	4.61
James Blanchard, Granby	6	370	30	0	4.86
Frederic Chabot, Drummondville	8	481	40	0	4.99
Jimmy Waite, Chicoutimi	11	576	54	*1	5.63

	Games	Mins.	Goals	SO.	Avg.
Eric Maguire, Longueuil	2	73	7	0	5.75
Stephane Beauregard, St. Jean	5	260	26	0	6.00
Eric Bohemier, Granby	3	129	13	0	6.05
Joel Drolet, St. Jean	4	219	24	0	6.58
Eric Vachon, Laval	2	80	10	0	7.50
Eric Metivier, Shawinigan	3	182	27	0	8.90

Individual President Cup Playoff Leaders

Goals .... Patrice Tremblay, Chicoutimi— 22
Assists.. Marc Fortier, Chicoutimi— 40
Points.. Marc Fortier, Chicoutimi— 51
Penalty Minutes .... Don McGrath, Longueuil— 96
Goaltender's Average ....Robert Desjardins, Longueuil— 3.52
Shutouts .... Jimmy Waite, Chicoutimi— 1

★★★

1986-87 QHL All-Star Teams

First Team	Position	Second Team
Robert Desjardins, Longueuil	Goalie	Jimmy Waite, Chicoutimi
Jean Marc Richard, Chicoutimi	Defense	Donald Dufresne, Longueuil
Stephane Quintal, Granby	Defense	Eric Desjardins, Granby
Marc Fortier, Chicoutimi	Center	Stephan Lebeau, Shawinigan
Patrice Lefebvre, Shawinigan	Right Wing	Luc Beausoleil, Laval
		Patrice Tremblay, Chicoutimi
Everett Sanipass, Granby	Left Wing	Benoit Brunet, Hull

★★★

1986-87 QHL Trophy Winners

Frank Selke Trophy (Most Gentlemanly Player).. Luc Beausoleil, Laval
Michel Bergeron Trophy (Top Rookie Forward)... Rob Murphy, Laval
Raymond Lagace Trophy (Top Rookie Defenseman or Goaltender)..................................... Jimmy Waite, Chicoutimi
Jean Beliveau Trophy (Leading Point Scorer).. Marc Fortier, Chicoutimi
Michel Briere Trophy (Regular Season MVP)...Robert Desjardins, Longueuil
Marcel Robert Trophy (Top Scholastic/Athletic Performer)............................... Patrice Tremblay, Chicoutimi
Mike Bossy Trophy (Top Pro Prospect)... Pierre Turgeon, Granby
Emile "Butch" Bouchard Trophy (Top Defenseman) .... Jean Marc Richard, Chicoutimi
Jacques Plante Trophy (Best Goalie)...Robert Desjardins, Longueuil
Guy Lafleur Trophy (Playoff MVP)... Marc Saumier, Longueuil
Robert LeBel Trophy (Best Team Defensive Average)... Longueuil Chevaliers
John Rougeau Trophy (Regular Season Champion).. Granby Bisons
President Cup (Playoff Champion).. Longueuil Chevaliers

Historical QHL Trophy Winners

Frank Selke Trophy
(Most Gentlemanly Player)

1970-71—Norm Dube, Sherbrooke
1971-72—Gerry Teeple, Cornwall
1972-73—Claude Larose, Drummondville
1973-74—Gary MacGregor, Cornwall
1974-75—Jean-Luc Phaneuf, Montreal
1975-76—Norm Dupont, Montreal
1976-77—Mike Bossy, Laval
1977-78—Kevin Reeves, Montreal
1978-79—Ray Bourque, Verdun
          Jean Francois Sauve, Trois Rivieres
1979-80—Jean Francois Sauve, Trois Rivieres
1980-81—Claude Verret, Trois Rivieres
1981-82—Claude Verret, Trois Rivieres
1982-83—Pat LaFontaine, Verdun
1983-84—Jerome Carrier, Verdun
1984-85—Patrick Emond, Chicoutimi
1985-86—Jimmy Carson, Verdun
1986-87—Luc Beausoleil, Laval

Michel Bergeron Trophy
(Top Rookie Forward)
(Prior to 1980-81 season, award was given to QMJHL Rookie-of-the-Year.)

1969-70—Serge Martel, Verdun
1970-71—Bob Murphy, Cornwall
1971-72—Bob Murray, Cornwall
1972-73—Pierre Larouche, Sorel
1973-74—Mike Bossy, Laval
1974-75—Dennis Pomerleau, Hull
1975-76—Jean-Marc Bonamie, Shawinigan
1976-77—Rick Vaive, Sherbrooke
1977-78—Norm Rochefort, Trois Rivieres
          Denis Savard, Montreal
1978-79—Alan Grenier, Laval
1979-80—Dale Hawerchuk, Cornwall
1980-81—Claude Verret, Trois Rivieres
1981-82—Sylvain Turgeon, Hull
1982-83—Pat LaFontaine, Verdun
1983-84—Stephane Richer, Granby
1984-85—Jimmy Carson, Verdun
1985-86—Pierre Turgeon, Granby
1986-87—Rob Murphy, Laval

Raymond Lagace Trophy
(Top Rookie Defenseman or Goaltender)

1980-81—Billy Campbell, Montreal
1981-82—Michel Petit, Sherbrooke
1982-83—Bobby Dollas, Laval
1983-84—James Gasseau, Drummondville
1984-85—Robert Desjardins, Shawinigan
1985-86—Stephane Guerard, Shawinigan
1986-87—Jimmy Waite, Chicoutimi

Jean Beliveau Trophy
(Leading Point Scorer)

1969-70—Luc Simard, Trois Rivieres
1970-71—Guy Lafleur, Quebec
1971-72—Jacques Richard, Quebec
1972-73—Andre Savard, Quebec
1973-74—Pierre Larouche, Sorel
1974-75—Norm Dupont, Montreal
1975-76—Richard Dalpe, Trois Rivieres
          Sylvain Locas, Chicoutimi
1976-77—Jean Savard, Quebec

1977-78—Ron Carter, Sherbrooke
1978-79—Jean-Francois Sauve, Trois Rivieres
1979-80—Jean-Francois Sauve, Trois Rivieres
1980-81—Dale Hawerchuk, Cornwall
1981-82—Claude Verret, Trois Rivieres
1982-83—Pat LaFontaine, Verdun
1983-84—Mario Lemieux, Laval
1984-85—Guy Rouleau, Longueuil
1985-86—Guy Rouleau, Hull
1986-87—Marc Fortier, Chicoutimi

Michael Briere Trophy
(Regular Season Most Valuable Player)

1972-73—Andre Savard, Quebec
1973-74—Gary MacGregor, Cornwall
1974-75—Mario Viens, Cornwall
1975-76—Peter Marsh, Sherbrooke
1976-77—Lucien DeBlois, Sorel
1977-78—Kevin Reeves, Montreal
1978-79—Pierre Lacroix, Trois Rivieres
1979-80—Denis Savard, Montreal
1980-81—Dale Hawerchuk, Cornwall
1981-82—John Chabot, Sherbrooke
1982-83—Pat LaFontaine, Verdun
1983-84—Mario Lemieux, Laval
1984-85—Daniel Berthiaume, Chicoutimi
1985-86—Guy Rouleau, Hull
1986-87—Robert Desjardins, Longueuil

Marcel Robert Trophy
(Top Scholastic/Athletic Performer)

1981-82—Jacques Sylvestre, Granby
1982-83—Claude Gosselin, Quebec
1983-84—Gilbert Paiement, Chicoutimi
1984-85—Claude Gosselin, Longueuil
1985-86—Bernard Morin, Laval
1986-87—Patrice Tremblay, Chicoutimi

Mike Bossy Trophy
(Top Pro Prospect)
(Originally called Association of Journalism of Hockey Trophy from 1980-81 through 1982-83.)

1980-81—Dale Hawerchuk, Cornwall
1981-82—Michel Petit, Sherbrooke
1982-83—Pat LaFontaine, Verdun
          Sylvain Turgeon, Hull (tie)
1983-84—Mario Lemieux, Laval
1984-85—Jose Charbonneau, Drummondville
1985-86—Jimmy Carson, Verdun
1986-87—Pierre Turgeon, Granby

Emile "Butch" Bouchard Trophy
(Top Defenseman)

1975-76—Jean Gagnon, Quebec
1976-77—Robert Picard, Montreal
1977-78—Mark Hardy, Montreal
1978-79—Ray Bourque, Verdun
1979-80—Gaston Therrien, Quebec
1980-81—Fred Boimistruck, Cornwall
1981-82—Paul Andre Boutilier, Sherbrooke
1982-83—Jean-Jacques Daigneault, Longueuil
1983-84—Billy Campbell, Verdun
1984-85—Yves Beaudoin, Shawinigan
1985-86—Sylvain Cote, Hull
1986-87—Jean Marc Richard, Chicoutimi

Jacques Plante Trophy
(Best Goalie)

1969-70—Michael Deguise, Sorel
1970-71—Reynald Fortier, Quebec
1971-72—Richard Brodeur, Cornwall
1972-73—Pierre Perusse, Quebec
1973-74—Claude Legris, Sorel
1974-75—Nick Sanza, Sherbrooke
1975-76—Tim Bernhardt, Cornwall
1976-77—Tim Bernhardt, Cornwall
1977-78—Tim Bernhardt, Cornwall
1978-79—Jacques Cloutier, Trois Rivieres
1979-80—Corrado Micalef, Sherbrooke
1980-81—Michel Dufour, Sorel
1981-82—Jeff Barratt, Montreal
1982-83—Tony Haladuick, Laval
1983-84—Tony Haladuick, Laval
1984-85—Daniel Berthiaume, Chicoutimi
1985-86—Robert Desjardins, Hull
1986-87—Robert Desjardins, Longueuil

Guy Lafleur Trophy
(Most Valuable Player During Playoffs)

1977-78—Richard David, Trois Rivieres
1978-79—Jean-Francois Sauve, Trois Rivieres
1979-80—Dale Hawerchuk, Cornwall
1980-81—Alain Lemieux, Trois Rivieres
1981-82—Michel Morissette, Sherbrooke
1982-83—Pat LaFontaine, Verdun
1983-84—Mario Lemieux, Laval
1984-85—Claude Lemieux, Verdun
1985-86—Sylvain Cote, Hull
          Luc Robitaille, Hull (tie)
1986-87—Marc Saumier, Longueuil

Robert LeBel Trophy
(Best Team Defensive Average)

1977-78—Trois-Rivieres Draveurs
1978-79—Trois-Rivieres Draveurs
1979-80—Sherbrooke Beavers
1980-81—Sorel Black Hawks
1981-82—Montreal Juniors
1982-83—Shawinigan Cataracts
1983-84—Shawinigan Cataracts
1984-85—Shawinigan Cataracts

1985-86—Hull Olympics
1986-87—Longueuil Chevaliers

John Rougeau Trophy
(Regular Season Champions)
(Originally called Governors Trophy from 1969-70 through 1982-83.)

1969-70—Quebec Remparts
1970-71—Quebec Remparts
1971-72—Cornwall Royals
1972-73—Quebec Remparts
1973-74—Sorel Black Hawks
1974-75—Sherbrooke Beavers
1975-76—Sherbrooke Beavers
1976-77—Quebec Remparts
1977-78—Trois Rivieres Draveurs
1978-79—Trois Rivieres Draveurs
1979-80—Sherbrooke Beavers
1980-81—Cornwall Royals
1981-82—Sherbrooke Beavers
1982-83—Laval Voisins
1983-84—Laval Voisins
1984-85—Shawinigan Cataracts
1985-86—Hull Olympics
1986-87—Granby Bisons

President Cup
(Playoff Champions)

1969-70—Quebec Remparts
1970-71—Quebec Remparts
1971-72—Cornwall Royals
1972-73—Quebec Remparts
1973-74—Quebec Remparts
1974-75—Sherbrooke Beavers
1975-76—Quebec Remparts
1976-77—Sherbrooke Beavers
1977-78—Trois Rivieres Draveurs
1978-79—Trois Rivieres Draveurs
1979-80—Cornwall Royals
1980-81—Cornwall Royals
1981-82—Sherbrooke Beavers
1982-83—Verdun Juniors
1983-84—Laval Voisins
1984-85—Verdun Junior Canadiens
1985-86—Hull Olympics
1986-87—Longueuil Chevaliers

National Collegiate Athletic Association

Year	Champion	Coach	Runner-Up
1948	Michigan	Vic Heyliger	Dartmouth
1949	Boston College	John Kelley	Dartmouth
1950	Colorado College	Cheddy Thompson	Boston University
1951	Michigan	Vic Heyliger	Brown
1952	Michigan	Vic Heyliger	Colorado College
1953	Michigan	Vic Heyliger	Minnesota
1954	Rensselaer Poly	Ned Harkness	Minnesota
1955	Michigan	Vic Heyliger	Colorado College
1956	Michigan	Vic Heyliger	Michigan Tech
1957	Colorado College	Thomas Bedecki	Michigan
1958	Denver	Murray Armstrong	North Dakota
1959	North Dakota	Bob May	Michigan State
1960	Denver	Murray Armstrong	Michigan Tech
1961	Denver	Murray Armstrong	St. Lawrence
1962	Michigan Tech	John MacInnes	Clarkson
1963	North Dakota	Barry Thorndycraft	Denver
1964	Michigan	Al Renfrew	Denver
1965	Michigan Tech	John MacInnes	Boston College
1966	Michigan State	Amo Bessone	Clarkson
1967	Cornell	Ned Harkness	Boston University
1968	Denver	Murray Armstrong	North Dakota
1969	Denver	Murray Armstrong	Cornell
1970	Cornell	Ned Harkness	Clarkson
1971	Boston University	Jack Kelley	Minnesota
1972	Boston University	Jack Kelley	Cornell
1973	Wisconsin	Bob Johnson	Denver
1974	Minnesota	Herb Brooks	Michigan Tech
1975	Michigan Tech	John MacInnes	Minnesota
1976	Minnesota	Herb Brooks	Michigan Tech
1977	Wisconsin	Bob Johnson	Michigan
1978	Boston University	Jack Parker	Boston College
1979	Minnesota	Herb Brooks	North Dakota
1980	North Dakota	Gino Gasparini	Northern Michigan
1981	Wisconsin	Bob Johnson	Minnesota
1982	North Dakota	Gino Gasparini	Wisconsin
1983	Wisconsin	Jeff Sauer	Harvard
1984	Bowling Green	Jerry York	Minnesota-Duluth
1985	Rensselaer Polytechnic Inst.	Mike Addesa	Providence College
1986	Michigan State	Ron Mason	Harvard
1987	North Dakota	Gino Gasparini	Michigan State

WESTERN COLLEGIATE HOCKEY ASSOCIATION

	W.	L.	T.	GF.	GA.	Pct.
North Dakota (40-8-0)	29	6	0	200	94	.829
Minnesota (34-14-1)	25	9	1	176	123	.729
Wisconsin (23-18-1)	17	17	1	127	134	.500
Denver (19-18-3)	16	16	3	150	149	.500
Northern Michigan (18-21-1)	16	18	1	131	144	.471
Colorado College (17-24-1)	12	22	1	143	151	.357
Minnesota-Duluth (11-27-1)	11	23	1	114	163	.329
Michigan Tech (11-28-1)	11	23	1	118	182	.329

1986-87 WCHA All-Stars

First Team	Position	Second Team
Ed Belfour, North Dakota	Goalie	Mike Richter, Wisconsin
Ian Kidd, North Dakota	Defenseman	Guy Gosselin, Minn.-Duluth
Rob Doyle, Colorado College	Defenseman	Todd Richards, Minnesota
Tony Hrkac, North Dakota	Forward	Tony Granato, Wisconsin
Bob Joyce, North Dakota	Forward	Corey Millen, Minnesota
Gary Emmons, Northern Michigan	Forward	Paul Ranheim, Wisconsin
		Rick Boh, Colorado College

WCHA Player of the Year: Tony Hrkac, North Dakota

WCHA Rookie of the Year: Dave Shields, Denver

WCHA Coach of the Year: John Gasparini, North Dakota

WCHA PLAYOFFS

Quarterfinals
(Two-Games, Total Goals Series)

Colorado College 4, Denver 2
Colorado College 3, Denver 2
(Colorado College wins series, 7-4)

Minnesota 9, Michigan Tech 4
Minnesota 8, Michigan Tech 5
(Minnesota wins series, 17-9)

North Dakota 5, Minnesota-Duluth 3
North Dakota 8, Minnesota-Duluth 1
(North Dakota wins series, 13-4)

Wisconsin 4, Northern Michigan 2
Wisconsin 6, Northern Michigan 2
(Wisconsin wins series, 10-4)

Semifinals
(Two-Games, Total Goals Series)

North Dakota 6, Colorado College 2
Colorado College 2, North Dakota 1
(North Dakota wins series, 7-4)

Wisconsin 2, Minnesota 1
Minnesota 8, Wisconsin 4
(Minnesota wins series, 9-6)

Championship Games

North Dakota 5, Minnesota 3
North Dakota 5, Minnesota 3
(North Dakota wins series, 10-6)

CENTRAL COLLEGIATE HOCKEY ASSOCIATION

	W.	L.	T.	GF.	GA.	Pct.
Bowling Green (33-10-2)	24	6	2	181	121	.781
Michigan State (33-10-2)	23	8	1	163	117	.734
Lake Superior State (22-16-2)	19	11	2	143	130	.609
Illinois-Chicago (21-17-1)	18	13	1	148	118	.578
Western Michigan (23-20-0)	16	16	0	155	144	.500
Ohio State (19-23-1)	12	19	1	132	168	.391
Michigan (14-25-1)	11	20	1	153	174	.359
Ferris State (16-27-0)	9	23	0	114	152	.281
Miami (O.) (8-31-0)	8	24	0	127	192	.250

Overall record in parentheses.

1986-87 CCHA All-Stars

First Team	Position	Second Team
Gary Kruzich, Bowling Green	Goalie	Bill Horn, Western Michigan
Wayne Gagne, Western Michigan	Defenseman	Brian McKee, Bowling Green
Don McSween, Michigan State	Defenseman	Jeff Norton, Michigan
Mitch Messier, Michigan State	Forward	Paul Ysebaert, Bowling Green
Brad Jones, Michigan	Forward	Bill Shibicky, Michigan State
Iain Duncan, Bowling Green	Forward	Rob Bryden, Western Michigan

CCHA Player of the Year: Wayne Gagne, Western Michigan.
CCHA Rookie of the Year: Nelson Emerson, Bowling Green.
CCHA Coach of the Year: Val Belmonte, Illinois-Chicago.

CCHA PLAYOFFS
Quarterfinals
(Best Two-of-Three Games Series)

Ferris State 6, Bowling Green 4
Bowling Green 5, Ferris State 0
Bowling Green 5, Ferris State 1
(Bowling Green wins series, 2-1)
Michigan State 8, Michigan 7 (OT)
Michigan State 6, Michigan 3
(Michigan State wins series, 2-0)
Lake Superior St. 8, Ohio State 5
Ohio State 5, Lake Superior St. 2
Ohio State 8, Lake Superior St. 4
(Ohio State wins series, 2-1)
Western Michigan 3, Illinois-Chicago 2 (OT)
Illinois-Chicago 6, Western Michigan 4
Western Michigan 5, Illinois-Chicago 1
(Western Michigan wins series, 2-1)

Semifinals
Michigan State 6, Western Michigan 3
Bowling Green 5, Ohio State 1

Consolation Game
Ohio State 7, Western Michigan 4

Championship Game
Michigan State 4, Bowling Green 3 (OT)

EASTERN COLLEGIATE ATHLETIC CONFERENCE

	W.	L.	T.	GF.	GA.	Pct.
Harvard (22-4-0)	22	0	0	106	43	1.000
Colgate (22-7-1)	15	6	1	114	85	.705
St. Lawrence (21-8-0)	15	7	0	109	73	.682
Yale (14-11-1)	14	7	1	77	71	.636
Clarkson (17-12-0)	13	9	0	84	68	.591
Vermont (18-12-0)	12	10	0	75	82	.545
RPI (11-16-1)	9	13	0	81	75	.409
Brown (11-14-0)	9	13	0	83	102	.409
Cornell (11-16-0)	8	14	0	84	94	.364
Princeton (8-17-1)	7	14	1	67	87	.341
Army (9-19-1)	6	16	0	64	109	.273
Dartmouth (2-22-1)	2	19	1	57	109	.114

Overall record in parentheses.

1986-87 ECAC All-Stars

First Team	Position	Second Team
Mike O'Neill, Yale	Goalie	Scott Yearwood, St. Lawrence
Randy Taylor, Harvard	Defenseman	Hank Lammens, St. Lawrence
Mark Benning, Harvard	Defenseman	Dave Basseggio, Yale
Joe Nieuwendyk, Cornell	Forward	Tim Barakett, Harvard
Lane MacDonald, Harvard	Forward	Pete Lappin, St. Lawrence
Bob Kudelski, Yale	Forward	John Messuri, Princeton

ECAC Player of the Year: Joe Nieuwendyk, Cornell.
ECAC Rookie of the Year: John Fletcher, Clarkson.
ECAC Coach of the Year: Tim Taylor, Yale.

ECAC PLAYOFFS

Quarterfinals

Harvard 6, Brown 2
Harvard 5, Brown 2
(Harvard wins series)
St. Lawrence 9, Vermont 1
St. Lawrence 3, Vermont 1
(St. Lawrence wins series)
Yale 4, Clarkson 4
Yale 4, Clarkson 3
(Yale wins series)
RPI 9, Colgate 1
Colgate 7, RPI 2
(RPI wins mini-game 2-0, wins series)

Semifinals

Harvard 4, RPI 1
St. Lawrence 7, Yale 0

Consolation Game

RPI 4, Yale 4

Championship Game

Harvard 6, St. Lawrence 3

HOCKEY EAST

	W.	L.	T.	GF.	GA.	Pct.
Boston College (31-8-0)	26	6	0	203	121	.813
Lowell (22-12-2)	20	10	2	146	136	.656
Maine (24-16-2)	19	12	1	159	117	.609
Boston University (19-15-3)	15	14	3	134	132	.517
Northeastern (13-21-3)	11	18	3	110	139	.391
Providence (7-23-3)	7	22	3	104	156	.266
New Hampshire (8-27-3)	5	24	3	105	179	.203

Overall record in parentheses.

1986-87 Hockey East All-Stars

First Team	Position	Second Team
Bruce Racine, Northeastern	Goalie	Dave Delfino, Lowell
Brian Leetch, Boston College	Defenseman	Jack Capuano, Maine
Eric Weinrich, Maine	Defenseman	Paul Ames, Lowell
Craig Janney, Boston College	Forward	Dan Shea, Boston College
Jon Morris, Lowell	Forward	Gord Cruickshank, Providence
Kevin Stevens, Boston College	Forward	John Cullen, Boston University

Hockey East Player of the Year—Brian Leetch, Boston College
Hockey East Coach of the Year—Bill Riley, Jr., Lowell
Hockey East Rookie of the Year—Brian Leetch, Boston College

HOCKEY EAST PLAYOFFS

Quarterfinals

Northeastern 3, at Boston University 2
Maine 5, Providence 2

Semifinals

Maine 5, Lowell 4
Boston College 9, Northeastern 3

Championship Game

Boston College 4, Maine 2

1986 NCAA Tournament

Quarterfinal Series
(Two-game, Total Goal Series)

North Dakota 3, St. Lawrence 1
North Dakota 6, St. Lawrence 3
(North Dakota wins series, 9-4)

Harvard 7, Bowling Green 1
Harvard 3, Bowling Green 0
(Harvard wins series, 10-1)

Minnesota 4, Boston College 1
Boston College 3, Minnesota 2
(Minnesota wins series, 6-4)

Michigan State 6, Maine 2
Michigan State 5, Maine 3
(Michigan State wins series, 11-5)

Semifinal Series
Played at Detroit, Michigan

North Dakota 5, Harvard 2
Michigan State 5, Minnesota 3

Consolation Game
Minnesota 6, Harvard 3

Championship Game
North Dakota 5, Michigan State 3
1987 NCAA Champion: University of North Dakota

1987 NCAA All-Tournament Team

Position	Player	College
Goalie	Ed Belfour	North Dakota
Defenseman	Ian Kidd	North Dakota
Defenseman	Chris Luongo	Michigan State
Defenseman	Don McSween	Michigan State
Forward	Tony Hrkac	North Dakota
Forward	Corey Millen	Minnesota
Forward	Bob Joyce	North Dakota

NCAA Tournament MVP: Tony Hrkac, North Dakota.

1986-87 College Hockey All-America Teams
FIRST TEAM
WEST

Position	Player	College
Goalie	Gary Kruzich	Bowling Green
Defenseman	Wayne Gagne	Western Michigan
Defenseman	Ian Kidd	North Dakota
Forward	Tony Hrkac	North Dakota
Forward	Bob Joyce	North Dakota
Forward	Mitch Messier	Michigan State

SECOND TEAM

Position	Player	College
Goalie	Ed Belfour	North Dakota
Defenseman	Don McSween	Michigan State
Defenseman	Rob Doyle	Colorado College
Forward	Gary Emmons	Northern Michigan
Forward	Tony Granato	Wisconsin
Forward	Brad Jones	Michigan

FIRST TEAM
EAST

Position	Player	College
Goalie	Bruce Racine	Northeastern
Defenseman	Brian Leetch	Boston College
Defenseman	Mark Benning	Harvard
Forward	Craig Janney	Boston College
Forward	Joe Nieuwendyk	Cornell
Forward	Lane MacDonald	Harvard

— 216 —

Position	Player	College
Goalie	Scott Yearwood	St. Lawrence
Defenseman	Eric Weinrich	Maine
Defenseman	Hank Lammens	St. Lawrence
Forward	Kevin Stevens	Boston College
Forward	Jon Morrison	Lowell
Forward	Peter Lappin	St. Lawrence

All-Time NCAA Tournament Records and Finishes

		Tournament					Finished	
	Visits	W.	L.	GF	GA	Pct.	1st	2nd
Michigan	13	21	6	173	91	.778	7	2
Wisconsin	8	15	5	90	52	.750	4	1
North Dakota	12	21	9	121	87	.700	5	3
Denver	11	17	9	121	73	.654	5	2
Minnesota	13	21	12	153	127	.636	3	5
*Northeastern	1	2	1	17	14	.625	0	0
†Michigan State	9	14	9	100	81	.604	2	2
Michigan Tech	10	13	9	118	85	.591	3	4
#RPI	6	8	6	52	50	.567	2	0
Boston University	15	16	16	136	151	.500	3	2
*Bowling Green	6	6	6	39	52	.500	1	0
Cornell	8	8	8	54	52	.500	2	2
Yale	1	1	1	7	5	.500	0	0
Providence	4	5	6	31	30	.455	0	1
Dartmouth	5	4	5	38	37	.444	0	2
Minnesota-Duluth	3	4	5	33	34	.444	0	1
Clarkson	8	7	9	48	67	.438	0	3
Colorado College	9	6	10	76	84	.375	2	2
Brown	3	2	4	28	38	.333	0	1
†Harvard	12	9	20	105	138	.317	0	2
Boston College	16	8	23	105	76	.258	1	2
Northern Michigan	2	1	3	10	19	.250	0	1
New Hampshire	4	2	8	35	56	.200	0	0
St. Lawrence	9	3	16	55	101	.158	0	1
#Lake Superior State	1	0	1	6	10	.025	0	0
Maine	1	0	2	5	11	.000	0	0
Western Michigan	1	0	2	4	11	.000	0	0

(Denver also participated in 1973 tournament but its record was voided by the NCAA in 1977 upon discovery of violations by the University. The team had finished second in '73.)

*Bowling Green and Northeastern played to a 2-2 tie in 1981-82.

†Harvard and Michigan State played to a 3-3 tie in 1982-83.

#Lake Superior State and RPI played to a 3-3 tie in 1984-85.

HOBEY BAKER MEMORIAL TROPHY (Top College hockey player in U.S.): Tony Hrkac, North Dakota.

Air Force Academy
Overall: 17-10

	Pos.	Class	Games	G.	A.	Pts.	Pen.
John Klimek	F	Sr.	27	16	27	43	22
John Manney	F	Jr.	27	20	21	41	12
Joe Delich	F	So.	27	10	21	31	27
Greg Gutterman	F	So.	27	15	13	28	20
Joe Doyle	F	So.	27	11	17	28	22
Tom Zupancich	D	Jr.	27	12	15	27	40
Jim Jirele	F	So.	26	13	9	22	6
John Anzelc	D	So.	27	6	15	21	33
Jeff Banks	F	So.	18	5	11	16	10
Keith Nightingale	D	Sr.	24	5	9	14	52
Jim Brunkow	D	Sr.	27	3	11	14	4
Mike Mason	F	Jr.	25	1	8	9	28
Kevin McManaman	D	So.	23	5	3	8	38
Chuck Juhala	F	So.	13	4	4	8	0
Joe Chapman	F	Sr.	22	4	3	7	14
Kurt Rohloff	F	Fr.	26	2	5	7	6
Jeff Verville	F	Jr.	15	3	1	4	4
Steve Chartrand	F	Fr.	16	1	3	4	4
Brian Raduenz	F	Jr.	11	1	2	3	2
Matt Watson	F	Fr.	14	1	2	3	2
Tony Lind	F	Fr.	5	1	1	2	12
Mike Travalent	F	So.	11	1	1	2	0

U.S. Military Academy (Army)

Overall: 9-19-1; ECAC: 6-16-0

	Pos.	Class	Games	G.	A.	Pts.	Pen.
Matt Wilson	F	Sr.	29	18	23	41	38
Rob Brenner	F	Sr.	29	15	21	36	15
Kevin Keenan	F	Sr.	28	13	19	32	26
Rich Sheridan	F	Fr.	29	8	14	22	40
Ed Melanson	F	Jr.	29	9	7	16	16
Scott Schulze	D	Fr.	29	4	11	15	18
Mike Chenette	F	Jr.	24	3	6	9	14
Mark Hudak	D	So.	29	1	8	9	42
Vinny Bono	D	Jr.	16	1	7	8	6
Neil Minihane	D	Fr.	25	1	5	6	34
Scott Custer	D	Jr.	21	0	6	6	20
Mark Hill	D	Jr.	26	3	2	5	57
John Schoeppach	F	Jr.	24	2	3	5	26
Mike Gengler	F	Fr.	25	3	1	4	8
Brian Cox	F	So.	25	3	0	3	6
Dan McCormick	F	Sr.	26	2	1	3	6
John Farnham	F	Fr.	12	1	2	3	10
Tim McWain	F	So.	24	0	3	3	16
Matt Quinn	D	Sr.	19	1	1	2	16
John Knieriem	F	So.	17	0	2	2	6
Chris Pietrzak	F	Jr.	10	1	0	1	4
Todd Traczyk	F	Fr.	7	0	1	1	4

Boston College

Overall: 31-8-0; Hockey East: 26-6-0

	Pos.	Class	Games	G.	A.	Pts.	Pen.
Craig Janney	F	So.	37	28	55	83	6
Kevin Stevens	F	Sr.	39	35	35	70	54
Dan Shea	F	Jr.	38	21	45	66	56
Ken Hodge	F	Jr.	37	29	33	62	30
Tim Sweeney	F	So.	38	31	16	47	28
Brian Leetch	D	Fr.	37	9	38	47	10
Greg Brown	D	Fr.	37	10	27	37	22
John Devereaux	F	Jr.	39	14	20	34	6
Steve Scheifele	F	Fr.	38	13	13	26	28
Chris Stapleton	F	Jr.	32	10	9	19	8
Mike Gervasi	F	Jr.	36	7	10	17	21
John McLean	D	Sr.	37	1	16	17	44
Paul Marshall	D	So.	36	4	10	14	30
Richard Braccia	F	So.	30	4	5	9	52
David Buckley	D	So.	34	3	5	8	9
Tim Ceglarski	F	Sr.	23	5	1	6	2
Shawn Kennedy	F	So.	24	2	4	6	10
David Whyte	F	Sr.	28	2	2	4	26
Rob Cheevers	F	Fr.	10	1	2	3	6
Bill Nolan	F	Fr.	16	1	1	2	12
Mike Mullowney	D	So.	30	0	2	2	22
Sean Delaney	F	Fr.	3	1	0	1	0

Boston University

Overall: 19-15-3; Hockey East: 15-14-3

	Pos.	Class	Games	G.	A.	Pts.	Pen.
John Cullen	F	Sr.	36	23	29	52	35
Ed Lowney	F	Sr.	37	22	22	44	6
Mike Kelfer	F	So.	33	21	19	40	20
Clark Donatelli	F	Jr.	37	15	23	38	46
Scott Young	F	So.	33	15	21	36	24
Mike Sullivan	F	Fr.	37	13	18	31	18
Jay Octeau	D	Sr.	37	5	23	28	40
Eric Labrosse	F	Jr.	37	10	12	22	56
Scott Sanders	F	Jr.	31	11	9	20	26
Ville Kentala	F	Fr.	35	4	11	15	24
Scott Shaunessy	D	Sr.	32	2	13	15	71
Jeff Sveen	F	Jr.	34	8	6	14	32
David Quinn	D	Jr.	27	1	11	12	34

	Pos.	Class	Games	G.	A.	Pts.	Pen.
Tom Ryan	D	Jr.	37	1	7	8	20
Jim Ennis	D	So.	26	3	4	7	27
David Thiesing	D	Sr.	37	2	5	7	18
Robert Regan	F	Fr.	17	1	3	4	6
Ian Wood	F	So.	19	1	3	4	4
Steve Shaunessy	D	Fr.	15	0	2	2	18
Matt Pesklewis	F	Fr.	24	0	2	2	28
Bob Deraney	G	Sr.	12	0	1	1	4
Kris Werner	D	Jr.	16	0	1	1	4

Bowling Green State University
Overall: 33-10-2; CCHA: 24-6-2

	Pos.	Class	Games	G.	A.	Pts.	Pen.
Paul Ysebaert	C	Jr.	45	27	58	85	44
Iain Duncan	LW	Sr.	39	28	40	68	141
Don Barber	LW	Jr.	43	39	34	63	107
Nelson Emerson	C	Fr.	45	26	35	61	28
Scott Paluch	D	Jr.	45	13	38	51	88
Greg Parks	C	So.	45	23	27	50	52
Brian McKee	D	Jr.	40	18	31	49	93
Andy Gribble	F	Jr.	45	18	18	36	26
Brent Regan	F	Jr.	43	12	17	29	22
Marc Potvin	RW	Fr.	43	5	15	20	74
Todd Flichel	D	Sr.	42	4	15	19	77
Joe Quinn	RW	Fr.	39	4	13	17	22
Mike Natyshak	RW	Sr.	45	5	10	15	101
Rob Urban	F	Sr.	29	5	8	13	58
Chad Arthur	F	So.	20	6	4	10	41
Clarke Pineo	LW	So.	21	3	5	8	6
Alan Leggett	D	So.	37	3	5	8	26
Kevin Dahl	D	Fr.	32	2	6	8	54
Tom Pratt	D	Sr.	41	1	7	8	46
Gary Kruzich	G	Sr.	38	0	8	8	19
Geoff Williams	F	Jr.	18	2	4	6	26
Thad Rusiecci	D	So.	26	2	4	6	37
Brian Meharry	F	Jr.	12	1	4	5	20
Steve Dickinson	F	So.	4	0	1	1	2

Brown University
Overall:11-15-0; ECAC: 9-13-0

	Pos.	Class	Games	G.	A.	Pts.	Pen.
Mark Rechan	F	Sr.	27	7	24	31	36
Dan Allen	F	Sr.	25	17	11	28	4
Mike Girouard	D	Sr.	27	8	16	24	72
Steve Climo	F	Sr.	26	10	13	23	43
Mike Rechan	F	Sr.	27	9	10	19	48
Mike Langton	F	So.	27	9	8	17	26
Rob Hardy	F	So.	24	7	9	16	20
Bruce McColl	D	Jr.	27	4	11	15	18
John Caragliano	D	Jr.	27	2	11	13	14
Gordie Ernst	F	So.	15	5	6	11	10
Kelly Burns	F.	Jr.	20	4	7	11	28
Mark LaChance	D	So.	21	0	11	11	22
Bob Kenneally	F	Fr.	21	4	6	10	10
Steve Crozier	F	Sr.	24	2	8	10	50
Rod Pritchard	F	So.	16	3	6	9	22
Bob Ernst	F	So.	21	4	4	8	4
Karl Burns	F	Jr.	25	3	4	7	32
Jim Lombardi	D	So.	19	0	5	5	8
Greg Murphy	D	Jr.	22	3	1	4	79
Rick Bonine	F	So	6	2	2	4	2
Joe Swirbalus	F	Jr.	10	0	3	3	4
Sean McNamara	D	Jr.	12	0	3	3	16
Matt Parker	D	Jr.	1	0	1	1	2
Dan Sheehan	D	Fr.	5	0	1	1	2

Clarkson University
Overall: 17-13-1; ECAC: 13-1-0

	Pos.	Class	Games	G.	A.	Pts.	Pen.
Luciano Borsato	F	Jr.	31	16	41	57	55
Stephen Williams	F	Jr.	30	28	13	41	20
Shawn LaVoy	F	So.	31	14	12	26	52
Mike Morrison	F	So.	31	7	17	24	80
Chris Mills	D	Fr.	30	3	14	17	32
Al Hill	F	Sr.	17	8	8	16	18
Mark Tretowicz	F	Fr.	31	5	11	16	16
Jeff Korchinski	D	Sr.	30	5	8	13	40
Rodger Huiatt	F	Jr.	31	8	4	12	16
Jay Rose	D	Jr.	29	2	10	12	74
Mike Ashe	D	So.	29	0	11	11	48
Brad James	D	So.	29	4	6	10	54
Pierre Morin	D	Fr.	30	1	8	9	16
Ron Reagan	F	Fr.	26	3	5	8	6
Jean Rouleau	F	Jr.	28	4	3	7	32
Steve Brennan	F	Fr.	29	3	3	6	17
Dan O'Brien	F	So.	29	3	0	3	18
Matt LaLonde	F	So.	26	2	1	3	12
Paul Donovan	F	Fr.	18	1	2	3	21
Scott Denicourt	F	Fr.	2	0	2	2	2
Dave Mellen	F	So.	12	0	2	2	14
Pat Phillips	F	So.	4	0	1	1	0

Colgate University
Overall: 23-9-1; ECAC: 15-6-1

	Pos.	Class	Games	G.	A.	Pts.	Pen.
Rejean Boivin	F	Jr.	33	19	28	47	18
Greg Drechsel	F	Jr.	33	20	21	41	55
Brad Martel	F	Jr.	33	15	24	39	20
Steve Spott	F	Fr.	33	21	13	34	34
Joe Gardner	F	Fr.	31	10	20	30	20
Scott Young	D	So.	33	13	15	28	113
Doug Davis	F	Sr.	33	8	19	27	14
Mark Holmes	F	Jr.	31	12	14	26	45
Harold Duvall	F	Sr.	32	9	17	26	65
Mike Bishop	D	So.	30	7	17	24	68
Shawn Lillie	F	Fr.	30	11	10	21	4
Scott Reston	D	Sr.	31	2	18	20	34
Lowell MacDonald	F	Sr.	29	5	13	18	20
Todd Wolf	D	So.	33	1	15	16	44
Brett Lawrence	F	Fr.	33	8	7	15	22
Rick Russell	D	Sr.	31	1	13	14	18
Peter Webb	D	So.	31	2	11	13	18
Paul Jenkins	D	Sr.	19	2	5	7	26
Gary Mitchell	F	Jr.	10	1	3	4	8
John McCarthy	F	Jr.	9	1	2	3	2
Karl Clauss	D	Fr.	12	1	1	2	0
Wayne Cowley	G	So.	31	0	2	2	6
Jeff Weber	F	Fr.	2	1	0	1	6

Colorado College
Overall: 17-24-1; WCHA: 12-22-1

	Pos.	Class	Games	G.	A.	Pts.	Pen.
Rick Boh	F	Sr.	38	22	42	64	37
Rob Doyle	D	Sr.	42	17	37	54	72
Doug Clarke	D	Jr.	37	11	37	48	73
Scott Schneider	F	Sr.	42	21	22	43	36
Gord Whitaker	F	Sr.	34	21	17	38	69
Tim Budy	F	So.	42	17	20	37	40
Cal Brown	D	Fr.	41	7	17	24	80
Keith Hoppe	F	Jr.	41	12	8	20	10
Doug Kirton	F	Fr.	38	10	10	20	42
Guy Gadowsky	F	So.	40	9	7	16	32
Chris Anderson	F	Fr.	42	6	9	15	10
Scott Campbell	D	Sr.	40	5	10	15	47

	Pos.	Class	Games	G.	A.	Pts.	Pen.
Dave Hardie	D	Sr.	42	0	11	11	50
Marty Ketola	F	Sr.	41	4	4	8	55
Tom Pederson	D	Jr.	35	2	6	8	25
Mark Olsen	D	So.	42	2	4	6	38
Paul Noad	F	Fr.	28	3	1	4	10
Kevin Hoffman	F	Fr.	40	2	1	3	24
Steve Grumley	F	So.	16	0	1	1	17
Derek Pizzey	G	So.	33	0	1	1	0

Cornell University
Overall: 11-16-0; ECAC: 8-14-0

	Pos.	Class	Games	G.	A.	Pts.	Pen.
Joe Nieuwendyk	F	Jr.	23	26	26	52	26
Chris Norton	D	Jr.	24	10	21	31	79
Andy Craig	D	Sr.	27	3	21	24	30
Casey Jones	F	Fr.	27	6	12	18	38
Chris Grenier	F	So.	27	7	10	17	2
Pete Marcov	F	Sr.	27	10	6	16	6
Darren Snyder	F	So.	23	10	6	16	36
Craig Donovan	D	Jr.	27	1	15	16	40
Dave Shippel	F	Sr.	27	7	8	15	28
Bob Levasseur	F	So.	25	6	7	13	95
Stewart Smith	F	So.	24	5	7	12	55
Ross Lemon	F	Fr.	21	3	4	7	30
Mark Major	F	Sr.	26	2	5	7	20
John Parry	D	Sr.	25	2	4	6	22
Paul Winters	D	Fr.	27	0	6	6	48
Neil Paterson	F	Fr.	17	2	2	4	18
Keith Howie	F	Sr.	6	1	3	4	4
Alan Tigert	D	So.	27	1	3	4	36
Pat Heaphy	F	Jr.	8	1	2	3	6
Dave Crombeen	F	Jr.	23	1	2	3	73
Jim Goerz	F	Fr.	17	2	0	2	12
Keith Donovan	D	So.	2	0	1	1	0
Mike Tallman	F	Fr.	6	0	1	1	0

Dartmouth College
Overall: 2-22-1; ECAC: 2-19-1

	Pos.	Class	Games	G.	A.	Pts.	Pen.
Dave Williams	D	Fr.	23	2	19	21	20
Mark Glover	F	So.	25	10	10	20	55
Paul Rai	F	Jr.	25	7	9	16	46
Doug Weiss	F	Jr.	25	6	9	15	40
Tom Finks	F	So.	24	11	3	14	26
Jamie Hanlon	F	Fr.	25	6	7	13	18
Ned Desmond	D	So.	24	4	9	13	28
Bill McInerny	F	Jr.	22	3	7	10	31
Jeff Miller	D	Fr.	25	1	8	9	10
Kevin McCann	F	Sr.	21	3	5	8	40
Andy Donahue	F	So.	18	0	7	7	10
Derek Tweddell	F	So.	25	4	2	6	12
Paul O'Hern	F	Jr.	25	3	3	6	37
Roger Chiasson	F	Fr.	23	1	3	4	8
Rob Goulet	D	So.	20	0	4	4	12
Butch Coughlin	D	So.	23	0	3	3	20
Mike Freedman	F	So.	22	1	1	2	6
Jack Bohn	D	Sr.	21	1	0	1	57
Ed Cepuran	F	So.	7	0	1	1	0
Joe Gualtieri	D	Fr.	15	0	0	0	12

University of Denver
Overall: 19-18-3; WCHA: 16-16-3

	Pos.	Class	Games	G.	A.	Pts.	Pen.
Dave Shields	F	Fr.	40	18	30	48	8
Daryl Seltenreich	F	Jr.	39	27	13	40	53
John McMillan	F	Sr.	39	16	21	37	37

	Pos.	Class	Games	G.	A.	Pts.	Pen.
Jeff Lamb	F	Sr.	40	10	24	34	58
Daryn McBride	F	Fr.	39	19	13	32	54
Bruce Hill	F	Jr.	38	14	16	30	28
Ed Cristofoli	F	So.	40	14	15	29	52
Scott Mathias	F	So.	40	11	13	24	22
Dave Hanson	F	Jr.	36	7	17	24	64
Derek Mayer	D	So.	38	5	17	22	87
Marc Rousseau	D	Fr.	39	3	18	21	70
Glen Evgevik	F	So.	40	10	8	18	32
Eric Murano	F	Fr.	31	5	7	12	12
Dave Gourlie	D	Jr.	37	3	9	12	34
Jim Onstad	F	Sr.	34	6	5	11	18
Eric Johnson	D	Sr.	40	3	8	11	48
Tom Moore	F	So.	13	2	2	4	4
Don McLennan	D	Fr.	35	2	2	4	38
Dean Williamson	F	Fr.	2	1	0	1	0
Doug Menzies	D	Sr.	8	0	1	1	12
Chris Gillies	G	So.	22	0	1	1	2
Chris Olson	G	Sr.	24	0	1	1	8

Ferris State College
Overall: 16-27-0; CCHA: 5-13-0

	Pos.	Class	Games	G.	A.	Pts.	Pen.
Paul Lowden	F	Sr.	43	32	29	61	14
Rod Schluter	F	Jr.	42	22	31	53	73
Pete Lowden	F	Sr.	43	14	31	45	20
Murray Winnicki	F	Jr.	36	9	32	41	24
Darin Fridgen	F	Jr.	33	18	13	31	78
Clark Davies	D	Fr.	42	5	20	25	42
Andy Black	F	So.	39	16	8	24	20
Gary Sweetnam	D	Jr.	39	2	20	22	83
Dean Cowling	F	So.	42	6	8	14	24
Bill Thomas	F	Fr.	43	5	9	14	42
Greg Cyr	D.	Fr.	43	2	10	12	42
Randy Robertson	D	So.	43	7	3	10	56
Tim Corkery	D	Fr.	40	3	7	10	120
Mike Sparago	F	Sr.	35	4	3	7	27
Dean Davies	D	So.	34	3	4	7	51
Phil Kaske	F	Jr.	16	3	3	6	12
Kevin MacIsaac	F	Jr.	20	3	3	6	52
Mike LaLonde	F	Fr.	42	2	4	6	8
Doug Miller	D	Fr.	24	1	2	3	46
Gilles Grondin	F	So.	17	0	1	1	12
Glenn Raeburn	G	So.	32	0	1	1	0
John Bergeron	D	Fr.	33	0	1	1	51

Harvard University
Overall: 28-6-0; ECAC: 20-2-0

	Pos.	Class	Games	G.	A.	Pts.	Pen.
Lane McDonald	F	Jr.	34	37	30	67	26
Allen Bourbeau	F	Jr.	33	23	34	57	46
Tim Barakett	F	Sr.	34	25	29	54	12
Randy Taylor	D	Sr.	34	3	35	38	30
Mark Benning	D	Sr.	31	3	29	32	30
C. J. Youn	F	Fr.	34	17	12	29	30
Steve Armstrong	F	Jr.	34	11	15	26	36
Don Sweeney	D	Jr.	34	7	14	21	22
Peter Chiarelli	F	Sr.	34	8	7	15	30
Tod Hartje	F	Fr.	34	3	9	12	36
Ed Krayer	F	So.	14	2	9	11	12
Josh Caplan	D	So.	32	1	10	11	24
Nick Carone	F	Jr.	33	3	6	9	38
John Murphy	F	Fr.	34	3	6	9	10
Rick Haney	F	Sr.	17	2	5	7	0
Chris Biotti	D	So.	30	1	6	7	23
Jerry Pawloski	D	Jr.	18	1	5	6	26
Craig Taucher	F	So.	15	3	2	5	8
Andy Janfaza	F	Jr.	31	3	2	5	26

	Pos.	Class	Games	G.	A.	Pts.	Pen.
Paul Howley	F	So.	8	0	3	3	4
Scott McCormack	D	Fr.	8	1	1	2	0
Dickie McEvoy	G	Sr.	24	0	2	2	0
Butch Cutone	D	Sr.	33	0	2	2	12
Gerald Green	F	Jr.	3	0	1	1	6

University of Illinois-Chicago
Overall: 21-17-1; CCHA: 18-13-1

	Pos.	Class	Games	G.	A.	Pts.	Pen.
Jeff Nelson	C	Jr.	39	23	31	54	6
Rob Klenk	W	Jr.	39	21	20	41	151
Sheldon Gorski	W	So.	39	18	20	38	50
Paul Tory	C	Jr.	34	17	21	38	73
Todd Beyer	C	Fr.	39	13	16	29	40
Tom Almquist	W	Sr.	38	8	20	28	75
Jeff Simmer	D	So.	37	4	21	25	51
Trent Rees	C	So.	37	6	18	24	12
Barry McKinlay	D	Fr.	33	9	14	23	35
Darin Alexander	D	Jr.	37	6	14	20	66
Darin Banister	D	Fr.	38	4	16	20	38
Paul Pulis	W	Sr.	24	10	9	19	32
Kevin Alexander	W	Fr.	39	9	9	18	18
Kurt Kabat	W	Fr.	37	12	5	17	47
John Mynatt	D	Sr.	39	4	11	15	58
Scott Wolter	W	So.	37	5	5	10	6
Jamie Husgen	D	Sr.	31	2	8	10	59
Dan Perry	W	So.	29	1	7	8	14
Harry Armstrong	D	Sr.	15	1	3	4	32
Steve Huglen	D	Sr.	13	1	1	2	22
Henry Reimer	W	So.	22	1	1	2	12
Brian Bellefeuille	W	Fr.	2	0	0	0	2
Jim Hickey	G	Sr.	10	0	0	0	0
Brad Ryan	G	Jr.	15	0	0	0	19
Dave DePinto	G	Fr.	17	0	0	0	2

Lake Superior State College
Overall: 22-16-2; CCHA: 19-11-2

	Pos.	Class	Games	G.	A.	Pts.	Pen.
Mike de Carle	F	So.	38	34	18	52	122
Dean Dixon	F	Sr.	40	19	24	43	56
Jim Roque	F	Sr.	38	13	26	39	30
Anthony Palumbo	F	So.	40	11	26	37	14
Mark Vermette	F	So.	38	19	17	36	59
Pete Stauber	F	Fr.	40	22	13	35	80
Paul Jerrard	F	Sr.	35	10	19	29	56
Jeff Jablonski	F	Fr.	40	17	10	27	42
Kord Cernich	D	Fr.	39	4	18	22	32
Mike Warus	F	Sr.	38	6	15	21	113
Jeff Dicaire	F	Jr.	39	11	8	19	36
Craig Hewson	F	Jr.	37	4	10	14	38
Grant Clark	D	Sr.	40	1	11	12	18
Terry Hossack	D	Jr.	30	2	7	9	46
Matt Cote	D	Sr.	36	1	8	9	30
Dan Keczmer	D	Fr.	38	3	5	8	26
Rene Chapdelaine	D	So.	28	1	5	6	51
Drew Famulak	F	Fr.	26	2	2	4	16
Ken Martel	D	So.	35	0	3	3	29
Rob Friesen	F	Fr.	6	1	0	1	2
Brian Michaud	F	Jr.	9	0	0	0	13

University of Lowell
Overall: 22-12-2; Hockey East: 20-10-2

	Pos.	Class	Games	G.	A.	Pts.	Pen.
Jon Morris	F	Jr.	35	28	33	61	48
Randy LeBrasseur	F	Fr.	35	20	19	39	30
Jim Newhouse	F	Jr.	31	12	24	36	17
Bill Dohaney	F	Jr.	33	13	22	35	45

	Pos.	Class	Games	G.	A.	Pts.	Pen.
Tony LoPilato	F	Jr.	31	13	19	32	56
Scott Drevitch	D	Jr.	35	3	25	28	24
Craig Charron	F	Fr.	36	11	16	27	48
Tim Foley	D	Jr.	35	10	14	24	36
Paul Ames	D	Sr.	34	7	16	23	43
Carl Valimont	D	Jr.	36	8	9	17	36
Gary Valimont	F	Jr.	26	7	8	15	20
John Borrell	F	So.	34	5	10	15	43
Conrade Thomas	F	Fr.	31	5	7	12	78
Jeff Flaherty	F	Fr.	28	4	5	9	37
Peter Heinze	D	Jr.	27	5	3	8	26
Scott MacPherson	F	Fr.	30	2	6	8	14
Fred Allard	F	So.	32	4	3	7	37
Gary Murphy	D	So.	21	3	4	7	13
Scott Stanlick	F	Fr.	22	2	2	4	2
Jyrki Maki	D	Jr.	25	2	2	4	8
Paul Mahan	F	Sr.	17	0	2	2	10
Mike Teolis	F	Fr.	1	0	1	1	0

University of Maine
Overall: 24-16-2; Hockey East: 19-12-1

	Pos.	Class	Games	G.	A.	Pts.	Pen.
Dave Capuano	F	Fr.	38	18	41	59	14
Mike McHugh	F	Jr.	42	21	29	50	40
Eric Weinrich	D	So.	41	12	32	44	59
Jack Capuano	F	Fr.	42	10	34	44	20
Mike Golden	F	Jr.	36	19	23	42	37
Guy Perron	F	Fr.	42	13	22	35	28
Dave Wensley	F	Jr.	31	16	17	33	22
Bob Corkum	F	So.	35	18	11	29	24
Jay Mazur	F	Sr.	39	16	10	26	61
Bruce Major	F	So.	37	14	10	24	12
Dave Nonis	D	Jr.	39	1	23	24	18
Todd Studnick	F	Jr.	33	9	7	16	30
Chris Lalonde	F	Fr.	40	8	8	16	49
Steve Santini	F	Sr.	41	9	5	14	12
Bob Beers	D	So.	38	0	13	13	45
Todd Jenkins	F	So.	40	6	6	12	38
Chris Cambio	F	So.	24	3	3	6	2
John Massara	F	Fr.	24	2	2	4	10
Vince Guidotti	D	Sr.	39	1	3	4	40
Claude Scremin	D	Fr.	15	0	1	1	0
John Baker	D	Sr.	18	0	1	1	0
Scott King	G	Fr.	21	0	1	1	0
Al Loring	G	So.	25	0	1	1	0

Miami (O.) University
Overall: 8-31-0; CCHA: 8-24-0

	Pos.	Class	Games	G.	A.	Pts.	Pen.
Mike Martinec	F	Sr.	39	12	35	47	29
Mike Orn	F	Jr.	38	22	23	45	70
Greg Dornbach	F	Jr.	39	11	28	39	42
Boyd Sutton	F	So.	39	19	18	37	44
Jeff Sisto	F	So.	37	21	12	33	18
Tom Neziol	F	Fr.	39	11	18	29	80
John O'Connor	F	Sr.	39	11	17	28	30
Mike Macoun	D	Sr.	38	5	15	20	99
Dan Beaudette	F	Fr.	31	5	9	14	26
Ron Saatzer	F	So.	31	5	8	13	44
Nate Kondo	D	So.	36	3	9	12	44
Steve Benson	D	Jr.	34	0	12	12	28
Paul Swift	F	Fr.	34	5	6	11	52
Craig Pestell	F	Jr.	33	5	5	10	75
Greg Island	D	Fr.	30	1	9	10	39
Rob Robinson	D	So.	33	3	5	8	32
Joe Tonello	D	Fr.	21	2	6	8	4
Chris Archer	F	So.	24	2	5	7	12
Steve McGrinder	D	Fr.	20	2	3	5	24

	Pos.	Class	Games	G.	A.	Pts.	Pen.
Tom Terwilllinger	D	Jr.	26	2	1	3	24
Jeff Johnson	F	So.	13	0	1	1	2
Brent Smith	G	Sr.	22	0	1	1	6

University of Michigan
Overall: 14-25-1; CCHA: 11-20-1

	Pos.	Class	Games	G.	A.	Pts.	Pen.
Brad Jones	F	Sr.	40	32	46	78	64
Brad McCaughey	F	Jr.	38	26	23	49	53
Jeff Norton	D	Jr.	39	12	36	48	92
Todd Brost	F	So.	40	16	31	37	43
Myles O'Connor	D	So.	39	15	30	45	111
Mike Moes	F	Fr.	39	11	15	26	16
Bruce Macnab	F	Sr.	33	9	16	25	24
Bryan Deasley	F	Fr.	38	13	11	24	74
Billy Powers	F	Jr.	38	13	10	23	18
Rob Brown	F	Fr.	40	7	12	19	24
Joe Lockwood	F	Jr.	39	13	5	18	62
Ryan Pardoski	F	Fr.	39	4	9	13	26
Brad Turner	D	Fr.	40	3	10	13	40
Todd Copeland	D	Fr.	34	2	11	13	59
Alex Roberts	D	Fr.	37	1	7	8	117
Jeff Urban	F	So.	28	3	4	7	18
Sean Baker	F	Jr.	31	3	3	6	24
John Bjorkman	F	Sr.	25	4	0	4	6
Randy Kwong	D	Fr.	38	0	4	4	38
Warren Sharples	G	Fr.	32	0	3	3	10
Mike Cusack	F	So.	17	1	1	2	43
Gary Lorden	D	Jr.	1	0	1	1	2
Tim Makris	G	Jr.	4	0	1	1	0
Glen Neary	G	Fr.	12	0	1	1	2

Michigan State University
Overall: 33-10-2; CCHA: 23-8-1

	Pos.	Class	Games	G.	A.	Pts.	Pen.
Mitch Messier	F	Sr.	45	44	48	92	89
Kevin Miller	F	Jr.	45	25	56	81	63
Bill Shibicky	C	Sr.	42	43	36	78	100
Kip Miller	F	Fr.	45	22	20	42	94
Brian McReynolds	F	So.	45	16	25	41	68
Brad Hamilton	D	So.	45	3	29	32	54
Don McSween	D	Sr.	45	7	23	30	34
Bruce Rendall	F	So.	44	11	14	25	113
Danton Cole	F	So.	44	9	15	24	16
Tom Tilley	D	Jr.	42	7	14	21	48
Chris Luongo	D	So.	27	4	16	20	38
Mike O'Toole	F	Fr.	43	2	13	15	74
Dave Arkeilpane	F	Sr.	42	6	8	14	20
Sean Clement	D	Jr.	41	3	11	14	70
Geir Hoff	F	So.	38	3	9	12	54
Steve Beadle	D	Fr.	38	0	9	9	12
Neil Wilkinson	D	Fr.	19	3	4	7	18
Don Gibson	D	Fr.	43	3	3	6	74
Norm Foster	G	Sr.	24	0	2	2	4
Dave McAuliffe	F	Fr.	10	0	1	1	0
Jim Lycett	D	Fr.	19	0	1	1	4
Bob Essensa	G	Sr.	25	0	1	1	0

Michigan Technological University
Overall: 11-28-1; WCHA: 11-23-1

	Pos.	Class	Games	G.	A.	Pts.	Pen.
Ally Cook	F	Sr.	39	13	29	42	22
John Archibald	F	Jr.	37	19	20	39	18
Brian Hannon	F	Sr.	38	19	18	37	34
Tom Bissett	F	So.	40	16	19	35	12
Todd Decker	F	Fr.	38	10	15	25	38

	Pos.	Class	Games	G.	A.	Pts.	Pen.
Randy Oswald	D	Sr.	39	3	17	20	67
Scott White	D	So.	36	4	15	19	58
Randy McKay	F	Jr.	39	5	11	16	46
Jim Carroll	F	Fr.	31	11	4	15	40
Shawn Harrison	F	Fr.	29	7	8	15	35
Kevin Fritz	F	Sr.	39	6	6	12	22
Ron Rolston	F	Fr.	37	4	8	12	26
Don Porter	F	Sr.	36	7	3	10	42
Kip Noble	D	Fr.	33	2	6	8	33
Marc Colvin	F	Jr.	27	2	4	6	26
Tom Hussey	F	Jr.	11	1	2	3	38
Charlie Henrich	D	Fr.	23	0	3	3	24
Jim Rokala	F	Fr.	12	1	1	2	10
Jeff St. Cyr	D	Fr.	38	0	2	2	82
Frank Furlan	G	Fr.	11	0	1	1	2
Kelly Murphy	D	Jr.	14	0	1	1	14
Steve Wendorf	D	So.	19	0	1	1	16
Russ Becker	D	Jr.	27	0	1	1	46

University of Minnesota
Overall: 34-14-1; WCHA: 25-9-1

	Pos.	Class	Games	G.	A.	Pts.	Pen.
Corey Millen	F	Jr.	42	36	29	65	62
Steve MacSwain	F	Jr.	48	31	29	60	24
Dave Snuggerud	F	Fr.	39	30	29	59	38
Todd Richards	D	Fr.	49	8	43	51	70
Gary Shopek	D	Jr.	46	12	31	43	71
Tom Chorske	F	Fr.	47	20	22	42	20
Jay Cates	F	So.	47	18	22	40	58
Paul Broten	F	So.	48	17	22	39	52
Tim Bergland	F	Jr.	49	18	17	35	48
Phil Hankinson	F	Fr.	43	16	12	28	10
David Grannis	F	So.	46	10	12	22	32
Gary Bloom	F	Fr.	44	6	11	17	28
Steve Orth	F	So.	37	8	7	15	18
Randy Skarda	D	Fr.	43	3	10	13	77
David Espe	D	Fr.	45	4	8	12	28
Eric Dornfeld	D	Jr.	45	3	8	11	53
Tony Pitlick	D	Fr.	45	0	9	9	88
Marty Nanne	F	Fr.	31	3	4	7	41
Todd Okerlund	F	Jr.	4	0	7	7	0
Craig Mack	D	Jr.	20	1	5	6	24
John Blue	G	So.	33	0	6	6	6
Tom Strot	F	Fr.	13	1	3	4	0
John May	F	Fr.	10	2	1	3	0
Eric Rude	F	Fr.	6	1	1	2	2
Mike Luckraft	D	Fr.	10	0	2	2	6
Peter Paulett	D	Fr.	4	0	1	1	0
Barry Nelson	F	Jr.	12	0	1	1	8
Robert Stauber	G	Fr.	20	0	1	1	2

University of Minnesota-Duluth
Overall: 11-27-1; WCHA: 11-23-1

	Pos.	Class	Games	G.	A.	Pts.	Pen.
Sean Toomey	F	Sr.	39	26	17	43	34
Brian Johnson	F	Sr.	39	20	20	40	14
Skeeter Moore	F	Sr.	39	15	25	40	48
Mike DeAngelis	D	Jr.	39	4	16	20	12
Jim Sprenger	D	Sr.	39	5	14	19	30
Bob Alexander	F	Jr.	37	12	6	18	40
Barry Chyzowski	F	Fr.	39	5	11	16	16
Guy Gosselin	D	Sr.	33	7	8	15	66
Dave Cowan	F	Sr.	31	2	9	11	24
Darin Illikainen	F	Jr.	32	5	4	9	20
Joe DeLisle	F	Jr.	38	4	4	8	60
Dan Tousignant	F	Fr.	27	3	3	6	22
Sandy Smith	F	Fr.	35	3	3	6	26
Tom Lorentz	F	So.	22	4	1	5	14
Dale Jago	D	Fr.	33	1	4	5	14
Pat Scanlon	F	Fr.	22	2	2	4	14

	Pos.	Class	Games	G.	A.	Pts.	Pen.
Bruce Fishback	F	Sr.	18	1	3	4	6
Tom Hanson	D	So.	25	0	4	4	12
Terry Shold	F	So.	11	1	1	2	2
Georg Thiele	F	Fr.	12	1	1	2	2
Rob Pallin	D	So.	10	0	2	2	4
Dennis Vaske	D	Fr.	33	0	2	2	40
John Hyduke	G	So.	2	0	1	1	2
Rick Hayko	G	So.	4	0	1	1	0
Ross Johnson	F	Fr.	18	0	1	1	6
Pat Janostin	D	So.	22	0	1	1	8

University of New Hampshire

Overall: 8-27-3; Hockey East: 5-24-3

	Pos.	Class	Games	G.	A.	Pts.	Pen.
James Richmond	F	Sr.	37	16	29	45	45
Steve Horner	F	So.	33	19	17	36	14
Tim Hanley	F	Jr.	37	11	23	34	34
David Aiken	F	Fr.	37	19	9	28	10
Jeff Lazaro	D	Fr.	38	7	14	21	38
Tim Shields	F	So.	34	11	8	19	8
Mike Rossetti	F	Jr.	23	9	10	19	46
Quintin Brinkley	F	Jr.	38	6	12	18	8
Dan Prachar	F	So.	35	7	7	14	29
Mark Johnson	F	Fr.	38	4	9	13	4
Chris Laganas	F	Sr.	33	5	6	11	8
Allister Brown	D	Sr.	33	0	10	10	38
Rick Lambert	F	Jr.	34	1	5	6	63
Kevin Schrader	D	So.	27	1	4	5	16
Chris Grassie	F	Fr.	27	0	5	5	18
Jeff Cournoyer	D	So.	26	1	3	4	14
Mike Roth	D	So.	22	1	2	3	11
Greg Boudreau	D	So.	31	0	3	3	41
Mark Dorval	F	So.	23	1	1	2	7
Mike Glennon	F	Jr.	16	0	2	2	20
Greg Rota	G	Sr.	34	0	1	1	8

University of North Dakota

Overall: 40-8-0; WCHA: 29-6-0

	Pos.	Class	Games	G.	A.	Pts.	Pen.
Tony Hrkac	F	So.	48	46	70	116	48
Bob Joyce	F	Jr.	48	52	37	89	42
Steve Johnson	F	Jr.	48	26	44	70	38
Ian Kidd	D	So.	47	13	47	60	58
Mickey Krampotich	F	Sr.	47	27	27	54	18
Scott Koberinski	F	So.	48	19	27	46	34
Malcolm Parks	F	Sr.	48	18	21	39	50
Lee Davidson	F	Fr.	41	16	12	28	65
Perry Nakonechny	F	Sr.	43	6	14	20	42
Tom Benson	D	Jr.	47	0	20	20	80
Scott Dub	F	Jr.	46	11	8	19	81
Brent Bobyck	F	Fr.	46	8	11	19	16
Mike LaMoine	D	So.	47	2	17	19	36
Russ Parent	D	Fr.	47	2	17	19	50
Grant Paranica	F	So.	42	5	10	15	38
Murray Baron	D	Fr.	41	4	10	14	62
Jeff Bowen	F	Sr.	45	5	8	13	42
Tarek Howard	D	Sr.	32	1	9	10	38
Bill Claviter	F	Sr.	20	2	2	4	10
Darryn Fossand	D	Fr.	16	1	2	3	8
Ed Belfour	G	Fr.	34	0	2	2	6
Scott Brickey	F	Fr.	5	0	1	1	4
Gary Kaiser	D	So.	9	0	1	1	18
Scott Brower	G	Jr.	15	0	1	1	4

Northeastern University

Overall: 13-21-3; Hockey East: 11-18-3

	Pos.	Class	Games	G.	A.	Pts.	Pen.
David O'Brien	F	Jr.	35	16	24	40	12
Kevin Heffernan	F	Jr.	36	14	22	36	30

	Pos.	Class	Games	G.	A.	Pts.	Pen.
Greg Pratt	F	Sr.	37	17	18	35	20
Dave Buda	F	So.	37	15	15	30	32
Harry Mews	F	Fr.	29	10	15	25	70
Claude Lodin	D	Jr.	27	2	23	25	33
Brian Dowd	D	Jr.	34	8	13	21	40
Tom Bivona	F	Fr.	37	8	9	17	28
Rico Rossi	F	So.	33	9	7	16	118
Joe MacInnis	F	Jr.	29	7	8	15	33
Andy May	F	Fr.	36	4	8	12	25
Roman Kinal	F	Sr.	26	5	5	10	17
Bill Whitfield	D	Sr.	36	2	6	8	6
Tom Mutch	F	Fr.	31	3	4	7	24
Martin Raus	D	So.	26	0	7	7	24
Mike McDougall	F	Jr.	31	1	5	6	29
Steve Schofield	D	So.	20	2	3	5	8
Gerry Kiley	D	Sr.	31	0	5	5	40
John Ridpath	D	Jr.	12	2	2	4	8
Jay Valade	F	So.	19	1	3	4	6
Bruce Racine	G	Jr.	32	0	2	2	0
Marty Haidy	F	Fr.	5	1	0	1	2
Jim O'Shaughnessy	F	So.	12	1	0	1	2
Chris Cunniff	F	Fr.	17	1	0	1	4
Peter Massey	F	So.	16	0	1	1	6

Northern Michigan University
Overall: 18-21-1; WCHA: 16-18-1

	Pos.	Class	Games	G.	A.	Pts.	Pen.
Gary Emmons	F	Sr.	35	32	34	66	59
Ron Chyzowski	F	Sr.	39	15	22	37	35
Kory Wright	F	Sr.	36	11	14	25	22
Darryl Olsen	D	So.	37	5	20	25	96
Joe West	F	Sr.	15	11	12	23	28
Dave Porter	F	Fr.	39	10	12	22	20
Phil Berger	F	So.	24	11	10	21	6
Tony Savarin	D	Jr.	36	7	14	21	30
Rod Poindexter	F	Jr.	37	10	10	20	37
Eric Lemarque	F	Fr.	38	5	12	17	49
Dave Moree	D	Sr.	33	1	16	17	32
Ralph Vos	F	Sr.	18	4	12	16	18
John Goode	D	So.	39	2	13	15	59
Mark Lanigan	D	Jr.	34	2	9	11	46
Phil Brown	F	Fr.	31	2	8	10	20
Jeff Gawlicki	F	Fr.	37	7	2	9	61
Dean Hall	D	Fr.	20	4	5	9	16
Troy Jacobsen	F	So.	27	2	7	9	24
Pete Podrasky	D	Fr.	34	2	7	9	12
Brad Werenka	D	Fr.	30	4	4	8	35
Glen Hartley	F	Sr.	29	3	5	8	11
Doug Garrow	F	Fr.	22	1	1	2	26
Dennis Jiannaras	G	Sr.	15	0	2	2	0
Cris Kleven	D	Fr.	9	0	1	1	0

University of Notre Dame
Overall: 10-19-1

	Pos.	Class	Games	G.	A.	Pts.	Pen.
Mike McNeill	F	Jr.	30	21	16	37	24
Tim Kuehl	F	Fr.	30	14	14	28	38
Matt Hanzel	F	So.	25	10	15	25	2
Tom Mooney	F	Jr.	30	9	14	23	42
Kevin Markovitz	D	Fr.	30	3	18	21	32
Pat Foley	D	Jr.	30	6	11	17	36
Bruce Guay	F	Fr.	29	7	8	15	39
Robert Bilton	F	So.	30	7	6	13	12
Rich Sobilo	F	Sr.	28	5	8	13	10
Robert Herber	F	So.	28	5	7	12	20
Lance Patten	D	Jr.	30	2	8	10	50
Tom Smith	F	So.	19	2	7	9	28
Tim Caddo	D	So.	26	2	4	6	12
Roy Bemiss	D	So.	24	2	3	5	53
Frank O'Brien	D	Jr.	27	1	4	5	22

	Pos.	Class	Games	G.	A.	Pts.	Pen.
John Nickodemus	F	Sr.	27	2	2	4	12
Michael Leherr	D	Fr.	29	2	2	4	26
Brian Montgomery	F	So.	21	1	2	3	8
Tom Fitzgerald	F	So.	15	2	0	2	2
Bruce Haikola	D	Fr.	11	1	0	1	0
John Welsch	F	Jr.	29	0	1	1	4

Ohio State University
Overall: 19-23-1; CCHA: 12-19-1

	Pos.	Class	Games	G.	A.	Pts.	Pen.
Rick Brebant	F	Jr.	42	35	51	86	50
Jeff Madill	F	Jr.	43	38	32	70	139
Mark Anderson	F	Jr.	43	21	26	47	74
Andy Forcey	F	So.	38	15	26	41	68
Derek Higdon	F	Fr.	42	13	20	33	79
Darcy Gryba	F	Jr.	42	14	17	31	34
Scott Syring	D	Sr.	43	5	22	27	74
Dave Beaudin	F	Sr.	36	5	19	24	58
Joe Tracy	F	Sr.	37	8	13	21	49
Scott Rex	D	Fr.	35	3	17	20	101
Steve Harder	F	Fr.	40	10	9	19	14
Doug Claggett	D	Jr.	43	4	10	14	20
Daryn Fersovich	F	So.	43	4	9	13	18
Sean Clifford	D	So.	42	3	8	11	107
Dan Wilhelm	F	So.	40	4	6	10	30
Don Rothgery	F	Sr.	43	4	5	9	79
Tom Wisloff	F	So.	38	3	6	9	26
Henry Dunn	D	Fr.	41	1	6	7	39

Princeton University
Overall: 8-17-1; ECAC: 7-14-1

	Pos.	Class	Games	G.	A.	Pts.	Pen.
John Messuri	F	So.	26	17	21	38	51
Greg Polaski	F	Fr.	26	21	13	34	10
Jaimie MacPherson	D	Sr.	26	5	20	25	16
Scott Howe	D	Sr.	26	3	21	24	59
Bart Blaeser	F	Fr.	25	8	15	23	16
Tim Driscoll	F	Sr.	26	9	7	16	44
John Rocco	F	Sr.	25	3	10	13	16
Jim Sourges	F	Fr.	26	2	9	11	6
Kelly Szautner	F	Jr.	25	6	1	7	14
Dave Umland	F	Jr.	25	3	3	6	16
Lenny Quesnelle	D	Jr.	26	1	3	4	6
Nate Smith	D	Fr.	25	0	3	3	10
Chris Hughes	F	So.	23	1	1	2	10
Todd Dow	F	Fr.	23	0	2	2	8
Ward Welles	F	Fr.	15	1	0	1	0
Kevin Sullivan	F	Fr.	25	1	0	1	10
Bill Brady	F	Sr.	2	0	1	1	6
Mark Khozozian	F	Fr.	25	0	1	1	14
John Allen	D	Jr.	26	0	1	1	32

Providence College
Overall: 7-23-3; Hockey East 7-22-3

	Pos.	Class	Games	G.	A.	Pts.	Pen.
Gord Cruickshank	F	Jr.	31	27	18	45	38
Rick Bennett	F	Fr.	32	15	12	27	34
Andy Mattice	F	Fr.	33	13	14	27	26
Tom Fitzgerald	F	Fr.	27	8	14	22	22
Shawn Whitham	D	Jr.	31	9	11	20	57
Andy Calcione	F	Sr.	30	4	9	13	16
Terry Sullivan	F	Sr.	33	6	5	11	16
Luke Vitale	F	So.	32	4	7	11	14
Jeff Serowik	D	Fr.	33	3	8	11	22
Jim Hughes	D	So.	21	2	8	10	31
John Butterworth	F	So.	25	4	3	7	32

	Pos.	Class	Games	G.	A.	Pts.	Pen.
Perry Florio	D	So.	23	1	6	7	58
Lance Nelson	F	Sr.	31	1	6	7	34
Jay Guden	F	Fr.	33	4	2	6	22
Joe DiGiacomo	D	Fr.	31	2	3	5	16
Todd Whittemore	F	Fr.	29	1	4	5	12
Mike Flanagan	D	Sr.	25	1	2	3	18
Steve Higgins	D	Fr.	31	0	3	3	8
Paul Saundercook	D	Fr.	32	1	1	2	21
Matt Merten	G	Fr.	24	0	1	1	4

Rensselaer Polytechnic Institute
Overall: 13-18-2; ECAC: 9-13-0

	Pos.	Class	Games	G.	A.	Pts.	Pen.
Brian Ferreira	F	Fr.	30	19	17	36	24
Tony Hejna	F	Fr.	33	12	18	30	18
Neil Hernberg	F	Sr.	33	14	13	27	54
Denis Poissant	F	Fr.	33	6	18	24	20
Bill Kopecky	F	Jr.	32	13	9	22	29
Chris Walsh	F	Jr.	29	12	10	22	16
Terry Butryn	F	Sr.	31	10	12	22	28
Trini Iturralde	F	Sr.	31	8	13	21	37
Mike Robinson	D	Sr.	33	6	15	21	53
Steve Moore	D	So.	32	3	16	19	47
Derek DeCosty	F	Fr.	29	3	11	14	50
Bill Flanagan	F	Fr.	24	4	8	12	18
Maurice Mansi	F	Jr.	22	3	7	10	19
Rob Schena	D	So.	32	1	9	10	34
Graeme Townshend	F	So.	31	7	1	8	56
Shannon Mulligan	F	Fr.	12	1	7	8	8
Jim Kropp	F	So.	22	1	4	5	12
Paul Frazier	F	Fr.	12	2	1	3	6
Arik Mathison	F	Fr.	11	1	2	3	10
Kevin Mazzella	F	Fr.	5	2	0	2	4
Rod Brescia	D	So.	13	0	2	2	20
Ryan Kummu	D	So.	20	0	2	2	34
Ken DeCubellis	D	Fr.	16	0	1	1	16
Matt Lanza	D	Fr.	18	0	1	1	31

St. Lawrence University
Overall: 24-11-0; ECAC: 15-7-0

	Pos.	Class	Games	G.	A.	Pts.	Pen.
Pete Lappin	F	Jr.	35	34	25	59	32
Dave Saunders	F	Sr.	34	18	34	52	44
Tim Lappin	F	Jr.	33	12	29	41	44
Gary Robertson	F	So.	33	16	16	32	24
Jamie Baker	F	So.	32	8	24	32	59
Rick Mulligan	F	Sr.	33	17	13	30	12
Brian McColgan	D	Jr.	34	3	21	24	26
Mike Hurlbut	D	So.	35	8	15	23	44
Pete McGeough	F/D	Jr.	30	7	14	21	90
Joe Day	F	Fr.	33	9	11	20	25
Hank Lammens	D	Jr.	35	6	13	19	92
Brad McKee	F	Jr.	28	9	8	17	49
Dave Witherall	F	So.	31	7	9	16	20
Russ Mann	D	So.	34	2	14	16	30
Doug Murray	F	Fr.	33	1	14	15	12
Mike Palletier	F	So.	21	6	8	14	20
Martyn Ball	F	Fr.	31	11	2	13	14
Rob White	D	Fr.	30	2	9	11	52
Kevin Wright	F	Fr.	28	4	4	8	8
Joe McEachern	D	Jr.	15	0	5	5	8
Steve Torkos	D	Fr.	2	0	1	1	0

United States International University
Overall: 17-17-1

	Pos.	Class	Games	G.	A.	Pts.	Pen.
Gary Bernard	F	Sr.	34	26	17	43	43
Jeff Dobek	F	Jr.	28	14	28	42	10

	Pos.	Class	Games	G.	A.	Pts.	Pen.
Jim Hau	F	Fr.	30	18	18	36	18
David Nash	F	Jr.	31	11	23	34	56
Mike McGrath	D	Sr.	35	10	22	32	81
Darren Clarkin	D	Sr.	34	7	22	29	62
Tom Genz	F	Jr.	28	11	16	27	10
Dewey Wahlin	D	Fr.	34	7	12	19	42
Mike Castellano	D	So.	35	6	11	17	89
Joe Schwartz	F	Fr.	35	9	7	16	53
Rick Swarbrick	F	Sr.	31	7	9	16	26
Blake Jurgens	F	Fr.	33	5	8	13	6
Brad Fenton	F	Fr.	33	6	6	12	12
Troy Buder	F	Jr.	23	4	7	11	27
Matt Shaw	D	So.	33	2	8	10	55
John Christofilos	F	Jr.	25	3	6	9	14
Peter Stensgard	F	Jr.	26	5	3	8	14
Matt Lundgren	F	Jr.	35	3	5	8	24
Chris Sonnesyn	D	So.	35	0	6	6	18
Joe Purtell	F	Fr.	8	1	2	3	0
Jim Plankers	D	Sr.	19	0	2	2	34
Jim Wilharm	D	So.	19	0	1	1	6
Gary Shepherd	G	Sr.	27	0	1	1	2
Rob Watson	G	Sr.	9	0	1	1	0

University of Vermont
Overall: 18-14-0; ECAC:12-10-0

	Pos.	Class	Games	G.	A.	Pts.	Pen.
Jeff Capello	F	Sr.	32	17	26	43	56
Kyle McDonough	F	So.	32	28	12	40	44
Shannon Deegan	F	Sr.	29	19	21	40	44
Ian Boyce	F	So.	32	8	23	31	30
Jim Purcell	F	Sr.	32	7	15	22	44
Toby Ducolon	F	Jr.	32	9	11	20	42
Jim Walsh	F	So.	32	7	7	14	26
Marc Lebreux	D	So.	12	4	8	12	10
Jerry Tarrant	F	So.	32	3	9	12	34
Dan Lambert	F	So.	32	7	4	11	8
Dave Weber	D	Fr.	28	3	8	11	25
Paul Seguin	D	Jr.	32	3	6	9	57
Jeff Schulman	D	So.	29	1	8	9	14
Bill Butler	D	Fr.	32	0	7	7	14
Richard Laplante	F	Jr.	3	2	4	6	6
Jeff Smith	F	Sr.	24	1	5	6	6
Rob Bateman	D	Fr.	32	2	3	5	78
Dennis Miller	D	So.	32	1	4	5	40
Brian McLaughlin	F	So.	15	0	4	4	4
Cory Bilodeau	D	Fr.	24	2	1	3	0
Joe Gervais	D	Jr.	22	1	2	3	14
Craig Staff	F	Sr.	5	0	1	1	0
Tom Draper	G	Sr.	27	0	1	1	0

Western Michigan University
Overall: 23-20-0; CCHA: 16-16-0

	Pos.	Class	Games	G.	A.	Pts.	Pen.
Wayne Gagne	D	Sr.	43	13	76	89	38
Rob Bryden	F	Sr.	43	46	32	78	82
Paul Polillo	F	Fr.	42	18	48	66	35
Jeff Green	F	Fr.	43	28	29	57	54
Henry Fung	F	Sr.	35	20	25	45	52
Mike Posma	D	Fr.	35	12	31	43	42
Bill Armstrong	F	Fr.	43	13	20	33	86
Jim Culhane	D	Sr.	43	9	24	33	163
Pat Ryan	F	Sr.	42	11	13	24	37
Shane Redshaw	F	Fr.	38	14	8	22	102
Andy Rymsha	F	Fr.	41	7	12	19	122
Ron Hoover	F	So.	34	7	10	17	22
Jeff Pack	D	Fr.	30	2	13	15	20
Eddie Smith	F	So.	34	5	5	10	72
Doug Melnyk	D	Fr.	43	2	7	9	40
Jeff Kick	F	Jr.	33	3	5	8	8

	Pos.	Class	Games	G.	A.	Pts.	Pen.
Scott Howe	D	Jr.	22	2	6	8	38
Lee Brodeur	F	Jr.	25	3	3	6	8
Dave Lobdell	D	Jr.	41	2	4	6	34
Todd Dries	F	Fr.	16	1	1	2	16
Bill Horn	G	So.	36	0	2	2	14
Rich Whitten	F	Fr.	20	1	0	1	2

University of Wisconsin
Overall: 23-18-1; WCHA: 17-17-1

	Pos.	Class	Games	G.	A.	Pts.	Pen.
Tony Granato	F	Sr.	42	28	45	73	64
Paul Ranheim	F	Jr.	42	24	35	59	54
Steve Tuttle	F	Jr.	42	31	21	52	14
Chris Tancill	F	Fr.	40	9	23	32	26
Gary Shuchuk	F	Fr.	42	19	11	30	72
Shaun Sabol	D	Fr.	40	7	16	23	98
Paul Stanton	D	So.	41	5	17	22	70
Todd Geisness	F	Sr.	40	9	6	15	20
Glenn Revak	F	Jr.	39	7	7	14	4
Pat Ford	F	Jr.	32	5	9	14	62
Bob Mendel	D	Fr.	42	1	7	8	26
Tony Scheid	F	Jr.	23	4	3	7	0
Garry Bunz	D	Jr.	35	0	7	7	134
Andy Akervik	F	So.	18	3	3	6	4
John Byce	F	So.	40	1	4	5	12
Tom Sagissor	F	Fr.	41	1	4	5	32
Paul Graveline	F	Sr.	33	2	2	4	19
Kurt Semandel	D	So.	37	1	3	4	20
Ken MacKenzie	D	Jr.	22	0	4	4	28
Steve Rohlik	F	Fr.	31	3	0	3	34
Greg Poss	D	So.	20	0	2	2	12
Eric Faust	D	Sr.	5	0	1	1	12
John Parker	F	Fr.	8	0	1	1	4
Mike Richter	G	So.	36	0	1	1	0

Yale University
Overall: 15-12-3; ECAC: 14-7-1

	Pos.	Class	Games	G.	A.	Pts.	Pen.
Bob Kudelski	F	Sr.	30	25	22	47	34
Julian Binavince	F	So.	29	11	15	26	30
David Baseggio	D	So.	29	8	17	25	52
Adam Snow	F	Sr.	30	8	17	25	18
Rich Geist	F	Sr.	28	9	14	23	41
Rob Baseggio	D	Jr.	30	4	18	22	66
David Tanner	F	Jr.	30	10	11	21	20
Scott D'Orsi	F	Fr.	30	4	9	15	30
Tom Walsh	F	So.	12	4	8	12	30
Billy Matthews	D	Fr.	29	2	5	7	20
John Moore	F	So.	30	4	2	6	38
Bill Zito	F	Sr.	29	3	3	6	58
Greg Harrison	D	Fr.	30	2	4	6	26
Erik O'Borsky	F	Fr.	27	1	5	6	24
Eric Thieringer	D	So.	15	0	4	4	20
Ralph Russo	D	Jr.	24	0	3	3	10
Tony Maxwell	F	Sr.	19	2	0	2	4
Greg Seitz	F	Fr.	12	1	1	2	2
Tom Dea	F	Sr.	28	1	1	2	20
Tom Bachner	F	So.	6	0	1	1	0
Scott Sarbacker	D	Jr.	20	0	1	1	16

COLLEGIATE GOALTENDING RECORDS

AIR FORCE ACADEMY	G.	W.	L.	T.	Min.	Goals	Avg.
John Moes	21	13	6	0	1163	67	3.46
Jack Sundstrom	14	4	4	0	480	36	4.50
(ARMY) U.S. MILITARY	G.	W.	L.	T.	Min.	Goals	Avg.
Paul DeGironimo	26	9	16	1	1485	104	4.20
Corey Averill	8	0	3	0	259	20	4.63
Jon Staples	2	0	0	0	24	4	10.00

BOSTON COLLEGE	G.	W.	L.	T.	Min.	Goals	Avg.
David Littman	21	15	5	0	1182	68	3.45
Shaun Real	20	16	3	0	1110	69	3.72
Jeff Walker	9	0	0	0	75	6	4.80
BOSTON UNIVERSITY	G.	W.	L.	T.	Min.	Goals	Avg.
Peter Fish	5	4	1	0	285	17	3.58
Bob Deraney	12	5	4	2	715	45	3.78
Terry Taillefer	22	10	10	1	1260	82	3.90
BOWLING GREEN STATE UNIVERSITY	G.	W.	L.	T.	Min.	Goals	Avg.
Gary Kruzich	36	28	7	2	1564	123	3.31
Paul Connell	7	4	1	0	324	23	4.26
BROWN UNIVERSITY	G.	W.	L.	T.	Min.	Goals	Avg.
Chris Harvey	22	9	13	0	1241	88	4.26
Michel Bayard	8	1	2	0	332	33	5.96
Dominic Alfonso	1	1	0	0	60	6	6.00
CLARKSON UNIVERSITY	G.	W.	L.	T.	Min.	Goals	Avg.
John Fletcher	23	11	8	1	1240	62	3.00
Jason Poirier	12	6	5	0	595	34	3.43
Erik Baker	1	0	0	0	20	4	12.00
COLGATE UNIVERSITY	G.	W.	L.	T.	Min.	Goals	Avg.
Wayne Cowley	31	21	8	1	1805	106	3.52
Scott Luce	3	2	1	0	152	10	3.94
COLORADO COLLEGE	G.	W.	L.	T.	Min.	Goals	Avg.
Derek Pizzey	33	14	19	0	1963	120	3.67
Matt Gilbreath	11	3	5	1	604	52	5.16
CORNELL UNIVERSITY	G.	W.	L.	T.	Min.	Goals	Avg.
Jim Edmands	18	7	7	0	953	60	3.78
Don Fawcett	3	1	2	0	138	9	3.91
Darin McInnis	9	3	6	0	522	41	4.71
Wayne Skelton	1	0	1	0	20	4	12.00
DARTMOUTH COLLEGE	G.	W.	L.	T.	Min.	Goals	Avg.
Tim Osby	12	2	8	1	622	46	4.44
Steve Laurin	15	0	14	0	883	75	5.09
Jeff Bower	1	0	0	0	24	5	12.50
UNIVERSITY OF DENVER	G.	W.	L.	T.	Min.	Goals	Avg.
Chris Olson	22	10	11	1	1327	92	4.16
Chris Gillies	19	9	7	2	1118	78	4.19
FERRIS STATE COLLEGE	G.	W.	L.	T.	Min.	Goals	Avg.
Glenn Raeburn	32	12	18	0	1738	128	4.42
Mike Williams	17	4	9	0	846	65	4.61
HARVARD UNIVERSITY	G.	W.	L.	T.	Min.	Goals	Avg.
Dickie McEvoy	24	19	5	0	1460	54	2.22
John Devin	10	9	1	0	600	23	2.30
UNIVERSITY OF ILLINOIS-CHICAGO	G.	W.	L.	T.	Min.	Goals	Avg.
Brad Ryan	15	8	5	1	865	46	3.19
Dave DePinto	17	9	7	0	955	64	4.02
Jim Hickey	10	4	5	0	552	44	4.78
LAKE SUPERIOR STATE	G.	W.	L.	T.	Min.	Goals	Avg.
Mike Greenlay	17	7	5	0	744	44	3.54
Randy Exelby	28	12	9	1	1357	91	4.02
Joe Shawhan	7	3	2	1	337	24	4.28
UNIVERSITY OF LOWELL	G.	W.	L.	T.	Min.	Goals	Avg.
Ken Stein	13	7	4	0	642	44	4.11
Dave Delfino	24	14	6	1	1281	88	4.12
Peter Harris	6	1	2	1	279	22	4.73
UNIVERSITY OF MAINE	G.	W.	L.	T.	Min.	Goals	Avg.
Scott King	21	11	6	1	1111	58	3.13
Al Loring	25	13	10	1	1448	90	3.73
MIAMI (O.) UNIVERSITY	G.	W.	L.	T.	Min.	Goals	Avg.
Steve McKichan	28	3	19	0	1351	130	5.77
Brent Smith	22	5	12	0	983	99	6.04
UNIVERSITY OF MICHIGAN	G.	W.	L.	T.	Min.	Goals	Avg.
Warren Sharples	32	12	16	1	1728	148	5.14
Glen Neery	12	1	9	0	573	55	5.76
Mike Rossi	3	0	0	0	29	3	6.14
Tim Makris	5	1	0	0	86	10	7.01

MICHIGAN STATE UNIVERSITY	G.	W.	L.	T.	Min.	Goals	Avg.
Bob Essensa	25	19	3	1	1383	64	2.78
Norm Foster	24	14	7	1	1383	90	3.90
MICHIGAN TECHNOLOGICAL UNIV.	G.	W.	L.	T.	Min.	Goals	Avg.
Dave Roach	30	10	18	1	1811	151	5.00
Frank Furlan	11	1	10	0	623	66	6.36
UNIVERSITY OF MINNESOTA	G.	W.	L.	T.	Min.	Goals	Avg.
John Blue	33	21	9	1	1889	99	3.14
Robert Stauber	20	13	5	0	1072	63	3.53
UNIVERSITY OF MINNESOTA-DULUTH	G.	W.	L.	T.	Min.	Goals	Avg.
John Hyduke	23	7	15	0	1359	99	4.37
Gordy Meahger	9	3	5	0	497	37	4.47
Mike Cortes	5	1	3	1	261	20	4.60
Rick Hayko	4	0	4	0	240	26	6.50
UNIVERSITY OF NEW HAMPSHIRE	G.	W.	L.	T.	Min.	Goals	Avg.
Greg Rota	34	7	22	3	1937	160	4.96
Denver Moorehead	2	0	1	0	80	11	8.25
UNIVERSITY OF NORTH DAKOTA	G.	W.	L.	T.	Min.	Goals	Avg.
Ed Belfour	34	29	4	0	2049	81	2.37
Scott Brower	15	11	4	0	803	44	3.29
Greg Strome	3	0	0	0	40	4	6.00
NORTHEASTERN UNIVERSITY	G.	W.	L.	T.	Min.	Goals	Avg.
Mike Errico	2	1	1	0	62	4	3.87
Bruce Racine	33	12	18	3	1966	133	4.06
Ken Baum	4	0	1	0	100	10	6.00
Dave Pecarara	4	1	1	0	137	15	6.57
NORTHERN MICHIGAN UNIVERSITY	G.	W.	L.	T.	Min.	Goals	Avg.
Mike Jeffrey	28	13	12	1	1601	102	3.82
Dennis Jiannaras	15	5	9	0	835	57	4.09
UNIVERSITY OF NOTRE DAME	G.	W.	L.	T.	Min.	Goals	Avg.
Jeff Henderson	6	3	2	1	370	17	2.76
Tim Lukenda	7	2	5	0	384	25	3.90
Lance Madson	18	5	12	0	1096	76	4.16
OHIO STATE UNIVERSITY	G.	W.	L.	T.	Min.	Goals	Avg.
Todd Fanning	24	11	10	1	1276	97	4.56
Roger Beedon	24	8	13	1	1322	114	5.17
PRINCETON UNIVERSITY	G.	W.	L.	T.	Min.	Goals	Avg.
Dave Shea	17	6	10	0	992	53	3.21
Dave Marotta	10	2	7	1	603	50	4.97
PROVIDENCE COLLEGE	G.	W.	L.	T.	Min.	Goals	Avg.
Matt Merten	24	6	14	2	1455	104	4.29
Mark Romaine	5	1	3	1	289	25	5.19
Ed Walsh	7	0	6	0	290	32	6.62
RENSSELAER POLYTECHNIC INSTITUTE	G.	W.	L.	T.	Min.	Goals	Avg.
Gavin Armstrong	26	11	13	1	1388	79	3.42
Steve Duncan	11	2	2	1	398	21	3.16
Shawn Sarbacker	4	0	2	0	126	6	2.85
ST. LAWRENCE UNIVERSITY	G.	W.	L.	T.	Min.	Goals	Avg.
Scott Yearwood	24	13	10	0	1465	72	2.94
Paul Cohen	14	11	1	0	639	42	3.94
UNITED STATES INTERNATIONAL U.	G.	W.	L.	T.	Min.	Goals	Avg.
Gary Shepherd	27	11	13	1	1488	88	3.55
Rob Watson	9	3	2	0	357	22	3.70
Dana Orent	5	3	2	0	280	25	5.36
VERMONT UNIVERSITY	G.	W.	L.	T.	Min.	Goals	Avg.
Phil Marrandette	1	0	0	0	20	1	3.00
Tom Draper	29	16	13	0	1662	96	3.47
Elias Delany	10	2	1	0	250	23	5.52
WESTERN MICHIGAN UNIVERSITY	G.	W.	L.	T.	Min.	Goals	Avg.
Bill Horn	36	19	16	0	2065	139	3.95
Kevin McCaffrey	12	4	4	0	539	48	5.36
UNIVERSITY OF WISCONSIN	G.	W.	L.	T.	Min.	Goals	Avg.
Mike Richter	36	19	16	1	2136	126	3.53
Dean Anderson	9	4	2	0	409	27	3.96
YALE UNIVERSITY	G.	W.	L.	T.	Min.	Goals	Avg.
Michael O'Neill	16	9	6	1	964	55	3.42
Mike Schwalb	14	6	6	2	857	58	4.06

National Hockey League Schedule
1987-88

*Denotes afternoon game.

THURSDAY, OCTOBER 8

Washington at Boston
Quebec at Hartford
Minnesota at Buffalo
Montreal at Philadelphia
New York Islanders at Los Angeles
Pittsburgh at New York Rangers
Toronto at Chicago
Detroit at Calgary
St. Louis at Vancouver

FRIDAY, OCTOBER 9

Pittsburgh at New Jersey
Detroit at Edmonton

SATURDAY, OCTOBER 10

Boston at Quebec
New York Rangers at Hartford
Buffalo at Montreal
New York Islanders at Vancouver
New Jersey at Toronto
Philadelphia at Minnesota
Chicago at Washington
St. Louis at Los Angeles
Winnipeg at Calgary

SUNDAY, OCTOBER 11

Hartford at Boston
Washington at Buffalo
Philadelphia at Chicago
Edmonton at Los Angeles

MONDAY, OCTOBER 12

Quebec at Montreal
Minnesota at New York Rangers
Detroit at Vancouver
Calgary at Winnipeg

TUESDAY, OCTOBER 13

Buffalo at Pittsburgh

WEDNESDAY, OCTOBER 14

Hartford at New Jersey
Toronto at Minnesota
St. Louis at Chicago
Calgary at Edmonton

THURSDAY, OCTOBER 15

Boston at Los Angeles
New York Islanders at Philadelphia
New York Rangers at Pittsburgh

FRIDAY, OCTOBER 16

Hartford at Washington
Quebec at Buffalo
Montreal at New Jersey
Toronto at Detroit
Edmonton at Calgary

SATURDAY, OCTOBER 17

Boston at Edmonton
New Jersey at Hartford
Buffalo at Quebec
Pittsburgh at Montreal
Philadelphia at New York Islanders
New York Rangers at Washington
Detroit at Toronto
Chicago at St. Louis
Winnipeg at Minnesota

SUNDAY, OCTOBER 18

Boston at Calgary
Pittsburgh at Philadelphia
Winnipeg at Chicago
Vancouver at Los Angeles

MONDAY, OCTOBER 19

Minnesota at Montreal
Washington at New York Rangers

TUESDAY, OCTOBER 20

Calgary at New York Islanders
Winnipeg at St. Louis

WEDNESDAY, OCTOBER 21

Boston at Vancouver
Hartford at Buffalo
Montreal at Toronto
Calgary at New York Rangers
New Jersey at Pittsburgh
Chicago at Detroit
Los Angeles at Edmonton

THURSDAY, OCTOBER 22

Minnesota at Quebec
Washington at Philadelphia

FRIDAY, OCTOBER 23

Montreal at Buffalo
New York Islanders at New Jersey
Chicago at New York Rangers
Pittsburgh at Detroit
Los Angeles at Winnipeg
Edmonton at Vancouver

SATURDAY, OCTOBER 24

Boston at St. Louis
Chicago at Hartford
Buffalo at Pittsburgh
Montreal at Washington
Calgary at Quebec
New Jersey at New York Islanders
New York Rangers at Philadelphia
Minnesota at Toronto
Vancouver at Edmonton

SUNDAY, OCTOBER 25

*Los Angeles at Winnipeg

MONDAY, OCTOBER 26

Calgary at Montreal
Philadelphia at New York Rangers

TUESDAY, OCTOBER 27

Edmonton at Quebec
Chicago at New York Islanders
Philadelphia at New Jersey
Los Angeles at Pittsburgh
Washington at Vancouver
Minnesota at St. Louis

WEDNESDAY, OCTOBER 28

Buffalo at Hartford
Edmonton at Montreal
New York Islanders at Toronto
Los Angeles at New York Rangers
Detroit at Winnipeg

THURSDAY, OCTOBER 29

Quebec at Boston
Toronto at Pittsburgh
St. Louis at Minnesota

FRIDAY, OCTOBER 30

Los Angeles at Buffalo
Montreal at Detroit
Washington at Winnipeg
Calgary at Vancouver

SATURDAY, OCTOBER 31

Boston at Montreal
Philadelphia at Hartford
Pittsburgh at Quebec
N. York Rangers at N. York Islanders

SUNDAY, NOVEMBER 1

New York Islanders at Boston
Hartford at Quebec
Chicago at Buffalo
Edmonton at New York Rangers
Los Angeles at Philadelphia
Vancouver at Winnipeg

MONDAY, NOVEMBER 2

St. Louis at Montreal

TUESDAY, NOVEMBER 3

St. Louis at Quebec
New Jersey at New York Islanders
New York Rangers at Calgary
Philadelphia at Pittsburgh
Vancouver at Washington
Minnesota at Detroit

WEDNESDAY, NOVEMBER 4

Boston at Hartford
Buffalo at Los Angeles
Montreal at Chicago
New York Rangers at Edmonton
Winnipeg at Toronto
Detroit at Minnesota

THURSDAY, NOVEMBER 5

Toronto at Boston
Pittsburgh at New York Islanders
St. Louis at New Jersey
Vancouver at Philadelphia
Edmonton at Calgary

FRIDAY, NOVEMBER 6

Hartford at Detroit
Quebec at Washington
Chicago at Winnipeg

SATURDAY, NOVEMBER 7

Pittsburgh at Boston
Quebec at Hartford
Buffalo at Edmonton
Philadelphia at Montreal
Detroit at New York Islanders
New York Rangers at Los Angeles
Washington at New Jersey
St. Louis at Toronto
Vancouver at Minnesota

SUNDAY, NOVEMBER 8

Buffalo at Calgary
New Jersey at Philadelphia
Minnesota at Chicago
Vancouver at Winnipeg

MONDAY, NOVEMBER 9

Boston at Quebec
Toronto at Montreal

TUESDAY, NOVEMBER 10

Washington at New York Islanders
New Jersey at New York Rangers
Philadelphia at St. Louis
Calgary at Winnipeg
Edmonton at Los Angeles

WEDNESDAY, NOVEMBER 11

Boston at Toronto
Montreal at Hartford
Buffalo at Vancouver
Washington at Pittsburgh
Detroit at Chicago
Calgary at Minnesota

— 235 —

THURSDAY, NOVEMBER 12

Montreal at Boston
New York Islanders at St. Louis
Winnipeg at New Jersey
Pittsburgh at Philadelphia

FRIDAY, NOVEMBER 13

Minnesota at Buffalo
Quebec at Vancouver
Los Angeles at Calgary

SATURDAY, NOVEMBER 14

Hartford at Boston
Chicago at Montreal
Quebec at Los Angeles
Winnipeg at New York Islanders
New York Rangers at Pittsburgh
*Detroit at New Jersey
*Toronto at Philadelphia
Minnesota at Washington
Edmonton at St. Louis

SUNDAY, NOVEMBER 15

Toronto at Buffalo
Winnipeg at New York Rangers
Edmonton at Chicago
Vancouver at Calgary

MONDAY, NOVEMBER 16

Hartford at Montreal

TUESDAY, NOVEMBER 17

Boston at Calgary
Los Angeles at New York Islanders
Pittsburgh at Vancouver
Detroit at Washington

WEDNESDAY, NOVEMBER 18

Boston at Winnipeg
Buffalo at Hartford
New York Islanders at Montreal
Quebec at Edmonton
Philadelphia at New Jersey
St. Louis at Toronto
Minnesota at Chicago

THURSDAY, NOVEMBER 19

Quebec at Calgary
New York Rangers at Minnesota
Los Angeles at Philadelphia
Toronto at St. Louis
Vancouver at Detroit

FRIDAY, NOVEMBER 20

Washington at Buffalo
New York Rangers at Winnipeg
Chicago at New Jersey
Pittsburgh at Edmonton

SATURDAY, NOVEMBER 21

Boston at Minnesota
Washington at Hartford
New Jersey at Montreal
New York Islanders at Philadelphia
Pittsburgh at Calgary
Los Angeles at Toronto
Vancouver at St. Louis

SUNDAY, NOVEMBER 22

Boston at Detroit
Los Angeles at Buffalo
Vancouver at Chicago
Edmonton at Winnipeg

MONDAY, NOVEMBER 23

Montreal at Quebec
New Jersey at Calgary

TUESDAY, NOVEMBER 24

Toronto at New York Islanders

WEDNESDAY, NOVEMBER 25

Boston at Washington
Montreal at Hartford

Buffalo at Philadelphia
Quebec at Pittsburgh
Toronto at New York Rangers
New Jersey at Edmonton
Winnipeg at Detroit
Chicago at Los Angeles
St. Louis at Minnesota
Calgary at Vancouver

THURSDAY, NOVEMBER 26

Winnipeg at Boston

FRIDAY, NOVEMBER 27

Hartford at Buffalo
Montreal at Minnesota
New Jersey at Vancouver
Pittsburgh at Washington
St. Louis at Detroit
Chicago at Edmonton

SATURDAY, NOVEMBER 28

Detroit at Boston
Hartford at Toronto
Montreal at Winnipeg
Philadelphia at Quebec
N. York Rangers at N. York Islanders
Washington at Pittsburgh
Minnesota at St. Louis
Calgary at Los Angeles

SUNDAY, NOVEMBER 29

Edmonton at Buffalo
N. York Islanders at N. York Rangers
New Jersey at Los Angeles

MONDAY, NOVEMBER 30

Boston at Montreal
Chicago at Calgary

TUESDAY, DECEMBER 1

Vancouver at Quebec
Edmonton at Washington
Toronto at Minnesota
Winnipeg at Los Angeles

WEDNESDAY, DECEMBER 2

Boston at Hartford
Vancouver at Montreal
New York Islanders at Pittsburgh
Edmonton at Detroit
Chicago at St. Louis

THURSDAY, DECEMBER 3

New York Rangers at Boston
Hartford at Philadelphia
Quebec at Buffalo
St. Louis at New Jersey
Toronto at Calgary
Winnipeg at Los Angeles

FRIDAY, DECEMBER 4

New York Islanders at Washington
Chicago at Detroit

SATURDAY, DECEMBER 5

Chicago at Boston
Buffalo at Hartford
Los Angeles at Montreal
New Jersey at Quebec
New York Rangers at St. Louis
Vancouver at Pittsburgh
Toronto at Edmonton
Minnesota at Calgary

SUNDAY, DECEMBER 6

Vancouver at Buffalo
New Jersey at Philadelphia
Los Angeles at Washington
Minnesota at Edmonton

MONDAY, DECEMBER 7

Detroit at Toronto

TUESDAY, DECEMBER 8

Boston at Philadelphia
Hartford at Quebec
Montreal at New York Islanders
Calgary at Washington
Minnesota at Vancouver

WEDNESDAY, DECEMBER 9

Washington at Hartford
Buffalo at Chicago
Montreal at New York Rangers
Los Angeles at New Jersey
Calgary at Pittsburgh
St. Louis at Detroit
Winnipeg at Edmonton

THURSDAY, DECEMBER 10

Los Angeles at Boston
New York Rangers at Philadelphia
St. Louis at Minnesota

FRIDAY, DECEMBER 11

Quebec at Winnipeg
New York Islanders at Pittsburgh
Calgary at New Jersey
Philadelphia at Detroit
Vancouver at Edmonton

SATURDAY, DECEMBER 12

*Buffalo at Boston
Los Angeles at Hartford
Detroit at Montreal
Quebec at Minnesota
New Jersey at New York Islanders
New York Rangers at Toronto
Pittsburgh at St. Louis
Chicago at Washington
Edmonton at Vancouver

SUNDAY, DECEMBER 13

Calgary at Buffalo
Philadelphia at Winnipeg
Toronto at Chicago

MONDAY, DECEMBER 14

Detroit at New York Rangers

TUESDAY, DECEMBER 15

Vancouver at Hartford
St. Louis at New York Islanders
Philadelphia at Pittsburgh
Washington at Toronto

WEDNESDAY, DECEMBER 16

Quebec at Montreal
New Jersey at New York Rangers
Washington at Detroit
Chicago at Minnesota
Winnipeg at Calgary
Edmonton at Los Angeles

THURSDAY, DECEMBER 17

Vancouver at Boston
St. Louis at Hartford
New York Islanders at Philadelphia
Pittsburgh at New Jersey

FRIDAY, DECEMBER 18

Montreal at Buffalo
Toronto at Washington
Minnesota at Detroit
Winnipeg at Edmonton

SATURDAY, DECEMBER 19

*St. Louis at Boston
Hartford at Edmonton
Buffalo at Montreal
Philadelphia at New York Islanders
New York Rangers at Pittsburgh
New Jersey at Minnesota
Chicago at Toronto
Calgary at Los Angeles

SUNDAY, DECEMBER 20
Boston at Chicago
Hartford at Vancouver
*Detroit at Quebec
Pittsburgh at New York Rangers
New Jersey at Winnipeg
*St. Louis at Washington
Los Angeles at Calgary

MONDAY, DECEMBER 21
Minnesota at Toronto

TUESDAY, DECEMBER 22
Buffalo at Boston
Hartford at Calgary
Washington at Quebec
New York Islanders at Winnipeg
Philadelphia at New York Rangers
Los Angeles at Edmonton

WEDNESDAY, DECEMBER 23
Buffalo at Detroit
Washington at Montreal
New York Islanders at Chicago
New Jersey at Pittsburgh
Minnesota at Philadelphia
Toronto at St. Louis
Los Angeles at Vancouver

SATURDAY, DECEMBER 26
Boston at New York Islanders
Quebec at Hartford
Montreal at Toronto
*New York Rangers at New Jersey
Philadelphia at Washington
Detroit at Pittsburgh
St. Louis at Chicago
Minnesota at Winnipeg
Edmonton at Calgary
Vancouver at Los Angeles

SUNDAY, DECEMBER 27
Boston at New York Rangers
*Hartford at Quebec
Pittsburgh at Buffalo
Detroit at Minnesota
Chicago at St. Louis

MONDAY, DECEMBER 28
Montreal at Calgary
New York Islanders at New Jersey
Washington at Toronto
Winnipeg at Los Angeles
Vancouver at Edmonton

TUESDAY, DECEMBER 29
Boston at Pittsburgh
Buffalo at Quebec
Montreal at Vancouver
N. York Rangers at N. York Islanders

WEDNESDAY, DECEMBER 30
Toronto at Hartford
Washington at New Jersey
Philadelphia at Edmonton
Detroit at St. Louis
Minnesota at Chicago
Winnipeg at Los Angeles

THURSDAY, DECEMBER 31
Boston at Buffalo
Quebec at New York Rangers
Philadelphia at Calgary
St. Louis at Detroit
Chicago at Minnesota
Winnipeg at Vancouver

FRIDAY, JANUARY 1
*Pittsburgh at Washington

SATURDAY, JANUARY 2
*Quebec at Boston
New Jersey at Hartford
Buffalo at Toronto

Montreal at Los Angeles
Pittsburgh at New York Islanders
New York Rangers at Minnesota
Philadelphia at Vancouver
*Edmonton at Washington
Calgary at St. Louis

SUNDAY, JANUARY 3
Quebec at Buffalo
Detroit at Winnipeg
Calgary at Chicago

MONDAY, JANUARY 4
Edmonton at Boston
St. Louis at New York Rangers
Los Angeles at New Jersey
Vancouver at Toronto

TUESDAY, JANUARY 5
Minnesota at New York Islanders
Washington at Philadelphia
Los Angeles at Pittsburgh

WEDNESDAY, JANUARY 6
Edmonton at Hartford
Buffalo at Montreal
Quebec at Chicago
Vancouver at New York Rangers
Minnesota at Toronto
St. Louis at Detroit
Winnipeg at Calgary

THURSDAY, JANUARY 7
Boston at Pittsburgh
Vancouver at New Jersey
St. Louis at Philadelphia

FRIDAY, JANUARY 8
Hartford at Buffalo
New York Islanders at Calgary
New York Rangers at Washington
Toronto at Chicago
Los Angeles at Detroit
Edmonton at Winnipeg

SATURDAY, JANUARY 9
Boston at St. Louis
Pittsburgh at Hartford
Philadelphia at Montreal
Vancouver at Quebec
New York Islanders at Edmonton
New Jersey at Minnesota

SUNDAY, JANUARY 10
New York Rangers at Buffalo
New Jersey at Philadelphia
Pittsburgh at Detroit
Washington at Calgary
Toronto at Winnipeg
Los Angeles at Chicago

MONDAY, JANUARY 11
Hartford at Boston
Chicago at New York Rangers
Washington at Edmonton
Los Angeles at Minnesota

TUESDAY, JANUARY 12
Buffalo at St. Louis
New York Islanders at Pittsburgh
Winnipeg at Vancouver

WEDNESDAY, JANUARY 13
Boston at Montreal
Hartford at Chicago
Quebec at New Jersey
Detroit at New York Rangers
Washington at Los Angeles
Toronto at Minnesota
Winnipeg at Vancouver
Calgary at Edmonton

THURSDAY, JANUARY 14
Montreal at Boston
Hartford at St. Louis

Buffalo at Philadelphia
Quebec at New York Islanders

FRIDAY, JANUARY 15
Toronto at New Jersey
Philadelphia at Pittsburgh
Minnesota at Detroit
Winnipeg at Edmonton
Calgary at Vancouver

SATURDAY, JANUARY 16
*Buffalo at Boston
Hartford at Los Angeles
New York Rangers at Montreal
Chicago at Quebec
New Jersey at New York Islanders
Pittsburgh at Toronto
Washington at St. Louis
Detroit at Minnesota

SUNDAY, JANUARY 17
New York Islanders at Buffalo
Philadelphia at New York Rangers
Washington at Chicago
Vancouver at Winnipeg

MONDAY, JANUARY 18
Edmonton at Montreal
Toronto at Detroit

TUESDAY, JANUARY 19
Hartford at Minnesota
Edmonton at Quebec
Pittsburgh at New York Islanders
New York Rangers at Los Angeles
New Jersey at Washington
St. Louis at Winnipeg
Vancouver at Calgary

WEDNESDAY, JANUARY 20
Boston at Buffalo
Pittsburgh at Chicago

THURSDAY, JANUARY 21
Minnesota at Boston
New York Islanders at Hartford
St. Louis at Montreal
Quebec at Toronto
Detroit at New Jersey
Edmonton at Philadelphia
Los Angeles at Calgary

FRIDAY, JANUARY 22
New Jersey at Buffalo
New York Rangers at Vancouver
Los Angeles at Winnipeg

SATURDAY, JANUARY 23
*Philadelphia at Boston
Minnesota at Hartford
Buffalo at Washington
Pittsburgh at Montreal
St. Louis at Quebec
Edmonton at New York Islanders
Chicago at Toronto
*Calgary at Detroit

SUNDAY, JANUARY 24
Detroit at Hartford
Montreal at Quebec
Minnesota at Philadelphia
Vancouver at Chicago
*Los Angeles at Winnipeg

MONDAY, JANUARY 25
Buffalo at New Jersey
Edmonton at Pittsburgh
Calgary at Toronto

TUESDAY, JANUARY 26
Los Angeles at Quebec
Winnipeg at Washington
Chicago at Detroit
Vancouver at St. Louis

WEDNESDAY, JANUARY 27

Hartford at Calgary
Montreal at Buffalo
New York Islanders at Minnesota
Winnipeg at Pittsburgh
Los Angeles at Toronto

THURSDAY, JANUARY 28

Quebec at Boston
New York Rangers at Philadelphia
Pittsburgh at New Jersey
Minnesota at St. Louis

FRIDAY, JANUARY 29

Hartford at Vancouver
New York Islanders at Buffalo
Montreal at Washington
Chicago at New Jersey
Toronto at Detroit
Calgary at Edmonton

SATURDAY, JANUARY 30

*New York Rangers at Boston
Hartford at Edmonton
Montreal at New York Islanders
Quebec at St. Louis
*Winnipeg at Philadelphia
Chicago at Pittsburgh
Detroit at Toronto
Minnesota at Los Angeles
Vancouver at Calgary

SUNDAY, JANUARY 31

*Winnipeg at Buffalo
*Philadelphia at Washington

MONDAY, FEBRUARY 1

Boston at Chicago
Hartford at Montreal
New Jersey at Calgary
St. Louis at Toronto

TUESDAY, FEBRUARY 2

Buffalo at Quebec
N. York Rangers at N. York Islanders
Washington at Pittsburgh
Los Angeles at Vancouver

WEDNESDAY, FEBRUARY 3

Montreal at Hartford
New Jersey at Edmonton
Detroit at Chicago
St. Louis at Minnesota
Calgary at Winnipeg
Vancouver at Los Angeles

THURSDAY, FEBRUARY 4

Montreal at Boston
New York Rangers at Quebec
Toronto at Philadelphia
Minnesota at Pittsburgh

FRIDAY, FEBRUARY 5

Toronto at Buffalo
New York Islanders at Washington
New Jersey at Vancouver
Calgary at Detroit
Chicago at Winnipeg

SATURDAY, FEBRUARY 6

*Boston at Quebec
Hartford at Pittsburgh
Buffalo at New York Islanders
Detroit at Montreal
New York Rangers at Washington
Philadelphia at St. Louis
Winnipeg at Minnesota
Edmonton at Los Angeles

SUNDAY, FEBRUARY 7

*New Jersey at Boston
Toronto at Hartford
*Chicago at Quebec
*Pittsburgh at New York Rangers

Calgary at Los Angeles

TUESDAY, FEBRUARY 9

All-Star Game at St. Louis

THURSDAY, FEBRUARY 11

Montreal at New Jersey
Quebec at Los Angeles
New York Islanders at Toronto
Washington at New York Rangers
Edmonton at Vancouver

FRIDAY, FEBRUARY 12

Boston at Edmonton
Buffalo at Winnipeg
New York Islanders at Washington
New Jersey at Detroit
Calgary at Philadelphia
St. Louis at Chicago

SATURDAY, FEBRUARY 13

Boston at Vancouver
Hartford at Montreal
Quebec at Minnesota
Philadelphia at Toronto
Pittsburgh at Los Angeles
Detroit at St. Louis

SUNDAY, FEBRUARY 14

*Buffalo at Chicago
Quebec at Winnipeg
*N. York Islanders at N. York Rangers
New Jersey at Toronto
*Calgary at Washington
Vancouver at Edmonton

MONDAY, FEBRUARY 15

*Hartford at Philadelphia
*Montreal at New York Rangers
*Detroit at Los Angeles

TUESDAY, FEBRUARY 16

Buffalo at St. Louis
Winnipeg at Quebec
Calgary at New York Islanders

WEDNESDAY, FEBRUARY 17

Boston at Montreal
Winnipeg at Hartford
Calgary at New York Rangers
Washington at New Jersey
Pittsburgh at Vancouver
Toronto at Edmonton
Detroit at Chicago
Los Angeles at Minnesota

THURSDAY, FEBRUARY 18

New York Islanders at Philadelphia
Los Angeles at St. Louis

FRIDAY, FEBRUARY 19

Philadelphia at Buffalo
New York Rangers at New Jersey
Pittsburgh at Edmonton
Washington at Winnipeg
Toronto at Vancouver

SATURDAY, FEBRUARY 20

Hartford at New York Islanders
Quebec at Montreal
Washington at Minnesota
Toronto at Los Angeles
*Chicago at Detroit
Calgary at St. Louis

SUNDAY, FEBRUARY 21

*Boston at New Jersey
New York Islanders at Hartford
Quebec at Buffalo
Vancouver at New York Rangers
*Detroit at Philadelphia
St. Louis at Pittsburgh
Calgary at Chicago
*Edmonton at Winnipeg

MONDAY, FEBRUARY 22

Toronto at Minnesota

TUESDAY, FEBRUARY 23

Boston at Hartford
Montreal at Quebec
Vancouver at New York Islanders
Philadelphia at Detroit
Winnipeg at Pittsburgh
Edmonton at St. Louis

WEDNESDAY, FEBRUARY 24

Vancouver at Montreal
Winnipeg at New Jersey
Washington at Los Angeles
Minnesota at Toronto
Edmonton at Chicago

THURSDAY, FEBRUARY 25

Hartford at Boston
St. Louis at Buffalo
Chicago at New York Islanders
Pittsburgh at New York Rangers

FRIDAY, FEBRUARY 26

Quebec at Detroit
New York Rangers at New Jersey
Calgary at Vancouver

SATURDAY, FEBRUARY 27

*Minnesota at Boston
Buffalo at Hartford
Winnipeg at Montreal
Detroit at Quebec
Washington at New York Islanders
Philadelphia at Los Angeles
St. Louis at Toronto

SUNDAY, FEBRUARY 28

Winnipeg at Buffalo
*Minnesota at New Jersey
*Pittsburgh at Chicago
Calgary at Edmonton
Los Angeles at Vancouver

MONDAY, FEBRUARY 29

Montreal at Quebec
St. Louis at New York Rangers

TUESDAY, MARCH 1

Hartford at Winnipeg
Buffalo at Detroit
St. Louis at New York Islanders
New Jersey at Washington
Philadelphia at Vancouver
Minnesota at Pittsburgh
Los Angeles at Edmonton

WEDNESDAY, MARCH 2

Hartford at Chicago
Quebec at Toronto
N. York Islanders at N. York Rangers
Washington at New Jersey

THURSDAY, MARCH 3

Toronto at Boston
Montreal at St. Louis
Philadelphia at Calgary
Minnesota at Detroit
Vancouver at Winnipeg

FRIDAY, MARCH 4

New York Rangers at Buffalo
Quebec at Washington
Philadelphia at Edmonton

SATURDAY, MARCH 5

*New Jersey at Boston
New York Rangers at Hartford
Montreal at Los Angeles
*New York Islanders at Pittsburgh
Winnipeg at Toronto
Detroit at St. Louis

Chicago at Minnesota
Edmonton at Calgary

SUNDAY, MARCH 6

Boston at Buffalo
*New York Islanders at Quebec
*Philadelphia at New Jersey
*Vancouver at Washington
Detroit at Chicago

MONDAY, MARCH 7

Pittsburgh at Calgary
Edmonton at Winnipeg

TUESDAY, MARCH 8

Boston at Detroit
Hartford at Quebec
Vancouver at New York Islanders
New Jersey at New York Rangers
Toronto at St. Louis

WEDNESDAY, MARCH 9

Los Angeles at Hartford
Buffalo at Minnesota
Montreal at Edmonton
Toronto at Chicago
Calgary at Winnipeg

THURSDAY, MARCH 10

Los Angeles at Boston
Quebec at New York Islanders
Washington at Philadelphia
Pittsburgh at St. Louis
Vancouver at Detroit
Winnipeg at Calgary

SATURDAY, MARCH 12

Boston at Quebec
Hartford at Montreal
Buffalo at Calgary
Detroit at New York Islanders
New York Rangers at Washington
*New Jersey at Philadelphia
*Pittsburgh at Minnesota
Chicago at Toronto
Edmonton at Vancouver

SUNDAY, MARCH 13

Washington at Boston
Quebec at Hartford
Buffalo at Vancouver
New York Islanders at Detroit
Philadelphia at Chicago
*Pittsburgh at Winnipeg
St. Louis at Los Angeles

MONDAY, MARCH 14

Montreal at Minnesota

TUESDAY, MARCH 15

Calgary at Hartford
Buffalo at Edmonton
Toronto at Quebec
Philadelphia at New York Rangers
Chicago at St. Louis

WEDNESDAY, MARCH 16

Montreal at Winnipeg
Washington at New York Rangers
Toronto at Pittsburgh
Detroit at Minnesota
Vancouver at Los Angeles

THURSDAY, MARCH 17

Calgary at Boston
Quebec at New Jersey
Chicago at Philadelphia
Minnesota at St. Louis

FRIDAY, MARCH 18

New York Islanders at Washington
Winnipeg at Edmonton
Los Angeles at Vancouver

SATURDAY, MARCH 19

*Buffalo at Boston
Hartford at St. Louis
Chicago at Montreal
Calgary at Quebec
New York Rangers at Toronto
Philadelphia at Pittsburgh
Detroit at Los Angeles

SUNDAY, MARCH 20

Boston at Buffalo
Hartford at New York Rangers
*New York Islanders at Winnipeg
*New Jersey at Washington
Pittsburgh at Philadelphia
St. Louis at Chicago
Edmonton at Minnesota

MONDAY, MARCH 21

Calgary at Montreal
New York Islanders at Minnesota

TUESDAY, MARCH 22

Boston at Philadelphia
Winnipeg at Hartford
Buffalo at New York Rangers
St. Louis at Washington
Toronto at Vancouver
Edmonton at Detroit

WEDNESDAY, MARCH 23

Quebec at Montreal
New York Islanders at Los Angeles
Washington at Pittsburgh
Minnesota at Chicago

THURSDAY, MARCH 24

Winnipeg at Boston
Hartford at Detroit
Edmonton at New York Rangers
New Jersey at St. Louis
Toronto at Calgary

FRIDAY, MARCH 25

New Jersey at Buffalo
Montreal at Pittsburgh
Philadelphia at Washington
Chicago at Vancouver

SATURDAY, MARCH 26

*Quebec at Boston
Minnesota at Hartford
Edmonton at New York Islanders
*New York Rangers at Detroit
Winnipeg at Philadelphia
Toronto at St. Louis
Chicago at Los Angeles
Vancouver at Calgary

SUNDAY, MARCH 27

Montreal at Hartford
Detroit at Buffalo
*Pittsburgh at Quebec
*New York Rangers at New Jersey

MONDAY, MARCH 28

Edmonton at Toronto
Chicago at Minnesota
St. Louis at Calgary

TUESDAY, MARCH 29

Buffalo at Quebec
Philadelphia at New York Islanders
Pittsburgh at New Jersey
Detroit at Washington
Winnipeg at Vancouver

WEDNESDAY, MARCH 30

New York Rangers at Chicago
Minnesota at Edmonton
Calgary at Los Angeles

THURSDAY, MARCH 31

Montreal at Boston
Hartford at Buffalo
Quebec at Philadelphia
Washington at New York Islanders
New Jersey at Pittsburgh

FRIDAY, APRIL 1

New York Rangers at Winnipeg
Toronto at Detroit
St. Louis at Edmonton
Minnesota at Vancouver
Los Angeles at Calgary

SATURDAY, APRIL 2

Boston at Hartford
Buffalo at Montreal
Philadelphia at Quebec
*New York Islanders at New Jersey
Pittsburgh at Washington
Detroit at Toronto

SUNDAY, APRIL 3

New York Islanders at Boston
Hartford at Pittsburgh
Montreal at Buffalo
Quebec at New York Rangers
New Jersey at Chicago
Washington at Philadelphia
*St. Louis at Winnipeg
*Minnesota at Calgary
Los Angeles at Edmonton

NOTES